Heredity, Family, and Inequality

Heredity, Family, and Inequality

A Critique of Social Sciences

Michael Beenstock

The MIT Press
Cambridge, Massachusetts
London, England

MIT Press books may be purchased at special quantity discounts for business or sales promotional use. For information, please email special_sales@mitpress.mit.edu or write to Special Sales Department, The MIT Press, 55 Hayward Street, Cambridge, MA 02142.

Set in Palatino by Toppan Best-set Premedia Limited. Printed and bound in the United States of America.

Library of Congress Cataloging-in-Publication Data

Beenstock, Michael, 1946–
Heredity, family, and inequality : a critique of social sciences / Michael Beenstock.
    p.   cm.
Includes bibliographical references and index.
ISBN 978-0-262-01692-6 (hbk. : alk. paper)
1. Nature and nurture—Econometric models. 2. Heredity. 3. Families. 4. Equality. 5. Social stratification. I. Title.
BF341.B3735   2012
155.2'34—dc23

                                                                2011024326

10 9 8 7 6 5 4 3 2 1

Contents

Preface

This book is based on a series of lectures I gave at the University of Otago (Dunedin, New Zealand) in 2008, when I was William Evans Visiting Professor. I became interested in the topic several years earlier when Israel's Central Bureau of Statistics merged the censuses of 1983 and 1995, making it possible to match families in those years. I thought it would be interesting to investigate the intergenerational relationship between the earnings and schooling of parents and the earnings and schooling of their children. Later I extended the investigation to the intragenerational relationship between the earnings and schooling of siblings. My main research question was whether the intergenerational correlation between these outcomes is causal or due to heredity. For example, do the children of more educated parents have more schooling (as the data clearly showed they did) because of "nature," through heredity, or because of "nurture," through parenting and the environment?

When I began my research, it was well known that economic outcomes are correlated between generations and within generations. However, the literature of economics had little to say about the causes of those correlations. I quickly discovered rich literatures in behavioral genetics and psychology that dealt with non-economic aspects of heredity, parenting, and family. It struck me that these literatures differed in style from what I was used to in economics. Whereas economists write down structural models to determine the theoretical underpinnings of observed behavior, their counterparts in behavioral genetics and psychology are more discursive. Also, whereas the holy grail in empirical economics is causality, in behavioral genetics and psychology empirical standards seemed looser.

As often happens, other economists began to take an interest in the topic. Several empirical and theoretical papers have appeared in economics journals since 2001. However, this economics literature is, on the whole, very different from the literatures in behavioral genetics and psychology. Indeed, one would not guess from the economics literature that behavioral genetics and psychology have a long and venerable history. I should also point out that behavioral genetics and psychology are mutually detached, and there is no sign that they recognize developments proposed by economists. In short, behavioral genetics, psychology, and economics have had little to do with one another. The interdisciplinary spirit seems dead. Unfortunately, there is nothing new in this, and I suppose that the same applies in other areas of scientific investigation.

One of the purposes of this book is to resurrect the interdisciplinary spirit. I genuinely believe that psychologists, sociologists, behavioral geneticists, economists, and criminologists have much to learn from one another. I think these disciplines would benefit greatly from scientific cross-fertilization. I am an economist, and I am naturally a prisoner of my intellectual upbringing. As economists go, however, I think I am unusually broad-minded. Not only do I stray within the discipline; I also roam between disciplines. Currently I work with geographers and earth scientists, and in the recent past I have worked with sociologists, criminologists, statisticians, and otolaryngologists. So I am used to seeing things from the points of view of other scientific disciplines.

Finally, I am not trying to reach hard empirical conclusions. I have no intention, for example, of coming down on one side or the other on the nature-vs.-nurture debate. On the contrary, my intention is to provide intellectual tools for testing hypotheses about nature and nurture. I hope my book will help people think more clearly and critically about these fascinating and controversial issues.

The book is dedicated to Ruchi.

Michael Beenstock
Jerusalem
August 2011

1   The Apple and the Tree: Galton Revisited

This book is about the roles of heredity, family, and social environment in the determination of outcomes among humans, including anthropometric, psychological, behavioral, and economic outcomes. Family here encompasses parenting and interactions between siblings; social environment encompasses cultural affiliation, peer groups, and other aspects of social intercourse that are outside the family. The specific outcomes, including health, longevity, fertility, personality, income, education, cognitive ability, and indeed almost the entire spectrum of human life, vary considerably. Chapter 2 reviews the extensive empirical literature, which shows that in virtually every aspect of life the outcomes of children are correlated with their parents' outcomes to some extent. The outcomes of siblings also are correlated. There is, of course, nothing new in these observations; the apples really don't fall far from the tree, nor do they fall far from one another.

The similarity between parents and their children and between siblings lies at the very heart of the human condition. We are naturally and even irresistibly curious to understand why we are similar and why we are different. However, there is a deeper reason why it is important to satisfy this curiosity, since heredity, family, and social environments are inextricably interwoven with the transmission of inequality and diversity between generations, and also within generations. Social and economic inequality are loaded political issues, and so are some of the theories that purport to explain the intergenerational transmission of inequality. If heredity is entirely responsible for the similarity between parents and children, the intergenerational transmission of inequality is fixed by nature. If, on the other hand, parents and environments matter too, the intergenerational transmission of inequality is not simply the inevitable consequence of some iron law of nature. If parents and environments can change the course of nature, why shouldn't governments too be able to intervene in the transmission of inequality from one generation to the next? As we shall see, the debate about nature vs. nurture has deep political and social implications. Indeed, it occasionally has lead to acrimony and even violence.

Numerous conflicting explanations and interpretations for intergenerational and sibling correlations have been proposed by psychologists, sociologists, behavioral geneticists, economists, and (latterly) geneticists. My main purpose here is to present a critique of the explanations and interpretations proposed by these intellectual stakeholders. I also want to provide an axiomatic framework for thinking about the complex interplay among heredity, family, and environments. This framework involves both theoretical and methodological components.

The theoretical component draws on game theory and control theory, which surprisingly have been ignored by psychologists, to form hypotheses about the behavior of parents and children. Yet it was no less a figure than John Bowlby, the developmental psychologist who founded Attachment Theory, who suggested that "models that promise to make great contributions to our understanding of the prototypic structures of instinctive behaviour are models developed by control theory."[1] The control theory Bowlby was referring to is the mathematical theory of dynamic optimization,[2] developed largely in the 1950s and the 1960s. Developmental psychologists did not take up Bowlby's challenge. They preferred to continue with their informal approach to theory.

The methodological component draws on econometrics, which has been ignored by behavioral geneticists and developmental psychologists (though not, of course, by economists and some sociologists). Econometrics is a discipline invented by economists to test hypotheses using observational (that is, non-experimental) data. Behavioral genetics has stuck to the methodological workhorses of comparing identical and fraternal twins, and comparing adopted and biological siblings, to identify the role of genetics and heredity in human outcomes. As we shall see, this methodology makes numerous heroic assumptions and throws away data for the vast majority of people, who are neither twins nor adoptees. I hope to persuade the reader that the way of thinking I propose will serve to deepen our understanding of the human condition. At the very least it should be helpful in critically appraising conflicting scientific claims about the roles of heredity, family, and environments in the human condition. These matters are profoundly controversial, so it is all the more important to have a clear head when assessing the pros and cons of various arguments.

As I have already mentioned, several disciplines are involved in our subject matter, including psychology, behavioral genetics, sociology, economics, and genetics. We might also add statistics to this list, since some statistical theories originated in the study of heredity. However, as often happens, these disciplines are segregated from one another and have developed more or less along parallel lines. Each discipline has its own scientific journals, conferences, and research foundations. Each discipline has its own intellectual passions and standards of scientific achievement. What passes for science in one discipline is often regarded with suspicion in another. There is almost no cross-fertilization among the various disciplines, which at universities are typically taught in separate departments. These disciplines have developed into intellectual subcultures in which ideas are jealously guarded and reputations vigorously defended. In the study of heredity, family, and environments, the interdisciplinary spirit seems to be dead.

1.1   Axiomatic Science

One of my purposes is ecumenical. I want to consider heredity, family, and environments in an interdisciplinary way. I know that this is a difficult mission, and that it is made all the more difficult by the fact that the disciplines concerned have many sacred cows. For example, the editor of a leading journal of developmental psychology wrote to me in 2008 to say that she is against the use of game theory in developmental theory, since this will degrade the subject just as surely as game theory has degraded political science and possibly economics too. She went on to say that game theory has been exploited by economists to engage in cultural imperialism and intellectual colonialism. She does not want this to happen to developmental psychology. She appears to be unaware that game theory was not invented by economists but by mathematicians and that game theory is used in numerous disciplines, including biology, zoology, and law, as well as in political science and economics.

There are economists, among them Edward Lazear (2000), who are self-confessed cultural imperialists. They are proud that economics is a beacon to the world and has managed to invade other disciplines, including sociology, political science, and (in Lazear's case) personnel management and labor relations. Lazear may be right in believing that the so-called success of economics among the social sciences is due to the fact that economic theory, like theory in the natural sciences, is highly axiomatic. In particular, the axiom of rationality has caused economic theory to be highly focused and empirically testable. Perhaps this explains why there is a Nobel Prize in economic science but none in political science, sociology, or psychology. It is noteworthy that, although since Marx economics has not been invaded by other disciplines, economics is unusually eclectic. It has borrowed many ideas from other disciplines, including mathematics, statistics, computer science, psychology, political science, and evolutionary biology. For example, it has borrowed the median voter model from political science (Downs 1957) and probabilistic choice theory from psychology (Luce 1959). If economics were to be invaded by some alien discipline, the invaders would probably be welcomed with open arms.

I mentioned in the preface that, although I am an economist and teach in an economics department, as economists go I am unusually inter-disciplinary. However, I will not pretend that I am intellectually unprejudiced. On the other hand, I hope I am not an economic imperialist. My critique is inevitably and unapologetically written from the standpoint of economics. Had I been trained in behavioral genetics or psychology, no doubt I might have seen matters differently. Although I see matters through the spectacles of economics, and I have striven to understand other disciplines, I apologize for being rather blunt. I am not saying that game theory, or anything else, is necessarily the right way to do things. I am not a crusader in favor of this idea or that, neither in terms of theory nor in terms of empirical methodology. I am simply suggesting that there is a need for scientific cross-fertilization between the disciplines involved. I would have liked to reply to the aforementioned editor that she should be more pluralistic and open-minded, and that only good can come from the sharing of ideas. Game theorists should not be afraid of developmentalism, but neither should developmentalists be scared of game theory, which is simply a compact vehicle or language for theorizing about conflict situations.

The tension between the axiomatic approach to social science and the informal approach has erupted before. Behavioral biology (not to be confused with behavioral genetics) is concerned with the behavior of wildlife. Much of behavioral biology, such as Jane Goodall's well-known 1986 study of chimpanzees in Africa, is descriptive. However, in the 1970s a new trend emerged in which the theory of wildlife behavior was axiomatized using mathematical concepts such as optimization and game theory. The unifying axiom drew on the Darwinian concept that wildlife behaves so as to maximize fitness. All forms of behavior, including foraging, fighting, and of course mating and kin selection, may be understood in terms of the promotion of fitness as embodied in the progeny of each generation. In his landmark 1975 book, Edward O. Wilson referred to this specialized branch of behavioral biology as "sociobiology." A year later, Richard Dawkins wrote of the "selfish gene." Sociobiology made extensive use of evolutionary game theory, and was premised on the assumption that animals, fish, insects, and indeed all forms of wildlife are driven and motivated by selfish genes, which express themselves in the maximization of fitness and in the urge to survive.

It was the last chapter of Wilson's book that caused an intellectual storm.[3] Wilson suggested that sociobiology might be applicable not only to the study of wildlife but also to the study of humans. Division of labor between the sexes, bonding between kin, the incest taboo, suspicion of strangers, xenophobia, overall male dominance, territorial aggression, and other aspects of human behavior are, according to Wilson, sociobiological phenomena. Although humans have free will, they are prisoners of their selfish genes. Indeed, this explains why, although cultures vary greatly, they converge toward common traits.

Wilson was accused of being a racist, a chauvinist, a reductionist, and a biological determinist. At the 1978 meeting of the American Association for the Advancement of Science, demonstrators chanted "Racist Wilson you can't hide, we charge you with genocide." In 1986 a group of twenty distinguished social scientists issued what came to be known as the Seville Statement on Violence, in which they disputed Wilson's suggestion that there was a link between biology and violence. The Seville Statement was adopted by strange bedfellows, including UNESCO and the American Psychological Association. Wilson's critics insisted that humans are not just another form of wildlife. It might be possible to reduce the behavior of fruit flies to a few equations, they argued, but not the complex behavior of humans.

I agree with Steven Pinker's (2002) analysis of the intellectual motivation of these critics. There is a fundamental cleavage between two views of human nature. The first assumes that we are born as *tabulae rasae*, or blank slates, and that what we become results from the accumulation of life's experience. According to this view, we differ from one another because we have been exposed to different experiences, environments, and parents. This idea is usually attributed to John

Locke,[4] who referred to the phenomenon as "white paper" in his *Essay Concerning Human Understanding*. The alternative view, which Locke called "innatism," dates back at least to Plato, who in the *Theaetetus* argued that we are born with instinctive knowledge of Forms and Ideas, which experience corrupts. In the *Republic* Plato suggests that, because the ruling class is genetically superior to the ruled, selective breeding and infanticide should be practiced in order to improve the fitness of the ruling class.[5] For Plato, heredity plays a major role in who we are, and the slate is deeply engraved at birth. Members of the "guardian" class, born with a rational temperament, become rulers. Members of the "auxiliary" class, born with a spirited temperament, become soldiers and law enforcers. The "appetitive" class includes everyone else; its members become laborers and simple traders. In more recent times, innatism has received renewed support from Charles Darwin and from Noam Chomsky. The slate is not blank; it is hard-wired with innate knowledge of grammar and instincts honed by evolutionary forces.

Locke was concerned specifically with knowledge and its origins. His argument that knowledge and ideas are not innate does not necessarily extend to such phenomena as personality and fitness. In fact, Locke didn't discuss the origins of human diversity. Although for Locke the slate was blank as far as knowledge was concerned, it was not necessarily blank as far as fitness was concerned. I doubt very much that Locke would have agreed with the extreme "blank-slaters" who deny that we are born with different abilities and fitness. The slate is blank as far as knowledge is concerned, but slates differ; some are fitter or harder than others.

We are born with different personalities, gifts, and preferences, which are partially inherited from our parents. According to this view, we are diverse because we are born differently. This does not rule out the importance of life's experiences, but it means that our chances in life are circumscribed by our endowment at birth. If, in contrast, the slate is blank, life's chances are unbounded, because we may draw on it what we will, both for good and for bad. Adolf Hitler might have been Albert Schweitzer, and vice versa. If, however, the slate isn't blank, such a thing is unlikely, though not necessarily impossible.

The blank slate takes an optimistic view of mankind because it means that the sky is the limit, that we are born equal, and that we are potentially equal in life. It also appeals to left-wing philosophy, because social intervention may turn us into better people and create a more equal society. Social engineering may improve the lot of mankind and reduce inequality. Indeed, perhaps this is what distinguishes mankind from other species. Innatism is less optimistic. According to it, we are constrained by our birth endowments, and the best intentions of social engineers might not be able to make up for the fact that we are born unequal. It is obvious why the blank slate is appealing. Indeed, this is where the critics of Wilson (1975), Dawkins (1976), and Harris (1998) are coming from.

What concerns me about the disgraceful episode mentioned above is not just the self-righteous outrage of the politically correct, or even the suggestion that culture may be driven by genes and evolutionary forces. It is the objection by social scientists—particularly sociologists, anthropologists, and psychologists—that social science, unlike sociobiology, cannot be axiomatized. The axiomatic treatment of theory in the social sciences is put down as reductionism. Therefore, it was both the political message of human sociobiology and (to a lesser extent) its axiomatic medium that upset Wilson's critics. The mathematical media and techniques of sociobiology, including optimization and game theory, were anathema to them.

A major theme of the present book is that psychology and sociology comprise numerous subdisciplines that do not share axioms. Indeed, the failure of psychology as a discipline stems from the fact that, in contrast to the natural sciences and economics, there are no agreed-upon axioms in psychology. I shall argue that good science is axiomatic, and that psychology will continue to stagger from one *ad hoc* theory to the next until it too becomes axiomatic. Each new *ad hoc* theory attracts attention for a while, earns fame for its proponents, then joins its predecessors, to be learned by bewildered students of psychology from ever-thicker textbooks. Indeed, psychology textbooks read like intellectual junkyards, with one defunct theory following another.

Laland and Brown (2002) relate that the essence of human sociobiology survived the onslaught, but in disguise. It was variously called instead "human behavioral ecology," "evolutionary psychology," and "gene-culture coevolution." The message might have survived, but the medium went into decline. Indeed, Laland and Brown suggest (p. 309) that evolutionary psychology would benefit from the use of mathematical techniques and from greater formalization. Although antagonism toward axiomatization runs deep among most social scientists, the same does apply to economics. Much of economic theory is based on the axiom that economic agents—be they consumers or producers, workers or investors, parents or children—rationally pursue their objective to maximize profits, utility, or whatever. Economics and sociobiology share a common denominator in their search for useful axioms on which to base theory, and in their exploitation of formal techniques such as game theory, optimization theory and mathematical statistics to develop theory. As we shall see in chapters 3 and 8, economics even attaches importance to fitness, and the theory of economic growth has evolutionary features.[6] Economics is therefore unashamedly reductionist; like all theory, it attempts to express the essence of complex phenomena in terms of a relatively small number of parameters. Einstein's famous formula, $E = mC^2$, is reductionist too. Reductionism is a virtue rather than a vice. Scientific progress is impossible without it; and reductionism is impossible without axiomatization.

Although rationality has roots that date back at least to Adam Smith, and is no longer controversial, economics has had cultural wars of its own.[7] One of these concerned the "mathematization" of economic theory that followed the publication of Paul Samuelson's pathbreaking 1947 book *Foundations of Economic Analysis*. In the end, the mathematical development of economic theory prevailed over the verbal idiom that had dominated economics until the middle of the twentieth century. Another controversy concerned the so-called Cowles Approach (named after the Cowles Commission at Yale University, where much of modern econometric theory was developed in the 1950s). Previously, empirical hypotheses were tested largely by generating experimental data. The data were gathered by asking individuals in surveys how they would behave in the face of various contingencies. Many distinguished economists, including John Maynard Keynes and Lionel Robbins, argued against econometrics. Debating with Jan Tinbergen, Keynes argued that the most economists could do with data was interpret the past. Tinbergen argued that data could be used to test hypotheses and predict the future. The Cowles approach used non-experimental data on how people actually behaved. In the end, econometric analysis of non-experimental data prevailed over experimentalism.[9]

These two intellectual revolutions in economics were recognized with Nobel Prizes. In 1969 the first Nobel Prize for economics was awarded to Jan Tinbergen and Ragnar Frisch, both econometricians. The second was awarded to Paul Samuelson in 1970. It is interesting that the econometricians preceded the theoreticians. These intellectual giants shaped the discipline of economics in the second half of the twentieth century and beyond.

I do not mean to say that I think all human behavior is rational, or that econometrics has all the methodological answers. It is easier to develop theory based on rationality than some behavioral alternative, because rationality is unique and well defined whereas the irrational alternatives are infinitely numerous and imprecise. In any case, a theory is tested by what it predicts empirically rather than by its axioms. If rationality helps us predict human behavior, which I think it does in many areas of economic life, well and good. If some other axiom leads to better empirical predictions, I will happily abandon the rationality principle.

More recently the rationality principle has come under attack both from within economics and from other disciplines. Behavioral economics was spearheaded by Daniel Kahneman[10] when he was a member of the psychology department at the Hebrew University of Jerusalem, where he did his seminal work with Amos Tversky. Behavioral economics claims that individuals behave irrationally, but seeks to find empirical laws that predict irrational behavior in the belief that individuals are systematic in their irrational behavior. Bounded rationality, on the other hand, assumes that individuals are not fully rational because the demands of rationality are too great, and it is impossible to be completely rational.

1.2 Francis Galton

It is appropriate to recall the scientific writings of Francis Galton (1822–1911), who singlehandedly set the agenda for the study of heredity and family for the twentieth century and even the twenty-first. Galton, like his first cousin, Charles Darwin, was a Victorian gentlemen who, having inherited his father's wealth, did not have to work for a living. He spent much of his life dabbling in diverse scientific matters, including statistical theory, meteorology, photography, optics, psychometrics, and even fingerprinting. Indeed, he had a major influence on Scotland Yard's decision to identify criminals through fingerprinting. At various times he was involved with prestigious scientific organizations, including the Royal Geographical Society and the Royal Society (in which he became a fellow in 1860). He received the Royal Medal in 1866, the Darwin Medal in 1902, and the Copley Medal in 1910. However, his personal conduct frequently led to acrimony with his scientific colleagues, as exemplified by what came to be known as the Stanley Affair.[11] Galton was aloof and had an elitist belief in the superiority of his own class, which almost surely led to his interest in eugenics (which he invented). He and his wife had no children. Perhaps it was this that led him to the belief that members of the elite had too few progeny, while the mediocre classes multiplied too rapidly for the public good.

"It was not the business of his particular kind of brain to push anything far," Keynes wrote of Galton. "His original genius was superior to his intellect, but his intellect was always just sufficient to keep him just on the right side of eccentricity."[12] One may question this judgment of Galton's theory of eugenics[13] and his belief that racism had a scientific basis, but it is true that Galton was better at posing questions than he was at answering them. Indeed, much of his boundless energy went into collecting data from the numerous surveys that he ran. He was an accomplished and even distinguished amateur who left it to those who were more intellectually capable to complete the job. A good example of this symbiosis is the work of Karl Pearson, who did much to develop Galton's statistical ideas. Nevertheless, geneticists from Wilhelm Ludvig Johannsen to James D. Watson held Galton's contribution to genetics in high regard. In 1903 Johannsen even dedicated a book to Galton.

1.2.1   Nature and Nurture

Scientific enquiry into human heredity begins in 1869 with the publication of *Hereditary Genius*, in which Galton claimed that the close relatives of distinguished men such as judges and statesmen were more likely to be distinguished than average members of their class. Perhaps our story really begins even earlier, in 1859, when Darwin published his theory of evolution in *On the Origin of Species by Means of Natural Selection*. Galton remarked in his autobiography, in reference to Darwin's theory of evolution, "I was encouraged by the new views to pursue many enquiries which had long interested me, and which clustered around the central topic of Heredity and the possible improvement of the Human Race." For Galton, distinguished men had distinguished progeny because of heredity; the mechanism was genetic, not social.

It was not as if Galton failed to consider that the mechanism might be social rather than genetic. Indeed, it was Galton who invented the dichotomy between "nature and nurture" when he argued in his 1874 book *English Men of Science: Their Nature and Nurture* that what was true for judges also applied to scientists. Bulmer (2003) and Watson (2003) have suggested that Galton might have been inspired by Shakespeare's play *The Tempest*, in which Prospero calls his adopted son Caliban "a devil, a born devil, on whose nature nurture can never stick." Indeed, Galton consistently rejected nurture as a significant influence on the outcomes of children. For Galton, nature was the major factor, and nature had a large hereditary component.

Galton's detractors argue that his rejection of the role of nurture reflected his elitism. If nurture mattered rather than nature, Galton would not have been essentially superior to members of the lower classes, who, but for chance, could have become like him. Or, even worse, had Galton not received such a privileged upbringing he might have ended up like members of the lower classes, who he clearly despised. It was important for Galton to believe that he was what he was thanks to pedigree—that is, because he had inherited distinguished genes from his equally distinguished ancestors.

The debate on nature vs. nurture continues to rumble on. As we shall see, the idea that heredity may play a significant role in human behavior is anathema to some (especially developmental psychologists) but is stock in trade for others (especially behavioral geneticists). In the twentieth century, behavioral genetics and developmental psychology continued along these parallel lines. On the whole, developmental psychologists shun the idea that children's outcomes are partly genetic. For them it is almost an article of faith that parents affect their children through their behavior but not through their genes. Behavioral geneticists, on the other hand, pay lip service to the role of the environment and parenting, which they then give short shrift, and attribute to heredity much if not all of the similarity between parents, children, and siblings.

1.2.2   Heredity

In 1869 genetics was an unknown science. Gregor Mendel had published the results of his pea experiments in German in 1866 in the *Proceedings of the Brünn Natural Science Society*. He sent 120 reprints to scientists and libraries in Europe and the United States. According to Plomin et al. (2001), one even landed on Darwin's desk. He also sent a copy to the distinguished botanist Karl Nägeli in Munich, and the two men corresponded at least ten times between 1867 and 1873. So it is not the case that Mendel's work lay concealed from the public eye. It remains one of the great mysteries in the history of science that his work had no impact and lay unnoticed until the turn of the twentieth century, when de Vries, Correns, and Tschernak simultaneously rediscovered his laws of heredity. Indeed, de Vries, Correns, and Tschernak had been unaware of Mendel's work, even though it was mentioned in the *Encyclopaedia Britannica*. Watson (2003) argues that Mendel was simply ahead of his time, but this is not persuasive—so were Newton, Einstein, and indeed all scientific revolutionaries. (Mendel referred to genes as "elements," and according to the *Oxford English Dictionary* it was not until 1913 that the word "gene" entered the vernacular.[14])

It is clear that Galton too was completely unaware of Mendel's work. Indeed, Galton invested much effort in discovering the mechanism for heredity. In his theory of pangenesis, Darwin had argued that heredity was transmitted in the bloodstream through hypothetical "gemmules," which can be thought of as miniature replicas of cells. He hypothesized that gemmules were transmitted intergenerationally but could remain dormant. Darwin's theory of heredity had nothing in common with Mendel's revolutionary theory. In fact, Darwin's theory harked back to Aristotle's homunculus theory, which had influenced thinking about heredity for nearly 2,500 years. According to Aristotle, embryos form when tiny components of body parts are passed from the male into the womb. Galton tested Darwin's theory by carrying out blood transfusions on different varieties of rabbits at London Zoo between 1869 and 1871. If Darwin was right, he expected that the transfused rabbits would breed progeny with features of the rabbits whose blood they had received. Since this did not happen, Galton rejected Darwin's theory of pangenesis, and the relationship between the cousins became strained.

Having rejected Darwin's theory of pangenesis, Galton hypothesized the existence of "stirps" in newly fertilized ova.[15] Stirps contain many more germs than there are cells, so only a small proportion develop into cells. Unused germs contribute to the stirp of the next generation. Galton's stirp theory of heredity was incomplete because it did not explain the selection process for unused germs. Had Galton been aware of Mendel's genetic theory of heredity, surely he wouldn't have wasted effort on his stirp theory, and he would have avoided going down several blind alleys.

The stirp theory also led Galton to a major missed opportunity in his suggestion to study the behavior of twins. As far as Galton was concerned, all siblings shared the same stirp, whether they were identical twins, fraternal twins, or simply siblings. Therefore, he did not understand that something genetic might be learned from comparing identical and fraternal twins. The comparison of outcomes for identical and fraternal twins is a major methodological workhorse in behavioral genetics. However, it turns out that Galton did not anticipate these developments in behavioral genetics when he studied twins reared together and twins reared apart. His purpose was to show that twins reared apart behaved similarly to twins reared together, and that their different environments made no difference to them. His sample of 94 sets of twins included 35 identical and 59 fraternal twins, but in view of his stirp theory this distinction could not have been of any significance to him.

However, Galton's comparison between twins reared together[16] and twins reared apart anticipated a second methodological workhorse of behavioral genetics: comparison of biological siblings and adopted siblings. It would have been enough for Galton to have used data on siblings reared together and apart, since, according to his stirp theory, siblings are as genetically similar as identical twins. Therefore, Galton's twin studies only partially anticipated twentieth-century behavioral genetics. Nevertheless, Galton must be regarded as the founding father of behavioral genetics.[17] This extends also to his disrespect for the role of nurture. (To be fair, behavioral genetics doesn't deny the role of nurture, but it makes no serious effort to take account of it in its statistical methodologies.) Indeed, we shall return to this theme on several occasions.

1.2.3 Regression and Correlation

Subsequently, Galton took a very different direction in his study of heredity turning from stirp theory (a deductive attempt to understand the fundamental biological mechanism that underpinned heredity) to inductivism. He hoped that by observing data on parents and their progeny he might be able to identify statistical laws that govern heredity. He began this endeavor by studying the sizes of the seeds of successive generations of sweet peas.[18] That choice was wise: sweet peas propagate asexually, so their progeny have only one parent. Examining data on 490 pairs of seeds, Galton noticed that the progeny of large seeds were larger than average but smaller than their parents, whereas the progeny of smaller seeds were smaller than average but larger than their parents. In the absence of appropriate statistics for measuring correlation and mean reversion, or regression toward the mean, Galton invented those concepts during the 1880s. Indeed, the letter *r*, which is still universally used today to symbolize the coefficient of correlation between two variables,[19] was first used by Galton in 1884. However, Galton calculated r by using groups of observations rather than individual observations. It was left to Pearson to invent the definition of r that is used today.

Galton also invented the theory of regression. He regressed the seed size of progeny on the seed size of their parents. The term "regression" is Galton's and is still used universally. It was also left to Pearson to refine Galton's ideas on regression. Whereas Galton used grouped data, Pearson used individual observations. He estimated the mean reversion coefficient at 0.33. Indeed, this is the first-ever beta coefficient to be estimated. It means that 0.33 of the excess size of the parent pea is inherited by its progeny. It also means that 0.33 of the deficit in size is inherited. Galton found that regression to the mean from below and above the mean is symmetrical.

It is amusing to note that Galton was puzzled by the fact that the slope of the regression line depends on the direction of the regression. When he reversed the regression, and the size of the parent pea was regressed on the size of the progeny he obtained what he thought was an inconsistent result. Indeed, he spent much time worrying about this phenomenon, which today every first-year student understands.[20]

Isaac Newton invented differential calculus to express his inverse square law of the theory of gravitation. Francis Galton invented regression theory to express his theory of heredity. However, the comparison is unfair. Newton's mathematical achievement surpassed Galton's statistical achievement. Had Galton refined regression theory along the lines subsequently developed by Pearson, the comparison might have been more apposite. I think this exemplifies what Keynes meant when he said that Galton was a genius but not an intellect, and that he didn't know how to push an idea as far as it needed to go.

Next, Galton turned his attention from sweet peas to the heights of human beings. He collected data on the heights of parents and children for 205 pairs. He was sufficiently aware of what today is called assortative mating. This did not matter for sweet peas, which propagate asexually. But Galton surmised that the stirps of children were influenced by the stirps of both parents. If taller men marry taller women there will be a double dose of tallness in the stirps of their children. Finding no correlation between the heights of husbands and wives, he ruled out assortative mating in his sample. His main result was that regression toward the mean applies to the heights of human beings.[21] The slope of the regression line was 0.66. This means that the children of parents who are 3 inches taller (shorter) than the average parent are expected to be 2 inches taller (shorter) than the average child. In other words, there is regression toward the mean. However, Galton referred to the phenomenon as "regression towards mediocrity" rather than simply "regression towards the mean." Apparently he attached importance to the downward mobility of those above the mean rather than to the upward mobility of those below the mean.

Galton correctly understood that mean reversion implies that genealogy doesn't matter over successive generations: "[T]he further his genealogy goes back, the more numerous and varied will his ancestors become, until they cease to differ from any equally numerous sample taken at haphazard from the race at large. Their mean stature will then be the same as that of the race; in other words, it will be mediocre."[22] To Galton the mean is mediocre and value laden. His later interest in eugenics was motivated by a desire to raise the mean through selective mating.

Chapter 4 of this book contains a detailed discussion of beta convergence and sigma convergence. Galton's mean reversion is beta convergence. If instead there been mean diversion, or regression away from the mean, there would have been beta divergence. This would have happened had Galton discovered that taller parents had even taller children instead of shorter ones. "Sigma convergence" refers to changes in inequality between one generation and the next. Parents have different heights, and children have different heights. If the heights of children are more similar than the heights of their parents, there is sigma convergence. If they are more dissimilar, there is sigma divergence. During the 1990s, even distinguished economists confused beta convergence and sigma convergence. They thought mistakenly that regression toward the mean implies that inequality must decrease over time. What has become known as Galton's Paradox clears up this confusion. Galton understood that the mere fact that there was regression toward the mean in the heights of children did not imply that eventually human beings would be equally tall. He understood that beta convergence was about mobility rather than equality.

Galton also investigated sibling correlations. He correlated the heights of siblings in his sample, and reported his findings in *Natural Inheritance* (1889). Since according to Galton's theory of heredity siblings shared similar stirps, they should be correlated on various outcomes, including height. He found that the correlation was between

0.48 and 0.67. He preferred the latter estimate, which was almost identical to his estimate of the intergenerational correlation coefficient. There is no inherent reason why the sibling and intergenerational correlation coefficients should be the same or even similar. Indeed, the sibling correlation should be at least as large as the square of the intergenerational correlation. Nevertheless, Galton was clearly on the right track in extending his investigation of heredity to siblings, and his work on siblings anticipated many of the developments discussed in this book.

It is important to appreciate that Galton discovered simple regression, i.e., regression between two variables. He did not discover multiple regression; Pearson did that. Therefore, when Galton regressed outcomes of children on outcomes for parents, and ignored the role of grandparents and higher-order ancestors, it was not because he disregarded the importance of higher-order ancestors. It was simply because he didn't know how to do multiple regression. In his sweet pea data he had several generations of seeds, which might have been used in a multiple regression analysis of heredity, but that was beyond his technical capability (and he was aware that it was). One can only speculate whether Galton might have rediscovered Mendel's laws through biometry had he used data on several generations of sweat pea seeds in a multiple regression analysis of heredity.

Not only was Galton a founding father of genetics and behavioral genetics; he was also a founding father of biometrics. He understood that the statistical analysis of heredity might reveal important clues to how genetic patterns are transmitted intergenerationally. In 1901 he was instrumental in launching *Biometrica*. That journal, whose purpose is the advancement of statistical methods in evolutionary biology, remains a leader in its field.

1.2.4 Psychology

Though not for want of trying, Galton is not recognized as a founding father of psychology. But he was a pioneer of psychometric measurement. Alfred Binet, who a century ago invented psychometric testing, paid generous tribute to Galton's efforts. In the 1880s Galton established an anthropometric laboratory, where he collected data on a broad range of phenomena, including weight, height, arm span, lung capacity, strength, reaction time, sight, hearing, and memory. Textbooks on psychology usually begin with Wilhelm Wundt, who is credited with the establishment of the first psychological laboratory in 1879, but don't mention Galton's laboratory.[23] Galton also experimented on himself with word association, introspection, and free association. He published his findings on psychometrics and free association in *Brain* in 1879 and in *Mind* in 1880. Sigmund Freud, a subscriber to *Brain*, referred in his writings to other papers published in the 1879 issues of *Brain*, but not to Galton's paper that dealt with unconscious mental processes. Later Galton summarized these efforts in two books, *Inquiries into Human Faculty and its Development* (1883) and *Record of Family Faculties* (1884). The former also included Galton's results on the effect of prayer. He carried out empirical tests to show that prayer made no difference to human outcomes. In Victorian Britain this claim naturally stirred a great deal of controversy, which might have distracted attention from the book's main message on psychology. A subsequent edition of the book omitted the material on prayer. Nevertheless, this story is a metaphor for Galton's belief in rationalism and empirical inquiry and his political incorrectness.

Diamond (1977) points out that there was a time when psychologists held Galton in high regard. Indeed, James McKeen Cattell, who together with William James founded the Functionalist School of psychology in the United States, had worked in Galton's anthropological laboratory. Galton had a major intellectual influence on Cattell, "who profited from his contact with Galton immeasurably more than from his contact with Wundt, and American psychology profited as a result."[24] In his later years Cattell thought that Galton was "the greatest man he knew." In Diamond's opinion, "Galton's innovative methods for the study of human capacities were accepted as part of psychology, and they helped to give American psychology its distinctive character. It seems unlikely that the same development would have taken place in anything like the same time span without Galton's influence."[25] Other acolytes of Galton included Joseph Jastrow, Lewis Terman, Edward Thorndike, and Edward Titchener.

Why did psychology turn its back on Galton? The answer lies, to some extent, in political and ideological developments that occurred in the twentieth century. In particular, Galton's emphasis of heredity became politically incorrect. Behaviorism, developed by William James in the 1920s, detached psychology from heredity in its egalitarian ideology that all humans are born as *tabulae rasae* with equal potential. Also, Galton became identified with eugenics, which was adopted by Hitler. It did not matter that Galton was interested in positive eugenics—that is, raising high intelligence rather than eliminating low. He was, of course, specifically against negative eugenics, which was concerned with eliminating the less fit. By 1950 Galton had become persona non grata and an embarrassment to the discipline.

1.3   The Disciplines

Let us now turn our attention to the main academic disciplines that are involved in the study of heredity, family, and environments. These include behavioral genetics, psychology, sociology, economics, and genetics, which are the main intellectual stakeholders. We shall see that each of these disciplines has focused rather narrowly on a certain set of issues.

1.3.1   Behavioral Genetics

Behavioral genetics (invented, as we have seen, by Galton) was rather slow to develop. I have noted that Galton did not invent the MZ-DZ twin methodology, which was in fact developed simultaneously in the 1920s in the United States and Germany. Indeed 1924 was a golden year for behavioral genetics: the first twin study and the first adoption study were published in that year. In both cases the outcome of interest was IQ. However, the first textbook on behavioral genetics was not published until 1960. Since then, behavioral genetics has grown exponentially and has achieved a number of scientific successes. It has shown that Huntington's disease, schizophrenia, and autism are genetic. The psychoanalyst Bruno Bettelheim had claimed that autism resulted from "refrigerator mothers" and "iceberg fathers." Behavioral genetics proved him woefully wrong.

Behavioral genetics applies designs developed in twin research and in adoption research to studies of mental illness and of behavioral responses to drugs. It is to be distinguished from genetics itself, whose concerns have included the basic science of heredity, the discovery of the double helix in DNA, and the decoding of the human genome. Whereas genetic research takes place in laboratories where data are generated, behavioral genetics uses data generated naturally through human behavior. The data on twins and adoptees are not generated under laboratory conditions but are generated spontaneously and naturally through the behavior of the twins and the adoptees themselves.

The empirical methodology of behavioral genetics is based on quasi-experimentation. In a real experiment the data are randomized. If one wants to test the hypothesis that some variable X has a causal effect on some outcome Y, control and trial groups are selected randomly. X is administered to the trial subjects but not to the control subjects, and the effect of X on Y is measured by the change in Y in the trial and control groups. (Since ethical and compliance problems preclude treating human beings like rats in an experiment, we have to think of other ways to mimic laboratory conditions.) Quasi-experimentation can serve as a substitute for real experimentation.

One type of quasi-experiment occurs when something happens in life that is almost surely random—for example, the birth of identical (MZ) twins or the birth of fraternal (DZ) twins. Since MZ twins are more genetically similar than DZ twins, the former may be regarded as a trial group and the latter as a control group for purposes of studying the effect of genetics on human outcomes. Whereas in a real experiment the experimenter can completely control for outside noise or disturbances, such as room temperature, the quasi-experimenter cannot do so. In particular, he has no control over numerous environmental factors that might affect the outcome of interest. Since these environmental influences may be extensive, the quasi-experiment is subject to outside contamination. This is the Achilles' heel of behavioral genetics.

A second type of quasi-experiment is based on adoption. Children adopted at birth or shortly after have no control over their adoptee status, nor do children not adopted at birth have any control over their status. Adopted children may be regarded as a control group; their siblings who are the biological children of the adoptive parents may be regarded as a trial group. Adoptees do not share the genes of their siblings, but they belong to the same family. Therefore, differences in the outcomes of mixed pairs of siblings (i.e., adopted and biological siblings) and pairs of biological siblings may be due to genetic differences between them, because the latter are genetically similar whereas the former are not.

For several reasons, quasi-experiments of the second type aren't free from outside contamination. Indeed, they are even less clean than twin quasi-experiments. First, parents cannot choose their biological children, but they can choose their adopted children, so the latter are not selected randomly. Moreover, adopted children have to be given up for adoption by their biological parents, and that is unlikely to be random. Therefore, whereas biological children are random events, adopted children are not. In technical terms, adopted children are *selective samples* rather than random samples. Matters would have been very different if children had been randomly taken away from their parents and forced into adoption. Furthermore, in this quasi-experiment too there is outside interference from the environment, which is an omitted variable that is not under the control of the quasi-experimenter. Parents might treat their biological children differently than their adopted children, or the interaction between biological siblings might differ from that between adopted siblings. Behavioral geneticists are aware of these problems and spend much time discussing them. Textbooks on behavioral genetics normally contain a chapter on environmental effects, but they don't treat these problems seriously, and their concerns are more lip service than expressions of a genuine methodological interest in solving the problems of non-random sampling and omitted-variable bias.

Arthur Goldberger (1997, 1999, 2005) repeatedly pointed out the great methodological irony in the fact that behavioral genetics has relatively little to do with genetics but has almost everything to do with behavior. It is by making very strong assumptions about behavior—including the role of the environment, the reaction of parents to their children, the reaction of children to their parents, the reaction of children to each other, the social choices of both parents and children, and indeed the entire rich spectrum of human interaction and social intercourse—that behavioral genetics identifies heredity. In short, behavioral genetics completely ignores social science and thereby tends to attribute to heredity what might in fact be attributed to environment inside the family and outside it. Just as it would be absurd for social scientists to ignore genetics in the study of heredity, it is equally absurd for behavioral genetics to ignore social sciences such as psychology, sociology and economics in the study of the environment in which children develop. Behavioral genetics has developed its own methodological bubble in which it remains cut off from ancillary disciplines. However, behavioral genetics is not alone in enveloping itself in its own bubble culture.

Behavioral genetics has imposed a methodological straitjacket upon itself by confining itself to data on twins and adoptees and ignoring ordinary parents and children. Twins and adoptees are only a small fraction of the population, and in any case families with adoptees and twins may not be representative of families as a whole. There are also genetic relationships inside ordinary families where the children are neither adopted nor twins. Therefore, behavioral genetics throws away a vast amount of data that might be informative about nature and nurture. I shall argue that this comes about because behavioral genetics insists on the methodology of quasi-experimentation and rules out the methodology of natural experimentation.

A natural experiment occurs when something happens spontaneously to randomize the variable (X) whose hypothesized causal effect on some outcome (Y) is being tested. In a laboratory, X is randomly administered to the control subjects and the trial subjects. In a natural experiment, something happens spontaneously or naturally to randomize X when there is no control over the selection of trial subjects and control subjects—i.e., when the treated, who receive X, and the untreated, who do not receive X, are not randomly assigned. Therefore, a natural experiment mimics a real or laboratory experiment in a way that a quasi-experiment does not. It is crucial that the outside event (Z) that randomizes X has no direct effect on the outcome Y.

An example serves to illustrate the basic idea. Wages and schooling are universally positively correlated. This does not necessarily mean that more schooling causes higher earnings. It might be the case that abler people manage to acquire more schooling because they have greater learning ability and have higher earnings because they have greater earning ability. Therefore, the positive correlation may be induced by a common unobserved factor, ability, which affects both earnings and schooling. In a laboratory experiment, schooling would be administered through random assignment to trial subjects and control subjects, but this is obviously not practicable in human studies.

During the Vietnam War, the US government decided against national conscription and instead drafted young men according to their Social Security numbers and the vicissitudes of the war. A young man with a higher Social Security number was more likely to be drafted. However, college students were exempt. Angrist (1990) showed, not surprisingly, that the probability of an individual's attending college varied directly with his Social Security number. Young men who had higher Social Security numbers, and thus were more likely to be drafted, were more likely to attend college so as to be exempt from conscription. There is no reason to believe that a person's Social Security number is directly related to his ability. Therefore, Social Security numbers serve to randomize college attendance, and thereby make it practicable to test the hypothesis that there is a causal effect of schooling on wages.

I shall have a lot more to say about natural experimentation in chapter 5. Here, two things should be noted. First, natural experiments are more informative about human beings than laboratory experiments. Just imagine what would happen if some people were forced into schooling regardless of whether they wanted it, while others were randomly denied it regardless of whether they needed it. Their behavior would be contaminated by Hawthorne effects (which are discussed in chapter 5). People behave differently under experimental conditions than they do in real life. Second, natural experimentation forms the basis of econometrics—or, if you prefer, econometrics forms the basis of natural experimentation.

In the context of behavioral genetics, natural experimentation would randomize the environment, or it would randomize who is adopted and who isn't adopted. Here the environment includes schooling, social grouping, parenting, sibsize, and indeed all the potentially important phenomena that behavioral genetics lumps together under the rubric "environment." Natural experimentation would also enable behavioral geneticists to use data on ordinary families and not just data on the small minority of families that happen to have twins and adoptees.

1.3.2   Psychology

In 1992, at its centennial conference, the American Psychological Association officially declared genetics to be among the themes that best represent the future of psychology. As might be surmised from psychology's negative attitude toward Galton, this was not a simple matter. Indeed, it is probably doubtful that the APA's declaration applied to developmental psychologists ("developmentalists" for short). Developmental psychology is concerned with the life cycle of human psychological development, from the cradle to the grave. Much of developmentalism is, however, devoted to infant and child development. Neuropsychologists and evolutionary psychologists have no trouble with behavioral genetics, but developmental psychologists do.

Some textbooks on psychology[26] are written in the spirit of the APA's declaration—the treatment of heredity and genetics versus nurture is balanced. However, most of the textbooks treat nature and heredity much more critically than nurture. There is a clear bias in favor of nurture. We are told at length about the methodological limitations of behavioral genetics, in which the results are always "not conclusive," whereas methodological limitations in the study of nurture are scarcely mentioned and the results are characterized as much more conclusive.

Hilgard's Introduction to Psychology serves to illustrate the point. Four "misunderstandings about heritability" are listed.[27] First, "Heritability refers to populations not to individuals. . . . To say that height has a heritability of 90% does not mean that 90% came from your genes and 10% came from your environment." In chapter 4 it is said that these numbers mean in fact that we inherit nearly 0.95 of our parents' height. This confusing comment spreads misunderstanding and is designed to suggest that heredity somehow does not apply to individuals and is weaker than it really is. Second, "Heritability is not a fixed number. . . . If everybody in our society were suddenly given equal educational opportunities, the variance of intellectual performance in the society would decrease." Here it is taken for granted that more equal environments would reduce inequality. This proposition wouldn't be true if intellectual performance was entirely genetic. The same environmental bias arises in the discussion of the third "misunderstanding about heredity": We are told about a "thought experiment" in which there are two bags of seeds, one of which is sown in a fertile field and the other in a field that isn't fertile. In both cases the plants grow to different heights because the seeds in each bag are not genetically identical. However, the average height is larger in the fertile field. The idea here is that, although genetics matters within fields, it does not matter between fields, or that, although IQ scores may vary due to nature within ethnic groups, they vary due to nurture between ethnic groups. This too is an empirical claim that requires investigation. Fourth, "Another incorrect claim about heritability is that a trait with high heritability cannot be changed by a change in the environment . . . between 1946 and 1982 the height of young adult males in Japan increases by 3.3 inches, mainly owing to improved nutrition. . . . In sum, heritability is about variances, not average levels." The untested assumption here is that it is the nutritional environment that matters rather than genetic modification or mutation.

Physics, chemistry, and biology are characterized by dominant paradigms. Indeed, they confirm Kuhn's (1970) theory of scientific revolutions, at least until the dominant paradigm begins to be challenged by new empirical data that it fails to explain. The transition to a new dominant paradigm is often protracted, painful, and confusing. Psychology has no dominant paradigm, not because it happens to be in a transitional phase, but because it never had a dominant paradigm. Miller writes: "There has never been a paradigm that was accepted by the entire field of psychology or even developmental psychology.

Today, there is still a questioning of basic assumptions about development."[28] Another way of putting it is that psychology has been in a
permanent state of transition for 120 years.

As we have seen, behavioral genetics has a dominant paradigm. So,
as we shall see, does economics (the neoclassical paradigm). Marxism,
institutionalism, and other schools of thought have been pushed out of
the discipline by the dominant paradigm. Students of economics, like
students of the natural sciences, don't have to study a variety of competing approaches to the subject. This does not mean that there is no
controversy. However, the protagonists share a common language and
a common intellectual framework in which they debate their disagreements. This applies to the way theory is developed and also to the way
empirical analysis is carried out. The intellectual rules of the game have
been dictated by the dominant paradigm.

Psychology, in contrast, has many schools of thought, including
functionalism, structuralism, behaviorism, cognitive psychology,
social psychology, evolutionary psychology, psychoanalysis, and neu-
ropsychology. These schools of thought coexist, and like old soldiers
they never die. I pity future students of psychology, who will have to
learn about more and more schools of thought as they are developed
during this century. There is a new school of thought about every 25
years. Nor are these schools nested in some broader paradigm. For
example, in the 1950s and the 1960s Keynesian economics and classical economics were rival paradigms. However, it turned out that
Keynesian macroeconomic theory and classical macroeconomic theory
were special cases of the neoclassical paradigm. Patinkin (1966)
showed that the two theories could be synthesized in what was called
the Neoclassical Synthesis. Such a synthesis has not happened in psychology. Even the different branches of psychology lack dominant
paradigms. For example, developmental psychology has the Piagetian
school, the Freudian School, the Jungian School, the Behavioral school,
and others.

I suspect that the failure of a dominant paradigm to emerge in psychology is due either to the fact that most psychological theory isn't
empirically testable or to the fact that the protagonists have beliefs that
they will continue to hold, regardless of the empirical evidence. As an
undergraduate student at the London School of Economics, I attended
a course on "Scientific Method" given by Karl Popper. Popper told us
that his interest in epistemology began when he was an assistant to the
psychoanalyst Alfred Adler.[29] "As for Adler, I was much impressed by

a personal experience. Once, in 1919, I reported to him a case which to me did not seem particularly Adlerian, but which he found no difficulty in analyzing in terms of his theory of inferiority of feelings, although he had not even seen the child. Slightly shocked, I asked him how he could be so sure. 'Because of my thousandfold experience,' he replied; whereupon I could not help saying: 'And with this new case, I suppose, your experience has become a thousand-and-one-fold.'" (Popper 1963, p. 35)

I am also reminded of a joke told by the comedian Jackie Mason. A depressed man goes to a psychologist for help. The psychologist asks him "Did your mother love you as a child?" The patient answers "Yes." "And did your father love you?" "Yes." "And what about your wife and your children?" "They love me too." The psychologist replies "Your problem is too much love."

I know that jokes don't prove anything. Indeed, there are numerous jokes about economics too. However, psychoanalytical theory, be it Freudian, Jungian, or Lacanian, is not empirically falsifiable. The same applies to behaviorism and cognitive psychology. It is this lack of falsifiability that prevents false theories from being discarded. They are metaphysical and should be regarded as sorts of secular religions. A Freudian is no more likely to give up his beliefs in the light of empirical evidence than a Catholic, a Buddhist, or an orthodox Jew. The natural sciences, behavioral genetics, and economics[30] are modernist disciplines. Psychology is very much a post-modernist discipline in which subjectivism and interpretation are all-important.

This means that the psychological study of heredity, family, and society is largely left to the subjective beliefs of the various protagonists. Such is specially the case in developmental psychology. Behavioral psychology maintains an axiomatic belief that we are all born as *tabulae rasae* with the same potential. Heredity doesn't matter. This political correctness has crept into cognitive psychology too. The hypothesis that IQ might have a racial component has led to the vilification of its proponents. To claim that black people are better athletes than whites is not contentious, but to claim that black people may have less cognitive ability is contentious.

Two other branches of psychology are pertinent to our enquiry: social psychology and evolutionary psychology. I have already mentioned that evolutionary psychology has emerged as the standard bearer of human sociobiology. Evolutionary psychologists think that human instincts have developed to increase the fitness of mankind.

This lays the foundation for an axiomatic treatment of psychology. However, evolutionary psychology is marginal to the discipline as a whole.

The same does not apply to social psychology, which is concerned with the two-way relationship between the group and the individual in the group. This covers peer-group effects and neighborhood effects, which constitute environmental influences, and which may induce correlation between siblings and between parents and children. Social psychology is rich in theory, but it is methodologically weak. The main methodological problem is that, because individuals choose their group affiliation, the correlation between the individual and his group is not informative about the effect of the group on the individual. This problem is discussed in depth in chapter 5.

1.3.3 Economics

Historically economics paid little attention to heredity. Nor did it take much of an interest in the family until the work of Gary Becker in the 1970s and the 1980s. Today, textbooks on the economics of the family abound. Those textbooks are concerned with the Quality vs. Quantity Theory of fertility and education, with the allocation of resources within the family, with bequests and savings, and with decisions about work and leisure by spouses and other household members. All these developments fall squarely within the neoclassical paradigm, but none of them are concerned with heredity per se. The Quality vs. Quantity Theory seeks to explain why the outcomes of parents and children are correlated, and why the outcomes of siblings are correlated, but without recourse to heredity. Behrman and Taubman (1976) probably were the first economists to apply the methodologies of behavioral genetics to economic phenomena, and their work prompted other economists to take a greater interest in heredity. Some economists, including Bruce Sacerdote (2007), continue to use behavioral genetics,[31] but most have applied various econometric techniques to the problem under investigation.

The relationship between behavioral genetics and economics may be summed up as follows: Whereas behavioral genetics treats the environment as a nuisance parameter in the identification of the effects of heredity, economics treats heredity as a nuisance parameter in the identification of the effects of environments. A nuisance parameter is a parameter of no direct interest to the investigator whose presence threatens to confound the estimation of the parameters of interest.

Behavior is a nuisance to behavioral geneticists because it threatens to conceal the effects of heredity, especially if behavior and heredity happen to be correlated. Heredity is a nuisance to economists because, though they aren't really interested in heredity, they understand that if they ignore it they may be misled into making false empirical claims about the effect of parenting, peer groups, and other environmental effects. Though economists take heredity seriously as a methodological threat, behavioral geneticists don't take behavior seriously as a methodological threat. Instead, behavioral genetics pays lip service to the specification of the environment, whereas economics is completely devoted to it.

Economists have been mainly, though not exclusively, concerned with the effect of parents on their children's schooling and earnings. This focus has been largely dictated by the scientific agenda set by the Quality vs. Quantity Theory, which is concerned with the interwoven determination of wages, education, and fertility. Indeed, the economics of education and the economics of fertility have become respectable specialties in their own right. In the last 10 years, labor economists in particular have broadened their interest into social phenomena that transcend economics, including the effects of neighborhoods on criminality and social behavior, the effects of smoking by pregnant women on birth weight, and the effect of birth weight on the developmental prospects of children. These developments, which are not manifestations of scientific imperialism, constitute fruitful applications of methodological developments in econometrics.

Labor economists devote much of their time to estimating the causal effect of schooling on wages. Indeed, this was what motivated Angrist's natural experiment. The return to schooling is typically estimated to be about 8 percent, which means that an extra year's schooling increases wages by 8 percent. This return varies by time and place according to conditions in the labor market. However, schooling, experience in the labor market, and other observable phenomena typically explain only about 30 percent of the variance in individual wages. This means that persons with the same observable characteristics in terms of schooling, age, etc. have considerably different wages. In other words, heterogeneity is very large. Economists tend to think that this heterogeneity has to do with individual ability,[32] which is also heterogeneous. Abler persons earn more simply because they have higher productivity thanks to their greater ability. However, ability cannot be directly observed and measured.

In their controversial 1994 book *The Bell Curve*, the psychologists Richard Herrnstein and Charles Murray attach major importance to IQ as a measure of cognitive ability. They use US data to show that almost every socioeconomic outcome depends *inter alia* on the child's IQ and on the parents' socioeconomic background. However, the former is more important than the latter. People with low IQ are more likely to be involved in crime and antisocial behavior; people with high IQ are more likely to be more educated and earn.[33] Most labor economists think that IQ has no effect on wages, or that the effect is small. Therefore, even allowing for IQ, wage heterogeneity remains stubbornly high, and economic achievement has almost nothing to do with cognitive ability as measured by IQ. There might be an indirect effect if persons with more cognitive ability acquire more schooling. However, since schooling explains only a small part of the variance of earnings these indirect effects will be very small too.

It is here that economics and heredity meet. If ability is inherited, maybe we can learn something about ability by taking into consideration the outcomes for parents. If abler parents have more favorable outcomes, it might be possible to proxy ability by conditioning on the outcomes of parents. A related idea is that, since siblings share their parents' genes, ability is likely to be positively correlated between siblings. Therefore, it might be possible to proxy ability by conditioning on the outcome of siblings.

It is largely through the quest for measuring ability that economists have backed into genetics. Another reason has to do with the availability of data on parents, children, and siblings. Until recently there were no matched economic data on parents and children. However, the Panel Study on Income Dynamics (PSID), conducted in the United States in the 1980s, matched wages and schooling for parents and children. Becker and Tomes (1986) note that these data show that the correlation between the earnings of parents and children is very small, of the order of 0.1. This suggests that the United States is the land of opportunity, since the outcomes of children have almost nothing to do with the outcomes of their parents. Each generation is almost an economic tabula rasa. Gary Solon (1992) and David Zimmerman (1992) overturned this result. They showed that, allowing for measurement error and associated attenuation bias, the intergenerational correlation coefficient for earnings is in fact about 0.4. The intergenerational correlation coefficient for schooling, as measured by years of education, was also about 0.4. Therefore, there is considerable intergenerational persistence in the United States. Indeed, as intergenerational data from other countries increasingly became available, it seems that there is less intergenerational mobility in schooling and earnings in the United States than in Europe. This contradicts the popular perception that the Old World is tradition bound and characterized by social immobility, while the New World is free of these shackles.

Although the intergenerational correlation coefficients for earnings and schooling are about 0.4, this means that only approximately 16 percent of the variances in earnings and schooling in the current generation are attributable to the earnings and schooling of parents in the previous generation. Nevertheless, the effect is large enough to become a focus of research attention. Not surprisingly, economists began to ask whether this correlation is induced by nature, by nurture, or by both. Specifically, economists are interested in the causal effect of the income of parents on the economic prospects of their children. Better-off parents are able to buy their children more and better education, which will increase their earning capacity. If this is true, the intergenerational transmission of economic inequality may be reduced by subsidizing less well-off families to help them educate their children.

The literature on the economics of inequality is very large. As we have just seen, economists have been concerned with the intergenerational transmission of inequality. However, in contrast to sociologists, surprisingly few economists have been concerned with the role of the family in propagating inequality intragenerationally. Exceptions include Eytan Sheshinski and Yoram Weiss (1982), who explore the implications of the Quality vs. Quantity Theory for the allocation of parents' resources between children. The Quality vs. Quantity Theory predicts that parents prefer to invest in the schooling of their brighter children because the return to investment varies directly with ability. As a result, inequality is increased because not only do abler children earn more because they are more able; they earn more because they have more human capital than their less able siblings. Matters will be different if parents care about inequality. Parents might practice reverse discrimination by investing more in their less able children to compensate for their lower ability.

1.3.4 Sociology

Sociology studies all aspects of society. Since the family is perhaps the most important of social institutions, it receives a great deal of attention. The same applies to the roles of schooling, neighborhoods, and culture (or environments, as I refer to them collectively here). There-fore, sociology is also an intellectual stakeholder. On the whole, sociol-ogy tends to be more eclectic and descriptive than the other disciplines. For example, in the study of the family, sociologists draw on psychol-ogy, behavioral genetics, and economics. From this point of view, soci-ology is the most interdisciplinary of the disciplines under review. On the other hand, it has contributed relatively little to the theoretical discourse concerning the causes of intergenerational and intragenera-tional correlations.

Not only has sociology been interdisciplinary and eclectic with respect to theory, it has also been interdisciplinary and eclectic with respect to empirical methodology. Empirical sociologists have drawn extensively on ideas developed by econometricians in the sphere of natural experimentation and the exploitation of longitudinal data. A number of sociologists have made important contributions to empirical knowledge concerning the effect of birth order and sibship on the out-comes of children, as well as the effects of low birth weight on these outcomes.

Criminologists too are intellectual stakeholders in the study of heredity and family. Criminal behavior is intergenerationally corre-lated, and there is a family dimension to criminality. Indeed, criminolo-gists have expended much effort on establishing this empirically. However, interpreting this phenomenon is difficult. The standard view in criminology is that the relationship is causal—the family is to blame. On the other hand, sociologists such as Robert Putnam attach more importance to social culture and the environment—society is to blame. Despite the vast amount of empirical study of these issues, there has been no serious research on this issue. Much of what passes for scien-tific research amounts to little more than advocacy for one theory or another. Some high-quality research has sought to identify the roles of family, genes, and environments. However, that research was not undertaken by criminologists or sociologists, but by labor economists.

1.3.5   Molecular Genetics

Since 2003, when the Human Genome Project was completed, molecu-lar geneticists have been trying to discover the genes responsible for a large variety of medical diseases. At first there was great optimism that genome-wide association studies would reveal the genetic origins of medical afflictions and would pave the way to genetically engineered treatments. Indeed, prestigious journals in genetics soon published articles claiming that the genes causing various afflictions had been discovered.

By 2010, that early optimism had waned. It turned out that what seemed at first to be major breakthroughs were not replicated when different data sets were used. Discoveries obtained using US data were not replicated with European data, and vice versa. Most if not all discoveries turned out to be false positives. In chapters 7 and 10 I argue that the methodology of genome-wide associations studies is inherently biased in favor of discovering false positives. Indeed, this methodology data-mines the human genome and the genetic markers (up to a million of them) used to map it. Since the number of human observations is typically several thousand, and is vastly exceeded by the number of genetic markers, it is inevitable that false positives will be frequent. Indeed, that could have been predicted in 2003.

What does molecular genetics have to do with our present study? Sets of socioeconomic data will soon become available that will include—in addition to individual data on schooling, earnings, deviancy, and IQ—molecular data. It will therefore be possible to carry out genome-wide association studies in which the human outcomes are social (schooling, IQ, etc.) rather than medical. Indeed, the authors of a study published in 2011 in *Molecular Psychiatry* claim to have discovered the genes for IQ. I discuss this study further in chapter 7, where I mention an earlier "discovery" of the genes for antisocial behavior that failed to replicate in other data. I also mention another false positive regarding the "discovery" of the genes for schooling.

Whereas behavioral genetics attempts to identify genetic causes of socioeconomic behavior when genotypes are not observed, molecular genetics does the same thing using observed genotypes. It sounds, therefore, as if molecular geneticists should have an easier task in identifying the genetic causes of human behavior than behavioral geneticists. However, that is not the case, for two main reasons. First, the human genome contains as many as 3 billion nucleotide base pairs, which are sampled through genetic mapping into the order of a million genetic markers. Although the sample is much smaller than the population, the number of markers vastly exceeds the number of human observations, which is typically about 10,000. Large though it may be, this is still not sufficient to carry out hypothesis testing. Second, the theory of genetics is underdeveloped; it does not predict which genes matter for which diseases. Without theory, it is not possible to test hypotheses, especially when the observations are vastly outnumbered by the number of genetic markers. Gold and oil prospectors use geological theory to direct them where to search. Their job would be impossible without the theory. Indeed, they probably would not prospect at all. Gene prospectors blindly comb the human genome without any theory to guide them, in the hope that they will make a lucky strike.

Molecular genetics is about to become a new and probably a major intellectual stakeholder in the study of heredity, family, and inequality. Indeed, we are on the verge of a major methodological revolution in the social sciences. Apart from replication failure, the handful of molecular studies in the social sciences show, as do their medical counterparts, that the proportion of phenotypic variance explained by genetics is small. Also, molecular genetics in the social sciences is more complicated than molecular genetics in medicine because environmental causes might be falsely attributed to genetics. For example, Crohn's disease is probably less susceptible to behavioral and social influences than is schooling or deviancy. Therefore, the disappointment with genome-wide association studies is likely to be even greater in the social sciences than in the medical sciences.

1.4   Issues

1.4.1   Nature vs. Nurture

The nature-vs.-nurture debate in developmental psychology became particularly acrimonious in 1998 after the publication of *The Nurture Assumption* by Judith Rich Harris. Much of Harris' next book, *What Makes Us Different?* (published in 2006) was devoted to her responses to her numerous critics. It is clear that people in general, not just developmental psychologists, are naturally fascinated by this debate. The very idea that heredity might be partially responsible for our behavior and achievement and not just for our physical features is apparently anathema to some. In *What Makes Us Different?* Harris relates, in a chapter titled "Monkey Business," how a leading developmental psychologist referred to experiments that apparently did not take place. The would-be experiment was to have forced adoption on monkeys. The offspring of aggressive monkeys were to be raised by passive monkeys, and vice versa. The putative result of the experiment was to show that the adopted monkeys raised by the aggressive parents were more aggressive than the adopted monkeys raised by the passive monkeys. This would have established that nurture matters and not nature, at least for monkeys.

Since Harris apparently wasn't asked to apologize by the leading psychologist in question, it must be assumed that either that the monkey experiment didn't take place or that, if it did, the results didn't establish that nurture matters rather than nature. The point of this story is not to take sides in the debate, but simply to show how politically loaded these issues are. Political correctness arises more forcefully and even violently if it is suggested that there might be racial differences in cognitive ability. Herrnstein and Murray (1994) recall the scientific denigration of the educational psychologist Arthur Jensen, who suggested in 1969 that the IQs of blacks in the United States were substantially below those of whites.[34] Herrnstein and Murray themselves became scientific pariahs for concluding, in regard to black-white differences in IQ, "It seems likely to us that both genes and the environment have something to do with racial differences. What might the mix be? We are resolutely agnostic on the issue; as far as we can determine, the evidence does not justify an estimate." (1994, p. 311)

Whereas Herrnstein and Murray compared different groups of the population in the United States, Lynn and Vanhanen (2002) compared different countries. They argue that there is a strong positive correlation between IQ and economic development. Unlike Herrnstein and Murray, Lynn and Vanhanen do not pull their punches. They claim that poor countries are poor because average mental ability is lower, and rich countries are rich because mental ability is higher. They rebut the criticism that international comparisons of IQ tests are meaningless owing to cultural differences, and argue that IQ has a strong genetic component. Indeed, they quote some of the results reported in chapter 2 of the present volume, which show that the IQs of identical twins are more correlated than the IQs of fraternal twins, which suggests that IQ is genetic. The economic backwardness of Africa is therefore explained in part by the fact that IQ in Africa is relatively low.

James Watson, the co-discoverer of DNA, was forced to relinquish the directorship of the Cold Spring Harbor Laboratory, after nearly 40 years, for suggesting that Africa's lagging economic development might have something to do with intelligence. For some reason, Lynn and Vanhanen have not attracted the attention of the politically correct. Perhaps it is because they are not Americans. Lynn is from Northern Ireland and Vanhanen is from Finland. One wonders: Had Wilson, Herrnstein, Murray, and Harris not been Americans, would they have attracted so much backlash from the politically correct? Perhaps their behavior is peculiarly specific to American academia.

1.4.2 Families Propagate Inequality and Diversity?

If the outcomes of children depend on the outcomes of their parents, inequality is transmitted from one generation to the next. This transmission mechanism is reinforced by assortative mating, which increases the average fitness of fitter parents and reduces the average fitness of less fit parents. Another mechanism through which the family induces inequality is sibling interaction. If siblings affect one another, inequality will be enhanced. The extent to which this happens varies directly with the number of siblings, since scope for interaction varies directly with sibship. Therefore, with everything else equal, a society with larger families will experience more inequality than a society in which fertility is lower. There would be more equality if conception was sexless, as in the case of Galton's sweet peas, because there would be no assortative mating. There would be even more equality if conception was immaculate so that children did not need parents to be born. There would be maximum equality if children could be born without parents and have no siblings!

Inequality is further enhanced if parents react to their children's ability by engaging in what in chapter 3 I call *endogenous parenting*, which in behavioral genetics is called the "genetic-environment correlation." This simply means that parents try to help their children according to their needs. Since normal parents behave this way, endogenous parenting increases inequality. In short, Dalton Conley (2004) was right in saying that inequality starts in the family.

The public interest in inequality is manifestly large. Inequality is regarded as a bad thing by many people, but not by everybody. Rawlsian justice doesn't prize egalitarianism. Nor do Hayek's or Nozick's concepts of social justice.[35] The point of my concern with the relationship between family and inequality, especially economic inequality, is simply to shed some new light on this overlooked source of inequality in society. Since we are all born different, there is natural inequality in society, and it is enhanced by the fact that we live in families.

"Inequality" is a loaded word, especially for egalitarians. A less loaded term for the same phenomenon is "diversity." Human beings, like fauna and flora, are inherently diverse. We are all different. We are diverse physically, emotionally, intellectually, in sports, in tastes, in social behavior, indeed in every aspect of life. Egalitarians do not care about inequality in height or temperament, but they care about economic inequality. Rather than use "inequality" when referring to economic diversity and "diversity" when referring to other forms of human inequality, I use "inequality" throughout.

1.4.3 Public Policy

If human outcomes are entirely determined by heredity or nature, policy interventions that are designed to change these outcomes are bound to fail. Is it possible, for example, to make society more nearly equal by helping poorer parents educate their children? More generally, is it possible to offset the forces of heredity by policy interventions that cut the link between the outcomes of parents and the outcomes of their children? The latter question is related to the former. There are many egalitarians who seek to create an artificially level playing field by preventing the fortunes and misfortunes of one generation from affecting the outcomes of the next. Inheritance taxes and death duties, for example, are motivated by such egalitarianism.

1.5 The Chapters Ahead

Chapters 1–7 are essentially narratives discussing various aspects of heredity, family, and inequality. Chapters 8–10 contain essential technical material; however, they are self-contained and may be read independently. I hope that technically minded readers will benefit from the material in chapters 8–10 just as much as general readers will benefit from the material in chapters 1–7. Chapters 1–7 are almost completely free of mathematics and accessible to all, but they do contain some technical material, which I do my best to explain.

Chapter 2 sets the empirical scene by presenting a comprehensive survey of intergenerational and sibling correlations for a broad range of outcomes. These outcomes are demographic (fertility, birth weight, longevity), cognitive (IQ, education), economic (earnings, wealth, consumption), physical (weight, height, health), behavioral (bad habits, deviancy, religiosity), and personal (personality). Chapter 2 shows that there seems to be no sphere of life in which the outcomes of parents and children, or the outcomes of siblings, are not correlated.

Where appropriate, chapter 2 distinguishes between short-term and long-term correlations, or between temporary and permanent correlations. This issue does not arise in the case of height (which doesn't depend on when it is measured), but it does arise in the case of weight (which depends on when it is measured). Weight fluctuates; height does not. The inherent variability of weight induces attenuation bias, which makes correlations involving weight look smaller than they really are. Attenuation bias also arises in the case of income, because income fluctuates, but it does not arise in the case of years of schooling.

Chapter 2 introduces the concept of "beta," which measures mean reversion in Galton's sense and which is related to the intergenerational correlation coefficient. No attempt is made in chapter 2 to interpret intergenerational and sibling correlations. Since correlations are not generally informative about causality, they are silent about the roles of nature and nurture and about the effects of parenting and environments. Nevertheless, as we shall see, this has not stopped some social scientists from interpreting their correlations as supporting one theory or another.

Chapter 3 is devoted to various theories that purport to explain why the outcomes of parents and children are correlated, and why the outcomes of siblings are correlated. The main ideas behind behavioral genetics are introduced and discussed critically. These include the decomposition of the variance of outcomes (to which behavioral genetics refers as *phenotype variance*) into the contribution of heredity (genotype variance), the contribution of shared and unshared environments, and the interaction between genes and environment. Chapter 3 also discusses the two methodological workhorses of behavioral genetics. The first involves the comparison between the outcomes of identical and fraternal twins. Because the former are genetically identical and the latter or not, behavioral geneticists maintain that the difference between sibling correlations for identical and fraternal twins is informative of the role of heredity. The second methodological workhorse involves comparing the outcomes of biological and adopted children. Since biological children share their parents' genes whereas adopted children do not, behavioral geneticists believe that the difference between the sibling correlation for biological children and adopted children is informative of the role of heredity and parenting.

One of the themes of chapter 3 is the need for axiomatic theory, which is based on a small number of axioms. However, this theory must be falsifiable, for otherwise it cannot be tested empirically. Axiomatic theory is not judged by the empirical validity of its axioms, but by its ability to predict. Chapter 3 makes the point that psychology in general and developmental psychology in particular are inherently non-axiomatic. This makes hypothesis testing in developmental psychology too difficult (or too easy), since it is not clear what would constitute falsifying evidence. (Recall Jackie Mason's joke.) By default, theory in psychology degenerates into *ex post* interpretation of events rather than *ex ante* prediction of falsifiable events. (Recall Karl Popper's criticism of Adler.)

In contrast, economic theory in general and the Quality vs. Quantity Theory in particular are axiomatic. A handful of axioms about rationality and preferences is used to develop falsifiable theory about the relationship between fertility and investments in children. This theory explains why the outcomes of parents and children might be correlated, and why the outcomes of siblings might be correlated. Chapter 3 therefore recalls the main features of the Quality vs. Quantity Theory.

The Quality vs. Quantity Theory is also a theory about the gene-environment correlation of behavioral genetics. For example, the Quality vs. Quantity Theory predicts that parents will invest more in the education of their abler children than in that of their less able children. The gene-environment correlation is positive because schooling and ability are positively related. Behavioral geneticists refer to this phenomenon as "the nature of nurture," since schooling, which is part of "nurture," is ultimately dependent on "nature" through the genotype for learning. If ability is inherited, behavioral genetics would claim schooling to be due to nature rather than nurture. Therefore, the nature of nurture induced by the gene-environment correlation attributes to nature what is ostensibly nurture. This petty-minded attribution aggrandizing nature at nurture's expense is not enlightening. What is enlightening is the structural way in which the Quality vs. Quantity Theory predicts that, with everything else equal, parents invest more in the education of their abler children.

I conclude chapter 3 by showing how developmental psychology theory might be axiomatized. In particular, I refer to the paper, mentioned above, that was vilified by the editor of one of the developmental psychology journals but fortunately was welcomed by a more broad-minded editor. Based on a few axioms, this paper develops a theory of parenting that provides the basis of a theory of child development. The idiom is, of course, completely different from that used in informal theories of child development, but it has something in common with evolutionary psychology and its emphasis on parental-investment theory. I also note that recently other axiomatic theories of parenting have begun to appear in the literature of economics rather than in that of developmental psychology.

As I have mentioned, intergenerational correlations imply that inequality or diversity is transmitted from one generation to the next, and sibling correlations imply that inequality is also transmitted within generations and not just between them. Therefore, inequality has both intergenerational and intragenerational features. Chapter 4 is devoted to the relationship between intergenerational and intragenerational inequality. If inequality is measured by the variance or standard deviation, the dynamics of inequality are usefully summarized by the relationship between "beta convergence" and "sigma convergence." The former is related to the concept of absolute mobility; the latter is related to the concept of horizontal inequality (measured in a given generation). The relationship between horizontal and vertical inequality (measured over generations) is elucidated in terms of the relationship between conditional and unconditional inequality. The former refers to inequality in the present generation given inequality in the previous generation; the latter refers to average inequality over all generations.

Apart from the standard deviation, inequality or diversity may be measured in a variety of ways, which are reviewed in chapter 4. A particularly fruitful way of measuring inequality is the Gini coefficient, which is explained. One of the advantages of the Gini coefficient is that it distinguishes between absolute mobility and relative mobility. In the case of height, for example, "absolute mobility" refers to the physical change in height between parents and children, whereas "relative mobility" refers to the change in the position of parents in their generation's distribution relative to the position of their children in their respective distribution. Upward absolute mobility may coexist with downward relative mobility.

Issues concerned with empirical methodology and hypothesis testing are discussed in chapter 5. The main problem is that data on parents, children, and siblings are observational, which makes it difficult to test various hypotheses discussed in chapter 3. At the heart of this problem is the absence of data on genotypes, which means that ability, personality type, and susceptibility are not observable. Generally speaking, if these unobservable phenomena are correlated with observable covariates, their estimated effects on the outcome of interest will be biased. In the language of econometrics, they are not identified. The identification problem arises not only because variables are unobservable but also because the outcome of interest is simultaneously related to another. For example, in studies of the effect of mothering on infants' crying, the behavior of the mothers is jointly determined with the crying of their infants. Therefore, mothering is not an independent variable, as age or height is.

Several methodological solutions have been proposed to solve this identification problem. These are reviewed in chapter 5. One proposed solution entails using longitudinal data, which in the present context means data on successive generations. This solution is not feasible, because the dynastic data that are required are not available. Indeed, even sets of data on parents and children for one generation are scarce. Matters are different, however, if there are several phenotypes but only one genotype, in which case the methodology of longitudinal data may be applied to observations on parents and children for one generation. Other methodologies include natural experimentation and instrumental-variables estimation, quasi-experimentation, and the generated-regressor methodology.

Specific identification problems arise when, for one reason or another, the sample is not random. For example, adopted children are unlikely to be a random sample of children as a whole. Specific identification problems also arise when individuals happen to be members of a peer group. Social psychologists, among others, are interested in identifying peer-group effects, in which the individual's behavior is affected by the behavior of the group as whole. However, individuals choose their group affiliations, so how can we take account of the fact that individuals behave like other members of their group when that is why they chose the group in the first place? Answers to these questions may be found in chapter 5.

Chapter 6 reviews empirical knowledge of what causes the outcomes of parents and children to be correlated, and of what causes the outcomes of siblings to be correlated. Theories regarding these causes are reviewed in chapter 3. What do we know about these causes? How much is nurture and how much is nature? And how much is the nature of nurture induced by the gene-environment correlation? Also, how much can be attributed to neighborhood and peer-group effects? In short, this chapter covers what we have all been waiting for. It should be the pinnacle of our study.

It is inherently easier to collect data and theorize than to test hypotheses, especially when the data are observational. Therefore, we should not be surprised that there isn't a great amount of empirical knowledge of the causes of intergenerational and sibling correlations. In fact the amount of such knowledge is quite modest. One reason for this is the scarcity of good data, especially data that enables identification through natural experimentation. A second reason is the sheer difficulty of undertaking high-quality empirical work in this area. In fact, we shall see in chapter 6 that there is much low-quality empirical work, especially in developmental psychology and behavioral genetics.

Nevertheless, there has been serious empirical work on the identification of neighborhood and peer-group effects, as well as the effects of parenting on the outcomes of children. These fascinating results are reviewed in chapter 6. Therefore, it is easier to say what we don't know, which is a lot, than what we know, which is little. Indeed, most of the outcomes or phenotypes mentioned in chapter 2 have not been properly researched. Chapter 6 therefore looks at the cup that is half full (or less). But it is also critical of what passes for science in some disciplines.

Chapter 7 completes the narrative part of the book by trying to answer the question "Where do we go from here?" I critically assess the likely contribution to social science of genome-wide association studies (GWAS), which have been popularized in medicine since the completion of the Human Genome Project in 2003. Medical scientists have been searching the human genome for genes associated with diseases that are suspected of having a genetic basis. In the next few years, socioeconomic survey data containing genetic markers obtained from respondents' DNA will become available. It will therefore be possible to use GWAS to search for genes associated with schooling, criminality, marital stability, earnings, and a range of socioeconomic phenomena. I have already mentioned that much of the scientific debate about the roles of nature and nurture stems from the fact that genetic endowments are not directly observable. Therefore, on the face of it, the extension of GWAS to the social sciences sounds like a major breakthrough.

But it isn't. I argue that, on the whole, genome-wide association studies have not led to major breakthroughs in medicine. Since the number of genetic markers (currently typically a million) vastly exceeds the number of observations (typically 20,000), searching the data for active markers accumulates type II errors and thereby increases the risk of finding false positives. In fact, claims by GWAS scientists that they have discovered the genes for various phenomena have typically not been replicated in other data. These claims have turned out to be false positives, as the theory of data mining predicts. There are exceptions to this, such as in the cases of diabetes 2 and Crohn's disease, but these should be regarded as lucky strikes rather than as evidence that genome-wide association studies work systematically. The hope was that if we let the data speak for themselves the actives genes would reveal themselves. But this is not how science progresses. The problem is that genome-wide association studies are based on induction, whereas successful science is based on deduction, as David Hume established. Gold diggers do not dig randomly; they use geological theory to direct them where to dig. Gene diggers are in urgent need of genetic theory to direct them where to dig. However, this theory is lacking.

Genome-wide association studies are likely to be even less successful in the social sciences than they are in medicine, because socioeconomic outcomes such as crime and economic success are probably more complex phenomena than Crohn's disease and diabetes. No doubt, as soon as the new genetic data become available, a wave of futile research will hit the social sciences, with all sorts of false claims about the genes responsible for an entire range of socioeconomic phenomena. Indeed, that has already begun.

Chapter 8, the first of the technical chapters, is devoted to statistical concepts that are used elsewhere in the book, especially in chapter 4. It is a self-contained chapter which may be read in its own right provided the reader has sufficient knowledge of mathematical statistics. Since genotypes are inherently random, a statistical or stochastic framework is required for investigating the relationship between phenotypes and genotypes. To that end, a simple data-generating process is proposed in which the phenotype of children depends on their genotype as well as the phenotype of their parents. This part of the data-generating process is a first-order autoregressive model. The autoregressive coefficient is, in fact, Galton's "beta," which expresses the causal effect of parents on their children's outcome. In the second part of the data-generating process, heredity is modeled by assuming that the genotype of children depends on their parents' genotypes and on a random draw from the gene pool. This part too is a first-order autoregressive model in which the autoregressive coefficient has a genetic interpretation. The data-generating process therefore comprises two related first-order autoregressive processes, which I refer to as the AR^2 *model*. If, in addition, the environments of children are correlated with their parents' environments (in terms of culture, religion, geography, professions, and so on), the AR^2 model becomes an AR^3 model.

The AR^2 and AR^3 models are used to solve for the transmission of inequality between generations. They form the basis for defining the concepts of beta and sigma convergence and for understanding the concepts of conditional and unconditional inequality. In the basic AR^2 model, parents don't mate assortatively, siblings don't interact with each other, birth order doesn't matter, and the model is homogeneous (the autoregressive parameters are the same for all children). Subsequently these assumptions are relaxed one at a time. The basic AR^2 model is a first-order model, since only parents matter for children. It is extended to the second-order case, in which grandparents also matter.

In the AR^2 model, there is only one phenotype. In a further extension, multiple phenotypes are assumed and comorbidity between them is modeled. A decomposition formula is obtained in which the intergenerational correlation for one phenotype is related to other phenotypes. For example, the intergenerational correlation coefficient for earnings is decomposed into the intergenerational correlation for schooling, since earnings depend on schooling. A decomposition formula involving the sibling correlation coefficient and the intergenerational correlation coefficient is also obtained.

The AR^2 and AR^3 models measure inequality by the variance or standard deviation. Chapter 8 concludes with a discussion of other metrics for measuring inequality. A particularly attractive and popular metric is the Gini coefficient, which attaches importance to the rank of phenotypes in their distribution and not just to the value of the phenotype itself. This gives rise to a richer framework for measuring intergenerational mobility. A decomposition formula is presented in which Galton's beta depends on relative mobility between generations, on the change in inequality as measured by Gini between generations, and on the growth of the phenotype between generations. Finally, Gini measures of mobility are compared with other measures, including Spearman's rank correlation and Bartholomew's mobility metric.

Chapter 9 requires knowledge of differential calculus and optimization theory and some elementary knowledge of game theory. The foundations of parenting theory may be found in the Quality vs. Quantity Theory. Therefore, in sections 9.2 and 9.3 the Quality vs. Quantity Theory is presented more formally than in chapter 3. At first parents are assumed not to discriminate between their children even if, as shown, discrimination is efficient. Subsequently parents discriminate by, for example, investing more in the education of their abler children.

In a further development, which is related to Becker's Rotten Kid Theorem, children react to discrimination by their parents.

Chapter 9 also extends the ideas behind the Quality vs. Quantity Theory to parenting in general and develops the axiomatic theory of parenting that is presented informally in chapter 3. Parents want their children to be happy because they are instinctively altruistic. A simple model is proposed in which children's happiness depends on parental attention. At first children are assumed to be passive, so parents decide how much attention they receive. Parents trade off time spent on their children with adult time. Subsequently, children are not assumed to be passive. They instinctively understand that their parents care for them, which they exploit. An asymmetric game is implied because children, especially infants, aren't altruistic toward their parents, but their parents are altruistic toward them. I refer to this game as the *Heartstrings Game* or the *Crying Game*.

The Heartstrings Game is extended to sibling rivalry and favoritism by parents. Finally, it is assumed that happier children develop more healthily. On the other hand, over-indulgent parents can spoil their children. This gives rise to a theory of child development in which parents trade off parenting today with parenting in the future. Parents have an enlightened self-interest in promoting the development of their children because more developed children are less demanding and less time consuming. They are also more rewarding. Therefore, parents have to take account of the future in the Heartstrings Game; their current actions are not independent of the future consequences of these actions for the development of their children. Not surprisingly, dynamic optimization theory is required to solve for optimal parenting over time.

Empirical methodology is discussed in chapter 10. That chapter begins with an analysis of attenuation bias induced by measurement error or data fluctuation. Next, it shows that the empirical estimates of the AR^2 model introduced in chapter 8 are generally biased and inconsistent. Various solutions to this problem are reviewed. The remainder of chapter 10 forms the basis of much of chapter 5. The identification problem arises mainly because genotypes are not observable. However, even if genotypes were perfectly observed there might still be an identification problem in observational data because genotypes and outcomes, such as wages and schooling or mothering and infant distress, are jointly determined.

Various solutions to the identification problem are reviewed. These solutions, long since featured in textbooks on econometrics, are quite standard. The main purpose of chapter 10 is to communicate these solutions to readers who are not aware of econometrics. The first of these solutions exploits panel data, if they exist. Panel data are synonymous with longitudinal data in which the same individuals or observation units are observed repeatedly. For example, siblings and parents may be observed repeatedly, as was done in the PSID. In principle, panel data exist for generations of the same family (great-grandchildren, grandchildren, children, parents, grandparents, great-grandparents). In practice such dynastic data are not available. Nevertheless, chapter 10 shows how, if such data were available, family-specific effects that would express unobserved family genotypes could be estimated.

In the absence of dynastic data there are a number of methodologies that may be used to solve the identification problem. The most important of these is the instrumental-variables estimator, which is based on the principle of natural experimentation. Closely related to natural experimentation is quasi-experimentation. A related solution is the generated-regressor methodology. These methodologies are compared and contrasted in chapter 10.

The identification problem is a monster with many heads and manifests in different ways. The so-called selection problem, in which the sample may not be random, is a special manifestation of this problem. For example, adopted children are put up for adoption by their parents and are unlikely to be randomly selected from the population of children. The so-called reflection problem, in which peer groups and neighborhoods are not randomly assigned, is another manifestation of the identification problem.

Not all identification problems have solutions. When one doesn't have a solution, the alternative to doing nothing or (worse still) ignoring the identification problem altogether is to appeal to "partial identification." Identified parameters (for example, beta estimated to be 0.6) are unambiguous. Partially identified parameters are ambiguous. Partial identification typically bounds parameter estimates between an upper and lower value—for example, beta is between 0.2 and 0.8. This ambiguity may be greater or smaller, depending on what information is available. It is shown in chapter 10 that in the worst possible scenario, where there are no instrumental variables at all, the data are still informative. This means that the intergenerational correlation coefficient alone bounds the causal effect of parents on the outcomes of their children. Partial identification is better than no identification at all. It is certainly better than pretending that identification exists when it doesn't.

Chapter 10 includes a methodological critique of behavioral genetics. The equal-environments assumption (EEA) plays a central methodological role in behavioral genetics. It stipulates, for example, that parents treat their adopted children as they treat their biological children, and that they treat their identical-twin children as they treat their fraternal-twin children. It also stipulates that identical twins relate to one another as fraternal twins do, and that adopted siblings relate to one another as biological siblings do. What if the EEA is wrong? How sensitive is the estimation of the role of heredity in behavioral genetics to infringements of the EEA? It is shown that the estimates of heredity in behavioral genetics are sensitive to these infringements. Indeed, a positive effect of heredity might be estimated when there is no effect at all. Worse still, a positive effect may be estimated when the true hereditary effect is negative. In short, behavioral genetics fails to identify the role of heredity in the correlation between siblings.

Chapter 10 concludes with a methodological critique of genome-wide association studies, now used in medical science and soon to be used in social science. The main focus is on the loss of statistical power in data mining, especially when the number of genes vastly exceeds the number of observations. Also noting that genome-wide association studies typically search the human genome one gene at a time, I show that such studies run the risk of missing active genes (false negatives) as well as the risk of identifying false positives.

2 Correlation within the Family

There are two main types of correlation within the family: the intergenerational correlation between parents and children and the intragenerational correlation between siblings. These correlations are obviously related, because siblings have common parents, common genes, and common environments. The relationship between the intergenerational and intragenerational correlation coefficient is discussed in detail in chapter 3. Here, note that if sibling outcomes are correlated only because siblings happen to have common parents, the sibling correlation should be equal to the square of the intergenerational correlation coefficient. Since, as we shall see, sibling correlations tend to be larger than the square of the intergenerational correlations, sibling outcomes aren't correlated merely because the parents are shared.

This chapter shows that the outcomes of parents and children are correlated for a broad range of phenomena. What Galton discovered for the heights of parents and children applies not only to anthropometric outcomes but also to economic, social, demographic, behavioral, and psychological outcomes. Indeed, intergenerational correlation seems to be an almost universal and pervasive phenomenon, touching every aspect of life. It is hard to find an outcome or a population in which the outcomes of parents and children are uncorrelated. The same applies to siblings.

This chapter serves to set the empirical scene for the book (which would have no purpose if intergenerational and sibling correlations were 0). In it I cite examples from the large empirical literature on sibling and intergenerational correlations. I do not pretend to be comprehensive. Breadth is more important to me than depth. My main purpose is to show how pervasive these correlations are in terms of the variety of phenomena for which the outcomes of parents, children, and siblings are correlated.

As statistics go, matched data between parents and children and between siblings are relatively rare. They are rare because matching requires effort and expense. In contrast, unmatched data on parents and children are plentiful. Matching requires establishing that individual A is the child or the sibling of individual B. In the case of survey data, this requires collecting data on parents and children or on siblings at the same time or in some coordinated way. It is obviously more difficult to do this than to survey individuals separately. In the case of data obtained from administrative records, a way must be found to match an individual in one data file with his parents or siblings in another. Typically, such matching isn't feasible, because family relationships between individuals in different data files are generally unknown.

Because matched data are rare, their coverage is haphazard both in terms of topic and in terms of country. It will not be surprising that the United States is over-represented in the data, or that most countries aren't covered at all. Furthermore, many topics or outcomes aren't covered, while earnings and schooling are over-represented. It is, of course, not possible to know whether the available matched data are representative of the population as a whole. If IQ is intergenerationally correlated in one country for which data happen to be available, does this mean that it will be intergenerationally correlated universally?

Two main types of samples are covered. For the most part, the correlations are derived from samples of parents, children, and siblings in which no account is taken of whether the children are biological or adopted or whether the siblings are fraternal or identical twins. Since adoption and identical-twin births account for only a small fraction of the population, it is unlikely that their presence will significantly affect these correlations. The sample sizes used to calculate these correlations tend to be relatively large, occasionally running into the hundreds of thousands. Secondly, I include correlations for twins, which have mainly but not exclusively been calculated by behavioral geneticists. In these cases the sample sizes tend to be relatively small because they require data on identical and fraternal twins. I also include correlations involving adopted children either between biological and adopted siblings or between adoptive parents and adopted children.

It is sad to have to warn that scientific results reported in the published literature may not be representative of scholarship as a whole. There is a danger (discussed further in chapter 6) of publication bias, since editors of scientific journals prefer to publish "positive" results rather than "negative" ones. If there is publication bias, a paper reporting correlated outcomes within the family stands a greater chance of publication than one that reports that family outcomes are uncorrelated. It is naturally difficult to quantify publication bias or even to establish its existence, because this requires data on the papers that editors have rejected. It also requires data on research that wasn't even submitted for publication because the authors believe that editors will reject it for lack of public interest. If the same syndrome applies to family correlations, it is not impossible that the "scientific" literature creates an exaggerated impression regarding the strength of family correlations.

2.1   Methodology

2.1.1   Correlation and Mean Reversion

Chapter 4 provides a detailed discussion of the relationship between Galton's intergenerational mean reversion coefficient (conventionally known as "beta") and the intergenerational correlation coefficient. As we shall see, some studies report results in terms of beta and others report them in terms of the coefficient of correlation. Therefore, it is necessary as a preliminary to define these and related statistical terms as simply as is possible.

The mean reversion model consists of a simple regression of the outcome of the child on the outcome of the parent:

$$Y_{ci} = \alpha + \beta Y_{pi} + u_i , \tag{1}$$

where Y denotes the outcome, subscript c indicates the child, subscript p indicates the child's parent, subscript i indicates the family, and u is the regression error. The latter captures other factors (apart from the outcome of the parent) that affect the outcome of the child, such as environment and luck. The coefficient β is Galton's beta, the coefficient of mean reversion. It measures the response of the child's outcome to the outcome of his parent. If $\beta = 0$, this response is 0; the outcome of the child is unrelated to the outcome of the parent. If $\beta = 1$, the outcome of the child increases one for one with the outcome of his parent. If β is between 0 and 1, there is mean reversion, since the outcome of the child increases by less than one-for-one with the outcome of the parent. This means that parents with larger-than-average outcomes have children whose outcomes are larger than average but closer to the mean. The same applies to parents that lie below the mean: their children's outcomes are smaller than average but are larger, on average, than the outcomes of their parents. This case is referred to as *beta convergence*.

The speed at which mean reversion occurs varies inversely with β. If β is negative, parents with large outcomes have children with smaller-than-average outcomes, and vice versa for parents with small outcomes. In this case there is regression past the mean. And if β > 1, parents with larger outcomes have children with even larger outcomes, and vice versa for parents with low outcomes. This case is referred to as *beta divergence*.

The relationship between the outcomes of children and their parents is illustrated in figure 2.1, where outcomes for children are measured on the vertical axis and outcomes for their parents are measured on the horizontal axis. Figure 2.1 is drawn for the case in which the average outcome for children is the same as for their parents, i.e., there is no intergenerational growth. This average outcome is denoted by Y*. Along the 45° line, the outcome of parents and children are identical by definition. Point a refers to the data on a specific child-parent dyad. Since point a lies below the 45° line, the outcome of the child is less than the outcome of his parent. The opposite applies for point b, which refers to another dyad and which is above the 45° line.

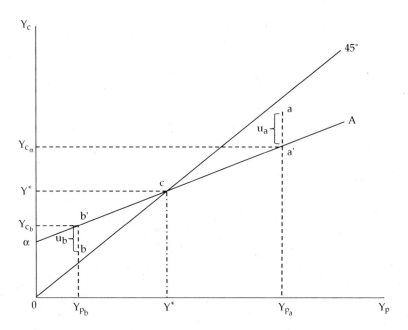

Figure 2.1
Intergenerational mean reversion

Equation 1 is estimated from data on parent-child dyads; points a and b are two examples. The estimated relationship is represented by line A in figure 2.1. Notice that line A must intersect the 45° line at c, since the average value of Y_c must equal the average value of Y_p for line A. If β is positive, this means that α must be less than Y^*, as drawn. Since line A is flatter than the 45° line, it must be the case that $\beta < 1$, because $\beta = 1$ in the case of the 45° line. Since dyad a is located above line A, u_a in equation 1 is positive. In this case the outcome of the child of dyad a is greater than expected from equation 1. The opposite applies in the case of dyad b, since point b lies below line A (i.e., u_b is negative). By definition the average of these residuals across all dyads must be 0.

Line A illustrates a typical case of beta convergence. It predicts that the outcomes of children are closer to the mean than the outcomes of parents. For example, in the case of dyad a the outcome of the parent is above the mean at Y_{pa}; the outcome for the child is expected to be above the mean at Y_{ca} but closer to the mean. In the case of dyad b, the outcome of the parent is below the mean at Y_{pb}; the child's outcome is expected to be below but closer to the mean at Y_{cb}. Finally, for dyad c the child's outcome is expected to equal the mean because the parents' outcome equals the mean. In practice the actual outcomes for these children differ from their expectations, but on average across all children these expectations are fulfilled.

If beta convergence is stronger (i.e., β is smaller), line A will be flatter, but it must pass through point c. If $\beta = 0$, A is a flat line, which means that, on average, there is no relationship between children's outcomes and their parents' outcomes. If $\beta = 1$ (i.e., there is no beta convergence), A turns into the 45° line, which means that, on average, children's outcomes equal their parents' outcomes. In the event of beta divergence, A is steeper than the 45° line. If there is regression past the mean, β is negative and line A slopes downward through point c. If there is intergenerational growth in the outcome, so that mean of the outcome for children exceeds the mean outcome for parents and the 45° line will start not at the origin in figure 2.1 but at a point like α. This will shift line A upward by a similar amount if β is unchanged.

Equation 1 is estimated by the ordinary least squares (OLS) method from a sample of N families or dyads of parents and children. The estimate of β (denoted $\hat{\beta}$) is defined as the covariance between the children's outcome and their parents' outcomes, denoted by $cov(Y_p Y_c)$, divided by the variance of the outcome of parents, denoted by $var(Y_p)$:

$$\hat{\beta} = \frac{\text{cov}(Y_c Y_p)}{\text{var}(Y_p)} . \tag{2}$$

The correlation coefficient between the outcome of parents and their children is defined as

$$r = \frac{\text{cov}(Y_c Y_p)}{\text{sd}(Y_c)\text{sd}(Y_p)}, \tag{3}$$

where sd denotes the standard deviation (square root of the variance). The standard deviation, commonly referred to as "sigma," measures inequality in the outcome. "Sigma divergence" arises when the standard deviation for children is greater than the standard deviation for parents, i.e., inequality is increasing. "Sigma convergence" arises when inequality decreases—that is, when the standard deviation for parents exceeds the standard deviation for children. The numerators in equations 2 and 3 are the same, but the denominators are different.

Equations 2 and 3 imply that r and $\hat{\beta}$ are related as follows:

$$r = \hat{\beta} \frac{\text{sd}(Y_p)}{\text{sd}(Y_c)} . \tag{4}$$

This equation states that if the standard deviation of the outcome among parents is the same as among their children, then the intergenerational correlation coefficient is equal to $\hat{\beta}$. This happens when inequality (as measured by the standard deviation) is the same for parents and children. If instead inequality happens to increase between generations (i.e., there is sigma divergence), the correlation coefficient will be smaller then $\hat{\beta}$. The opposite happens if there is sigma convergence.

The mean reversion model in equation 1 is linear, and the coefficient of correlation is linear too. Therefore, the coefficient of correlation measures the degree of *linear* correlation. If the mean reversion model is nonlinear because the size of β varies with the outcome of the parent, the correlation coefficient will understate the explanatory power of the mean reversion model. This will happen if, for example, β is greater for parents with larger outcomes and smaller outcomes and lower for parents with intermediate outcomes. This case is illustrated by curve B in figure 2.2, line A in which is comparable to line A in figure 2.1. If the outcomes are measured in logarithms and beta convergence is linear in logarithms, beta convergence must be nonlinear in the outcomes themselves.[1] This case is illustrated by curve C in figure 2.2. Of course, there are many other nonlinear possibilities.

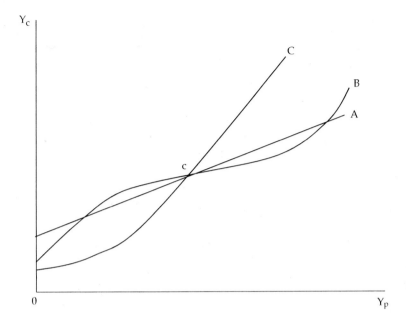

Figure 2.2
Nonlinear beta convergence

In this context, if two variables happen to have a perfectly circular relationship the coefficient of correlation is 0, so $R^2 = 1$ and $r = 0$. This goes to show that explanatory power and correlation are quite different concepts. It also means that R^2 is generally greater than the square of the correlation coefficient, since a nonlinear model may explain the data better than a linear one. If the model is linear, as in equation 1, then $R^2 = r^2$.

2.1.2   Attenuation Bias

The data on the outcomes of parents and children may not be representative of what we ideally want to measure. Typically there is a single observation on parents and a single observation on children, since survey questionnaires usually ask parents and children "What is your income, or whatever, now?" Or, if the data come from administrative records, these records refer to a given point in time. Two quite separate problems arise. First, the data may contain measurement error, either because there are genuine mistakes in reporting or because of deception. For example, reported income may be incorrect because individuals don't recall their income correctly or because they brag that they are richer than they really are. Second, the current value of the outcome that is reported might be different from what it normally is. For example, the result of an IQ test might have been unusually high or low. If parent are weighed after Christmas and their children are weighed after Lent, reported weights will tend to be less representative. It would have been preferable if the results of several tests or weighings had been averaged, but such data aren't usually available.

Both of these problems induce "attenuation bias," which means that the estimated relationships calculated from the data typically understate the truth. A detailed discussion of this issue may be found in section 10.1, where the solutions to the problem are discussed. A simple and intuitive discussion of attenuation bias will be provided here.

Let Y_p^* and Y_c^* denote the true phenotype values for parents and children respectively. However, the data contain error denoted by v_p and v_c. These errors are expected to be 0, which implies that the data are unbiased. Also, they are assumed to be independent of the truth; for example v_p is independent of Y_p^*. They are also assumed to be mutually independent, so v_p and v_c are unrelated. The standard deviations of these measurement errors are denoted by $sd(v_p)$ and $sd(v_c)$. If these standard deviations are 0, Y_p and Y_c are measured with perfect accuracy. The noise-to-signal ratio is defined as $var(v)/var(Y^*)$. The data are therefore equal to $Y_p = Y_p^* + v_p$ and $Y_c = Y_c^* + v_c$. Since $var(Y) = var(Y^*) + var(v)$, it must be the case that the data have a greater variance than the truth.

It is simple to show (see section 10.1) that, if the data contain measurement error, the intergenerational correlation coefficient (r) is less than the true intergenerational correlation (r^*), and β is less than its true value (β^*). The relationships between false β and β^* and between the false intergenerational correlation (r) and the true intergenerational correlation (r^*) are as follows:

$$\beta = \beta * \frac{var(Y_p^*)}{var(Y_p)},$$ (5a)

$$r = r * \frac{sd(Y_c^*)sd(Y_p^*)}{sd(Y_c)sd(Y_p)}.$$ (5b)

If the data do not contain measurement error, $var(Y) = var(Y^*)$, in which case measured β is equal to true β and measured r is equal to true r. If there is measurement error, the numerators are larger than the denominators, in which case the ratios in equations 5 are less than 1. Consequently, measured β must be less than true β and measured r must be less than true r—that is, the estimates of β and the intergenerational correlation coefficient are "attenuated." Notice that attenuation bias is negative, but it cannot change the sign—for example, it cannot turn a positive correlation into a negative one. Notice also, that if β and r^* are negative, attenuation makes these parameters look less negative than they really are. Notice, further, that attenuation bias in β depends on measurement error in data only for parents; it does not depend on measurement error in data on children. In contrast, attenuation bias in the intergenerational correlation coefficient is induced by measurement error in data on parents and children. This means that it is a more serious matter if data on parents contain measurement error than it is if data on children are mismeasured.

In table 10.1 the implications of measurement error for β and the intergenerational correlation coefficient are illustrated numerically. Suppose, for example, that in truth the variance for parents and children are the same, and that the intergenerational correlation is 0.5. Since parents and children have the same variance, equation 4 implies that true β must be 0.5 too. Suppose that the noise-to-signal ratio for parents is 0 while that for children is 16 percent. The estimate of β will be 0.5, as it should be because there is no measurement error in the data on parents. However, the estimate of the intergenerational correlation is only 0.464 instead of 0.5. If data on parents are also mismeasured and the noise-to-signal ratio happens to be 20 percent, the estimate of β is 0.417 instead of 0.5 and the estimate of r is 0.424.

Figure 2.3 plots the ratio of the measured correlation relative to the true correlation against the noise-to-signal ratio. When the noise-to-signal ratio is 0, the measured correlation is equal to the true correlation, in which case the curve in figure 2.3 starts at 1. It subsequently tends to 0 as the noise-to-signal ratio tends to infinity. In the latter case, the true variance, var(Y^*), is 0.

Attenuation bias may not apply to outcomes (such as height) that naturally do not fluctuate over time. If, however, height is misreported because people do not know their true height, or because they misrepresent it, attenuation bias will apply in this case too. The solution to the problem of attenuation bias is to find some "instrumental variable" that is correlated with the outcome (Y) but which is not correlated with the transient component of the outcome (v). For example, height might serve as an instrumental variable for weight, since height is correlated with weight; however, there is no reason to believe that weight is

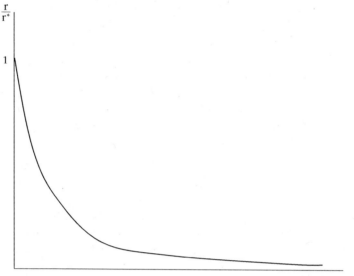

Figure 2.3
Attenuation bias.

correlated with transient weight (v), since the amount of weight people put on after Christmas isn't related to how tall they are.

2.2 Demography

Three demographic outcomes are (in life-cycle order) birth weight, fertility, and longevity. Is birth weight intergenerationally correlated? Do more fertile mothers have more fertile daughters or sons, and if so is there mean reversion or beta convergence in human fertility? Do longer-lived parents have longer-lived children? The answers to all three questions seem to be positive, and beta convergence turns out to be nonlinear in the cases of fertility and longevity. Because these three outcomes don't fluctuate, the question of attenuation bias doesn't arise (unless the data are misreported).

2.2.1 Birth Weight
Data on the intergenerational correlation coefficient for birth weight are rare. In fact I have only managed to find two studies, both of which suggest that this correlation is positive and very statistically significant.

Black et al. (2007) report that in a sample of nearly 64,000 Norwegian women born between 1967 and 1988 who had a baby by 2004, the birth weight of the first-borns is positively correlated with the mother's birth weight. The intergenerational birth weight elasticity is 0.15, meaning that a 10 percent increase in mother's birth weight is associated with an increase in first-born's birth weight of 1.5 percent. Indeed, the relationship is similar to curve C in figure 2.2, since it is estimated using logarithms. Surprisingly, however, this correlation is 0 for later-born children.

Behrman and Rosenzweig (2004) report that the birth weights of 1,207 identical female twins drawn from the Minnesota Twin Registry are positively correlated with their mothers' fetal growth, defined as the ratio of birth weight to length of gestation. This correlation means that a one-pound increase in mother's birth weight is associated with an increase in 2.3 ounces in the birth weight of her child. This estimate is quite similar to Black et al.'s estimate for first-borns.

2.2.2 Fertility

It is surprising that the relationship between the fertility of children and the fertility of their parents has received relatively little empirical attention. The problem of data collection is comparatively simple, since the fertility of parents is easily measured by sibship. If a women reports that she has two siblings, her mother's fertility is 3. Perhaps the most interesting study is the one by Booth and Kee (2009), who used data from the British Household Panel Survey on 2,103 women between the ages of 45 and 65 years. They find that β is nonlinear; there is a U-shaped relationship between completed fertility of daughters and completed fertility of their mothers. This means that for daughters of parents at the tenth percentile in terms of fertility β is 0.043, at the 25th percentile $\beta = 0.041$, at the 50th percentile $\beta = 0.055$, and at the 90th percentile $\beta = 0.149$. Fertility rapidly reverts toward the mean, because β is relatively small, but it reverts more slowly for women whose mothers were more fertile. Even at the 90th percentile, at which the completed fertility of the mother is about 5, the expected fertility of daughters is only 2.5, assuming average fertility of 2. In contrast, a daughter of a mother who had only one child is expected to have 1.95 children. Thus, fertility mean reverts very strongly at the bottom end of the fertility distribution.

I mentioned in chapter 1 that there is a natural temptation for scientific investigators to provide causal interpretations of their observations. Booth and Kee are no exception. They see beta convergence in fertility as a cultural phenomenon. The daughters of more fertile mothers imbibe their pro-birth culture and, as a result, have more children. Booth and Kee do not take account of the fact that the regression error in their model (which, like u in equation 1, is the fertility residual) may be partly genetic. If fecundity is inherited, and more fecund mothers are more fertile, this will induce positive intergenerational correlation in fertility. Therefore, the estimates of Booth and Kee might be induced by genetics rather than culture. I shall return to this issue in chapter 5.

To study the relationship between their incompleted fertility and sibship as a measure of mothers' completed fertility, Murphy and Knudsen (2002) used a cohort of 148,294 Danish women born in 1968–69 and observed at the end of 1994. These women were only 26 years old at the time of the study. Nevertheless, expected fertility varies directly with the fertility of the mother, rising from 0.17 for mothers of one or two children to 0.7 for mothers of six. Here too, beta convergence is strong and nonlinear. It is, of course, possible that completed fertility might turn out quite different. If the daughters of less fertile mothers delay having children while the daughters of more fertile mothers do the opposite, the fertility of the former daughters may eventually catch up with the fertility of the latter. If, however, we assume that birth timing doesn't depend on mother's fertility, incompleted fertility at 26 years would be correlated with completed fertility. In this case Murphy and Knudsen's results may be extrapolated to completed fertility.

In an attempt to identify the genetic component in the heredity of fertility, Pluzhnikov et al. (2007) studied fertility among Hutterites in Canada. The Hutterites are genetically homogeneous and eschew birth control, Pluknikov et al. argue that the intergenerational correlation in fertility among Hutterites has a genetic interpretation. The intergenerational correlations are 0.31 for sons and 0.23 for daughters. These correlations are much larger than those reported by Booth and Kee and by Murphy and Knudsen.

Using data from the Contemporary Danish Twin Study, Rodgers et al. (2001) report that the correlation for fertility for 576 sets of female MZ (identical) twins is 0.31 while for 964 sets of female DZ (fraternal) twins it is only 0.13. The correlations for male twins are 0.29 ($N = 646$) and 0.13 ($N = 1,032$) respectively. The methodology of behavioral genetics would suggest that this demonstrates that fertility is genetically inherited, and that this result does not vary by sex. I shall discuss this issue in greater detail in chapter 3. Here, I note that if DZ twins interact more closely than MZ twins, their outcomes will be more correlated because they try to become more similar. Therefore, the difference between MZ and DZ twins might have nothing to do with genetics and everything to do with social behavior. Also, husbands or fathers are assumed to have no effect on the fertility of their wives or partners. Given the fertility of mothers, does the fertility of daughters depend at all on the fertility of husbands' parents?

2.2.3 Longevity
To calculate the intergenerational correlation in longevity requires data on age at death for parents and children. Matched age-at-death data on parents and children are extremely difficult to obtain. Matters are yet more problematic if the data are required to be randomly sampled and representative of the population as a whole. For the most part, however, small and non-representative samples have been used to study sibling correlations for longevity. A rare and recent exception is some work carried out by some of my colleagues at the Hebrew University of Jerusalem.

Lach, Ritov, and Simhon (2008) have constructed a nationally representative database on age at death for parents and children in Israel. This formidable task involved matching children to their fathers using the Population Registry. The study is based on 552,019 fathers, born since 1901, who had died by March 31, 2004. There is an obvious censoring problem, since 93.5 percent of the children of these dead fathers were still alive in 2004. Censoring naturally increases for the later birth cohorts. Thus, by 2004, 98.1 percent of the children born to the 1901–1909 cohort of dead fathers had died themselves. This proportion is only 9.8 percent for the 1940–1949 cohort of dead fathers.

The correlation between age at death of fathers and their children is only 0.06. However, this greatly understates the rate of beta convergence, since mean reversion in longevity turns out to be highly nonlinear. It also ignores information on the censored observations, i.e. children who had not died by 2004. An octogenarian in 2004 will live at least 80 years, and possibly longer, but is given no representation in the correlation coefficient. If such octogenarians (and even centenarians) happen to be the offspring of long-lived parents, censoring will induce downward bias in the intergenerational correlation in longevity. Common sense suggests, therefore, that data on the survivors and not just the deceased should be used to calculate the relationship between the longevity of parents and their children. Lach et al. therefore use

Table 2.1
Mean life expectancy and father's age at death. Source: Lach, Ritov, and Simhon 2008.

Father's age at death	Daughters' life expectancy	Daughters' β	Sons' life expectancy	Sons' β
40	69.56	0.6	67.47	0.29
50	75.25	0.53	70.98	0.36
60	79.82	0.41	73.88	0.24
70	82.51	0.22	75.30	0.11
80	83.85	0.10	76.26	0.09
90	84.91	0.13	77.99	0.21
100	86.26	0.17	81.85	0.47

survival analysis to estimate β for longevity in which the censored observations are used too.

The results obtained by Lach et al. are reported in table 2.1.[2] Children have greater life expectancy if their fathers live longer. The children of fathers who die young are expected to outlive their fathers. However, the opposite happens if their fathers die old. If the father dies at the age of 70, his son is expected to outlive him by 5.3 years. If instead he dies at the age of 80, his son is expected to live about 3.75 years less than his father. Since short-lived fathers have children who outlive them, whereas the opposite applies to long-lived fathers, longevity is clearly mean reverting.

Table 2.1 also reports β, the coefficient of mean reversion. Since β < 1, there is mean reversion, or beta convergence, in longevity. However, the rate of mean reversion is not constant, and therefore beta convergence is nonlinear. The children of short-lived parents revert more slowly to the mean than children of long-lived parents. For exceptionally long-lived fathers, this pattern reverts; β is 0.17 for daughters and 0.47 for sons if the father lived to the age of 100.

I have given almost exclusive attention to the study by Lach et al. simply because there is little else to report on the intergenerational correlation for longevity. There are several studies of the sibling correlation in longevity, but they are limited to twins. McGue et al. (1993) report that in a sample of more than 500 twins the correlation in longevity was 0.23 for MZ twins and 0 for DZ twins, which suggests that longevity is entirely genetic. Perhaps the behaviors or the bad habits of MZ twins are more correlated than those of DZ twins, as indicated in table 2.6, and longevity varies inversely with bad habits. For example,

MZ twins are more likely to be correlated in smoking and drinking, which explains why they are more correlated in longevity. This constitutes a behavioral interpretation of the results of McGue et al. On the other hand, Christensen et al. (2006) claim that for Nordic twins genetics explains only 20–30 percent of adult longevity.

2.3   Cognitive Ability

2.3.1   IQ

To judge by the stormy reception of Herrnstein and Murray's 1994 book *The Bell Curve*, what probably is one of the most contentious issues in heredity concerns the genetic transmission of intelligence. Somehow, intelligence seems to stir more emotions than other outcomes. However, IQ seems to have almost no effect on labor-market outcomes. Indeed, it might not matter for anything other than access to programs that include IQ in their entry requirements.

Since the publication of *The Bell Curve*, labor economists in particular have re-examined the data that Herrnstein and Murray used. Their measure of IQ is the Armed Forces Qualification Test (AFQT), a psychometric test applied by the US military. One of the many criticisms of Herrnstein and Murray's work is that the only control for family background they used was the SES (socioeconomic status of parents) statistic, an ad hoc concoction of parents' attributes. Korenman and Winship (2000) use data on IQ differences between siblings to control for family background, for neighborhoods, and for other shared experiences. They confirm Herrnstein and Murray's estimates regarding the role of IQ in explaining a broad range of socioeconomic outcomes among Hispanic, black, and white Americans, but they find that family background matters more than Herrnstein and Murray claimed.

Using similar data, Neal and Johnson (1996) claim that black-white wage differences are almost entirely explained by black-white differences in AFQT test scores. Neal and Johnson argue that, because AFQT scores depend on the schooling and occupational status of parents, sibship, and school characteristics, the AFQT is not a measure of IQ but a measure of pre-labor-market investment in human capital.[3] Accordingly, investments in the human capital of young blacks will help close the black-white wage gap. Although Neal and Johnson's results ostensibly confirm Herrnstein and Murray's empirical findings, their interpretation is radically different because they do not think that AFQT scores measure IQ.

If IQ is inherited, and if schooling and occupational status are positively correlated with IQ, it might simply be the case that Neal and Johnson's results regarding the empirical determinants of AFQT scores have a genetic interpretation. Take, for example, Neal and Johnson's negative association between AFQT scores and sibship. If the AFQT measures IQ, there is no reason why it should depend on sibship, according to Neal and Johnson. AFQT scores are lower in larger families because there are fewer resources available to invest in the education of each child. On the other hand, the Quality vs. Quantity Theory predicts that abler parents have fewer children because they expect their children to be abler. (See chapter 3 below.) Therefore, the negative effect of sibship on AFQT scores might be intermediating the effect of the unobserved IQs of parents on their children's IQs. In other words, parents with lower IQs have larger families and also have children with lower IQs. Had Neal and Johnson controlled for the IQs of parents, the interpretation of their results for AFQT scores might have been different. Indeed, all the controls that they intended to demonstrate that the AFQT does not measure IQ happen to be correlated with the unobserved IQs of parents. Therefore, Neale and Johnson's claim that the AFQT does not measure IQ but measures pre-labor-market investments in human capital is not persuasive.

Herrnstein and Murray's rationale for not controlling for education is that education (years of schooling) is endogenous and in any case largely depends on IQ. Neal and Johnson also don't control for education, on the ground that it is endogenous—that is, abler workers will acquire more schooling and therefore will earn more. However, many labor economists control for both education and IQ. Ashenfelter and Rouse (2000) use data similar to those used by Herrnstein and Murray to show that IQ as measured by AQFT scores does not affect the return to schooling. Altonji and Dunn (1996) show that AQFT scores have no effect on earnings in sibling comparisons once schooling is used as a control. Cawley et al. (2000) show that when g is calculated from AFQT scores[4] the relationship between earnings and IQ is considerably weakened. In summary, after schooling is controlled for, the effects of IQ as measured by the AFQT weaken or disappear.

An exception to the aforementioned empirical consensus is Gould (2005), who uses similar data to show that IQ has an independent effect on wages, controlling for schooling.[5] The return to a year's schooling among white males in the United States is about 10 percent in the professional and service sectors and 0 in the blue-collar sector. The return to IQ is 8 percent in the blue-collar sector and varies between 4 percent and 11 percent in the other sectors. Gould also shows that occupational status varies directly with schooling and IQ. Therefore, the effect of IQ on wages is twofold: it enables people to get better jobs, and given their choice of occupation, it enables them to earn more. To obtain this result it is necessary to take account of the occupational choices of workers and the roles that IQ and schooling play in these choices. Although IQ has a statistically significant effect on wages, the size effects are small and the contribution of IQ to wage inequality is probably of the order of 1 percent. Therefore, IQ is not quantitatively important in explaining wage inequality.

Let us now turn to the empirical correlations for IQ within and between generations. Bouchard and McGue (1981) report that the correlation between the IQ of parents and their children lies in the range 0.42–0.72. The higher estimate applies when the average of both parents' IQ is used, which suggests that there is assortative mating between parents. Indeed, the correlation between the IQs of spouses is 0.33. Bouchard and McGue also suggest that these correlations have a genetic interpretation, since the sibling correlation for IQ among identical twins is 0.85, while for fraternal twins the sibling correlation is 0.6. Indeed, the more distant the genetic relationship, the weaker the correlation. The correlations between first-degree, second-degree, and third-degree relatives are 0.45, 0.3, and 0.15 respectively.

Note that the correlations for siblings reared apart tend to be smaller. For example, the correlation between MZ twins is 0.86 when they were reared together and 0.72 when they were reared apart. Note also that the correlation between adopted and biological siblings is slightly smaller than the correlation between adopted siblings raised apart. These differences seem to suggest that shared environments induce correlation in IQ, but genetic distance matters more.

These estimates are rather higher than the β coefficients reported by Black et al. (2008) for a sample of 24,754 Norwegian parent-child dyads. Using sons' IQ at the age of 18, the mean reversion coefficient is 0.32, which suggests quite rapid regression to the mean. The correlation coefficient is 0.38, which according to equation 4 implies that IQ is more unequal among parents than among children. In fact, the standard deviation of IQ among parents is 19 percent larger than the standard deviation of IQ among their children. The intergenerational correlation coefficient for IQ reported by Daniels et al. (1997) confirms the findings of the previous two studies. According to Jencks (1972), the IQs of

Table 2.2
Family correlations: cognitive ability (IQ).

	Correlation	Location	Relation
Bouchard & McGue (1981)	0.40	US	Parent-child
	0.72		Parents-child
	0.85		MZ twins
	0.72		MZ twins reared apart
	0.6		DZ twins
	0.47		Siblings
	0.24		Siblings (apart)
	0.31		Half siblings
	0.29		Biol. and adopted sibs
	0.34		Adopted siblings
	0.33		Spouses
	0.15		Cousins
	0.45		First-degree relative
	0.3		Second-degree relative
	0.15		Third-degree relative
Black et al. (2008)	0.38	Norway	Parent-child
Daniels et al. (1997)	0.5	US	Parent-child
	0.41		Single parent-child
Jencks (1972)	0.5	US	Spouses
	0.48		Parent-child
	0.21		Father-adoptee
	0.24		Mother-adoptee
	0.52		Siblings
	0.26		Biol.-adopted sibs
	0.81	US, UK, Denmark	MZ twins reared apart
	0.2	US	Biol.-adoptive parents

adoptive parents and biological parents are correlated (0.2).[6] Also, the IQs of adopted children at the time of their placement are correlated 0.34 with the schooling of adopting mothers. Adoption, like marriage, appears to be assortative.

Note should be taken of the "Flynn Effect," according to which IQ test scores are universally increasing over time (Flynn 2002). Although cognitive ability may be increasing over time, the trends in scores on IQ tests are implausibly large. They point to severe measurement error. For example, between 1952 and 1982 IQ test scores increased by 21 percent in the Netherlands. Did cognitive ability really increase by that much in a single generation?

2.3.2   Schooling

Whereas intergenerational data on IQ are scarce except in the United States, the opposite applies to education, as can be seen in table 2.3. In some studies the intergenerational association is measured by the correlation coefficient; in others it is measured by β. Recall that according to equation 4 the two measures are identical if inequality in schooling, as measured by the variance, is the same for parents and children. My data from Israel show, however, that inequality in schooling is considerably less among children than among their parents. (Table 2.3 is not comprehensive or exhaustive; the country coverage is limited owing to absence of data, and the United States remains heavily over-represented.)

Table 2.3 shows that β or the correlation coefficient is typically about 0.3. In some studies the sex mix makes a difference; in others it does not. All the studies show that adopted children are less correlated with their adoptive parents than are biological children. Indeed, in Sweden the correlation between adopted children and their biological parents is about as large as the correlation with their adoptive parents. The sum of these two correlations is suggestively similar to the correlation for biological children.

Behrman and Taubman (1989) show that, as in the case of IQ discussed above, the correlation in schooling varies directly with genetic proximity. The sibling correlations between identical and fraternal twins are 0.75 and 0.55 respectively. The correlations between first-degree and second-degree relatives are 0.34 and 0.13 respectively. The schooling correlation for spouses is 0.54, which strongly suggests assortative mating in education.

My 2008 study (Beenstock 2008) suggests (table 2.3) that the intergenerational correlation for schooling in Israel lies in the range 0.27–0.35, depending on the sex composition of the dyad. Daughters' schooling is more correlated with their parents' schooling than sons' schooling. The same data set indicates (table 2.5) that schooling is more correlated among siblings (i.e., within generations) than between generations. The sibling correlations range between 0.35 and 0.56.

2.4   Economic Outcomes

Owing to the availability of data, earnings and income are the most intensively and widely investigated economic phenomena. Results for several countries are reported in table 2.4. However, a word of caution

Table 2.3
Intergenerational relationships for years of schooling.

	Correlation	β	Location	Relation
Olneck (1977)		0.45	Kalamazoo	Father-son
Behrman & Taubman (1985)		0.31	US	Father-child
Lillard & Willis (1994)		0.19	Malaysia	Father-son
		0.23		Father-daughter
Couch & Dunn (1995)		0.27	US	Father-son
Mulligan (1997)		0.32	US	Father-son
Hertz et al. (2007)	0.30		Denmark	
	0.33		Finland	
	0.35		Norway	
	0.40		Sweden	
	0.36		Holland	
	0.31		UK	
	0.46		US	
Plug (2004)	0.39		Wisconsin	Father-daughter
	0.54			Father-son
	0.27			Father-adoptee
	0.28			Mother-adoptee
Björklund et al. (2006)	0.24		Sweden	Father-son
	0.24			Father-daughter
	0.11			Father-adoptee
	0.07			Mother-adoptee
	0.11			Biol. father-adoptee
	0.13			Biol. mother-adoptee
Behrman & Rosenzweig (2002)	0.33		US	Mother-daughter
	0.45			Father-son
Sacerdote (2007)	0.33		US	Biol. children
	0.14			Adoptees
Beenstock (2008)	0.29		Israel	Father-son
	0.35			Father-daughter
	0.27			Mother-son
	0.34			Mother-daughter

Table 2.4
Intergenerational associations: economic outcomes.

	Outcome	Correlation	β	Country	Relation
Corak & Heisz (1999)	Earnings	0–0.4		Canada	
Björklund et al. (2006)	Earnings	0.24		Sweden	Father-child
		0.10			Father-adoptee
		0.05			Biol. father-adoptee
Chadwick & Solon (2002)	Earnings[b]	0.53		US (PSID)	Son
		0.43			Daughter
Altonji & Dunn (1991)	Earnings	0.37		US (NLSY)	Siblings
Solon (1991)	Earnings[b]	0.45		US (PSID)	Siblings
			0.41		Father-son
Sacerdote (2007)	Income	0.28		US	Biol. parents
		0.11			Adoptive parents
Black et al. (2008)	Income		0.19–0.23	Norway	Parent-son
Jäntti & Österbacka (1996)	Income		0.22	Finland	
Björklund & Jäntti (1997)	Earnings[a]		0.27	Sweden	Father-son
Peters (1992)	Earnings[a]		0.14	US (NLSY)	Father-son
			0.13		Father-daughter
Atkinson et al. (1983)	Earnings		0.44	UK (York)	Father-son
Beenstock (2008)	Earnings[b]	0.14–0.4		Israel	Parent-child
Mulligan (1997)	Wealth[b]		0.43–0.5	US	Parent-child
	Consumption[b]		0.77	US	Parent-child
Menchik (1979)	Wealth	0.5	0.759	Connecticut	Parent-child
Bevan (1979)	Wealth	0.019–0.107		UK	Parent-child

a. yearly averages
b. instrumental variables

is in order before interpreting these correlations and betas. Because income or earnings fluctuate, they have permanent and transient components. In this they are very different from schooling, which does not fluctuate. Whereas reported schooling is unlikely to change from year to year, the same does not apply to income. If the individual has become unemployed, his earnings are 0; if the economy is in a recession, his earnings may be lower than they would be otherwise. Therefore, reported earnings have permanent and transient components (as discussed above), and attenuation bias will tend to induce correlations and betas that are under-estimated. Unless otherwise noted (see notes a and b to table 2.4), the reported estimates suffer from attenuation bias.

Solon (1991), who corrects for attenuation bias by applying the method of instrumental variables, estimates the intergenerational correlation coefficient for earnings at 0.45 for the United States.[7] The uncorrected counterpart is about 0.2, which suggests that attenuation bias is potentially large. Black et al. (2008), who do not correct for attenuation bias, estimate the intergenerational correlation coefficient for income at about 0.2 for Norway. That is quite low. Since attenuation bias is always negative, the true intergenerational correlation coefficient is presumably higher than 0.2. The same applies to the correlations reported for Finland and Sweden.

All the reported correlations and betas in table 2.4 are linear except those of Corak and Heisz (1999), who find that in Canada the intergenerational correlation coefficient for earnings is highest (0.4) for rich and poor parents and decreases to 0 for parents with average earnings. The beta convergence curve is nonlinear and looks like curve B in figure 2.2. This means that there is less mobility among the rich and poor, so that the children of rich parents are more likely to be richer and the children of poor parents are likely to be poorer. On the other hand, there is much more mobility as we move away from the extremes of the earnings distribution. I did not find such nonlinear effects in a large sample for Israeli parents and children (Beenstock 2008). However, I did find that the correlation was stronger for older children. The correlation coefficient (corrected for attenuation bias) for children in their early twenties is only about 0.14, but it climbs to 0.4 for children in their mid thirties. Apparently it takes time for the apple to fall not far from the tree.

The studies by Björklund et al. (2006) and Sacerdote (2007) involve comparisons of biological and adopted children. The intergenerational correlations for adoptees are half the size of their counterparts for biological siblings. The correlations reported by Björklund et al. for earnings are similar to their counterparts for schooling in table 2.2. However, whereas in the case of schooling the correlation for adopted children and their biological fathers is 0.11, in the case of earnings it is only 0.05.

Because of data availability, the main economic outcome that has been investigated is earnings or income.[8] An exception is Mulligan (1997), who calculates the intergenerational correlation coefficient for consumption in the United States at 0.77, which is much larger than the correlation for income or earnings. This means that children are more similar to their parents in terms of how much they consume than how much they earn. Economic theory predicts that consumption is driven by permanent income rather than current income. If that is so, it suggests that the intergenerational correlation for permanent income is about 0.77. The same economic theory predicts that wealth and permanent income should have the same correlation with consumption. However, it turns out that the intergenerational correlation coefficient for wealth[9] is somewhat lower, at 0.5.

2.5   Sibling Correlations for Schooling and Earnings

Sibling correlations for earnings and schooling are reported in table 2.5. For reasons that will be discussed in chapter 3, the correlation coefficient between siblings is likely to be larger than the square of the intergenerational correlation. This results from the fact that not only do siblings share the same parents, they belong to the same household and share each others' company. This is true for earnings in Sweden and perhaps the United States and Israel, but not for Norway. The sibling correlations for schooling are considerably larger than their intergenerational counterparts in Israel, where sisters are most correlated for schooling and least correlated for earnings. The data from Toronto are interesting because they show that although siblings are correlated with respect to economic outcomes, neighbors are uncorrelated. This suggests that the correlation between siblings stems from what is happening in the family rather than in the neighborhoods of these families.

2.6   Bad Habits

Though I don't wish to go into a discussion of what constitutes a bad habit, table 2.6 indicates that outcomes such as smoking, drinking, and

Table 2.5
Sibling correlations: schooling and earnings.

	Outcome	Correlation	Country	Relation
Björklund et al. (2002)	Earnings	0.43	US	Brothers
		0.23	Denmark	
		0.26	Finland	
		0.14	Norway	
		0.43	Sweden	
Solon (1991)	Earnings[a]	0.45	US (PSID)	Siblings
Altonji & Dunn (1991)	Earnings	0.37	US (NLSY)	Siblings
Sieben et al. (2001)	Schooling	0.38–0.47	W. Germany	Siblings
		0.27–0.30	E. Germany	
		0.41–0.52	Holland	
Björklund & Salvanes (2010)	Schooling	0.40–0.42	Norway: living with same mother	Brothers
		0.43–0.48		Sisters
Björklund et al. (2009)	Schooling	0.46–0.48	Sweden	Bio brothers
Conley & Glauber (2008)	Schooling	0.63	US: same biological mother	Brothers
		0.75		Sisters
Mazumder (2008)	Schooling	0.62	US: same household	Brothers
		0.60		Sisters
Oreopoulos (2003)	Income	0.284	Canada	Brothers
	Earnings	0.280		Brothers
	Welfare years	0.24		Brothers
	Earnings	0.043		Neighbors
	Welfare years	0.071		Neighbors
Behrman & Taubman (1989)	Schooling	0.75	US	MZ twins
		0.55		DZ twins
		0.34		First-degree relatives
		0.15		Second-degree relatives
		0.54		Spouses
Beenstock (2008)	Earnings[b]	0.30	Israel	Brothers
		0.18		Sisters
		0.24		Brother-sister
	Schooling	0.42		Brothers
		0.56		Sisters
		0.35		Brother-sister

a, b. See table 2.4.

Table 2.6
Associations for negative behavior.

	Outcome	Correlation	β	Country	Relation
Medlund et al.	Smoking	0.75		Sweden	MZ twins
(1977)		0.63			DZ twins
Shields &	Smoking	0.79		US	MZ twins reared apart
Shields (1962)					
Sacerdote (2007)	Obesity	0.16		US	Biol. siblings
		0.04			Adopted siblings
	Smoking	0.29			Biol. siblings
		0.15			Adopted siblings
	Drinking	0.35			Biol. siblings
		0.32			Adopted siblings
	Obesity		0.11		Mother-biol. child
			0		Mother-adoptee
	Drinking		0.24		Mother-biol. child
			0.21		Mother-adoptee
	Smoking		0.11		Mother-biol. child
			0.13		Mother-adoptee

obesity are correlated both intergenerationally and intragenerationally. Indeed, the intragenerational correlation tends to exceed its intergenerational counterpart. In the case of smoking, siblings are more correlated than parents and children, and within siblings there seems to be a clear trend: MZ twins are most correlated and adopted siblings least correlated. Interestingly, Sacerdote's intergenerational beta coefficients are the same regardless of whether the child happens to be biological or adopted. Siblings also appear to more correlated for drinking, but in this case it makes no difference whether siblings are adopted or not. This does not apparently apply to obesity; adoptees are uncorrelated with their biological siblings and their adoptive mothers.

2.7 Anthropometrics and Morbidity

Perhaps it comes as no surprise that height is more correlated than weight since, unlike height, weight has transient components. In any case one cannot influence one's height while the same does not apply to weight. Indeed, the correlations for height are about twice their counterparts for weight. However, the sibling and mother-child correlations are 0 when adoptees are involved for both weight and height.

Table 2.7
Anthropometric correlations.

	Outcome	Correlation	Country	Relation
Matheny (1990)	Weight	0.88	Sweden	MZ twin
		0.50		DZ twin
Sacerdote (2007)	Weight	0.28	US	Biol. siblings
		0.03		Adopted siblings
	Height	0.44		Biol. siblings
		0.02		Adopted siblings
		0.49[a]		Mother-biol. child
		0		Mother-adoptee
Martin (2008)	Weight/height	0.48[a]	US	Parents-child
		0.24[a]	(NLSAH)	Parent-child
		0.42		Siblings
		0.73		MZ twins
		0.22		Half-siblings

a. β

This pattern repeats the one reported above for obesity. Indeed, biosiblings are more correlated for weight than they are for obesity.

Martin (2008) used data from the US National Longitudinal Study of Adolescent Health (often referred to as "Add Health"), which reports the body mass index (BMI) for children defined as weight divided by height. NLSAH also includes data on the obesity of parents. If both parents are obese, their child's BMI is 0.48 larger; if only one parent is obese, it is 0.24 larger. These effects aren't strictly beta coefficients, since they do not refer to BMI for parents. Nevertheless, they clearly suggest that there is an intergenerational association in excess weight, since BMI and obesity are different measures of excess weight. Martin's sibling correlation coefficients (see table 2.7) refer to BMIs and clearly suggest that BMI is correlated among siblings and is greatest among MZ twins.

Table 2.8 includes a selective number of health-related outcomes. Textbooks on behavioral genetics, such as Plomin et al. 2001 and Rutter 2006, are replete with numerous health-related examples in which the outcomes of parents, children, and siblings are correlated. Sacerdote (2007) reports that asthma is correlated among biological siblings but not between adopted siblings, which suggests that asthma has a genetic basis. The same applies to schizophrenia where the sibling correlation varies directly with family closeness. Gottesman's study (reported here in table 2.8) is one among many.

Table 2.8
Health correlations.

	Outcome	Correlation	Country	Relation
Sacerdote (2007)	Asthma	0.22	US	Biol. sibling
		0.08		Adopted siblings
Gottesman (1991)	Schizophrenia[a]	0.48	US	MZ twin
		0.17		DZ twin
		0.09		First-degree relative
		0.04		Second-degree relative
		0.01		Unrelated

a. probability

Neuroticism displays the classical pattern, with MZ twins most correlated and parents and adoptees least correlated. Loehlin's results for extroversion, shown here in table 2.9, display almost the same pattern as his results for neuroticism. MZ twins are most correlated and adoptees are least correlated. Interestingly, DZ twins reared apart are just as uncorrelated as adoptees. A perhaps surprising feature of Loehlin's results is that DZ twins are twice as correlated as other siblings and it makes no difference whether siblings are biological or adopted.

2.8 Crime and Deviancy

Empirical research into the intergenerational transmission of criminal and delinquent behavior has been motivated largely by the desire to test rival hypotheses about its nature. Glueck and Glueck (1950) emphasized the importance of family, and especially parents, as a factor in the determination of juvenile delinquency. A similar conclusion was reached by West and Farrington (1977). Subsequently, criminologists have suggested that labeling might be responsible for this correlation. If the courts label parents as criminals, this might induce their children to become criminals. Also, these studies seek to determine the effects of child rearing on the deviant behavior of their children, as well as the effects of poverty and neighborhoods. In table 2.10, however, our concern is limited to the descriptive data in these studies on the correlations between parents and children and between siblings in terms of their deviant behavior.

Table 2.9
Personality correlations.

	Outcome	Correlation	Country	Relation
Loehlin (1992)	Extroversion	0.51	US	MZ twins
		0.38		MZs reared apart
		0.18		DZ twins
		0.05		DZs reared apart
		0.20		Biol. siblings
		0.07		Adopted siblings
		0.16		Parents-biol. child
		0.01		Parents-adoptee
Carmichael & McGue (1994)	Extroversion	0.03	US	Parent-child
	Neuroticism	0.27		Parent-child
Crook (1937)	Neuroticism	0.29	UK	Parent-child
Insel (1974)	Extroversion	0.24	US	Parent-child
	Neuroticism	0.21		Parent-child
Loehlin (1992)	Neuroticism	0.46	US	MZ twins
		0.38		MZs reared apart
		0.20		DZ twins
		0.23		DZs reared apart
		0.09		Biol. siblings
		0.11		Adopted siblings
		0.13		Parents-biol. child
		0.05		Parents-adoptee
Loehlin (2005)	Extroversion	0.14	US	Parent-child
	Neuroticism	0.13		
	Agreeableness	0.11		
	Conscientiousness	0.09		
	Openness	0.17		

It should be pointed out that the samples do not represent the general population. For example, the two London studies mentioned in table 2.10 are based on data from the Cambridge Study in Delinquent Development (CSDD), which sampled 411 8-year-old boys living in the inner city of South London in 1961–62. This is a predominantly working-class area, which at the time was exclusively white and had few immigrants. The sample boys were subsequently followed up and continue to be followed up today. The CSDD contains data on the boys' parents as well as their children, so it spans three generations (Farrington et al. 2008). In 1994 the conviction rates for the boys'

Table 2.10
Correlations for deviant behavior.

	Outcome	Correlation	Country	Relation
Rowe & Farrington (1997)	Criminal convictions	0.43	UK	Father-son
		0.52		Mother-daughter
		0.22		Father-daughter
		0.31		Mother-son
		0.47		Brothers
		0.57		Sisters
		0.27		Siblings— different sex
		0.55		Parents
Thornberry et al. (2003)	Antisocial behavior	0.31	US	Father-child
		0.22		Mother-child
Hagan & Palloni (1990)	Delinquency	0.22	UK	Parent-child
Mednick et al. (1984)	Criminality		Denmark	Parent-biol. child
				Parent-adoptee

mothers and fathers were 13.6 percent and 27.7 percent respectively. By 2004 the conviction rate among the boys themselves stood at 41.1 percent. In 2006 the conviction rates for the boys' sons and daughters stood at 25.5 percent and 6.4 percent respectively. These extraordinarily high conviction rates are many times the conviction rates in the population as a whole. It is questionable whether inferences obtained from the CSDD are limited to a specific population (white working-class inner-city male Londoners) or whether they apply more generally. Therefore, the intergenerational correlations reported in table 2.10 that are based on the CSDD may be of only parochial interest.

Rowe and Farrington (1997) use data from the CSDD for the first two generations (boys and their parents) to show that criminal conviction rates are correlated across generations and within generations. The highest correlations are for mothers and daughters and between sisters. There may also be evidence of assortative mating since the correlation among parents is 0.55. However, part of this correlation may be induced by the bad influence that spouses have on each other. Farrington et al. (2008) show that a similar pattern applies to transmission of criminal convictions from the boys to their children in the third generation.

Hagan and Palloni (1990) use the CSDD to study youth delinquency among the boys. Needless to say, the reservations mentioned above about the CSDD apply to this study too. Youth delinquency is measured by seven items including self-reports of shoplifting, breaking and entering, and other crimes. The correlation between this measure of youth delinquency and criminal conviction among parents is 0.22. Hagan and Palloni also report that the beta (mean reversion) coefficient estimated from a Poisson regression is 0.23. This estimate takes account of numerous other covariates, including parenting, economic status, and delinquency among friends. Hagan and Palloni give a causal interpretation to their findings, as if variables such as parenting and the choice of friends are randomly assigned and do not depend on the behavior of the boys in the CSDD. I shall return to this issue in chapters 4 and 5.

In Thornberry et al. 2003, "antisocial behavior" covers 24 items, including vandalism, petty theft, and aggravated assault, among youths in the Rochester Youth Development Study (RYDS), which, like the CSDD, involves three generations. The intergenerational correlations are similar in magnitude to Hagan and Palloni's and refer to a similar phenomenon.

2.9   Religious Practice

Can it be that there is something akin to a gene for religious belief and observance? Some evolutionary psychologists, including Dawkins (1976), think that, just as genes control physical and mental outcomes, "memes" control moral or cultural outcomes. Indeed, memes, like genes, have adopted and evolved over time. The data shown here in table 2.11 compare the correlations for church attendance and belief in God among more than 2,200 pairs of twins in North Carolina. On the whole, identical twins are more correlated for church attendance than fraternal twins, although the differences aren't large. The methodology of behavioral genetics would suggest that there is a meme for church attendance, because identical twins are more correlated for church attendance than are fraternal twins. The same applies to belief in God among males but apparently not among females.

Even if these correlations might not have a genetic, or memetic, interpretation, they are very large. These data suggest, therefore, that the sibling correlations for religious observance and belief in God are large regardless of whether siblings happen to be identical or fraternal twins.

Data on sibling correlations for religiosity are scarce. Intergenerational correlations are more available. This is because in surveys on

Table 2.11
Sibling correlations for religiosity. Source: Eaves et al. 2008.

	Identical twins		Fraternal twins	
	Male	Female	Male	Female
Church attendance	0.91	0.9	0.79	0.87
Belief in God	0.81	0.55	0.74	0.65

Table 2.12
Intergenerational and life-cycle beta coefficients for frequency of church, mosque, or synagogue attendance and prayer. Source: Branãs-Garza et al. 2010. The coefficients are estimated for an ordered logit model. Asterisked coefficients aren't statistically significant. The coefficients are estimated jointly. "Life-cycle" refers to respondent at age 12.

	Father		Mother		Life-cycle	
	Male	Female	Male	Female	Male	Female
Church attendance	0.372	0.165	0.277	0.459	0.285	0.394
Prayer	0.295	–0.064*	0.075*	0.160	0.366	0.478

religiosity it is natural to ask whether a subject was raised in a religious home. Perhaps the most informative data on this matter are those from the International Social Survey Program, in which more than 35,000 people from 34 countries were surveyed in 1998. Table 2.12 reports conditional beta coefficients for frequency of prayer and attendance at a house of worship. Interestingly, the conditioning variables include beliefs in heaven and hell. It comes as no surprise that frequency of prayer and attendance at church vary directly with the strength of these beliefs. What concern us here, however, are the conditional beta coefficients, which indicate that there is considerable intergenerational mobility in religiosity. Recall that a coefficient of 1 means complete immobility and a coefficient of 0 means complete mobility. All the coefficients in table 12.2 are less than 0.5, and some of them are less than 0.2. In the case of prayer, there are even two beta coefficients that aren't statistically significant from 0: those for son-mother dyads and daughter-father dyads. The beta coefficients for church attendance vary between 0.46 (for daughter-mother dyads) and 0.16 (for daughter-father dyads) and tend to be greater than their counterparts for prayer.

The last two columns in table 12.2 refer to life-cycle beta coefficients, since they refer to current religiosity with respect to religiosity at age 12. If respondents' religiosity at age 12 was identical to their parents' religiosity, the life-cycle beta coefficients should be identical to their intergenerational counterparts. The fact that they differ indicates that at the age of 12 religiosity of children differed from that of their parents. The life-cycle beta coefficients are less than 0.5, but they tend to be larger than their intergenerational counterparts.

Since 2007 the Central Bureau of Statistics in Israel has undertaken a survey of religiosity for the general population. In table 2.13 I calculate the intergenerational mobility matrix for the Jewish population in Israel. Adult respondents were asked to define their current religiosity in terms of the five categories in table 2.13, which are in decreasing order of religiosity. They were also asked to categorize the religiosity of their home when they were 15 years old. As the table shows, 8 percent defined themselves as ultra-orthodox Jews and 41.8 percent defined themselves as secular Jews.

Table 2.13 reports the percentage who changed their religiosity relative to the religiosity in the home in which they were raised. For example, 68.4 percent of those raised in an ultra-orthodox home were still ultra-orthodox in 2008, 11.2 percent became religious, and 5.5 percent became completely secular. At the other extreme, 75.1 percent of those who were raised in a secular home were still secular in 2008, 14.9 percent became traditional, and only 0.3 percent became ultra-orthodox. On the whole, the table suggests that there is more downward mobility than upward mobility in religiosity. Although this means that Jews in Israel are becoming less religious, it should be recalled that fertility is greater among religious Jews than among less religious Jews. But for this, the proportion of religious Jews would decrease, since according to table 2.13 they are becoming less religious.

A major social and political issue in Israel concerns the increasing percentage of ultra-orthodox Jews in the population, which is visible in table 2.13. This share increased from 6.4 percent when respondents were 15 years old and living with their parents to 8 percent in 2008. The ultra-orthodox are exempted from serving in the army, in return for which they aren't allowed to work until they are 40 years old.[10] They therefore become a burden on the social security budget. The proportion of 18-year-olds receiving this army exemption increased from 2 percent in 1950 to about 11 percent in 2009. The table shows that the ultra-orthodox population has been making gains at the expense of religious Jews. Indeed, there is a clear trend of polarization in which the middle ground is losing out to the ultra-orthodox at one extreme and to the secular at the other.

Table 2.13
Intergenerational transition matrix for religiosity among Jews in Israel (percentages). Source: Social Survey 2008, Central Bureau of Statistics; calculations by M. Beenstock.

	Ultra-orthodox	Religious	Traditional-Religious	Traditional	Secular	Current share	Home share
Ultra-orthodox	68.4	11.2	9.8	5.0	5.5	8.0	6.4
Religious	3.4	70.7	13.1	5.5	7.2	9.8	15.9
Traditional-religious	1.6	24.9	55.6	10.6	7.2	13.9	18.5
Traditional	0.7	11.9	23.3	47.4	16.3	26.4	21.2
Secular	0.3	3.6	5.9	14.9	75.1	41.8	37.9

The retention rates along the diagonal of the mobility matrix range from 47 percent to 75 percent, which suggests that there is relatively little intergenerational mobility in religiosity among Jews in Israel. The Bartholomew index of mobility (defined in subsection 8.5.6 below) is only 0.21. Since this index varies between 0 (no mobility) and 1 (complete mobility), table 2.13 indicates that intergenerational mobility in religiosity is small.

I apologize if the material in the above tables reads rather like a shopping list. I wanted to show that the empirical evidence indicates that the apples do not fall far from the tree for a broad range of phenomena. Also, I wanted to show that siblings are correlated too, indicating that the apples do not fall far from one another. In fact, it turns out that siblings are more correlated than one would expect simply on account of their sharing common parents. If only parents mattered, the sibling correlation should equal the square of the intergenerational correlation coefficient. However, the sibling correlation typically exceeds that by a substantial margin, which suggests that something else is going on that induces correlation between siblings. One possibility is that siblings share environments that aren't shared by their parents. Another is that siblings interact with each other. I shall return to this issue in chapters 3 and 6.

Many scientific investigators attribute causal interpretations to the intergenerational correlations that they measure. Just because, for example, deviancy happens to be intergenerationally correlated does not mean that children are deviant because their parents are deviant. If it did, the cycle of crime could be broken by reforming parents, or by removing children from their parents' bad influence. It might be the case that the relationship is not causal at all. For example, intergenerational correlation is induced by environmental factors shared by both parents and children.

Another possibility is that deviancy is inherited—that there is a gene for deviancy. This is the "nature" view in the nature-vs.-nurture debate. It is the view that is typically espoused by behavioral geneticists. For example, Mednick et al. (1984) report that criminality is more intergenerationally correlated between biological parents than between adoptive parents. If this interpretation is correct, then short of genetic engineering there is absolutely nothing that can be done to break the intergenerational transmission of deviance.

Parents have a causal effect on their children if the answer to the following question is positive: Suppose that by chance a parent turned to crime, perhaps because he agreed to participate in a randomized trial conducted by some desperate criminologists or because he was mistakenly targeted by the Mafia. Whatever the random reason happened to be, were the children of such "random criminals" more disposed to crime than other children? If not, there is no causal effect of parents on the criminal behavior of their children. Randomization disconnects the criminal behavior of parents from genetic, environmental, and other confounding influences.

Environments have a causal effect on the behavior of children if the answer to the following question is positive: Suppose by chance a parent with young children moves from a "bad" neighborhood to a "good" one. This might have happened because the parent applied for housing assistance and, when he reached the top of the waiting list, an appropriate house happened to be available in a good neighborhood. Were the children of these fortunate parents less disposed to crime than the children of parents who moved to worse neighborhoods or remained in bad neighborhoods? If not, there are no causal environmental effects on criminal behavior. In chapter 6 I discuss precisely this question.

Empirical correlations are informative about the facts but not about their causal explanations. Causal explanation requires hypothesis testing, which involves decomposing the intergenerational correlation coefficient into its component parts: heredity, parent behavior, sibling behavior, and various environmental influences. If the answers to the two questions above are negative—that is, if there is no causal effect of parenting, and there are no causal environmental effects—then the intergenerational correlation must be genetic by default. This challenging task of hypothesis testing is a central topic in this book. First, however, I should discuss the main hypotheses that purport to explain why the outcomes of parents and children are correlated, and why the outcomes of siblings are correlated.

3   Theory: What Explains the Intergenerational and Sibling Correlations?

This chapter critically reviews various theories that purport to explain intergenerational and sibling correlations. These theories have been developed in a variety of disciplines, including behavioral genetics, psychology, sociology, and economics. In short, most of the social sciences have been involved in one way or another in attempting to explain these correlations. Behavioral genetics is a completely dedicated discipline, exclusively concerned with explaining these correlations. The other disciplines have much broader agendas, covering a vast range of other issues. Indeed, in psychology, sociology, and economics these correlations are of significant although not of central interest. As was pointed out in chapter 1, these disciplines have largely developed along parallel lines; there has been almost no interdisciplinary cross-fertilization.

3.1   Axiomatic vs. *Ad Hoc* Theory

3.1.1   The Family

Since intergenerational and sibling correlations result from the behavior of parents, children, and siblings, common sense suggests that any theory that purports to explain them should include a theory of the participants' behavior. This means that the theory should refer to the collective behavior of families, not just to the individual behavior of their members. More accurately, it should refer to the behavior of the participants in the context of the family. It is challenging enough to develop a theory for individual family members. It is much more challenging to develop a theory that explains their behavior as a family and the complex interactions that are likely to take place between parents and children and those that are likely to take place between siblings. In short, families are complex organizations, and an integral and indispensable component of any theory that purports to explain the correlations between parents, children, and siblings must also be a theory of the family.

The family has traditionally been an important focus of interest for psychology and sociology. Psychology, especially developmental psychology, is concerned with the development of the child in a family setting. However, the focus is on the child rather than the family. Social psychology is concerned with the child's development in the context of his broader social environment, including his peers and the cultural context. The family per se does not constitute a focus of interest in psychology. In sociology it is just the opposite: the family per se is a major focus of interest, and the behavior and development of the individual in the family are less important. Therefore, whereas psychology is micro-oriented, in that it is mainly concerned with the individual in the family rather than with the family per se, sociology is, on the whole, macro-oriented, in that it is mainly concerned with the family as a whole rather than with the individual.

Economics discovered the family relatively recently.[1] In fact, before 1970 the family was hardly mentioned in economics. Since then, labor economics has attached importance to the household as a decision-making unit in decisions about work, leisure, and consumption.[2] Previously, economics treated the family as just a collection of individuals in which the whole was simply the sum of its parts. Secondly, population economics is concerned with fertility and with investments in child development. A celebrated contribution is the Quality vs. Quantity Theory of fertility, originally proposed by Becker and Lewis (1973), which will be elucidated below. Third, the economics of the family, including marriage, divorce, and the behavior of children, has developed as a subdiscipline in its own right.

The only discipline that has ignored the potential importance of the family is behavioral genetics. This is particularly surprising since behavioral genetics is exclusively concerned with correlations between siblings, and despite the claim that "because behavioral genetics is an interdisciplinary field that combines genetics and the behavioral sciences, it is complex" (Plomin et al. 2001, p xviii) I shall argue that in practice behavioral genetics is not interdisciplinary. Indeed, the name "behavioral genetics" is a misnomer: behavioral genetics has almost nothing to say about human behavior, though it has a lot to say about genetics.[3] In behavioral genetics the family is lumped together as part of an amorphous environment. A recurring criticism in this book is that behavioral genetics pays lip service to the role of the environment in determining outcomes. In practice, behavioral genetics attributes the differences between sibling correlations to heredity and genetics. By default, the family and other potential influences on sibling correlations are assumed to be non-existent. For example, the difference between the correlations for identical twins and those for fraternal twins is simply assumed to be genetic. The same applies to the difference between the correlations for biological siblings and those for adopted siblings.

Perhaps parents relate to identical twins differently than to fraternal twins or other children. Perhaps identical twins interact differently than fraternal twins, both with each other and with other members of their family. Perhaps parents who adopt differ from parents who do not adopt, and relate to their biological children differently than to their adopted children. Perhaps adopted children differ from orphans who aren't adopted. Perhaps biological siblings interact with each other differently than they do with adopted siblings. Perhaps parents have a say in what children they adopt, but they certainly cannot choose their biological children. Perhaps adoption agencies place adoptees non-randomly in families that seem suitable. This incomplete list of rhetorical perhapses goes largely ignored in behavioral genetics.

It is not as if behavioral geneticists are unaware of the potential roles of the family and other environmental phenomena on correlations within the family (see, e.g., Plomin et al. 2001, chapter 15). This criticism is not about theory. It is a methodological criticism of the way the contribution of heredity to sibling correlations is estimated in behavioral genetics. As I will explain below, the equal-environments assumption in behavioral genetics is tantamount to the claim that the role of the family and other aspects of the environment may be ignored in estimating the contribution of heredity to sibling correlations. Since the equal-environments assumption (EEA) is of central methodological importance, and without it behavioral genetics as we know it would be meaningless, textbooks on behavioral genetics go out of their way to explain why the EEA is empirically valid. These claims in favor of the EEA are critically reviewed below and again in chapter 5. It should be noted here that the various justifications that have been proffered for the EEA do not, on the whole, relate to the long list of perhapses, which have the family as their common denominator.

Another recurrent criticism in this book is that, just as behavioral genetics gives behavior and the environment short shrift, developmental psychology has given heredity short shrift. This criticism does not apply to all branches of psychology; however, the central importance of developmental psychology cannot be compared to the marginal importance of evolutionary psychology. The tabula rasa constitutes a basic axiom for much of modern psychology. This axiom, which dates back to Aristotle, and which 2,000 years later was re-invented by Locke and Rousseau, asserts that all knowledge is acquired through experience of the world. This view was challenged by Darwin and Galton, who attached central importance to biology and heredity. The slate is not entirely blank, but is to some extent affected by heredity. Thus was born the nature-nurture debate. Since then, psychology has gravitated alternatively to nature and nurture. With the rise of behaviorism in the early twentieth century Watson and Skinner returned psychology to the tabula rasa, and nature was demoted in favor of nurture. This demotion was further consolidated by Piaget, who hypothesized that children develop as "inquiring scientists"—i.e., that through trial and error they figure out how the physical and social worlds operate. Piaget acknowledged that some children do this job better than others, depending on their intelligence and cultural background. However, intelligence is not inherited.

Psychoanalytical theory doesn't attach importance to heredity either. Indeed, Freud scarcely mentioned heredity. This does not mean that Freud believed that the slate is blank. On the contrary, he believed that we are born with instincts and drives. However, the development of the child is assumed to be largely driven by nurture. There are, of course, major branches of psychology, such as cognitive psychology, in which the issue of heredity does not arise. The same applies to sociology. However, there probably is an ideological objection to the role of heredity in human outcomes in psychology and in sociology. It is politically incorrect to claim that heredity counts and nature matters. Idealistic beliefs that we are all born with equal potential and that the genes of parents do not matter for the outcomes of their children prevail. Only the environment is said to matter. The psychologist J. B. Watson put it in terms reminiscent of the Jesuits: "Give me a dozen healthy infants, well-formed and my own specified world to bring them up in, and I'll guarantee to take any one at random and train him to be any type of specialist I might select—doctor, lawyer, artist, merchant-chief, and, yes, even beggar-man." (Watson 1930, p. 104) Watson's fantasy arguably served as the basis for a great deal of psychology in the twentieth century.

3.1.2 Axiomatic Theory

Apart from discussing theories of the intergenerational and sibling correlations, there is another theme to this chapter. I shall distinguish between two types of theory: *ad hoc* theory and axiomatic theory. *Ad hoc* theory is based on some mechanical rule of human behavior. Take, for example, Erik Erikson's theory of development. Erikson suggested eight age-related stages of development spanning from infancy to old age. At each stage there is a developmental hurdle that, if not satisfactorily surmounted, jeopardizes the development process as a whole. For instance, stage 3 typically occurs between the ages of 4 and 6 years, when the child learns to balance initiative and guilt. If a child's parents aren't too controlling or strict, the child develops high standards and doesn't feel guilty about taking initiatives of his own. Nor does he doubt his ability to measure up to those initiatives. During stage 4, which usually lasts from the age of 6 years until puberty, the child masters cognitive and social skills. If that goes well, the child develops a sense of confidence: if it goes badly, he feels inferior and inadequate. The probability of successfully passing through stage 4 depends on how well the child came out of stage 3. But the probability of successfully passing through stage 3 depends on how well the child came out of stage 2, and so on.

Erikson's theory is *ad hoc* because it entails mechanical rules that relate the probability of passing through a later stage to how well the child passed through an earlier stage. Why should failure in stage 3 jeopardize stage 4? Suppose in stage 3 the child has excessively strict parents and he feels guilty about taking initiatives. How does this make it harder for the child in stage 4 to balance industry with inferiority? The *ad hoc* answer is of the just-so variety. It does not stem from an axiomatic treatment of the transition from stage 3 to stage 4. It may or may not be *a priori* plausible that what happens in stage 4 should be related to what happened in stage 3. Once the axioms are stated clearly, it may make theoretical sense that stage 4 depends on stage 3; but without such axioms, one has to take Erikson's theory or leave it.

Erikson's theory is inductive because it is empirically driven by observations rather than by axioms. In contrast, axiomatic theory is deductive. It begins with a set of axioms, which are used to develop a theory that predicts behavior. For example, the central axiom of sociobiology is that animals, and perhaps humans too, maximize survival. That simple axiom leads to numerous empirical predictions about mating, fertility, and family roles. Entropy is an axiom in physical chemistry and in statistical mechanics. A central axiom of economics is that individuals maximize utility and firms maximize profits. These axioms lead to predictions about economic behavior. Theoretical physics is entirely axiomatic. For example, Relativity Theory is based on axioms concerning the property of light. Many of the aforementioned axioms are quite abstract. For example, in economics utility is unmeasurable. Nanoscience is based on axiomatic phenomena that are unobservable. The issue is not whether the axioms themselves are right or wrong. The issue is whether they enable the development of fruitful theories that lead to successful predictions that have empirical content. Therefore, axioms should be judged by the empirical success of the theories that are derived from them. If the predictions of a theory aren't refuted by the data, it is as if the axioms upon which the theory is based are reasonable. If the predictions of a theory are refuted by the data, the axioms should be criticized and replaced. To argue about the validity of the axioms themselves is pointless.

A recurrent theme in this book is that most of the theory about intergenerational and sibling correlations is *ad hoc*. Popper (1963, p. 61) notes that "a 'good' theory is not *ad hoc*, while a 'bad' theory is." This criticism is especially applicable to psychology and sociology. I noted in chapter 1 that psychology and sociology embrace numerous subdisciplines that do not share axioms. For example, psychoanalytical theory shares almost nothing in common with cognitive theory, which shares almost nothing in common with behavioral theory. I have always pitied psychology students because they are required to learn a bewildering array of theories, and the theories differ considerably. In contrast, students of economics, like students of the natural sciences, are exposed to a unified set of axioms which are common to all economic theory, including labor economics, public economics, the theory of international trade, growth economics, and macroeconomics. Even where there are major scientific disagreements, especially in macroeconomics, it is not because the protagonists are using entirely different axioms.[4] The axioms are the same, but there is ambiguity in the interpretation of the data. The fact that there is a common set of axioms enables, for example, Keynesian economists and neoclassical economists to engage in dialog and to understand why they disagree. The same does not apply to developmental psychologists and social psychologists, or to adherents of different schools of developmental psychology (e.g., Lacanians and Jungeans). In summary, psychology and sociology are fractionalized because there are no agreed-upon axioms. In contrast, the natural sciences and economics aren't fractionalized, because there are agreed-upon axioms that integrate diverse bodies of theory.

3.1.3   Mathematical vs. Verbal Idioms

The Quality vs. Quantity Theory is an axiomatic theory of human fertility. Its axioms of utility maximization and rationality lie at the foundations of economics as a whole, as well as at the foundations of the economics of the family, including marriage, divorce, and bequests. One purpose of this chapter is to extend this axiomatic theory to the two-way interaction between parents and children, and to the two-way interaction between siblings. Axiomatic theory tends to suit the mathematical idiom rather than a verbal idiom. This is because the axioms are sharply defined and are unambiguous. I mentioned in chapter 1 that in the backlash to the proposal that sociobiology might be applied to humans as well as to animals there was also a methodological objection. Sociobiology adopted a mathematical idiom, using differential calculus, optimization techniques, and game theory. That idiom differs radically from the verbal idiom traditionally used in psychology and sociology. The verbal idiom makes it easier to engage in woolly thinking, whereas the mathematical idiom enforces sharpness, rigor, and unambiguity. The mathematical idiom also enables the development of theory that would be either impossible or very difficult with a verbal idiom. It is probable that all the logical conclusions reached using the formal methods of optimization theory and game theory can be stated verbally; it is doubtful that they could have been reached verbally. Mathematics streamlines logical argument; it forces would-be theoreticians to be sure that B follows from A and that C is consistent with A and B.

The natural sciences adopted the formal idiom long ago. Imagine what theoretical physics would be like today had Newton and others insisted on using the verbal idiom to develop their theories. The Inverse Square Law of gravity could have been developed verbally, but it was easier to use differential calculus jointly invented by Leibniz and Newton. Quantum mechanics and nanoscience could not have been developed using the verbal idiom. On the whole, the social sciences have clung to the verbal idiom and have criticized the mathematical idiom as reductionist. An important exception to this is economics. As was pointed out in chapter 1, originally economics was just as verbal as other social sciences, but during the twentieth century formalism became victorious over verbalism (Weintraub 2002). Perhaps the watershed came in 1947, when Paul Samuelson published *Foundations of Economic Analysis*, in which he complains: "Moreover, I have come to feel that Marshall's dictum that 'it seems doubtful whether anyone spends his time well in reading lengthy translations of economic doctrines into mathematics, that have not been made by himself' should be exactly reversed. The laborious literary working over of essentially simple mathematical concepts such as is characteristic of much of modern economic theory is not only unrewarding from the standpoint of advancing the science, but involves as well mental gymnastics of a peculiarly depraved type." (Samuelson 1947, p. 6)

The depravity to which Samuelson referred concerns making lengthy verbal statements of ideas that can be written more succinctly in a few lines of mathematics. Because mental gymnastics is difficult, the chances of making logically incorrect statements increase when the idiom is verbal. Finally, even the best mental gymnast may not be able to express verbally ideas which can be stated mathematically. In the interests of deterring depravity, economics students have long since been required to learn mathematics and statistical theory to an advanced level. In this respect they have joined their peers in the natural sciences.

There is no doubt that the mathematical idiom is reductionist in the sense that it forces theoreticians to simplify. However, this is a strength rather than a weakness. All good theory simplifies. It seeks to explain important aspects of natural and human behavior rather than all aspects. Good theoretical models are simpler than the world they seek to explain. The arrogant theorist who tries to explain everything is destined to explain nothing. The modest theorist who seeks to explain some important phenomena while ignoring other possibly related phenomena is likely to be more successful. Good theory distills the essential drivers of behavior; it does not purport to explain all behavior. Also, as was pointed out by Popper (1963, p. 241), good theory tends to be simple, because simple theories are easier to test.

Not all psychologists have shunned formalism. As I pointed out in chapter 1, Bowlby (1969) suggested that the mathematics of dynamic optimization might contribute to the understanding of instinctive behavior. Bowlby himself did not bring this vision to fruition, nor have later generations of developmental psychologists. Nevertheless, since van Geert (1991) some psychologists have explored the use of mathematical techniques to model growth and development. They have used nonlinear mechanics and other concepts borrowed from the physical sciences to simulate how stressors, parenting, and capacity constraints might affect child behavior over time.[5] These modeling exercises have been *ad hoc* in the sense that a system of plausible feedback equations has been specified for the mutual reactions of parents and children, and the dynamic properties of the system has been investigated. Van Geert and others did not, however, intend to undertake an axiomatic treatment of the behavior of parents and children, which is an objective of the present chapter.

3.1.4 Body-Mind Dichotomy

This axiomatic treatment, as we shall see, gives rise to feedback equations between parents and children and defines equilibrium trajectories for children and parents in the sense of Tschacher and Haken (2007). Tschacher and Haken, like other *ad hoc* theorists, are troubled by the body-mind dichotomy in which mechanical theories about bodily behavior are divorced from the mental processes of the brain or mind that govern the body. Popper (1963, p. 294) pointed out that the body-mind problem "is due to a faulty way of talking about minds, i.e. it is due to talking as if mental states exist *in addition* to behavior." Indeed, in axiomatic theory the body-mind dichotomy turns out to be false. Body and mind are bridged, since the intentions, wishes, and goals in the minds of parents and children are axiomatized while the implications of these axioms for the body in terms of crying, parenting, and development are derived.[6]

Another dichotomy that is bridged concerns agent-based modeling versus variable-based modeling[7] (Smith and Conrey 2007). Axiomatic theory focuses on agents (such as parents, children, and siblings) and on the static and dynamic interactions of these agents. Although the theory is agent-based, what results is a variable-based model in which the two variables are infant development and parenting. The structural parameters in the variable-based model may, however, be traced back to the axioms in the agent-based model.

In summary, axiomatic theory is fundamentally different from *ad hoc* theory. Axiomatic theory is better suited to the mathematical idiom than to the verbal idiom. Axiomatic theory tends to be simple, since it is based on only a few axioms. When applied to human behavior, axiomatic theory bridges the body-mind problem. The axioms refer to the mind, whereas the predictions of the theory based on these axioms refer to the body. Axiomatic theory is more falsifiable than *ad hoc* theory because it is simple.

3.1.5 Theory vs. Interpretation

Scientific theory must be empirically falsifiable; if theory is not falsifiable, it is not scientific (Popper 1963). Scientific hypotheses are about causal effects of actions on outcomes. Take, for example, the hypothesis that Y varies inversely with X. If X increases, Y should decreases because the theory predicts an adverse causal effect of X on Y. If Y does not decrease when X increases, the theory is false. If Y decreases, the theory is corroborated. Corroboration does not mean that the theory is true, since sooner or later all theories are falsified. Scientific progress is measured by our knowledge of what is false.

Many so-called scientific theories are not scientific at all, because they cannot be falsified empirically. They are *ex post* interpretations of empirical events rather than *ex ante* predictions of these events. A good example of what I mean is the Stages of Growth Theory (Rostow 1960). Rostow used empirical data to identify three stages of economic development; the pre-industrial stage, the "takeoff" stage, and the maturity stage. When I first read about the Stages of Growth Theory, I could not help picturing an airplane accelerating down a runway, taking off, and then settling into steady flight. In fact, I used this analogy when I was an undergraduate. I wrote that, whereas there is a theory of aerodynamics that explains why airplanes do not crash on takeoff, Rostow does not offer a theory that predicts why "takeoff" into economic development should happen. He is simply interpreting the past, rather than predicting the future. To judge by the disappearance of Rostow's "theory" from modern textbooks on economic growth (Barro and Sala-I-Martin, 2003), maybe I was right. The theory of economic growth, like economic theory in general, is axiomatic. Rostow's stages were not derived from axioms; they were simply based on ad hoc interpretation of the data.

I think something similar can be said of Erikson's theory of the stages of human development. It is not a scientific theory that can be falsified empirically. Instead, it is an *ex post* interpretation of human development. When psychology textbooks criticize psychoanalytical theory for being non-scientific (see, e.g., Atkinson et al. 2000, pp. 462–464), they mean that it cannot be falsified by data. If, like religion, theory cannot be falsified, it is metaphysical rather than scientific. In the "Keynes-Tinbergen Debate," Keynes, who revolutionized macro-economics in the 1930s, argued that economic theory was essentially interpretative. (See Hendry and Morgan 1995.) It cannot predict the future, but it may explain the past. Tinbergen, who pioneered macro-econometrics in the 1930s, argued that economic theory was inherently falsifiable since its predictions could be tested empirically. We shall return to this debate in chapter 5. In the meantime, note that just because a theory is not scientific since it is not falsifiable, this does not necessarily mean that it has no value. The study of history has evident value even if it is largely interpretative. Just as people may find solace in religion or in transcendental meditation, they may also find solace in psychoanalysis. A world without metaphysics would be very dull. However, we should be clear about the demarcation line between science, which is predictive and falsifiable, and metaphysics, which is not.

3.2   Behavioral Genetics

Behavioral genetics is concerned with how genes affect outcomes or phenotypes. It is not directly concerned with explaining why the outcomes of children are correlated with the outcomes of their parents. However, children inherit their parents' genes, and if genes affect behavior then the outcomes of children should be correlated with the outcomes of parents. Although heredity plays an important background role in behavioral genetics, intergenerational correlations have not been a focus of interest in behavioral genetics. Instead, behavioral genetics has focused on correlations between siblings, especially twins or adopted siblings. The reason for this is that identical twins are more genetically similar than fraternal twins, and adopted siblings are genetically different from biological siblings.

By comparing the degree of correlation in the outcomes of pairs of identical twins against the degree of correlation in the outcomes of pairs of fraternal twins, behavioral geneticists hope to learn something about how genes affect outcomes. If the outcomes of identical twins are more correlated than the outcomes of fraternal twins, perhaps this has something to do with how genes affect outcomes. The same applies to comparisons between the correlation in the outcomes of pairs of biological siblings and the correlation in the outcomes of pairs of adopted siblings. If the outcomes of biological siblings are more correlated than the outcomes of adopted siblings, genetics may have something to do with it. Behavioral genetics is dedicated to the estimation of heritability, which is defined as the percentage contribution of genotypes to the variance of phenotypes. For example, if the variance of IQ in the population is 40 and the contribution of genotypes is 25, heritability is 62.5 percent.

I shall argue that the fact that identical twins are more correlated than fraternal twins does not necessarily mean that the difference between them is due to genes. Also, the fact that biological siblings are more correlated than adopted siblings does not necessarily mean that the difference between them is due to genes. The reason for this is that the effects of parents, family, and social milieu, or what behavioral genetics lumps under the "environment," are potential confounders. If the environment (especially the parents) relates to identical twins differently than to fraternal twins, identical twins might be more correlated simply because their parents and family relate to them more similarly. In short, the methodology of behavioral genetics assumes that only genes matter, because it ignores the effect of environments on outcomes.

This, as we shall see, is a methodological criticism. It does not mean that behavioral genetics assumes that only genes matter and that environments do not matter. On the contrary, behavioral genetics typically estimates that roughly half of what we observe is due to genes and the other half is due to environments. My point is that these proportions are generally incorrect because behavioral genetics makes questionable methodological assumptions to obtain these estimates. It might be that genes explain more or less than 50 percent. It might even be the case that genes explain 0 percent, in which case outcomes have nothing to do with genes.

3.2.1 Elementary Statistics

To evaluate the scientific contribution of behavioral genetics, it is important to understand some elementary statistical concepts. Behavioral genetics decomposes outcomes (such as schooling and height) into a genetic component (denoted by G) and an environmental component. The latter has a shared component (denoted by E) and an unshared component (denoted by R). In the case of siblings the shared component is induced by shared parents and family backgrounds. The unshared component arises because siblings are exposed to environmental influences that are separate and specific. For example, siblings might attend different schools. The outcome or phenotype is assumed to be the linear sum of these components: $Y = G + E + R$. People vary in their outcomes (Y) since, e.g., their heights differ. They vary by their genotypes (G) and by their shared and unshared environmental exposures (E and R). Some are genetically predisposed to be taller than others; hence people vary by G. They also vary by E and R, since, e.g., nutrition might affect growth and nutrition varies between individuals.

The statistical concept of variance is traditionally used to measure the extent to which we differ. Unless we all have the same height, some of us must be taller than average and some of us must be shorter. The average height is defined as the mean height. The variance is defined as the average squared deviation from the mean. Since the square of something is always positive (the square of 2 is 4 but so is the square of –2), the variance attaches the same importance to someone who is 2 centimeters shorter than the mean and someone who is 2 centimeters taller. Since squares increase nonlinearly (the square of 4 = 16 is 4 times the square of 2 = 4, yet 4 is only twice as large as 2), the more a person deviates from the mean, the disproportionately greater is his contribution to the variance. The variance is just one among many ways to measure dispersion or inequality. (Other measures are considered in subsection 8.5.1.)

Since Y, G, E, and R vary by individual, each of these variables has a variance. The variances are denoted here by var(Y), var(G), var(E), and var(R). The standard deviation (sd) is simply the square root of the variance. Next, we must define the statistical concept of covariance, which measures the degree to which one variable (such as G) varies when some other variable (such as E) varies. The covariance between G and E, referred to as cov(GE), measures the degree of statistical association between G and E. It is defined as the average of the deviations from the mean for G multiplied by the deviations from the mean for E. The correlation coefficient between, say, G and E is the covariance between G and E divided by the product of their standard deviations, or

$$r_{GE} = \frac{\text{cov}(GE)}{\text{sd}(G)\text{sd}(E)},$$

which in behavioral genetics is referred to as the *gene-environment correlation*.

If parents take account of their children's genotypes, the gene-environment correlation will not be 0. For example, if parents behave more sensitively toward their less genetically fit children, the gene-environment correlation will be negative. If brighter children attend better schools, the gene-environment correlation will be positive. The same considerations apply to unshared environments, so r_{GP} will not generally be 0.

Intuitively, the decomposition $Y = G + E + R$ implies that the variance of Y is related to variations in G, E, and R. In fact, the variance of Y equals the sum of the variances of G, E, and R plus twice the covariance between these variables—that is,

$$\text{var}(Y) = \text{var}(G) + \text{var}(E) + \text{var}(R) + 2\,\text{cov}(GE) + 2\text{cov}(GR) + 2\text{cov}(ER).$$

This is the formula for the analysis of variance (ANOVA). If G, E, and R happen to be independent, i.e., they are uncorrelated, the covariance terms will be 0, in which case the ANOVA model simplifies to

$$\text{var}(Y) = \text{var}(G) + \text{var}(E) + \text{var}(R).$$

3.2.2   Gene-Environment Correlations and Interactions

The definition of heritability in behavioral genetics, usually denoted by h^2, is defined as the ratio of the genetic variance to the variance of the outcome:

$$h^2 = \frac{\text{var}(G)}{\text{var}(Y)}.$$

It is tempting to say that h^2 expresses the relative importance of genetics in the outcome, and that if $h^2 = 1$ the outcome is entirely explained by genetics and if $h^2 = 0$ the outcome is entirely explained by environment. This would be correct if the covariance between G and E and the covariance between G and R were 0. However, if these covariances are not 0, h^2 is not informative of the relative importance of genetics and environment in the outcome, because the shares of the contributions of genes and the environment do not add up to 1. The counterpart of h^2 for the environment is e^2 ("environmentability"), defined as $\text{var}(E)/\text{var}(Y)$.

The simple point that h^2 may not measure heritability is illustrated numerically in table 3.1, where R is ignored for simplicity. In case 1, the genotypic variance is assumed to be equal to the variance of the environment, and the gene-environment correlation is assumed to be 0. In this case it is obvious that heritability is equal to ½ because G and E have the same variance. Case 2 shows that matters are different when the gene-environment correlation is not 0. If it is ½, heritability decreases

Table 3.1
Heritability and the gene-environment correlation.

Case	Var(G)	Var(E)	r_{EG}	Heritability	e^2
1	1	1	0	0.5	0.5
2	1	1	0.5	0.33	0.33
3	1	1	–0.5	1	1
4	1	1	–0.7	1.67	1.67
5	2	1	0	0.66	0.34
6	2	1	0.5	0.45	0.23

to ⅓. Notice that the contribution of the environment to the variance of the outcome (e^2) is also ⅓. This means that the contribution of the gene-environment correlation to the variance of Y is ⅓ too. If the gene-environment correlation is negative, heritability and e^2 increase (case 3) and may even exceed 1 (case 4). In this case more than a 100 percent of the phenotype variance is attributable to heritability. In cases 5 and 6, the genotype variance is larger than the variance of the environment, so that given the gene-environment correlation, heritability is larger and e^2 is smaller. Table 3.1 shows that heritability has no obvious meaning unless the gene-environment correlation happens to be 0.

In behavioral genetics the gene-environment correlation is typically assumed to be 0 by default. However, in a minority of cases the gene-environment correlation is sometimes taken explicitly into consideration. (See, e.g., Jencks 1972. It is probably no coincidence that Jencks is a sociologist and not a behavioral geneticist. Sociology attaches more importance to the role of behavior than behavioral genetics does.)

Another phenomenon that is typically assumed to be 0 by default is what is known in behavioral genetics as "the gene-environment interaction." The equation $Y = G + E$ is linear and additive. If there is gene-environment interaction, this equation becomes $Y = G + E + GE$, which is nonlinear and no longer additive in G and E. The gene-environment correlation captures the idea that, say, a person with a genetic predisposition to hay fever is less likely to visit flower gardens. The gene-environment interaction captures the idea that a person with a genetic predisposition to hay fever will sneeze more if he visits flower gardens. It is obvious that gene-environment correlations and interactions should be behaviorally related, although in behavioral genetics they are usually treated as separate phenomena.

Table 3.2
Heritability and the gene-environment interaction (based on equation 72 in chapter 10).

Case	Var(G)	Var(E)	r_{EG}	Heritability	e^2
1	1	1	0	0.33	0.33
2	1	1	0.5	0.27	0.27
3	1	1	-0.5	057	0.57
4	1	1	1	0.33	0.33
5	2	2	0	0.25	0.25
6	2	1	0.5	0.34	0.17
7	1	2	0.5	0.17	0.34

In subsection 10.13.1, I derive the definition of heritability when there is gene-environment interaction. In that case, it turns out that heritability depends on the gene-environment correlation, as illustrated in table 3.2. Case 1 in table 3.2 may be compared with case 1 in table 3.1, since the gene-environment correlation is 0. The gene-environment interaction reduces heritability from 0.5 in table 3.1 to 0.33 in table 3.2. This is because the gene-environment interaction increases the variance of the phenotype. Case 2 in table 3.2 shows that when the gene-environment correlation is positive heritability decreases to 0.27, which is smaller than its counterpart in case 2 in table 3.1. Heritability increases when the gene-environment correlation is $-\frac{1}{2}$ instead of $\frac{1}{2}$ (case 3), but it is smaller than its counterpart in case 3 in table 3.1. Case 5 shows that heritability varies inversely with the variances of G and E. Heritability decreases to $\frac{1}{4}$ from $\frac{1}{3}$ in case 1. In contrast, in table 3.1 heritability is independent of these variances. Case 6 shows that heritability increases from 0.27 to 0.34 when the variance of G increases to 2. However, this is less than case 5 in table 3.1. Case 7 shows that if the variance of E increases heritability decreases to 0.17. Therefore, cases 6 and 7 are symmetrical.

Tables 3.1 and 3.2 make the simple point that heritability is highly sensitive to assumptions about the gene-environment correlation and the gene-environment interaction. For the most part, however, behavioral geneticists tend to assume that the gene-environment interaction and the gene-environment correlations are 0. What, one might ask, is the point of calculating a parameter such as heritability when almost any estimate can be concocted from the data with whatever arbitrary behavioral assumptions that one is prepared to make?

Behavioral genetics does not distinguish between the environment itself and the environment's effect on outcomes. If the outcome is sneezing and the environment is flower gardens, behavioral genetics focuses on the contribution of flower gardens to sneezing. Therefore, if John, who is not sensitive to pollen, sneezes ten times after spending an hour in a flower garden, and Mary, who is sensitive to pollen, sneezes ten times after spending 5 minutes in the flower garden, in behavioral genetics the environmental contribution to sneezing is the same for John and Mary. In subsection 10.13.2, I calculate the relationship between the variance of the effect of the environment on phenotypes (E represented by sneezing in flower gardens) and the variance of environmental exposure (E^* represented by time spent in flower gardens) and the variance in the sensitivity to the environment (sensitivity to pollen). It is easy to show that the variance between environmental exposure (time spent in flower gardens) and what behavioral genetics defines as the variance of E (sneezing) are very different phenomena. In fact the relationship between them depends on the sensitivity-environment correlation, as illustrated in table 3.3.

In table 3.3 it is assumed that the variance of the actual environment, denoted by E^*, is 1. The variance of sensitivity to the environment (denoted by a) is also assumed to be 1. The influence of the environment on the outcome of individual i is therefore

$$E_i = (\alpha + a_i)E_i^* .$$

For convenience, E^* and a are assumed to be random variables with standard normal distributions and α is set equal to 1. Table 3.3 attaches importance to the sensitivity-environment correlation (i.e., the correlation between a and E^*) (column 2), the correlation between a and the square of E^* (column 3), and the correlation between the square of a and the square of E^* (column 4). If individuals sensitive to pollen avoid flower gardens, the sensitivity-environment correlation will be negative. If this response is nonlinear (e.g., the degree to which individuals

Table 3.3
The relationship between environmental variance and its influence (based on equation 74a in chapter 10).

Case	r_{aE^*}	$r_{aE^{*2}}$	$r_{a2E^{*2}}$	Var(E)
1	0	0	0	1
2	±0.5	0	0	0.75
3	0	0.5	0	5
4	0	0	0.5	2.5
5	±0.5	0.5	0.5	6.25

avoid flower gardens varies with their sensitivity to pollen), the correlations in columns 3 and 4 will not be 0.

In case 1 in table 3.3, all three correlations are assumed to be 0, in which case the variance of environmental influence is equal to 1. In this case the variance of E equals the variance of E^*. In case 2 the sensitivity-environment correlation is assumed to be 0.5 and the variance of E decreases to 0.75. What matters is the absolute value of this correlation, so it makes no difference whether the correlation is positive or negative. In subsequent cases in table 3.3 the other correlations are changed. In case 5, all correlations are assumed to be 0.5 and the variance of environmental influence (E) is more than six times the true variance in environmental exposure.

The counterpart of table 3.3 for the sibling correlation between environmental effects may be found in table 10.1 in chapter 10. It is evident in that table that, in general, the sibling correlations between environmental effects (E) and the actual environment (E^*) are quite different in magnitude. In fact, the former may be positive while the latter is negative, and vice versa. Behavioral genetics makes strong assumptions about the sibling correlation for environmental effects. Specifically, it is assumed that the sibling correlation for E is the same for MZ and DZ twins and for biological and adopted siblings. Since these correlations depend on the parameters that feature in table 3.3, this assumes that all the parameters featured in table 3.3 are the same for MZ and DZ twin siblings. They are also the same for biological and adopted siblings.

The distinction between environmental influence and environmental exposure does not arise in behavioral genetics, because the two are implicitly assumed to be the same. Either sensitivity is assumed to be implicitly the same or some implicit behavioral assumptions are made. This would not matter if environmental choices were independent of environmental sensitivities (case 1 in table 3.3). For example, pollen-sensitive individuals visit flower gardens as much as their less sensitive counterparts. However, since behavioral genetics pays lip service to the role of behavior in the determination of what happens to us, its failure to address this elementary distinction comes as no surprise.

3.2.3   The Achilles' Heel of Behavioral Genetics: The Equal-Environments Assumption

None of the difficulties cited above would arise if empirical data were available for G and E. It would then be a simple and straightforward matter to work out the relative contributions of nature (genetics) and nurture (environment) to the outcome of interest. The trouble is that there are no such data. Perhaps one day, when the human genome is fully decoded and all the relevant genetic markers have been identified, G will be observable; but it is improbable that E will be completely observable even then. Behavioral genetics tries to solve this problem by comparing data on people who differ in the degree to which they are genetically similar. The classic case is the comparison between pairs of identical (MZ) twins and pairs of fraternal (DZ) twins, since identical twins are genetically more similar than fraternal twins.

In what follows, r_G denotes the sibling correlation for genotypes and r_E denotes the sibling correlation for environments.[8] As will be discussed in greater detail in chapter 10, the difference between the correlation between MZ and DZ twins is informative about heritability provided the following assumptions are made:

(i) MZ twins are perfectly genetically correlated, i.e., $r_G = 1$.

(ii) DZ twins are genetically correlated, with $r_G = 0.5$.

(iii) The sibling correlations for environments do not depend on zygosity, so r_E is the same for both types of twins.

(iv) The gene-environment correlation is 0.

(v) Siblings are equally sensitive to environments.

Since the arbitrary implications of assumptions iv and v have already been discussed, I focus on the first three assumptions. Assumptions i and ii are genetic. The former assumes that MZ twins are genetically identical, which they are. However, they may not be identical epigenetically. Epigenetic drift causes MZ twins to be less correlated as they age. Therefore, the assumption that $r_G = 1$ implicitly assumes that there is no epigenetic drift. Assumption ii is correct if parents do not marry assortatively. If spouses positively select each other, r_G for DZ twins will exceed 0.5 since the genotypes of spouses are positively correlated. The opposite happens if there is negative selection in marriage; that is, if opposite genotypes marry.

The most problematic of the assumptions is assumption iii, referred to in behavioral genetics the *equal-environments assumption*. The EEA means that sibling correlations for environments are the same for MZ and DZ twins. The environment embraces parents, siblings, extended family, schools and neighborhoods. Take parenting, for example. The EEA implies that parents relate to their MZ twins as they do to their DZ twins. They dress their identical twins as they do their fraternal

Table 3.4
Heritability in comparisons of MZ and DZ twins (based on equation 81 in chapter 10).

Case	r_G (MZ)	r_G (DZ)	r_E (MZ)	r_E (DZ)	h^2
1	1	0.5	1	1	0.6
2	1	0.5	0.5	0.5	0.6
3	1	0.5	0.7	0.5	0.2
4	1	0.5	0.5	0.7	0.69
5	0.9	0.5	0.5	0.5	0.75
6	1	0.4	0.5	0.5	0.5
7	1	0.5	0.8	0.5	0

twins, and disregard in every respect the fact that their twins are identical. The EEA also assumes that fraternal twins relate to one another as identical twins do, and that their other siblings completely ignore the fact that their twin siblings happen to be identical. So do school teachers, uncles, aunts, and cousins. In short, the EEA assumes away the rich fabric of human nature by making strong behavioral assumptions.

Goldberger (1977, 1979, 2005) has repeatedly criticized behavioral genetics for ignoring human nature. It is, he has said, all about genetics; it gives no weight to behavior. Indeed, minor changes in the EEA can make large changes to estimates of heritability, as table 3.4 illustrates.

In table 3.4 it is assumed that the phenotype correlation between MZ siblings is 0.8 and that between DZ siblings is 0.5. The fact that MZ twins are more correlated than DZ twins seems to suggest that genetics is involved, since MZ twins are more genetically similar than DZ twins. Cases 1 and 2 show that heritability is 0.6 regardless of the assumptions made about the correlations between sibling environments. What matters is that the equal-environments assumption assumes that these correlations are the same. Cases 3 and 4 show that if the EEA is incorrect, the implications for heritability may be considerable. In case 3, MZ siblings are assumed to have more correlated environments than DZ siblings, as a result of which heritability decreases. The opposite happens in case 4. In case 5, MZ twins are assumed to be imperfectly correlated genetically, possibly owing to epigenetic drift, but they are more correlated than DZ twins. This raises heritability from 0.6 to 0.75. Case 6 shows that if the genetic correlation between DZ twins is 0.4 instead on 0.5 in case 2, heritability decreases from 0.6 to 0.5. Case 7 makes the point that judicious contravention of the EEA can return an estimate of heritability of 0!

Assumption iv is in fact unnecessarily strong. It may be shown that all that is required is to assume that the gene-environment correlations for MZ and DZ twins are the same. I will refer to this as the *equal-gene-environments assumption* (EGEA). A special case of the EGEA is assumption iv according to which the gene-environment correlations for MZ and DZ twins are assumed to be identically equal to 0. Even if the EEA happened to be valid, there is no reason why the EGEA should be valid, and vice versa. Just as the EEA embodies numerous behavioral assumptions, so does the EGEA. More generally, the methodology of behavioral genetics breaks down because both the EEA and the EGEA are too radical.

It is clear that violation of the EEA and violation of the EGEA play havoc with what we might learn from comparing the correlations for identical twin and for fraternal twins. In fact, we can learn almost nothing.[9] By ignoring the behavioral forces that underlie the differences between the gene-environment correlations of the two types of twins and the differences between the environment correlations, behavioral genetics is rather like *Hamlet* without the prince. Behavioral genetics simply assumes that behavior doesn't matter, and then carries on as if all that really matters is genetics. A "behaviorist" who believes that genetics doesn't matter and that environment alone matters might just as easily have assumed that the EEA and the EGEA are invalid, to obtain the desired result that heritability is zero and genetics makes no difference. By making arbitrary assumptions, one can "cook" the results at will. There is obviously no scientific merit in this kind of pseudo-scientific game.

The same criticism applies *a fortiori* to the other workhorse of behavioral genetics: comparing the outcome correlations for pairs of biological sibling pairs and pairs of adopted siblings. However, in this case matters are much worse, because whereas parents cannot choose their biological children, whose births may be regarded as random events, adoption is not a random event. The selection process through which a child is adopted consists of a chain of non-random events. First, parents who give up their children for adoption are unlikely to be a random sample of parents as a whole. Second, adoption agencies don't place children randomly among parents seeking to adopt. Third, parents seeking to adopt may not be like parents as a whole. Apart from these considerations, which do not arise with MZ-DZ comparisons, the EEA and the EGEA are even less plausible in the case of adopted children, because parents may relate to their adopted children

Table 3.5
Heritability in comparisons of adopted and biological siblings (based on equation 85 in chapter 10).

Case	r_E (biological)	r_E (adopted)	r_G	Heritability
1	0.5	0.5	0.5	0.6
2	0.6	0.6	0.5	0.6
3	0.6	0.5	0.5	0.52
4	0.5	0.2	0.5	0
5	0.5	0.5	0.6	0.5

differently than to their biological children, and because dyads of adopted and biological siblings may interact differently than dyads of biological siblings. This selectivity problem is discussed in depth in chapter 5.

In table 3.5 it is assumed that the phenotype correlation for biological siblings happens to be 0.5 and that the correlation between adopted and biological siblings is 0.2. In case 1, where the EEA is assumed to apply, biological siblings are assumed to be genetically correlated 0.5, in which case heritability is 0.6. Case 2 shows that because of the EEA it makes no difference what is assumed about the correlation between the environments of biological and adopted siblings. Heritability is always 0.6, just as in cases 1 and 2 in table 5.4. Case 3 shows that heritability decreases if the environments of biological siblings are more correlated than those of adopted siblings. In fact, heritability is 0 in case 4, which is the counterpart to case 7 in table 5.4. Finally, case 5 shows that the estimate of heritability decreases to 0.5 if the genetic correlation between biological siblings increases to 0.6 (owing to assortative mating, for example).

In summary, the methodology of behavioral genetics is postmodern. By making strong and arbitrary behavioral assumptions, and even genetic assumptions, it creates a narrative to interpret the data. In the words of Goldberger (1979, p. 336): "Implausible assumptions are needed to identify the parameters and produce estimates, and thus keep the model-fitters happy. But estimates produced in that manner do not merit the attention of the rest of us."

3.2.4   Behavioral Genetics: The Case for the Defense
My contention is that behavioral genetics has not taken the EEA and the EGEA seriously enough. Standards of corroboration in behavioral

genetics fall far short of standards in other disciplines in which similar methodological problems arise, and unobserved behavior threatens to be a major confounder. Textbooks on behavioral genetics follow a standard format. They begin by appealing to the EEA and the EGEA as being plausible. Subsequently, a number of studies are cited as "establishing" that the EEA is not grossly violated. Take the EEA first. Plomin et al. (2001, p. 80) deal with the matter summarily: "The EEA has been tested in several ways and appears reasonable for most traits." To establish the EEA it would be necessary to collect data on the environments of MZ and DZ twins. These data might then be used to calculate the correlations between the environments for MZ twins and DZ twins. If the two correlations were not statistically significantly different from each other, we could conclude that the EEA was valid for this sample of data. Since the environment is multi-dimensional, this statistical test should refer to all the variables that are used to represent the environment. This will typically involve a joint test that the EEA is valid in a multivariate context. In any case, just because the EEA happens to be valid in one sample of data does not necessarily mean that it is valid generally.

There are also many environmental variables that aren't observable. Indeed, the most crucial environmental variables may be the least observable ones. Parents' treatment of their children is generally unobserved, as is how the general public reacts to different types of twins. Therefore, even if for some observable measures of the environment satisfy the EEA, it cannot be taken for granted that the same applies for unobserved aspects of the environment.

Then there is the gene-environment correlation, which is either ignored or assumed to be equal for MZ and DZ twins. The treatment of this problem in behavioral genetics is bizarre. For example, chapter 15 of Plomin et al. 2001 is entirely devoted to the contribution of behavioral genetics to the understanding of the gene-environment correlation. There are two pertinent issues here. First, if the gene-environment correlation is not 0, the methodology of behavioral genetics breaks down because the EGEA is violated. Therefore, admitting that the gene-environment correlation is important is a methodological own goal. Second, behavioral genetics congratulates itself on making important discoveries: "The first discovery is that environmental influences tend to make children growing up in the same family different, not similar. Because environmental influences that affect psychological development aren't shared by children in the same family, they are called *nonshared environment*. The second discovery is equally surprising:

Many environmental measures widely used in psychology show genetic influence. This research shows that people create their own experiences, in part for genetic reasons. This topic has been called the *nature of nurture*, although in genetics it is known as the *genotype-environment correlation*." (Plomin et al. 2001, p. 298)

Did it really take behavioral genetics to teach us that our experiencing different environments makes us different? The same applies to discovery 2. Gifted children select environments according to their gifts. Athletically gifted children may attend sport clubs, musically gifted children may learn to play a musical instrument, geniuses attend top schools, and criminally adept children may join the Mafia. Not only has this been understood for centuries; it forms the methodological basis of the theory of program evaluation[10] and other disciplines in the social sciences in which selectivity into treatments or environments is a confounding issue.

Perhaps in behavioral genetics the gene-environment correlation is regarded as an integral element of genetics. Maybe this is what lies behind the nature of nurture. If this is true, why do methodological texts on behavioral genetics (see, e.g., Purcell 2001, p. 353) assume that the gene-environment correlation is 0? Secondly, there is an implicit assumption in behavioral genetics that the gene-environment correlation is one-way causality from genes to the environment, and not the other way around. It is assumed that genes select environments, but not that environments select genes. The former may be true for the gifted, but there are many examples in which environments select genes. For example, in corrective actions, such as Head Start programs, the initiative is taken by the environment rather than by the genes.

3.2.5   The Relationship between Sibling and Intergenerational Correlations

Behavioral genetics focuses mainly on correlations between siblings; it pays little or no attention to intergenerational correlations. The reason for this is that the methodology of behavioral genetics is based on quasi-experiments such as the accident of twin births or adoption. I shall argue in chapter 5 that the methodological insistence on quasi-experiments throws away data on the vast majority of mankind. After all, only a fraction of the population happens to be twins or adoptees. Apart from throwing away possibly informative data on ordinary siblings, the insistence on quasi-experiments also throws away potentially informative data on parents and children.

That sibling correlations depend in part on intergenerational correlations is attributable to the fact that siblings share parents. This parental contribution to sibling correlations has genetic components as well as behavioral components. But even in the hypothetical case that siblings had no parents their outcomes might still be correlated, because siblings interact and influence one another. I will refer to this component of the sibling correlation as the *pure sibling correlation*. In subsection 8.3.2 it will be shown that the correlation between siblings depends on the square of the intergenerational correlation as well as on the pure sibling correlation. If the pure sibling correlation is 0, the sibling correlation is equal to the square of the intergenerational correlation. In this case the sibling correlation must be smaller than the intergenerational correlation because the square of a correlation is always smaller than the correlation itself. For example, if the intergenerational correlation is 0.4 the sibling correlation must be 0.16.

Using equation 53 in chapter 8, we may illustrate the relationship between the sibling correlation and the intergenerational correlation when the pure sibling correlation is not 0. Table 3.6 explores the relationship between these correlations. In case 1 the pure sibling correlation is 0, so the sibling correlation is 0.16. When the pure sibling correlation equals the intergenerational correlation (case 2), the sibling correlation exceeds its components. Cases 3 and 4 show that the sibling correlation is more sensitive to the pure sibling correlation than it is to the intergenerational correlation. Case 5 shows that if the pure sibling correlation is sufficiently negative, the sibling correlation will be negative. Notice that, because the sibling correlation depends on the square of the intergenerational correlation, the sign of the intergenerational correlation does not affect the sibling correlation. However, the sign of the pure sibling correlation matters.

Table 3.6
Relation between sibling and intergenerational correlations (based on equation 53 in chapter 8).

Case	Intergenerational correlation	Pure sibling correlation	Sibling correlation
1	0.4	0	0.16
2	0.4	0.4	0.496
3	0.6	0.4	0.616
4	0.4	0.6	0.664
5	0.4	−0.4	−0.176

3.3   Developmental Psychology

Judith Rich Harris' two books (1998, 2006) have caused a stir in the world of psychology and especially in developmental psychology. Behavioral genetics has found a champion in Harris, who now gets mentioned favorably in textbooks on behavioral genetics.[11] She gets somewhat less favorable mentions in textbooks on psychology. Gazzaniga and Heatherton (2006, p. 465) write: "Although Harris's theoretical stance has received a great deal of criticism, it has stimulated a fresh look at the social lives of children and the importance of peers." In *Hilgard's Introduction to Psychology* she even gets a special box page, where she is cited as one of the contemporary voices in psychology.[12]

Harris' main achievement has been to shake developmental psychology out of its intellectual and scientific lethargy by challenging some of its developmental platitudes. The first belief she challenges is that parents are mainly responsible for determining the outcomes of their adult children. A second developmental belief that she challenges is that genes do not matter. By appealing to behavioral genetics, Harris argues that genes matter. Parents matter for children because of their genes, not because of their parenting. Finally, Harris has brought developmental psychology into contact with social psychology and evolutionary psychology.

My central claim is that developmental psychology is replete with *ad hoc* theory, and that in any case much of it not falsifiable. Indeed, this criticism also applies to Harris' (2006) Three Systems Theory. Developmental psychology seems to stagger from one *ad hoc* theory to the next. New theories have little in common with incumbent and previous theories. What is missing is agreement on common axioms. Each theory is more or less self-contained. It is never clear whether these theories are meant to be descriptive or prescriptive. In their textbook on developmental psychology, Siegler et al. (2003, pp. 164–165) muse:

. . . you may have wondered, "Why not construct a theory that combines the strengths of all four theories?" Such a theory would convey the panoramic overview of Piaget's theory, the precise description of cognitive processes and change mechanisms of information processing theories, and the insights about early competence and the contributions of the social world of core-knowledge and sociocultural theories.

The question can be answered in two ways. One is that the theories have many contradictory features that would be difficult if not impossible to reconcile within a single coherent theory. They differ greatly in their views of children's nature, of whether development included discontinuities, of whether children possess domain-specific learning mechanisms, and of the role of the social world. Creating a formal unified theory from among them is probably impossible.

On the other hand, creating formal theories that incorporate insights from all four theories is not only possible—it is what most researchers do. They borrow wisdom from wherever they can find it.

In short, in developmental psychology *ad hoc* theories are constructed of bits and pieces taken from disparate paradigms that do not share axioms. The natural sciences do not work in this way, nor does economics.

3.3.1   Psychoanalytical Theory

Developmental psychology, or psychology as a discipline, does not set out to explain why the outcomes of parents and children are correlated, or why the outcomes of siblings are correlated. In these respects developmental psychology and behavioral genetics have very different agendas. Nevertheless, because developmental psychology attributes a central role to parents in the development of their children, this assumption is bound to induce correlation between what happens to parents and what happens to children. Also, the fact that siblings share parents has implications for the correlation between sibling outcomes.

This is particularly true for psychoanalytical theory. In Freud's view, development depends on how the individual handles his basic psycho-sexual drives, which are largely unconscious. He has to negotiate five developmental stages (oral, anal, oedipal, latency, and genital). How the individual navigates these stages shapes his personality for life. If at any stage fundamental needs aren't satisfied, the individual becomes fixated on those needs, and he spends the rest of his life trying to compensate for them. Since his mother plays a unique role in satisfying these needs, mothers are crucially important for the development of their children. In Erikson's view, development also depends on how the individual handles a series of age-related developmental crises. In this model too parents, especially mothers, play a central role.

The same applies in Attachment Theory (Bowlby 1969) and in Object Relations Theory (Winnicott 1960). In the former, infants have an evolutionary need to attach to a stable secure base of caring, typically the mother. Bowlby drew his ideas from Freud, especially regarding the effect on later development of the crucial early relationship between mother and infant. He also drew on the ethological theory of Konrad Lorenz, who discovered the imprinting process through which newborn goslings attached themselves to the first mother-like figure they saw. The future development of an infant who is denied attachment, or whose mother jeopardized the attachment process, is at risk. According to object-relations theory, the future development of an infant whose mother isn't "good enough" is at risk.

Object Relations Theory would predict that if a mother is "good enough" then her children are likely to be "good enough." Attachment Theory would predict that a mother who handled the attachment process more successfully is likely to have children who are better at attachment. Children whose mothers sabotaged one of Freud's or Erikson's stages are more likely to repeat the same error when they become parents. Psychoanalytical theory therefore explains why the outcomes of parents, children, and siblings might be correlated.

3.3.2 Behavioral Theory

Learning theory too implies that the outcomes of parents, children, and siblings are likely to be correlated. According to the behaviorism of William James and Robert Skinner, parents can induce behavior in their children that matches their own behavior. This means that parents can largely determine their children's values, their career choices, who they marry, and other outcomes. According to Skinner, parents can also adversely affect the development of their child through "intermittent reinforcing" that makes negative behavior resistant to change. Parents who give in intermittently to inappropriate demands from their children inculcate the very behavior that they hope to stamp out.

In James and Skinner's learning theories, parents play a critical role, which induces correlation in the outcomes between parents, children, and siblings. The same obviously does not apply to social learning theory (Bandura 1965) or indeed to social psychology as whole, where what happens outside the family matters the most. In terms of the parent-environment dichotomy, these theories clearly attach importance to the social environment in which the child develops. The greater the importance of social learning, the less correlated the outcomes of parents, children, and siblings should be.

In the bioecological model (Bronfenbrenner 1979), the child's environment consists of a series of nested structures in which the immediate environment (the "microsystem") includes parents and other family members, schools, and neighborhoods. The emotional development of the child is hypothesized to depend on the quality of component parts of the microsystem and on the quality of the "mesosystem" that connects the elements of the microsystem. When the mesosystem is less supportive, negative outcomes are more likely. Note that whereas in learning models and psychoanalytical models the child is assumed to be passive, in the bioecological model he is assumed to be active. For example, the child can affect the quality of the relationship between his parents, even to his own detriment. The "exosystem" includes the extended family, welfare services, and the parents' workplaces—components of the environment with which the child has no direct contact. Finally, the "macrosystem" comprises the outer envelope of social institutions, including law and order, social class, and the state of the economy.

The bioecological model of development is not so much a theory as a way of organizing thinking about the environment in all its various forms and facets. Because it includes everything, the bioecological model says nothing. Indeed, according to the "chronosystem" the model may change over time as a result of changes in social values, in technology, and in other aspects of the macrosystem and the exosystem. Nothing is constant. The point to be made here is that parents play a small role in this all-embracing bioecology. Moreover, the role they play is not independent of their child or of the meso, exo, and macrosystems.

3.3.3 Evolutionary Psychology

Evolutionary psychology[13] too gives parents a central role in determining the outcomes of their children. Evolutionary psychology applies Darwinian concepts of natural selection and adaptation in human behavior. As was noted in chapter 1, the intellectual origins of evolutionary psychology stem from sociobiology in that survivalism is a unifying axiom. Indeed, it has been suggested that "evolutionary psychology is simply sociobiology rebranded to make it politically more palatable" (Workman and Reader 2008, p. 17). Humans are hypothesized to be motivated by the urge to preserve their genes in the gene pool of the species. According to the important evolutionary concept of "parental-investment theory," parents invest time, energy, and money in raising their offspring (Björklund and Shackelford 1999; Trivers 1972, 1974, 1985). This theory induces correlation in the outcomes of parents, children, and siblings because parents who invest more in their children are likely to have been fitter. In this way fitness is transmitted from parents to children.

Evolutionary psychology has been criticized for being metaphysical. It offers a series of just-so interpretations (Gould and Lewontin 1979) for such phenomena as altruism by parents toward their children. The obsessive concern to give everything an evolutionary explanation is rather like wondering why God (if He exists) allows so many bad things to occur. Perhaps evolution has honed us to love our children in order to preserve the species. Perhaps humans mature more slowly than other species because this imparts adaptive benefits that will be helpful in adulthood. Perhaps human adulthood is relatively compli- cated because it promotes longevity through economic and social prog- ress. Humans write books; spiders do not. Moreover, human societies that became settled and centralized had greater powers of survival (Diamond 1999). This list of perhapses is not important, just as surely as it doesn't really matter whether man descends from apes or not. The critics of evolutionary psychology have missed the important point, which is that parental-investment theory is the starting point for an axiomatic theory of parenting and family.

The axioms that underpin parental-investment theory also underpin economic theories of the correlation among parents, children, and sib- lings. As we shall see, however, economics has not been overly con- cerned with the possibly evolutionary justification of these axioms. Since we judge axioms not by their pedigree but by their ability to develop falsifiable theory, it is pointless to debate whether these axioms have evolutionary origins. In the rest of this chapter and in chapter 9, the axioms of evolutionary psychology are extended and developed to provide an axiomatic theory of parenting and sibling behavior. However, the final result bears only superficial resemblance to the original.

Evolutionary psychologists see themselves as attacking the "Stan- dard Social Science Model," according to which humans are born as blank states, their behavior is infinitely malleable and is determined by learning, socialization, indoctrination, and culture, and culture is an autonomous force existing independently of people. (See Workman and Reader 2008, p. 12.) This model—espoused by anthropologists such as Margaret Mead, sociologists such as Emile Durkheim, and psychologists such as Albert Bandura—provides no role for evolution- ary forces or even nature in the broad sense. "Standard Social Science Model" is an unfortunate title, because it is not standard to all the social sciences. It is certainly not espoused by economists or even by most psychologists. The model that Judith Harris attacks is very different, for example, from the so-called Standard Social Science Model. She tilts at a very different windmill: a model in which parents are assumed to be the main influence on their children. Psychology, in this case evolutionary psychology, seems to need windmills to tilt at in order to establish its separate identity.

3.3.4   Back to Harris

I began this subsection by recalling Harris' attack on the platitudes of developmental psychology. I entirely agree with her that scientific disciplines tend to become self-serving and introverted and that there is insufficient cross-fertilization between them. Indeed, that is why I am writing this book. She is right in claiming that developmental psychology became stuck in a rut in which nurture by parents was assumed to be crucial and that nature was unimportant. But behavioral genetics too has gotten stuck in a rut—one in which behavior is not taken seriously. Scientists, like other people, have vested interests. Thus, we should not be particularly hard on developmental psychologists, or on behavioral geneticists.

Harris herself is a good example of my criticism of methodological *ad hoc*ery. She attacks developmental psychology, praises behavioral genetics, and then proposes a new theory of development that is just as arbitrary as the objects of her criticism. She takes behavioral genetics at face value and attributes 45 percent of why people are different to genes and only 9 percent to shared environments, or parenting and family (Harris 2006, pp. 40–41). This leaves about half of the variance unexplained. Harris is right in calling a spade a spade and in criticizing both developmentalists and behavioral geneticists for referring to the unexplained variance as the contribution of non-shared environments to the variance. It may be non-shared environments, or it may simply be model error or data error.

The rest of Harris' book is concerned with explaining the unexplained variance. Her main thesis is that humans are largely formed by society:

The disposition to acquire a language is one of the things that fit humans for society. So is the disposition to figure out what other people are thinking. Three other things that fit humans for society are their disposition to form and maintain personal relationships, their disposition to adjust their behavior to the norms and customs of their society, and their disposition to compete with other members of their society and, if possible, outdo them in some way. (Harris 2006, p. 244)

Harris calls these three things the "relationship system," the "socialization system," and the "status system." What happens to us in these three systems determines about 50 percent of why no two individuals are alike:

Each of the three systems . . . gives people a way of adjusting to or making use of a particular aspect of their social environment. Nature—that is evolution—has endowed humans with dispositions fit for society. These dispositions enable people to behave appropriately in different social contexts and with different social partners. People make long-term adjustments in behavior that adapt them to their culture; they thus become more alike in some ways. People also find different ways of competing with their rivals; they thus become less alike in other ways. The result is that no two people have the same personality. No two are alike. (ibid., p. 428)

The three dispositions and systems are features of social psychology, a branch of psychology that developed largely after World War II. Social psychology has little in common with other branches of psychology. It is mainly concerned with the power of society over the individual, the power of individuals over society, our perceptions of our social reality, and how we construe the world. Harris' theory, like so many other so-called theories, is not falsifiable. Like Erikson's stages theory, it is more concerned with *ex post* interpretation than with *ex ante* prediction. Harris cites the story of identical twins Conrad and Perry. Perry was held back in fifth grade; Conrad was not. Conrad became a successful businessman; Perry became a homeless alcoholic. "The cruel experiment the world performed on Conrad and Perry," Harris writes, "produced results that were consistent with my theory." (ibid., p. 262) Harris' theory doesn't necessarily predict that Perry would end up as he did. Why didn't it predict that repeating fifth grade gave Perry an advantage over his peers? Maybe repeating fifth grade had nothing to do with his fate.

Harris does not make unambiguous and testable predictions of the type "If X then Y." Her theory is no more testable that those she criticizes, and is just as arbitrary and opinionated. "Though my theory is, in principle, testable," she writes, "these methodological and ethical problems are not going to be easy to solve." (ibid., p. 263) I doubt that her theory is testable in principle, but I have no doubt that it is untestable in practice. I return to this issue in chapter 5. "It is hoped," Harris writes on page 260, "that this book will inspire scientists to conduct research on three mental systems whose existence they might not have suspected, or suspected only vaguely." Perhaps not.

3.3.5 Wilson's Vision of Social Science

In the closing pages of *Sociobiology*, Wilson speculates about the future of social science:

Consider the prospects for sociology. The science is now in the natural history stage of its development. There have been attempts at system building but, just as in psychology, they were premature and came to little. Much of what passes for theory in sociology today is really labeling of phenomena and concepts, in the expected manner of natural history. . . . Sociology is drawing closer each day to cultural anthropology, social psychology, and economics and will soon merge with them. . . . The transition from purely phenomenological to fundamental theory in sociology must await a full neurological explanation of the human brain. . . . Having cannibalized psychology, the new neurobiology will yield an enduring set of first principles for sociology. (1975, pp. 574–575)

The phenomenological theory to which Wilson refers in this passage is what I call *ad hoc theory*, which interprets the past without predicting the future. The first principles to which Wilson refers are what I call *axioms*. This criticism is as applicable to psychology as it is to sociology. No doubt the promise of neurobiology is great indeed. Already departments of psychology as we have known them are being closed down, and are being transferred out of social science faculties to the natural science faculties so that psychology and brain sciences will be more proximate. The question is whether we really have to wait 100 years, as Wilson predicted, to set the first principles or axioms of sociology, and for that matter, psychology. I think not. After all, economics has progressed as an axiomatic science without knowing how the brain works. Indeed, so-called neuroeconomics, which uses fMRI imaging to discover the location of economic decision making in the brain, has made no significant contribution to economic theory, and is unlikely to do so in the future.

My suggestion is that, just as economic theory is axiomatic, there is a need to axiomatize psychology and sociology. This does not have to take 100 years (of which 36 years have already passed), or however long it takes to discover how the workings of the human brain. Indeed, later in this chapter and in chapter 9 I discuss concrete proposals how to do this. In any case, we might wait 100 years only to be disappointed. The promises of neurobiology may not live up to their expectations, just as the promises of physiology have left us in the dark about cancer.

3.4 Economics

Gary Becker opened his landmark *Treatise on the Family* with this remark: "Aside from the Malthusian theory of population change, economists hardly noticed the family prior to the 1950s, when they began to recognize spouses, children, and other family members." (1990, p. 2) Jacob Mincer (1962; see also Long 1958) argued persuasively that the participation of married women in the labor force is determined not only by their earning potential but also by the earnings of their husbands, the number of children they have, and other family characteristics. A modern economic analysis of fertility began to replace the Malthusian analysis, and the demand for children has been shown to depend on family income, the value of parents' time (especially that of mothers), the "quality" of children, and other family variables (Becker 1960, 1965; Easterlin 1968). Studies of investment in human capital treated private expenditure on education as parental investments in the productivity of children (Schultz 1963; Becker 1964).

To set the scene, I present the economic theory of fertility to which Becker refers, which is referred to as the *Quality vs. Quantity Theory* (QQT). This theory exemplifies the axiomatic approach that economics takes toward theory. It develops from simple axiomatic assumptions. It seeks to explain jointly fertility and parental investments in their children. It also exemplifies the formal nature of economic theory. The idiom is formal rather than verbal. The QQT is testable and therefore falsifiable. Later in this chapter, I consider other aspects of family behavior apart from those concerned with fertility and investment in education. A detailed theoretical discussion of these issues may be found in chapter 9.

Becker references the sociobiologists Edward O. Wilson and Robert L. Trivers in *A Treatise on the Family*. Indeed, in chapter 9 he tries to bridge the gap between the QQT and sociobiology by applying the QQT to nonhuman species. "Indeed," he notes, "modern biology is relying increasingly on explicit maximizing models similar to those used by economists. Still, the economic approach does appear to provide a unified treatment of human and nonhuman behavior while recognizing that cultural forces are major determinants of human behavior and biological forces are decisive determinants of nonhuman behavior." (p. 322) Evolutionary psychology, which grew out of sociobiology, does not refer to economics, despite the common intellectual denominators of the QQT and evolutionary psychology.

According to the QQT, parents have children because they enjoy them. Economists do not delve deeply into the ultimate reasons why people enjoy consuming various goods and services. They don't ponder whether these reasons are evolutionary. Instead, they simply accept that we humans are hedonistic—that we enjoy goods, such as food and cars, and services, such as entertainment and holidays. We also enjoy having children. Maybe one of the reasons for wanting children is survivalism. If so, humans are motivated by survivalism and hedonism. Having more children means having less of something else. Therefore, in economics, individuals trade off survivalism and hedonism. With everything else equal, if parents decide to have more children, they will be less able to afford rival goods and services. Also, their careers may suffer—especially the careers of mothers.[14]

Therefore, children are costly. The costs include the cost of investing in their quality, and especially in their education. Indeed, according to the QQT, parents face a double tradeoff. First, they trade off consumption with family size (that is, number of children). Second, they trade off consumption and family size with the quality of their children, especially as measured by their investment in education.

The axioms of economics are very simple:

1. Individuals derive satisfaction or "utility" from consumption of goods and services.

2. Utility varies directly with consumption, so more is preferred to less.

3. However, utility increases at a decreasing rate—the so-called law of diminishing marginal utility.

4. Individuals have preferences between various goods and services. The law of diminishing marginal utility implies that different combinations of goods consumed deliver the same utility. For example, if more of good A is consumed but less of good B, utility will be unchanged.

5. Individuals seek to maximize their utility.

Similar axioms apply to firms, but since firms are tangential to the QQT the axiomatic theory of the firm is ignored. The same applies to the theory of markets, which deals with the interaction between consumers and firms. However, there are implicit market interactions that take place within families. These interactions concern the assignment of tasks between spouses and between siblings. These simple related axioms are all the axioms the QQT requires.

3.4.1 The Quantity vs. Quality Theory

The utility of parents is hypothesized to depend mainly on the number of children, the human capital invested in each child, and the consumption of goods and services. The QQT classifies the first component as quantity and the second as quality. The law of diminishing marginal utility is assumed to apply to each of these three components. This means that different combinations of the three components deliver the same utility. If human capital invested and consumption of goods and services are held fixed and the number of children is reduced, the level of utility must fall. This may be offset by an increase in the quality of children. Therefore, given their consumption, parents may be just as happy with less quantity and more quality. By the same reasoning, they may be just as happy with more quantity and less quality.

Parents spend their income on raising their children, investing in their quality, and purchasing goods and services for consumption. The investment in quality consists of education, which enhances the human capital of children. Since wages tend to vary directly with human capital, parents help their children become better off by investing in their quality. Parents are assumed to maximize utility by allocating their budget among the three components. In doing so, it is assumed, parents are egalitarian, investing the same amount in each child. As we shall see, investing the same amount in each child is inefficient. However, it may minimize envy between siblings.

The unit cost to parents of raising children is assumed to be given. Therefore, the total cost of raising children is simply this cost per child multiplied by the number of children. In practice, this cost may be greater for the first child than for subsequent children, since subsequent children use the hand-me-downs from their elder siblings. Also, the unit cost to parents of child quality is assumed to be given. Higher quality, such as that produced by better schooling, is more expensive. Therefore, the outlay on quality per child is quality multiplied by the unit cost of quality, and the total outlay on quality is the latter multiplied by the quantity of children. Finally, the price of consumption goods to parents is given.

The QQT hypothesizes that parents, given their budget, choose the quantity of their children, the quality of their children, and their consumption so as to maximize their utility. In short, they jointly determine their fertility, the investment in schooling per child, and their standard of living in a way that maximizes their utility. Clearly matters are more complicated than this. If fertility increases, the family's budget

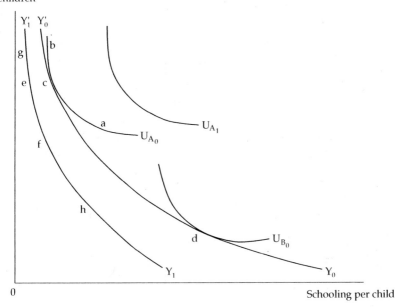

Children

Figure 3.1
The Quality vs. Quantity Theory.

probably will be tighter, since it will be more difficult for the mother to go out to work. Also, more children mean more sleepless nights and perhaps more aggravation. However, the purpose of any model is to be simpler than reality and to distill the most essential decision-making process (in this case, that of parents). In any case, forgone income and sleeplessness are two of the costs of raising children.

As an illustration of the basic predictions of the QQT, suppose that parents' consumption is given. Therefore, all that remains for them to decide is the number of children (represented on the vertical axis in figure 3.1) and the quality of each child as measured by schooling (represented on the horizontal axis). The preferences of family A are represented by the curve U_{A0}, along which different combinations of quantity and quality deliver the same level of utility. The law of diminishing marginal utility guarantees that the shape of the curve U_A is convex toward the origin. There is a continuous set of such curves such that curve U_{A1} delivers more utility than curve U_{A0} because the quantity of children, the quality of children, or both are greater along U_{A1}.

These curves are known as "indifference curves." In figure 3.1, combinations a and b deliver the same utility, so family A is indifferent between them. Curve U_{A1} must lie above curve U_{A0}, i.e., indifference curves cannot cross each other, for otherwise preferences would be inconsistent. This is known as the principle of *intransitivity*. Another principle is *ordinality*. Curve U_{A1} delivers more utility to family A than curve U_{A0}, but by an unknown amount. In short, the indifference curves are ordinal rather than cardinal.

Parents vary in their preferences. For example, in figure 3.1 the preferences of the parents in family B are represented by curve U_{B0}, along which are plotted different combinations of quality and quantity that deliver the same level of utility for family B. The shape of curve U_B is visibly different from the shape of the indifference curves for family A. On the whole, family B prefers quality to quantity, whereas family A prefers quantity to quality. The indifference curves of family B cannot cross each other; however, the indifference curves of family B must cross those of family A, since the two families have different preferences.

Suppose families A and B have the same income and the same consumption. For example, their monthly income is $10,000 and their spending on goods and services, excluding outlays on children, is $7,000 per month. This leaves $3,000 per month to spend on rearing and educating the children. The main question is how they should allocate this $3,000 between quantity and quality. Curve YY' in figure 3.1 is a "budget curve," which plots all the combinations of quantity and quality that the families can afford, i.e., all the combinations of quality and quantity that can be obtained for $7,000 per month. It slopes downward because if parents spend more on quality they can afford less quality. It is curved because each child receives the same schooling. This means that when the number of children decreases, schooling per child may be increased disproportionately. If schooling were to become more expensive, the budget curve would be steeper than in figure 3.1, because, for a given quantity of children, parents would not be able to afford as much quality. If child rearing were to become more expensive, the budget curve would be flatter, because, for a given investment in schooling per child, parents would not be able to afford as many children. The slope of the budget curve therefore reflects the relative cost of raising children to the cost of educating them. Better-off parents have budget curves that lie to the right of YY' because they can afford more education per child, or because, given the cost of education per child, they can afford more children.

Since families A and B have the same income, their budget curves are the same. Family A maximizes utility at c; family B maximizes utility at d. Neither family can obtain more utility. Therefore, family A has more children but invests less in the education of each, while the opposite holds for family B. This confirms that family A prefers quantity to quality that and the opposite holds for family B. The difference in behavior is due to the difference in preferences, since the budget curves of the two families are exactly the same.

Suppose that the cost of education increases so that the budget curve is Y_1Y_1' instead of Y_0Y_0'. Notice that Y_1Y_1' lies to the left of Y_0Y_0', because $7,000 buys less quality and quantity. Notice also that, because the cost of schooling (quality) has risen, the horizontal distance between the two budget curves gets larger as quantity gets smaller, so the budget curve becomes steeper. Family A will maximize utility at a point like e, in which case fertility is reduced and each child receives less schooling than at c. In this case both quantity and quality decrease. We cannot rule out the possibility that family A will maximize utility at a point, such as f, at which quantity decreases but quality increases. However, this is a pathological case, since when the price of something increases the demand for it falls. At f the price of schooling increases and the demand for schooling increases. We cannot rule out a point, such as g, at which quantity increases and quality decreases. At g, parents cut back on quality and increase quantity because quality has become relatively expensive.

Similar arguments apply to family B, which maximizes utility at a point such as h, at which quantity is increased at the expense of quality. Since family B has chosen less quantity and more quality than family A, family B is likely to be more responsive to the increase in the cost of quality. Although families differ in terms of their preferences between quantity and quality, they respond similarly to economic incentives, such as the cost of child rearing and the cost of schooling. If the cost of child rearing happened to increase instead of the cost of schooling (that is, if quantity were to become relatively expensive), the budget curve would shift to the left and become flatter. Family A would reduce quantity in favor of quality, but family B might do the same.

This is the QQT in a nutshell. It is a theory of fertility that integrates parental investment theory. Its empirical validity should not be judged by its axioms. In fact, utility is unobservable, just as quarks are unobservable to physicists. Instead, the QQT's empirical validity should be judged by its ability to predict, which is discussed in detail in chapter 6. Is it the case, for example, that Israel's child benefit system (that is, fiscal transfers to families according to the number of children) increases fertility, as predicted by the QQT, because it gives parents an incentive to have more children? Recent evidence from Israel (Gottlieb et al. 2009) suggests that the answer is Yes.[15] In 2003 the rates of the child benefit were cut for the fourth child and for any additional children. Fertility has subsequently declined among large families. In the 1990s Druze families in the Golan Heights became eligible for the child benefit, and their fertility increased relative to the population as a whole. Similar effects were observed when Bedouins became eligible for the child benefit. More educated women have greater earning power. The QQT predicts that more educated women should have lower fertility because the cost of child rearing in terms of forgone earnings is larger. There is widespread evidence that the decline in fertility is positively correlated with the education of women.

The QQT predicts that the schooling of parents will be positively correlated with their children's schooling. With everything else equal, since earnings vary directly with education, the budget curves of educated parents will lie further to the right in figure 3.1, so they can afford to invest more in their children's schooling. Also, more educated parents may have a preference for quality over quantity—that is, they are more like family B than family A, and they invest more in the schooling of their children.

The QQT also predicts that the incomes of parents and children will be positively correlated. First, since the schooling of parents and children are correlated, and since earnings vary directly with education, the earnings of parents and children will be correlated. Secondly, if ability is inherited, abler parents think that their children are abler too. Since abler children benefit more from schooling, abler parents have an incentive to invest more in quality—that is, they are like family B, while less able parents are like family A. They therefore have fewer children, but invest more in them. Therefore, abler parents who are more educated and earn more have children who are more able and more educated and who earn more as a result.

The QQT also predicts that the earnings and the schooling of siblings should be positively correlated. This stems from the assumption that parents are egalitarian and help their children unconditionally and indiscriminately: if they have more than one child, they do not invest in one child at the expense of another. In chapter 9 the QQT is extended to the case where parents invest more in their more able children because the return to investment varies directly with ability. Another possibility is that parents might practice reverse discrimination, investing more in their less able children despite the fact that the return is lower, because they want to give them a boost. However, as will be discussed later in this chapter and at greater length in chapter 9, envy among siblings might deter parents from discriminating between their children.

The most important point is that the QQT is an axiomatic theory of intergenerational and sibling correlations. It is concerned with outcomes such as earnings and schooling, but, as we shall see, its theoretical vision can be extended to other outcomes in which parents make decisions that affect their children.

3.4.2 The Rotten Kid Theorem

The QQT serves as a prototype for an axiomatic theory of parenting. This has been noted before (Foster 2002), but the QQT has been criticized for assuming that children are passive. In the QQT parenting is a one-way process: parents invest in their children out of altruism, love, or whatever, but children are assumed merely to accept the resources transferred to them by their parents—to cooperate rather than resist. The reason for this is the so-called Rotten Kid Theorem (Becker 1990, pp. 9–12 and chapter 8), which states that under certain conditions it is not in children's self-interest to be "rotten" toward their parents. It isn't that children are unselfish and inherently compliant. Rather, children understand that their parents are powerful, and that they are the beneficiaries of their parents' altruism. It is therefore in the self-interest of the beneficiaries to promote the well-being of their benefactors. In short, it doesn't pay to bite the hand that feeds you. If benefactor A is altruistic toward beneficiary B, then B has a selfish interest in A's welfare because what is good for A is also good for B. It might look as though B cares about A, but this is "cupboard love," which should not be confused with true love or altruism by B toward A. An altruist is defined as someone whose utility varies directly with the utility of a beneficiary. Normally, the utility of the beneficiary does not vary directly with the utility of the benefactor. If it did, then A and B would be mutual altruists. One hopes that children will eventually, in adulthood, become mutual altruists with respect to their parents and siblings. However, this is unlikely to apply to infants.

The Rotten Kid Theorem also applies when there are multiple beneficiaries. Suppose sibling 1 obtains $100 at the expense of sibling 2, who loses $150 as a result of sibling 1's actions. The family then is worse off by $50. An altruistic parent, seeing that sibling 2 is worse off, gives sibling 2 $120 at the expense of sibling 1. This leaves sibling 1 $20 worse off, sibling 2 $30 worse off, and the family as a whole $50 worse off. It is not in sibling 1's self-interest to be rotten to sibling 2. Matters would be different if siblings were envious. For example, sibling 1 may be willing to lose $20 provided sibling 2 loses more than him. Altruists' utility varies directly with the utility of their beneficiaries. The opposite applies to enviers. The utility of the envier varies inversely with the utility of the envied. And just as altruism may be mutual, so may envy. Families in which everyone is envious of everyone else are viper's nests of mutual self-destruction.

The main insight of the Rotten Kid Theorem is that power in the family is asymmetric. Parents are more powerful than children because children depend on parents more than parents depend on children. On the other hand, parents are more altruistic toward their children than are children toward their parents. Indeed, infants aren't altruistic toward their parents at all, whereas parents are very altruistic toward their infant children. The Rotten Kid Theorem doesn't apply only to parents and children; it applies to any situation in which selfish beneficiaries are dependent on a benefactor. The benefactor may be a spouse, a jailer, a PhD supervisor, or the state.

However, the theorem makes a number of strong assumptions. The first is that all goods and services are tradable, i.e., they can be bought and sold in the marketplace. For example, schooling, which plays a central role in the QQT, can be bought and sold. So, of course, can consumer goods in general. But the time of parents cannot be bought and sold. The infant that cries for his mother cannot, of course, buy "mummy time" in the marketplace. Nor can mummy sell this time. There may be an internal market for mummy time within the family because siblings and daddy compete for her time and attention, but this is quite a different matter. Mummy time is not like babysitting, which may be bought and sold. Second, the Rotten Kid Theorem is entirely static. This is the appropriate point at which to introduce some terminology from game theory.[16] Here the word "game" refers to any situation in which people are mutually responsive. Parents and children may be regarded as players in the game of Happy Families. The plays in this game are the actions of parents and those of children. Plays may be simultaneous (as in judo) or sequential (as in chess). Also, games may be "one-shot" (i.e., never to be repeated) or they may be "repeated." A repeated game is played many times. In a one-shot game the players may ignore the future because the game will not be repeated. But in repeated games the players must take account of their current plays or behavior on the outcomes of future games—that is, they must behave strategically. For example, in a one-shot game it may pay to lie, but in a repeated game reputation and truthfulness may matter. In a one-shot game cowardliness may not matter, but in repeated games it may be necessary to be tough if deterrence affects the outcomes of subsequent games.

The Rotten Kid Theorem refers to a one-shot two-stage game. There is only one round in the game, so the future does not matter, and parents play after children. The fact that parents play after children gives them a last-move advantage: they can offset their children's actions. Matters would be very different if children had the last call instead of parents, and if the game were repeated. Happy Families is, of course, a repeated game, played every day and night throughout childhood. This means that parents have to take account of their current actions on future plays, i.e., they must take into account the developmental needs of their child. It also means that children have to take account of their current actions on future plays. Children who need more attention from their parents might have to over-react, so that their parents are more conciliatory in the future. Happy Families is not necessarily a two-stage game in which parents have the last word or play. Parents may have the last word when it comes to paying for certain market goods, such as schooling; however, the child may have the last word or cry, which may cause the parent to concede or give in.

Another limitation of the Rotten Kid Theorem is that it assumes that there are no merit goods. A merit good is a good that parents believe their children should have, even if they do not want it for themselves. For example, parents may want their children not to smoke, or they may want their children to do well at school. Merit goods consumed by children feature directly in the utility function of parents as well as in the utility of their children. This means that the altruism of parents is no longer unconditional. If children use their pocket money to buy cigarettes, alcohol, and drugs, their parents are likely to be less generous. All parents can do is tax goods that they think are harmful and subsidize merit goods. By making altruism conditional, parents encourage their children to consume fewer harmful goods and more merit goods. However, children do not behave exactly as their parents wish, and in this sense the Rotten Kid Theorem breaks down. (In an example presented in chapter 9, schooling is a merit good. Parents subsidize their children's education, but they cannot force them into living out their parents' fantasies.)

In short, the Rotten Kid Theorem is a heuristic construct that simplifies the development of the QQT. Since we live only once, this construct may be reasonable in some contexts, such as schooling. Certain aspects of life may be like a one-shot game, since a person has only one childhood. However, childhood involves many repeated games. More generally, Happy Families is a repeated simultaneous game in which merit goods are present. Therefore, any axiomatic theory of parenting should not take the Rotten Kid Theorem for granted. Chapter 9 contains a detailed theoretical discussion of parenting that draws on the QQT but relaxes the Rotten Kid Theorem. In the remainder of this section, I distill the main insights from this theory.

3.4.3 Parenting Theory

Parents allocate their time between caring for their children and pursuing their own activities. They derive utility from their "adult time," but because they are altruistic they also derive pleasure from the utility of their child. Parents vary in their degree of altruism. More altruistic parents get more pleasure out of their children's utility than more selfish parents, who prefer to spend more time on themselves. Children derive utility from the attention they receive from their parents. More responsive children are more easily gratified when their parents pay them attention. Children vary in their gratifiability. Infant children are assumed not to be altruistic. The law of diminishing marginal utility applies to the utility of parents and to the utility of their children. At first, I shall assume that there is only one child in the family. Later, I shall introduce a sibling.

This axiomatic model assumes that the personality traits of parents and children are hard-wired. Parents vary in altruism and in patience. Children vary in gratifiability, in resilience, and in envy. The model distinguishes between these traits, which are fixed, and state variables (such as the happiness and development of the child, and the happiness and adult time of parents), which vary. The axioms and the parameters of the model constitute a theory of mind, whereas the solution to the model predicts the behavior of the body. The theory axiomatizes the mind, which in turn predicts how the mind controls the body.

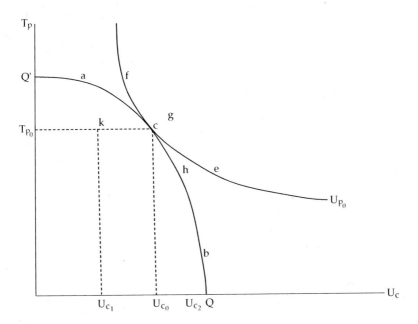

Figure 3.2
Parenting with passive children

However, there is feedback from body to mind, since the emotional development of the child alters his mind.

At first, the Rotten Kid Theorem is assumed to apply, and the child is assumed to be passive. Parents decide how much time or attention to devote to their child and how much to spend on themselves. They do so to maximize their utility. The solution to the parenting problem is illustrated in figure 3.2, where the vertical axis measures the amount of time parents spend on themselves (T_P) and the horizontal axis measures their child's utility (U_C). Curve QQ' plots the inverse relationship between parent time and the utility of their child; the more time parents spend on themselves the less time they spend on their child. Since the happiness or utility of the child varies directly with the attention he gets from his parents, curve QQ' slopes downward. If parents devoted all their time to their child, the child's utility would be equal to Q. At Q' the parents devote no time to their child, whose utility is minimal.

Because of the law of diminishing marginal utility, curve QQ' is concave toward the origin, i.e., it bulges outwards as drawn. There are three reasons for this. First, the marginal utility of altruism to parents varies inversely with the time the parents devote to their child. Second, the marginal utility of parent time increases as the parents devote more time to their child. Third, the marginal gratification effect of parental attention varies inversely with the time the parents devote to their child. At point a on QQ' the child is more gratifiable than at point b, since a small reduction in parent time has a bigger effect on the happiness of the child at point a than at point b.

Curve QQ' is drawn for an individual child. Children differ by their gratifiability, in which case different children have different QQ' curves. If a child is absolutely more gratifiable, his QQ' curve will lie to the right of its position in figure 3.2. This means that the same amount of parental attention makes the child happier. If the child is relatively more gratifiable, curve QQ' will be flatter, since an extra minute of parent time has a larger effect on the child's happiness. If the child is very ungratifiable, curve QQ' will lie closer to the origin and will be flat.

Different combinations of parent time and child utility deliver the same utility for parents. The indifference curves for parents appear as they do in figure 3.1. Points c, f, and e on curve U_{P0} all deliver parents the same level of utility. On curve QQ', parents maximize their utility at point c, where there is a tangency between curve QQ' and U_{P0}. It is inefficient for parents to choose point a or point b, because their utility would be less than at point c. Parents therefore spend T_{P0} of their time on themselves and the rest of their time on their child (T_{C0}), and the utility or happiness of their child is U_{C0}. Less altruistic parents would pick point a, at which parents spend more time on themselves and less time on their child, and the child would be less happy. More altruistic parents would pick point b, at which they spend more time on their child, as a result of which the child is happier, and they spend less time on themselves. If their child is relatively more gratifiable, parents may pick point f, at which they spend more time on themselves; if their child is relatively less gratifiable they might pick a point such as e. If their child is absolutely more gratifiable so that curve QQ' shifts to the right, the parents may be able to reach point g, at which the parents have more utility, the child has more utility, the parents spend more time on themselves, and the whole family is happier because the child has a more gratifiable personality.

Thus far the child is passive. He makes do with whatever attention his parents bestow on him at point c in figure 3.2. He obviously would prefer more attention. Ideally, he wants his parents to be completely devoted to him so that he reaches a point like b on curve QQ', or, better still, reaches Q, at which his parents spend no time on themselves. Can he do better than point c by being active rather than passive? The answer is "Yes, provided he is prepared to be 'rotten' toward his parents." The child can manipulate his parents into giving him more attention so that they spend less time on themselves, as a result of which the utility of the child will be greater than U_{C0}. He does so by crying or undertaking other attention-seeking behavior. The parents are misled into thinking that curve QQ' has become flatter, so that when they allocate T_{P0} time to themselves they now think that the happiness of the child is only U_{C1} instead of U_{C2}. This induces them to devote more time to their child, and they re-optimize at a point such as h on curve QQ', at which their true happiness is in fact U_{C2}. By exploiting his parents' altruism, the child gets more attention.

The game played between parents and children is inherently asymmetric. Parents have power over children, but children have power over parents. In a sense, parents are prisoners of their own altruism. Children understand this, either instinctively or though experience. They understand that their parents care for them. Parents give their children the benefit of the doubt precisely because they are altruistic (especially when the children are infants). Because infants bear no altruism toward their parents, they are prepared to act "rottenly." It isn't that they want to hurt their parents. They simply want their parents to give them more attention. In short, children are selfish beneficiaries who exploit the altruism of their benefactors. There is a two-stage game played between parents and children. In the first stage, parents pick point c in figure 3.2. If the child thinks he can do better than this, in the second stage he "cries" and he manipulates his parents to choose, e.g., point h. The last word, or cry, is the child's, not the parents'.

In the Heartstrings Game or the Crying Game (described in detail in chapter 9), it is assumed that children do not like crying. Therefore, at point h in figure 3.2 the utility of the child is less than U_{C2}, because the child incurs a psychological cost by crying. He obviously would prefer point h to point c if he could get there without crying, but that isn't possible. If the cost of crying exceeds the difference between U_{C2} and U_{C0}, the child will be better off at point c; crying will not be worthwhile. In this case the child is passive; he behaves as if the Rotten Kid Theorem is valid. More generally, the child will figure out his optimal amount of crying so that the extra attention that he gets from his parents exceeds the crying cost by some maximal amount.

Just as children vary in their gratifiability, they also vary by their psychological costs of crying. Crybabies cry more because these costs are lower, and they get more parental attention in return. Therefore, the solution to the Heartstrings Game, such as point h in figure 3.2 will be further toward point b for children why are crybabies.

3.4.4   Sibling Rivalry

I now introduce a second child into the family so that parent time is divided between the two siblings. To set the scene, it is assumed that parents have no favorites; they are strictly egalitarian. What matters to them is the sum of their children's utilities. They give equal weight to the siblings' utilities or happiness. At first, it is assumed that the siblings aren't envious—that they don't care how much attention a brother or a sister receives from the parents. Not surprisingly, in the solution to the Heartstrings Game each sibling ends up with less parental attention than in the single child case, and the parents end up with less parent time because the combined attention they give to their two children exceeds what they give to a single child. Matters become more interesting when siblings are envious and when parents have favorites. Envy triggers a crying war as each sibling tries to distract attention from his brother or sister. The siblings end up by getting more parental attention, but the cost of crying typically exceeds the benefit. As in arms races, it would have been better not to have entered the race in the first place. Also, envy punishes favoritism by parents. If sibling A is favored, sibling A will cry less, but sibling B will cry more because he is envious of A. The combined crying of the two siblings might increase, and parents might end up having to compensate B. Egalitarianism may therefore be in the collective self-interest of parents and indeed of the family as a whole.

3.4.5   Child Development

The Heartstrings Game that has been described is a one-shot game. This is obviously a heuristic abstraction meant to reveal the complex psychological interactions that parenting entails. Parenting is not a one-shot game—after today there is tomorrow, then the day after tomorrow, and so on. In repeated game situations, rival siblings might learn that cooperation pays with the result that they fight less over their parents' attention. This cooperation is not the result of a formal peace agreement, but a kind of cease-fire that each side realizes is in its own interest. Also, parents might learn in repeated games that it may be wiser to be egalitarian. Parents can be stupid too. Also, in repeated games crybabies might be found out. Parents realize that their child is acting out. On the other hand, the child has a strategic interest in establishing that he is tough and that he will cause trouble if his parents take him for granted. The child will invest in the development of appropriate body language if it makes him better off.

These and related issues that arise in repeated games are interesting, but they do not change in a fundamental way the insights learned from the study of one-shot games. However, there is one issue that does change matters in a fundamental way. If the emotional development of the child depends on the parenting he receives, the parents must consider the future when they play the Heartstrings Game. The solution to today's one-shot game has implications for the future. For example, very selfish parents who today pick point a in figure 3.2 and pay little attention to their child may find that in the future their child is less gratifiable because he is less emotionally developed. In contrast, parents who are very altruistic and pick point b in figure 3.2 reap the rewards of their own generosity because their child is more emotionally developed as a result of the attention he receives. The basic axiom here is that emotional development varies directly with the happiness of the child. Everything else equal, children who are paid more attention by their parents develop more resilience.

Just as surely as the axiom of utility maximization doesn't require empirical justification, this developmental axiom doesn't have to be tested. This axiom means that parents matter since parents contribute to their child's happiness. At this point one could cite numerous developmental researches based on sad natural experiments in which children who lost their parents and were subsequently adopted were either totally or partially impaired emotionally. Studies in this category include research by Rutter (2007) on Romanian children discovered in an orphanage in 1989 after the Ceauşescu government fell and research by Bowlby (1969) on children orphaned during World War II. Such evidence doesn't necessarily establish that happier children develop more healthily.

Curve QQ' in figure 3.2 changes over time as the child develops. As the child develops, curve QQ' becomes steeper, since the child becomes less dependent on his parents for gratification. As his resilience develops. the child can increasingly gratify himself; his happiness or utility depends decreasingly on the attention he gets from his parents. In the

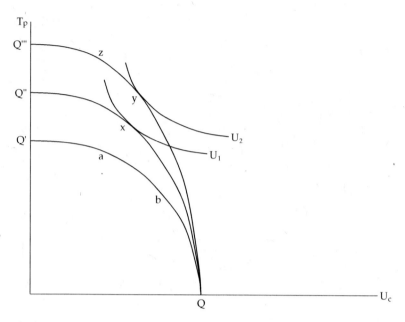

Figure 3.3
Parenting and infant development.

limit, curve QQ' will be vertical if the child's utility is completely independent of parental attention. However, the degree to which curve QQ' steepens over time varies directly with the child's previous happiness, which depends in part on the parental attention he received when he was younger.

Curve QQ' in figure 3.3 replicates its counterpart in figure 3.2. Suppose that if parents choose point a the curve subsequently becomes QQ". The resilience of the child has increased because he is older, and the new resilience curve is therefore steeper than the old one. Suppose the parents had been more altruistic and had chosen point b, at which the child would have been happier than at point a. The child's resilience curve (QQ''' in figure 3.3) would be subsequently steeper than QQ". Because he was happier, his resilience is increased. In this case the parents will subsequently be able to maximize their utility at a point like y. Had parents been more selfish, they would have maximized utility at a point such as x on curve QQ". The parents are better off at y than at x because their utility is U_2 instead of U_1. At y the parents have more time for themselves than at x, and their child is happier too. So the parents are twice blessed. Even if they happened to choose point z on curve QQ''', a point at which their child is not happier, they are still better off than at x.

Figure 3.3 demonstrates that previous parenting decisions affect parents' subsequent opportunities. Selfish parents may be better off in the short term at point a than at point b, but they are subsequently worse off at x than at y. In short, parents face an intertemporal tradeoff: if they allocate more time to their child in the short term, they will not have to allocate as much time to the child subsequently. Therefore, in the Heartstrings Game parents must consider the consequences of their actions for the future resilience of the child. This means that the Heartstrings Game must be played dynamically rather than statically, as in the one-shot game.

Parents can also spoil their children. As will be discussed in more detail in chapter 9, over-attentive parents may harm the subsequent resilience of their child. Children have to learn to cope on their own, and parents who do everything for their children may impede their development. This means that after some point the resilience curve may become flatter instead of steeper as parents pay more attention. Parents have to strike a fine balance between giving their child too little attention (and thus inhibiting his development) and giving him too much attention (thereby spoiling him). It is in the enlightened self-interest of parents to choose their current actions in such a way as to promote the development of their child, because this eases the job of parenting in the future. Parents may find that they have to be cruel to be kind, both with respect to themselves and with respect to their child. In short, current parenting is an investment in future adult time as well as in the future happiness of the child.

How should this repeated game be played out? What is the optimal parenting policy over time? Parents face a dynamic optimization problem that takes account of how current actions affect future outcomes and actions. Optimal control theory is used in chapter 9 to find the optimal parenting policy. In each period the Heartstrings Game is played in which parents take account of their current actions on the future. Here there is yet another asymmetry between parents and children in addition to various other asymmetries that have been mentioned. Children consider only the present, and their gratification is instant. In contrast, parents have to be farsighted, because they are responsible for the development of their child. Parents may be farsighted to a greater or lesser degree. Impatient parents care more for the present and less for the future. For example, in figure 3.3 impatient

parents might choose point a even though in the future they will pay
a price for this; they prefer combination a and x over b and y. Patient
parents, in contrast, might choose combination b and y even though
point b might be less preferable than point a in the short term. Therefore, the developmental path of the child depends, apart from everything else, on the impatience of parents. Children whose parents are
more patient have more favorable developmental prospects.

The solutions to the optimal control problem are discussed in detail
in chapter 9. Unfortunately, they are rather technical and difficult to
summarize. However, the basic insights and intuitions are conveyed
in subsection 9.6.3, where parents heuristically consider the present
(period 1) and the future (period 2). For convenience, the main results
are summarized here, and figure 3.4 repeats figure 9.6. In this figure,
the horizontal axis measures the utility of parents in period 1 (the
present) and the vertical axis measures the utility of parents in period
2 (the future). Point A denotes the utility coordinates for parents when
they devote none of their time in the first period to their child. Along
curve AcB in the direction from A to B, parents increase the time they
devote to their child in the first period. At B they devote all of their
time. As they devote time to their child, their child is happier in the

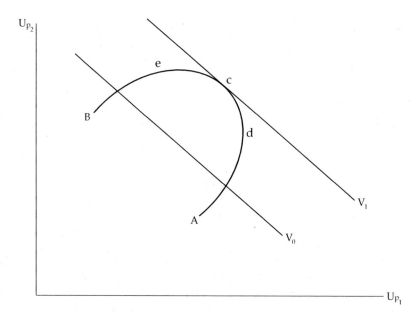

Figure 3.4
Parenting in the two-period model.

first period, which makes parents happier in the first period. If the child is happier in the first period, this will promote his development and his resilience will be greater in the second period, which in turn will make parents happier in the second period. Therefore, curve AcB may initially slope upward; time devoted to the child increases parents utility in both periods. After point d, however, the slope of the curve becomes vertical because the marginal utility of time spent on themselves increases, and after a further point the slope turns negative. This happens when parents stall their child's development through spoiling. Finally, the curve may bend backward at point e so that utility in both periods falls as parents devote more time to their child in the first period.

Curve AcB constitutes the inter-temporal "utility possibility frontier" for parents. It is inefficient for parents to be inside this frontier, and it is impossible for them to be beyond it. Where will efficient parents choose to be on curve AcB? To answer this we assume that the life-cycle utility of parents is simply a weighted sum of the utilities in the two periods. The weight on the first period is 1, but the weight in the second period is less than 1 because parents are impatient. Along curve V_0 life-cycle utility is constant. There is an entire family of such curves that have the same negative slope. Those that lie below deliver less life-cycle utility, and those above it deliver more. The slope of these curves is steeper for more impatient parents since future utility is worth less to them.

Parents will choose a point on the utility possibility frontier that maximizes their lifetime utility. The highest attainable lifetime utility is V_1. Therefore, parents choose point c on the utility possibility frontier, at which the tradeoff between utility in the two periods must be negative. Notice that the utility possibility frontier has inflection points at d and e. At d the curve begins to slope downward, and at e it begins to slope backward. Therefore, rational parents will choose to be in the range dce and will rule out solutions between A and d and between B and e. If parents are more impatient, the V curves will be steeper and the tangent between V_1 and the utility possibility frontier will lie closer to d, implying that parents devote less time to their child in the first period. Parents who are completely impatient and do not care about the future have vertical V curves and will maximize utility at d. Parents who care only for the future have horizontal V curves and maximize utility at e. Normal parents maximize utility between d and e. The shape of the utility possibility frontier depends on all the parameters of the model, which obviously determine the point of tangency.

Since the time parents devote to their child in period 1 increases along the utility possibility frontier in the direction from A to B, we can calculate how much time parents devote to their child at c in period 1. Through reverse engineering we can calculate the happiness of the child in period 1 in terms of the time parents spend on their child in period 1 and the utility of parents in period 1. The happiness of the child in period 2 can also be calculated, because it varies directly with the happiness of the child in period 1 and the amount of time parents devote to their child in period 2. The two-period model therefore predicts what happens to the developmental path of the child, as well as predicting the actions of parents over time.

3.4.6   Intergenerational and Sibling Correlations

Just as the QQT predicts that the schooling and earnings of parents, children, and siblings should be correlated, so does the axiomatic parenting theory (APT) predict that the outcomes of children, parents, and siblings should be correlated. Matters are slightly more complex in the APT than the QQT because children aren't necessarily passive; the Rotten Kid Theorem doesn't hold. The APT predicts, for example, that the resilience of siblings should be correlated because they experience common if not identical parenting. The APT does not predict that this correlation should be perfect—siblings have different degrees of gratifiability, different capacities to cry or act out, and different abilities to develop. Also, their parents might not be even-handed and might discriminate between them. Nor does it predict that the correlation should necessarily be large—apart from parents, there are influences outside the family that might affect the development of the child. What is important in this chapter's frame of reference is that the APT establishes an axiomatic link between the outcomes of siblings.

This link stems from parenting. Siblings' outcomes may be correlated because their gratifiability and their developmental potential are correlated for genetic reasons. Or siblings' outcomes may be correlated because siblings share neighborhoods, ethnicity, and cultural capital. The point of APT is to establish that, even in the absence of heredity and other environmental factors, the outcomes of siblings are expected to be correlated through parenting.

The same applies to the correlation between the outcomes of parents and children. The APT establishes an axiomatic link between the outcomes of parents and children. Suppose for argument's sake that gratifiability isn't inherited and that parents and children don't share environments. Suppose also that two families, A and B, are identical in every respect. Parents A and parents B have identical preferences and are equally altruistic, and child A is identical to child B in gratifiability other considerations. This means that the parents share identical indifference curves and curve QQ' in figure 3.2 is the same for both families. Therefore, in the one-shot game both parents will optimize at same point, such as c.

Suppose that the only difference between the two families is that parents A happen to be less resilient than parents B. It might be argued that altruism varies directly with resilience because more resilient parents have more emotional space for their children. If this were true, parents B would optimize at b in figure 3.1 whereas parents A would optimize at c because more altruistic parents have steeper indifference curves. Child B would be happier than child A because he gets more attention, as a result of which he develops more rapidly. Since the two children are otherwise identical, child B ends up more resilient than child A. In this way correlation is induced between the resilience of parents and children.

But suppose we assume that the preferences of parents aren't affected by their resilience and that parents are equally altruistic. Suppose that more resilient parents are more patient and more able to consider the future than their less resilient counterparts. Parents B are consequently more patient than parents A. Therefore, parents B choose point b figure 3.3 while parents A choose point a, as a result of which parents B subsequently attain point y while parents A only manage point x. The resilience of child B is greater than that of child A because the latter's resilience curve is QQ" while the former's is QQ'''. This establishes an axiomatic relationship between the resilience of parents and that of children.

Therefore, we may add the axiomatic parenting theory to the list of theories that predict that the outcomes of parents, children, and siblings should be correlated. In contrast to other *ad hoc* theories, the APT is axiomatic, suits a formal rather than a verbal idiom, and (as we shall see in chapter 6) is falsifiable.

3.4.7 Post-QQT Parenting Theory

The axiomatic theory of parenting just described may be compared with recent developments in what might be called "post-QQT theory." Lizzeri and Siniscalchi (2008) propose a learning-by-doing model in which children learn from their mistakes. Children cope with problems as best they can with their imperfect understanding of what is the best solution. They learn through experience along Lockean lines. Over time, as they mature, they cope better and make fewer mistakes. In the absence of parents, children would have to learn the hard way on their own. Parents are assumed to have a better understanding than their children regarding the best actions to take in the face of the problems faced by their children. The parent-child relationship is asymmetric because parents are more experienced than their children. Parents can intervene to help their children solve their problems.

Parents don't want their children to suffer from the mistakes that they make, but parents understand that children must make mistakes in order to learn from experience. Parents therefore face a delicate tradeoff between over-protection and sheltering (which will spoil their child) and a "Spartan" policy of deliberate exposure (which leaves children to learn the hard way). Lizzeri and Siniscalchi solve for the optimal parenting policy, which balances the forces of exposure and sheltering. This theory echoes the solution to the parents' dilemma discussed above in connection with the Crying Game. The main difference is that in Lizzeri and Siniscalchi's model children are passive and don't induce responses by their parents, whereas in the Crying Game children are active and act out to get their parents to respond.

Lizzeri and Siniscalchi show that, with all else equal, parents intervene more as the difference between how children solve their problems and how parents perceive the best solution increases. By way of illustration, suppose the solution to a child's problem is an action measured on a scale of 1 to 10. The child's parents think the best action is 3, but the child's action is 8, so the action gap is 5. The parents shelter the child by taking a countervailing action of, say, −3 to close the gap so that the final action is 5. The child is sheltered by his parents' intervention, and suffers less, but he also learns less from his experience. Had the child's action been closer to 3, the parents would have intervened less. The greater the correlation between the child's action (8) and his parents' perception of this action (3), the smaller the parental intervention will be.

The smaller the correlation, the greater will be the parental intervention, as a result of which the outcome of the child will be closer to what his parents want. Lizzeri and Siniscalchi think that the perceptions of parents and children regarding what action should be taken are partly genetic in origin. For example, if calmer parents have calmer children, it is more likely that the children's actions and their parents' perceptions of the best action will be closer to 3. In the case of excitable children and parents it will be closer to 8. The more genetically dissimilar parents and children are, the larger the action gap will be. Repeated intervention by parents to close the gap ends up with children being more like their parents. Therefore, if parents and children are genetically similar, parents need to intervene less and their phenotypes are correlated owing to heredity. If parents and children are genetically different, parents intervene more, and as a result their phenotypes are correlated. Essentially, parents force their phenotypes on their children through their intervention. If heredity can't be relied upon to achieve this, the environment set by the parents will do the job instead.

For example, bookish parents may have bookish children even if bookishness isn't a genetically transmitted characteristic. If bookish parents see that their children are naturally bookish, they need not intervene to turn them into bookworms. If, however, parents see that their children aren't adopting bookish ways, they intervene to get them more involved in bookish ways. Parents have to work hard to make sure that their children turn out like themselves. Lizzeri and Siniscalchi argue that this creates the misleading impression that nature matters more than nurture. The irony is that nurture by parents has to work hard to create the illusion that nature matters rather than nurture. Lizzeri and Siniscalchi join Goldberger (1979) in criticizing behavioral genetics for ignoring the science of human behavior. Incidentally, they also argue that the equal-environments assumption of behavioral genetics is violated by their theory because parents are expected to intervene differently between MZ and DZ twins since their action gaps are generally different. Also, they are expected to intervene more with adopted children than with biological children because the action gap is expected to be larger among the former than among the latter.

My model of parent-child interaction may be given a genetic interpretation too. In the Crying Game, parents vary in altruism and in ability to gratify their children, and children vary in selfishness and in gratifiability. Suppose that gratifiability and parents' ability to gratify happen to be genetically related. In that case, less parenting would be needed, because a small amount of parenting goes a long way toward gratifying the child. Suppose, on the other hand, that the altruism of parents and the selfishness of their children are negatively correlated. More altruistic parents want to devote more time to their children, who are less demanding. The former increases parenting, but the latter reduces it.

Another example of "post-QQT theory" is Akabayashi's (2006) model of parents' maltreatment of children. In this model, maltreatment occurs not because parents are cruel or inadequate, but because they misunderstand their children. Parents help children acquire human capital, which serves as a measure of child developmental status. Parents promote their child's development by devoting time to help him acquire human capital, but development also depends on the child's development effort. Parents can't observe this effort directly, nor can they observe their children's human capital or developmental status directly. Instead, they obtain noisy signals through an outcome that depends on human capital as well as on the child's effort. Parents may reduce but not eliminate this noise by spending more time with their children. If parents think their child isn't making a sufficient effort, they punish him; otherwise, they reward him. Parents are altruistic and children are myopic, as in the Crying Game model. However, children's myopia varies inversely with their development as measured by their human capital.

In this model there is tension between parents' assessment of their children's developmental status and developmental effort and parents' investment in their children's development. If parents assess children's developmental status correctly, they supply more or less parenting according to their children's needs. Emotionally needy children will receive more parental attention and will close the developmental gap between them and more resilient children, who receive less parental attention. Along this developmental path, parents apply the carrot and the stick intermittently and mildly to keep their children on a healthy developmental path. In normal families, children become less myopic as they develop, and eventually it is no longer necessary for parents to invest in their children's development because the marginal effect of parenting tends to 0.

Matters are different in pathological families. Suppose parents initially over-estimate their children's resilience because, for example, the children have had a lucky run of positive outcomes, which misleads the parents into thinking that they are more developed than they really are. Because the parents mistakenly believe that their children are more resilient than they are, they reduce their investment in the children's development. Subsequently, the outcomes of the children deteriorate for two reasons. First, their luck runs out. Second, their developmental status is impaired because the parents have cut back their investment in their development. When parents perceive these outcomes, they mistakenly believe that their children are shirking—that is, their developmental effort is insufficient. Disappointed, the parents respond by applying the stick, and by reducing their investment even more, which makes matters worse. While this process is going on, the parents appear to be maltreating their children.

Altruistic parents, not aware that they are making a mistake, practice such maltreatment with the best of intentions. They aren't abusive, but they appear to be, at least for a while. Eventually they perceive their error and cease their seemingly abusive behavior. Akabayashi characterizes this equilibrium with child maltreatment as a local equilibrium rather than a global one. My guess is that such equilibria are localized indeed, and that concerned parents rapidly become aware of their mistake and cease their punitive behavior. Akabayashi is certainly not saying that child maltreatment is a stable equilibrium in the long run.

The paper by Lizzeri and Siniscalchi, the paper by Akabayashi, and perhaps my 2010a paper can hardly be counted as a new trend in axiomatic parenting theory. Two things they have in common are that (as in the QQT) parents care about their children's developmental status and that child development is treated as entirely axiomatic. My work focuses on the two-way interaction between parents and children and on the intertemporal tradeoffs parents make when raising their children. Lizzeri and Siniscalchi focus on the way parents try to create children in their own image in the belief (perhaps mistaken) that they know what is best for their children. Akabayashi deals with a problem I tried to avoid in my own work: parents don't know their children's true developmental status and instead make inferences about their developmental status from their observed behavior. As we saw, the latter may create the misleading impression that children are shirking. My solution was to assume that parents give their children the benefit of the doubt when they cry.

It is doubly surprising that the paper by Lizzeri and Siniscalchi and that by Akabayashi were published in economics journals. First, the papers have nothing to do with economics. Second, one has to ask why they were not published in journals on developmental psychology, where their impact on developmental psychologists obviously would have been greater. This is yet another manifestation of interdisciplinary fractionalism.

Behavioral genetics is a discipline that is completely dedicated to explaining why the outcomes of siblings are correlated. By making a number of very strong assumptions, behavioral genetics interprets the difference between correlations for identical and fraternal twins as evidence of genetically induced behavior. The same applies to the difference between the correlations for biological siblings and adopted siblings. Behavioral genetics obtains "results" by ignoring behavioral confounders. In short, behavioral genetics ignores behavior and assumes that what we observe is genetic by default.

Developmental psychology also has much to say about the correlations between parents, children, and siblings. The problem is that much of developmental theory is phenomenological; it is concerned with describing the past rather than predicting the future. This stems from the fact that developmental theory is *ad hoc* rather than axiomatic. Indeed, there is an unusually large variety of developmental theories that do not share axioms. The empirical falsifiability of these theories is questionable because they do not make unambiguous predictions that can be tested.

Evolutionary psychology has drawn extensively on sociobiology, which is concerned with social behavior in nonhuman species. Sociobiology stresses the axiom of survivalism and the corollary of parental-investment theory. Evolutionary psychology has joined a long list of other approaches to psychology, but currently it is not in the mainstream. Coincidentally, many of the insights of evolutionary psychology have been imported by economics and generalized. This has given rise to an axiomatic theory of parenting in the form of the Quantity vs. Quality Theory of fertility. The QQT doesn't only predict human fertility, it also predicts parents' investments in children, especially in terms of their education. Essentially, the QQT integrates survivalism with hedonism in human behavior.

The QQT serves as an archetype for the axiomatic theory of parenting that uses formal mathematical methods such as static and dynamic optimization theory, and game theory to promote its development. In the APT parents have power over children, but so do children over parents. The APT axiomatizes the power play between parents, children, and siblings. The APT predicts that the developmental outcomes of siblings should be correlated, and that developmental outcomes should be correlated within generations. It also predicts that developmental outcomes should be correlated between generations.

4   Inequality, Diversity, and Family

Families induce inequality and diversity. Imagine a world in which humans are created spontaneously without parents. If you like, children are formed at God's whim, perhaps to replace people who have died. So children have no biological parents. Suppose also that children have no caregivers and they raise themselves. The concept of the family doesn't exist. The genes of each child are determined by a random draw from the gene pool. Since these children will never become parents, they cannot pass on their genes to the next generation. In this bleak world, we should find that inequality and diversity do not propagate between generations, because each generation has absolutely nothing to do with the previous generation. People are taller or shorter, richer or poorer, happier or sadder, but this has nothing to do with family.

We may gradually humanize this bleak world. First, we can assume that children have one parent but reproduction is asexual. Parents therefore do not need to find a mate in order to reproduce, but at least children have a biological parent. This biological parent may not, however, care for its child. At birth, parents abandon their children, who are left to their own devices and raise themselves. In this case each child inherits genes from its parent, which establishes a connection between the parent and the child. In such a world we should begin to observe that inequality propagates between generations; the outcomes of the child for height, economic success, and happiness may now be correlated with the outcomes of the parent. If the parent does not abandon the child to its own devices, and raises it, a further connection is established between the child and the parent. Parenting may therefore induce further intergenerational correlation.

Suppose next that we allow reproduction to be sexual, so that in order to become a parent an individual must find a mate. However, we assume that people mate randomly. The child now has a mother and a father, and he shares both their genes. He is also affected by their parenting if they decide to raise him. This broadens the connection between generations simply because the child has two parents instead of just one. Inequality (or diversity) is transmitted from one generation to the next through both parents. If we allow parents to be yet more human and mate assortatively rather than randomly, the connection between the generations is further strengthened because the genes of parents are likely to be positively correlated. This reinforces the propagation of inequality between generations.

Finally, we allow parents to have more than one child. Suppose they have two children. Siblings share their parents' genes, and they share parenting. However, they also share each other's company as long as they aren't separated. Because they share each other's company, sibling correlation is induced through the pure sibling correlation, as was discussed in chapter 3. Therefore, siblings further increase the correlation between generations. Parents affect their children, who affect each other. The influence of parents propagates and multiplies through their children. If they have more than two children, the scope for sibling interaction increases and the family turns into a more powerful vehicle for propagating inequality. Therefore, the family may play a central role in determining inequality within generations as well as between generations.

This chapter elucidates the conceptual role that the family plays in the propagation of inequality and diversity intergenerationally (between generations) and intragenerationally (within generations). It draws on the insights and the technical material presented in chapter 8. The main arguments are illustrated intuitively and accessibly by carrying out simple numerical illustrations of models featured in chapter 8 in the spirit of tables 3.1–3.6, which illustrated the relationship between the intergenerational and sibling correlations.

Intuitively, mobility and inequality are interwoven: if there were no mobility between generations, inequality would persist from one generation to the next. Suppose that the heights of parents and their children are identical, so that there is no intergenerational mobility in height; the heights of parents and children are perfectly correlated. In this case the inequality of heights among children will be identical to the inequality of heights among their parents, and inequality will be transmitted perfectly from one generation to the next. Suppose, at the other extreme, that the heights of children are completely uncorrelated with the heights of their parents, so that there is complete intergenerational mobility. In this case the inequality of height among children has nothing to do with the inequality of heights among their parents, and inequality is not transmitted at all from one generation to the next.

When there is partial or imperfect mobility between generations, intragenerational inequality varies systematically over time. This means that inequality tends to persist, but it eventually settles down to some long-term, or normal, level of inequality. This is referred to as *structural inequality*, since it is the level of inequality toward which inequality tends given the structure of society. There are different concepts of mobility as well as different concepts of inequality. The concept of mobility alluded to in the previous paragraph is *absolute* mobility because it is concerned with the absolute heights of children compared with their parents' height. *Relative* mobility, in contrast, is concerned with the rank or position of children in their distribution relative to the position of parents in their distribution. If the rank or position of children in their distribution is that same as the rank of their parents, there is perfect relative immobility. If these ranks are independent, there is perfect relative mobility. Absolute and relative mobility are conceptually different, but they might be correlated. A society may be upwardly mobile in absolute terms but downwardly mobile in relative terms. In this case taller parents have shorter children who are taller than average, and shorter parents have taller children who are shorter than average. However, the children of taller parents may rank higher in their distribution than did their parents, and the children of shorter parents may rank lower in their distribution than did their parents.

Just as mobility has different meanings, so inequality may be measured in different ways. The most common statistical measure of inequality is the variance or standard deviation, which is the square root of the variance. However, other measures are arguably superior to the variance. If inequality is measured by the Gini coefficient, it turns out that intergenerational inequality may be decomposed into relative and absolute mobility, as well as "leveling up" or "leveling down." In the case of income, for example, leveling up occurs when children are, on average, better off than their parents. The Gini coefficient also ensures that inequality decreases if a dollar is transferred from a richer person to a poorer person.

Egalitarianism is a political doctrine that penalizes inequality as a matter of public policy. Individuals may or may not value equality privately. Egalitarianism is concerned with the political process: laws are passed to reduce inequality. Egalitarianism seems to be confined to economics. No one seems to care about anthropometric inequality, such as inequality in height or in athletic ability, as a matter of public policy. Individuals may privately wish to run faster or look more beautiful, and they may attend jogging clubs or beauty parlors, but no one expects the government to pass laws that handicap people in the interest of equality just because they can run fast or happen to be beautiful. Matters are very different when it comes to income and wealth. Egalitarian economic policy, which involves the transfer of income from those who are better off to those who are less well off, is enshrined in the progressive income-tax systems that have been adopted by most countries. Indeed, distributive justice, which is concerned with income inequality, has become a major issue in philosophy (Rawls 1972) and in the social sciences (including much of economics).

Surprisingly, economics has largely ignored the role of the family as a source of inequality. Instead, economics has been mainly concerned with intragenerational inequality; more narrowly, it has been concerned with "horizontal inequality," meaning inequality at a point in time. Typically, these measures of inequality refer to income in a certain year as collected by national statistical authorities, such as the Current Population Survey in the United States or the Office of National Statistics in the United Kingdom. "Vertical inequality," in contrast, is concerned with inequality over the life cycle; it refers to some average income rather than income in some specific year. Studies show (Beenstock 2004) that vertical inequality is smaller than horizontal inequality because current income is inherently more random than average or life-cycle income. Owing to a lack of data,[1] horizontal measures of inequality vastly outnumber vertical measures of inequality, which might explain why economics has been narrowly concerned with the determinants of horizontal inequality. Reasons for this lack of data were given in chapter 2. It is cheaper to conduct a horizontal survey than it is to conduct a vertical survey, since the latter must be longitudinal. Longitudinal surveys involve all the complications and administrative costs of tracking people over time, and of preventing sample attrition due to dropping out.

Whereas longitudinal data are scarce, intergenerational data are rare collector's items. Indeed, tables 2.3 and 2.4 list many of the intergenerational data sets that are available. Matters might have been different had longitudinal data and intergenerational data been more available.

Perhaps this explains why economics has under-emphasized the role of the family in the transmission of inequality. Sociology, on the other hand, has been more prone to see the family as a source of inequality (Conley 2004). It is my hope that the present chapter will prove useful regardless of the case for or against egalitarianism.

4.1 A Brief History of Egalitarianism

The preoccupation with economic inequality and egalitarianism is a relatively recent phenomenon (Phelps Brown 1988). Indeed, it is largely a twentieth-century phenomenon. Equality before the law has preoccupied philosophers throughout the ages, but economic inequality had been accepted as a fact of life, just as surely as anthropometric inequality had been accepted as a natural state. Rousseau, in his *Discourse on the Origins and Basis of Inequality among Men* (1755), probably was the first to place economic inequality on the philosophical agenda. Rousseau saw the bleak familyless world described above as a desirable State of Nature in which inequality would be entirely natural and minimal. Parents would mate randomly, and children would be subsequently abandoned to their own devices.[2] However, the institution of the family serves to propagate and entrench inequality. Short of dismantling the family and other social institutions, Rousseau suggested, public policy should counterbalance the family so that inequality should be as close as possible to what it would be in a State of Nature. This lead him to make the following suggestion in his *Political Economy* (1755): "It is, therefore, one of the government's most important tasks to prevent extreme inequality of wealth, not by taking treasures away from those who possess them, but by removing the means of accumulating them from everyone; nor by building poorhouses, but by protecting citizens from becoming poor." (Rousseau 1992, p. 154). However, later (ibid., p. 168) he writes: "Such taxes, which help the poor and burden the rich, must be used to prevent the continual increase of inequality of fortunes. . . ." At first Rousseau did not attack the institution of private property, but in his *Project for Corsica* (1765) he did. He was appalled by the rich wasting food while the poor starved.

Rousseau's position may be contrasted with that of his Scottish contemporaries Adam Smith and David Hume. Smith and Hume too were appalled by the huge economic cleavages in their societies. Smith held a Malthusian view: unskilled workers were doomed to subsistence, while owners of capital and land would reap the rewards of economic progress. If the economic position of unskilled workers improved, the population of unskilled workers would increase as Malthus predicted, forcing unskilled wages back to the level of subsistence. According to Smith, the lot of the unskilled would improve only if they acquired education. In the meantime, private property had to be protected against potential threats from the unskilled poor, who might rise up against the rich and confiscate their property. Smith, unlike Rousseau, was a conservative.

Rousseau's manifesto was not, however, taken up for more than 100 years. It was not taken up by the American Revolution of 1776, or by the French Revolution (despite the call for liberty, equality, and fraternity). In both of these revolutions, equality was limited to equality before the law; it did not encompass economic equality. It is difficult to find a clear statement of economic egalitarianism in the writings of other philosophers of the eighteenth and nineteenth centuries. Even Karl Marx was not an egalitarian. He did not propose communism on egalitarian grounds, but on moral grounds. He thought that bourgeois life was morally feckless, not because it perpetuated inequality, but because it degraded man. To Marx egalitarianism was a bourgeois invention designed to prop up capitalist decadence. Nor were early socialists such as Robert Owen egalitarian.

The philosophical roots of egalitarianism may also be found in Utilitarianism. In *Principles of the Civil Code*, Jeremy Bentham propounded an idea that in fact dates back to Hume, who argued in *Of Justice* (1753) that a pound is worth more to a poor man than to a rich man. This logically means that the greatest happiness of the greatest number would be achieved by complete equality. Indeed, this simple logic lies at the heart of modern egalitarianism (Atkinson 1970; Squire and van der Tak 1984), which makes interpersonal comparisons about utility and welfare. This contrasts with the utility theory applied in chapter 3, in which interpersonal comparisons of utility were strictly avoided, and indeed were unnecessary. The law of diminishing marginal utility may apply to individual income, such that the marginal utility of income is positive but varies inversely with the level of income for each individual. This means that each individual prefers a steady income stream to one that fluctuates. However, it does not mean that utility can be summed across individuals, unless arbitrary value judgments are made about interpersonal comparisons.

In 1996 James Mirrlees was awarded the Nobel Prize in economics for his work on optimal tax policy. Mirrlees saw the tax system as a way of redistributing income from the rich to the poor. But, like Hume, he understood that if tax rates were too high the incentives to work and to innovate might be adversely affected. In the worst possible scenario, complete inequality might destroy the cake to be allocated. Mirrlees' main contribution was concerned with the design of tax systems that allow for optimal or minimal inequality, which trades off the size of the economic cake with the distaste for inequality. All this goes to show how egalitarianism pervaded much of economic theory in the twentieth century.

According to Phelps Brown (1988), the turning point in favor of egalitarianism came at the turn of the twentieth century for two main reasons. First, the application of economic egalitarianism required sophisticated administrative capabilities and a strong civil service, which were not previously available, to operate the income-tax system and the welfare system. Second, the spread of universal suffrage gave political voice to the working classes. The political parties that emerged to represent the economic interests of the working class adopted egalitarian political agendas.

The spread of egalitarianism in the twentieth century was challenged on philosophical grounds as well as on economic grounds. According to Friedrich Hayek (1960, p. 86), "equality before the law and material equality are therefore not only different but are in conflict with one another," because the confiscation of income means that the law discriminates between individuals on the basis of their ability to earn. In principle, this is the same as discrimination on the basis of any other arbitrary characteristic, such as hair color. Hayek also saw the family as a source of inequality: "The most important factors to be considered in this connection are the family, inheritance, and education, and it is against the inequality which they produce that criticism is mainly directed." (ibid., p. 89) Apart from legal objections to egalitarianism, Hayek voiced moral objections, since "most of the strictly egalitarian demands are based on nothing better than envy" (ibid., p. 93).

There are two aspects to envy. First, if A is richer than B, B envies A and seeks to transfer income from A to B. In this case, B is better off and there is more equality because A has less and B has more. Second, B dislikes the fact that A is better off and is prepared to pay to change the situation. He is prepared to take a cut in income just to see that A is brought down to his income level. In this case there is more equality, but B is worse off. Incomes have been leveled down. In any case, B might be rich, but A happens to be richer. Transferring income from the very rich to the rich increases equality, but this is hardly of social importance even to would-be egalitarians. Presumably, egalitarians are motivated by transfers to the poor. Transferring $100 from Bill Gates or Warren Buffet to George Soros may be egalitarian, but it is quite a different matter when the poor benefit from the transfer.

Perhaps a more sensible concept of social justice is based on John Rawls' difference principle. However, this is very different from egalitarianism, and it attaches no social importance to various measures of economic inequality, such as the variance or the Gini coefficient. Rawls (1972) invites us to contemplate (hypothetically, of course) our future the moment before we are born, when we are still under the veil of ignorance. We do not know whether we will be richer or poorer but understand that we all stand an equal chance of being one of the poorest. We also stand an equal chance of being one of the richest. Suppose that while under the veil of ignorance we were asked to vote for a social insurance policy that would benefit the poorest at the expense of everyone else. As in all forms of insurance, individuals are happy to pay insurance premiums to cover the risk of adverse contingencies. We all prefer that our house not burn down, but if it does, at least there is redress through the insurance policy. We all prefer not to be among the poorest, but if we are, at least we obtain redress from the social insurance policy. Moreover, we should prefer social arrangements that maximize the lot of the poorest, just as surely as we would prefer an insurance policy that provides the best deal in the event that the contingency insured against is realized. This is the *maximin* principle of distributive justice, so called because it maximizes minimum incomes.

Rawlsian distributive justice is not based on envy, but on the principle of social insurance. It does not tax the rich to reduce inequality. If A gets richer and inequality increases, this is of no consequence if it does not make the poorest worse off. In fact, the poorest may be better off as a consequence. An optimal redistributive policy is one that maximizes the condition of the poorest, since but for the grace of God each one of us might have been one of the poorest.

Rawls' distributive justice draws attention to measures of poverty rather than to measures of inequality. Since the poorest comprise the bottom percentiles of the distribution of income, they reside by definition in the left-hand tail of the distribution. Rawlsians are therefore not interested in various measures of inequality, such as the variance or the

Gini coefficient, which refer to the entire distribution, but only in a small component of the distribution. Various measures of poverty may be defined in terms of poverty lines, and in terms of the proportion of the population who happen to fall below the poverty line. Sen's (1976) index of poverty, for example, is based on the proportion below the poverty line but gives greater weight to people who are deeper in poverty. Even among the poorest there are gradations in the depth of poverty.

Should poverty be measured in absolute terms, or in relative terms? The fact that social security systems are national rather than international would suggest that what matters is relative poverty for a given society rather than absolute poverty. It is, no doubt, better from this point of view to be born in a rich country than in a poor one. Should poverty be measured horizontally, or vertically? How should equivalence scales be calculated for children? Since measuring poverty lies beyond the scope of our present terms of reference, I do not take the matter any further here.

Rawlsian distributive justice has been criticized for violating the "entitlement principle" (Nozick 1974), according to which an individual is entitled to income he has created through fair endeavor and effort. To some extent this is a restatement of Hayek's criticism of egalitarianism, since it involves unequal treatment before the law. The main point is that after Rawls egalitarianism makes even less sense than it made before. Tax systems are becoming less progressive as governments increasingly rely on non-progressive indirect taxes, such as a value-added tax, to raise revenue. Also, proponents of "flat taxes" are making the case for a single rate of income tax, which would simplify the tax system and under which income taxation would cease to be progressive. Adoption of flat taxation by policy makers would ring the death knell for egalitarianism. Flat taxes are in operation in a number of former Soviet Bloc countries. The twentieth century bore witness to the rise of egalitarianism. Perhaps the twenty-first century will bear witness to its decline.

4.2   Beta Convergence and Sigma Convergence

Chapter 2 introduced the concepts of intergenerational mean reversion, or beta convergence, and the intergenerational correlation coefficient. In what follows, these concepts are denoted by β and r respectively. Let us now explore the implications of these concepts for the transmission of inequality between generations. Suppose that for some outcome, such as height, r happens to be 0.4 and β happens to be 0.6. This logically means that inequality in height, or whatever, must be increasing from one generation to the next. To prove this proposition, solve equation 4 in chapter 2 for the standard deviation for children:

$$\text{sd}(Y_c) = \frac{\hat{\beta}}{r}\text{sd}(Y_p).$$ (1)

This equation shows that the standard deviation for children is related to the standard deviation for their parents through the ratio of $\hat{\beta}$ to r. Since the standard deviation measures inequality, it is in this way that inequality is transmitted from the parents' generation to the generation of their children.[3] This shows that the family transmits inequality from one generation to the next. If $\hat{\beta} = 0.6$ and $r = 0.4$, equation 1 states that inequality among children, as measured by the standard deviation, is 50 percent bigger than inequality among parents, because the ratio of $\hat{\beta}$ to r is 1.5.

If $\hat{\beta}$ happens to be smaller than r, it must be the case that inequality among children is smaller than inequality among parents. Finally, if $\hat{\beta} = r$, it must be the case that inequality among children is equal to inequality among parents. This means that $\hat{\beta}$ and r are informative about the intergenerational dynamics of inequality.

Some numerical illustrations are provided in table 4.1, where the standard deviation for parents (sd_p) is assumed initially to be 1.863. Case 1 shows that if $\hat{\beta} < r$ the standard deviation for children is 1.5, so inequality decreases from one generation to the next. Since the standard deviation is decreasing, and since the standard deviation is usually denoted by σ (sigma), case 1 is said to be sigma convergent. Case 2 shows that when these children become parents, their children's standard deviation will be 1.21 if $\hat{\beta}$ and r don't change. This

Table 4.1
Beta and sigma convergence illustrated. (The intergenerational mean reversion coefficient is denoted by β, and the intergenerational correlation coefficient by r. The standard deviation s for children and parents are denoted by sd_c and sd_p respectively.)

Case	β	r	sd_p	sd_c
1	0.6	0.745	1.863	1.5
2	0.6	0.745	1.5	1.21
3	0.6	0.6	1.863	1.863
4	0.6	0.5	1.863	2.236
5	1.1	0.745	1.863	2.751

demonstrates that sigma convergence implies beta convergence. Case 3 shows that if $\hat{\beta} = r$, σ remains unchanged; it neither converges nor diverges. Matters are different in case 4 because $\hat{\beta} > r$, so σ is divergent; it increases from 1.863 to 2.236. Case 4 establishes that beta convergence does not necessarily imply sigma convergence. However, case 5 establishes that beta divergence implies sigma divergence: when $\hat{\beta} > 1$, it must be the case that σ increases, because r has an upper limit of 1.

In summary, although beta convergence doesn't necessarily imply sigma convergence, sigma convergence implies beta convergence, and beta divergence implies sigma divergence.

Beta measures absolute immobility between generations. If $\hat{\beta} = 1$, the outcome for children is expected to be the same as their parents' outcome, in which case there is no intergenerational mobility. If $\hat{\beta} = 0$, the outcome for children is expected to be independent of the parents' outcome, in which case there is complete intergenerational mobility. If $\hat{\beta}$ lies between 0 and 1, the outcome for children is expected to be smaller than the outcome of their parents; mobility is therefore partial, and $\hat{\beta}$ is convergent since there is regression toward the mean. If $\hat{\beta} > 1$, the outcome for children is expected to be greater than their parents' outcome, and there is beta divergence since there is regression away from the mean. If $\hat{\beta}$ is negative, the outcome of children is expected to be inversely related to the outcomes of their parents, so there is regression past the mean.

These concepts can be illustrated with an empirical example for Israel. In table 2.4 it was reported that the intergenerational correlation coefficient for permanent earnings is 0.199. The estimate of β using the same data is 0.105. According to equation 1 above, this implies that the ratio of the standard deviations for children's earnings relative to the standard deviation for their parents' earnings is 0.53. Therefore, sigma convergence occurred between the two generations, because the standard deviation among children is 0.53 of its counterpart for parents. There had been a substantial reduction in permanent wage inequality between the generations.

Equation 1 in chapter 2 may be used to calculate the proportion of the variance of the outcome for children that is explained by the outcome of parents. The variance among children is equal to[4]

$$\mathrm{var}(Y_c) = \hat{\beta}^2 \, \mathrm{var}(Y_p) + \mathrm{var}(u). \tag{2}$$

The first term on the right-hand side is the explained variance among children due to the outcome of parents, and var(u) is the residual or unexplained variance. The latter comprises all the determinants of the outcome for children, which are independent of parents, including genes, the environment, luck, and other phenomena. It is easy to show that the explained variance as a percentage of the total variance, conventionally symbolized by R^2 and known as the coefficient of multiple determination, is equal to r^2:

$$R^2 = \frac{\hat{\beta}^2 \, \text{var}(Y_p)}{\text{var}(Y_c)}.$$
(3)

In behavioral genetics[5] this is referred to as "heritability." Notice that the explanatory power of parents varies directly with $\hat{\beta}$ and var(Y_P) and varies inversely with var(u). Note that solving equation 3 for r by taking its square root brings us back to equation 1, because the standard deviation is the square root of the variance. Thus, equation 2 is consistent with equation 1. Knowledge of $\hat{\beta}$ alone doesn't tell us much about explanatory power, but it is informative about the degree of mean reversion.

Equation 2 may be used to investigate the intergenerational dynamics of inequality. Suppose that, as in case 1 in table 4.1, $\beta = 0.6$, $r = 0.745$, and the standard deviation for parents is 1.863. Since the variance is the square of the standard deviation, the variance for parents is 3.471. We assume throughout that var(u) = 1. According to equation 2, the variance for children equals 0.36 × 3.471 + 1 = 2.249, the square root of which is 1.5. Note that this is precisely the standard deviation for children according to equation 1, which features in case 1 in table 4.1. We can use equation 3 to calculate R^2 = 0.36 × 3.471/2.249 = 0.555. This means that the intergenerational mean reversion model explains 55.5 percent of the variance of the outcome for children. Note that in case 1 we have $r = 0.745$. Since R^2 must equal r^2, we check whether this holds, which it does. Thus, everything adds up as it should.

Next, equation 2 may be used to simulate the dynamic development of inequality from one generation to the next. The starting point is case 1 in table 4.1. The results are reported in table 4.2, which records the simulated value of inequality, as measured by the standard deviation, over successive generations. The solutions for generations 1 and 2 are taken from case 1 in table 4.1. Over subsequent generations the standard deviation decreases until it eventually settles down at 1.25. However, by generation 5 it has nearly reached this level. This measure of long-term or structural inequality is referred to in chapter 8 as the *unconditional standard deviation*. It is structural in the sense that this is

Table 4.2
Conditional and unconditional inequality. (Inequality is measured by the standard deviation derived from equation 2.)

Generation	1	2	3	4	5	∞
$\beta = 0.6$	1.863	1.5	1.345	1.285	1.262	1.25
$\beta = 0.4$	1.863	1.247	1.117	1.095	1.092	1.091

the level of inequality to which society tends. It is unconditional in the sense that it doesn't depend on what happened to inequality in generations 1–5. In fact, the unconditional standard deviation is equal to the square root of the variance of u divided by $1 - \beta^2$. Since in case 1 $\text{var}(u) = 1$ and $\beta^2 = 0.36$, the unconditional variance is 1.563, and the unconditional standard deviation is the square root of this, which is 1.25. Therefore, structural inequality varies directly with the variance of u and with β. For example, if β is 0.4 instead of 0.6, structural inequality is 1.091 instead of 1.25. Table 4.2 shows that inequality reaches this level by generation 4, whereas when $\beta = 0.6$ it takes longer to get there. This shows that the speed of convergence varies inversely with β.

Structural inequality is the underlying level of inequality. Over the generations average inequality is equal to structural equality. In the short term, however, inequality in a given generation might differ from structural inequality, because of random events that affect inequality in that generation. In chapter 8 short-term inequality is referred to as *conditional inequality*. Inequality in earlier generations in table 4.2, such as generation 3, are conditional measures of inequality, since they depend on, or are conditioned by, the initial level of inequality in generation 1. To see this, suppose that when $\beta = 0.6$ the initial level of inequality were 1.25 instead of 1.863. In this case inequality would have remained at 1.25 in successive generations. Therefore, if the initial level of inequality happens to be greater than its long-run level, as in table 4.2, inequality converges from above onto the long-run or unconditional level of inequality. Had the initial level of inequality been less than 1.25, convergence would have been from below. Therefore, if there is beta convergence because β is between 0 and 1, σ may increase or decrease over time, but it converges to its unconditional value. Had β been greater than 1, σ would have tended to infinity over time because $\beta^2 > 1$ in equation 2.

Table 4.2 demonstrates that if σ is convergent the dynamics of inequality depend on three separate phenomena. The first is the role of family, expressed by β. If parents don't matter, $\beta = 0$ and inequality simply depends on the variance of u. The second phenomenon is the variance of u, which depends on all the other factors affecting outcomes apart from parents, including uninherited genes, or the variance of the gene pool, as well as environmental factors. The third phenomenon is the initial level of inequality, which may differ from its long-run counterpart for various reasons.

Suppose hypothetically that children are born without parents. In this case β is trivially 0 and inequality is entirely determined by the variance of u. In table 4.2 the variance of u is 7.56, in which case its standard deviation is 2.75. Had β been 0, long-run inequality would have been only 2.75, whereas it is 3.44 if $\beta = 0.6$. This shows that families induce inequality. Indeed, the contribution of being born to parents is the difference between 3.44 and 2.75. This contribution is smaller when $\beta = 0.4$ because parents are less important.

Suppose β is 0.4 instead of 0.6 because children have parents but parents do not raise their children. Children raise themselves in the sense of Rousseau, and the effect on β of parenting is 0.2. Table 4.2 shows that long-run equality would decrease from 3.44 to 3. Therefore, in a State of Nature inequality would have been 2.75. The genetic effect of having parents raises inequality to 3, and parenting raises it further to 3.44. Therefore, the total contribution of parents is to raise inequality from 2.75 to 3.44.

4.2.1   Assortative Mating[6]

So far it has been implicitly assumed that children have only one parent. Common sense suggests that the combined influence on children of two parents will be greater than the influence of one parent. If children had three or more parents, their combined influence would be even greater. In equation 2 the variance for parents is one of the three parameters determining the variance for their children. What happens to this variance when there are two parents instead of just one? If parents carry equal weight, the combined variance should be twice as large. This would be correct if parents do not mate assortatively. If they mate assortatively, the combined variance will be more than twice as large.

To demonstrate this, let the combined effect of two parents be the sum of the effects of each parent so that $Y_p = Y_f + Y_m$, where the subscript f refers to fathers and the subscript m refers to mothers. The variance of Y_p is equal to $\text{var}(Y_f) + \text{var}(Y_m) + 2r_{mf}\text{sd}(Y_m)\text{sd}(Y_f)$, where r_{mf} denotes the correlation between Y_f and Y_m. If the variances for mothers and fathers are the same and are equal to var(Y_{mp}), the variance of Y_p simplifies to $2(1+ r_{mf})$var(Y_{mp}). If there is no assortative mating, so that $r_{mf} = 0$, the variance of Y_p is twice the variance of Y_{mp}, as common sense suggests. If there is positive assortative mating, so that r_{mf} is positive, the variance of two parents is more than twice the variance of one parent. If, instead, there is negative assortative mating, so that r_{mf} is negative, the variance of two parents will be less than twice the variance of one parent. If r_{mf} is sufficiently negative, the variance with two parents may be less than that with one parent, because the two parents offset each other. If $r_{mf} = -1$ (i.e., if fathers and mothers are perfectly negatively correlated), the variance of two parents will be 0, and parents do not matter for children. At the other extreme, if mothers and fathers are perfectly positively correlated, the combined variance of two parents is four times that of one parent.

Therefore, when there are two parents we modify equation 2 to

$$\text{var}(Y_c) = \hat{\beta}^2 2(1+ r_{mf}) \text{var}(Y_{mp}) + \text{var}(u). \tag{4}$$

Since the coefficient of var(Y_{mp}) is larger in equation 4 than in equation 2, the intergenerational transmission of inequality is strengthened. Suppose, for example, that $r_{mf} = 0$ and $\beta = 0.6$, as in table 4.2. Long-term inequality would have been 1.89 instead of 1.25. Having two parents instead of one strengthens the effect of parenting on long-term inequality. If, in addition, there were positive assortative mating and $r_{mf} = 0.2$, long-term inequality would increase further to 2.71.

Evidence on assortative mating suggests that couples are positively correlated. Therefore, assortative mating intensifies the intergenerational transmission of inequality. If we take case 1 in table 4.1 as the base line, we can now decompose underlying inequality into the contributions of different aspects of family life. In the complete absence of parents, the underlying level of inequality is 1, since var(u) = 1. If there is one parent, inequality increases to 1.25. If there are two parents but there is no assortative mating, inequality increases further to 1.89. If, in addition, parents mate assortatively with correlation 0.2, inequality increases yet further to 2.71. Underlying inequality will, of course, be greater than this if the correlation between parents exceeds 0.2. It will also be greater if $\beta > 0.6$.

4.2.2   AR^2 and AR^3 Models of Intergenerational Transmission[7]

The discussion so far has been entirely based on Galton's model of mean reversion, expressed by equation 1 in chapter 2. Since the outcome of children depends on the outcome of parents through β and a random variable, this constitutes a first-order intergenerational autoregressive model, denoted by AR(1). An AR(2) model would include the outcomes of two previous generations, i.e., grandparents as well as parents. In subsection 8.1.3 it is shown that whereas in AR(1) models sigma convergence is monotonic, as in table 4.2 (σ converges from below or above without overshooting its unconditional value), in AR(2) models matters may be different. Sigma may converge with overshooting. In terms of the first case in table 4.2 this would mean that the standard deviation falls below 1.25 for some generations before eventually stabilizing at that level.[8]

In Galton's AR(1) model, u in equation 2 is assumed to be independent between generations. In section 8.2 Galton's model is generalized to allow two forms of intergenerational dependence. In the first, u is given a genetic interpretation and is assumed to be an AR(1) process. This means that genotypes of children depend through heredity on their parents' genotype plus a random draw from the gene pool. The mean reversion coefficient for genotypes is denoted in chapter 8 by ρ. In the second form, u is given an environmental interpretation and is assumed to be an AR(1) process. This means that the environments of children depend on their parents' environment plus a random draw from the environment pool. The mean reversion coefficient for environments is denoted in chapter 8 by ϕ. If both of these AR(1) processes are present, this gives rise to the AR^3 model described in subsection 8.2.2, so called because it comprises three related AR(1) processes. If only one of these AR(1) processes is present, this gives rise to the AR^2 model discussed in subsection 8.2.1. Obviously, the AR^3 model is more complicated than the AR^2 model, which is more complicated than Galton's AR(1) model. In these more complicated models, such as the AR^2 model, the phenotypes of children depend on their genotypes as well as on their parents' phenotypes, and the genotypes of children depend on their parents' genotypes.

The intergenerational transmission of inequality is naturally more complex in the AR^2 and AR^3 models than in Galton's AR(1) model. Sigma convergence doesn't depend only on β, as in Galton's model; it also depends on ϕ and ρ. The speed of convergence varies inversely with ϕ and ρ, just as we saw that it varied inversely with β in Galton's AR model. Not only does the convergence path depend on these parameters; so does the long-run or unconditional level of inequality. Table 4.3 illustrates the relationship between long-run inequality and

Table 4.3
Unconditional (structural) inequality in the AR^2 Model, calculated using equation XX in chapter 8 with unit variance for the gene pool. Structural inequality is measured by the unconditional standard deviation.

Case	β	ρ	Structural inequality
1	0.6	0	1.25
2	0.6	0.3	1.57
3	0.5	0.3	1.41
4	0.5	0.2	1.30

Table 4.4
Unconditional inequality in the AR^3 model, calculated using equation 34 in chapter 8 with unit variances for the gene pool and the pool of environments.

Case	β	ρ	φ	Structural inequality
1	0	0	0	1
2	0.6	0	0	1.25
3	0.6	0.3	0	1.426
4	0.6	0.3	0.3	1.574
5	0.5	0.3	0.3	1.411
6	0.5	0.3	0.2	1.277
7	0.5	0.2	0.3	1.277

β and ρ in the AR^2 model. Table 4.4 does the same for the AR^3 model, in which φ is also one of the parameters.

The first case in table 4.3, in which ρ = 0, serves as a base line. This is essentially the same case as in table 4.2, where β = 0.6, except that the variance of the gene pool has been normalized to unity in table 4.3. In this base case, structural inequality as measured by the long-run standard deviation is 1.25, which exceeds 1 because β is positive but less than 1. Case 2 shows that if ρ is 0.3 instead of 0 the standard deviation increases to 1.57. This demonstrates that inequality increases when genotypes are inherited. Case 3 shows that if ρ is fixed, reductions in β reduce inequality. Finally, case 4 shows that if β is fixed, reductions in ρ reduce inequality. Notice, however, that inequality is more sensitive to β than to ρ. If β and ρ are 0, the standard deviation is unity, and the family has no effect on structural inequality.

In the AR^3 model there are two underlying random variables: the random draw from the gene pool and the random draw from the pool of environments. For simplicity, these random draws have been assumed to be independent, i.e., the gene-environment correlation is 0. The two random variables are assumed to have unit variances. Because there are two random variables, the variance would be 2 in the absence of family (i.e., if β, ρ, and ϕ are 0), in which case the standard deviation is 1.4142, as in case 1 in table 4.4. Case 2 in table 4.4 may be compared to case 1 in table 4.3, since in both cases β is 0.6 and the other parameters are 0. Structural inequality as measured by the standard deviation is larger in table 4.4 than in table 4.3 because in the AR^3 model there are two random variables whereas in the AR^2 model there is only one. Case 3 in table 4.4 may be compared with case 2 in table 4.3. Here too there is more inequality in table 4.4 than in table 4.3, for the same reason. Case 4 shows that if β and ρ are fixed, inequality varies directly with ϕ, i.e., with the correlation between the environments of parents and children. Increasing ϕ from 0 to 0.3 raises the standard deviation from 1.426 to 1.575. Case 5 shows that reducing β from 0.6 to 0.5 reduces the standard deviation from 1.575 to 1.411. Cases 6 and 7 show that reducing ϕ or reducing ρ from the same level reduces the standard deviation by the same amount. This would not happen, however, if the variances of the gene pool and environments were not assumed to be equal as in table 4.4. Nor would it happen if the initial levels of ρ and ϕ were not assumed to be equal as in case 5.

In summary, tables 4.3 and 4.4 show that structural inequality varies directly with β, ρ, and ϕ, but especially with β. These three parameters are quintessentially to do with the family. Therefore, the family is a source of structural inequality. For example, comparing cases 1 and 4 in table 4.4 shows the family increases structural inequality as measured by the standard deviation by as much as 56 percent.

4.2.3   Intergenerational Impulse Responses

Suppose that Jim has a lucky draw from the gene pool and consequently his phenotype is increased. In terms of Galton's AR model, this means that Jim's u is positive, since the mean of the gene pool distribution is 0 by definition. If u is positive, Jim's phenotype (Y) is increased by the same amount. What does this lucky draw imply for Jim's children? How does it propagate over subsequent generations? Jim's children benefit in two ways. First, because Jim's phenotype increased, his children's phenotype will increase via β. Second, because Jim's u was positive, his children's u will be greater than they otherwise would have been, since genotypes are inherited. Therefore, Jim's children's phenotype will benefit for both reasons. However, because of mean reversion the effect of Jim's good luck on his children is expected to be less than the effect on Jim. The first-order intergenerational impulse is defined as the effect of Jim's good luck (or bad luck) on his children, the second-order impulse response refers to the effect of Jim's good luck on his grandchildren, and so on. Higher-order impulse responses tend to be smaller than their lower-order counterparts. After many generations, the impulse response dies out and Jim's good luck is dissipated among his descendants. Galton understood all this.

In Galton's model the impulse responses depend entirely on β. If β is 0.6, the first-order impulse response is 0.6, the second-order impulse response is $0.6^2 = 0.36$, the third-order impulse response is $0.6^3 = 0.216$, and so on. In short, the intergenerational impulse responses die away geometrically, or propagation is geometric. In the AR^2 model, the impulse responses depend, not surprisingly, on β and ρ. Equation 24 in chapter 8 provides the formula for these impulse responses, which are illustrated in table 4.5 for different values of β and ρ.

In case 1, $\rho = 0$ (that is, genotypes are not inherited), which is equivalent to Galton's AR model. Incidentally, the same intergenerational impulses would apply if ρ were 0.6 and β were 0. Comparing case 2 to case 1 shows that, because $\rho = 0.3$, the intergenerational impulses are much more persistent. Apart from being larger, they decrease more slowly. For example, in case 1 the second-order impulse response is 40 percent smaller than the first-order impulse response, whereas in case 2 it is only 30 percent smaller. Case 3 shows that when β is reduced from 0.6 to 0.5 the impulse responses are lower and decrease more rapidly. The same result would have been obtained if the roles of β and ρ had been reversed, i.e., if in case 2 ρ had been 0.6 and β had been 0.3. Finally, case 4 illustrates how a reduction in ρ affects the impulse responses.

Table 4.5
Intergenerational impulse responses for the AR^2 model (based on equation 24 in chapter 8).

Order	Case 1: $\beta = 0.6, \rho = 0$	Case 2: $\beta = 0.6, \rho = 0.3$	Case 3: $\beta = 0.5, \rho = 0.3$	Case 4: $\beta = 0.5, \rho = 0.2$
1	0.6	0.9	0.8	0.7
2	0.36	0.63	0.49	0.39
3	0.216	0.405	0.272	0.203
4	0.13	0.251	0.144	0.103
5	0.078	0.153	0.075	0.052

In the AR^3 model the impulse responses also depend on ϕ. The formula for these impulse responses is given in equation 28 in chapter 8. Just as the impulse responses die out more gradually in the AR^2 model the larger are β and ρ, they die out more gradually in the AR^3 model the larger is ϕ. The larger these parameters are, the more Jim transmits his phenotype, genotype, and environment to his descendants. This makes his good or bad luck propagate longer over the generations.

4.2.4   The Gini Coefficient[9]

Thus far we have used the variance to measure inequality. Although the variance is widely used as a measure of dispersion or inequality, it has a number of shortcomings (discussed in greater detail in section 8.5). One of these is that if two equally unequal distributions are merged, common sense suggests that inequality is not affected. However, the combined variance is generally different from its component parts. Another shortcoming is that, although the variance has a natural lower limit of 0 when there is perfect or complete equality, the variance has no natural upper limit. Several other measures of inequality are considered in chapter 8. It turns out that there is no perfect measure of inequality. However, it is arguable that the least imperfect measure is the *Gini coefficient*, invented by the Italian statistician Corrado Gini in 1912. It is for this reason that the Gini coefficient is so widely used to measure income inequality, or other forms of economic and social inequality. The Gini coefficient equals 0 when there is complete equality and equals 1 when there is complete inequality. The main shortcoming of the Gini coefficient is that if a dollar of income is transferred from a better-off individual to one who is less well off, the decrease in measured inequality is greater if the parties are closer to the mean. In contrast and perhaps more appropriately, the variance decreases the more the parties deviate from the mean.

Unlike the variance and other measures of inequality, the Gini coefficient attaches importance to both the levels of individual outcomes and the ranks of the individual in the distribution. For example, A's income may be $1,000, which is at the 30th percentile in the distribution. This means that 30 percent of the population is worse off than A and 70 percent is better off. B's income may be $1,300, which is at the 35th percentile of the distribution. So B is better off than A and his position in the distribution is higher, with 5 percent of the population separating B from A. Whereas the variance merely compares the incomes of A and B to mean incomes, the Gini coefficient also takes account of how many people have incomes between those of A and B. Indeed, the Gini coefficient, usually denoted by G, is equal to

$$G = 2\frac{\text{cov}(YR)}{\bar{Y}}, \tag{5}$$

where $\text{cov}(YR)$ is the covariance between individual incomes (Y) and their rank (R), and where $\bar{Y}$ is the mean income. This equation shows that if mean income increases, inequality decreases proportionately, provided the covariance remains unchanged. It also shows that if mean income remains unchanged but the covariance increases, inequality increases proportionately. If incomes and ranks are more correlated, there is more inequality.

We saw that the variance integrates absolute mobility into the dynamics of inequality but gave no expression to the role of relative mobility. The Gini coefficient, in contrast, integrates relative and absolute mobility into the dynamics of inequality. Moreover, it also integrates the intuitive concepts of leveling up and down. A society may become more equal because the poor get richer through leveling up or because the rich get poorer through leveling down. The counterpart to equation 1 for the Gini coefficient as a measure of inequality rather than the standard deviation is

$$G_c = \frac{\beta_G}{r_G}\frac{Y_p}{Y_c}G_p, \tag{6}$$

where β_G is β estimated from a Gini regression of the outcome for children on the outcome for parents, r_G is the Gini correlation between the income of children and parents, Y_p is the average outcome for parents, and Y_c is the average outcome for children. (Gini regressions and correlations are defined in section 8.5.) Like β in equation 1, β_G measures absolute immobility. In chapter 8 it is explained that the Gini estimate of β is more reliable than its more popular least squares counterpart because ranked data contain less measurement error than outcomes themselves. B may be better off than A, but it is naturally harder to be sure by how much B is better off than A. Unlike r in equation 1, r_G measures relative immobility, since the Gini correlation uses information on rank. Therefore, the ratio of β_G to r_G in equation 6 measures absolute immobility relative to relative immobility. If absolute and relative immobility happen to be the same, this ratio is equal to 1. The second ratio in equation 6 has no counterpart in equation 1. It is less than 1 if there is intergenerational leveling up and greater than 1 if there is intergenerational leveling down.

The counterpart to sigma convergence and divergence is Gini convergence and divergence. The former occurs if inequality among children, as measured by the Gini coefficient, is less than for their parents. If the opposite happens, there is Gini divergence. If there is no leveling up or down because the average for children is the same their parents', and if relative and absolute immobility are the same, equation 6 states that the Gini coefficient for children must be the same as the Gini coefficient for parents. In this case inequality among children is the same as inequality among parents, so there is neither Gini convergence nor Gini divergence. Equation 6 shows that Gini divergence occurs when there is leveling down and when absolute immobility exceeds relative immobility.

The implications of equation 6 for the intergenerational transmission in inequality are illustrated in table 4.6, in which the Gini coefficient for parents is assumed to be 0.3. In case 1 the Gini coefficient for children is also 0.3, so inequality among children is the same as among parents. In case 2 absolute immobility is reduced, which reduces the Gini coefficient to 0.2, so the inequality among children is less than the inequality among parents. There is Gini convergence because inequality is decreasing, which is the counterpart to sigma convergence, when inequality is measured by the Gini coefficient. The opposite happens in case 3, where relative immobility increases, so there is Gini divergence. Case 4 is Gini convergent; it shows that when there is leveling up the Gini coefficient for children falls to 0.27. When, instead, there is

Table 4.6
Beta convergence and Gini convergence illustrated. The Gini estimate of the mean reversion coefficient is denoted by β_G and the Gini correlation coefficient between the outcomes of parents and children by r_G. The mean outcomes for children and parents are denoted by Y_c and Y_p and the Gini coefficients for parents and children by G_p and G_c.

Case	β_G	r_G	Y_p	Y_c	G_p	G_c
1	0.6	0.6	100	100	0.3	0.3
2	0.4	0.6	100	100	0.3	0.2
3	0.6	0.4	100	100	0.3	0.45
4	0.6	0.6	100	110	0.3	0.27
5	0.6	0.6	110	100	0.3	0.33
6	1.1	0.6	50.9	100	0.3	0.28

leveling down, the Gini coefficient among children increases to 0.33, so there is Gini divergence.

Whereas sigma convergence implies beta convergence, Gini convergence doesn't imply beta convergence. For example, in case 6 in table 4.6, β exceeds 1, so there is beta divergence. Nevertheless, there is Gini convergence, since the Gini coefficient for parents is 0.3 whereas its counterpart for children is 0.28. The reason for this difference is that leveling up and leveling down do not affect the intergenerational transmission of inequality when inequality is measured by the variance, but the same does not apply when inequality is measured by the Gini coefficient.

4.2.5   An Empirical Illustration of Intergenerational Sigma Convergence and Gini Convergence

I have used empirical data for earnings among 12,900 dyads for parents and their children in Israel to calculate β, σ, and the Gini coefficient (Beenstock 2010). Since reported earnings are subject to measurement error, estimates of β tend to suffer from attenuation bias. As was explained in chapter 2, the remedy for this is to use instrumental variables that are correlated with earnings but are not likely to be correlated with measurement error. The results reported in table 4.7 use such instrumental variables, and the instrumental-variables (IV) estimate of β is 0.105. The ordinary least squares estimate of β is 0.04, so the attenuation bias is indeed negative, as expected. The Gini regression estimate for β is 0.124 instead of 0.105. We expect the Gini estimate to be larger than the IV estimate, since the rank of parents' income is likely to be measured more accurately than reported income. And this is precisely what happens. However, the IV and Gini estimates indicate a high

Table 4.7
Intergenerational beta and sigma convergence for earnings in Israel.

	Gini	Variance
β	0.124	0.105
Correlation	0.218	0.2
Y_p	100	100
Y_c	51.84	51.84
sd_p	Na	1.469
sd_c	Na	0.771
G_p	0.215	NA
G_c	0.236	NA

degree of absolute intergenerational mobility, since β is much closer to 0 than to 1. The Gini estimate of β suggests that income is less absolutely mobile than does the IV estimate.

The Gini correlation coefficient between the incomes of children and their parents is 0.218, which is slightly larger than the more familiar Pearson correlation coefficient, which is equal to 0.2. Since the Gini correlation coefficient is a measure of relative immobility, and the Gini estimate of β is a measure of absolute immobility, table 4.7 suggests that relative and absolute immobility are quite different. In fact relative immobility exceeds absolute immobility. This means that there was more movement in the ranks of parents and children in their respective distributions than there was in income itself. Therefore, β_G divided by r_G in equation 6 is equal to 0.124/0.218, which is 0.568. This may be compared with β divided by r in equation 1, which according to table 4.7 is equal to 0.105/2, which is 0.525. Note that this number is not greatly different from 0.568.

The data in table 4.7 show that average income at constant prices for parents greatly exceeded average income of their children. This comparison is somewhat unfair because when the data were collected the children were in their twenties and early thirties whereas their parents were observed when they were older. It is well known that wages vary directly with age since age is correlated with experience. Therefore, the incomes of children appear low simply because they were insufficiently experienced when they were observed. Nevertheless, Y_p divided by Y_c in equation 6 is 1.929, which when multiplied by 0.568 is equal to 1.096. Therefore, the coefficient of the Gini coefficient for parents in equation 6 is 1.096. Since the Gini coefficient for parents was 0.215, we should expect that Gini divergence occurred between the generations. Indeed, the Gini coefficient for children is greater than it was for their parents and is equal to 0.236.

We may therefore decompose the increase in inequality as follows: Because absolute immobility, as measured by β_G is less than relative mobility, as measured by r_G, there would have been Gini convergence. In fact, on this account the Gini coefficient for children's income would have been 0.568 times the Gini coefficient for parents, or 0.122. However, because income leveled down between the generations, this convergent effect was more than offset by a divergent effect. In fact, on this account the Gini coefficient for children would have been 1.929 times the Gini coefficient for parents, or 0.415. Since this divergent effect was slightly stronger than the convergent effect, inequality among children increased slightly relative to inequality among their parents.

The fact that the coefficient on the standard deviation for parents in equation 1 is 0.525 implies that earnings were sigma convergent. Since the standard deviation of the logarithm of earnings among parents was 1.469, its counterpart for children was 0.776. This comparison, like the one mentioned above, is somewhat unfair, because the variance of earnings tends to increase with age. The reason for this is that it takes time for workers to prove themselves in the labor market, and it takes time for employers to discern workers' productivity. Therefore, younger workers appear to be more homogeneous than more mature workers. Consequently, wage inequality tends to be smaller among younger workers than among older ones.

4.3   Sibling Interaction[10]

We have seen how parents increase the underlying level of inequality above what would otherwise prevail under the State of Nature. However, it was assumed that parents have only one child. We will now see how the family induces further inequality when parents have more than one child. For these purposes, let us return to the State of Nature, in which siblings have no parents but they have each other. Whenever there is human intercourse, there is mutual influence, which induces inequality.

Suppose that in the State of Nature child 1 and child 2 choose to be siblings randomly. This random selection mirrors reality: children don't choose to have siblings; their parents decide. In the State of Nature children differ and they share a common, natural degree of inequality, represented here by the standard deviation for their outcomes, assumed for illustrative purposes to be 2. When the State of Nature is disturbed because children form sibling pairs, inequality will tend to increase. Subsection 8.3.1 contains a formal discussion of the effect of sibling interaction on the transmission of inequality within generations and between them. The main logic that underlies this discussion is presented here.

Assume that that the outcome for sibling 1 depends, as in the case of a single child, on his parents' outcome via β, and also depends on the outcome of sibling 2 via a sibling interaction coefficient λ (lambda). And, as in the case of a single child, the outcome of sibling 1 depends on his random draw from the gene pool. In the case of a single child this draw was denoted by u. Since here there are two siblings, these draws are denoted by u_1 and u_2.

The outcome for sibling 2 depends on his parents' outcome via β, on the outcome of sibling 1 via λ, and on his draw from the gene pool (u_2). For the sake of simplicity it is assumed that the models which determine the outcomes of siblings 1 and 2 are symmetrical. This means that the β and λ coefficients for siblings 1 and 2 are identical. In the absence of symmetry these coefficients would vary by sibling. For example, if birth order mattered, the older sibling might be more affected by his parents than his younger sibling, in which case the β coefficient for sibling 1 would be larger than its counterpart for sibling 2. Also, sibling interaction might be asymmetrical (for example, sibling 1 might have more of an influence over his younger sibling than vice versa), in which case the λ coefficient for sibling 2 would be greater than that for sibling 1. Sibling interactions may also vary between brothers and sisters, and β coefficients may be different for mothers and fathers. Fathers and sons may share different betas than mothers and daughters or fathers and daughters. Also, λ may differ between brothers, between sisters, and between brothers and sisters. Finally, owing to personality differences, the β and λ coefficients may differ between siblings, so that β and λ are not the same for sibling 1 as for sibling 2.

The sibling interaction coefficient, λ, measures the size of the effect of siblings on each other. This effect may be benign (in which case λ is positive) or malign (in which case λ is negative). In asymmetrical situations, the effect of sibling 1 on sibling 2 may be benign but the effect of sibling 2 on sibling 1 might be malign. Or it may be the case that sibling 1 affects sibling 2 but sibling 2 does not affect sibling 1—i.e., that sibling interaction is a one-way street. Here, however, we assume symmetry, so sibling interaction is either mutually benign or mutually malign. Although in theory λ is unbounded, it is reasonable to assume that its absolute value is less than 1. This means that sibling 1 affects sibling 2 less than sibling 1 affects himself. It is therefore assumed that λ lies between –1 and 1.

When there are two siblings, the counterpart to equation 2 is

$$\text{var}(Y_c) = a\,\text{var}(Y_p) + b\,\text{var}(u),\qquad(7)$$

where

$$a = \frac{\beta^2(1+\lambda)^2}{(1-\lambda^2)^2}$$

and

$$b = \frac{1+\lambda^2}{\left(1-\lambda^2\right)^2}.$$

Equation 7 (a simplified version of equation 45 in chapter 8) has a simple intuitive interpretation. Notice that when $\lambda = 0$ equation 7 reverts to equation 2 because $a = \beta^2$ and $b = 1$. Therefore, when there are two siblings instead of one and when siblings aren't mutually influential, it makes no difference whether children happen to be siblings or singletons. Inequality within and between generations is exactly the same as in the case of singletons. If sibling interaction is positive (if λ is positive), a is greater than β^2, in which case the intergenerational transmission of inequality is stronger when children are siblings than when they are singletons. Also, when sibling interaction is positive, b is greater than 1, in which case intragenerational inequality is greater when children are siblings than when they are singletons. If intragenerational inequality is increased and if the intergenerational transmission of inequality is stronger, it must be the case that the unconditional, or long-term, structural level of inequality increases on both of these accounts. In short, when children are siblings instead of singletons, structural inequality is increased, and the increase varies directly with sibling interaction as measured by λ.

Some numerical simulations of equation 7 may serve to illustrate these phenomena. Our starting point is case 1 in table 4.1, where β is 0.6, the standard deviation for parents is 2, and the standard deviation of u is 2.75. Recall that this case represents the level of inequality that would prevail under the State of Nature. Also recall, from table 4.2, that the unconditional or structural level of inequality under case 1 is 3.44 when children are singletons, or when $\lambda = 0$. Therefore, case 1 in table 4.8 is identical to case 1 in table 4.1. In case 2 in table 4.8, sibling interaction is positive and $\lambda = 0.2$. This raises a from 0.36 to 0.563 and b from 1 to 1.128. If the standard deviation among parents is 2, equation 7 implies that the standard deviation among children is 3.28 instead of 3. This amounts to an increase in inequality among children of 9.3 percent due to sibling interaction. This increase may be broken down into the contribution due to the increase in a (that is, the stronger intergenerational transmission of inequality), which adds 0.81 or 9 percent to the variance, and the contribution due the increase in b (that is, the greater intragenerational inequality), which adds 0.97 or 10.8 percent to the variance. Therefore, the majority of the increase in inequality among

Table 4.8
Simulating the effect of sibling interaction on inequality. Here λ denotes the sibling interaction coefficient, a and b are coefficients determined by equation 7, and sd* denotes structural inequality as measured by the standard deviation. Also see caption of table 4.1.

Case	λ	a	b	sd_p	sd_c	sd*
1	0	0.36	1	1.863	1.5	1.25
2	0.2	0.563	1.128	1.863	1.755	1.607
3	−0.2	0.250	0.722	1.863	1.261	0.981
4	0.1	0.444	1.031	1.863	1.604	1.362
5	0.4	1	1.643	1.863	2.261	∞

children is coming from the increase in intragenerational inequality rather than the transmission of intergenerational inequality.

In the absence of sibling interaction, we saw in table 4.2 that conditional inequality is 1.5 while structural, or long-term inequality was 1.25, as shown in the last column of table 4.8. The long-term level of inequality for case 2 is 1.607, i.e., sibling interaction increases structural inequality by 29 percent, while conditional inequality increases from 1.5 to 1.755. This happens because both a and b increase as a result of sibling interaction. Sibling interaction fans the fires of inequality by increasing intragenerational inequality, which in turn propagates intergenerationally. Case 3 considers malign sibling interaction. Both a and b decrease relative to case 1. For both of these reasons, conditional and structural inequality are lower in case 3 than in cases 1 and 2. Finally, in case 5, a equals 1, thereby inducing beta divergence. Also, b increases to 1.643. For both of these reasons, conditional inequality increases to 2.261, but structural inequality is infinite, because beta divergence implies sigma divergence, as already discussed.

When there are three siblings, a and b in equation 7 become[11]

$$a = \left(\frac{\beta[1 + 2\lambda(1+\lambda)]}{1 - 3\lambda^2 - 2\lambda^3} \right)^2$$

and

$$b = \left(\frac{1 + 2\lambda(1+\lambda)}{1 - 3\lambda^2 - 2\lambda^3} \right)^2.$$

We continue to assume that $\beta = 0.6$ and $var(u) = 1$. If λ is fixed, a and b are always larger when there are three siblings instead of two, because

Table 4.9
Structural inequality and number of siblings.

Case	Sibship	λ	Inequality
1	1	0	1.25
2	2	0.1	1.362
3	3	0.1	2.606
4	3	0.15	3.331

the scope for sibling interaction naturally varies directly with the number of siblings.

Table 4.9 shows the simulated value for structural inequality (measured by the standard deviation). "Case 1" in this table refers to case 1 in table 4.2. Since there is only one child, λ is implicitly 0. "Case 2" refers to case 4 in table 4.8. Case 3 shows that when there are three siblings structural inequality increases from 1.641 to 2.606. The larger scope for sibling interaction has a pronounced effect on structural inequality. If the sibling interaction coefficient is 0.15 instead of 0.1, structural inequality with three siblings increases from 2.606 to 3.331 (case 4). Table 4.9 shows that structural inequality varies directly and disproportionately with the number of siblings. This nonlinear relationship between inequality and sibship stems from the fact that the scope for sibling interaction expands disproportionately when sibship increases. When there are two siblings, the scope is 2, because sibling 1 interacts with sibling 2 and vice versa. When there are three siblings, the scope is 6. When there are four siblings, the scope is 12. When there are N siblings, the scope is $N(N - 1)$. Thus, the scope for interaction increases with the square of the number of siblings, and inequality increases accordingly.

Case 4 in table 4.9 shows that structural inequality, besides being very sensitive to sibship, is very sensitive to the extent to which siblings interact. Indeed, this sensitivity varies directly with sibship. Therefore, we should expect that, everything else equal, societies with larger families should experience greater inequality.

In a State of Nature, structural inequality depends on the standard deviation of the gene pool and other random factors, which in the numerical example is 1. When reproduction is asexual and β is 0.6, structural inequality increases to 1.25. If reproduction is sexual, inequality increases further to 1.89, and if parents mate assortatively with correlation 0.2, inequality increases further to 2.71 in the numerical example. If we add to this the effect of sibling interaction when there are two siblings and λ is 0.1, inequality increases further to 2.95; if there are three siblings, it increases to 5.65. Structural inequality is more than five times as great as in a State of Nature. These numerical illustrations naturally depend on the assumptions about β (0.6), λ (0.1), and assortative mating ($r_{mf} = 0.2$). The larger these parameters, the greater would be the increase in inequality relative to the State of Nature. Although these numbers are arbitrary, they nevertheless illustrate the potentially powerful role of the family in the propagation of structural inequality.

4.4 Propagation of Inequality with Multiple Phenotypes[12]

Thus far the analysis has been univariate; there was a single outcome or phenotype under consideration. For example, the outcome might have been income, schooling, or health status, or indeed any other outcome affected by parenting and sibling interaction. We saw how the family potentially propagates inequality in this univariate context. However, this understates the effect of family on inequality. We shall see that in the bivariate case, in which two outcomes are dependent, the family promotes inequality with greater force. More generally, in the multivariate case in which several outcomes affect each other, inequality is induced by the family with even greater force. Since this phenomenon doesn't depend on sibship, it is assumed that parents have only one child.

The two outcomes in the bivariate case are referred to as Y and X. For example, Y might be income and X might be schooling. As an illustration of the argument, we take the simplest possible case, in which the outcome of the child depends, as before, on the outcome of parents, and the phenotype (Y) of the child depends on his X. However, in the interest of simplicity, X doesn't depend on the phenotype. Thus, if Y represents income and X represents schooling, the child's income depends on his schooling, as human capital theory predicts, but his schooling doesn't depend on his income. Typically, schooling precedes working life, so this one-way-street assumption is plausible.

The models for Y and X are therefore

$$Y_c = \beta_Y Y_p + \gamma X_c + u \tag{8}$$

and

$$X_c = \beta_X X_p + v, \tag{9}$$

where, as before, u denotes the genotype for Y and β_Y denotes β for Y. The genotype for X is denoted by v and β for X is denoted by β_X. Since these genotypes might be correlated, their correlation coefficient is denoted by r_{uv}. Because Y depends on X, equation 2 becomes

$$\mathrm{var}(Y_c) = \beta_Y^2\,\mathrm{var}(Y_p) + \gamma^2\beta_X^2\,\mathrm{var}(X_p) + \mathrm{var}(u) + \gamma^2\,\mathrm{var}(v) + 2\gamma r_{uv}\mathrm{sd}(u)\mathrm{sd}(v). \tag{10}$$

Note that if $\gamma = 0$ equation 10 reverts to equation 2 because in this case Y_c doesn't depend on X_p. Equation 10 states that inequality in Y among the generation of children varies directly with inequality in both Y and X in the previous generation. Therefore, in the bivariate case the inter-generational transmission of inequality is transmitted through two channels instead of one. It is transmitted through inequality in Y among parents as well as inequality in X among parents. Also, apart from depending as before on the variance of u, inequality in Y varies directly with the variance of v, the genotype for X. This means that on both these accounts inequality in Y in the bivariate case is naturally greater than in the univariate case. If, in addition, the genotypes for Y and X are correlated so that r_{uv} is not 0, the final term in equation 10 influences the variance of Y. The direction of influence is positive if γr_{uv} is positive.

To see how the intergenerational transmission of inequality is strengthened in the bivariate phenotype case relative to the univariate case, let us return to the numerical example in table 4.2. We assume that β for Y and β for X both happen to be 0.6, that the standard deviations of Y_p is 1.863 (as in table 4.1), and that the standard deviations of u, v, and X are 1. The first case in table 4.10 is identical to its counterpart in table 4.2 because $\gamma = 0$, so conditional inequality is 1.5 and structural inequality is 1.25. When $\gamma = 0.2$, as in case 2, the standard deviation among children increases from 1.5 to 1.518 and structural inequality increases from 1.25 to 1.284. In case 2 the genotype correlation is assumed to be 0. If it happens to be 0.4, as in case 3, conditional inequality among children increases to 1.57 from 1.518, and structural inequality increases from 1.284 to 1.377. Case 4 shows that when γ increases structural and conditional inequality increase to 1.55 and 1.669 respectively. If, however, γ is negative, case 5 shows that conditional and structural inequality decrease. Notice that cases 4 and 6 are equivalent.

Table 4.10
Simulating the intergenerational transmission of inequality with two phenotypes. The effect of X on Y is denoted by γ, and r_{uv} denotes the correlation between the genotypes for X and Y. Also see caption of table 4.8.

Case	γ	r_{uv}	$sd(Y_c)$	$sd^*(Y)$
1	0	0	1.5	1.25
2	0.2	0	1.518	1.284
3	0.2	0.4	1.570	1.377
4	0.4	0.4	1.669	1.55
5	−0.4	0.4	1.465	1.184
6	−0.4	−0.4	1.669	1.55

Assuming that the genotype variances are the same obviously affects the calculations in table 4.10. Had we assumed that inequality in X among parents is larger, or that β is greater for X than for Y, or that the variance of v exceeds the variance of u, inequality among children would be larger than what is reported in table 4.10. Nevertheless, table 4.10 illustrates how phenotypic dependence increases inequality when the phenotypes are positively related and decreases inequality when the phenotypic dependence is negative.

Inequality (or human diversity) and the family are inextricably interwoven phenomena. This chapter has shown how various aspects of the family contribute to inequality. Two different types of inequality are distinguished. Inequality in the current generation is transmitted to the next generation. I referred to this as *short-term* or *conditional* inequality. It is short-term because inequality in the next generation lasts for only one generation. It is conditional because inequality in the next generation depends on, or is conditioned by, inequality in the current generation. Inequality in the generation after the next will be different again. Eventually, over many generations, inequality (or diversity) tends to settle down at what I referred to as *structural* or *unconditional* inequality. This is the level of inequality that is expected after the intergenerational transmission of short-term inequality has fully worked itself through. It is unconditional because it doesn't depend on inequality in the current generation. I also refer to this as *long-term* inequality, because it is the level of inequality that, on average, is expected to be ground out over all generations.

The dynamic process through which short-term inequality (or diversity) tends toward long-term inequality is referred to as *sigma convergence.* The interwoven concepts of short-term inequality, long-term inequality, and sigma convergence have been elucidated by using numerical examples based on statistical models discussed in greater detail in chapter 8. Several family phenomena are studied, and their contribution to inequality and diversity are illustrated numerically. These include the effect of the genotypes of parents on their children's genotypes, the effect of the phenotypes of parents on their children's phenotypes, the mutual effect of sibling phenotypes on each other, the effect of phenotypes on each other, and the effect of the environments of parents on the environments of their children. All these phenomena magnify families' propagation of inequality. Moreover, these phenomena are not additive but multiplicative. Therefore, the effect of any two such phenomena on inequality is more than the sum of their individual effects.

Much of the debate about the causes of economic inequality has ignored the potential role of family as a root cause of inequality. During the second half of the twentieth century, economic inequality increased in most of the industrialized countries, and especially in the United States, the United Kingdom, and even Israel. Some economists have attributed this to skill-biased technical change, according to which technical changes and the "digital divide" increased the productivity of skilled workers relative to lower-paid unskilled workers. Other economists have attributed growing economic inequality to globalization, which is increasingly requiring unskilled workers in the industrialized countries to compete with low-paid unskilled workers in the developing countries, especially China and the countries of Southeast Asia.

If families induce inequality, can it be that the aforementioned increase in economic inequality had something to do with family? During the second half of the twentieth century, fertility fell substantially across the industrialized world, and especially in Catholic Europe. Also, the institution of the traditional family weakened and suffered. The number of single-parent families increased disproportionately. Mothers increasingly went out to work. In terms of the model proposed in this chapter, these trends should have worked to reduce economic inequality rather than to increase it. On the face of it, the model seems to be wrong. This does not mean that the model *is* wrong. It means that the increase in inequality is all the more remarkable because it occurred despite the trend to smaller families and weaker family ties. This theoretical model has yet to be tested empirically. Everything else equal, has inequality increased less in countries in which fertility decreased more?

5 Empirical Methodology

5.1 Observational and Experimental Data

Empirical hypothesis testing is conducted using two main types of data: experimental and observational. The former are generated under laboratory conditions by empirical investigators; the latter are generated spontaneously by nature or human behavior. Examples of observational data include planetary movements, meteorological data, economic data such as gross domestic product, demographic data such as fertility and population, and sociobiological data such as the behavior of animals and insects. In theory, empirical investigators using experimental data have complete control over their data because they are actively involved in constructing the data. In contrast, empirical investigators using observational data have no control whatsoever over their data. They are passive observers and users of data that have come spontaneously into existence through some unknown "data-generating process" (DGP).

Empirical investigators who use experimental data are lucky compared to their less fortunate colleagues who use observational data. This is not to belittle the challenges involved in designing and running good laboratory experiments. To test whether phenomenon A has a causal effect on outcome B, experimentalists carefully construct a "treatment" or "trial" group to which A is applied and a "control" group to which A is not applied. The experimenter makes sure that these two groups are entirely chosen at random, and that all potential confounders are controlled for in the laboratory. Therefore, if the outcomes for the two groups are different, it can only be because of A. The outcomes B for the two groups are subsequently compared. If B for the control group and B for the treatment group are not statistically significantly different from each other, the null hypothesis that A causes B can be rejected. Alternatively, the null hypothesis cannot be rejected, in which case the null hypothesis is corroborated. These experiments may involve chemicals, plants, animals, or any other subjects or objects that have no choice in participating in the experiment.

Matters are very different for an empirical investigator using observational data. The investigator has obtained a sample of data in which phenomena A and B just happen to assume various values. The data typically include other variables; call one of them C. Since the data are observational, the investigator doesn't know their DGP; unlike his experimenter colleague, he doesn't exercise control over their generation. Therefore, if A and B happen to be correlated the investigator can't be sure that A is causing B or vice versa. Nor can he be sure that A is affecting B through C. And if A and B don't happen to be correlated, that doesn't necessarily mean that A doesn't cause B, for it might be the case that the effect of A on B is intermediated through C, so that, given C, A causes B.

Hypothesis testing with observational data is inherently more difficult than hypothesis testing with experimental data. Investigators using observational data have to be more ingenious than their counterparts who have access to experimental data. Indeed, an entire discipline has developed that is concerned with hypothesis testing with observational data. This discipline, invented by economists, is known as *econometrics*.

Whereas social scientists typically test their hypotheses using observational data, natural scientists typically test their hypotheses using experimental data. There are, however, many branches of natural science in which experimentation is not feasible, and the only available data are observational. Among them are astronomy, meteorology, and cosmology. Chemists, physicists, and biologists may carry out experiments in their laboratories. In many cases these experiments and laboratories are very expensive, such as the particle accelerator at CERN in Geneva. Although the vast majority of empirical investigation in the social sciences is conducted with observational data, social scientists have also generated their own experimental data. Psychology has a particularly strong experimental tradition; it dates back to the 1860s, when Gustav Fechner and Wilhelm Wundt showed that the marginal effect of a stimulus varies inversely with its size. Bardsley et al. (2010) point out that the founding fathers of neoclassical economics, such as William Stanley Jevons and Francis Ysidro Edgeworth, saw in these experimental findings a scientific justification for marginal utility theory. Indeed, Jevons himself carried out experiments to test marginal utility theory, which were reported in the second volume of *Nature* in 1871. Bardsley et al. also assert that experimentalism in the social sciences was originally suggested by no less an authority than David Hume (in his *Treatise on Human Nature*). Indeed, the subtitle of the Treatise is "An attempt to introduce the experimental method of reasoning in moral subjects." However, Bardsley et al. misinterpret Hume. In his introduction to the Treatise, Hume clearly argues the opposite:

> Moral philosophy has, indeed, this peculiar disadvantage, which is not found in natural, that in collecting its experiments, it cannot make them purposefully, with premeditation, and after such a matter as to satisfy itself concerning every particular difficulty which may arise. When I am at a loss to know the effects of one body on another in any situation, I need only put them in that situation, and observe what results from it. But should I endeavour to clear up after the same manner any doubt in moral philosophy, by placing myself in the same case with that which I consider, 'tis evident this reflection and premeditation would so disturb the operation of my natural principles, as must render it impossible to form any just conclusion from the phaenomenon. We must therefore glean up our experiments in this science from cautious observation of human life, and take them as they appear in the common course of the world, by men's behaviour in company, in affairs, and in their pleasures. (1739, pp. vviii–xix)

Clearly Hume is aware that experiments involving people are fundamentally different from experiments involving matter. People do not behave naturally and spontaneously under experimental conditions. Indeed, Hume anticipated the methodological criticism of experiments involving people. The experiments to which Hume refers in the final sentence involve, in his words, "observational data generated as they appear in the common course of the world." They are not data generated in a laboratory, as Bardsley et al. suggest. In summary, Hume opposed experimentalism in the social sciences (moral philosophy) and proposed that we cautiously learn what we might from observational data.[1]

The methodological break between economics and psychology came in 1906 when Vilfredo Pareto attacked the use of experiments to test hypotheses in economics.[2] In the 1940s and the 1950s, there were sporadic experiments that were concerned mainly with rational choice behavior. Experimentalism naturally became less attractive as econometric theory was developed in the first half of the twentieth century, especially by Elmer Working (1927), by P. G. Wright (1928), and by Olav Reiersøl (1941). These pioneers were economists who couldn't find methodologies for non-experimental data in the literature on statistics, so they invented their own. (Reiersøl invented the instrumental-variables estimator.)

In the last 30 years there has been a renaissance of experimentalism in economics. Indeed, in 2002 Daniel Kahneman and Vernon Smith were awarded the Nobel Prize in economic science for their work on experimental economics. The ongoing debate about the scientific contribution of experimental economics has relevance for testing hypotheses concerning family and heredity. Let us distinguish between two types of experiment: private and social. In private experiments, students or some other non-representative sample of the population are invited to serve as guinea pigs in an experiment. A typical example is the "ultimatum game," in which students are offered the opportunity of sharing, say, $10. If student A proposes that he should get $8, Student B may either accept $2 or reject the opportunity so that A and B get nothing. In contrast, social experiments involve real-life situations. One typical example is a de-worming experiment among school children in Kenya (Miguel and Kremer 2003). In randomized field trials, some children are offered de-worming treatment, which is not offered to the population at large. There is an obvious double-edged compliance problem: the trial children cannot be forced to de-worm, while the control children might obtain de-worming treatment by indirect means. Randomized trials are "quasi-experiments," not proper experiments. In proper experiments there are no problems of compliance; rats in a proper experiment have no choice but to comply, whereas human beings in a randomized trial may choose not to comply. There are also moral problems with randomized trials: potentially helpful treatments are withheld in the name of science, and there is unavoidable discrimination against the control group in favor of the trial group. Despite these methodological and moral problems, random field trials have grown in popularity.[3]

It is ironic that social experimentation and randomized trials have grown in popularity. Not so long ago, social experimentation became unpopular and even fell into disrepute. During the 1960s and the 1970s there were a number of social experiments in the United States covering a wide variety of issues, including the effects of negative income taxes on employment and welfare claims, the effects of time-of-use pricing of electricity on peak loading, the effects of housing allowances on the demand and supply of housing, the effects of Head Start programs, the effects of health insurance on health spending, and the effects of public health programs. These experiments were very expensive, and the results were generally disappointing. There was a widespread feeling that it would have been better to spend the money on conventional research into the same phenomena. In 1981 the National Bureau of Economic Research held a conference to consider the matter (Hausman and Wise 1985). On the whole, social experimentation was regarded as an expensive failure.

The empirical study of intergenerational and sibling correlations is also based exclusively on observational data, since it is not feasible to carry out experiments to test hypotheses concerning the causal mechanisms that underlie the intergenerational and intragenerational (sibling) correlations that we observe. Take, for example, the correlation in fertility between sisters that was discussed in chapter 2. This correlation could be induced by several competing phenomena. One possibility is that sisters interact in the sense of chapter 3 and they influence each other's behavior. A second possibility is that sisters share genes that affect their fertility. Since their fecundity is correlated, so is their fertility. A third possibility is that children copy their parents' behavior, including their fertility. Since sisters have common parents, their fertility is correlated because both sisters copy their parents. There may be other phenomena too, including the effect of shared environments, but the list is already long enough.

Suppose we wanted to conduct an experiment to test the first of the three hypotheses mentioned above. What would we have to do? We would have to generate treatment and control groups for pairs of sisters, selected at random. One of the control sisters would be required not to get pregnant. One of the treatment sisters would be required to get pregnant. If the incidence of pregnancy among the other treatment sisters is greater than the incidence of pregnancy among the other control sisters, the data do not refute the hypothesis that there is a causal effect of fertility between sisters.

Obviously it is not feasible to carry out such an experiment. Even if in some other context it were possible to get people to participate in the experiment, the participants probably would be unrepresentative of the population as a whole. One can think of numerous ingenious experiments that would test hypotheses concerning nature vs. nurture, but they are all infeasible. Just imagine designing an experiment to test the hypothesis (which also arose in chapter 2) that there is a causal effect of the longevity of parents on the longevity of their children. Parents in the trial group would be asked to die, and parents in the control group to survive!

Suppose, however, that in some contexts experimentation happens to be feasible. Just because it is feasible this does not necessarily mean that it is also desirable. It might be the case that human beings behave differently under experimental conditions than they do naturally. The experiment might make them self-conscious, since they are aware that they are serving a scientific purpose. They might want to please the investigator by providing the result that he wants according to the null hypothesis. Contrary subjects might provide results that refute the null hypothesis. Or, if not aware of the null hypothesis, they might think that, since this is just an experiment, they do not have to take things seriously, as they would in real life. In the literature on experiments involving humans, these phenomena are known collectively as Hawthorne Effects, so named after the Hawthorne Works,[4] a factory (near Chicago) in which time-and-motion experiments designed to boost productivity were carried out in the 1930s.

Experimenters with rats and similar animal life assume that Hawthorne effects don't apply to animals. They also take it for granted than when rats are randomly assigned to treatment and control groups the rats can't influence their selection. But perhaps some rats are better at avoiding selection than others. If these more wily rats have better outcomes than their less wily colleagues, the difference between the outcomes for the two groups of rats will not deliver what the experimenter thinks it will.

Experimentalism in the social sciences is on the increase, but in my opinion it is of doubtful scientific value. If there were no alternative to experimentalism, there would be more of a case for taking experimentalism seriously. But there is an alternative. In fact there are several alternatives. The first is "natural experimentation," in which nature mimics laboratory experiments. A laboratory is simply a man-made device for randomizing treatments to ensure that the allocation of treatment has nothing to do with the outcome of interest. A natural experiment randomizes treatments through real-life events; it induces some people to take the treatment under investigation, while others elect not to take the treatment. Moreover, the life events that serve as natural experiments have no direct effect on the outcome of interest. Natural experiments mimic laboratory experiments by randomizing treatment status in a way that isn't correlated with the outcome of interest. There is, however, an important difference between laboratory and natural experiments as far as human subjects are concerned. Because natural experiments occur spontaneously, Hawthorne effects don't arise in natural experiments. In natural experiments, people behave naturally and spontaneously because they are not aware that they are providing experimental information.

A disadvantage of natural experiments is that, unlike laboratory experiments, they can't be contrived at will, since natural experiments occur spontaneously in the course of life. Indeed, there may be no natural experiments available to facilitate the empirical testing of some (or even many) hypotheses. This is a common and frustrating occurrence in cosmology, astronomy, and meteorology, fields in which laboratory experimentation is not feasible: null hypotheses remain in epistemological limbo until some natural experiment happens to occur, such as a supernova explosion that redeems the situation and makes it feasible to test the null hypothesis. Such an event occurred in 1919: a solar eclipse corroborated Einstein's theory about the behavior of light.

Natural and laboratory experiments test the null hypothesis unambiguously. If the null hypothesis is that A causes B, both natural and laboratory experiments seek to falsify or corroborate it. If the hypothesis is corroborated, the quantitative effect of A on B is estimated. Although all statistical testing is probabilistic, these tests and estimates are inherently unambiguous. If the hypothesis happens to be corroborated, we may be 99 percent or even 99.9 percent sure that the hypothesis can't be rejected. This level of probability varies directly with the sample size in the experiment and inversely with the randomness of the outcome of interest. In principle, if the sample were infinitely large and if there were no randomness in the outcome of interest, we could be 100 percent sure that the null hypothesis was false or not. Therefore, in the limit there is no ambiguity.

Even if natural experimentation is not feasible, there is still something for the user of observational data to do. An alternative methodological paradigm that has developed in the last decade is based on the principle of "partial identification," which is inherently ambiguous.[5] Partial identification uses observational data to test causal hypotheses ambiguously. For example, suppose that we have observational data on variables A and B and that the null hypothesis is that A causes B positively. Under partial identification it is possible to conclude from the data that the causal effect of A on B can't be greater than some upper limit or less than some lower limit. If the effects that fall between these limits are positive, we can't refute the null hypothesis. In this case the null hypothesis is corroborated but we still cannot say how large the causal effect of A is on B. However, we can rule out that the effect is greater than the upper limit or bound and less than the lower limit or bound. Herein lies the ambiguity. On the other hand, if the upper bound is positive and the lower bound is negative we can't be sure whether A causes B positively, whether it causes B negatively, or whether it causes B at all. In this case there is ambiguity about the test of the null hypothesis.

Partial identification comes in a variety of shapes and forms. It might not be possible to corroborate the null hypothesis, but it might be possible to show that it is false. I use observational data to test the null hypothesis that treatment helps drug addicts (Beenstock 2010c). I can't corroborate this hypothesis, but I can establish that the data are inconsistent with it. In short, I can't show that treatment works, but I can show that it doesn't seem to work. It may not be empirically possible to establish that nature matters, but it may be possible to establish that nature does not matter. In many cases such partial identification is of sufficient and even major public interest. That treatment programs for drug addicts aren't working is of obvious policy interest.

Unambiguous hypothesis testing is obviously preferable to ambiguous hypothesis testing. However, in the absence of natural experiments, and in view of the reluctance to undertake laboratory experiments with humans, partial identification is an attractive methodological option in hypothesis testing with observational data. Partial identification is like the cup that is half full. In the absence of empirical data, it is not possible to test the null hypothesis, in which case there is maximal ambiguity. We can't reject or accept the null hypothesis; we can know nothing empirically. At the other extreme, when experimental data are available that are generated in a laboratory, or are generated naturally, there is no ambiguity; the null hypothesis may be falsified or corroborated. Between these two extremes, partial identification uses observational data to learn something about the empirical world. Observational data are obviously more informative than no data at all, but they are inevitably less informative than experimental data.

5.2   Intergenerational Mean Reversion

In chapter 2 I introduced Galton's intergenerational mean reversion model, in which the outcome or phenotype for the child is hypothesized to depend on the outcome for the parent.[6] In chapter 4 I extended this model into the AR^2 model, in which the phenotypes of children depend on their genotypes and their parents' phenotypes, and the genotypes of children depend on their parents' genotype through heredity. The following equations recall the AR^2 model:

$$Y_c = \alpha + \beta Y_p + u_c,$$ (1)

$$u_c = \rho u_p + \varepsilon_c,$$ (2)

where Y denotes the phenotype, u denotes the genotype, c and p indicate children and parents, and ε is a random draw from the gene pool. Equation 1 states that children's outcomes depend on their genotypes (u) and their parents' outcomes via β. Equation 2 states that the genotype of the child depends on his parents' genotype via ρ, as well as via ε. In terms of the nature-nurture dichotomy, ρ captures nature through heredity, β captures nurture, and ε is also part of nature since it is the non-inherited genotype.

The parameter of interest is assumed to be β, which measures the causal effect of the outcome of the parents on the outcome of the child. For example, if Y denotes education, equation 1 states that, with everything else equal, more educated parents have more educated children. In this example, u denotes learning ability or a genotype for learning. Equation 2 states that the learning ability of the child is partly inherited.

In chapter 10 I will show that empirical estimates of β tend to be biased upward.[7] This bias is induced by the fact that ordinary least squares (OLS) regression assumes that in equation 1 u_c is independent of Y_p. However, it is obvious from equation 2 that Y_p and u_c are positively related, since Y_p varies directly with u_p (because phenotypes for parents depend on their genotypes) and u_c varies directly with u_p (because genotypes are inherited). Therefore, OLS estimates of β are generally biased.

Table 5.1 illustrates how this bias[8] depends on β and ρ. In case 1, $\rho = 0$ and the true value of β is 0.5. Since $\rho = 0$, the genetic relationship between parents and children cannot distort the estimate of the causal effect of the outcome of parents on the outcome of children. Therefore, the regression bias is 0, and the estimate of β is expected to be its true value of 0.5. This happens because the phenotype of parents is independent of the genotype of their children—that is, u_c and Y_p are independent in equation 1.

This independence is removed in case 2. Since $\rho = 0.2$, the genotype of children must depend on the phenotype of their parents. In the case of education, children inherit their parents' learning ability, and abler parents acquire more education; therefore the learning

Table 5.1
Bias in β.

Case	β	ρ	Bias
1	0.5	0	0
2	0.5	0.2	0.136
3	0.2	0.5	0.436
4	0.6	0.2	0.114
5	0	0.5	0.5
6	−0.2	0.5	0.533

ability of children (u_c) and the education of their parents (Y_p) are dependent. Since this dependence is positive, β is over-estimated and the bias is positive. In fact the bias is 0.136, so β is expected to be 0.636 instead of its true value of 0.5. This biased estimate entangles the true values of β and ρ. The naive investigator who thinks that β is 0.636 will over-estimate the causal effect of parents on children. In fact, as a percentage of its true value the bias in case 2 is 27.2 percent, which is large.

Case 3 reverses the values of ρ and β in case 2. The bias more than doubles, and the estimate of β is 0.636—more than three times its true value. Note that the estimate of β in cases 2 and 3 are identical. This happens because the values of ρ and β have been interchanged in the two cases. In general, the bias varies directly with ρ and inversely with β. For example, in case 4 β is increased from 0.5 to 0.6 while ρ is unchanged at 0.2. The bias in case 4 decreases to 0.114 from 0.136 in case 2. In case 5 the true value of β is 0 but ρ is 0.2. In such cases the bias is always equal to ρ, so the bias is equal to 0.2. The naive investigator may think that the outcome of parents has a causal effect on their children's outcomes, but the truth is that there is no such effect. The estimate of $\beta = 0.2$ is entirely the result of genetic dependence of children on their parents. Finally, case 6 shows that when $\beta = -0.2$ and $\rho = 0.5$ the bias is 0.533, which means that the estimate of β is 0.333.

In the jargon of econometrics, β is not "identified." This means that the unbiased estimate of β cannot be disentangled from its estimated value. For example, in case 2 the estimate of β is 0.636, but its true estimate of 0.5 cannot be disentangled. In case 1, in contrast, β is identified because its estimate is not confounded by ρ, which is 0. In case 4, ρ is identified because β is 0. In the general case, when β and ρ are non-zero, β is not identified, nor is ρ.

How might we solve this identification problem? Experimentalists would conduct an experiment in which the phenotype of parents was increased in the trial group and left unchanged in the control group. Subsequently the outcomes of the two groups of children would be compared. Experiments identify β because they disconnect what happens to the phenotype of parents from the genotypes of their children. In short, experiments break the link between the genotypes of parents and children; they short-circuit heredity. As I have argued, even if such experimentation were feasible it probably would be undesirable.

So how might this identification problem be solved when the data are observational rather than experimental? There are several ways, which I discuss in detail in chapter 10. Here I outline the main ones.

5.2.1 Dynastic Data

Suppose that we have longitudinal data on successive generations of parents and children—that is, on grandparents, on great-grandparents, and indeed on the dynasty as a whole. Suppose also that β and ρ don't vary from one generation to the next. With such dynastic data it would be possible to identify beta because it is possible to estimate ρ. To see this, suppose that at first we ignore ρ and estimate β from the dynastic data. This estimate of β will be biased. The regression residuals constitute biased estimates of the genotypes because β is biased. Next, we use these residuals to estimate ρ, as in equation 2. Since the residuals are biased, so must be the estimate of ρ. Thus far, we have obtained biased estimates of β and ρ, which will be referred to as β_0 and ρ_0.

Equations 1 and 2 imply the following relationship[9] between the outcomes of children and the outcomes of parents and grandparents:

$$Y_c = \alpha(1-\rho) + (\beta+\rho)Y_p - \beta\rho Y_g + \varepsilon_c, \tag{3}$$

where Y_g denotes the outcome or phenotype of grandparents. Notice that the coefficient on Y_g is negative, so that, conditional on their parents' outcome, the outcomes of children vary inversely with their grandparents' outcomes due to heredity. What is important in equation 3 is that the residual is equal to ε_c, the child's draw from the gene pool. Since this is entirely random and is not related to the genotypes and phenotypes of parents and grandparents, the residual in equation 3 is independent of Y_p and Y_g, and the classical regression assumptions[10] are satisfied.

Next, substitute ρ_0 into equation 3 for ρ; then regress $Y_c - \rho_0 Y_p$ on $Y_p - \rho_0 Y_g$, which gives a new estimate of β. The new estimate (referred to as β_1) differs from the initial estimate (β_0) because β_0 is biased. β_1 would be unbiased if ρ_0 were unbiased, but such is not the case. However, β_1 is less biased than β_0 because the latter entirely ignores heredity whereas the former does not. The remaining steps are designed to refine the estimate of ρ as follows: Substitute β_1 into equation 1 for β; then compute a new set of residuals, and use them to estimate ρ_2 in equation 2. Substitute this estimate of ρ_2 into equation 3 for ρ, which is used to estimate β_2. Follow this iterative procedure until ρ and β converge on their final estimates. In this way, dynastic data identify both β and ρ.

In the absence of dynastic data this identification methodology is obviously not feasible. However, at a minimum it requires three successive generations. This is clearly visible in equation 3, which delivers estimates of $\beta + \rho$ from the coefficient on Y_p and estimates of $\beta\rho$ from the slope coefficient on Y_g. It is a simple matter to solve separately for β and ρ from these estimates. For example, if $\beta + \rho = 0.8$ and $\beta\rho = 0.15$ it must be the case either that $\beta = 0.5$ and $\rho = 0.3$ or that $\beta = 0.3$ and $\rho = 0.5$. Identification is ambiguous and partial.

If the data are available for only two generations, identification isn't even partial. There is no identification, because it is not possible to estimate ρ. It requires at least three generations to learn anything about heredity. Most intergenerational data refer to two generations, although some refer to three generations. Dynastic data are very rare.[11]

5.2.2   Natural Experiments

Since most intergenerational data refer to only two generations, we have to ask how, in the absence of dynastic data, β might be identified in observational data. The main answer lies in natural experimentation. Natural experiments arise when, in the course of life, events happen to affect the outcome for parents (Y_p) that are completely unrelated to their genotype. For example, if parents were exposed to different educational regimes and policies that affected their schooling in a way that didn't depend on their learning ability, there may be exogenous or independent variation in the parents' schooling. In immigrant societies, parents are exposed to different educational policies in their source countries. Two otherwise similar individuals will have different amounts of schooling simply because they were raised in different countries. Or two otherwise similar individuals may have differential access to schooling, perhaps because of distance from educational facilities. The individual who happened to be closer to educational facilities is likely to acquire more schooling because the cost of access is lower.

Natural experiments are based on the instrumental-variables (IV) estimator.[12] In the present context, the instrumental variables are those that are hypothesized to affect the outcome of parents but that don't directly affect the outcomes of their children. Examples of such variables include distance from schools and schooling policy in immigrants' source countries. To implement the IV estimator, regress the outcome for parents on these instrumental variables; then estimate equation 1 using the predicted values of Y_p that are obtained. Since these predicted values depend on the instrumental variables, which by definition are independent of parents' genotypes, they must be independent of u_c in equation 2. The instrumental variables serve to randomize the outcomes for parents, as would an actual experiment. However, because the experiment is entirely natural and spontaneous, the trial subjects and the control subjects behave in a normal and representative manner.

The IV estimator is unbiased. Therefore, in case 2 in table 5.1 the IV estimate of β is expected to be 0.5. This implicitly means that $\rho = 0.3$, but there is no way of verifying this because ρ cannot be estimated when the data refer only to parents and children. Nevertheless, the instrumental variables deliver unbiased estimates of β even when ρ cannot be estimated.

A generalization of the IV estimator is the *generalized method of moments* (GMM) estimator,[13] which has become popular since its development in the 1980s. Suppose that there are several (n) instrumental variables. As we saw, the IV estimator involves regressing the outcome for parents on all n instrumental variables. The GMM estimator, in contrast, exploits the n moment conditions, one for each instrumental variable, according to which the covariance between u_c and the instrumental variable is 0. GMM optimally weights together the n estimates of β that are obtained. The IV estimator of β is a special case of the GMM estimator. Therefore, the GMM estimator is an optimal estimator for implementing natural experiments. If, however, there is only one natural experimental variable, the GMM and IV estimators are identical.

5.2.3 Generated Regressors[14]

Suppose that the genotype for parents (u_p) in equation 2 happens to be known or observed. If equation 2 is substituted into equation 1 for u_c, we obtain

$$Y_c = \alpha + \beta Y_p + \rho u_p + \varepsilon_c. \tag{4}$$

This equation states that the outcome for children depends on the phenotype for parents via β, and it depends on the genotype of parents via ρ. The important thing to note about equation 4 is that its residual ε_c is entirely random and is equal to the child's draw from the gene pool. Therefore, Y_p and u_p are completely independent of ε_c, in which case both β and ρ are identified. This shows that the identification problem arises because u_p is generally unknown.

It is therefore tempting to proxy u_p in some plausible way, to substitute this proxy into equation 4 for u_p, and then to estimate β and ρ directly from equation 4. In the schooling example, u_p might be proxied by the IQ of parents or some other measure of their learning ability. Another strategy is to think of u_p in equation 4 as a missing regressor, and to generate it via some auxiliary hypothesis. For example, in several papers[15] I use "Mincer residuals" from wage regressions for parents to proxy their unobserved ability. Mincer models date back to the work of Jacob Mincer in the 1960s. Mincer hypothesized that wages vary directly with human capital and ability. Therefore, the residuals from such Mincer regressions contain information on unobserved ability. This generated-regressor methodology identifies β.

The generated-regressor methodology naturally requires instrumental variables to serve in the generating regression. Identification requires that the generated regressor for u_p should not be perfectly correlated with Y_p, for otherwise it would not be possible to estimate β and ρ in equation 4. This means that instrumental variables that are used in the generating regression may be correlated, but imperfectly, with the outcome for parents.

5.2.4 Partial Identification[16]

Suppose that, for one reason or another, none of the previous methods of identification is feasible. Dynastic data, or at least data on three successive generations, aren't available. The data solely refer to children and their parents, as they do in most cases. Suppose also that there are no convincing natural experiments, so that identification using IV estimation or GMM isn't feasible either. Finally, suppose that there are no convincing generated regressors, because the instrumental variables required to generate them aren't available. In short, β is not identified.

Although β may not be identified, it may nevertheless be possible to say something about β. For example, it may be possible to conclude from the observational data that β cannot be larger than some upper value or less than some lower value. Presumably there is something to be learned from the availability of data, since any data must be better and more informative than no data at all. The concept of partial identification applies to situations in which full or complete identification is not feasible. It is obviously preferable to identify β completely, so in case 2 in table 5.1 β is estimated to be 0.5. But if this is not feasible, it might be possible to conclude from the data that β lies within some range—say, between 0.2 and 0.7. At least the data in this case would rule out the possibility that β can be less than 0.2 or greater than 0.7, so at least something has been learned from the data. However, partial identification is inherently ambiguous, since it doesn't reveal what β is. Indeed, β might take any value between 0.2 and 0.7. Nor would it be meaningful or appropriate to say that β probably is 0.45, the average of 0.2 and 0.7. Such a calculation implicitly assumes that each value of β 0.2 and 0.7 is equally probable. We simply cannot know whether that is the case.

Partial identification is like the cup that is half full. A full cup is obviously preferable, but a half-empty cup is better than an empty one. So what in fact can be gleaned from raw observational data? To simplify matters, in what follows the outcome variable Y is dichotomized into a dummy variable that takes the value of 1 if the outcome is high and above some threshold and takes a value of 0 otherwise, i.e., if Y is low. If β is positive, we expect that parents who have high outcomes or high phenotypes are likely to have children with high outcomes. For example, tall parents are more likely to have tall children, and educated parents are more likely to have educated children. Suppose that in the data we observe the following:

(i) 60 percent of parents have high outcomes and 40 percent have low outcomes.

(ii) 80 percent of the children of the high-outcome parents have high outcomes.

(iii) 20 percent of the children of the low-outcome parents have high outcomes.

These data hint that the high-outcome parents are more likely than low-outcome parents to have high-outcome children. However, this doesn't establish that there is a causal effect from the outcomes of parents on the outcomes of their children. It might simply be the case that what we observe in the data is due to inherited ability—i.e., that abler parents have abler children and the outcomes of parents and children depend on ability. In short, what the data reveal depends on both ρ and β, not only on β.

Ideally we would want to conduct the following impossible experiment: What would the outcomes have been of the children with high-outcome parents had their parents been low-outcome parents? The answer to this question is the counterfactual for the children of the high-outcome parents. Since a child can't be raised twice by different parents, the answer to this question is entirely speculative and the counterfactual is unknowable. Perhaps all these children might have had low outcomes. On the other hand, we can't rule out the opposite— that they would have all had high outcomes. For it might be the case that low-phenotype parents have high genotypes. Therefore, had these children been born to these high-genotype parents they might have inherited their favorable genes, and they might have achieved high outcomes even though their parents happened to have low outcomes.

The same applies to the counterfactual for the children of low-outcome parents. We cannot know what would have happened to these children had they been born to and raised by high-outcome parents. They might all have achieved high outcomes thanks to the causal effect of the outcome of parents on the outcomes of their children. On the other hand, it might be the case that high-phenotype parents have low genotypes, so that in their counterfactual their children all have low outcomes. In the former case what matters is β; in the latter case what matters is ρ.

To appreciate what might be learned from these empirical data, it is important to understand the concepts of conditional and unconditional probability and expectations. Suppose that if it is cloudy today the temperature is expected to be $20°$, and if it is not cloudy the temperature is expected to be $30°$. These are conditional expectations: they are conditional on the absence or presence of clouds. Suppose that the probability that it will be cloudy today is 0.7. Therefore, the temperature is expected to be $27°$, which is an average of the two expectations weighted by the probability of it being cloudy or not. This is an unconditional expectation because whether or not it is cloudy the weather forecast is that it will be 27° today. It is obvious that we cannot calculate unconditional expectations without conditional expectations.

Our observational data reveal conditional expectations or probabilities; they do not reveal unconditional expectations or probabilities. Conditional on having high-outcome parents, the probability that the child has a high outcome is 0.8 according to the data. To calculate the unconditional probability of a high outcome for these children we need to know the conditional probability when the same children have low-outcome parents. Since this is an unknown counterfactual, we can't calculate the unconditional probability. Suppose that God told us that this conditional probability is in fact 0.7—that is, 70 percent of the children born to high-outcome parents would have had high outcomes had they been born to low-outcome parents. Since the probability of being born to high-outcome parents is 0.6 in the data, and therefore the probability of being born to a low-outcome parent is 0.4, we can now calculate the unconditional probability that these children have high outcomes: $0.6 \times 0.8 + 0.4 \times 0.7 = 0.76$.

Our observational data also reveal the conditional probability of high outcome for the children born to low-outcome parents to be 0.2. Since their counterfactual is unknown, we cannot calculate their unconditional probability. Suppose God told us that this conditional probability is in fact 0.4. The unconditional probability may be calculated as $0.4 \times 0.2 + 0.6 \times 0.4 = 0.32$. To estimate the causal effect of parents' outcome status on the outcomes of their children, we need to know the unconditional probabilities. The unconditional probability of a high outcome is 0.76 for the children of high-outcome parents and 0.32 for the children of low-outcome parents. Therefore, β is equal to $0.76 - 0.32 = 0.44$; that is, the causal effect of high-outcome status of parents increases the probability of high-outcome status for children by 0.44. This effect is not biased by unobserved hereditary phenomena, because we have been able (with God's help) to calculate the unconditional probabilities for both types of children.

Notice that the conditional probabilities differ for the two types of children when the condition is the same. When the condition is high-outcome status for parents, the two conditional probabilities are 0.8 and 0.4. They need not be identical, because the unknown genotypes of the two sets of parents might be different. Because 0.8 is greater than 0.4, this indicates that the first group of parents have more favorable genotypes. When the condition is low-outcome status for parents, the conditional probabilities are 0.7 and 0.2. Here too, because 0.7 exceeds 0.2, there is an indication that the first group of parents have more favorable genotypes. It is essentially in this way that the conditional probabilities enable us to remove bias induced by heredity.

Without God's help, what can we do? As will be explained in greater detail in subsection 10.12.2, we can bound the unknown counterfactual outcomes. We can't rule out the possibility that none of the children of high-outcome parents would have had high outcomes in their counter-factual, since for these children the outcome status of the parents is crucial. But neither can we rule out the possibility that all of them would have had high outcomes, since for these children heredity is crucial and they are genetically better off in their counterfactual. There-fore, their counterfactual probabilities are naturally bounded between 0 and 1. Using these bounds to calculate the unconditional probability for this first group of children bounds this probability between 0.48 ($0.6 \times 0.8 + 0.4 \times 0$) and 0.88 ($0.6 \times 0.8 + 0.4 \times 1$). The probability of a child's obtaining a high outcome if he is born to a high-outcome parent lies between 0.48 and 0.88.

We may also bound the outcomes of the children of low-outcome parents between 0.08 ($0.4 \times 0.2 + 0.6 \times 0$) and 0.68 ($0.4 \times 0.2 + 0.6 \times 1$). The probability of a child's obtaining a high outcome if he is born to a low-outcome parent lies between 0.08 and 0.68. The causal effect of the outcome of the parents on the outcomes of the children ranges between 0.8 (because $0.88 - 0.08 = 0.8$) and –0.2 (because $0.48 - 0.68 = -0.2$). Therefore, β ranges between 0.2 and 0.8. Identification is partial because we cannot pin down the actual value of β. We may confi-dently rule out that β exceeds 0.8 and that it is less than 0.2. Thus, we have learned something from the data. Beta naturally takes a value between 1 and –1. It is equal to 1 if high-outcome status for parents guarantees high-outcome status for children, and it is equal to –1 if high-outcome status for parents guarantees low-outcome status for children. Therefore, in the absence of empirical data the ambiguity in β is equal to 2 (i.e. the ambiguity is $1 - (-1) = 2$). The empirical data have reduced the ambiguity to $0.8 - (-0.2) = 1$. So the cup is precisely half full, or half empty.

Notice that in this case ambiguity prevents us from ruling out negative values of β, since β may take any value not more negative than –0.2. Therefore, because heredity clouds what we observe, we cannot rule out the possibility that the outcomes of children vary inversely with their parents' outcomes. The intergenerational correlation coefficient may be positive despite the fact that β is negative, as in case 6 in table 5.1.

A naive investigator using our hypothetical observational data and ignoring heredity would have estimated β as the difference between 0.8 and 0.2, which is 0.6. This implicitly assumes that children are randomly assigned to parents in terms of their genotypes, since it attributes all the difference between the outcomes of the two sets of children to differences in outcomes status of their parents. This means that the two sets of parents have identical genotypes, so that the effects of heredity on the outcomes of the two sets of children are identical. This naive estimate of β (0.6) falls in the upper part of its bound, since it is closer to 0.8 than it is to –0.2. It implicitly assumes that heredity doesn't matter in the data. If we were sure of this, there would have been no identification problem to solve, in which case there would have been no ambiguity.

Table 5.2 illustrates the range of ambiguity under different assumptions about the data. Case 1 is the above example. The table shows that the lower and upper bounds for β increase when the proportion of high-phenotype parents with high-phenotype children (column 2) increases and when the proportion of high-phenotype parents increases (column 4).

Naive investigators come in different varieties. A less naive investigator might suspect that heredity matters but that a placebo effect applies to parental outcomes. In clinical trials the treatment group is supplied with the real pill while the control group is given a placebo under the assumption that the placebo makes no difference; it has a neutral effect. In our example, the placebo is having parents with low outcomes. This means that the counterfactual for the children of high-outcome parents cannot be better than 0.8 but can be worse. This

Table 5.2
Partial identification of β (based on equations 68 in chapter 10).

Case	Proportion of high-phenotype children		Proportion of high phenotypes	β low	β high
	High-phenotype parents	Low-phenotype parents			
1	0.8	0.2	0.6	–0.2	0.8
2	0.8	0.3	0.5	–0.25	0.75
3	0.8	0.3	0.75	–0.225	0.775
4	0.5	0.5	0.5	–0.5	0.5

bounds their counterfactual probability of obtaining a high outcome to between 0 and 0.8 instead of between 0 and 1. Their unconditional probability of obtaining a high outcome is bounded between 0.48 and $0.6 \times 0.8 + 0.4 \times 0.8 = 0.8$; thus, the lower bound hasn't changed but the upper bound has decreased. The counterfactual for the children of low-outcome parents is bounded between 0.2 and 1, since they can't be worse off. This means that their unconditional probability of a high outcome is between $0.4 \times 0.2 + 0.6 \times 0.2 = 0.2$ and $0.4 \times 0.2 + 0.6 \times 1 = 0.8$. The upper bound for β is $0.8 - 0.2 = 0.6$; the lower bound is $0.48 - 0.8 = -0.32$. The placebo assumption has reduced the ambiguity about β from 1 to 0.92 (i.e., $0.8 - (-0.32) = 0.92$).

Another naive investigator might assume that in the counterfactuals all children are bounded between 0.2 and 0.8. This gives an upper bound for β of $0.8 - 0.2 = 0.6$ and a lower bound of $0.6 - 0.44 = 0.16$. The ambiguity about β is reduced further to $0.6 - 0.16 = 0.44$. And because the lower bound of β is now positive, there is no ambiguity about the direction of causation from the outcome status of parents on the outcome of their children.

5.2.5   Multiple Outcomes[17]

Thus far we have been concerned with a single outcome or phenotype when there is also one genotype. If there are multiple phenotypes but there continues to be only one genotype, it may be possible to identify β from observational cross-section data on parents and their children. Equation 4 showed that the identification problem arises from the lack of data on the genotype of parents (u_p). The generated-regressor methodology was motivated by the desire to proxy that missing variable in some plausible way.

Suppose now that instead of just one outcome as in equation 4 there are N outcomes, denoted by Y_n. In each of these, outcome n for children (Y_{cn}) is hypothesized to depend on their parents' outcome (Y_{pn}) via β for this outcome (β_n). Therefore, an equation like equation 4 is hypothesized for each phenotype:

$$Y_{cni} = \alpha_n + \beta_n Y_{pni} + \rho_{in} u_{pi} + \theta_n \varepsilon_{ci} + e_{ni}. \tag{5}$$

This equation states that phenotype n for children depends on phenotype n for parents and it depends on the single genotypes that children inherit from their parents. Since the genotype of the child might affect his outcomes differentially, we allow ρ and θ to vary by outcome. In the case of two outcomes, such as schooling and earnings, the effect of the child's genotype on his schooling might be different from its effect on his earnings. The final term, e_n, denotes a random error or residual, which varies by outcome.

What is important here is that there isn't a separate genotype for each outcome or phenotype. There is only one genotype, which affects outcomes or phenotypes differentially. For example, there aren't separate genotypes for schooling and earnings; there is a single genotype that affects both schooling and earnings. If there were separate genotypes, the identification strategy would break down. Because there are multiple outcomes but there is a single genotype, this unobservable genotype may be estimated as it expresses itself through the various outcomes. Specifically, the methodology of panel-data econometrics described in subsection 10.5.1 may be used in this context. This methodology estimates the specific effect for each individual (represented by $\rho_{in}u_{pi} + \theta_n\varepsilon_{ci}$ in equation 5) and a specific effect for each outcome (represented by α_n in equation 5).

When there is only one outcome (that is, when $N = 1$), these specific effects cannot be estimated. They are relegated to the error term, which is correlated with the outcome for parents. This induces bias in the estimate of β, and, as has been discussed, its identification becomes problematic. Here, however, the specific effects are estimated rather than relegated to the error term. What remains of the error term is e_{cn} (which is independent of Y_{pn}, for there is no reason to suspect that these random variable should be correlated). Accordingly, β_n in equation 5 is identified. The more outcomes there are (i.e., the greater is N), the easier it is to estimate these specific effects, and the better is β identified.

5.3   Environments

In chapter 3 I criticized behavioral genetics for trivializing the role of environments in hypothesis testing. I distinguished between exogenous and endogenous environments—that is, between environments over which the individual has no choice and environments that are chosen. If all environments were exogenous, their causal effects on outcomes would be identified. Matters are very different when environments are endogenous. Not only are their causal effects not identified; neither are the causal effects of exogenous environments, unless exogenous and endogenous environments happen to be uncorrelated.

Identification failure is contagious. In chapter 3 much time and effort was devoted to developing what might be called a theory for endogenous environments. For example, parents set environments for their children by taking into consideration their own genotypes as well as the genotypes of their children. Also, as they mature, children begin to choose their own environments.

When environments are endogenous, they tend to be correlated with phenomena the investigator doesn't observe, including the unobserved genotypes of the children and perhaps those of the parents. In this section, we consider the identification of endogenous environmental effects on the outcomes of children. For the sake of simplicity, assume that the outcomes of parents do not matter for their children; ignore all the methodological problems discussed in the previous section, just as in the previous section the effect of environmental variables on outcomes was ignored. In general we need to consider the joint methodological implications of both sets of issues, and indeed those of other issues yet to be discussed. However, we shall continue to deal with one issue at a time.

Incidentally, we can think of the outcome of parents (Y_p) as part of the child's environment. If the child's parents are more educated, the family environment is likely to be more pro-schooling. Children don't ask to be born, they don't select their parents, and they cannot decide their parents' schooling. This doesn't mean, however, that parents' schooling is part of the exogenous environment of their children. If that were the case, the identification problem of the previous section would not have arisen. The issue here is what in econometrics is called "weak exogeneity." It is true that parents' schooling is predetermined as far as children are concerned, because most parents acquire their schooling while their children are too young to be of any influence, or even before they are born. However, because of unobserved genotypes, the outcomes of parents are not independent of what empirical investigators don't observe about the children in the data. As we saw, Y_p is not independent of u_c. Therefore, the outcomes of parents cannot be assumed to be weakly exogenous.

In what follows, Y continues to represent some outcome of interest and X denotes the environment. Since the issue is generic, I omit subscripts for children, parents, siblings, and so on. The model is linear and simple:

$$Y_i = \gamma + \delta X_i + u_i, \tag{6}$$

where u denotes the residual error. The main methodological task is to estimate δ, which is the causal effect of the environment on the outcome.

If the environment is weakly exogenous, X and u are independent by definition, in which case δ is identified. In this case, observational data may be used to regress Y on X to obtain an unbiased estimate of δ.

If X is not weakly exogenous, it must be the case that X and u are not independent. In chapter 3 several reasons were suggested why X and u might not be independent. The most important of these is the so-called gene-environment correlation, through which the genotype of the child affects his environment. For example, if Y measures musical achievement and X measures music lessons, then u embodies the genotype for music, or musical ability, and δ measures the causal effect of music lessons on musical achievement. If musically gifted children are more likely to invest their time in music lessons, this induces positive dependence between X and u. There are many other similar examples. In one, Y measures sporting achievement, X measures training, and u embodies the unobserved genotype for sport. In another, Y measures crying by the infant, X measures the strictness of his mother, and u embodies the infant's sensitivity. In all these cases, we expect that X depends on u.

Suppose that observational data are used to regress Y on X in order to estimate δ. The bias in the estimate of δ is equal to the covariance between X and u divided by the variance of X. If the covariance between X and u is 0 because X is independent of u, the bias is 0. Otherwise the direction of the bias depends on the sign of the covariance between X and u. If X varies directly with u, the bias is positive and δ is overestimated. In table 5.3 it is assumed that the true value of δ is 2. In case 1 the covariance between X and u is assumed to be 0, in which case the OLS regression estimate of δ is 2 and the bias is 0. Since the variance of X is assumed in these synthetic observational data is assumed to be 1, it must be the case that the covariance between Y and X is 2, since

Table 5.3
Bias in environmental effects.

Case	Var(X)	Cov(YX)	Cov(Xu)	Estimated δ	Bias
1	1	2	0	2	0
2	1	2	1	3	1
3	1	0	1	1	1
4	2	4	1	2.5	0.5
5	1	2	2	4	2

the estimate of δ is defined as the covariance between Y and X divided by the variance of X.

Case 2 is identical to case 1 except for the fact that the covariance between X and u equals 1. Since the bias is equal to the covariance between X and u divided by the variance of X, the bias equals 1 and the estimate of δ is 3 instead of 2. So δ is over-estimated by 50 percent. A naive investigator who ignores the gene-environment correlation thinks δ is 3 when it is in fact 2. If the true value of δ happens to be 0, as in case 3, because the environment has no causal effect on the outcome, our naive investigator would reach the mistaken conclusion that δ is 1. In case 4 the true value of δ continues to be 2. Since the variance of X is doubled, the covariance between X and Y must have doubled from 2 to 4 as indicated in table 5.3. The covariance between X and u, however, remains unchanged at 1. The bias is less than in case 2 because the variance of X has increases, thereby diluting the bias. The estimate of δ is therefore 2.5 instead of 3, but this is still too large. Finally, case 5 demonstrates that if the covariance between X and u increases, the bias increases, and the estimate of δ is twice as large as it should be.

What if the estimate of δ happens to be biased? The biased estimate of δ is the total or overall effect of X on Y, including what behavioral geneticists refer to as "the nature of nurture." The latter refers to the dependence of measures of nurture, such as X, on genotypes. In fact the bias in table 5.3 quantifies the nature of nurture. For example, in case 2, when X increases by 1 in the data, Y increases by 3, since the estimate of δ is 3. The reply is that ignoring the bias makes for bad science. An experiment in which the bias is ignored isn't a test of a hypothesis; it's merely a description of the data. Here the hypothesis is that outcomes depend on environments, and that δ (for example) is positive. In the case of sports, the research question is this: Does training improve achievement, and if so, by how much? In case 3 the answer is that training has no effect on sporting achievement, and the apparently positive effect of training is a statistical illusion induced by the fact that "sporty types" happen to train more.

Good science decomposes the estimate of δ into a causal effect (which in the previous example is the effect of training on sporting achievement) and the bias (which in the previous example is the gene-environment correlation). For example, in case 2 in table 5.2 good science will report that the effect of training on sporting achievement is 2 (e.g. that an extra hour's training reduces running times by

2 seconds) and that the gene-environment correlation is 1. To make this decomposition, it is necessary to identify δ.

5.3.1 Identification

The methods for identifying δ in observational data are essentially the same as those for identifying β in equation 1. Suppose that the observational data happen to be longitudinal, and that as a result we have repeated observations on Y and X for individual i. In this case equation 6 becomes

$$Y_{it} = \gamma + \delta X_{it} + u_{it},\tag{7}$$

where $u_{it} = \varepsilon_i + e_{it}$ and where t denotes the time period to which the data refer. Importantly, the residual error is decomposed into a genetic component (ε, which varies by individual but not by time) and random component (e). The assumption here is that genotypes don't vary over time. The dependence of X on u is largely induced by X's dependence on ε rather than by its dependence on e. In cross-section data it is not possible to distinguish between ε and e. However, when the data are longitudinal the genetic component ε may be estimated as a specific effect using panel-data econometrics. This means that the residual is e because ε is estimated rather than relegated to the residual. Since X and e are independent, δ is identified.

If longitudinal data aren't available, identification may be carried out by means of natural experimentation in which instrumental variables (referred to as the Z variables) must directly affect the X variables (i.e., the environments) but must not directly affect the outcome, Y. Because the Z variables don't directly affect the outcome, it must be the case that the Z variables are independent of the unobserved component of Y, i.e., u in equation 6. Although X depends on u through the gene-environment correlation, the instrumented value of X created through the dependence of X on Z is independent of u. Therefore, the instrumented value of X identifies δ, because it is independent of u. The instrumented value of X is equal to the predicted value of X obtained by regressing X on Z.

In short, the instrumental variables (the Z variables) decompose X into a component that is independent of u and a component that is dependent on u. The former component is used to identify δ. The instrumental variables serve to randomize X in such a way that the instrumented component of X is independent of the outcome, Y. This mimics what would happen in a laboratory experiment in which the experimenter varied X randomly in order to see how X affected Y. The only difference is that the Z variables happen naturally and spontaneously, and the individuals involved in the natural experiment are completely unaware that nature is treating them as guinea pigs.

In the sporting example, the observational data consist of, say, track times (Y) and time spent training (X). The main research question is Do track times vary inversely with training, and if so by how much? In the null hypothesis, δ is expected to be negative. Athletic genotypes vary in the data, but they are unobserved and are therefore embodied in u. More athletic genotypes have smaller u's because they can naturally run faster. If athletic genotypes train more, X varies inversely with u, which induces negative bias in the estimate of δ. Since δ is expected to be negative, this bias will make δ appear more negative than it really is. The truth may be that training makes no difference (i.e., $\delta = 0$), but the naive investigator mistakenly concludes that training is effective. Alternatively, athletic genotypes may train less. They may say to themselves "Because I can naturally run fast, I don't need to train so much." Individuals with less athletic ability chose to train more to make up for what they don't have naturally. In this case, X varies directly with u, and the bias is positive, which will make δ less negative than it really is. In fact the estimate of δ may be 0 or even positive, creating the misleading impression that training doesn't matter or even that it is counter-productive.

To identify δ by natural experimentation, we seek instrumental variables that directly affect training and don't directly affect track times. Such instrumental variables serve to randomize training in a way that has nothing to do with track times. The instrumented component of training may then be used to identify the causal effect of training on track times. Suppose that the time it takes to get to the training ground reduces the demand for training. Individuals who happen to live close to a training ground are more likely to train than individuals who happen to live far away. Since there is every reason to expect that distance from a training ground will affect the amount of training, but there is no reason to expect that the location of training grounds and domiciles are related to athletic ability, distance might serve as an instrumental variable. Of course, it would be necessary to check that athletic individuals didn't choose to live near training grounds; otherwise domiciles and athletic ability would be dependent, and distance could no longer serve as an instrumental variable.

A natural experiment that I particularly like involves the effect of fertility on the labor supply of women. It is well known that, with education controlled for, female labor supply varies inversely with fertility. However, this doesn't mean that fertility causes women to work less. The causality may be the other way around: women with low productivity, who consequently earn less, choose to have more children, according to the Quality vs. Quantity Theory. Therefore, women, who in any case work less because their wages are low, decide to invest more of their effort in family life. Women who can command high wages because their productivity is high decide to invest more in their careers; they work more and have fewer children. So the causal effect of fertility on the labor supply of mothers is not identified.

In a laboratory experiment we would vary fertility randomly and then observe the labor-supply response of the mothers in the experiment. Clearly laboratory experimentation isn't feasible. Labor economists have suggested two natural experiments. The first involves multiple births. They show that completed fertility is greater among mothers who have twins. This is especially true of women whose first birth does not involve twins. A mother might have intended having two children, but if the second birth involves twin, her completed fertility is three instead of two. Since twin births are random, they serve to randomize fertility. If women with twins supply less labor, this identifies the causal effect of fertility on their labor supply.

Another natural experiment involves births when parents have sex preferences.[18] Suppose that parents prefer to have at least one child of each sex. The probability of having a third child will depend on the sexes of the first two children. This probability will be lower if the second child is the opposite sex of the first child. If both children are of the same sex, the probability of a third child is increased; if the first three children all are of the same sex, the probability of a fourth child is increased; and so on. Demographers have shown that fertility behaves as predicted by this model. Indeed, there are also preferences between boys and girls. Fertility is lower the more boys there are. Since the sex of the next child is entirely random, the sex order of births serves to randomize fertility as if in an experiment. However, this experiment is natural and is not contrived in a laboratory. Fertility is instrumented by the sexes of the first two children, and instrumented fertility is used to investigate the causal effect of fertility on mothers' labor supply.

Another type of natural experiment is based on the methodology of regression discontinuity design (RDD). RDD arises when X in equation

6 happens to jump for reasons not related to the outcome or to the unobserved genotypes (u). This idea is best illustrated by another favorite example[19] in which the objective is to investigate how class size affects children's academic performance. The methodological concern is that class size doesn't vary randomly between pupils. Pushier parents may persuade schools to place their children in smaller classes, or they may send their children to schools in which classes are smaller. If pushier parents have abler children, then smaller classes will contain abler pupils. This would create the misleading impression that grades are better in smaller classes. In short, class size is an environmental variable, such as X in equation 6, and the effect of class size on grades (Y) is not identified. We expect δ to be negative, but its estimate is biased downward because parents are pushy.

In Israel the maximum class size is 40. Suppose that enrollment in a school happens to be 40 or less in a certain grade, so that there is only one class with 40 or fewer pupils. If enrollment happens to increase to 42, the school is required to open a second class and to put 21 pupils in each class; if enrollment exceeds 80, the school has to open a third class; and so on. This makes class size a discontinuous variable that jumps whenever enrollment reaches a multiple of 40. If, as seems reasonable, enrollment doesn't depend on the pushiness of parents, enrollment serves to randomize class size and may be used to instrument class size. Therefore, enrollment identifies the causal effect of class size on grades.

Convincing natural experiments are not always available, in which case there are no instrumental variables that serve to randomize the environment and identify δ. In this last resort, the partial identification methodology discussed in the previous section may be used to bound the causal effect of environments on outcomes.

5.4 Selectivity[20]

In chapter 3 we saw that one of the main methodological workhorses of behavioral genetics involves the comparison of adopted and biological siblings. I criticized this methodology on the grounds that adoptive parents are selective and may not be representative of parents as a whole. And adopted children may be selective too. Not only may adopted children not be representative of children as a whole; the matching of adoptive children to their adoptive parents may be far from random. Parents don't select their biological children, nor do biological children select their parents. Matters are quite different and much more complicated in the case of adoptions. In this section I show how ignoring selectivity may bias results. I also discuss methodological solutions to the problem of selection bias.

Let Y_A denote an outcome for adopted children and Y_B denotes the outcome for biological children. The objective is to estimate β in equation 1. The identification problem surrounding β arose from the fact that biological children are genetically related to their parents via ρ. All the children are B-types. If the children are adopted, they aren't genetically related to their parents, in which case $\rho = 0$ for A-types. Therefore, if equation 1 is estimated using observational data on adopted children, β is identified. Strictly speaking, β_A is identified, which is the causal effect of the outcome of adoptive parents on the outcome of their adopted children.

This result would be true only if adopted children are randomly assigned to parents. This means, unreasonably, that the adoption agency doesn't consider which parents will be most appropriate for specific children who are available for adoption, i.e., it doesn't match children to parents. Nor do parents match themselves to children, i.e., they have no say in which children they adopt. Also, parents are randomly selected, including parents who aren't seeking to adopt. In this unlikely set of circumstances, β_A is identified. However, this tells us nothing about β_B, which is the causal effect of the outcome of parents on the outcomes of biological children. β_A and β_B might differ because parents treat their adopted children differently than their biological children, and because the responses of adopted children to their adoptive parents might differ from than the responses of biological children to their biological parents. Therefore, although β_A is identified, β_B is not.

If, as is more likely and more general, adopted children aren't randomly assigned to parents, and adoptive parents aren't randomly selected, β_A ceases to be identified. The reason for this is that in terms of equation 1 the adoption decision might not be independent of the genotypes of the adopted children and the adoptive parents. It is true that in the case of adoptions ρ is 0. But if the adoption agency matches children to parents and if parents match themselves to children, u_c and u_p will be correlated once more. For example, if the agency allocates weaker children to stronger parents, u_c and u_p will be negatively correlated. Consequently, β_A is not identified. One identification problem is simply replaced by another. In the case of biological children, the identification problem is genetic in origin. In the case of adopted children, the identification problem is induced by selectivity in adoption.

Just as we saw that we may bound β_B, we may bound β_A by partial identification. Suppose that 60 percent of adopted children are placed with high-outcome parents, and that 80 percent of these children have high outcomes, whereas 20 percent have high outcomes among the 40 percent of children placed with low-outcome parents. There are two unknown counterfactuals: What would have happened to the first group of adopted children had they been placed with low-outcome parents? What would have happened to the second group of children had they been adopted by high-outcome parents? There is, of course, a third possibility: What would have happened had they been not adopted and had been raised in an institution? To simplify matters, I assume that none of the children are institutionalized.

Since the proportions are exactly the same as those used previously, we may bound β_A between 0.8 and –0.2. The ambiguity in β_A is the same as the ambiguity in β_B, because we don't know how the adoption agency matched children to parents. If the children matched to· low-outcome parents had been adopted by high-outcome parents, the probability of their obtaining a high outcome might have increased or decreased. It will increase if parents and children are matched better in the counterfactual; it will decrease otherwise. It might be argued that because the adoption agency is good at matching parents to children, counterfactual matches are bound to be inferior. However, this is a placebo-type argument that cannot be taken for granted. Therefore, ambiguity is just as large with observational data on adoptions as it is with data on biological parents and children.

Perhaps the selection problem for adoptions can be solved through natural experimentation. This would require instrumental variables that directly affect the allocation of children to parents but don't directly affect the outcome. These instrumental variables must be independent of the genotypes of the adoptive parents, i.e., they must be independent of u_p. For example, color is an instrumental variable if black children are more likely to be adopted by black parents. Since there is no reason to believe that skin color is correlated with genotype, color may serve as an instrumental variable. If white parents raise black children differently than white children and black parents raise white children differently than black children, or if white children respond differently to black parents than to white parents and black children respond differently to black parents than to white parents, color cannot serve as an instrumental variable. Indeed, perhaps the adoption agency took these possibilities into consideration when it tried to match white children to white families and black to black.

On the face of it, the prospects of solving the identification problem for β_A through natural experimentation are even more remote than the prospects of solving it for β_B in the case of biological children. Therefore, observational data on adoptions are more problematic than observational data on biological parents and children. Behavioral genetics is mistaken in believing that the opposite is true. This mistake stems from the ideological prejudice in behavioral genetics that genetics matters and behavior doesn't.

A well-known solution to the identification problem in face of selection bias is based on the methodology of incidentally truncated regression (ITR), originally developed by Heckman (1976). Indeed, this methodology identifies β_A unambiguously. A variable is said to be "censored" when it is partially observable—for example, the variables exceeds a certain value, but we don't know by how much. A variable is said to be "truncated" when it is not observed at all. Since all the data we have are on adopted children, and we have no data on the children who weren't adopted, the variable for children not adopted is truncated.

To motivate this methodology, assume that not all the children available for adoption are adopted, and that some of them are raised in institutions. Estimating β_A in equation 1 involves regressing Y_A on Y_P using the data on the children who were adopted. The children raised in institutions don't have adoptive parents, so Y_P doesn't exist for them. If adopted and institutionalized children are chosen at random, β_A is identified. However, there is every reason to believe that the institutionalized children are negatively selected, since the agency could not successfully place them. Therefore, β_A ceases to be identified. In fact, if adopted children are positively selected β_A tends to be over-estimated.

ITR hypothesizes the existence of a latent variable—a variable that exists but is not directly observable. The latent variable is adoptability (A^*), which makes some children more attractive for adoption, and which isn't directly observed but instead is indirectly revealed when some children are adopted and others are not. The latent variable depends on observed (A) and unobserved characteristics (a) of the children. So $A^* = A + a$. Observed characteristics (A) might include color and sex. The unobserved component (a) is hypothesized to be a standard normal random variable that is correlated with u_c in equation

1 with correlation coefficient r_{au}. This is the correlation between the genotype of the child and his unobserved adoptability, which is positive if adopted children are positively selected. If A^* is positive, the child is sufficiently attractive in the market for adoption and is adopted. Otherwise he is raised in an institution.

To implement ITR the following two-step procedure is used.[21] First, a probit regression is estimated in which the dependent variable is adoption status, which takes a value of 1 if the child is adopted and 0 otherwise, and in which the independent variables include color, sex, and age. The independent variables might also include the outcome of the adoptive parent, Y_p, since the adoption agency might take the status of parents into consideration when matching children to families. Let z denote the predicted value from the probit model. Next, calculate the standard normal density of z and divide it by the predicted probability of adoption (equal to the cumulative standard normal density of z), and denote this ratio by ξ. This ratio is known as the conditional hazard of adoption. In the second stage, ξ is added as a regressor in equation 1:

$$Y_{Ai} = \alpha_A + \beta_A Y_{pi} + r_{ua}\sigma_{uA}\xi_i + u_{Ai}. \tag{8}$$

Notice that the coefficient of ξ is equal to the correlation coefficient between a and u multiplied by the standard deviation of the residuals. Using the estimate of the latter, equation 8 identifies r_{ua}. If indeed adopted children are positively selected, we expect r_{ua} to be positive. Since ξ may depend on Y_p, ξ and Y_p in equation 8 will be correlated. Naive estimation of β_A ignores the issue of selectivity, which is equivalent to relegating ξ to the residual. Since Y_p and ξ are generally correlated, naive estimation by OLS regression induces correlation between Y_p and the residual, in which case β_A is not identified. β_A is overestimated if ξ and Y_p are positively related; β_A is under-estimated if they are negatively related. By specifying ξ in equation 8, ITR extricates ξ from the residual error and treats it as a generated regressor that measures adoptability. Because Y_p and ξ are independent of u_A in equation 8, β_A is identified and the problem of selection bias is resolved.

If r_{ua} just happens to be 0, so that unobserved adoptability and genotypes are independent, equation 8 shows that naive estimation identifies β_A, because in this special case ξ makes no difference. The truncated regression methodology might reveal that r_{ua} is in fact 0, but we could not have known this in advance. By assuming that selectivity is ignorable, behavioral genetics implicitly assumes that r_{ua} is 0. If it is 0, all is

Table 5.4
Selection bias in adoption data.

Case	r_{ua}	$\text{Cov}(Y_p\xi)$	$\text{Cov}(Y_A\xi)$	β_A
1	0	0.5	0.4	0.8
2	0.5	0.5	0.775	0.55
3	0.1	0.5	1.15	0.03
4	0.5	0.2	0.64	0.7
5	-0.5	0.2	-0.32	0.9

well and good. But if it is not 0, the opposite is true, as is illustrated in table 5.4.

Suppose the naive estimate of β_A is 0.8 when the variance of parents' outcomes equals 1 and the covariance between Y_A and is therefore 0.8. The variances of ξ and u are normalized at 1 for convenience. Case 1 shows that because r_{ua} is 0 the naive estimator delivers the true value of β_A, which is 0.8. Notice that when r_{ua} is 0 and the covariance between Y_p and ξ is 0.5, the covariance between Y_A and ξ must be 0.4. This is because r_{ua} is the regression coefficient of ξ. In case 2 selection is not ignorable, because r_{ua} is assumed to be 0.5. If the covariance between Y_p and ξ is 0.5, it must be the case that the covariance between Y_A and ξ is 0.775. The estimate of β_A is 0.55 according to the ITR coefficient. The naive estimate of 0.8 exceeds its unbiased estimate. In case 3 r_{ua} is assumed to be 0.1, which implies that when the covariance between Y_p and ξ is 0.5 the covariance between Y_A and ξ is 1.15, which in turn gives 0.03 as the estimate of β_A. Therefore, the naive estimate of 0.8 greatly exceeds the true unbiased estimate of 0.03. Cases 4 and 5 are other examples in which OLS regression estimates of β_A and ITR estimates are different.

In table 5.4 bias is caused by the fact that there is sample selection in adoption and the fact that the matching of adopted children to families isn't random. In table 5.1 bias is caused by the fact that genotypes aren't observed, which induces omitted-variable bias. The former bias is just as problematic as the latter. Indeed, table 5.4 understates the problematic nature of studies based on adoptions because it considers only one aspect of the selection problem—namely, selectivity as to what children are adopted and what children are raised in institutions. Other aspects include selectivity in terms of which parents want to adopt, which parents are selected by the adoption agencies, and which adopted children are matched with which adoptive parents. Therefore, far from making empirical investigations methodologically easier, as behavioral genetics claims to do, adoption studies are far more problematic than studies based on data on biological parents and children. Biological parents do not select their children, nor do biological children select their parents. It is true that heredity is a methodological problem in the case of biological data, but it is easier to handle than the many layers of selectivity that arise in adoption studies.

We have seen how ITR may solve the selection problem when there is one layer of selectivity, i.e., when some children are adopted and others are not. This methodology may be extended to more layers of selectivity, for example, when selectivity applies to adoptive parents as well as adopted children. A latent variable is hypothesized for parents that measures their desire to adopt (D^*), which is analogous to A^* (which refers to the adoptability of children). D^* has observable (D) and unobservable components (d), so $D^* = D + d$. The unobservable component, d, is assumed to be a standard normal random variable. In this case it is also necessary to estimate a probit regression for adoptive parents in which the dependent variable takes a value of 1 if the parents adopted and 0 otherwise, and the independent variables refer to the observable variables that influence parents' decision to adopt or not. Just as we calculated ξ from the probit model for selection among children, we may calculate ξ_p from the probit model for parents. Equation 8 is then estimated with both ξ and ξ_p.

A crucial identifying assumption in the ITR methodology is that the random variables in the model, such as genotypes (u) and adoptability (a), are bivariate normal random variables. We are all different, but these differences are normally distributed. If these differences happen to have some distribution other than the normal, the methodology ceases to identify the parameters of interest, such as β_A. Indeed, studies show that results may be sensitive to the specification of the normal distribution, when some other distribution is appropriate. The methodology can be implemented with other parametric assumptions. For example, if a and u have logistical distributions rather than normal distributions, it is necessary to estimate a logit regression for selectivity instead of a probit regression.

5.5   Reflection

So far, our attention has been focused mainly on the intergenerational correlation between parents and children rather than the intragenerational correlation between siblings. Let us now turn to methodological issues that particularly arise in the intragenerational context, though they may also arise in intergenerational contexts.

The outcome of interest for an individual (Y) may be hypothesized to depend on the outcome of his sibling (Y_S) or on the outcome of his peer group. This hypothesis is conceptually different from the hypothesis in equation 1, which is concerned with dependence of children's outcomes on the outcomes of their parents. Because parents are older than their children, the outcome of parents is predetermined; Y_p typically happens before Y_c. In contrast, the outcomes for siblings (Y and Y_S) are simultaneous; they happen more or less at the same time.

Since I am my sibling's sibling, it is going to be very difficult to identify the causal effect of one sibling on the other. To a large extent, one sibling is a reflection of the other. This is rather like looking at one's reflection in the mirror. When I raise my hand, I see my mirror image raise its hand simultaneously. I know by experience that I am causing the image to raise its hand, and not the other round. However, infants must wonder about this. The proverbial man from Mars who has never seen a mirror before will be puzzled too. My reflection in the mirror is entirely dependent on me. My sibling is not, because he is a separate person. However, to unravel the causal effects that siblings have on each other is going to be almost as difficult as for our Martian to figure out whether the image is affecting the person or the other way around.

This so-called reflection problem is just another type of identification problem. Our objective is to identify the sibling interaction coefficient denoted by λ in chapter 3. The problem of identifying λ is not inherently different from the problem of identifying β in equation 1 or δ in equation 6. The outcomes of siblings might be correlated for several separate reasons. First, siblings have common parents, which will induce correlation between them since the outcomes of children depend on their parents' outcomes as well as common parenting. Second, siblings share genes that they inherit from their parents. This does not apply to adopted siblings, but, as we have seen, selectivity replaces genetics as a source of correlation. Third, siblings share exogenous environments, such as their culture or their school. Fourth, siblings might choose similar or correlated endogenous environments, such as peer groups, clubs, and friends. Finally, siblings might be correlated because sibling interaction takes place between them via λ.

The first factor can be controlled for by specifying the outcome for parents in the model. The third factor can be controlled for by specifying variables that represent the exogenous environments. Matters are more complicated with the second and fourth factors. The second factor, induced by common heredity, is methodologically similar to the identification problem discussed in relation to equation 1 for β and equation 2 for δ. The fourth factor is methodologically similar to the identification problem regarding the causal effect of endogenous environments in equation 6. Therefore, identifying the sibling interaction coefficient (λ) requires solving methodological issues that have already been discussed. However, even if these methodological issues are successfully resolved, there is a new methodological problem to be solved: the reflection problem.

To see this, suppose, just for argument's sake, that none of the four factors that might induce sibling correlation apply. Therefore, if there happens to be sibling correlation, it can only be the result of sibling interaction. In fact the hypothesis to be tested is

$$Y_i = \varphi + \lambda Y_{si} + v_i, \tag{9}$$

where v is the residual error. Because the four factors that might induce sibling correlation don't apply, they cannot induce dependence between sibling outcomes (Y_s) and v. For example, if common parents had mattered, both v and Y_s would have been dependent on Y_p, which turns v and Y_s into dependent random variables. This dependence between v and Y_s would mean that λ wouldn't be identified. Nevertheless, even if the four factors don't apply, v and Y_s are dependent, because sibling interaction is mutual. Therefore, Y_s and v must be dependent, because if Y depends on Y_s through sibling interaction then Y_s must depend on Y. Since Y depends on v in equation 9, Y_s must depends on v too. Therefore, even if all four factors that might induce sibling correlation aren't present, the reflection problem means that λ is not identified.

Table 5.5 simulates reflection bias for various values of the sibling interaction coefficient (λ) when equation 9 is estimated by OLS regression.[22] In case 1, λ is 0, so there is no reflection bias. Therefore, λ is estimated correctly at 0. Notice that this result did not apply in table 5.1's case 5, in which $\beta = 0$, and in table 5.3's case 3, in which $\delta = 1$. In case 2 the reflection bias is half as large as λ itself, so λ is considerably over-estimated. Case 3 shows that the reflection bias is symmetrical when λ is negative, i.e., when sibling interaction is malign instead of benign. Reflection bias reaches an absolute maximum of 0.3 when $\lambda = 0.5$, so that in case 4 λ is over-estimated at 0.8. In case 5 reflection bias decreases but λ continues to be over-estimated. However, when $\lambda = 1$ (case 6) reflection bias is 0 once more and λ is estimated

Table 5.5
Reflection bias.

Case	λ	Reflection bias	Estimated λ
1	0	0	0
2	0.1	0.098	0.198
3	–0.1	–0.098	–0.198
4	0.5	0.3	0.8
5	0.8	0.175	0.975
6	1	0	1
7	2	–0.2	0.8

correctly at 1. Finally, case 7 shows that when λ exceeds 1 reflection bias is negative and λ is under-estimated at 0.8.

Therefore, when sibling interaction is benign and damped (i.e., for values of λ between 0 and 1) λ is over-estimated. When sibling interaction is malign and damped (i.e., when λ is negative but less than 1) λ is not sufficiently negative. When sibling interaction is benign and explosive (i.e., when λ exceeds 1) λ is under-estimated. Finally, when sibling interaction is malign and explosive (i.e., when λ is less than –1) λ is insufficiently negative. In each of these cases, naive investigators who ignore reflection bias will reach mistaken empirical conclusions about the strength of sibling interaction.

The reflection problem would also arise if, instead of referring to sibling dyads, the data referred to friends and peers. For example, Y_S might be the outcome of friends or peers.[23] Since I am my friend's friend or my peer's peer, reflection is suspected in our mutual behavior, just as it is in the behavior of me and my sibling. In fact matters are more complicated because the problem of selectivity arises. I cannot choose my siblings, but I choose my friends and peers.

The solutions to the reflection problem are broadly similar to the methodological solutions to other identification problems that have been discussed. The main solution involves natural experimentation in which sibling outcomes (Y_S) are hypothesized to depend directly on instrumental variables (Z) that don't directly affect Y in equation 9. Because Y doesn't depend on Z, u and Z are independent, in which case these instrumental variables identify λ. The natural experiment requires the investigator to propose a variable or phenomenon that affects one sibling but not the other. For example, an illness that afflicted one sibling but not the other would serve to randomize sibling outcomes, as in an experiment. However, we would have to be persuaded that this illness affected the outcome directly.

Longitudinal data, which helped identify β and δ, aren't likely to help us identify λ. The reason for this is that the identification problem in the case of sibling interactions (λ) stems from the fact that siblings outcomes are simultaneously determined. In the case of β, the identification problem stems from the fact that the genotypes of parents are unobserved and the genotypes of children and parents are expected to be correlated. Longitudinal data enabled us to control for the unobserved genotypes of children, and the generated-regressor methodology enabled us to control for the unobserved genotypes of parents. The reflection problem doesn't arise because some important phenomenon is unobserved; it arises because siblings mirror each other's behavior.

If natural experimentation isn't feasible, it is always possible to bound λ by partial identification, just as β in equation 1 and δ in equation 6 were bounded. Suppose that 80 percent of high-outcome people have siblings with high outcomes and 20 percent of low-outcome people have siblings with high outcomes. Let these conditional probabilities be P_1 and P_0 respectively. The proportion of the population with high outcomes (P) is equal to the probability of having a high-outcome sibling (p) multiplied by P_1 plus the probability of having a low-outcome sibling ($1 - p$) multiplied by P_0. Since the population consists of sibling pairs, it must be the case that $P = p$, i.e., the probability of having a high-outcome sibling is equal to the proportion of high-outcome people in the population. We may therefore solve for P in terms of the conditional probabilities[24] P_1 and P_0. Therefore, 50 percent of the people have high outcomes, and the probability of having a high-outcome sibling is 0.5. Calculating the bounds for the sibling interaction coefficient implies that λ cannot be greater than 0.7 or less than –0.3. This means that having a high-outcome sibling cannot raise the probability that a person will also have a high outcome by more than 0.7 if the interaction is benign and positive. However, we can't rule out the possibility that the interaction is malign and negative. In this case, having a high-outcome sibling can't increase the probability that a person will have a low outcome by more than 0.3. Not only is the causal sibling interaction quantitatively ambiguous, it is also qualitatively ambiguous. Once more, the cup is half full or half empty.

5.6 Calibration

At the beginning of this chapter it was pointed out that many natural scientists, because they are unable to generate experimental data, have to test their hypotheses with observational data, especially in cosmology, astronomy, meteorology, and climatology. They too fall back onto natural experiments to test their hypotheses. However, in some of these disciplines *calibration* has been used to make empirical inferences about causal effects.

Calibrators build mathematical models of whatever it is they wish to study. For example, climatologists build general circulation models (GCMs) in which the laws of atmospheric physics are used to specify the relationships between the variables in the model, such as atmospheric temperatures and concentrations of greenhouse gases. These relationships typically are quite complicated and involve nonlinearities and dynamic responses. Calibrated models entail state or endogenous variables (which are determined by the model) and control or exogenous variables (which are determined outside the model). In GCMs, the state variables include temperatures and atmospheric greenhouse-gas concentrations; the exogenous variables include carbon emissions and solar irradiance.

Once a model has been assembled on a computer, it is calibrated to the past. This means that parameter values are chosen for the model so that the model tracks past data. For example, climatologists[25] calibrate their GCMs to track data over the past 1,000 years. If the laws of physics used to construct the model are correct, the model should track the past data perfectly. However, the laws of physics are no more than hypotheses, so the model tracks the past imperfectly and even poorly (Kaufmann and Stern 2004). Calibrators adjust the parameters in the model until the model tracks the past to a reasonable degree of satisfaction. As we shall see, this is the Achilles' Heel of the methodology of calibration.

Once a model has been calibrated to the past, the next step is to use it to project the future. For example, GCMs are used to project temperatures over the rest of the twenty-first century and beyond. These projections require assumptions about the exogenous variables that aren't determined by the model. GCMs require assumptions about solar irradiance and carbon emissions that, in turn, depend on world economic activity and the consumption of energy. In the base projection, the most likely scenario for the exogenous variables is used to simulate the model into the future.

To study the effect of some variable of interest (such as carbon emissions) on some outcome of interest (such as global temperature), the base projection is perturbed by setting carbon emissions at a different level over the future. The GCM solves for a new projection of temperature, which is compared to its base projection. If the latter is higher than the former, the conclusion is that carbon emissions cause global warming. The model enables the calibrator to play God by changing one variable at a time, as if in an experiment. Indeed, the model may be used to carry out counterfactual simulations in which history is reconstructed under the assumption that the exogenous variables behaved differently than they behaved in practice. The GCM may be used to reconstruct the past under the counterfactual assumption that the cooling of the sun during the late Middle Ages did not in fact occur. This counterfactual simulation will shed light on the causes of the Little Ice Age during the sixteenth and seventeenth centuries.

Calibration suffers from a number of methodological problems. First, there is *observational equivalence*: there may not be a unique way to calibrate models to past data. Therefore, two or more different models might track the past similarly, but their projections of the future might be quite different. For example, two calibrated GCMs might track past temperature and greenhouse-gas concentrations in similar ways, but their future projections might differ widely. One model might predict considerable global warming, while another might predict that the world will not get warmer, even when both models are fed with common assumptions about carbon emissions and solar irradiance. The basic problem here is that the parameters of the model are not uniquely identified. The observational data simply don't enable us to discriminate between rival models. In technical terms, the number of independent moments in the data is less than the number of unknown parameters in the model. Therefore, the model is under-identified.

Second, the measures of goodness of fit that are used to calibrate models are typically rather loose and even vague (Kaufmann and Stern 2004). Calibrated models usually comprise numerous state variables, some of which are tracked better than others. Two calibrators might build different models simply because one happened to give greater tracking priority to one set of variables than to another. Or calibrators might set different standards of goodness of fit—for example, one calibrator might be satisfied if the model tracks the ups and downs of a variable qualitatively, while his more ambitious counterpart might insist that his model tracks the data quantitatively. Strictly speaking, calibrated models, like all models, should be required to track the data without bias, and the tracking errors should be entirely random. Therefore, calibrated models might differ simply because their calibrators have set different and arbitrary standards of goodness of fit.

Third, most calibrated models involve the use of non-stationary data, the means and variances of which vary over time. Trending data are necessarily non-stationary because their mean increases over time if the trend is positive and decreases if the trend is negative. It is well known that non-stationary variables may be spuriously correlated.[26] For example, two completely unrelated trending variables may even appear to be highly correlated when in truth they have nothing to do with each other. Calibrators don't test whether the correlations generated by their model are spurious or genuine. For example, a GCM in which global temperature turns out to be correlated with carbon emissions may be picking up a genuine greenhouse-gas effect or a spurious one.[27]

How might calibration be relevant to the study of intergenerational and sibling correlations? Social scientists are increasingly turning to calibration to make empirical inferences using observational data. For example, calibration was introduced into macroeconomics[28] during the 1980s. Like GCMs, macroeconomic models are constructed using observational time-series data, and they consist of a series of dynamic simultaneous equations, which may be nonlinear and stochastic. To the best of my knowledge, calibration hasn't infiltrated other social sciences, such as sociology and psychology. However, this is due in part to the non-axiomatic nature of those disciplines. Calibration is feasible only when there are "well-defined" laws (such as those of physics or economics) that can be specified in the model. There are no comparable well-defined laws in sociology or psychology. This raises the question whether the laws of economics can be compared to the laws of physics (Sims 1996). The physical sciences are arguably more "exact" than the economic sciences, and the laws of the latter probably are less empirically reliable than the laws of physics. However, even the laws of physics aren't empirically accurate. If the laws of atmospheric physics were accurate and consensual, there wouldn't be so much disagreement about the causes of global warming. The same applies to the laws of cosmology and astronomy.

There are indications that calibration is being used to study inter-generational correlations and heredity. Bowles and Gintis (2002) observe that the intergenerational correlation for income in the United States is approximately 0.41, which is broadly in line with the estimates reported in chapter 2. Using the decomposition methodology discussed in chapter 3, Bowles and Gintis decompose this correlation into environmental, genetic, and wealth-related components. They have a direct estimate of the wealth component: 0.12. The genetic component is based on the difference between the income correlations for identical and fraternal twins, which according to their calibrations contributes 0.09 to the intergenerational correlation. Since these two components account for an intergenerational correlation of 0.21, and the overall correlation is 0.41, the balance of 0.2 is attributed to the contribution of the environment. Bowles and Gintis calibrate this balance to a correlation between parent's income and their environment of about 0.74, which is much higher than their calibrated correlation between children's income and their environment.

Note that the only non-calibrated component refers to wealth. The genetic and environmental components are calibrated to the data. Roughly half of the intergenerational correlation is attributed to the environment simply because the genetic contribution is calibrated at 0.09. The results from this kind of reverse engineering might have been quite different if the genetic contribution had been treated as the residual or balancing item instead of the environmental contribution.

Grawe and Mulligan (2002), who also use calibration, criticize the work of Bowles and Gintis for drawing its inspiration from behavioral genetics and for being mechanistic rather than behavioral. I noted the irony that behavioral genetics is devoid of behavioral theory in chapter 3, where I presented a behavioral or economic model in which parents invest in their children's schooling. That model predicts that parents' investment in schooling varies directly with the ability of their children. It also predicts that if the capital market is imperfect parents will be credit-constrained in the sense they may not be able to raise sufficient capital to pay for their children's schooling. This constraint will be particularly binding for the parents of abler children. Since ability is inherited, abler children are likely to have better-off parents, who can afford to pay for their children's schooling. Therefore, the credit constraint is less binding than it would have been had ability not been inherited.

Grawe and Mulligan use a similar model to simulate the intergenerational correlation for earnings. First they assume that the capital market is perfect, so the parents aren't credit constrained. The simulations show that the intergenerational correlation is positive because ability is inherited. Abler parents earn more, and they have abler children who earn more because they are both more able and more educated. Grawe and Mulligan's simulation shows that when there are credit constraints the intergenerational correlation increases. This happens because better-off parents can afford to help their children buy schooling. Therefore, apart from inherited ability, the income of parents strengthens the intergenerational correlation coefficient. To be fair, Grawe and Mulligan don't formally calibrate their model to real data. Nevertheless, they conjecture that the intergenerational correlation may be higher in the United States than in Sweden or Canada because schooling is more highly subsidized in those countries than in the United States.

Social scientists test their hypotheses mainly by using observational data. They are far less fortunate than their colleagues in the natural sciences, who can test their hypotheses under laboratory conditions. Disentangling causality in correlated observational data is difficult but not impossible. The discipline of econometrics was invented, mainly by economists, to test causal hypotheses using observational data. A parameter is said to be "identified" when it can be estimated without bias using observational data. Identification problems arise under a variety of circumstances:

Explanatory variables happen to be missing. For example, genotypes and environmental variables are unobserved. These omitted variables may be correlated with observed covariates. Estimates of the effects of the observed variables on outcomes don't have a causal interpretation because they are biased due to their correlation with omitted unobservable variables.

Variables happen to be jointly determined. For example, sibling outcomes are mutually influential because of sibling interaction. Estimates of the effect of siblings on each other don't have a causal interpretation.

The sample isn't random. For example, adopted children aren't randomly assigned to parents. Estimates of the effects of genes and environments on the outcomes of adoptees are generally biased.

The main solution to the first two identification problems is the instrumental-variables estimator, which is based on the methodology of natural experimentation. A natural experiment is like a laboratory experiment except it occurs spontaneously. Just as laboratory experiments randomize trial subjects and control subjects, so do natural experiments. They induce variations in the causal variable of interest, which are independent of the outcome. These variations identify the causal effect of the variable of interest on the outcome because they mimic the random variations that take place in laboratory experiments.

As we shall see in chapter 6, natural experimentation is feasible in many contexts in the case of environmental phenomena, but not in the case of genetic phenomena. This means that it is easier to estimate the causal effect of environmental phenomena on outcomes than it is to estimate genetic effects. In short, it is much easier to identify the role of nurture than it is to identify the role of nature. Social scientists who are primarily concerned with the roles of nurture and environment have a much easier job than behavioral geneticists whose primary concern is with the roles of nature and genetics.

If longitudinal data on several successive generations happen to be available, panel-data methods may be used to solve the first type of identification problem. The specific effect may be regarded as an estimate of unobserved genotypes that run in families. If data on three successive generations happen to be available, it is possible to estimate the causal effect of environments and genes on the outcomes of interest, even in situations where natural experimentation is not feasible. A related method is the generated-regressor methodology, which proxies unobserved genotypes of parents with an estimate. This method also identifies the causal effect of genes and environments on outcomes. If several outcomes depend on common unobserved genotypes, panel-data methods may be used to estimate the causal effects of genes and environments. The specific effects may be regarded as estimates of the unobserved genotypes, which therefore solve identification problems of the first kind.

Identification problems of the second kind cannot be solved using panel data. The only feasible solution is natural experimentation, which requires specifying instrumental variables. To identify the causal effect of sibling 1 on sibling 2, instrumental variables are required that affect sibling 1 but don't affect sibling 2. These instrumental variables serve to randomize the outcome of sibling 1, which mimics laboratory randomization.

If for one reason or another it isn't possible to apply these methodological solutions to solve the identification problem, it is always possible to partially identify the causal effects of interest. Instead of delivering point estimates of causal effects, partial identification is inherently ambiguous because it provided bounds for causal effects. This means that one can rule out that the effect is larger than some upper value or less than some lower value. This is obviously inferior to a point estimate, but half a loaf is better than none.

The third identification problem is due to sample selectivity and is conceptually different from the previous two problems. There are two methodological solutions to this problem. The first solution parameterizes what we don't observe about selection and outcomes. Specifically, unobserved "adoptability" (which determines the probability of adoption) and unobserved "ability" (which determines the outcome of adopted children) are assumed to be correlated, normally distributed random variables. The second solution is based on natural experimentation in adoption. Some instrumental variable, which by definition is independent of the outcome of interest, is hypothesized to determine adoption status. The instrumental variable randomizes adoption status in a way that is independent of the outcome. It therefore mimics random assignment in adoption. Although the first method doesn't require instrumental variables, it is preferable if instrumental variables are also used in explaining the probability of adoption.

6 Empirical Knowledge on the Causes of Correlations within the Family

In this chapter, I take stock of what we know and what we don't know about the causal mechanisms that underpin the correlation between the outcomes of parents and children and that induce correlation between the outcomes of siblings. There are potentially three types of mechanism that induce these correlations. The first is genetic: the outcomes of children and parents are correlated because of heredity. The second is behavioral: the behavior of parents induces intergenerational dependence. The third is behavioral too: parents and children may share environments. It should be abundantly clear by now that correlation doesn't tell us anything about causal effects, and that identifying causal effects from observational data is difficult but not impossible. One of the themes in this chapter is that different disciplines set different standards of identification. In some disciplines, such as criminology and developmental psychology, the standards are low. The standards aren't much higher in behavioral genetics, and strong identifying assumptions are made to obtain results from the data. Since much of the literature of economics adopts the methodology of behavioral genetics, the same criticism applies to that discipline. However, recently labor economists in particular have began to enter the field, and the standards of identification in labor economics are very high. Indeed, these standards form the methodological basis of much of chapters 5 and 10 of this book.

There cannot, of course, be one set of scientific standards for developmental psychologists and behavioral geneticists and another set for labor economists. What passes for science has to satisfy best methodological practice, which, like everything else, tends to develop and improve over time. The scientific standards in developmental psychology and behavioral genetics fall far short of the cutting edge. Methodological standards vary within the discipline of economics too. As was mentioned in chapter 5, the adoption of calibration by economists (especially by macroeconomists) has been controversial and in my opinion constitutes methodological regress rather than progress. In the last 30 years, what might be called best practice has been developed mainly by microeconomists and by labor economists. This best practice sets high standards of identification for testing hypotheses of causal effects using observational data.

Because of publication bias, the published scientific literature may not be a fair representation of knowledge. This problem begins with editors of scientific journals, who typically prefer to publish "positive" results rather than "negative" ones. They prefer to publish research that corroborates hypotheses rather than research that falsifies them. It has always struck me as odd that most published empirical papers have happy endings, and that the hypothesis under investigation almost always turns out to be corroborated. One rarely comes across published research with a bad ending in which the maintained hypothesis is rejected. Manski et al. (2001) report that in the field of drug and alcohol abuse a paper showing that treatment works was much more likely to be published than one showing the opposite. Yet falsification is epistemologically more important than corroboration. Science progresses by discovering false theories so that we can develop new and better theories.

Hypothesis testing with observational data typically entails a protracted process of specification search (Leamer 1978) in which empirical investigators estimate numerous models using different methods, data definitions, and samples. This may sound like data mining,[1] but, as Leamer explains, there can be methodological justification for it. The process of specification search involves a variety of misspecification tests that distinguish meaningless data-mined models from genuine specification-searched models. For example, data-mined models typically fail to predict because they inflate the probability of false positives. They might appear impressive, and their t statistics suggest statistical significance, but they break down as soon as they have to explain data outside the sample. The process of specification search gives empirical investigators discretion in the results they report. It is easy to abuse this discretion.

Empirical investigators might naturally predispose their results to be positive and therefore attractive to editors. I am not referring here to willful fabrication of results, but to the moral hazard that is involved in how they are selected, presented, and written up. Also, empirical investigators are naturally reluctant to submit for publication papers that falsify, because they understand that editors of scientific journals are unlikely to be interested in them. Evidence of publication bias may show up in a variety of ways. For example, standard errors should, on average, be larger in smaller samples. However, if editors are stricter with results based on small samples, researchers may be tempted to report results that have lower standard errors if their sample is small. Also, statistical significance should be independent of the sizes of effects. Researchers may be tempted into reporting highly significant small effects to persuade editors to publish their results. Based on these and related indicators, Stanley (2005, p. 44) reports that "thus far, every area of economic research . . . has uncovered publication bias." Economics probably isn't alone in doing so. Publication bias regarding genome-wide association studies has become epidemic. Until editorial policy changes and editors attach as much importance to falsification as they do to corroboration, scientific research will remain biased in favor of corroboration. The naive consumer of the published scientific literature most probably obtains an over-optimistic impression from meta-analyses.

Publication bias probably is present in the empirical studies reviewed in this chapter. Therefore, meta-perceptions of the literature probably are optimistic. As we shall see, however, there is almost no hard evidence regarding the causal effects that parents have on their children. Empirical results from behavioral genetics are given almost no weight in this chapter because behavioral genetics is devoid of behaviorism. Since behavior is assumed not to matter, empirical revelations are given a genetic interpretation by default. The results of behavioral genetics may be suggestive and even fascinating, but they don't meet the minimal standards of identification that have been set for the purposes of this chapter. They fall too far short of the best methodological practice.

Reasons for this seemingly sweeping generalization were discussed at length in chapter 3. To repeat, in the case of adoption studies the strong behavioral assumptions are the following:

Adopted children are randomly assigned to parents, so parents have no say in who they adopt.

Children available for adoption are a random sample of children, so they are like children in general.

Parents wishing to adopt are like any other parents.

Adoption agencies allocate children to adoptive parents without considering the personalities of parents and children.

In studies of MZ twins, the equal-environments assumption is simply too strong as an identifying assumption. It essentially assumes that the differences between identical and fraternal twins and the differences between adopted and biological siblings aren't confounded by the behavior of parents and children and by their environments. Therefore, parents are assumed to relate to MZ twins as they would to their other children, and MZ twins are assumed to relate to each other as they would to other siblings.

The chapter has three sections. The first focuses on intergenerational correlations in which a chronological or life-cycle approach is taken, which begins with life itself *in utero*. Subsequently, infancy, then childhood, and finally adulthood are considered. The second is concerned with environmental effects, including neighborhood and peer group effects on outcomes such as criminal behavior and schooling. The third deals with the intragenerational (sibling) correlations. It will become apparent that empirical investigation into the causes of the intergenerational correlation has received much more attention than the causes of sibling correlation. As was pointed out in chapter 3, if parents and children are correlated, so must siblings be correlated. Indeed, the sibling correlation is related to the square of the intergenerational correlation. Although there is more to the sibling correlation than the intergenerational correlation, sibling interaction is under-researched in comparison to parent-child interactions. As we shall see, it is methodologically harder to test hypotheses about the effects of siblings on each other than it is to test hypotheses about the effects of parents on their children.

As has been mentioned, there are three causal mechanisms that underpin the correlation between parents and children. However, only the second and the third may be meaningfully investigated with observational data. The first mechanism, heredity, cannot be meaningfully investigated, because it is not possible to carry out natural experiments in which the causal effects of heredity are identified. On the other hand, natural experiments and other solutions are available that, to some degree, identify the behavioral causal mechanisms of parenting and environments. Therefore, the empirical material below deals first with parenting and subsequently with environmental mechanisms of intergenerational transmission.

The methodological failure of behavioral genetics means that there can be no separate section on heredity. Perhaps as the Human Genome Project develops and empirical data on specific genotypes are generated, this unfortunate state of affairs will change. However, as will be argued in the next chapter, the prospects don't seem good. In the meantime, heredity may only be identified indirectly. If indeed there are three mechanisms, the second and the third imply the first. If there are estimates of the separate contributions of parenting and environments to the sibling correlation, the contribution of heredity may be calculated as the residual, since the whole is the sum of its parts. This solution is far from satisfactory, but it may be better than nothing.

6.1   Intergenerational Causal Effects: Parenting

Parenting, or rather mothering, begins before we are born.

6.1.1   *In Utero*

Ideally we are looking for natural or quasi-experiments that provide "smoking-gun" evidence regarding genetic, parental, or environmental effects on children. Such evidence carries the same level of conviction that a controlled laboratory experiment might have carried, had it been feasible. Consider the claim that smoking by pregnant women induces lower birth weights. If, as is claimed, birth weight affects cognitive ability,[2] a mother affects her child's future even before it is born. The implication is that if pregnant women didn't smoke, their babies would weigh more at birth, as a result of which their cognitive ability would be enhanced and their life chances improved. There are two related claims. The first is that there is a causal effect from smoking to birth weight. The second is that there is a causal effect from birth weight to cognitive ability. Let us consider these claims in turn.

There seems to be little doubt that pregnant women who smoke heavily have babies that weigh less. However, this correlation may not be causal. If mothers who smoke while pregnant happen to be mothers who neglect their health and generally don't take good care of themselves (e.g., they over-eat, under-exercise, and drink too much alcohol), the low birth weight of their babies may simply reflect the characters of the mothers. Even if these pregnant women didn't smoke, they might still have underweight babies because they generally neglect themselves. The combination of smoking while pregnant and low birth weight is induced by a third factor, the personality or character of the mother, which affects both smoking and birth weight.

Imagine an experiment in which some pregnant women are forced to smoke while others are forced not to smoke. If the birth weights of the babies of the mothers who smoked are less than the birth weights of the babies whose mothers didn't smoke, this would constitute smoking-gun evidence (excuse the pun) in favor of the hypothesis that smoking causes low birth weight. Such experiments obviously aren't feasible. Even if they were, the results of the experiment probably would be spoiled by Hawthorne effects, since the experiment itself induces pregnant women to behave self-consciously and unnaturally. In addition, the women who were forced to smoke will include women who in any case would have smoked. However, it will also include women who wouldn't have smoked. These women might try to compensate for the fact that they are coerced into smoking by exercising more, eating less, or even faking their smoking. Some of the women forced not to smoke wouldn't have smoked in any case. Some of the women prevented from smoking might compensate by drinking more alcohol or by using drugs.

Sexton and Hebel (1984) carried out a quasi-experiment in which pregnant smokers participating in pre-natal care were randomized into a treatment group that received extensive counseling about smoking cessation and a control group that didn't receive counseling. The proportion of smokers among women in the treatment group was 23 percentage points less than among the women in the control group, as a result of which the treatment women's babies weighed 92 grams more than the babies of the control women. Permutt and Hebel (1989) use these data to estimate (by instrumental variables) the causal effect of smoking on birth weight at –400 grams (t statistic 2.56). This quasi-experiment is very different, of course, from the hypothetical experiment described in the previous paragraph. In a real experiment there is no problem of compliance, whereas in a quasi-experiment there is. What might be learned from the results of quasi-experiments turns on the counterfactuals for non-compliers. No doubt some women attended counseling reluctantly and women not offered counseling might have sought it elsewhere. Although the result is only marginally significant,[3] these data suggest that smoking while pregnant causes low birth weight.

Evans and Ringel (1999) have a natural experiment for the same issue. They note that because the taxation of tobacco in the United

States is decided by state legislatures rather than by the federal government, rates of cigarette taxation vary by state. Indeed there is a substantial incentive to cross state lines to save money on purchases of cigarettes. Evans and Ringel show that, with schooling, age, and other variables equal, pregnant women are more likely to smoke in states where cigarettes are cheaper than in states where cigarettes are more expensive. Indeed, there is widespread evidence that the demand for cigarettes varies inversely with cigarette prices.[4] If state cigarette taxes are set for reasons not related to birth weights of children born in the state (e.g., to raise tax revenue), they constitute a natural experiment, since they serve to randomize smoking as in an experiment. Evans and Ringel show that the birth weights of children born to otherwise similar women are lower in states where pregnant women are more likely to smoke because cigarettes are cheaper in their state. This result establishes, smoking-gun fashion, that the lower birth weights have something to do with smoking rather than with the women. The causal implication is that smoking while pregnant increases the risk of an underweight baby.

The women in this natural experiment were completely unaware of the role of cigarettes taxes in randomizing smoking, so they behaved perfectly naturally, and there were no Hawthorne effects. Indeed, the state legislators probably weren't aware of the effect of cigarette taxes on smoking. Matters would be very different if state legislators raised cigarette taxes in states where there is an unusually high incidence of low-birth-weight babies, in the hope that this policy would discourage smoking by pregnant women and thus lower the incidence of low-birth-weight babies. In this case the natural experiment would founder because the instrument is correlated with the outcome of interest. Evans and Ringel guard against this unlikely prospect by exploiting information on differences in cigarette taxes over time and information on differences in these taxes between states.[5]

Lien and Evans (2005) extend the work of Evans and Ringel using the differences-in-differences methodology.[6] They show that smoking rates among pregnant women decreased after cigarette taxes were sharply increased in Arizona, Illinois, Michigan, and Massachusetts in 1993 and 1994. Using the tax changes as instrumental variables, Lien and Evans find that smoking reduces birth weight by 182 grams (with a t statistic of 3.1) and increases the probability of low birth weight by 0.068 (with a t statistic of 2.62).[7]

In chapter 2 it was noted that anthropometric outcomes, such as weight, height, and body mass, are correlated between and within generations. Indeed, this is where Galton began, as we saw in chapter 1, by studying the heights of parents and children. We also saw in chapter 2 that birth weights seem to be intergenerationally correlated, which suggests that birth weight may be partly genetic. However, if there is a causal effect from mothers' weight when pregnant on the birth weights of their children, and if there is a causal effect of mothers' birth weight on their weight when pregnant, the intergenerational correlation in birth weight is behavioral rather than hereditary. The correlation between adult weight and birth weight is affected by parenting.

If parents invest more in the nutrition of their lighter babies and less in their heavier babies, the correlation between adult weight and birth weight will be attenuated. In the limit, there may be no correlation at all if parents succeed in making up for the weight deficits of their lighter babies by giving them compensatory nutrition. Not only may mothers close birth-weight deficits neonatally and during infancy, they may also close them *in utero*. Mothers may influence fetal development by resting and by cutting back on bad habits. If aware that her fetus is undersize, a mother may act to promote fetal development, in which case birth weight is partly influenced by parenting. This is true of regular births, but it obviously cannot apply to twin births. Since a mother can't discriminate between the fetal development of twins, the birth-weight differences between twins cannot be due to the behavior of mothers.

Conley and Bennet (2000) compare two models for birth weight. In the first model, the probability of low birth weight varies directly with the low birth weights of mothers and fathers. This model suggests that low birth weight is transmitted genetically from one generation to the next; it is inherited. In the second model, the probability of low birth weight depends on fixed effects[8] for mothers, which can be estimated because their data include the birth weights of their siblings. This test exploits information on the differential birth weights of siblings. In the second model it is the identity of the mother that matters rather than her birth weight, which suggests that mothers' behavior rather than heredity is affecting birth weights. Unfortunately, Conley and Bennet don't test which model is statistically superior.[9] Nevertheless, their results cast doubt on the heredity theory of birth weight, since the fixed effect washes out the effect of mothers' birth weights on the birth weights of their children.

Cesur and Rashad (2008) use data on 47,500 births to show that birth weights vary inversely with mothers' weight gains during pregnancy, and that they vary directly if mothers subsequently breast-fed their babies. The latter suggests that mothers who breast-feed take better care of themselves during pregnancy. Birth weight also varies directly with birth order, which suggests that mothers learn from experience. (Cesar and Rashid don't control for the birth weights of mothers.) Cesur and Rashad also show that birth weight depends on a wide range of other factors that are outside a mother's control, such as length of gestation and type of delivery. These and other variables account for only one-third of the variance in birth weights. The rest of the variance is due to randomness or nature. Thus, it seems that birth weight is about two-thirds nature and one-third nurture and environment.

Behrman and Rosenzweig (2001) investigate the relationship between birth weight and mother's birth weight controlling for smoking and alcohol consumption. They use a sample of about 1,600 identical twin sisters drawn from the Minnesota Twin Registry. At first they ignore the special nature of the data and treat the sisters as if they were not related. Like Evans and Ringel, they use state cigarette and alcohol taxes as instrumental variables for smoking and alcohol consumption while pregnant. They find that birth weight varies directly with the birth weight of the mother and varies inversely with her smoking and drinking. However, when they take account of MZ-twin status, these effects disappear. This result is reminiscent of Conley and Bennett's insofar as the mother's birth weight ceases to matter when family dependence in the data is taken into consideration. Behrman and Rosenzweig results also cast doubt on the claim that smoking and drinking while pregnant lowers birth weights.

Does smoking when pregnant cause low birth weight? Evans and Hebel think so, but Conley and Bennet and Behrman and Rosenzweig disagree. The former use quasi- experimentation and natural experimentation; the latter use various panel-data methods. Maybe this is just a methodological coincidence. However, since Behrman and Rosenzweig also showed that that their panel-data method wipes out the Evans-Ringel-type conclusion, perhaps the ubiquitous correlation between smoking while pregnant and low birth weight is a statistical illusion induced by heredity or by dysfunctionality. The fact that there is no clear evidence that smoking while pregnant adversely affects birth weight stands in contrast to the view promulgated in government-required health warnings on cigarette packets.

6.1.2 Causal Consequences of Birth Weight

The next step is to consider the evidence that cognitive and other developmental outcomes depend causally on birth weight.[10] Many studies show that low birth weight predicts adverse cognitive and scholastic outcomes that persist beyond childhood into adulthood. However, this relationship may not be causal; it may simply be that there is a factor that determines both birth weight and cognitive outcomes. For example, birth weight and cognition might be genetic, in which case the common factor is heredity. Behrman and Rosenzweig (2004) show that birth weight causally increases school attainments, adult height, and even earnings, but not body mass index. Since Behrman and Rosenzweig use data on the birth weights of identical twin sisters, their results control for genetic differences as well as for differences *in utero*.

The methodology of Behrman and Rosenzweig (BR) may be summarized as follows: Let Y_{1i} and Y_{2i} denote the outcomes for siblings in family i, and let their birth weights be denoted by B_{1i} and B_{2i}. The model to be estimated is as follows:

$$Y_{1i} = \alpha + \beta B_{1i} + u_{1i}, \tag{1}$$

$$u_{1i} = v_{1i} + e_{1i}, \tag{2}$$

$$Y_{2i} = \alpha + \beta B_{2i} + u_{2i}, \tag{3}$$

$$u_{2i} = v_{2i} + e_{2i}. \tag{4}$$

The regression residual (u) consists of two components: a correlated component (v) induced by the fact that siblings belong to the same family, and an uncorrelated component (e). The parameter of interest is β, which measures the causal effect of birth weight on the outcome. If birth weight is partly genetic and outcomes depend on genotypes, we might suspect that B and u are not independent, in which case ordinary least squares (OLS) estimates of β will be biased. The same applies if birth weight is influenced by parenting during pregnancy, and parenting affects outcomes. Let $y_i = Y_{2i} - Y_{1i}$ and $b_i = B_{2i} - B_{1i}$ denote sibling differences in outcomes and birth weights in family i. Subtracting equation 1 from equation 3 leads to the BR model:

$$y_i = \beta b_i + w_i, \tag{5}$$

$$w_i = v_{2i} - v_{1i} + e_{2i} - e_{1i}. \tag{6}$$

Since MZ twins are genetically identical and shared the same uterus, v_{2i} equals v_{1i}, in which case $w_i = e_{2i} - e_{1i}$. Therefore, w_i is independent of b_i. Equation 5 is the BR estimator of β, which is unbiased. Matters would be different if v_2 did not equal v_1. In this case w would depend on $v_2 - v_1$, as a result of which w and b would no longer be independent, and the BR estimator of β would be biased. This happens in the case of ordinary siblings, who are genetically different and shared different wombs. It also happens in the case of DZ twins, who shared the same womb but are genetically different. On the other hand, epigenetic drift implies that v_2 is not equal to v_1 for MZ twins, in which case b and w cease to be independent, in which case the BR estimator of β will be biased.

Behrman and Rosenzweig find that the heavier twin (at birth) surpasses the lighter one in schooling attainment, adult height, and earnings. Since MZ twins share the same genes and the same uterus, the differences almost surely have to do with the differences in birth weights. In fact these birth-weight effects would be larger than they seem if parents made neonatal nutritional investments in lighter twins to compensate for their disadvantage relative to their heavier twin sisters. Berman and Rosenzweig also note that when they ignore the fact that their data refer to identical twin sisters, and assume that they are unrelated, the causal effect of birth weight on schooling and other outcomes is substantially under-estimated. This suggests that heredity conceals the true causal effect of birth weight on future outcomes.

Behrman and Rosenzweig's results establish, in smoking-gun fashion, that there is a long-run causal effect of birth weight on cognitive and even economic development. They conclude from this that parents should invest in the fetal development of their children, because birth weight matters for their long-term life prospects. This conclusion is based on two principles. First, the birth-weight difference in a pair of MZ twins is entirely due to fetal nutrition failure. This rules out the possibility that the lighter twin is in some sense weaker *ab initio* and that epigenetic drift cannot begin in the womb. Perhaps the lighter twin is congenitally weaker, which is why his birth weight is lower and his lifetime outcomes are inferior to those of his heavier twin. Second, the life prospects of non-twins may be extrapolated from those of identical twins. However, cognitive and other outcomes might also depend on the way siblings inter-relate as well as on parenting, as was discussed in chapter 3. If MZ twins relate more intensively than do fraternal siblings, and if parents and teachers relate to identical twins differently

Table 6.1
Effect of birth weight on outcomes. Source: Black et al. 2007, table 3.

	Non-twins			Twins		
Outcome	OLS	Family fixed effects	N	OLS	Twin fixed effects	N
One-year mortality	–123.5	–186.7	1,253,546	–279.6	–41.1	33,366
Height (men)	11.03	7.33	203,741	7.48	5.68	5,832
IQ (men)	0.91	0.58	184,045	0.48	0.62	4,920
High school	0.16	0.04	536,020	0.07	0.09	13,106
Earnings (log)	0.09	0.08	239,906	0.09	0.12	5,952

than to other children, extrapolation may not be valid. In the limit, the relationship between birth weight and cognitive outcomes might apply only for MZ twins.

Results similar to those of Behrman and Rosenzweig have been found for Norway by Black et al. (2007), who estimate the causal effect of birth weight on a variety of outcomes, including high school completion, IQ (in males), and earnings. Black et al. apply the methodology of Conley and Bennett, which exploits data on siblings to estimate family fixed effects, and the methodology of Behrman and Rosenzweig, which exploits data on twins. Some of their results are reported here in table 6.1. Notice that in all cases the sample sizes (N) are very large and that all the estimates reported are statistically significant at the 5 percent level of significance and less.

The first result of Black et al. that should be discussed here is that first-year mortality varies inversely with birth weight. In the case of non-twins, the OLS estimate of –123.5 reported in table 6.1 is estimated using 1.25 million observations. Not surprisingly, many of these non-twins have siblings. When this family relationship is taken into consideration, the effect of birth weight on one-year mortality increases to –186.7. This means that something is going on in families that strengthens the relationship between birth weight and one-year mortality. One explanation for this is that less capable parents happen to have heavier babies.[11]

When the sample is restricted to twins, the OLS estimate is twice as negative (–279.6 instead of –123.5), meaning that the association between birth weight and one-year death rates among twins is much stronger than among non-twins. However, the relationship between differences in mortality rates among twins and differences in their birth weights is weaker (–44.1 instead of –279.6) but still statistically significant. This means that ignoring the status of twins leads to a huge overestimation of the effect of birth weight on one-year mortality. This leaves us with two unbiased estimates of the causal effect of birth weight on one-year mortality, one for non-twins (–186.7) and one for twins (–41.1). Which of these is correct? Both of them may be correct if twins are different from non-twins. Table 6.1 suggests that twins are less sensitive to their birth weights than singletons. This means that results for twins cannot be simply extrapolated to non-twins.

According to table 6.1, IQ, high school completion, and earnings vary directly with birth weight. The causal effects are derived from the family fixed-effects estimators. In some cases, especially in the case of twins, these causal effects are larger than their OLS estimates. For example, a 10 percent increase in birth weight raises twins' earnings by about 1 percent, whereas according to the OLS estimate the increase is only 0.75 percent. The OLS estimate is biased downward because it ignores the fact that twins are related.

The twins referred to in table 6.1 include all twins irrespective of their zygosity. When the sample is limited to DZ twins, the reported effects in table 6.1 don't change significantly. This suggests that zygosity is unimportant. What matters is that twins share wombs, not that they share genes. Newcombe et al. (2007) obtain similar results using data on 1,116 pairs of twins in the United Kingdom. They too find that the heavier twin does better. They estimate that an increase in birth weight of 100 grams raises IQ by 0.3 points regardless of whether the twins are MZ or DZ. What matters is a common womb rather than zygosity.

Cesur and Rashad (2008) carry out multivariate regressions in which pedagogic scores for children in mathematics, vocabulary, and other outcomes are regressed on birth weight, controlling for the child and the mother. These controls include the mother's education, age, and marital status, the child's age and place in the birth order, and various controls for the family, such as family income. Cesur and Rashad instrument birth weight using their birth-weight model described above. Whereas birth weight is a strong predictor of pedagogic outcomes, their instrumental-variables estimates are only marginally significant, which suggests that birth weight is positively correlated with unobserved learning ability, and that correlation between birth weight and pedagogic outcomes is largely non-causal. Cesur and Rashad also find that breast-fed babies do better and high-birth-order children do worse. Their identifying instruments are pre-natal care, gestation, mother's age, and weight gain during pregnancy. Since these variables are likely to be correlated with mothering, and children with better mothers might do better at school, Cesur and Rashad's evidence of the causal effect of birth weight on pedagogic outcomes does not have smoking-gun status. Cesur and Rashad show that it is not just low birth weight that matters—heavy babies also do worse than babies of average weight.

Conley and Bennett (2000) use a different identification strategy to show that low birth weight has a causal effect on high school graduation. Instead of using instrumental variables, they estimate fixed effects for mothers, which control for unobserved mothering ability. Their fixed-effects estimator quadruples the size of the adverse effect of low birth weight on the probability of graduation relative to a model that ignores the effect of mothering, implying that mothering ability is positively correlated with birth weight. This effect is marginally statistically significant, with a t statistic of 2.88. Behrman and Rosenzweig remark that because Conley and Bennett use data on ordinary siblings rather than twins, parents might have taken action to influence their birth weights. If the fetus is detected to be undersize, parents might take remedial action in the form of investments in fetal development. Therefore, lighter birth weight may be telling us something about pre-natal care by parents, rather than something about the endowments of children. Parents might also invest in the fetal development of twins, but in this case they obviously cannot discriminate between the two fetuses.

On balance it seems that lower birth weight adversely affects anthropometric outcomes, attainment at school, and even earnings. These effects aren't large, but they are statistically significant. However, the levels of statistical significance aren't large. If this literature has been affected by publication bias, the low levels of statistical significance are a cause for concern.

6.1.3   Mothers and Infants

Developmental psychologists study the effects of mothering on infants. Typically, this is carried out by video-taping interactive sessions between mothers and their infants at discrete intervals. Each session may last for up to several hours, and the intervals may be monthly or quarterly. The mothers know that they are being filmed, since their consent is required. Data on the behavior of mothers and infants—for example, the number of times the mother smiled or was harsh and the number of times her infant cried or gurgled—are coded for each session. Since mother-infant dyads are observed repeatedly, panel or longitudinal data on mothers' smiling and infants' crying or fussing are accumulated over time.

Do mothers behave naturally when they are under observation, or do they play to the camera by mitigating their behavior, especially when their infant is being difficult? This is an obvious question. In the following discussion, I assume for argument's sake that mothers behave perfectly naturally, despite the temptation to behave otherwise,. Another obvious question is whether mothers who consent to be observed are representative of mothers as a whole. If consenting mothers happen to be unusually capable, the sample will be biased against finding adverse developmental effects of mothering, since less capable mothers are under-represented and may even be not represented at all. For argument's sake, I assume that consenting mothers are representative of mothers as a whole, even though this is improbable.[12]

Studies of the effect of mothering on infant development date back at least to Etzel and Gewirtz (1967), who claimed that infants cried less if their caregivers were less responsive. According to this view, infants cry because their mothers spoil them. The opposite view, that infants cry less if their mothers are responsive, was proposed by Bell and Ainsworth (1972). Crockenberg and Smith (1982) came down firmly on the side of Bell and Ainsworth and against Etzel and Gewirtz. Responsive mothering calms infants; it doesn't spoil them. According to Ziv and Cassidy (2002), Crockenberg and Smith launched a generation of research focused on two supplementary questions. The first concerns the dependence of the responsiveness of mothers to their infant's characteristics. For example, van den Boom (1994) suggested that irritable infants receive insensitive care. More generally, mothers respond more if they perceive their infant to be more rewarding and attractive. The second concerns the reaction of infants to mothering. It is argued by some—e.g. Feldman, Greenbaum, and Yirmia (1999)—that irritable infants are more responsive to caregiving. If this is true, the payoff to mothering is greater among irritable infants.

The main criticism of this genre of research is that it assumes that infants don't cry strategically. Instead, infants are assumed to be passive players in a game in which mothers or caregivers are dominant players. There is an implicit assumption that there is no reverse causality from infants to mothers; all the causality is from mothers to infants. Crockenberg and Smith measure the responsiveness of mothers by how long they allow their infant to cry before intervening. They have two outcome variables for infants: crying/fussing and the time-to-calm. They also have two measures of caregiving by mothers: time-to-intervene when the baby cries or fusses and involved contact. Crockenberg and Smith investigated the relationship between these infants' outcomes at 3 months to mothers' caregiving at 1 month, controlling for infants' crying at 1 month as well as other covariates. Their main research question is this: Given everything else, including neonatal irritability, do infants cry less and calm more quickly at 3 months if their mothers intervened more promptly when they cried at 1 month? Their answer is No. In the case of crying, the only statistically significant variables are mothers' attitude (self-assessed responsiveness and flexibility) and parity, which reduce crying. In the case of time-to-calm, the only significant variables are parity (which is associated with more rapid calming) and neonatal irritability (which prolongs time-to-calm).

Crockenberg and Smith also investigated mothers' caregiving when their infant was 3 months old, as measured by involved contact and time-to-intervene, controlling for (among other things) time to intervene at 1 month and infants' crying at 1 month. Crockenberg and Smith are more successful at predicting mothers' behavior at 3 months than at predicting their infants' behavior at 3 months. In the case of mothers' involved contact at 3 months, the predictors are, in order of statistical significance, parity (negative), involved contact at 1 month (positive), infants' alertness at 3 months (positive), mothers' attitude (positive), and neonatal irritability (positive). In the case of time to intervene, at 3 months the only statistically significant predictors are mothers' attitude (negative) and neonatal irritability in excess of one standard deviation for boys (positive).

The Crockenberg-Smith (CS) model may be written as follows:

$$Y_{3i} = \alpha + \beta Y_{1i} + \gamma X_{1i} + \delta A_i + \varphi Y_{0i} + u_i , \tag{7}$$

$$X_{3i} = \eta + \pi Y_{1i} + \lambda X_{1i} + \theta A_i + \phi Z_{3i} + \psi Y_{0i} + v_i , \tag{8}$$

where Y_{3i} denotes the outcome for infant i at 3 months, Y_{1i} denotes the outcome at 1 month, and Y_{0i} denotes neonatal irritability. X denotes mothers' time to intervene when their baby is fussing or crying, A denotes mothers' self-reported attitude to involved contact and flexibility toward fussy infants,[13] and Z_3 denotes infants' alertness at 3 months.

The random variables u and v denote the residual errors of the CS model. Equation 7 embodies several related hypotheses about crying or time-to-calm among 3-month-old infants. First, these outcomes vary directly with their counterparts when the infants were 1 month old (i.e., β is positive), and they vary directly with neonatal irritability (i.e., ϕ is positive). Second, these outcomes vary inversely with caregiving and mothers' attitude (i.e., γ and δ are negative). The main parameter of interest is γ, which measures the causal effect of caregiving at 1 month on crying or time-to-calm at 3 months. A secondary parameter of interest is δ, which is the effect of mothers' attitude on the outcome of their infant.

Equation 8 embodies the following hypotheses: First, mothers who gave more care at 1 month give more care at 3 months (i.e., λ is positive). Second, mothers' caregiving at 3 months varies directly with their attitude (i.e., θ is positive). Third, mothers are expected to give less care if their infant is sleeping; therefore ϕ is expected to be positive. Finally, if mothers give more care if their baby had more neonatal irritability, then ψ will be positive.

Crockenberg and Smith report[14] that when Y_3 is measured by fussing and crying the only variable that is statistically significant in equation 7 is mothers' attitude; δ is statistically significant and negative, as expected. When Y_3 is measured by infants' time-to-calm, the only significant variable is neonatal irritability (i.e., ϕ is positive). Importantly, γ is not statistically significant; mothers' caregiving at 1 month makes no difference to infants' crying or time-to-calm at 3 months. Crockenberg and Smith had more luck with equation 8. When X is measured by mothers' involved contact, there are three significant covariates in equation 8: mothers' attitude (i.e., θ is positive), infants' fussiness at 1 month (i.e., π is positive), and neonatal irritability (i.e., ψ is positive). When X is measured by time-to-calm, however, the only significant covariate is neonatal irritability.

The CS model is concerned with prediction and sequencing rather than causality.[15] The fact that what happened at 1 month predicts what happened at 3 months doesn't mean that there is causal effect of the former on the latter. Simply because event A precedes event B does not mean that A causes B. The fact that cooking predicts eating doesn't mean that cooking causes eating; it simply means that cooking comes before eating. The cause of both cooking and eating is, of course, hunger. For an effect to be causal, a ban on cooking would have to reduce eating. Banning cooking doesn't eliminate hunger, so the ban would simply induce individuals to eat uncooked foods. Therefore, the result that infants' crying at 1 month predicts mothers' involved contact at 3 months doesn't necessarily mean that this is causal. It may simply mean that mothers who care more have fussier babies; babies are fussier at 1 month because they instinctively expect their mothers to care more at 3 months, so the causality is reversed.[16]

It comes as no surprise that mothers with a more caring attitude in fact care more in terms of involved contact and time-to-intervene. These variables are mutually reflective. However, the result that fussiness varies inversely with mothers' attitude doesn't demonstrate that a mother's attitude has a causal effect on fussiness. Mothers completed the questionnaire that was the basis for generating data on their attitude after their babies were born, and thus after they had observed their babies' neonatal irritability. Therefore, their attitude might be influenced by neonatal irritability. "Nice" mothers might intonate a more positive attitude if their baby is irritable, in which case attitude and neonatal irritability would be positively related. This means that in equation 7 attitude (A) will be positively correlated with the residual (u), in which event the estimate of δ would be biased upward. Since δ is hypothesized to be negative, this seems to suggest that Crockenberg and Smith underestimate the effect of mothers' attitude on infants' fussing, in which case their main thesis is even stronger than they convey. The reverse would apply if mothers' attitude is negatively related to neonatal irritability. In this case the negative estimate of δ reported by Crockenberg and Smith would be spurious; mothers' attitude doesn't reduce fussing. Instead, irritable babies fuss more, and their mothers intonate that their attitude is less flexible. The fact that fussing isn't affected by neonatal irritability suggests that its statistical influence is captured by the mother's attitude. This suspicion is strengthened by the fact that these statistical roles are reversed in the case of time-to-calm; neonatal irritability is statistically significant instead of mother's attitude.

The result that infants' alertness induces mothers to care more probably isn't identified. Infants may be more alert because their mothers pay them more attention. So this result too confuses (partial) correlation with causation. Generally speaking, the CS model suffers generically from failure to identify the parameters of interest and confuses prediction with causation.

The same criticism applies to numerous studies in developmental psychology. For example, Jahromi et al. (2004) investigated the effects of mothers' soothing after their infant was inoculated at the ages of 2 and 6 months. Mother and baby were observed from a minute before inoculation to 4 minutes after inoculation. The main research question concerned the effect of various measures of soothing on the change in distress of the baby 5 seconds later. Here too there is confusion between prediction and causation. That a mother performed a soothing act before the response of the child doesn't necessarily mean that the response was caused by the soothing. A further confusion is that mother-infant dyads were observed repeatedly during each inoculation. Since each dyad was observed for up to 4 minutes at intervals of 5 seconds, there are as many as 48 observations per dyad. These longitudinal observations are unlikely to be independent, since the behavior of mother and infant in the next 5 seconds is likely to depend on current soothing and distress. It cannot be ruled out that the soothing is responding to the distress just as much as the distress is responding to the soothing. Jahromi et al. don't address these identification problems.

6.1.4 Parents and Children

In chapter 3 I discussed how behavioral genetics challenged developmental psychology, which previously had ignored the role of heredity. In her defense of developmental psychology, Eleanor Maccoby concedes that this challenge "deserves to be taken seriously." "Nonetheless," she continues, "I believe they are out of date with respect to both the genetic studies and the parenting-effects studies they cite. . . ." (2000, p. 5) Maccoby also asserts that "there is clear evidence that parents can and do influence children" (ibid., p. 1). She refers here to the long-term influence of parenting on the behavior of children when they are teenagers and adults, rather than the very short-term effects that I have discussed so far. Maccoby cites a number of studies that in her opinion firmly establish this claim, including Patterson and Fogatch 1995, Loeber and Dishion 1983, and Kochanska and Thompson 1997.

Patterson and Fogatch studied 80 Oregon schoolchildren, between the ages of 9 and 12 years, who were referred to social services on the grounds of anti-social behavior. Referees and their parents were randomly assigned to an average of 20 hours of Parent Training Therapy (PTT) intended to give parents skills in raising their children. Parents and their referred children were interviewed before and after PTT by professional assessors who did not know which parents had been selected for PTT. Because 11 families failed to complete the follow-up interview, the net number of observations is 69. The interview data were converted into "before" and "after" measures of parents' skills at disciplining, monitoring, and problem solving. Data were also collected on the aversive behavior of the referred children. Although it isn't clear from their paper,[17] Patterson and Fogatch conclude (p. 280) that "overall, the findings were consistent with the idea that both child adjustment and parenting practices changed during treatment."

Patterson and Fogatch don't mention that if the 11 dropout families happened to have been negatively selected, the sample would have ceased to be random and the beneficial effects of the PTT program would have been biased upward. For argument's sake, let us assume, unreasonably, as Patterson and Fogatch implicitly do, that dropout is random, in which case their results suggest thus far that PTT benefited parents and their children during the brief period of treatment.

Two years later, data were collected from administrative records on two outcomes for the referred children: arrests and out-of-home status (i.e., living with foster parents or with relatives). Twenty-seven of the children were out of home, and 13 had been arrested. Patterson and Fogatch investigated whether the PTT children were less likely to be arrested and to be out of home. They estimated logit models for the two outcomes in which the covariates are "before" and "after" measures of parental skills. For example, they found that "after" measures of problem-solving skills significantly reduced the probability of arrest. They also found that the probability of arrest varied inversely with "before" measures of parental monitoring skills. In estimating separate logit models for each type of parental skill, Patterson and Fogatch made the unlikely assumption that these skills are independent of each other. Nor did they include standard controls such as the education of parents, the sex of the child, and other variables that might affect the probability of arrest. For argument's sake, let us assume unreasonably that these skills are independent and that the omitted covariates do not matter.

PTT cannot, of course, affect "before" measures of parental skills. The only result in which "after" measures of parental skills reduce the probability of arrest is for problem solving.[18] However, this effect is not identified, because it assumes that there is no reverse causality from the aversive behavior of children on parental skills. Parents of difficult children probably develop skills that parents of well-behaved children don't develop. To overcome this problem, Patterson and Fogatch should have exploited the fact that PTT was randomized; they should have regressed the change in parental skills on PTT status, then used the predicted value of the change in parental skills in their logit models of arrest. This would have delivered an estimate of the causal effect of PTT on the probability of arrest.

The work of Patterson and Fogatch (1995) is hardly (*pace* Maccoby) "robust" evidence in favor of parental effects inside and outside the home. In fact, the methodology is weak. Maccoby (2000, p. 6) also cites work by Loeber and Dishion (1983) as showing "strong predictive power of family interaction processes over much longer time spans." However, the evidence adduced by Loeber and Dishion fails to distinguish between correlation and causality. Dysfunctional parenting may predict subsequent criminality, but this doesn't mean that dysfunctional parenting causes criminal behavior among children. Dysfunctional parents may smoke more too, but this doesn't mean that smoking by parents causes delinquency among their children.

Finally, Maccoby cites Kochanska and Thompson (1997), who discuss the role of parents in the development of their children's moral conscience, and who cite two longitudinal studies undertaken by Kochanska. In the first of Kochanska's studies, mother-child dyads were observed when the child was a toddler and then again at pre-school age. The mothers and the children were graded on their mutual responsiveness. The children also were graded on their internalization of their mothers' values. Kochanska found that internalization of values varies directly with mutual responsiveness. She implicitly assumes that mutual responsiveness between mothers and children is independent of their personalities. Her results don't establish that parenting inculcates values in children. They may simply show that children who approve of their mothers' values happen to be more open to mutual responsiveness in the first place. Causality isn't established, because Kochanska doesn't try to identify the causal effect of parenting on the development of the moral conscience of the child. Indeed, she seems to be unaware that there is an identification problem. In the second of Kochanska's studies, 58 mother-toddler dyads were observed. The toddlers were graded on their fearfulness, and their mothers were graded on their discipline style. Between the ages of 8 and 10 years, the children's consciences were assessed. Kochanska found that among fearful children less disciplinary parenting promotes the development of moral conscience. Kochanska implicitly assumes that the disciplinary style of parents is independent of the temerity of their children. If parents happen to be softer with their more timorous children, it might simply be the case that timorous children have more developed consciences, and, in addition, their parents happen to behave more gently toward them. The children's consciences have nothing to do with parenting, but parenting has much to do with the children's personalities.

The evidence that Maccoby highlights in defense of developmental psychology is far from the smoking-gun variety. In fact it is methodologically weak. It systematically confuses correlation and predictability with causality. The overall impression is that empirical standards in developmental psychology are very lax. What passes for a causal effect in developmental psychology would not be accepted outside the discipline.

6.1.5 Parenting, Family, and Schooling

I showed in chapter 2 that schooling is correlated intergenerationally. I also showed that IQ is correlated intergenerationally. Therefore, the intergenerational correlation in schooling might simply be induced by heredity in IQ. Since more intelligent people acquire schooling more easily, we naturally expect that IQ be positively correlated with schooling. Gould (2005) used data for 1978 from the National Longitudinal Survey on 1,555 young men, which included the IQ test scores reported on high school transcripts. Gould also used data on 1,318 men from the National Longitudinal Survey of Youth, which included data for 1992 on AQFT test scores used by the US military as a measure of IQ. Although Gould's main purpose was to show that wage inequality has little to do with inequality in IQ, his results imply that IQ has a positive effect on schooling.[19] Because intelligence is inherited, correlation is induced between the schooling of parents and that of children. Heredity may have something to do with the intergenerational correlation in schooling. Do parents have any influence on the schooling of their children, in addition to or despite the contribution of heredity?

According to the Quality vs. Quantity Theory (discussed in chapter 3), parents determine their children's schooling. In this subsection I review the evidence regarding the effects of parenting on the educational outcomes of their children. Several interwoven issues are involved here. The first concerns the relationship between sibship and schooling. It is well known that sibship and schooling vary inversely with each other. However, this does not mean that sibship has a causal effect on schooling. Indeed, according to the QQT sibship and schooling are joint decisions made by parents, who trade off quality and quantity. The QQT predicts that on the whole parents who have more children invest less in the education of each child. Therefore, sibship and schooling should be negatively correlated, which they are.

However, several studies establish that this negative correlation disappears when account is taken of the determinants of sibship. Guo and VanWey (1999) use National Longitudinal Survey of Youth data for 1986 and 1992 to show that schooling achievement in the United States varies inversely with sibship. However, they use the difference-in-differences (DID) methodology to identify the causal effect of sibship on school achievement and to show that the change in schooling achievement between 1986 and 1992 is unrelated to sibship. They conclude from this that there is no causal effect of sibship on intellectual development, and that the negative correlation between schooling achievement and sibship is not causal. Strictly speaking, Guo and VanWey find that changes in pedagogic achievement aren't causally affected by sibship, but this doesn't necessarily rule out that sibship adversely affects the level of pedagogic achievement.

Black et al. (2006) show that in Norway, as elsewhere, schooling and sibship vary inversely with each other. Their sample includes all Norwegians over the age of 25 in 2000—nearly 1.5 million. They use the methodology of natural experimentation to identify the causal effect of sibship on schooling. First, they use twin births as an exogenous or random source of family size. They show that twin births increase sibship by 0.7–0.8, and this effect is very statistically significant. However, this exogenous variation in sibship has no effect on schooling. Another natural experiment is based on the idea that parents prefer to have children of both sexes. If their first two children happen to be of the same sex, they are more likely to have a third child. Since the sex of the second child is random, it serves as a source of exogenous variation in sibship. Indeed, Black et al. show that if the sex of the second child is the same as that of the first child, this turns out to increase sibship by 0.09 and is highly significant. This exogenous variation in sibship turns the negative relationship between schooling and sibship into a positive one! A third natural experiment is based on birth order. Since children cannot determine their birth order, it is entirely random from their point of view. Black et al. show that schooling varies inversely with birth order even after allowing for family fixed effects. They also show that the causal effect of sibship on schooling is 0 once birth order is taken into consideration.

Angrist et al. (2010) report similar findings for Israel. They too randomize sibship by twin births and the sex pattern of births. They also show that sex patterns matter for higher-order births because there is a preference for boys over girls, as I noted in Beenstock 2007. In Israel as elsewhere, sibship and schooling vary inversely with each other. However, Angrist et al. conclude that this effect is not causal; the instrumental-variables estimate of sibship on schooling is 0. Nor do they find that sibship has a causal effect on labor-market outcomes.

These results seem puzzling. On the one hand, the negative correlation between sibship and schooling seems to support the QQT. On the other hand, when sibship is randomized the QQT is rejected. The results imply that sibship and ability are negatively correlated.[20] The QQT predicts that fertility varies inversely with ability (Beenstock 2007). This prediction is supported by the negative correlation between ability and schooling. Therefore, fertility varies inversely with ability, but sibship has no effect on schooling. Quality adversely affects quantity, but quantity doesn't affect quality. The QQT is a one-way street.

We saw how Behrman and Rosenzweig (2004) used data on birth-weight differences of MZ twins to identify the causal effect of birth weight on developmental outcomes. They applied the same idea (Behrman and Rosenzweig 2002) to identify the causal effect of mothers' schooling on the schooling of their children. The main research question here is: Does the schooling of mothers increase their children's schooling? There are two causal channels involved. First, if mothers are more educated they might be able to help their children at school. In terms of the QQT, this reduces the investment cost of education, which according to the discussion in chapter 3, increases the demand for schooling among children. Second, role-model theory predicts that the demand for schooling increases among children who wish to emulate their more educated parents. Behrman and Rosenzweig assume that the schooling differences between MZ-twin mothers, like birth-weight differences, are randomly chosen by nature, and therefore have nothing to do with the unobserved ability of mothers. Behrman and Rosenzweig treat these schooling differences as if they were generated in a laboratory experiment, but of course the experiment in this case is natural.

Whereas this might be persuasive in the case of birth weight, matters are very different in the case of schooling because it ignores epigenetic drift. Differences in schooling, unlike differences in birth weight, aren't simply determined by nature. They also depend on the behavior of the MZ twins' mothers as well as their fathers. One twin might be more competitive than the other, and acquire more schooling. Parents might invest more in one twin than in the other. In short, MZ twins aren't identical, even if they happen to be genetically identical. Epigenetic drift has no time to manifest at birth; however, by the time schooling is completed, sufficient time has transpired for epigenetic drift to express itself.

Using data from the Minnesota Twin Registry, Behrman and Rosenzweig find that the positive correlation of the mothers' schooling with their children's schooling disappears once account is taken of the fact that the mothers are MZ twins. Specifically, there is no positive correlation between the schooling differences of MZ mothers and the schooling differences of their children. This suggests that the observed positive correlation is entirely due to heredity and there is no causal effect of mothers' schooling on the schooling of their children. Matters are different, however, in the case of MZ fathers; there is a positive causal effect of fathers' schooling on the schooling of their children.

Behrman and Rosenzweig's methodology has been applied in various other countries, with largely similar results. Holmlund et al. (2008) report similar results for Norwegian twins, and Bingley et al. (2009) for Danish twins.[21] Since these studies ignore epigenetic drift, it is difficult to categorize them as smoking-gun evidence. If the differences in schooling of MZ-twin parents are also induced by unobserved environmental effects, such as neighborhoods, and the environments of parents and children happen to be correlated, these estimates will be biased and the causal effect of parents' schooling on their children's schooling will not be identified. In terms of equation 5, v_2 does not equal v_1, in which case b and w are not generally independent. In short, although unobserved genotype effects may be "differenced away," the same doesn't apply to environmental effects, unless they happen to be identical. If they aren't identical, the unshared environments of MZ parents may be correlated with the unshared environments of their children.

The same, incidentally, applies to numerous studies involving adoptees[22] in which it is heroically assumed that adoptees are randomly assigned to parents. In short, as was discussed in greater methodological detail in chapter 5, studies based on adoption are riddled with selection biases of various kinds. It is for this reason that I don't discuss them in any detail here.

Another methodology for identifying the causal effect of parents' schooling on the schooling of their children involves natural experimentation. For example, an educational reform, such as an increase in the age at which a student is required to attend school, increases parents' post-reform schooling. This natural experiment revolves around the question whether the children of pre-reform parents obtained less schooling than the children of post-reform parents. If so, this suggests a causal effect of parents' schooling on the schooling of their children. For example, Oreopoulos et al. (2006) studied the effects of compulsory-schooling laws in the United States, which varied by state. They found that the effect of the legislation was limited to a reduction in the probability of grade repetition.[23]

Whereas most of the previous investigators tend to conclude that the intergenerational correlation for education has little to do with nurture and is mostly induced by nature, the opposite conclusion is reached by Gould and Simhon (2011). Their basic idea is that the death of a parent provides an opportunity to distinguish between intergenerational correlations induced by nature rather than nurture. If mothers die in childbirth, any correlation between them and their children must be due to nature, because the mothers did not survive to nurture their orphaned child. If, however, the intergenerational correlation for such orphaned children is zero, the intergenerational correlation for non-orphaned children must be induced by nurture rather than nature.

The logic behind this argument is the same as the logic of behavioral genetics, in which comparisons are made between MZ and DZ twins and biosibs and adopted siblings. For children orphaned at birth, the correlation with their parents has to be genetic. Indeed, it is surprising that the study of orphans doesn't feature as one of the methodological work horses in behavioral genetics.

In chapter 10 the methodological criticisms of behavioral genetics are extended to the case of orphans. For example, the equal-environments assumption (EEA) is unlikely to apply to orphans and non-orphans, just as it is unlikely to apply to MZ and DZ twins or to biosibs and adopted siblings. Orphans may suffer from trauma, or society might relate to orphans differently, or orphaned siblings may relate to each other differently from other siblings. Surviving spouses might relate to their children differently than other parents either because they remarry or because they are single parents. Furthermore, orphans might be genetically less fit than other children because they inherit the genes that were responsible for the premature deaths of their parents.

Gould and Simhon modify Galton's AR model as follows:

$$Y_{ci} = \alpha + D_i \{ \delta + \beta_m Y_{mi} + \beta_f Y_{fi} + \theta_m A_i Y_{mi} + \theta_f A_i Y_{fi} + \gamma A_i \}$$
$$+ \beta_M Y_{mi} + \beta_F Y_{fi} + u_i, \tag{9}$$

where subscripts m and f refer to mothers and fathers respectively, A denotes the child's age when its mother died, and D is a zero-one dummy variable equal to 1 if the mother died before her child reached a certain age ($A^* = 18$ years). For children whose mothers did not die before they were aged A^*, beta for mothers and beta for fathers are denoted by β_M and β_F respectively. $A = 0$ if the mother dies in childbirth. In this case, beta for mothers is $\beta_m + \beta_M$ and beta for fathers is $\beta_f + \beta_F$. For children whose mother died up to age A^*, beta for mothers is $\beta_m + \beta_M + \theta_m$ and beta for fathers is $\beta_f + \beta_F + \theta_f$. If A is greater than A^* the mother lived long enough to nurture her child. In this case, beta for mothers is β_M and beta for fathers is β_F. If nurture by mothers matters, θ_m is expected to be positive. If fathers engage in more nurturing after the death of their wife or partner, θ_f is expected to be negative. In this case, fathers try to make up for the loss of nurturing due to the death of their wife, or children seek compensatory nurturing from their father.

The parameters δ and γ in equation 9 are intended to capture potential traumatic effects on the outcome of the child due to the loss of the mother. The traumatic effect is hypothesized to depend upon the age at which the child was bereaved and is equal to $\delta + \gamma A$. If the child is bereaved at birth, the traumatic effect equals δ. Equation 9 is specified if mothers die. It has a counterpart if fathers die.

Gould and Simhon use data on some 12,500 Jewish children in Israel whose mother or father died during the period 1974–1986 before the children were 18 years old. The outcome variable for children (Y_c) is their high school matriculation status, defined as a zero-one dummy variable, and Y_m and Y_f are represented by the years of schooling of mothers and fathers. The matriculation exam takes place in the eleventh and twelfth grades, when the child is typically about 18 years old. Gould and Simhon control for environmental variables by specifying school fixed effects. Other controls include mother's and father's age at the time of the child's birth, gender, number of siblings, birth order, and birth cohort. Equation 9 and its counterpart for fathers are estimated by the OLS method. The main results (based on model 6 in table 4 of Gould and Simhon 2011) are the following:

(i) $\beta_f = 0$. The child's matriculation status does not depend on its mother's years of schooling if she died in childbirth.

(ii) $\theta_f > 0$. The longer the mother survives, the stronger is the relationship between matriculation status and mother's schooling.

(iii) $\beta_m > 0$. The child's matriculation status varies directly with father's schooling if his wife died in childbirth.

(iv) $\theta_m < 0$. The relationship between matriculation status and father's schooling varies inversely with the age at which his child lost its mother.

(v) $\delta > 0$. Children orphaned before they are 18 years old are more likely than other children to matriculate.

(vi) $\gamma < 0$. The previous effect varies inversely with the age at which the child was orphaned. This means that children orphaned as teenagers are less likely to matriculate than other children.

(vii) Approximately symmetrical effects are obtained for children who lose fathers. However, mothers do not substitute for fathers' lost nurturing.

Results i and ii suggest that the observed relationship between matriculation status and mother's schooling is related to nurture rather than nature. Otherwise, why should β_f be zero and θ_f be positive?

Results iii and iv suggest that fathers nurture more if their spouse dies; they try to make up for the lost nurturing of mothers. However, because $\theta_f = 0.002$ and $\theta_m = -0.001$, fathers make up only half the lost nurturing of deceased mothers. Another way of looking at these results is that fathers nurture less if their spouses survive.

Results v and vi imply that the traumatic effect of losing a mother is only adverse if she dies when the child was a teenager. This traumatic effect is greatest, not surprisingly, if she died just before her child was about to take the matriculation exam.

Table 6.2 shows that for children who are not bereaved beta for mothers and fathers are respectively 0.0209 and 0.0185. This means that an extra years' schooling for parents increases the probability of matriculation by 0.0209 in the case of mothers and 0.0185 in the case of fathers. However, if mothers die in childbirth their beta is almost zero. Beta for fathers increases in this case from 0.0185 to 0.0319. Table 6.2 shows that the longer mothers survive, the greater is their beta, but the lower is beta for fathers. If they survive until the matriculation exam (at aged 18) their beta increases to 0.036, while beta for fathers falls to 0.0139.

Given everything else, if mothers die in childbirth, the trauma effect is 0.1859—that is, the probability of matriculation increases very

Table 6.2
Effect of bereavement on beta. Based on Gould and Simhon 2011 (table 4 model 6 for mothers, table 14 model 6 for fathers).

Death of	β mother		β father		Trauma effect	
	Mother	Father	Mother	Father	Mother	Father
Not bereaved	0.0209	0.0209	0.0185	0.0185	n.a.	n.a.
Age 0	–0.0065	0.0209	0.0319	0.0064	0.1859	0.0769
Age 5	0.0035	0.0209	0.0269	0.0094	0.1069	0.0459
Age 10	0.0135	0.0209	0.0219	0.0124	0.0279	0.0149
Age 15	0.0235	0.0209	0.0169	0.0154	–0.0511	–0.0161
Age 18	0.036	0.0209	0.0139	0.0172	–0.0985	–0.0347

substantially. However, this effect eventually turns negative if mothers die when their children are teenagers. If mothers die when their child is about to take the matriculation exam the probability of matriculation is reduced by 0.0985.

If fathers die, beta for mothers is not affected. However, beta for fathers is zero if the child is bereaved at birth. The longer fathers survive the greater is their beta. However, this increase is less for fathers than for mothers. The same applies to traumatic effects, which are also half the size of their counterparts for mothers. These results suggest that for beta and traumatic effects mothers are more important than fathers.

Gould and Simhon admit that the parameters of equation 9 are not identified, for all the usual reasons (see chapter 5). In equation 9 the residual (u) is likely to be positively correlated with Y_f and Y_m if abler parents have abler children. Also, A in equation 9 will be positively correlated with u if fitter parents survive longer, and fitness and ability are positively correlated. One might asked, therefore, why bother to highlight their findings here? The answer lies in the curious result that θ_f is positive and θ_m is negative, which strongly suggests that surviving parents try to compensate for the nurturing of their dead spouse. This pattern is arguably too much of a coincidence. There is no genetic interpretation for this result, but there is an obvious behavioral one. Also, it is difficult to think of omitted unobserved variables, such as ability or fitness, that could account for this curious coincidence.

Some of my own research on this topic has involved the causal effect of parents' schooling on the schooling of their children in Israel. As I emphasized in chapter 5, identifying this effect and related causal effects would be much easier if data on the genotypes of parents and children were available. If such data were available, they could be used as covariates to control for the effect of genotypes on outcomes of interest. For example, in equation 1, v represented unobserved genotypes. Because we suspected that birth weight and v are not independent, the causal effect of birth weight on the outcomes (β) wasn't identified. Had data been available for v, it would have been specified alongside birth weight in equation 1. Consequently, the regression residual (u) would equal e, which is independent of both birth weight and v. In this case, β would have been identified, as well as the effect of genotype (v).

The problem, of course, is that genotype data aren't available. Suppose, however, that they could be proxied or generated in a convincing fashion. In the example above, v is unknown but there is a convincing proxy for v. Proxies, by definition, contain measurement error; therefore, the proxy for v is a noisy measure of true v. If the proxy is an unbiased estimate of v, the generated-regressor theorem described in chapters 5 and 10 states that the proxy may be used instead of the real thing. Indeed, even if the proxy is biased, it is possible to correct the bias.[24] The clock that runs five minutes slow may still be worth using provided you know that it is usually five minutes behind.

Israel's Central Bureau of Statistics has matched census data on parents in 1983 to their children in 1995. In 1983 the children were living in their parents' households. By 1995 these children were 12 years older. The youngest children in 1983 were still living as teenagers in their parents' households in 1995. However, the teenagers of 1983 were young adults in 1995. They had completed their education, and many of them were working. I proxied parent genotypes as follows: I estimated standard wage regressions for parents using cross-section data from the 1983 census in Israel (Beenstock 2010a). Apart from years of schooling, age, and sex, the covariates include continent of origin for first-generation and second-generation immigrants and years since immigration. The covariates also include dummy variables for non-Jews and ultra-orthodox Jews. The residuals from this regression reflect unobserved ability, or earnings genotypes. The R^2 is 0.33, which is quite standard and which implies that two-thirds of the wage inequality is due to inequality in unobserved ability. Apart from this, the model indicates that the return to a year's schooling is 9.9 percent, the age curve is ∩-shaped, men earn more than women, Jews earns more than non-Jews, ultra-orthodox Jews earn less than other Jews, European immigrants earn more, and immigrants from Asia and Africa earn the least.

I also estimated schooling regressions for parents (represented by heads of households), controlling for a range of demographic variables, among them birth cohort, sex, and continent of origin. The residual from this regression reflects learning genotype. R^2 is 0.216, which implies that nearly 80 percent of schooling inequality is induced by inequality in learning ability. The distributions of these proxies for earning ability and learning ability turn out to be non-normal; there is excess kurtosis (fat tails), especially in schooling, and the distributions are skewed to the left (that is, the mean is greater than the mode).

I use these proxies as controls in schooling and earnings regressions for children in 1995. Some of the results are shown here in table 6.3. The elasticity of children's schooling with respect to their parents' schooling is 0.081, meaning that a 1 percent increase in parents' schooling causes an increase in children's schooling of 0.081 percent. This causal effect may be small, but its t statistic is large: 7.95. The effect is causal because these estimates control for the two proxies for learning ability and earning ability, which are statistically significant. Without these controls the estimates reported in table 6.3 would not have been identified, because unobserved genotypes for parents would have been correlated with parents' schooling. The causal elasticity of children's schooling with respect to their parents' earnings is estimated at 0.059. Therefore, better-off parents can afford to buy their children more schooling.

Table 6.3
The causal effect of parents' schooling on children' schooling in Israel: Generated-regressor methodology. Source: Beenstock 2008, tables 7 and 8. All estimates are statistically significant at $p < 0.05$ except youngest of four.

	Schooling (log)	Earnings (log)
Male	−0.044	0.364
Non-Jew	−0.059	
Singleton	0.018	
Elder of two	0.017	
Eldest of three	0.019	
Youngest of four	−0.047	
Parents' schooling (log)	0.081	
Parents' earnings (log)	0.059	
Children's schooling		0.115
N	12,173	12,173
R^2	0.2535	0.3506

Among the other interesting results in table 6.3 are that boys get 4.4 percent less schooling than girls, that non-Jews get 5.9 percent less schooling than Jews, and that first-borns get about 1.8 percent more schooling than other siblings. The youngest child in a family of four gets 4.7 percent less schooling than older siblings, but the t statistic for this effect is only 1.1. There is a first-born advantage in schooling, but otherwise birth order does not seem to matter. The return to schooling is 11.5 percent, which is slightly high by international standards. Males earn much more than females. The gender wage gap is unusually large because in 1995 the children were young. Since they were matched to their parents' households in 1983, in 1995 the oldest adult children were only in their early thirties.

Table 6.3 indicates that there is a causal effect of parents' schooling and income on the schooling of their children. Since children's wages in 1995 vary directly with their schooling, there is an indirect causal mechanism between parents schooling and income and the earnings of their children. Children are thrice blessed by more educated parents. First, there is a direct causal effect of parents' education on their children's education. Second, the earnings of more educated parents are larger, which also has a direct causal effect on children's schooling. Third, the causal return to children's schooling on their earnings is 11.5 percent.

It was noted in table 2.3 that the intergenerational correlation for schooling in Israel is about 0.29. The causal component of this according to table 6.3 is of the order of about 0.17.[25] Therefore, parenting accounts for about half of the intergenerational correlation in schooling. The balance is accounted for by heredity and environmental effects. It was noted in table 2.4 that the intergenerational correlation in earnings in Israel is between 0.14 and 0.4. The causal component of this due to parenting, discussed in the previous paragraph, is small largely because the variance of schooling explains only about 1.3 percent of the variance of the logarithm of earnings.[26]

Using the same proxies for unobserved earning and learning genotypes to represent ability, I find that abler parents tend to be less fertile (Beenstock 2007). Table 6.4 reports results obtained using data from the censuses of 1983 and 1995. Two sets of results are reported. The first (household heads) controls for the ability of the head of household. The second (couples) controls for the ability of the head of household and his or her spouse. Typically, but not always, the head of household is a man.

The first result in table 6.4 for household heads shows that according to the census data of 1983, women in households with abler household

Table 6.4

Effect of ability on fertility in Israel. Source: Beenstock 2007, p. 446. This table shows Poisson regression coefficients in which the dependent variable is the number of children born to the female in the household. Other covariates include schooling, income, years married, remaining years of fertility, and ethnic status. Absolute t statistics are in parentheses.

	1983 census		1995 census	
	Household heads	Couples	Household heads	Couples
Ability of household head	−0.253 (4.42)	−0.014 (1.97)	−0.008 (1.95)	−0.009 (1.92)
Ability of spouse		−0.042 (4.79)		0.0 (0.06)
Observations	33,849	23,614	68,069	64,653

heads tended to have fewer children. Since ability as measured by the generated-regressor methodology is measured in logarithms, the coefficient of −0.253 has the dimension of an elasticity. This means that if the ability of the head of household increases by 1 percent, the fertility of the female in the household decreases by a quarter percent. Recall that this effect takes account of the fact that abler household heads may be married to more educated spouses, who marry later and consequently have fewer children. Therefore, the effects reported in table 6.4 hold all other factors constant.

The second result in table 6.4 for couples is based on data from the 1983 census and controls for the ability of spouses as well as that of household heads. The number of observations falls to 23,614 because it isn't always possible to apply the generated-regressor methodology to couples. The effects of both couples' ability on fertility are negative. The effect of the spouse's ability detracts from the statistical significance of the effect of the household head's ability. As noted above, there is assortative mating in terms of ability, which induces colinearity in the ability of couples. This result suggests that what really matters is the ability of the spouse (usually the wife), rather than the ability of the household head (usually the husband). However, the household head's ability seems to matter too.[27] Therefore, the results so far lend support to the QQT, which predicts that abler parents have fewer children because they wish to invest more in the education of their children, who they expect will be abler like themselves.

Finally, table 6.4 shows that when the same models are estimated using data from the 1995 census, the evidence that fertility varies inversely with ability is much weaker. The coefficients on the ability of household heads continue to be negative, but they are smaller and less statistically significant than their counterparts from the 1983 census.

6.1.6 Income

In chapter 2 we saw that incomes are correlated intergenerationally. According to the model in the previous subsection, this happens for three reasons. First, there is the causal effect of parenting. Better-off parents can afford to buy more schooling for their children, who subsequently earn more because more human capital has been invested in them. Second, there is a genetic effect. Abler parents have, on average, abler children. Since abler workers have higher productivity and therefore earn more, this channel induces correlation between the incomes of parents and their children. Third, there is a contextual channel of correlation induced by ethnicity. Since earnings and schooling depend on the individual's continent of origin as well as on his or her father's continent of origin, the earnings and the schooling of first-generation immigrants are correlated with the earnings and the schooling of second-generation immigrants. In immigrant societies, such as Israel, this third channel is particularly important. However, as we saw, the first channel—the effect of parental investments in their children's schooling—accounts for only a small part of the correlation between the incomes of parents and their children.

Mayer (1997) has investigated the effects of parents' income on the outcomes of their children, including the children's incomes, in the United States. On the whole, she concludes that it pays to have better-off parents. One shortcoming of Mayer's work is that she didn't control for the unobserved ability of parents, which might be correlated with the unobserved ability of their children. Therefore, the correlation between the outcomes of children with their parents' money might simply be induced by heredity. Abler parents are better off, so their children are better off because they too are abler. To check this, Shea (2000) used data on 3,033 children and their 1,271 fathers from the Panel Study on Income Dynamics to investigate the causal relationship between parents' income and the income and schooling of their children. The latter variables are highly correlated with parents' income, as noted in chapter 2, but of course this may not be causal. To test for causality, Shea used an instrumental-variables design in which the instruments include whether the parents were members of a trade union, the wage premium in the industry in which they worked, and whether or not they were involuntarily laid off through plant closures. Since union members tend to have higher wages, trade union status of parents would serve as an instrumental variable if union status of their children is independent of that of their parents. As Shea points out, however, these instrumental variables are correlated intergeneration- ally, so they are imperfect instruments. To overcome this, he deducts from children's earnings the wage premium attributable to their trade union status and their industry. These instrumental variables wipe out the correlation between parents' income and the income and schooling of their children. This means that there is no causal effect, according to Shea, of parents' income on the incomes and schooling of their children. Therefore, parents' money doesn't matter after all. If that is so, why are children's incomes and schooling correlated with their parents' income? The technical answer lies in heredity or in unobserved environments shared by parents and children, which induce correlation between the outcomes of parents and children. The substantive answer is that if the capital market is perfect, parents' money shouldn't matter for school- ing, since parents can borrow to finance their children's education and older children can borrow to finance their own educations.[28]

Shea's finding that parents' money doesn't matter at all conflicts with my results, which show that parents' money matters modestly. It may be the case that what is true for the United States is not true for Israel and vice versa. The capital market may function better in the United States than in Israel, so that parents' money matters in Israel, but not in the US. Several recent adoption studies (Plug and Vijverberg 2003; Plug 2004 and 2006; Sacerdote 2002, 2007) support Shea's finding that there is no causal effect of parenting on their children's schooling and earnings. As I have mentioned repeatedly, adoption studies are methodologically problematic. Therefore, we might discount this evi- dence that parents' money doesn't matter. The fact that the intergenera- tional correlation for adopted children is 0, whereas that for biological children is positive, doesn't establish that parenting doesn't matter. It may simply mean that adopted children are negatively selected, that the interactions between adopted and biological children are different, or that parents relate to their adopted children differently than they relate to their biological children.

6.1.7   Other Outcomes

A variety of phenotypes have been considered that are causally affected by parenting. However, numerous outcomes mentioned in chapter 2 that are intergenerationally correlated have not been discussed here. These include fertility, longevity, criminality, IQ, health, bad habits, personality, and religiosity. The reason they haven't been discussed is there has been no serious research on the effect of parenting on these outcomes. For example, the intergenerational correlations for deviant behavior reported in table 2.10 are fascinating, but criminologists and sociologists haven't attempted to disentangle the causal effects of parenting, heredity, and environments. Perhaps there is a gene for deviant behavior, or perhaps the environment is to blame and parenting has no effect. The same applies to the other phenomena that I have not discussed.

6.2   Environmental and Peer Effects

Empirical knowledge of the causal effects of environments on outcomes is even weaker and patchier than empirical knowledge of the causal effect of parenting. Social psychologists are quick to claim that peer-group effects are powerful and widespread, but they haven't been able to identify such effects empirically. In light of the dismal state of empirical research in developmental psychology, perhaps Harris (2006) was right to reject the empirical claims of developmental psychologists that parenting matters. Parenting might matter, but not on the basis of the evidence brought by developmental psychologists. On the other hand, Harris' claim that peer-groups play a major role in personality development is based on no serious research at all. That a teenage boy happens to behave similarly to his peers doesn't mean that there is a causal effect from the peer group to the individual member of the group. It doesn't mean that if the teenager had a different peer group with different behavioral norms and values he would have behaved differently. It might simply be that individuals choose groups that appeal to them, and that correlations with peers reflect self-selection rather than causality.

The basic methodological problem, discussed in chapter 5, is the reflection problem, so called because the peer group may be a reflection of its members. Teenagers, and adults too, choose their peer groups; they select the groups that best suit them. Or, like Groucho Marx, they reject groups or clubs that are willing to accept them. In short, it cannot be assumed that peer groups are randomly assigned to their individual members, just as it cannot be taken for granted that adoptees are randomly assigned to their adoptive parents.

If our peer groups are reflections of ourselves, how can we identify the causal effect of peer groups, or that of neighborhoods? In a laboratory experiment, we would randomly assign individuals to peer groups and then compare the outcomes of the control subjects and the trial subjects. Since such experiments aren't feasible, perhaps natural experiments are available in which peer-group membership is randomized spontaneously with respect to the outcome of interest.

I have selected a number of interesting natural experiments that, in different ways, illustrate the causal effects of environments on various outcomes. Although most of these studies have nothing to do with economics, their authors are labor economists. Maybe this is a hopeful sign that interdisciplinary boundaries are at last being breached.

6.2.1 Subsidized Housing Programs

In the past 10 years, labor economists have used the methodology of natural experimentation or quasi-experimentation to investigate the causal effect of environments or peer groups on a variety of different outcomes. These experiments fall into two groups: experiments that focus on subsidized housing programs for the poor and experiments that focus on the initial location of immigrants.

The Moving to Opportunity (MTO) Program, sponsored by the US Department of Housing and Urban Development, has been in operation since 1994 in Baltimore, Boston, Chicago, Los Angeles, and New York. Eligible families must have low incomes and live in high-poverty census tracts. Applicants are randomly rejected. Successful applicants are given vouchers to rent housing. The successful applicants are randomized into two groups. The first may use their voucher unrestrictedly. The second may use their voucher in "good" neighborhoods, i.e., housing tracts with poverty rates less than 10 percent in 1990. Between 1994 and 1997, about 4,600 mainly black families volunteered for MTO.

MTO is a quasi-experiment because individuals choose whether to volunteer and, if they get a voucher, whether to use it. A volunteer who receives a voucher to live in a "good" neighborhood might nevertheless find that using it is too expensive. Comparing the outcomes of volunteers who moved to "good" neighborhoods with those who remained in poor neighborhoods sheds light on the causal effect of neighborhoods.

Kling et al. (2005) obtained data from administrative records for arrests and delinquency among children of MTO volunteers. They found that, especially in the case of adolescent girls, crime and

Table 6.5
Causal effect of "good" neighborhoods (GN) on deviancy. Source: Kling et al. 2005, p. 100.

	Age	Comparison	Males	Females
Arrests	15–25	GN vs. control	0.391	–0.545
Arrests	15–25	Voucher vs. control	0.138	–0.024
Delinquency	15–20	GN vs. control	0.005	–0.016
Delinquency	15–20	Voucher vs. control	0.025	–0.008
Problem behavior	15–20	GN vs. control	0.160	–0.039
Problem behavior	15–20	Voucher vs. control	0.060	–0.015

delinquency rates were lower among the families that moved to "good" neighborhoods. Table 6.5, which summarizes the estimated causal effects, is based on comparisons between families that were offered restricted vouchers and families that were offered no voucher at all ("good" neighborhood vs. control) and between families that were offered unrestricted vouchers and families that were offered no voucher at all (voucher vs. control). The causal effect is expected to be larger in the former case than in the latter, because unrestricted voucher recipients aren't required to move to "good" neighborhoods (GN).

The estimated causal effects shown in table 6.5 are consistently negative for females and, as expected, are larger in absolute value for GN vs. control comparisons than they are for voucher vs. control comparisons. However, only one of these effects turns out to be statistically significant. In the case of males, the estimated causal effects of neighborhoods are positive, but only one of these is statistically significant. Moving from "bad" to "better" neighborhoods reduces criminal behavior among girls[29] and increases problem behavior among boys. Despite their claim to the contrary, Kling et al.'s results do not clearly establish the empirical importance of neighborhood effects, since the majority of anti-social outcomes aren't significantly affected by the MTO program.

Whereas MTO is a quasi-experiment, the Metro Toronto Housing Corporation (MTHC) has provided an opportunity for a natural experiment. MTHC provides public housing located across Toronto. Until 1995 applicants for MTHC housing were selected on the basis of a socioeconomic points system. Eligible applicants joined a waiting list. When they eventually reached the top of the list they were offered the first available unit with the correct number of bedrooms. They could refuse the offer once. If they refused the second offer they were removed from the list. Most applicants accepted the first offer. In this way applicants were randomly assigned to neighborhoods. Presumably there are many local authorities that operate public housing schemes, such as MTHC, in which applicants are randomly assigned to neighborhoods.

That MTHC assigned a family to a specific neighborhood doesn't necessarily mean that the family remained in that neighborhood. Families are always at liberty to move elsewhere if they find the MTHC housing sufficiently unattractive. However, if they move they forfeit the MTHC housing subsidy. Therefore, compliance is partial. Oreopoulos (2003) used administrative data records to match adults who were between 29 and 36 years old in 1999 to MTHC housing projects. These matches consist of individuals who as children moved with their family into MTHC housing. The most interesting outcome is their earnings. Did children who randomly moved to better neighborhoods through MTHC earn more as adults? The answer is No. There is no difference in the average earnings during 1997–1999 of MTHC beneficiaries who were assigned to "good" neighborhoods and the earnings of their MTHC counterparts who were assigned to "bad" neighborhoods. This is true whether or not controls are specified for family background, such as sibship, and for pre-MTHC neighborhood quality.[30]

Interestingly, however, the earnings of demographically similar individuals living in "good" neighborhoods were about 25 percent higher than the earnings of their counterparts from "bad" neighborhoods. Naive social psychologists might claim that this constitutes evidence of powerful neighborhood effects. However, this illusion results entirely from selection bias in neighborhood choices. Individuals choose their neighborhoods. Oreopoulos' results imply that high-productivity workers choose to live in better neighborhoods. After controlling for selectivity, the apparent neighborhood effect vanishes completely.

The same applies to other outcomes apart from earnings. The probability of being on welfare is lower for demographically similar individuals living in better neighborhoods. Ostensibly, therefore, there is a favorable neighborhood effect on welfare-beneficiary status. However, this effect vanishes once neighborhoods are randomized in terms of MTHC status. The same is true of unemployment benefit. Taken together, the evidence from MTHC in Toronto and from MTO in the United States suggests that neighborhood effects aren't causal; they are the statistical reflections of the location choices of the individuals who live in these neighborhoods.

6.2.2   Immigrants

Since 1985, Sweden's Immigration Board has assigned refugees to an initial municipality of residence. At first, the idea was to prevent ethnic concentrations by distributing asylum seekers over the country as a whole, but with the growing number of asylum seekers, the Immigration Board increasingly placed refugees on the basis of housing availability. At first, asylum seekers were sent to refugee centers in various parts of Sweden. Some 3–12 months later, their refugee status was either confirmed or denied. If it was confirmed, the Immigration Board took account of the refugees' location preferences. Municipal officers skimmed off the refugees who were "best" in terms of qualifications, language skills, and other criteria. Therefore, refugees were assigned according to their observed characteristics. What is important here is that refugees didn't directly choose a municipality, especially if they were unqualified and didn't speak Swedish. Also, the Immigration Board didn't have personal contact with refugees, so assignment wasn't decided after a personal interview. Instead, faceless bureaucrats looked at refugees' papers and, with a stroke of a pen, assigned them to a certain municipality. Once assigned, refugees were provided with housing, social assistance, and courses in Swedish. Receipt of social assistance wasn't conditional on residing in the assigned municipality. Therefore, as far as the refugees themselves are concerned, they were randomly assigned to municipalities by the Immigration Board.

During 1987–1989, 3,094 refugees were placed in immigrant enclaves and 3,324 were placed in municipalities that did not have concentrations of immigrants. After 8 years in Sweden, nearly half of these refugees had left their assigned municipality. Therefore, there was substantial mobility, and compliance was imperfect. However, according to Edin et al. (2003) there is no correlation between observed characteristics, such as qualifications, and location. This was true for locations after 8 years in Sweden as well as for assigned municipalities. Edin et al. make the case that the initial assignment of refugees doesn't depend on their preferences.

Edin et al. investigate the causal neighborhood effect on earnings due to living in ethnic enclaves. Given a host of demographic controls, such as age, sex, family status, and country of origin, Edin et al. report that refugee earnings vary inversely with ethnic concentration in their neighborhood. On the face of it, residence in immigrant enclaves adversely affects refugee earnings. This negative effect is not, however, causal, because it takes no account of the way in which refugees choose where to live. If, for example, refugees lacking in self-confidence or ambition choose to live in immigrant enclaves, and earnings vary directly with self-confidence and ambition, this will induce a negative correlation between earnings and enclaves. Using the municipality of initial assignment as an instrumental variable, Edin et al. show that the causal effect is in fact positive, especially if refugees have less than 10 years of schooling and live in "quality" enclaves (enclaves where average incomes are high). This means that the negative correlation between ethnic concentration and earnings is overturned and becomes positive when initial municipality is treated as a natural experiment. If, indeed, refugees have no influence over their initial municipality, initial municipality serves to randomize the location of refugees. This natural experiment shows that refugees do better not worse in immigrant enclaves, especially for uneducated refugees living in high-income enclaves.

Ethiopian Jews trace their origins back to Menelik I, King of Ethiopia and son of King Solomon and the Queen of Sheba. In 1973 and 1975 the Chief Rabbis of Israel recognized Ethiopian Jews as one of the ten lost tribes, which gave them the right to immigrate to Israel. The first Ethiopian immigrants arrived in 1977 against a background of severe drought and civil strife in Ethiopia. Colonel Mengistu, a Marxist-Leninist, had deposed King Haile Selassie in 1974. Under Operation Moses, the Israeli government sought surreptitiously to bring all the Ethiopian Jews to Israel, either directly or indirectly via Sudan. After the operation was discovered, Mengistu broke off diplomatic relations with Israel, leaving about 20,000–30,000 Ethiopian Jews stranded in Sudan and Ethiopia. After the resumption of diplomatic relations in 1989, legal immigration from Ethiopia resumed.

On May 21, 1991, Mengistu was deposed in a coup and forced to flee Ethiopia. The Israeli government decided to exploit the chaos to airlift 14,000 Jews who remained in Ethiopia ("Operation Solomon"). Within 36 hours they were all airlifted to Israel. On arrival the immigrants were placed in immigrant absorption centers in various parts of the country. These placements were haphazard, and many were housed in mobile homes. Matters were exacerbated by the fact that in the early 1990s half a million immigrants had arrived from the former USSR. Gould et al. (2004) use Operation Solomon as a natural experiment, since the initial location of the immigrants had nothing to do with immigrants' locational preferences. Some were lucky and were located near good schools and in better-off neighborhoods; others were less lucky. Gould et al. investigate the long-term consequences of elementary school quality and neighborhood quality on high school outcomes of Ethiopian children who came to Israel under Operation Solomon. Elementary school quality is measured by average math and verbal scores in 1991; outcomes are measured by survival in high school. Neighborhood quality is measured by a socioeconomic index of the elementary school (based on average income and welfare dependency of pupils' parents), and matriculation rates in the neighborhood.

The main positive result is that Ethiopian children who initially attended an elementary schools that was strong in mathematics were more likely to attend a good high school and then to graduate.[31] Also, the probability of attending tenth grade varies directly with elementary school quality. This effect, however, is only marginally significant.[32] The probability of attending eleventh and twelfth grades is not affected by elementary school quality. Nor is the probability of matriculating[33] unless the elementary school was strong in math. Despite the authors' enthusiasm, only 7 out of 57 different tests are statistically significant, and their t statistics never exceed 2.33.

6.2.3   Roommates

At Dartmouth, a liberal-arts college in New Hampshire, freshmen have been allocated to dorms randomly since 1993. Roommates cannot choose each other and are randomly selected. Since this allocation process is entirely random, one would expect the grade-point averages of roommates to be uncorrelated, since roommates aren't sorted by ability or any other criterion. Sacerdote (2001), who controlled for ability using the SAT scores of 1,589 students graduating in 1997–98, as well as controlling for other background variables and dorm fixed effects, found that a student's freshman-year GPA varied directly with the roommate's GPA.[34] Because roommates are randomly assigned, Sacerdote interprets this as a causal peer-group effect. This is true despite the fact that choice of major is uncorrelated between room-mates. This suggests that the peer-group effect transcends disciplines, perhaps working through example or rivalry rather through knowl-edge spillovers.

Sacerdote also found that fraternity or sorority affiliations were cor-related between roommates and even between dorm-mates, which sug-gests that peer effects are social as well as pedagogic. Although these effects are marginally significant, their explanatory contribution is very small. For example, the contribution of peers to fraternity choice is of the order of 1 percent, whereas the contribution to freshman-year GPA is no more than a few percentage points. Therefore, these peer-group effects are modest and explain little of what is happening. In any case, the roommate effect on freshman-year GPA disappears by the senior year. Having a good roommate may make a difference in the first year, but it makes no difference by the senior year.[35]

6.3   Sibling Correlations

In chapter 4 it was shown that, because siblings share parents, genes, and environments, their outcomes are expected to be correlated. There-fore, most of the sibling correlation may be attributed to phenomena that we have already considered. In other words, having identified the effects of parents on their children, the effects of environments, and genetic effects, we may calculate what they imply for the sibling cor-relation. However, because siblings also share each other's company and interact with each other, the sibling correlation is not simply a derivative of the intergenerational correlation.

6.3.1   Imputing the Sibling Interaction Coefficient

In chapter 8 it is shown[36] that the sibling and intergenerational correla-tion coefficients are related as follows:

$$r_{cs} = b + (1-b)r_{cp}^2, \tag{9}$$

where r_{cs} denotes the sibling correlations, r_{cp} denotes the intergenera-tional correlation, and $b = 2\lambda/(1 - \lambda^2)^2$, with λ denoting the sibling interaction coefficient. Note that when $b = 0$ the sibling correlation is simply the square of the intergenerational correlation coefficient. In this case, the sibling correlation must be smaller than the intergenerational correlation coefficient.

Equation 9 can be used to calculate the sibling correlation under the assumption that the intergenerational correlation coefficient is 0.4. Results are reported in table 6.6. Note that the sibling correlation varies, as expected, with sibling interaction. If the sibling interaction is suffi-ciently strong, as in case 4, the sibling correlation exceeds the intergen-erational correlation. Roughly speaking, doubling the sibling interaction coefficient doubles the sibling correlation. In cases 5 and 6 the sibling interaction is negative rather than positive. The sibling correlation decreases as expected and eventually becomes negative.

Table 6.6
Relationship between sibling and intergenerational correlations. (The intergenerational correlation is 0.4.)

Case	b	Sibling correlation
1	0	0.16
2	0.05	0.244
3	0.1	0.326
4	0.2	0.483
5	–0.05	0.077
6	–0.1	–0.0063

The important new parameter that arises in the case of explaining the sibling correlation coefficient is the sibling interaction coefficient λ, since all other effects are subsumed in the intergenerational coefficient. This coefficient is rather like the roommate effect discussed above, except that, instead of referring to interactions between roommates, λ refers to interactions between siblings. Like roommates at Dartmouth, siblings are randomly assigned. From this point of view the prospects of identification might sound promising. On the other hand, siblings are correlated because they share parents, genes, and environments, whereas Dartmouth roommates aren't correlated. This makes identifying λ extremely difficult if not impossible. This probably explains why there is almost no empirical work on sibling interactions. In short, sibling interaction is a type of peer effect.

Estimating λ would require randomizing siblings in some way. In a hypothetical laboratory experiment, siblings would be placed at random in some families, and the outcomes of the treated families would be compared with the outcome of the controls (i.e., families in which siblings were not planted). Even in such a "cuckoo experiment" it would be difficult to identify λ, because these sibling cuckoos would affect incumbent children indirectly; e.g., parents would be less able to afford to invest in their education. Matters would be different in our hypothetical experiment if parents received money to cover the costs of the planted sibling. Perhaps something like this happened during World War II, when children evacuated from London and other blitzed cities were placed with foster families. I am not aware of any such studies, and in any case evacuation might not have been random. I have been unable to find a serious empirical investigation of sibling interaction in the literature. Of course there have been numerous studies of sibling correlations, many of which were reported and discussed in chapter 2 above. However, siblings might be correlated for many other reasons apart from sibling interaction. Therefore, these studies are not informative about sibling interaction, although their authors sometimes think otherwise.

In view of the difficulty of estimating and identifying the sibling interaction coefficient, it is tempting simply to impute b through reverse engineering. According to equation 9, b may be imputed, or "backed out," using information on the sibling and intergenerational correlation coefficients.[37] For example, according to case 4 in table 6.6, if the sibling correlation is 0.483 and the intergenerational correlation is 0.4, b must be equal to 0.384 according to equation 9, which means that λ is 0.18. In table 2.5 the sibling correlation between brothers for schooling in Israel is 0.42, whereas according to table 2.3 the intergenerational correlation between fathers and sons for schooling is 0.29. The imputed value of λ from equation 9 is 0.17 (case 1 in table 6.7). This means that if a child who happens to be more able acquires an additional year's schooling, his sibling's schooling increases by 17 percent of a year (about 2 months). This effect is essentially similar to the roommate effect. This effect is symmetrical, so having a less able sibling would reduce schooling by about 2 months.

Table 6.7 reports sibling interaction coefficients for other phenotypes based on sibling and intergenerational correlations reported in chapter 2. The third column provides the source in chapter 2. Case 2 refers to criminal convictions in London, where the sibling correlation slightly exceeds the intergenerational correlation. The implicit sibling interaction coefficient is 0.153. The sibling correlation exceeds its intergenerational counterpart for all the phenotypes in table 6.7; therefore, the sibling interaction must be positive according to equation 9. The sibling interaction coefficients vary between 0.083 and 0.187. In fact they are surprisingly similar except for extroversion. These results suggest that sibling interaction seems to be positive, which means that for benign outcomes it is preferable to have abler siblings.

Tempting though it may be to reverse-engineer the sibling interaction coefficient in this way, it should be recalled that equation 9 assumes that the only reason why the sibling correlation does not equal the square of the intergenerational correlation coefficient is the fact the that siblings interact with each other. In chapter 8 it is shown that the sibling correlation may differ from the square of the intergenerational correlation coefficient for other reasons. For example, if heredity matters, the sibling correlation will be larger than the square of the

Table 6.7
Implicit sibling interaction coefficients. (Since equation 53 in chapter 8 involves λ^4, the sibling interaction coefficient is an approximation.)

Case	Phenotype	Table	Location	Sibling correlation	Intergenerational correlation	Sibling interaction
1	Schooling	2.3, 2.5	Israel	0.42	0.29	0.170
2	Criminal convictions	2.10	London	0.47	0.43	0.153
3	Schooling	2.3, 2.5	Sweden	0.47	0.24	0.187
4	Earnings	2.4	US (PSID)	0.45	0.41	0.148
5	Extroversion	2.9		0.2	0.16	0.083

intergenerational correlation coefficient even if siblings do not inter-act.[38] The same applies if environments matter. Therefore, the difference between the sibling correlation and the square of the intergenerational correlation coefficient doesn't necessarily tell us anything about sibling interaction. It would do so only if strong identifying assumptions were made, namely that the intergenerational correlation is not induced by heredity and environments but it is induced only by the causal effect of parents' outcomes on the outcomes of their children. Since this is against the methodological spirit of my book, I must sadly abandon the estimates of the sibling interactions in table 6.7.

6.3.2 Structural Estimation of the Sibling Interaction Coefficient

I mentioned that I have been unable to find a single serious study of sibling interaction in the literature. This is not quite true; I tried to do so myself (Beenstock 2008). (I leave it to others to decide whether this amounts to a serious attempt.) In table 6.3 I reported some results for schooling and earnings in Israel in which the generated-regressor methodology was used to control for unobserved ability of parents. I suggest that the reader refer back to table 6.3 and the associated discussion of the generated-regressor methodology. Suppose, for argument's sake, that these results are fair and good.

The models for schooling and earnings were estimated using data from Israel on 12,173 young adults in 1995. It turns out that some of these young adults happened to be siblings. In fact, as many as 2,102 of them were siblings. This is no coincidence; the data are from the matched census file in which the censuses of 1983 and 1995 were matched. It was therefore possible to identify siblings in 1995 because their household in 1983 is known.

The residuals from the models reported in table 6.3 contain information on unobserved ability in schooling and earnings. Recall that the models in table 6.2 control for the unobserved ability of parents as represented by the generated regressors for parents' ability to learn and earn. Therefore, the residuals in table 6.3 reflect the uninherited ability of children. The abilities of siblings are expected to be correlated owing to heredity. However, uninherited ability is expected to be uncorrelated. This means that, in the absence of sibling interactions, the residuals of siblings for schooling and earnings should be uncorrelated. In fact, they should be just as uncorrelated as the residuals for unrelated individuals. But such is not the case; the residuals of siblings are correlated, while the residuals of unrelated individuals are

Table 6.8
Sibling interactions in schooling and earnings. Source: Beenstock 2008, p. 343.

Relationship	Number of pairs	Outcome	Sibling residual correlation	Sibling interaction
All siblings	2,102	Schooling	0.308	0.158
All siblings	1,342	Earnings	0.305	0.156
Brothers	616	Schooling	0.419	0.220
Brothers	385	Earnings	0.372	0.193
Sisters	461	Schooling	0.293	0.150
Sisters	309	Earnings	0.350	0.181
Siblings 1 & 3	616	Schooling	0.240	0.122
Siblings 1 & 3	340	Earnings	0.330	0.170
Siblings 1 & 4	114	Schooling	0.443	0.234
Siblings 1 & 4	66	Earnings	0.362	0.187
Age gap 1–3 years	726	Schooling	0.341	0.176
Age gap 3–4 years	310	Schooling	0.223	0.113
Age gap 6+ years	306	Schooling	0.323	0.166

uncorrelated, as expected. These correlated residuals imply that siblings, like roommates, interact.

Table 6.8 reports the sibling correlations derived from these residuals as well as the sibling interactions that are implied by these correlations.[39] The correlation coefficient between sibling residuals for schooling is 0.308, which implies that the sibling interaction coefficient is 0.158. All the sibling interaction coefficients reported in table 6.8 are statistically significant and positive, and vary within a narrow range. Indeed, they resemble the sibling interaction coefficients reported in table 6.7. Since schooling and earnings are measured in logarithms, the sibling interaction coefficients are elasticities. The sibling interaction coefficient for schooling therefore means that if the schooling of a child happens to increase by 1 percent, his sibling's schooling increases by 0.158 percent. Since not all siblings work, the number of sibling pairs for earnings is smaller than it for schooling. In the case of brothers, sibling interaction is slightly larger for schooling than for earnings; the opposite applies for sisters.

In some cases, three or four siblings are matched in 1995. There are 616 matches for first and third siblings in the case of schooling, and there are 114 matches between first and fourth siblings. There seems to be no evidence that sibling interaction varies inversely with birth order. Recall that birth-order effects for schooling have already been specified in table 6.3. Therefore, this effect is not affected by sibship. Finally, sibling interaction doesn't appear to weaken with the age gap between siblings.

The correlation between sibling residuals has been interpreted here as sibling interaction. If, however, siblings share environments that aren't captured by the variables specified in the model, this omission will induce correlation between sibling residuals. Recall that the models in table 6.3 control for cultural background and ethnicity through dummy variables for continent of origin (if not born in Israel) and father's continent of origin (if born in Israel). It is possible that these dummy variables and other controls for parents don't capture environmental effects fully. If that is so, the effects reported in table 6.8 express the importance of unmeasured shared environments as well as that of sibling interactions. The potentially important omission here is the schools attended by siblings, for which there are no data. My own sense is that the effects reported in table 6.8 are almost certainly sibling interactions, but I am naturally prejudiced.

I have tried to take stock of what we know and what we don't know about the empirical phenomena that induce correlation between the outcomes of parents and children, on the one hand, and the outcomes of siblings, on the other. There are four main mechanisms or channels that are involved in these correlations:

(i) Heredity—Since children inherit their parents' genes, the outcomes of parents and children will be correlated if genes or genotypes matter for outcomes or phenotypes. Because siblings share their parents' genes, the same mechanism will induce correlation in sibling outcomes.

(ii) Parenting—The way parents raise their children affects their children's behavior and outcomes. If upbringing depends on the phenotype of parents, correlation is induced between the outcomes of parents and children. If the upbringing of siblings is correlated because siblings share parents, this mechanism will also induce correlation in sibling outcomes.

(iii) Environments and peer groups—If parents and their children share environments, and environments matter for outcomes, the outcomes of parents and children will be correlated. The outcomes of siblings will be correlated for the same reason, both because siblings share parents and because siblings share environments. The same applies to common peer groups.

(iv) Sibling interaction—Even if the previous three channels don't exist, sibling outcomes will be correlated if siblings interact with each other and are mutually influential.

These four channels have been studied variously by empirical investigators from three main disciplines. Behavioral geneticists have been mainly concerned with heredity, and developmental psychologists have been mainly concerned with parenting. More recently, labor economists and quantitative sociologists have taken an interest in parenting and environmental or peer-group effects. Behavioral genetics tends to ignore the effect of parenting on outcomes and assumes by default that the differences between sibling correlations (MZ twins vs. DZ twins and adopted siblings vs. biological siblings) must be genetic in origin. Developmental psychologists go to the other extreme and ignore the potential effect of heredity on outcomes and assume by default that intergenerational correlations are induced by parenting. Both of these empirical literatures are tendentious and methodologically flawed.

Here, rather than repeat the criticisms of behavioral genetics that I voiced in chapters 3 and 10, I focus on the empirical literature in developmental psychology. Several seminal empirical papers are critically discussed. These papers are concerned with parenting, and especially the effect of mothers on infant and child development. The burden of statistical proof is set very low. Also, there is an implicit assumption that causality is one-way: parents affect children, but children don't affect parents. For example, if a mother is strict with her child, it is implicitly assumed that she does not respond to her child's personality. In short, potential reverse causality and feedback from children to parents is ignored. In addition, mothers and infants are assumed to be genetically independent. Sadly, there is little that may be learned from the empirical literature in developmental psychology.

The same criticism doesn't apply to some fascinating work undertaken by labor economists and sociologists. These empirical investigators have the same agenda as developmental psychologists, in that they are interested in the effect of parenting on children as well as in peer-group effects and environmental effects. However, their methodological approach is completely different. And, although they aren't directly interested in heredity, they understand that heredity must be taken into consideration to prevent confounding.

For them heredity is a "nuisance parameter" that has to be dealt with even if it is of no direct interest. These methodologies are based on natural experimentation and the exploitation of longitudinal data. The methodological chasm between this literature and the literatures of behavioral genetics and developmental psychology cannot be overstated.

This literature, however, doesn't cover all the phenomena mentioned in chapter 2. In fact, it covers only the small fraction of those phenomena that are mainly concerned with the following questions:

(i) Does birth weight depend on mothers' behavior during pregnancy? In particular, does smoking during pregnancy reduce birth weight?

(ii) Does the development of the child depend on birth weight during childhood, as a teenager, and as an adult?

(iii) Do parents affect their children's schooling?

(iv) Do outcomes such as crime, delinquency, schooling, and earnings depend on the neighborhood in which a child was raised?

(v) Do peer groups have a causal effect on individual behavior?

(vi) Do siblings mutually influence each other's education and earnings?

I shall not try to summarize the answers to these questions. In any case, the answers aren't always unambiguous. However, some general comments are appropriate. First, these questions are underresearched. The literature is small, sometimes very small. Therefore, even in the absence of ambiguity it would be difficult to make strong generalizations. Nevertheless, there seems to be a persuasive consensus that birth weight affects long-term outcomes even if there is no consensus on whether or not smoking affects birth weight. Second, empirical size effects tend to be small, and their statistical significance is not very large. If this pattern has something to do with publication bias discussed at the beginning of this chapter, it is worrying. I was struck by the fact that peer-group effects and neighborhood effects are either small or not statistically significant. Individual and group outcomes are correlated, but this doesn't seem to imply that peer-group effects are important. Third, very little is known about sibling interactions. In fact, the issue has attracted almost no serious scholarly attention.

Therefore, despite the wealth of information on sibling and intergenerational correlations reported in chapter 2, very little is known about the behavioral and genetic phenomena that induce them. There is nothing new in this asymmetry. The same asymmetry occurs in all branches of scientific inquiry; there are many facts but few persuasive explanations. On the other hand, it is important to relate to the cup that is partially filled, even if this part is small. The increasing involvement of labor economists and quantitative sociologists is a hopeful development from this point of view.

7 Where Do We Go from Here?

7.1 What Have We Learned?

In chapter 6 I tried to take stock of what we have learned and what we have not learned about the effects of heredity, family, and neighborhoods on social and economic outcomes. Unfortunately, the balance is not impressive. Much of the empirical literature in developmental psychology and behavioral genetics is methodologically weak and tendentious. Indeed, this has been a constant theme of the book. It is often argued that if a similar result is obtained from a large number of studies, there must be a germ of truth in the result. This might be persuasive if the studies are based on different methodologies. In this case the common meta-result would be robust methodologically and empirically. However, if the same flawed methodology is repeatedly applied to broadly similar data, the results will be similar because they share a common flaw.

Social scientists have asked themselves the following question: Given that genotypes are unobserved, how might we identify the causal effects of environments on outcomes? Social scientists aren't directly interested in genetics; they are naturally interested in how environmental phenomena such as parents, siblings, and neighborhoods affect social and economic outcomes. They have exploited methodological developments in econometrics, including natural experimentation, to try to answer these questions. Several examples of such research featured in chapter 6. My reading of this line of research is that neighborhood effects and peer effects are either weak or non-existent. Parents and siblings matter more, but not as much as one might think. In view of my skepticism regarding publication bias, perhaps even these findings should be taken with a grain of salt.

So far, therefore, it doesn't seem that environmental influences are very large. Of greater scientific importance, to my mind, is the trend among social scientists to design empirical research with care, mindful of the risks of confusing correlation with causality. Just because such research hasn't established that environments are of great importance doesn't mean that human diversity is primarily genetic. If hypothesis A is rejected, it doesn't mean that hypothesis B is correct by default. Suppose, for argument's sake, that there is no empirical evidence in favor of the genetic theory of human outcomes. No one would claim that it must be the case that environments matter instead.

In contrast to social scientists, behavioral geneticists have not asked themselves the following question: Given that environments might be correlated with genotypes, how might we identify the causal effect of genotypes on outcomes? Instead they have taken the easy way out by assuming that behavior doesn't matter. Had social scientists taken this easy way out, they would have assumed that genetics doesn't matter. Something like this has occurred in empirical developmental psychology; genetics has been ignored by default. Therefore, developmental psychology and behavioral genetics occupy opposite methodological poles. The latter ignores behavior and environmental selection, while the former ignores genetics.

Because genotypes are unobserved whereas environments are at least partially observed, it has been harder to establish whether genes matter than it has been to establish whether parents, neighborhoods, and other environmental phenomena matter. Unfortunately, the natural experiments that have informed the debate about the effect of environments on social and economic outcomes aren't available when it comes to genetics. A natural experiment in the former case involves some random change in the environment—e.g., reaching the top of the list for some housing program. A natural experiment in the latter case would involve some random change in genotype, which is inherently impossible. It is true that MZ-twin and DZ-twin births are a source of quasi-experimental data because MZ twins are genetically more similar than DZ twins. However, as was explained in chapter 5, quasi-experiments and natural experiments are inherently different, and quasi-experiments are much less informative than natural experiments. Specifically, as we saw in chapter 3, violation of the equal-environments assumption means that quasi-experiments involving twins are almost entirely non-informative.

It is for this reason that we can say even less about the effect of genotypes on phenotypes than the little we can say about the effect of environments. Thus, despite the vast number of academic outpourings, we know very little about the roles of family and environments in social and economic outcomes, and even less about the role of genes. However, this doesn't prevent protagonists on both sides of the nature-vs.-nurture debate from persisting with empirical claims that go well beyond the limitations of the data and the methodologies used to analyze them.

7.2   Academic Solipsism: Bridge Building

In 1976 Arthur Goldberger began a one-man campaign against the methodological workhorses of behavioral genetics. As was shown in chapter 3, and as will be discussed in greater detail in chapter 10, behavioral geneticists make, by omission, very strong assumptions about human behavior, including the following:

Identical twins relate to one another as fraternal twins do.

Parents relate to identical twins as they do to fraternal twins.

Adopted siblings relate to one another as biological siblings do.

Parents relate to adopted children as they do to their biological children.

Parents who adopt behave as natural parents do.

Adoption agencies place adopted children randomly.

Children placed for adoption are like children as a whole.

There is no epigenetic drift.

The gene-environment correlation is 0.

More sophisticated behavioral geneticists relax the last assumption, but the other assumptions are necessary, for otherwise the methodological workhorses do not deliver estimates of heritability. It has been shown that relaxing these assumptions generally produces radically different estimates of heritability. Since heritability ranges between 0 and 1, any estimate in this range is as good as another, including 0.

These criticisms have made absolutely no difference to behavioral genetics, which continues to ignore the role of human behavior in the observed correlations between the phenotypes of identical and fraternal twins, on the one hand, and between adopted and biological siblings, on the other. Behavioral genetics is all about genetics and has almost nothing to do with behavioral science. The present book probably will make no difference either.

Academic disciplines are often like religions in which debate takes place quite freely just as long as it doesn't raise existential questions. These disciplines have their own scientific journals, research funds, conferences, and textbooks. The like-minded meet and talk. As long as no one asks whether the emperor is naked, everything is all right. But it isn't.

My criticism of behavioral genetics may be welcomed by developmental psychologists and others, but for the wrong reasons. As we have seen, developmental psychology has been attacked from within and without because it has been founded on the blank-slate view of mankind. Results from behavioral genetics, especially regarding heritability, have proved troublesome for developmental psychology. It would be convenient, therefore, if these estimates of heritability could be written off as nonsense. More generally, it would be convenient for the blank-slaters if they could ignore the attack that behavioral genetics has made on their view of human nature. We have seen how deeply some blank-slaters felt about the geneticist challenge that came from diverse sources in the second half of the twentieth century. They shamefully persecuted their challengers.

My methodological criticism of behavioral genetics is not an argument against the role of heredity in determining human outcomes; far from it. It is simply a call for methodological improvements in the way research on heredity is conducted. I have argued that the basic flaw of behavioral genetics is that the parameters of interest, especially heritability, aren't identified. This means that observational data don't pin down such parameters as heritability. This is a conceptual failure. It cannot be put right by some minor fixes to behavioral genetics. It calls for a more fundamental methodological change. I have discussed (in chapters 5 and 10) various methodological solutions to the identification problem—solutions that have proved useful in sociology, economics, political science, and epidemiology. Perhaps they will eventually disseminate to behavioral genetics. Perhaps part of the problem is that behavioral genetics is taught not in faculties of social science but in faculties of natural science.

Developmental psychology, on the other hand, is taught in faculties of social science. However, this hasn't made much difference to its methodological progress. We saw in chapter 6 how empirical research in developmental psychology fails to distinguish between causality and correlation. We saw how in many cases it is taken for granted that just because action A happened before action B, it must be the case that A is causing B. There is a conceptual confusion between sequencing and causality. It is not considered that A might anticipate B, in which case there is reverse causality from B to A. Indeed, this conceptual confusion is widespread.

The question is how to break the methodological isolationism of developmental psychology and behavioral genetics in particular. My answer is to teach econometrics in these disciplines, since econometrics is concerned with identifying causal effects in observational data. It is a pity that econometrics entails the prefix "econ." This makes it sound as though it is a special subject intended for economists. However, econometrics is no more concerned with economics than biometrics is concerned exclusively with biology. In the 1930s the founding fathers of econometrics made a strategic marketing error when they named their discipline as they did. It is true that many of these founding fathers happened to be economists, but not all of them were. Over time, econometricians have increasingly hailed from other disciplines. It is also true that econometrics is compulsory in university programs in economics. However, this is an accident of history. There is no reason why sociologists, political scientists, psychologists, and behavioral geneticists shouldn't be required to learn econometrics. Indeed, econometrics is relevant to any discipline that is concerned with testing causal hypotheses with observational data.

I believe that making the study of econometrics compulsory in the social sciences as a whole would transform the way in which empirical research is carried out. I suppose that it is too late to rename econometrics "sociometrics" as a part of a marketing effort to break disciplinary boundaries. Programs in the social sciences typically include courses on research methods, but those courses usually don't go beyond an introduction to statistics in which the study of causality is not treated in depth. What distinguishes econometrics from statistics is its overarching focus on testing causal hypotheses with observational data. In short, econometrics has an ecumenical function in bridging the gap between the social sciences. This is especially true of micro-econometrics, which is concerned with testing causal hypotheses when the data refer to individuals.

We saw in chapters 3 and 6 that many economists publish fascinating papers on subjects that have nothing to do with economics. This includes theoretical work on the axiomatic theory of parenting and empirical work on a variety of topics in criminology, social psychology, and sociology. Though these developments must be welcomed for breaching interdisciplinary walls, it is odd that these papers haven't appeared in scholarly journals of criminology, social psychology, and sociology. Instead, they have been published in journals of economics. It is to be welcomed that editors of economic journals are sufficiently broad-minded to publish papers on non-economic topics. But surely it would have made more sense had these papers been published in the relevant disciplinary journals. They would have then had a greater impact on developmental psychologists, criminologists, and sociologists. Since members of each discipline read their own discipline's journals, criminologists (for example) are unlikely to read the work of the adventitious labor economists.

It is, of course, very difficult to publish across disciplinary boundaries. The temptation for economists to submit their work on non-economic topics to economics journals is obvious. The reasons are largely cultural and stylistic. Each discipline has its own idiosyncrasies. Economists understand what the editors of economics journals expect of them; they don't understand what the editors of journals in other disciplines expect. The same applies to non-economists who have written important material on economics: it is easier for them to publish in journals in their own discipline. To break the disciplinary mold, it is important that editors be ecumenical and authors be more adventurous. The former is more important than the latter.

7.3   Molecular Genetics and Social Science

In chapters 5 and 10 I mentioned that much of the empirical debate about heredity and about nature vs. nurture stems from the fact that genotypes aren't observed. These genotypes are a crucial missing variable in the empirical analysis of phenotypes and outcomes. Empirical investigators are forced to work in the knowledge that this missing variable might confound their empirical results. In chapters 3 and 5, I fantasized about what would happen if these data were not missing, and I explained how they could be used to eliminate many of the methodological uncertainties that arise because they are missing. I then described the generated-regressor methodology, in which genotypes are estimated from an auxiliary model. These generated regressors are intended to proxy the real thing. In chapter 6 I used this methodology to control for unobserved genotypes in the study of the causal effect that parents have on their children's schooling and earnings. The generated-regressor methodology is, of course, no substitute for real data on genotypes.

I mentioned in my preface that in 2008 I was a Visiting Professor at the University of Otago in Dunedin, New Zealand. While there, I became aware of the Dunedin Multidisciplinary Health and Development Study (DMHD), which has followed just over 1,000 children born in the mid 1950s in Dunedin. This longitudinal study has suffered from surprisingly little sample attrition despite the fact that the children are now in their mid fifties and many have emigrated from New Zealand. Many of the Dunedin 1,000 now have children of their own, and some have grandchildren. Samples of these first- and second-generation children have also been included in the DMDH, as well as the parents of the original sample. This means that the DMDH spans three generations and is on its way to including a fourth generation.

The DMDH includes a broad range of social, economic, and health data. Unusually, it also includes DNA data. Caspi et al. (2002), who used these data to study the role of genotypes in violent behavior, found that maltreated children with high levels of the MAOA gene were less likely to be anti-social. Paradoxically, in Dunedin I lectured on the generated-regressor methodology as a substitute for missing genotype data while the real thing was close by.

It is possible that we are about to witness a major change in the study of heredity, since the DMDH is ceasing to be unique. There are many medical databases containing molecular data. Unlike the DMHD, they don't include social and economic data. However, this is beginning to change. Three molecular data bases on twins (TwinsUK, the Netherlands Twins Registry, and the Austrian Twins Registry) have been linked to behavioral variables. The Framingham Heart Study and the Rotterdam Study are medical databases that include some behavioral data (Beauchamp et al. 2011). The (US) Longitudinal Study of Adolescent Health has collected saliva samples and genotyped about 2,500 individuals for six genetic markers. The (US) Health Retirement Survey will provide more than a million genetic markers for about 13,000 individuals in 2011. The Wisconsin Longitudinal Study has genotyped nearly 7,000 individuals. Maybe a new age is dawning.

To estimate the likely scientific contribution of molecular genotyping in the social sciences, it makes sense to consider the experience with molecular genotyping, or genomics, in the medical sciences. Since the completion of the Human Genome Project, in 2003, there has been a vast outpouring of empirical research into the genetic causes of a broad range of medical phenotypes. As we shall see, this experience has turned out to be disappointing, especially in view of the high hopes held in the early 2000s. Since medical outcomes for which genetic markers have been identified (such as Crohn's disease and diabetes) are less complex phenomena than social outcomes (such as violence and academic success), social scientists are likely to have a more difficult time making scientific progress than have their counterparts in the medical sciences.

7.3.1 Basic Genetic Concepts

A human cell contains 23 pairs of chromosomes. Each chromosome contains quantitative trait loci (QTL), which are the underlying genetic phenomena of interest. QTLs are located at unknown locations in the chromosomes. Chromosomes in humans are about 160 centiMorgans (cM) in length. Since each cM of human chromosomes contains 10 million base pairs that link DNA helixes, the total number of base pairs is enormous (3 billion). QTLs aren't directly observed. The trouble is that, owing to recombination and crossover, genetic markers aren't the same as QTLs. Genome mapping samples the chromosome at discrete intervals measured in centiMorgans. Suppose chromosomes are sampled every 5 cM. If the QTLs happen to be located at 5-cM intervals, each marker measures a QTL. In general, however, the chances of such "direct hits" are very small. It is obvious that if markers are measured at finer intervals, say 2 cM instead of 5, it is more likely that markers will overlap with QTLs.

In genetic mapping it is fortunate that a miss isn't as a good as a mile. QTLs "cast a shadow" in their vicinity. Therefore, direct hits aren't essential; near misses in the relevant vicinity measure unobserved QTLs. Direct hits obviously provide better measures than near misses, which in turn provide better measures than complete strays. Suppose that in reality a QTL is located at a distance of 3 cM along the chromosome, and markers are measures at intervals of 2 cM. The first marker falls 1 cM short of the QTL; the second overshoots it by 1 cM. However, both markers contain information about the QTL, because the QTL casts a shadow in the neighborhood of its location. The finer the mapping, the better will be the quality of the data, because the distance between markers and QTLs will, on average, be smaller. Markers are therefore noisy measures of QTLs.

There are two main types of marker: SNPs (single nucleotide polymorphisms, commonly known as snips) and SSRs (simple sequence repeats). The former have proved more popular than the latter. The number of markers has grown during the last decade. If in 2005 the typical number of markers was a few hundred thousand, by 2011 this number had reached a million. It should be obvious by now that, as the number of markers increases, the probability of detecting QTLs increases; however, it does so at a decreasing rate, because markers are correlated. Therefore, increasing the number of markers from 500,000 to a million doesn't double fidelity. Markers are correlated because they are related to each other through the QTLs they are supposed to measure. Also, because QTLs are related, more distant markers will be correlated.

Since mice breed rapidly, it is relatively easy to construct mouse populations that are genetically homogeneous. This is typically achieved after 20 generations of brother-sister mating. (People might think that brother-sister mating creates genetic problems. It doesn't with mice.) Mice have only 20 chromosomes whereas humans have 23, and mice chromosomes are only half the length of human chromosomes. Also, the rate of crossover among mice is about half of what it is among humans, which means that markers and QTLs are more likely to be correlated among mice than among humans. Mouse genetics has become a popular field of study in its own right because it is easier to investigate mice than other mammals.

7.3.2 Genome-Wide Association Studies as Data Mining

Estimation always requires more observations than unknown parameters to be estimated. For example, to estimate an unknown parameter such as an average requires at least two observations. Since there is only one way to estimate an average from two observations, there are no "degrees of freedom" to this parameter estimate. The number of degrees of freedom naturally increases with the number of observations, since there are more ways of estimating the unknown parameter the greater is the number of observations. The quality or fidelity of the parameter estimate therefore varies directly with the number of observations.

In genome-wide association studies (GWAS), the number of potential parameters is as large as the number of genetic markers, which vastly exceeds the number of observations that are available. The problem is rather like finding a needle in an enormous haystack. Data mining proceeds by repeatedly using groups of markers in which the number of markers is sufficiently less than the number of observations. Various search algorithms are available that carry out this search process in a statistically efficient fashion. Stepwise regression isn't feasible, since it requires that the number of markers be less than the number of observations.[1] The trouble with this search methodology is that it uses up degrees of freedom, and as a result statistical power is sacrificed.

The medical literature of the last ten years has been replete with studies claiming to have discovered the genes causing various diseases. This development may be about to spread to the social sciences. Genome-wide association studies use data on hundreds of thousands of genetic markers, or even a million, to find statistical associations with outcomes of interest. For example, Beauchamp et al. (2011) used data from the Framingham Heart Study on 300,000 genetic markers in a sample of 7,500 in an attempt to discover the "gene for schooling." However, they failed to replicate their results using data from Rotterdam. This failure joins a large list of similar failures in medicine. After the completion of the Human Genome Project, hopes ran high that scientists would soon discover the genes responsible for a wide variety of diseases. It simply seemed to be a matter of combing through the data until the guilty gene revealed itself. Editors of leading scientific journals were quick to publish findings which later turned out to be false positives. For example, the results of Caspi et al. mentioned above haven't been replicated elsewhere. Failure to replicate turned out to be the rule rather than the exception.

This disappointing development has been attributed, in part, to publication bias. Editors preferred to publish papers reporting positive results rather than papers reporting negative results. However, I think that the cause of this disappointment runs much deeper, and that it was predictable. Genome-wide association studies were bound to disappoint because they were based on data mining, which re-uses the same data to test a large number of hypotheses. It is well known that sampling error in testing just one hypothesis results in errors of two types: rejecting the null hypothesis when it is true (type I error or false negatives) and accepting the null hypothesis when it is false (type II error, or false positives). Let P_I and P_{II} denote the probabilities of committing type I and type II errors. The significance level of a test, or its "size," is in fact P_I, which is typically set at 0.05. This means that there is at most a 5 percent chance of rejecting a correct hypothesis—that is, of a false negative. The "power" of a test is defined as $1 - P_{II}$. It is the probability of not accepting a false positive. A test is "most powerful" if it has greater power than other tests of the same size. A test is unbiased if its power is greater than or equal to its size, and it is consistent if its power tends to 1 as the sample size grows to infinity.

Unfortunately, size and power vary inversely with each other. Therefore, if we want to reduce the probability of rejecting correct hypotheses, or false negatives, we increase the probability of false positives. A simple numerical example serves to illustrate this point. Suppose that a random variable is normally distributed in the population and the null hypothesis to be tested is that the population mean is 10. According to a rival hypothesis the population mean is 15. In a sample of 20 observations the mean is 12 and the standard deviation is 2. Since there are 20 observations, the number of degrees of freedom is 19. If the size of the test is 0.05 (one tail), the critical value of the t statistic is 2.093. Suppose the calculated t statistic[2] is 4.472, so the sample mean exceeds its hypothesized value by a substantial margin. In fact the p value is close to 0. Thus, we reject the null hypothesis.

When size is fixed at 0.05 (5 percent) and according to the rival hypothesis the population mean is 15 instead of 10, P_{II} is equal to 0.073 (7.3 percent).[3] Therefore, the probability of a false positive is 0.073 and the power of the test is $1 - 0.073 = 0.927$; the probability of not accepting a false positive is 92.7 percent, as in case 1 in table 7.1. Case 2 in table 7.1 shows that if the size is reduced to 1 percent, i.e., the probability of rejecting a correct hypothesis is only 1 percent, the probability of accepting a false positive increases to 10.93 percent from 7.3 percent, and the power of the test falls to 89.07 percent Therefore, size and power vary inversely with each other. The extent to which they do so depends on the difference between the predictions of the null hypothesis and its rival.

Table 7.1
The conflict between size and power.

Case	N	Size: P_I	t^*	P_{II}	Power
1	20	0.05	2.093	0.073	0.9270
2	20	0.01	2.539	0.1093	0.8907
3	25	0.05	2.064	0.071	0.9290
4	∞	0.025	1.96	0.0643	0.9357

Case 3 in table 7.1 shows that if the sample size increases from 20 to 25 and the size of the test remains at 0.05, the critical value of the t statistic decreases to 2.064 from 2.093. This reduces P_{II} from 0.073 to 0.071, and the size of the test increases. This shows that when the sample size is larger the probability of accepting false positives decreases, as one would expect. Case 4 shows that asymptotically (when the sample size is infinitely large) the power of the test is 0.9357. The important point is that power varies directly with the size of the sample. However, for normally distributed populations the sensitivity of power to sample size may not be great, as the example in table 7.1 indicates.

If different data sets are used to test n independent hypotheses, the probability of accepting false positives naturally increases. In fact this probability has a binomial distribution. The mean number of false positives is nP_{II} and its variance is $n(1 - P_{II})$. Therefore, the expected number of false positives and its variance increase linearly with the number of hypotheses. The probability of x false positives in testing n hypotheses can be determined from the binomial distribution:

$$P_{IIn} = \frac{n!}{x!(n-x)!} P_{II}^x (1 - P_{II})^{n-x}. \tag{1}$$

Suppose therefore that n scientists participate in a GWAS consortium. Each scientist has his own data, and they work independently of one another. Each scientist has his own hypothesis, which is independent of his colleagues' hypotheses. The participating scientists agree on a common size to test their hypotheses. Suppose further that the power of this test $(1 - P_{II})$ is 0.9 for each scientist. Setting x to 0 in equation 1 gives the probability of not accepting a false positive for the GWAS consortium as 0.9^n. If there are 20 scientists in the consortium, the probability of their joint efforts' not accepting a false positive is 0.122. In other words, the likelihood that the GWAS consortium accepted a false positive is nearly 88 percent. This illustration shows that type II errors accumulate quite rapidly when scientists agree to collaborate in international research projects.

The GWAS consortium just discussed is not, however, the only way of organizing GWAS research. An alternative is to pool data in order to make the sample as large as possible. Indeed, the motivation for this is clear from table 7.1, which shows that with larger samples statistical power increases for given size. For normal populations, however, this gain tends to reach a maximum quite rapidly, as is evident from the table. If, however, the effect we are looking for is very small, or if it affects only a small proportion of the population, matters are different.

The GWAS database has N observations, which is assumed for present purposes to be very large. It is data-mined n times. In this case the n experiments aren't independent, because the same data are used repeatedly. Therefore, we can't use the binomial distribution to calculate the probability of false positives. Because the experiments are dependent, it is intuitively obvious that the number of false positives will tend to be larger than in the consortium model. This does not necessarily mean that a consortium is better than pooled genome-wide association studies. Pooling increases the number of degrees of freedom. On the other hand, pooling reduces statistical power. Pooling's advantages and disadvantages should be assessed before embarking on alternative GWAS arrangements.

To compensate for the loss of statistical power, many GWAS investigators[4] use Bonferroni p values rather than standard p values. Suppose that an investigator carries out n independent experiments to determine whether some outcome is affected by n separate covariates. If the nominal significance level is 0.05, there is a one-in-twenty chance that an experiment will appear significant when it is not. Bonferroni p values test the null hypothesis that none of the n covariates affects the outcome. If there is only one experiment, the critical value of z for normally distributed random variables is 1.96 at $p = 0.05$. If there are n independent experiments, the critical value is determined by the standard normal distribution at $p^* = p/n$. For example if $n = 5$ and $p = 0.05$, $z^* = \Phi(p^* = 0.01) = 2.57$. Therefore, in each of the five separate experiments, if z exceeds 2.57 the experiment is statistically significant. If z exceeds 1.96 but is less than 2.57, naive investigators will incorrectly conclude that the marker in question is statistically significant.

Bonferroni p values penalize investigators for running several experiments rather than just one experiment, and thereby reduce the probability of false positives. If the experiments are independent, all is well. If, however, the experiments aren't independent, the Bonferroni p values are too strict or conservative, and that increases the probability of false negatives, i.e., rejecting a true result. Since genetic markers are correlated, Bonferroni p values which are commonly used in genome-wide association studies are too conservative. Siegmund and Yakir (2007) have compared Bonferroni p values with p values that take into account the correlation between genetic markers in mouse genetics.

Table 7.2
Bonferroni and correct p values for mouse genetics. Source: Siegmund and Yakir 2007, p. 114. Nominal size: $p = 0.05$.

	80 cM	40 cM	25 cM	20 cM	10 cM	5 cM	1 cM
Bonferroni	0.0461	0.0468	0.0468	0.0419	0.0373	0.0286	0.0104
Correct	0.0478	0.0472	0.0495	0.0464	0.0476	0.0483	0.0470

Their results are reported in table 7.2 for different levels of fineness in genetic mapping. The mapping is least fine and the number of markers is smallest when markers are measured at 80-centiMorgan intervals; the mapping is most fine when markers are measured at 1-cM intervals. The calculations in table 7.2 take account of the fact that markers are correlated and that they are imperfectly correlated with quantitative trait loci.

As expected, the Bonferroni p values vary inversely with the number of markers, which varies inversely with the measurement interval. Even at 80 cM the Bonferroni and corrected p values are less than 0.05. Notice, however, that the Bonferroni value is less than the correct value because the latter takes account of the dependence between markers. When the markers are measured at intervals of less than 20 cM, the Bonferroni p values fall rapidly relative to their correct counterparts. For example, when the interval is 1 cM the Bonferroni p value is too conservative by 0.0366 ($0.047 - 0.0104$). The fact that the correct p values don't vary by the measurement interval stems from the fact that among mice the markers are highly correlated. Table 7.2 illustrates the magnitude of excess conservatism in Bonferroni p values in the case of genome-wide association studies for mice.

The tests discussed so far are for single markers. Suppose that there are two markers: X and Z.[5] Bonferroni genome-wide association studies estimate separate models for X and Z. A different test is for the joint significance of several markers. To test whether X and Z are jointly significant, it is standard to carry out an F-test, or Wald test, in which the residual sum of squares of a model in which X and Z are specified is compared to the residual sum of squares when X and Z aren't specified. A Bonferroni test would be more conservative, since it is based on the statistical significance of X and Z separately. An F-test might not reject the hypothesis that X and Z are statistically significant, whereas a Bonferroni test might do the opposite. Bonferroni and Wald tests are identical when X and Z happen to be independent.

Since they are generally dependent, Bonferroni correction is too conservative.

Suppose that the truth is that, of the n GWAS experiments, the nth experiment is correct. Bonferroni correction gives weight to the $n - 1$ rejections in judging the single acceptance or success. If $n = 1,000,000$ and the nominal size of the test is set conventionally at $p = 0.05$, the critical Bonferroni value for the normally distributed case is $z = 5.45$. The standard value is, of course, $z = 1.96$. Therefore, the Bonferroni p value is close to 0 instead of 0.05. Experience with genome-wide association studies suggests that Bonferroni correction reduces false positives, and replication success rates which previously had been very low have increased to the order of about 50 percent as a result. If Bonferroni correction was in fact appropriate, replication success rates should have been greater than this, especially since Bonferroni correction is supposed to be too conservative. It is therefore important to look at the cup that is half empty and not the cup that is half full in judging the use of Bonferroni correction. Why are success rates in replications so low, especially in view of the fact that Bonferroni correction is far too conservative? Something has gone wrong.

Bonferroni correction is equivalent to giving a light sentence to a convicted murderer simply because a large number of defendants were found not guilty of murder. The basic issue here is that it is inappropriate to treat the nth experiment as part of an induced test. It isn't that Bonferroni correction is too conservative; it is simply conceptually inappropriate. The methodologically correct way to penalize the loss of power in data mining is to the compute the correct p values for the null hypothesis (White 2000). Unfortunately this involves numerical simulation. White considers a situation in which $N = 1,560$ and $n = 3,500$, so the number of experiments greatly exceeds the number of observations. He shows that naive p values are about one-third of their corrected counterparts. For example, a naive p value of 0.1 works out at about 0.33 when it is corrected for data mining. These differences are large, and the penalty for data mining and associated loss of power is considerable.[6] White shows that the penalty increases with the number of experiments (n), but it increases at a decreasing rate.

Siegmund and Yakir (2007) specifically analyze the penalty or correction for mouse genetics. If genetic markers happen to be perfectly linked to QTLs, genes and markers are the same. However, markers are merely proxies for QTLs. The closer the location of markers to QTLs, the better is the proxy. Although the locations of markers in chromosomes are known, the locations of QTLs are unknown. In chapters 2 and 8 I discussed how noisy data hinder hypothesis testing. The imperfect linkage between markers and QTLs is another example of this phenomenon, which Siegmund and Yakir take account of in their analysis.

In mouse genetics, the parameters of interest are normally distributed, and the null hypothesis is that phenotypes are independent of genotypes. Therefore, in the case of a single marker, if its z statistic exceeds 1.96 we may reject the null hypothesis at $p = 0.05$. If markers are measured at 10-centiMorgan intervals, there are eight markers per chromosome, making a total of 160 markers. Siegmund and Yakir show that depending on assumptions made about the proximity of markers to QTLs, the critical value of z rises from 1.96 to 3.56 to preserve an effective test size of 0.05. The associated test power is about 0.7,. Since this correction is asymptotic, it is assumed that the sample size approaches infinity. In finite samples the correction is likely to be larger, however, Siegmund and Yakir didn't work out the finite-sample case. For mice they report that to preserve an effective size of 0.05 the sample size should be 135 when markers are measured at intervals of 1 cM, and that the sample size should increase to 154 when the interval is 20 cM. In crude terms this works out at about 0.87 observations per marker when the interval is 10 cM. The increase in the critical value of z from 1.96 to 3.56 is qualitatively similar to White's result that the penalty for data mining is large. In fact the nominal p value of $z = 3.56$ is close to 0.

So much for mouse genetics. Mice are genetically much simpler than humans. The human genome comprises 3 billion nucleotide base pairs, but since they are correlated the number of markers required to represent them is less. The current standard is to use about a million markers, but even this might be inadequate. What happens in genome-wide association studies for humans, in which the number of markers may be as large as a million? The main question for genome-wide association studies is this: What will happen to the data-mining penalty when N runs into the tens of thousand and n runs into the hundreds of thousands and even millions? There is, of course, no alternative to working this out. In White's example, the ratio of n to N is 2.24 and the ratio of the corrected p value to the naive p value is slightly larger. In genome-wide association studies, the ratio of n to N may be as large as 20, ten times what it is in White's example. However, because the penalty varies inversely with n, this does not mean that naive p values should be penalized by a factor of 10 times 3. However, even if it were 2 times 3, this would be a very substantial increase in the penalty.

The Health Retirement Survey mentioned above will include about 13,000 observations—probably far too few to justify undertaking genome-wide association studies, especially for social and economic outcomes. There may be genes for specific diseases. However, social and economic outcomes such as schooling and wages are more complex phenotypes than, say, Crohn's disease and multiple sclerosis. Environmental factors probably play a much larger role in social and economic outcomes than they do in medical outcomes. If genome-wide association studies have been disappointing in medicine, the prospects of their succeeding in the social sciences are even remoter. Type II errors will accumulate as these data are mined, as a result of which the probability of failing to reject false positives will be prohibitively large.

There have been some scientific successes in genome-wide association studies, especially in the cases of diabetes type 2, Crohn's disease, and height. However, these successes don't prove that genome-wide association studies work. There is always a chance, as in blind man's buff, that such a study will get lucky. In 100 genome-wide association studies, we might expect there to be a small number of successes, due to sheer luck. This is what has happened. On the whole, however, genome-wide association studies have failed, because they were methodologically flawed from the start.

7.3.3   GWAS Replication Tests

The new gold standard in genome-wide association studies is replication (Kraft et al. 2009). The previous one was Bonferroni correction. Suppose that a result obtained from GWAS1 is successfully replicated in GWAS2. Let PV1 and PV2 denote the p values of GWAS1 and GWAS2 respectively. If GWAS1 and GWAS2 are independent, Fisher's inverse χ^2 meta-statistic (Hedges and Olkin 1985) may be used to set the critical p value of GWAS2 for it to constitute an unsuccessful replication. The meta-statistic is $-2[\ln(\text{PV1}) + \ln(\text{PV2})]$, which has a χ^2 distribution with 4 degrees of freedom. For example, if PV1 = 0.05 and PV2 = 0.05 the meta-statistic equals 11.93. The critical value of χ^2 ($p = 0.05$) is 9.488; therefore GWAS1 and GWAS2 are jointly significant with p value less than 0.05 (approximately 0.02). Therefore, the p value of the meta-statistic is less than the p values of the individual genome-wide association studies. If PV1 is 0.05 and PV2 is 0.18, the meta-statistic is 9.42, just below its critical value of 9.488. In other words, the p value for GWAS2 would have to be greater than 0.18 for the replication to be unsuccessful.

Meta-statistics create the illusion of being less demanding than the usual demands of individual GWAS tests. The meta-statistic may be used to determine the consistency of two or more replications with GWAS1. Or it may be used to determine the joint significance of an entire range of GWAS results provided that they are independent.

Suppose that GWAS2 fails to replicate GWAS1. Liu et al. (2008) have suggested that this might happen simply because the markers in GWAS2 are poorer proxies for QTLs than the markers in GWAS1. This is a legitimate concern that requires an estimate of marker-QTL noise. Siegmund and Yakir have worked this out for mouse genetics, but I am not aware of such calculations for human genetics. Suppose the p value of GWAS2 is 0.22 instead of its critical meta-statistic value of 0.18. Suppose further that marker-QTL noise has an effect of 0.05 on p values in human genetics. Noise-corrected PV2 is 0.17, which is marginally significant.

An alternative statistical methodology is based on Bayesian learning (Kraft et al. 2009). Let $P(H)$ denote the probability that the phenotypic model (H) estimated from GWAS1 is true. Let D denote the data in GWAS2. $P(D/H)$ denotes the probability of observing the data in GWAS2 conditional on H from GWAS1. Bayesians refer to $P(H)$ as the *prior probability* and to $P(D/H)$ as the *likelihood*. The posterior probability that H from GWAS1 is correct is equal to $P(H/D) = P(D/H)P(H)$. The posterior probability is the probability that the model from GWAS1 is correct given the results from the replication in GWAS2. This posterior probability is what we want to know. For example, if the p value of GWAS1 is 0.05, the prior probability that H obtained from GWAS1 is correct is 0.95. If a similar kind of result is obtained from GWAS2, the likelihood will be 0.95. Therefore, the posterior probability that H is correct is $0.95^2 = 0.9025$. Since the likelihood is generally less than 1, the posteriors must be smaller than the priors. If, for example, we want to be 80 percent sure that the results from GWAS1 are correct, the likelihood of GWAS2 must be larger than 0.842. Therefore, if the likelihood from GWAS2 is 0.7, the posterior probability that H is correct is 0.665, which falls well short of 0.8, and GWAS2 fails to replicate GWAS1.

The Bayesian meta-statistic is very different from the inverse χ^2 meta-statistic. In fact it is more conservative. It sets a stricter standard for the likelihood of GWAS2 than its inverse χ^2 counterpart, which sets a more lenient standard for PV2. The difference between the two types of tests is conceptual. In the latter there are no priors. Each GWAS is of equal importance. There is no particular importance to the order of GWAS1 and GWAS2. In the Bayesian case, GWAS1 is the prior for GWAS2. The Bayesian approach to hypothesis testing is more ideological than the classical approach. In the classical approach, there is no role for priors, because all hypotheses are regarded as being equally false. Bayesians claim to have some information about the truth *a priori*. For example, Ioannidis (2005), who is a Bayesian, refers to a parameter *R* which is the *a priori* probability of finding a true relationship in the data. In classical statistics, *R* is entirely foreign, since it is inherently unknowable. I am not a Bayesian, because I do not believe in the concept of *a priori* knowledge.

7.3.4 Single-Genotype Tests in Multiple-Genotype Models

Phenotypes are unlikely to depend on single genotypes. Indeed, successful GWAS research shows that phenotypes such as height, diabetes 2, and Crohn's disease depend on several genotypes, each of which makes a small contribution to the phenotypic variance of the order of perhaps 5 percent. The combined genotypic variance is typically of the order of perhaps only 30 percent. Therefore, at best, GWAS models do not explain very much. Meanwhile, the search for missing genotypes goes on.

The majority of GWAS investigators search for genotypes one at a time, or marker by marker. (See, e.g., Beauchamp et al. 2011.) If the correct GWAS model has only one genotype, the marker-by-marker method doesn't matter. In section 10.15.1 below it is shown that searching for genotypes one at a time may mislead if the true model has multiple genotypes. In fact, it may miss empirically important genotypes and select unimportant genotypes. As an illustration of this point, suppose the true model contains two genotypes X and Z (as in subsection 10.15.1) with coefficients (size effects) equal to 0.33 each. Therefore, $Y = 0.33X + 0.33Z + u$, where u is the residual error of the GWAS model, which is estimated using 100 observations. The standard deviations of Y, X, and Z are assumed to equal 1 and the correlations between them are assumed to equal 0.5. This implies that the standard deviation of u is 0.816, and that the t statistics of the coefficients (0.33) are both equal to 3.273, which comfortably exceeds the critical value of 1.96. In addition, the F statistic is 24.25, which comfortably exceeds its critical value of 2.68 ($p = 0.95$). Therefore, the coefficients of X and Z are jointly and severally statistically significant. Finally, the R^2 for the GWAS model is 0.33.

Table 7.3
Testing genotypes marker by marker

Case	Coefficient of Z	Standard deviation of Z	t statistic of X
1	0.33	1	5.67
2	1	4	1.22
3	1	2	2.31
4	0.5	4	2.31

Suppose that a GWAS investigator attempts to estimate the true model using one genotype at a time. Suppose he begins with genotype X. If he regresses Y on X, the slope coefficient equals 0.5, since the regression coefficient equals the correlation coefficient when Y and X have the same standard deviation as assumed. Notice that this estimate exceeds its true coefficient of 0.33 as a result of omitted-variable bias. $R^2 = 0.25$, and the t statistic is 5.77. Therefore, in this example, marker-by-marker GWAS would include X as one of the empirical markers. Under the simplifying assumptions of symmetry (correlations equal to 0.5 and standard deviations equal to 1), the t statistic of Z is also 5.77. Therefore, in this particular example it makes no difference whether a genome-wide association studies commences with Z or with X.

As is explained in section 10.14, the t statistic depends on the standard deviation of Z and the square of its coefficient. Table 7.3 assumes different values for these parameters and calculates the t statistic for X. Case 1 assumes that these parameters are as in the true model. The t statistic exceeds its critical value of 1.99. Suppose that, as in case 2, the coefficient of Z is 1 and the standard deviation of Z is 4. In this case the t statistic is less than its critical value, and X would be incorrectly rejected as a genotype for Y. Cases 3 and 4 are marginal cases.

These simulations show that the marker-by-marker GWAS methodology could reach the erroneous conclusion that either or both of X and Z are not genotypes for Y when the opposite is true. Also, suppose that in the true model X is not a genotype for Y. However, because of omitted-variable bias it appears to be statistically significant according to its t statistic. This illusion arises because X is correlated with Z, and Z is a true genotype for Y. Therefore, the marker-by-marker GWAS method runs the risk of inducing false positives as well as false negatives.

7.3.5 Principal Components and Stratification
Mouse populations are genetically homogeneous by construction. Human populations are not. Immigrant societies, such as the United

States, are genetically more heterogeneous than insular societies, such as Japan. According to the "out of Africa" thesis, African populations are the most homogeneous, while populations furthest from Africa in the migratory chain are the least homogeneous. Phenotypes might be diverse simply because of genetic diversity in the population. Therefore, to identify the causal effect of genotypes on phenotypes it is essential to control for genetic diversity. Indeed, it is well known that GWAS research that ignores genetic diversity and population stratification runs the risk of identifying spurious genotypes (Lander and Schork 1994). In mouse populations the need for stratification doesn't arise, which is one reason why mouse genetics is so popular.

It has been suggested (Price et al. 2006) that principal-components analysis (PCA) be used to stratify GWAS data. Specifically, PCA is used to extract orthogonal combinations of markers. Since markers are correlated, it might be possible to reduce hundreds of thousand of markers to a small number of principal components. Various statistical tests are available (Schott 2006) to determine the principal components that aren't statistically significant. The statistically significant PCs are then used to control for genetic diversity in the data. These PCs may be used to form ancestry-adjusted genotypes, as explained in section 10.15.2. Following Price et al., Beauchamp et al. use the first ten principal components as measures of population heterogeneity. Subsequently, in the marker-by-marker methodology described above, the principal components are used as covariates to capture population stratification and thereby to reduce the risk of spurious markers.

Since the principal components are weighted sums of markers, and the object of genome-wide association studies is to discover genotypic markers, there is an obvious danger that statistically significant principal components might in fact be picking up genotypic effects rather than stratification effects. This happens because the same data are used to proxy stratification and to test genotypic hypotheses. Matters would have been different had stratification been proxied by other variables—such as variables related to ancestry. Suppose, for example, that stratification is ostensibly measured by the first principal component on the grounds that there are only two population strata,[7] and it just happens that this component weights markers as in the true genotypic model. Subsequently, the investigator searches for significant markers conditional on this first principal component. The search is bound to be fruitless because all the statistically significant markers are already included in the first principal component. In short, stratification and genotyping are not identified because they cannot be disentangled from the data. Separate instrumental variables are required to distinguish stratification from genotyping.

Furthermore, it is not obvious why the first principal components should express population stratification rather than genetics. In homogenous populations there will be statistically significant principal components because markers are correlated over the genome. If the most important principal components happen to be genetic, it will obviously be incorrect to use them for purposes of constructing ancestry-adjusted genotypes. The truth is that without external validation of the principal components we don't know which are genetic and which are induced by population stratification. Because theory predicts that markers are correlated, my hunch is that the most important principal components are genetic. In comparison, the effect of stratification is likely to more diffuse and less statistically important.

7.3.6   Sample Selectivity in Molecular Data

Another shortcoming of genome-wide association studies is that the samples are typically not random. People have to agree to donate their DNA data. Therefore, donors of DNA data are inevitably self-selected. Presumably compulsory donation of DNA data will never be legal in democracies. People may be required to complete questionnaires if they happen to fall in the samples of the official statistical bodies. For example, in Israel the law requires people who fall into the sample of the Central Bureau of Statistics to complete a questionnaire. Judging by the widespread public opposition to the establishment of biometric databanks, I doubt very much that this law will ever be extended to include molecular data.

Why should anybody object to donating DNA data? Why is the transfer of molecular data different from the transfer of economic or social data? Apart from the deeper invasion of privacy that is involved, people might feel that data on their DNA might be abused in the future. Perhaps one day I might be told that, since I have the gene for bank robbery, I should report to the nearest police station. Worse still, someone might try to clone me.

The crucial question for genome-wide association studies is this: Will sample selectivity bias the results? The answer (see section 10.11) is Yes if DNA-data donors are less likely or more likely to have active markers than people who do not supply DNA data. If I suspect that bad genes run in my family, I may be less likely to donate my DNA data. Alternatively, if heart disease runs in my family, I may be more disposed to donate my DNA data in the interests of science. In short, sample selectivity in molecular data bases might make it even more difficult to carry out genome-wide association studies.

7.3.7   Deductive vs. Inductive GWAS

If I am right that there is no scientific future in genome-wide association studies as currently practiced, what is the alternative? The answer to this question is as old as the debate on induction vs. deduction. Inductivists, including Plato, Aristotle, and Francis Bacon, believed that if scientists observed the world for long enough it would give up its secrets. In his *Enquiry Concerning Human Understanding*, David Hume refuted this view and replaced it with deductivism. I have discussed the deductivist view of epistemology in chapter 3. The data will not reveal the truth no matter how long we may gaze at them. The role of data is to be used in testing hypotheses that are derived from deductive thinking. This involves setting axioms, forming hypotheses, and then using data to try to falsify these hypotheses.

The methodology of genome-wide association studies is entirely inductive. Deductive GWAS involves theoretical work that uses axioms to form hypotheses about the relationships between specific genetic markers and phenotypes. Until this groundwork is done, genome-wide association studies will remain an empirically frustrating enterprise that occasionally strikes gold. Gold diggers and oil explorers use geological theory to decide where to prospect. Gene diggers need to prospect where genetic theory predicts specific relationships between genotypes and phenotypes. Gold diggers don't dig at random, nor should gene diggers. But that is exactly what has been happening since the completion of the Human Genome Project. Gene diggers are in urgent need of theory to point where they might meaningfully prospect. Until this theory exists, the future for genome-wide association studies doesn't seem bright.

These methodological problems are likely to be much greater in the social sciences than in medicine. Searching for the genes that contribute to phenomena such as schooling achievement, criminality, and economic success makes little sense. However, as soon as data sets containing molecular data become available to social scientists, a generation of them will tread the futile path of their predecessors in the medical sciences.

Indeed, this process has already started. IQ tests were carried out on a sample of 3,782 middle-aged to elderly British adults for whom some 600,000 genetic markers were obtained. Using GWAS, Davies et al. (2011) claim to have discovered the genes for IQ. These genes account for 51 percent of the variance in fluid intelligence and 40 percent of the variance in crystallized intelligence—that is, heritability is 0.51 and 0.4 respectively. The significance levels as measured by p values are respectively 0.00000051 and 0.000057. Therefore, these results are virtual certitudes. The authors subsequently try to replicate their results on a sample of 670 Norwegians. The p values increase respectively to 0.028 and 0.009. Since these p values are less than 0.05, the authors think their replication is successful; the genes that determine IQ in Norway are, they claim, the same as the genes that determine IQ in Britain. We shall ignore the fact that their paper probably would not have been published had these p values been slightly larger.

However, it is clear that matters are not so simple. The Norwegian p values are many times larger than their British counterparts. This might happen for three main reasons. First, the Norwegian sample is smaller than the British sample. However, finite sample theory suggests that 670 observations suffice to rule out this possibility. Second, the residual variance in Norway is larger than its counterpart in Britain; that is, IQ is more heterogeneous among Norwegians than among Britons once genes are taken into consideration. More intelligent Norwegians are more intelligent than more intelligent Britons, and less intelligent Norwegians are less intelligent than less intelligent Britons. Perhaps, but unlikely. Third, the GWAS model fits Norwegians less well than it fits Britons because the genetic determinants of IQ in Norway differ from their counterparts in Britain. Something has been lost in translating the British IQ model to Norway. Technically the Norwegian p values are "significant," and the replication is successful, but this misses the point. A more convincing replication would involve estimating separate GWAS models for Britain and Norway and then comparing the two. This would involve replicating the Norwegian model in Britain and not just replicating the British model in Norway. Replication should be mutual rather than one-way. In any case, the authors report that the p values for people born in Aberdeen in 1936 are 0.11 and 0.16. Therefore, the model does not replicate in Aberdeen despite the fact that the GWAS model is estimated from English and Scottish data.

The authors do not use any socioeconomic controls in their GWAS model. As in behavioral genetics, the authors assume by default that only genetics matters. In the case of medical research this may or may not make sense, but in the case of IQ it is well known, as was discussed in chapters 2 and 3, that cultural and social factors are related to IQ scores. If these factors are correlated with genotypes, as they probably are, the authors will falsely attribute to genetics and nature what really belongs to environments and nurture. The authors should have controlled for schooling, ethnicity, and so on, instead of only using molecular data. Their paper constitutes an unfortunate start along the futile path mentioned above. No doubt it is the first in what will turn out to be a torrent.

7.4   Does Heredity Matter?

In the case of genetic counseling, the answer is obviously Yes. However, for most decisions regarding public policy the answer is No. Suppose for the sake of argument that heritability and genes account for as much as 70 percent of human diversity. This still leaves a large role for environments to affect human outcomes. For example, a vocational training program designed to help the unemployed find work might be beneficial regardless of whether heritability is 20 percent or 70 percent.

Matters would be different if heritability were 100 percent. In this polar case, changes in environments wouldn't affect outcomes. Everything would be genetically predetermined. The rich would remain rich and the poor would remain poor, and there would be nothing the environment could do to alter that. There would be no point to vocational training or other workfare interventions; they would be doomed to fail. The unemployed would be destined to remain unemployed. The poor would be destined to remain poor, and the rich destined to be rich. Criminals would be destined to be criminals, and the depressed would be destined to remain depressed. There would be no point to social or private intervention. The genetically fit wouldn't need help, and the genetically unfit would be unhelpable. But this doesn't mean that there is nothing to be done in societies that are averse to inequality. The tax system may be used to transfer income from the genetically fit rich to the genetically unfit poor.

But not even the most avid innatists (as Locke called them) think that heritability is 100 percent, or even close to it. The blank-slaters might insist that the slate be 100 percent blank, but the innatists don't insist that the slate is 100 percent inscribed. Therefore, extreme innatism is of no practical importance, and has never been on the scientific agenda. The innatist position is, almost by definition, pluralistic; heredity matters and environments matter to different degrees, depending on the outcome. Therefore, there is nothing in innatism that limits the importance of social interventions, or that challenges developmental psychology or indeed any other discipline. The justification of social interventions such as welfare and workfare (programs to help socially weak groups find work), and therapies in deterring crime, drug addiction, unemployment, depression, or whatever, doesn't depend on heredity.

The negative reaction of developmental psychologists to innatism came about only because development psychology adopted blank-slatism on ideological rather than scientific grounds. However, innatism no more proscribes developmental psychology than it proscribes workfareism. Psychodynamic theory might be right or wrong regardless of innatism. The slate doesn't have to be completely blank for a theory in developmental psychology to be empirically relevant.

In short, blank-slaters' insistence that the slate be completely blank has discredited their own cause. This insistence was driven by the view that if the slate isn't 100 percent blank then it must be 100 percent inscribed and therefore there must be no role for innatism. Any concession to innatism, however small, runs the risk of sliding into total innatism. The political or ideological incorrectness of innatism stems from a profound lack of scientific confidence on the part of its blank-slatist opponents. The false dichotomy between nature and nurture is fundamentally an expression of intellectual inferiority among the standard bearers of neo-Lockean ideas.

It is a pity that so much energy has been expended and even anger vented on this false dichotomy. In chapter 4 I drew attention to the implication that if heredity matters, economic inequality is transmitted from one generation to the next. This doesn't mean that economic inequality is historically predetermined. It doesn't mean that universal schooling and other social interventions can't affect economic inequality. It means instead that because of inherited diversity there can't be complete economic equality. However, this doesn't rule out the possibility that economic inequality cannot be reduced.

Therefore, blank-slaters have nothing to fear from innatism. Their political and scientific credos aren't threatened by innatism. Indeed, it is hard to comprehend why the dichotomy between nature and nurture has survived for so long, and why it continues to arouse so much passion.

8 Statistics

8.1 Genotypes

A simple stochastic, or statistical, model is proposed for analyzing the relationship between the genetic endowments (genotypes) of parents and their children. The model is stochastic because genetic endowments are inherently probabilistic. At first the model is presented for the case of parents with a single child, i.e., there are no siblings. It is also assumed for simplicity that parents do not mate assortatively. Subsequently, the basic model is extended in a number of directions. First, the genetic endowments of grandparents are taken into account. Second, parents have more than one child, in which case account is taken of the interactions that take place between siblings. Third, parents are assumed to mate assortatively.

The basic tool that underpins the stochastic model is the autoregressive (AR) process, a workhorse in time-series analysis.[1] In an AR process, outcomes at t depend on previous outcomes at $t - 1, t - 2, \ldots,$ $t - j$; they also depend on a random variable drawn from some statistical distribution. The AR process is relevant here because the outcome at t may be represented by the genetic endowment of the child, while the outcome at $t - 1$ refers to the endowment of the child's parent. The outcome at $t - 2$ would refer to the genetic endowment of grandparents, while $t - 3$ refers to great-grandparents, and so on. Also, the random component in the AR process has a genetic interpretation since each child is born with a genetic endowment drawn randomly from the gene pool. The gene pool is represented by the statistical distribution of possible genetic draws. In short, time periods in the AR model are treated as generations of fixed lengths or durations.

AR models express a specific type of mobility since an outcome in one generation depends only imperfectly on the outcome in the previous generation. The AR model predicts mean reversion in the outcome, so that the children of parents who are less fit (with weaker-than-average genetic endowments) are expected to be fitter than their parents, while the genetic endowments of children of fitter parents (with stronger-than-average endowments) are expected to be less fit than their parents. This phenomenon, known as "beta convergence" and discussed in chapter 2, is the same as mean reversion. Therefore, according to the AR model, fitter parents tend to have children who are fitter than average but are not as fit as their parents, while less fit parents have children how are less fit than average but are fitter than their parents. A detailed analysis of mobility will be presented in section 8.5. For now, note that AR models refer to absolute mobility, which is concerned with absolute changes in fitness between the generations. They do not refer to relative mobility, which is concerned with rank of parents and children in their respective distributions.

AR models also imply that the variance of outcomes among children is related to the variance among parents. Since the variance measures inequality or diversity, this means that genetic inequality or diversity in the current generation is related to inequality or diversity in previous generations. Two distinct types of variance should be distinguished. The "conditional variance" is defined as the variance in the current generation conditional on what the variance actually was in the previous generation. The "unconditional variance" is defined as the average variance expected over all generations. The conditional variance may therefore be regarded as the short-term variance, since it refers only to the current generation, whereas its unconditional counterpart may be regarded as the long-term variance, since it refers to all generations.

In stationary processes the unconditional moments of the distribution do not depend on time.[2] For example, the long-term or unconditional mean and variance average out to a constant over time. By contrast, in non-stationary processes either the unconditional mean and/or the unconditional variance change over time. This chapter refers exclusively to stationary AR processes. This means that the unconditional mean and variance of genetic endowments do not change over time. If, however, the gene pool happened to improve over the generations because weaker strains are removed by natural selection, the assumption of stationarity would no longer be appropriate. The same would be implied if the variance of the gene pool varied over time. Evolutionary forces such as these would take a very long time to express themselves, far beyond the time frame of available empirical data on parents and children. Therefore, the assumption of stationarity is a heuristic device; it is not intended to preclude evolutionary phenomena.

For stationary AR processes, the conditional mean must converge to the unconditional mean. Stationary AR processes are beta-convergent. This means that inequality is mean reverting from one generation to the next because short-term inequality must eventually tend to long-term inequality with the passing of generations. This concept is known as "sigma convergence" since the standard deviation is expected to converge to its long-term average, which is constant by the assumption of stationarity.

8.1.1 Intergenerational Autoregressive Processes: First Order

Let G denote genetic endowment or genotype. The following subscripts are used to label variables:

c	children
p	parents
g	grandparents
gg	great-grandparents
i	family
t	generation
j	ancestor order

For example, G_{ci} refers to the genotype of a child in family i. His parent's genotype is G_{pi}, and his grandparent's genotype is G_{gi}. Parents are the child's first-order ancestors, in which case j = 1. For great-grandparents, j = 3. The current generation of children is referred to as generation t. Therefore, their parents' generation is labeled t − 1, their grandparents' generation is labeled t − 2, and so on, in which case $G_{c-j} = G_{t-j}$. L^j denotes the jth-order intergenerational lag operator.[3] For example, $L^j G_t = G_{t-j}$ is the jth lag of the genotype of the current generation of children, which refers to the jth-order ancestors of the current generation of children. The laws of algebra apply to L. For example, $L^a L^b = L^{a+b}$.

The intergenerational AR model for G is specified as follows[4]:

$$G_{ci} = \rho G_{pi} + \varepsilon_{ci} . \tag{1}$$

Here ρ is an AR parameter of heredity that links children's genotype to their parents' genotype, and ε is a random variable that is identically and independently distributed (iid) with a mean of 0 and a variance of σ^2. This random variable (ε) may be interpreted as a genetic mutation because it is drawn randomly from nature's gene pool. In the present context, the iid assumption means that the variance of ε is constant or identical between generations[5] and is always equal to σ^2 over the generations, and it means that ε_c is independent of ε_p. Hence, successive generations draw ε from the same gene pool, and each draw is completely independent of the draws of parents, grandparents, and so on. The mean of ε is 0. If ε is positive, the random draw from the gene pool is fortunate; if it is negative, the random draw is unfortunate. Genotypes therefore comprise two components: ρG_p (which is inherited) and ε (which is not inherited). Because there is no intercept term in equation 1, G is normalized at 0. It would make no difference to what follows if G were normalized to be positive or negative.

At this point it is not necessary to state how ε is distributed. If it happens to be normally distributed, ε will be symmetrically distributed around its mean of 0. Symmetric distributions that are not normal have fat or thin tails. They are fat-tailed when there is excess kurtosis,[6] in which case extreme positive and negative draws of ε are more probable than under the normal distribution. With thin-tailed distributions, extreme draws of ε are less probable than under the normal distribution. However, ε may be asymmetrically distributed[7] (e.g., the lognormal distribution), in which case the distribution is skewed to the left or the right. If it is skewed to the right, there is a bigger probability of drawing some large positive value of ε than of drawing some large negative value.

Figure 8.1 illustrates some possible distributions for ε. Curve A plots the normal distribution, which has the classic bell-curve shape. Curve B plots a fat-tailed distribution; it is symmetric, but the tails are visibly fatter than they are in curve A. Curve C plots an asymmetric distribution that is skewed to the right. In curve C there is a smaller probability of drawing very negative ε's and a larger probability of drawing large positive values.

In equation 1 the AR coefficient ρ expresses the genetic link between parents and children, which is typically bounded between 0 and 1. If $\rho = 0$, there is no hereditary linkage between parents and children. If $\rho = 1$, children are expected to inherit completely their parents' genetic endowment. Partial heredity implies that ρ is a positive fraction. Presumably ρ

Frequency

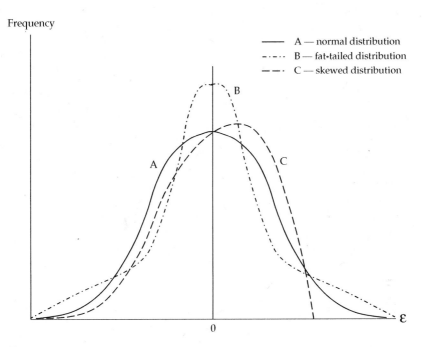

——	A — normal distribution
– · · ·	B — fat-tailed distribution
— · — ·	C — skewed distribution

Figure 8.1
Distribution of the gene pool.

cannot be negative, but if it were negative it would imply regression past the mean instead of toward the mean. The expected value of G_{ci} is equal to ρG_{pi}, or $E(G_{ci}) = \rho G_{pi}$, since according to equation 1 $E(\varepsilon_{ci}) = 0$. This means that, *ex ante*, we expect children to have genetic endowments that are similar to their parents' to a greater or a lesser extent. Since ρ is a positive fraction, this means that children whose parents have positive G (i.e., are fitter) are expected to have positive G too, but their G is expected to be less than their parents' G. It also means that children whose parents have negative G (i.e., are less fit) are also expected to have negative G, but their G is expected to be greater than their parents' G. Therefore, fitness tends toward the mean from one generation to the next. On average G is always 0, because on average $\varepsilon = 0$.[8]

This is the concept of mean reversion or regression toward the mean originally conceived by Galton (1885). It is also sometimes called *beta convergence*. It means that parents who are fitter than average are expected to have children who are fitter than average, but less fit than their parents. The converse applies symmetrically to parents who are less fit than the average. Although equation 1 implies mean reversion, what happens to children's fitness *ex post* depends on their luck in the draw from the gene pool. If ε_c exceeds $(1 - \rho)G_p$, then G_c will be greater than G_p, which will be greater than 0.

The AR process can usefully be expressed as an infinite moving average process in terms of the history of genetic draws. This is known as a *Wold representation*. The Wold representation[9] for equation 1 is obtained by applying equation 1 to determine genotypes for parents as $G_{pi} = \rho G_{gi} + \varepsilon_{pi}$, which is used to substitute for G_p in equation 1:

$$G_{ci} = \rho_2 G_{gi} + \rho\varepsilon_{pi} + \varepsilon_{ci} . \tag{2}$$

Equation 2 includes the genetic endowment of grandparents and parents' draw from the gene pool (ε_p). Next, G_g in equation 2 may eliminated by using equation 1 for grandparents. This replaces the first term in equation 2 with $\rho^3 G_{gg}$. Repeated substitution using the "chain rule" gives the Wold representation for equation 1:

$$G_{ti} = \sum_{j=0}^{\infty} \rho^j \varepsilon_{i(t-j)} , \tag{3}$$

where t refers to the child's generation and j to his ancestors. Equation 3 states that the genetic endowment of the current generation is a geometrically weighted average of the genetic draws of ancestors as well as the current draw. Because ρ is a fraction, the weight (ρ^j) varies inversely with ancestry; the weight of ancient ancestors tends to 0. Equation 3 also establishes that the unconditional expected value of G_t is 0, because the expected value of the history of genetic draws is 0, i.e., $E(G) = 0$. The conditional counterpart of equation 3 is, of course, equation 1, according to which $E(G_t/G_{t-1}) = \rho G_{t-1}$.

An alternative solution technique is to write equation 1 using lag operators. Let L denote an intergenerational lag operator such that $LG_c = G_p$. Writing equation 1 using the intergenerational lag operator and indexing the current generation by t gives $(1 - \rho L)G_{ti} = \varepsilon_{ti}$. The solution for G_{ti} is obtained by dividing both sides of the previous equation by $1 - \rho L$:

$$\frac{\varepsilon_t}{1 - \rho L} = \sum_{j=0}^{\infty} \rho^j \varepsilon_{(t-j)}.$$

This generates the solution in equation 3. Equation 3 may be used to obtain the intergenerational impulse responses, which refer to the effect on the genotype of the current generation of a draw from the gene pool j generations ago. These impulse responses are equal to ρ^j, which decays geometrically with j.

Because ρ is a fraction, G is a "stationary" random variable. As mentioned, variables are stationary when their unconditional moments, such as the mean and the variance, do not depend on time. Variables that have time trends cannot be stationary, because by definition their means aren't constant over time. The mean increases if the time trend is positive and decreases if it is negative. Variables that do not grow (or decrease) over time have constant means, but if their variance depends on time they are non-stationary. This happens when $\rho = 1$. In this case, equation 3 is the sum of all past ε's, and since each ε has a constant variance equal to σ^2 and is independent of other ε's, the variance of G_t equals tσ^2. Since this variance depends linearly on time, G is non-stationary.

8.1.2 Inequality Dynamics in AR Processes

The fact that children are expected to revert toward the mean does not imply that individuals become more similar with successive generations. If the children of fitter parents are, on average, less fit, and the children of less fit parents are fitter, this does not mean that eventually everybody ends up being equally fit. This is known as Galton's Paradox. Inequality is measured here by the variance of G; the greater the variance, the more the inequality. It is easily demonstrated that inequality does not disappear by using equation 1 to calculate the variance of G over successive generations. The conditional variance[10] of G among children according to equation 1 is

$$\text{var}(G_c) = \rho^2 \, \text{var}(G_p) + \sigma^2. \tag{4}$$

This equation states that inequality or diversity among the generation of children varies directly with inequality or diversity among the generation of parents plus the inequality of the gene pool. It describes the dynamics of inequality between generations. Notice that it is a first-order difference equation that relates the variance of G in one generation to the variance in the previous generation. This difference equation has a single root: $0 < \rho^2 < 1$. Therefore, the difference equation is stable, and its general solution is as follows:

$$\text{var}(G_t) = A\rho^{2j} + \text{var}(G^*), \tag{5a}$$

$$\text{var}(G^*) = \frac{\sigma^2}{1-\rho^2}, \tag{5b}$$

$$A = \frac{\text{var}(G_0) - \text{var}(G^*)}{\rho^2}. \tag{5c}$$

The dynamic solution for inequality in generation t is given by equation 5a, where A is an arbitrary constant determined by equation 5c. The parameter A depends on the initial difference between the variance in the current generation, var(G_0), and the unconditional variance, var(G^*). The unconditional variance is obtained by substituting var(G_c) = var(G_p) = var(G^*) into equation 4 and solving the result for var(G^*) as in equation 5b. Since $\rho^2 < 1$, equation 5a predicts that the variance tends over time to var(G^*). Notice that because $\rho^2 < 1$ equation 5b states that the long-term, or unconditional variance of G is greater than the variance of ε (σ^2). Therefore, heredity magnifies the effect on inequality of the underlying inequality that is engendered by the variance of the gene pool. In the special case when $\rho = 0$, var(G^*) = σ^2. However, more generally var(G^*) > σ^2. At the other extreme, when $\rho = 1$, equation 4 implies that the variance of G increases linearly with time and will eventually equal infinity. However, it is assumed here that these extreme cases do not apply, for otherwise genotypes would not be stationary.

Substituting equation 5c into equation 5a gives

$$\text{var}(G_t) = [\text{var}(G_0) - \text{var}(G^*)]\rho^{2(t-1)} + \text{var}(G^*). \tag{6}$$

This equation demonstrates that if initially at t = 0 (the current generation) inequality exceeded its long-term counterpart, i.e., var(G_0) > var(G^*), inequality would converge to its long-term value from above, as represented by curve 1 in figure 8.2. If, however, var(G_0) < var(G^*), convergence is from below, as represented by curve 2 in figure 8.2. Equation 6 shows that the speed of convergence varies inversely with ρ^2. If, e.g., var(G_0) > var(G^*), and ρ^2 is greater than in curve 1, the convergence process is depicted by curve 3. Curve 4 is discussed in the next subsection.

8.1.3   Second-Order Autoregressive Processes: AR(2)

Equation 1 assumes that grandparents, great-grandparents, and so on aren't directly important. Of course, grandparents matter indirectly, since they matter directly for parents. Indeed, according to equation 3 all ancestors matter indirectly, but more recent ancestors matter more than more remote ones. In this section, equation 1 is extended to grandparents, so that children inherit their genotypes directly from

Variance (V)

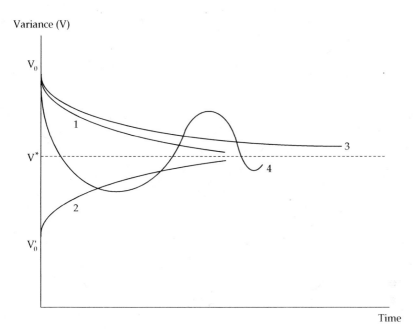

Figure 8.2
Sigma convergence.

grandparents as well as from parents. If recessive genes skip a generation, it would be necessary to specify grandparents in the model. Equation 1 becomes

$$G_{ci} = \rho_p G_{pi} + \rho_g G_{gi} + \varepsilon_{ci} , \tag{7}$$

where G_g denotes the genotypes of grandparents and ρ_g denotes the
heredity coefficient for grandparents. Equation 7 is a second-order
autoregressive model (abbreviated AR(2)), because the genotype
for children depends directly on the genotypes of two previous
generations.

Equation 7 is a second-order stochastic difference equation with
characteristic equation $\lambda^2 - \rho_p\lambda - \rho_g = 0$ and therefore has two roots or
eigenvalues equal to

$$\lambda = \frac{\rho_p \pm \sqrt{\rho_p^2 + 4\rho_g}}{2}. \tag{8}$$

The roots, denoted by λ_1 and λ_2, will be less than 1 in absolute value if
$\rho_p + \rho_g < 1$ and will be real if $\rho_p^2 + 4\rho_g > 0$. If parents are more important

than grandparents, ρ_p will be larger than ρ_g. With the current generation indexed by t, the Wold representation[11] for the genetic endowment of dynasty i in generation t is

$$G_{it} = \frac{1}{\lambda_1 - \lambda_2} \sum_{j=0}^{\infty} (\lambda_1^{1+j} - \lambda_2^{1+j}) \varepsilon_{i(t-j)}. \tag{9}$$

This equation, which is the counterpart to equation 3 for the AR(1) model, states that the genetic endowment of a child born to dynasty i in generation t depends on the entire history of genetic draws (ε) from the gene pool over all previous generations. The impulse response for a draw j generations ago is

$$\frac{\lambda_1^{j+1} - \lambda_2^{j+1}}{\lambda_1 - \lambda_2},$$

which tends to 0 as j tends to infinity because λ_1 and λ_2 must less than 1 in absolute value by definition of stationarity. The conditional expected value of G_{it} is non-zero, because it depends on the history of the ε's for dynasty i. However, the unconditional expectation is 0, because all the ε's are expected to be 0 *ex ante*.

The conditional variance of G for children (generation t) can be derived from equation 7:

$$\mathrm{var}(G_t) = \rho_p^2 \mathrm{var}(G_{t-1}) + \rho_g^2 \mathrm{var}(G_{t-2}) + 2\rho_p \rho_g \mathrm{cov}(G_{t-1} G_{t-2}) + \sigma_t^2. \tag{10}$$

Notice that equation 10 includes the covariance between parents and grandparents, which is naturally positive and increases inequality. In addition, inequality in the current generation varies directly with inequality in the previous two generations. Equation 7 can be used to calculate the intergenerational covariance between G_t and G_{t-1}:

$$\mathrm{cov}(G_t G_{t-1}) = \rho_p \, \mathrm{var}(G_{t-1}) + \rho_g \, \mathrm{cov}(G_{t-1} G_{t-2}). \tag{11}$$

Equation 11 uses the fact that ε_t is independent of G_{t-1} and G_{t-2}. Equations 10 and 11 are simultaneous first-order difference equation in the variance of G_t and the intergenerational covariance, $\mathrm{cov}(G_t G_{t-1})$. Their matrix representation in terms of lag operators is

$$\begin{bmatrix} 1 - \rho_p^2 L - \rho_g^2 L^2 & -2\rho_p \rho_g L \\ -\rho_p L & 1 - \rho_g L \end{bmatrix} \begin{bmatrix} \mathrm{var}(G_t) \\ \mathrm{cov}(G_t G_{t-1}) \end{bmatrix} = \begin{bmatrix} \sigma_t^2 \\ 0 \end{bmatrix}. \tag{12}$$

The first row in equation 12 expresses equation 10; the second row expresses equation 11. The general solution for var(G_t) from equation 12 is (using matrix algebra)

Table 8.1
The relation between heredity and unconditional variance in the AR(2) model.

Case	ρ_p	ρ_g	$Var(G^*)$
1	0.5	0.2	1.71
2	0.6	0.2	2.38
3	0.5	0.3	2.24

$$\text{var}(G_t) = \frac{(1-\rho_g L)\sigma_t^2}{(1-\rho_p^2 L - \rho_g^2 L^2)(1-\rho_g L) - 2\rho_p^2 \rho_g L^2} \, . \tag{13}$$

Because the denominator of equation 13 involves L^3, var(G_t) is a third-order autoregressive process, and the numerator is a first-order moving average process. It is therefore an ARMA(3,1) model.[12] Consequently, var(G_t) has three roots or eigenvalues. Equation 13 can be used to determine the complete intergenerational dynamics of var(G) as in equation 6 for the first-order AR model. To obtain the unconditional variance, set $L = 1$ and $\sigma_t = \sigma$ in equation 13 to obtain

$$\text{var}(G^*) = \frac{1-\rho_g}{(1-\rho_p^2 - \rho_g^2)(1-\rho_g) - 2\rho_p^2 \rho_g}\sigma^2 \, . \tag{14}$$

According to equation 14, as in the AR(1) case in equation 5b, the unconditional or long-term variance of G, or var(G^*), exceeds the variance of the gene pool (σ^2). The relationship between var(G^*) and ρ_p and ρ_g is illustrated in table 8.1, where it is assumed that $\sigma^2 = 1$. Table 8.1 shows that var(G^*) exceeds σ^2, and as expected, it varies directly with ρ_p and ρ_g. In contrast with the AR(1) case, where the convergence process for genetic inequality (illustrated in figure 8.2) must be monotonic, the convergence process is not necessarily monotonic in the AR(2) case. Indeed, if the roots are complex because $\rho_p^2 + 4\rho_g < 0$, the convergence process will be oscillatory as in curve 4 in figure 8.2, and overshooting will occur, i.e., inequality crosses over its long-run solution before eventually converging on it.

8.1.4 Assortative Mating
So far we have treated parents as if they were a single unit. In reality, however, G_p is made up of paternal and maternal components, denoted by G_m and G_f. Hence,

$$G_p = G_m + G_f \, . \tag{15}$$

Since the genotypes of fathers and mothers are random variables, the variance of G_p is equal to

$$\text{var}(G_p) = [\text{var}(G_m) + \text{var}(G_f) + 2\text{cov}(G_m G_f)]. \tag{16}$$

This equation shows that the variance of parents' genotypes increases with the covariance between the genetic endowments of spouses. This covariance will be 0 if spouses mate randomly. However, assortative mating theory suggests that the covariance will be positive, because fitter partners are mutually attracted. The covariance may be expressed in terms of the correlation coefficient between the genotypes of spouses:

$$\text{cov}(G_m G_f) = r_{mf}\text{sd}(G_m)\text{sd}(G_f), \tag{17}$$

where r_{mf} denotes the correlation between spouses' genotypes and sd refers to standard deviations. According to assortative mating theory, r_{mf} is positive, in which case $\text{var}(G_p)$ is increased by assortative mating. Since according to equation 4 inequality varies directly with $\text{var}(G_p)$, assortative mating strengthens the transmission of genetic inequality from one generation to the next. Notice also that, given r_{mf}, the covariance varies directly with the standard deviations of male and female genotypes. This means that the greater the variance of spouses' genotypes, the more assortative mating increases inequality. If the gene pools for men and women are identical, i.e., $\text{var}(G_m) = \text{var}(G_f) = \text{var}(G)$, equation 16 simplifies to

$$\text{var}(G_p) = 2(1 + r_{mf})\text{var}(G). \tag{18}$$

This equation reveals how assortative mating increases the variance of parents' genetic endowments through the parameter r_{mf}.

8.2   Phenotypes

Phenotypes, or outcomes, are hypothesized to depend causally on three main variables: genotypes, parental outcomes, and the "environment." A data-generating process (DGP) describes the stochastic process through which the outcome of interest is generated. The DGP for genotypes of children is specified as follows:

$$Y_{ci} = \alpha + \beta Y_{pi} + G_{ci} + e_{ci}, \tag{19a}$$

$$e_{ci} = \varphi e_{pi} + \mu_{ci}, \tag{19b}$$

where G_c is determined as in equation 1 and e expresses environmental and contextual phenomena that affect the outcome. For now it is assumed, for simplicity, that e is independent of G_c, so that there is no gene-environment interaction or correlation. However, equation 19b indicates that the environments of parents and children are correlated via φ, which for stationarity is less than 1 in absolute value. In equation 19b, μ_c is an iid random variable with variance σ_μ^2, which represents the idiosyncratic component of the child's environment.

According to equation 19a, Y for children has a genetic component since it depends on their genotypes, has a parental component via β, and depends on environments via e. The parental component is causal in the sense that if Y_p happened to change it would induce changes in Y_c. For example, if Y denotes income, it may be the case that better-off parents help their children become better off (through investments in schooling, as discussed in chapter 3). If Y denotes smoking, role modeling would suggest that if children see their parents smoking they might be induced to smoke too, which is separate from the genetic channel. Of course, they might also inherit their parents' genetic susceptibility to nicotine. The scale parameter α determines the value of the phenotype to which Y mean-reverts intergenerationally. If $\alpha = 0$, Y mean-reverts to 0.

8.2.1 The AR^2 Model

In what follows, I simplify by ignoring e in equation 19a. Since equation 19a is AR(1) and equation 1 is AR(1), I refer to this as the *AR^2 model*. (It should not be confused with the AR(2) model introduced in subsection 8.1.3.) With the subscript i dropped for convenience, equation 1 can be written in terms of the lag operator as

$$(1 - \rho L)G_c = \varepsilon_c. \tag{20}$$

To obtain the general solution for G_c, divide both sides of equation 20 by $1 - \rho L$:

$$G_c = \frac{\varepsilon_c}{1 - \rho L} + A\rho^j, \tag{21}$$

where A denotes an arbitrary constant of integration determined by initial conditions. Multiplying both sides of equation 21 by $1 - \rho L$ gets us back to equation 20. Equation 21 is identical to equation 3.

Substituting equation 21 into equation 19a, indexing generation c by t, and using the lag operator gives

$$(1 - \beta L)Y_t = \alpha + \frac{\varepsilon_t}{1 - \rho L} + A\rho^t. \tag{22}$$

Multiplying equation 22 by $1 - \rho L$ gives

$$(1 - \rho L)(1 - \beta L)Yt = (1 - \rho)\alpha + \varepsilon_t . \tag{23}$$

This is a second-order stochastic difference equation with two roots or eigenvalues equal to ρ and λ. Using partial fractions once more to factorize the inverse of $(1 - \rho L)(1 - \beta L)$ gives the following as the general solution for Y_t:

$$Y_t = \frac{\alpha}{1 - \beta} + \frac{1}{\beta - \rho} \sum_{j=0}^{\infty} (\beta^{1+j} - \rho^{1+j})\varepsilon_{t-j} + A_1\beta^t + A_2\rho^t . \tag{24}$$

Since β and ρ must be fractions for stationarity, the last two terms vanish over time. Equation 24 is the Wold representation, which is analogous to equation 9. It states that the phenotype of the current generation depends on the random draws from the gene pool of all ancestors. However, the weights of ancestors decline and tend to 0 because β and ρ are fractions. These weights are the intergenerational impulse responses. The first-order impulse response is the weight of parents' draw from the gene pool is $(\beta^2 - \rho^2)/(\beta - \rho)$ because $j = 1$. The jth-order impulse response is $(\beta^{j+1} - \rho^{j+1})/(\beta - \rho)$. In the long run, the phenotype tends to $\alpha/(1 - \beta)$.

8.2.2   The AR³ Model
In subsection 8.2.1, e was ignored for simplicity. The AR^2 model turns into an AR^3 model when e is no longer ignored. This is because equation 19b is AR(1) too. Ignoring terms involving arbitrary constants of integration, equation 22 becomes

$$(1 - \beta L)Y_t = \alpha + \frac{\varepsilon_t}{1 - \rho L} + \frac{\mu_t}{1 - \varphi L} , \tag{25}$$

which can be rewritten as

$$(1 - \rho L)(1 - \varphi L)(1 - \beta L)Y_t = (1 - \rho)(1 - \varphi)\alpha + (1 - \varphi L)\varepsilon_t + (1 - \rho L)\mu_t . \tag{26}$$

Equation 26 has three eigenvalues (β, ρ, and φ), all of which are fractions. By partial fractions, the inverse of the lag polynomial coefficient of Y_t can be expressed more conveniently as

$$\frac{1}{(1 - \rho L)(1 - \varphi L)(1 - \beta L)} = \frac{A}{1 - \rho L} + \frac{B}{1 - \varphi L} + \frac{C}{1 - \beta L} , \tag{27}$$

where

$$A = \frac{\rho}{(\rho - \beta)(\rho - \varphi)},$$

$$B = \frac{\varphi}{(\varphi - \beta)(\varphi - \rho)},$$

$$C = \frac{\beta}{(\beta - \phi)(\beta - \rho)}.$$

Substituting equation 27 into equation 26 and solving for Y_t gives the general solution of the AR^3 model[13]:

$$Y_t = \frac{\alpha}{1 - \beta} + \left[A \sum_{j=0}^{\infty} \rho^j + B \sum_{j=0}^{\infty} \varphi^j + C \sum_{j=0}^{\infty} \beta^j \right] [\varepsilon_{t-j} - \varphi \varepsilon_{t-j-1} + \mu_{t-j} - \rho \mu_{t-j-1}]. \quad (28)$$

Equation 28 relates the phenotype in the current generation to the history of random draws from the gene pool (ε's) and random shocks to the environment (μ's). It is the counterpart to equation 24 for the AR^3 model. Notice that, unlike equation 24, equation 28 includes ε_{t-j-1}. For example, the jth-order intergenerational impulse response for environmental shocks is

$$B\phi^{j-1}(\varphi - \rho) + C\beta^{j-1}(\beta - \rho).$$

The impulse responses for genetic shocks are

$$A\rho^{j-1}(\rho - \varphi) + B\varphi^{j-1}(\varphi - 1) + C\beta^{j-1}(\beta - \varphi).$$

8.2.3   The Unconditional Phenotypic Variance

The unconditional phenotypic variance measures the long-term inequality in the distribution of the phenotype. To obtain the unconditional variance for Y in the AR^2 model, the solution method used for the AR(2) process is applied. Equation 19a is used to formulate the conditional variance for Y_t:

$$\text{var}(Y_t) = \beta^2 \, \text{var}(Y_{t-1}) + \text{var}(G_t) + 2\beta \text{cov}(Y_{t-1} G_t). \quad (29)$$

Note that, because they are ignored in the AR^2 case, terms in e don't feature in equation 29. Equation 1 is used to formulate the variance of G_t:

$$\text{var}(G_t) = \rho^2 \, \text{var}(G_{t-1}) + \sigma_{\varepsilon t}^2. \quad (30)$$

Equations 1 and 19a are used to calculate the covariance between G_t and Y_{t-1}:

$$\text{cov}(Y_{t-1}G_t) = \beta\rho\,\text{cov}(Y_{t-2}G_{t-1}) + \rho\,\text{var}(G_{t-1}). \tag{31}$$

The preceding equation uses the fact that ε_t is independent of G_{t-1} and Y_{t-2}. Equations 29, 30, and 31 are simultaneous first-order difference equations. Their matrix representation in terms of lag operators is

$$\begin{bmatrix} 1-\beta^2 L & -1 & -2\beta \\ 0 & 1-\rho^2 L & 0 \\ 0 & -\rho L & 1-\beta\rho L \end{bmatrix} \begin{bmatrix} \text{var}(Y_t) \\ \text{var}(G_t) \\ \text{cov}(Y_{t-1}G_t) \end{bmatrix} = \begin{bmatrix} 0 \\ \sigma_{\varepsilon t}^2 \\ 0 \end{bmatrix}. \tag{32}$$

The general solution for var(Y_t) from equation 32 is

$$\text{var}(Y_t) = \frac{(1+\beta\rho L)\sigma_{\varepsilon t}^2}{(1-\beta^2 L)(1-\rho^2 L)(1-\beta\rho L)}. \tag{33}$$

Like equation 13, equation 33 is an ARMA(3, 1) process in the variance of Y_t. The three roots or eigenvalues are β^2, ρ^2, and $\rho\beta$. Since equation 33 is a third-order autoregressive process, it states that the phenotypic variance for children depends on the phenotypic variances of their parents, grandparents, and great-grandparents. To obtain the unconditional variance, set $L = 1$ and $\sigma_{\varepsilon t} = \sigma_\varepsilon$:

$$\text{var}(Y^*) = \frac{(1+\beta\rho)\sigma_\varepsilon^2}{(1-\beta^2)(1-\rho^2)(1-\beta\rho)}. \tag{34}$$

The relationship between the unconditional variance and β and ρ is illustrated in table 4.3.

Using the same solution procedure, it can be shown that the unconditional variance of Y in the AR^3 case is

$$\text{var}(Y^*) = \Gamma_1 \sigma_\varepsilon^2 + \Gamma_2 \sigma_\mu^2, \tag{35a}$$

where

$$\Gamma_1 = \frac{(1-\varphi^2)(1-\beta\rho)(1-\beta\varphi) + 2\beta\rho(1-\varphi^2)(1-\beta\varphi)}{(1-\beta^2)(1-\rho^2)(1-\varphi^2)(1-\beta\rho)(1-\beta\varphi)} \tag{35b}$$

and

$$\Gamma_2 = \frac{2\beta\varphi(1-\rho^2)(1-\beta\rho) + (1-\beta\varphi)(1-\rho^2)(1-\beta\rho)}{(1-\beta^2)(1-\rho^2)(1-\varphi^2)(1-\beta\rho)(1-\beta\varphi)}. \tag{35c}$$

The relationship between the unconditional variance and β, ρ, and φ is illustrated in table 4.4. When $\varphi = 0$, equation 35a reverts (as expected) to equation 34.

Several results follow from equations 35. First, heredity increases inequality, since the coefficient of σ^2_ε varies directly with ρ. Second, because the unconditional variance varies directly with β, causal dependence of children on their parents' outcome increases inequality. Third, since the coefficient of σ^2_μ varies directly with φ, inequality varies directly with the correlation between the environments of parents and children. Fourth, inequality varies directly with the variance of the gene pool (σ^2_ε) and the variance of the environment (σ^2_μ). If these variances are 0, var(Y^*) = 0 and there is complete equality. If $\beta = \varphi = \rho = 0$, then var($Y^*$) $= \sigma^2_\varepsilon + \sigma^2_\mu$.

As can be seen in the denominator of equation 35b, there are five real roots to the variance in the AR³ case: β^2, ρ^2, φ^2, $\beta\rho$, and $\beta\varphi$. Since the roots are real, var(Y) converges over the generations to var(Y^*) without overshooting. However, the convergent path need not be monotonic. Therefore, if, for example, var(Y) happened to be initially larger than var(Y^*), it would converge to var(Y^*) from above. This results from the fact that the equations in the system are individually first-order AR processes. If one or more of the equations happened to be a higher-order process (such as equation 7, in which grandparents matter directly), the roots may be complex, in which case the convergence process may involve overshooting.

8.2.4 Decomposing the Intergenerational Correlation

The intergenerational correlation coefficient between the outcomes of children (Y_c) and their parents (Y_p) may be derived using cross-section data on pairs of parents and children. The intergenerational correlation coefficient is defined as

$$r_{cp} = \frac{\text{cov}(Y_c Y_p)}{\text{sd}(Y_c)\text{sd}(Y_p)}. \tag{36}$$

According to equation 19a, cov($Y_c Y_p$) is equal to

$$\text{cov}(Y_c Y_p) = \beta\,\text{var}(Y_p) + \text{cov}(Y_p G_c) + \text{cov}(Y_p e_c). \tag{37}$$

Substituting equation 37 into equation 36 and reorganizing gives the decomposition for the intergenerational correlation:

$$r_{cp} = \frac{\text{sd}(Y_p)}{\text{sd}(Y_c)}\left(\beta + \frac{\text{cov}(Y_p G_c)}{\text{var}(Y_p)} + \frac{\text{cov}(Y_p e_c)}{\text{var}(Y_p)}\right). \tag{38}$$

The preceding equation has four components. The first refers to sigma convergence. If phenotypic inequality decreases between generations, the standard deviation of Y_p exceeds the standard deviation of Y_c, which increases the intergenerational correlation. Second, the intergenerational correlation varies directly with β, which represents the contribution of parenting or nurture to the intergenerational correlation coefficient. The third refers to the contribution of genes to the intergenerational correlation coefficient. This involves the regression coefficient of G_c on Y_p, which according to equation 25 is expected to be positive. The greater this regression coefficient, the larger is the genetic component of the intergenerational correlation coefficient. The fourth component in equation 27 is environmental or contextual and is equal to the regression coefficient of e_c on Y_p, which according to equation 26 is positive unless $\varphi = 0$.

Equation 38 refers to the conditional intergenerational correlation coefficient, since Y_c is conditional on Y_p. It therefore refers to the short-run intergenerational correlation. Its long-run or unconditional counterpart is obtained by substituting equations 35 into equation 37 and then substituting the result into equation 36:

$$r_{cp}^* = \beta + \frac{\rho}{(1-\beta\rho)(1-\rho^2)}\frac{\sigma_\varepsilon^2}{\text{var}(Y^*)} + \frac{\varphi}{(1-\beta\varphi)(1-\varphi^2)}\frac{\sigma_\mu^2}{\text{var}(Y^*)}, \qquad (39)$$

where $\text{var}(Y^*)$, the unconditional phenotype variance, is defined in equation 35a. The intergenerational correlation coefficients obtained from repeated cross-section data on parents and children would eventually converge on r_{cp}^* as defined in equation 39. Whereas equation 38 has four components, equation 39 has only three. The first component has disappeared because sigma has fully converged in equation 39, so that the standard deviations of Y for parents and children are equal. Apart from this, the three remaining components correspond to the other three components in equation 38. As before, the parenting component is equal to β. The genetic and environmental components are complicated, since, according to equations 35, $\text{var}(Y^*)$ varies directly with ρ, β, φ, σ_ε^2, and σ_μ^2.

The relationship between beta convergence and sigma convergence discussed here should be distinguished from the discussion in subsection 8.5.3. Here we have been concerned with the dynamics of inequality over many generations, whereas the discussion in subsection 8.5.3 refers to the relationship between beta and sigma between one generation and the next.

8.3   Siblings

8.3.1   Data-Generating Process with Two Siblings

Siblings may interact at least at two levels. First, they may influence each other so that their outcomes or phenotypes are mutually dependent. For example, there may be spillovers in educational achievement—siblings may help each other to obtain better grades. These spillovers may be negative or positive—siblings may be bad rather than good influences. Or spillover may be asymmetric—perhaps sibling 1 has a positive influence on sibling 2, but sibling 2 has a bad influence on sibling 1. Finally, spillover may be one-way, so that sibling 1 affects sibling 2 but sibling 2 does not affect sibling 1. In the two-sibling data-generating process (DGP), these interactions directly affect outcomes and environmental choices.

The DGP for sibling 1 is as follows:

$$Y_1 = \beta_1 Y_p + \lambda_1 Y_2 + G_1 + e_1 , \tag{40a}$$

$$G_1 = \rho G_p + \varepsilon_1, \tag{40b}$$

$$e_1 = \varphi_1 e_p + \pi_1 e_2 + \mu_1 , \tag{40c}$$

where the subscripts 1 and 2 stand for the two siblings. The DGP for sibling 2 has the same structure as that for sibling 1, except that the structural parameters differ. For example, if $\beta_2 > \beta_1$, the outcome for parents is more important for sibling 2 than for sibling 1. Equation 40a extends equation 19a, and λ_1 denotes the sibling interaction coefficient for phenotypes. Equation 40b is the same as equation 1, except ρ may vary by sibling. Equation 40c extends equation 19b by allowing for sibling interaction in environmental choice via π_1. If λ and π are positive, sibling interaction is benign; if they are negative, it is malign. If $\lambda_1 = \lambda_2$ and $\pi_1 = \pi_2$, sibling interaction is symmetric. If $\lambda_2 = \pi_2 = 0$, it is one-way from sibling 1 to sibling 2. The DGP for sibling 2 is the same as equations 40 except subscripts 1 and 2 are reversed. For example, $G_2 = \rho_2 G_p + \varepsilon_2$, where $E(\varepsilon_1 \varepsilon_2) = 0$. However, if siblings happen to be identical twins, $E(\varepsilon_1 \varepsilon_2) > 0$, because the siblings' genotypes are correlated.

Equation 40c for siblings 1 and 2 determines e_1 and e_2. Solving these simultaneous equations generates their "reduced forms," in which e_1 and e_2 are related to μ_1, μ_2, and e_p:

$$e_1 = \frac{(\varphi_1 + \pi_1 \varphi_2) e_p + \pi_1 \mu_2 + \mu_1}{1 - \pi_1} , \tag{41a}$$

$$e_2 = \frac{(\varphi_2 + \pi_2\varphi_1)e_p + \pi_2\mu_1 + \mu_2}{1 - \pi_2}. \tag{41b}$$

The environments for both children depend on their parents' environments as well as on their sibling's idiosyncratic components (μ_1 and μ_2). Notice, for example, that the effect of parents is magnified by sibling interaction; there is a "multiplier" effect. The direct effect of e_p on e_1 is φ_1, but the total effect in equation 41a is larger than φ_1.

The semi-reduced forms from equation 40a are

$$Y_1 = \frac{(\beta_1 + \lambda_1\beta_2)Y_p + G_1 + \lambda_1 G_2 + e_1 + \lambda_1 e_2}{1 - \lambda_1\lambda_2}. \tag{42a}$$

and

$$Y_2 = \frac{(\beta_2 + \lambda_2\beta_1)Y_p + G_2 + \lambda_2 G_1 + e_2 + \lambda_2 e_1}{1 - \lambda_2\lambda_2}. \tag{42b}$$

These are semi-reduced forms because the G's and the e's have not been substituted out in terms of equations 40b and 40c. The sibling multiplier effect is also featured in equations 42 since $1 - \lambda_1\lambda_2 < 1$. The full reduced form for Y_1 is obtained by substituting equation 40b into equation 42a for G_1 and G_2 and substituting equations 41a and 41b for e_1 and e_2:

$$Y_1 = \frac{(\beta_1 + \lambda_1\beta_2)Y_p + (\rho_1 + \lambda_1\rho_2)G_p + \varepsilon_1 + \lambda_1\varepsilon_2}{1 - \lambda_1\lambda_2}$$
$$+ \frac{1}{1 - \lambda_1\lambda_2}\left(\frac{\varphi_1 + \pi_1\varphi_2}{1 - \pi_1} + \lambda_1\frac{\varphi_2 + \pi_2\varphi_1}{1 - \pi_2}\right)e_p$$
$$+ \frac{1}{1 - \lambda_1\lambda_2}\left[\frac{1}{1 - \pi_1} + \frac{\lambda_1\pi_2}{1 - \pi_2}\right]\mu_1 + \frac{1}{1 - \lambda_1\lambda_2}\left[\frac{\pi_1}{1 - \pi_1} + \frac{\lambda_1}{1 - \pi_2}\right]\mu_2. \tag{43}$$

Compare the preceding equation with equations 19. Y_1 varies directly with Y_p, G_p, and e_p, but because of sibling interaction the interpretations of the coefficients are very different. Also, in equation 43 Y_1 depends on the genetic draw of sibling 2 (ε_2) as well as on sibling 2's environmental draw (μ_2). The reduced form for Y_2 is not reported, but it has the same form as equation 43 with labels 1 and 2 interchanged. In the symmetric case, the reduced forms are identical and simplify to

$$Y_c = \frac{\beta(1 + \lambda)Y_p + \rho(1 + \lambda)G_p + \varepsilon_c + \lambda\varepsilon_s}{1 - \lambda^2} + \frac{\varphi(1 + \pi)(1 + \lambda)e_p + (1 + \lambda\pi)\mu_c + (\pi + \lambda)\mu}{(1 - \lambda^2)(1 - \pi)} \tag{44}$$

The conditional variance of Y_c generated by the preceding equation is as follows:

$$\text{var}(Y_c) = a\,\text{var}(Y_p) + b\,\text{var}(G_p) + c\,\text{var}(e_p) + d\sigma_\varepsilon^2$$
$$+ f\sigma_\mu^2 + h\,\text{cov}(Y_pG_p) + k\,\text{cov}(Y_pe_p), \tag{45}$$

where

$$a = \left(\frac{\beta(1+\lambda)}{1-\lambda^2}\right)^2,$$

$$b = \left(\frac{\rho(1+\lambda)}{1-\lambda^2}\right)^2,$$

$$c = \left[\frac{\phi(1+\pi)(1+\lambda)}{(1-\lambda^2)(1-\pi)}\right]^2,$$

$$d = \frac{1+\lambda^2}{(1-\lambda^2)^2},$$

$$f = \frac{(1+\lambda\pi)^2 + (\pi+\lambda)^2}{[(1-\lambda^2)(1-\pi)]^2},$$

$$h = \frac{\beta\rho(1+\lambda)^2}{(1-\lambda^2)^2},$$

and

$$k = \frac{\beta\varphi(1+\pi)(1+\lambda)^2}{(1-\lambda^2)^2(1-\pi)}.$$

Equation 45 is identical to equation 34 except for the fact that there is sibling interaction in the former but not in the latter. When there is no sibling interaction (that is, when $\lambda = \pi = 0$), equation 45 reverts in principle to equation 34. Sibling interaction magnifies the sizes of the parameters and therefore increases inequality. For example, $a = \beta^2$ when there is no sibling interaction and $c = \varphi^2$. There would be more equality if all children were singletons. A society with smaller families will tend to be more egalitarian because there is less scope for sibling interaction. Numerical illustrations of equation 45 are presented in table 4.8.

If there are three siblings, the scope for sibling interaction is larger. To illustrate this, let us simplify the data-generating process to

$$Y_1 = \beta Y_p + \lambda(Y_2 + Y_3) + \mu_1, \tag{46}$$

in which the outcomes for the three siblings are mutually dependent due to trilateral sibling interaction. The outcome for each child depends on the sum of the outcomes of his siblings. The DGPs for siblings 2 and 3 are assumed to be symmetrical. The reduced form is obtained by solving equation 46 for Y_1, Y_2, and Y_3. Since the DGP is symmetric, the reduced forms will be symmetric too for Y_c:

$$Y_c = \frac{\beta[1 + 2\lambda(1 + \lambda)]Y_p + \mu_c + \lambda(1 + \lambda)(\mu_{s1} + \mu_{s2})}{1 - 3\lambda^2 - 2\lambda^3}, \tag{47}$$

where s1 and s2 label the two siblings of c. Here the coefficient of Y_p is larger than its counterpart in equation 44 because the multiplier effect with three siblings is larger. If, for example, $\lambda = 0.2$, the multiplier effect is 1.5 with two children and 1.71 with three. With only one child, the multiplier is, of course, 1. This suggests that the sibling multiplier is convex in the number of children. Matters would be different, however, if λ varied with the number of siblings. Numerical illustrations based on equation 47 are presented in table 4.9.

8.3.2 Decomposing Sibling Correlations

What does the model imply for the correlation between siblings when that correlation is induced because they share parents and interact with each other? Simplifying equation 44 by assuming that $\rho = 0$ and ignoring the environmental components yields

$$Y_c = aY_p + \frac{\varepsilon_c + \lambda\varepsilon_s}{1 - \lambda^2}, \tag{48}$$

where

$$a = \frac{\beta(1 + \lambda)}{1 - \lambda^2}.$$

The sibling correlation coefficient is defined as

$$r_{cs} = \frac{\text{cov}(Y_c Y_s)}{\text{sd}(Y_c)\text{sd}(Y_s)} = \frac{\text{cov}(Y_c Y_s)}{\text{var}(Y_c)}. \tag{49}$$

According to equation 48, the sibling and intergenerational covariances are equal to

$$\text{cov}(Y_c Y_s) = a^2 \text{var}(Y_p) + b\sigma_\varepsilon^2, \tag{50a}$$

where

$$b = \frac{2\lambda}{(1-\lambda^2)^2} ,$$

and

$$\text{cov}(Y_c Y_p) = a \, \text{var}(Y_p) . \tag{50b}$$

Substituting equation 50a into equation 49 provides the decomposition for the sibling correlation:

$$r_{cs} = a^2 \frac{\text{var}(Y_p)}{\text{var}(Y_c)} + b \frac{\sigma_\varepsilon^2}{\text{var}(Y_c)} . \tag{51}$$

Equation 51 shows that the sibling correlation has several components. First, it varies directly with a^2, which in turn varies directly with β and λ. Second, it varies directly with sigma convergence. Third, it varies directly with b, which varies directly with the sibling interaction coefficient λ. Finally, it varies directly with the share of genes in the variance. If $a = 0$, the sibling correlation is equal to b, the "pure sibling correlation" that might have been hypothetically observed had siblings been born without parents. The pure sibling correlation is entirely induced by sibling interaction.

The intergenerational correlation according to equation 50b is

$$r_{cp} = a \frac{\text{sd}(Y_p)}{\text{sd}(Y_c)} . \tag{52}$$

Substituting equation 52 into equation 51 re-expresses the decomposition for the sibling correlation in terms of the intergenerational correlation[14]:

$$r_{cs} = r_{cp}^2 + b \frac{\sigma_\varepsilon^2}{\text{var}(Y_c)} = b + r_{cp}^2 (1-b) . \tag{53}$$

This equation establishes that the sibling correlation depends on the square of the intergenerational correlation and on b. Note that when $b = 0$ it states that the sibling correlation is equal to the square of the intergenerational correlation. The implications of equation 53 for the relationship between the sibling and intergenerational correlation are illustrated numerically in table 3.6. Equation 38 may be used to decompose r_{cp} in equation 53. Therefore, all the components of the intergenerational correlation apply to the decomposition of the sibling correlation.

If there is no sibling interaction because $\lambda = 0$, according to equation 53 the sibling correlation is simply equal to the square of the intergenerational correlation. However, this result applies specifically to the DGP in equation 48. Suppose instead that there is no sibling interaction but the DGP is symmetric for both siblings:

$$Y_c = \beta Y_p + \rho G_p + \varepsilon_c. \tag{54}$$

In this equation, the outcomes of children depend on their genotype and their parents' phenotype. Their genotype is partly inherited. Using the DGP to determine $\mathrm{cov}(Y_c Y_p)$ and $\mathrm{cov}(Y_c Y_p)$ as in equations 50 and substituting the results into the definition of the correlation coefficient gives the following solutions for the intergenerational and sibling correlation coefficients, respectively:

$$r_{cp} = \beta \frac{\mathrm{sd}(Y_p)}{\mathrm{sd}(Y_c)} + \rho \frac{\mathrm{cov}(Y_p G_p)}{\mathrm{sd}(Y_c)\mathrm{sd}(Y_p)}, \tag{55a}$$

$$r_{cs} = \frac{\beta^2 \,\mathrm{var}(Y_p) + 2\beta\rho\,\mathrm{cov}(Y_p G_p) + \rho^2 \,\mathrm{var}(G_p)}{\mathrm{var}(Y_c)}. \tag{55b}$$

According to equation 55a, the intergenerational correlation has an autoregressive component induced by β and a genetic component induced by ρ. The same components feature in equation 55b, but in a more complicated way. Substituting the square of equation 55a into equation 55b and reorganizing gives the following relationship between the sibling and intergenerational correlations:

$$r_{cs} = r_{cp}^2 + (1 - r_{Y_p G_p}^2) \frac{\rho^2 \,\mathrm{var}(G_p)}{\mathrm{var}(Y_c)}. \tag{56}$$

Here, as in equation 53, the sibling correlation depends on the square of the intergenerational correlation coefficient. The second component in equation 56 is induced by the fact that siblings share their parents' genes. This component is 0 if there is no heredity ($\rho = 0$), and it varies directly with ρ and $\mathrm{var}(G_p)$ and inversely with $\mathrm{var}(Y_c)$ and the correlation between Y_p and G_p. In general, the sibling correlation is equal to the square of the intergenerational correlation plus components induced by their sharing of parents, environments, and each other's company.

8.3.3 Birth Order
If the λ coefficients depend on birth order, the DGPs for siblings are asymmetric. If sibling 1 is older than sibling 2 and older siblings have

a greater effect on their younger sibling, λ_1 will be larger than λ_2. If the age gap between siblings is large, we might expect less sibling interaction than if it is small. Or sibling interaction may be stronger within sexes than between them. This would weaken sibling correlations, especially for siblings of different sexes born far apart. The same does not apply to ρ, since this is a genetic or heredity parameter, and heredity should not depend on birth order. However, there is every reason to suspect that β might depend on birth order. If parents help their first-borns more than they help their second-borns, β_1 will be greater than β_2.

In addition to the variables already mentioned, sibling outcomes will be correlated if age and birth order affect the outcome of interest. Suppose that the outcome of interest (Y) depends linearly on age (A) as follows: $Y = aA + u$, where u is independent of age and is entirely random with variance σ^2. Let A_1 denote the age of the elder sibling. The age of the younger sibling is $A_2 = A_1 - x$, where $x > 0$ denotes the age gap. Since Y varies directly with age, at a given instant in time the expected value of Y is larger for first-borns simply because they are older, i.e.,

$$E(Y_1) - E(Y_2) = aE(x) > 0.$$

The variances of Y by birth order are

$$\operatorname{var}(Y_1) = a^2 \operatorname{var}(A_1) + \sigma^2 \tag{57a}$$

and

$$\operatorname{var}(Y_2) = \operatorname{var}(Y_1) + a^2 [\operatorname{var}(x) - 2\operatorname{cov}(A_1 x)]. \tag{57b}$$

For two reasons, the variance for second-borns is not the same as the variance for first-borns. First, the age gap is a random variable, which naturally increases the variance. The covariance term $\operatorname{cov}(A_1 x)$ will be negative in cohort data if parents who start their families when they are older reduce the birth gap by having children more frequently as they make up for lost time. Only if birth spacing is not a random variable, and x is fixed across families, will the sibling variances be identical.

The sibling correlation for Y (assuming that u_1 and u_2 are independent) is

$$r_{cs} = a^2 \frac{\operatorname{var}(A_1) - \operatorname{cov}(A_1 x)}{\operatorname{sd}(Y_1)\operatorname{sd}(Y_2)}. \tag{58}$$

Note that this component of the sibling correlation arises because siblings have different ages when observed at a given point in time. Controlling for sibling ages, however, would neutralize the effect of age.

8.3.4 Discriminatory Parenting and Sibling Heterogeneity

Parents may wish to invest more in their abler children because the return to investment varies directly with ability. In this case, further inequality between siblings is induced, since abler siblings attract more parental investments. On the other hand, parents may adopt an egalitarian policy by investing more in their less able children to compensate them for their innate disadvantages. This subsection explores the implications of discriminatory parenting for the sibling correlation coefficient. Parents' differential treatment of children will be discussed in section 9.4.

To simplify matters, it is assumed that siblings do not interact. Also, all variables are assumed to have zero expected values so that covariances between random variables are equal to the expected value of their products. The phenotypic models are

$$Y_1 = \pi_1 P_1 + G_1 \tag{59a}$$

and

$$Y_2 = \pi_2 P_2 + G_2 , \tag{59b}$$

where P denotes parental investment and G denotes genotype. Since siblings are genetically similar, $\text{cov}(G_1 G_2) = \rho$. The returns to parenting are denoted by π_1 and π_2, which are random variables with covariance $\text{cov}(\pi_1 \pi_2) = \phi$. This parameter may also have a genetic component so that ϕ is positive if returns to parenting are correlated. If P_1 and P_2 differ, parents are discriminatory. (This will be discussed in chapter 9.)

If parents are perfectly egalitarian so that $P_1 = P_2 = P$, equations 59 imply that the sibling covariance has two genetic components, ρ and ϕ:

$$\text{cov}(Y_1 Y_2) = \rho + \phi P^2 . \tag{60a}$$

If parents aren't egalitarian and $\pi_1 = \pi_2 = \pi$ (i.e., the returns to parenting are perfectly correlated between siblings), the covariance between sibling phenotypes is equal to

$$\text{cov}(Y_1 Y_2) = \rho + \pi^2 \text{cov}(P_1 P_2) + \pi[\text{cov}(P_2 G_1) + \text{cov}(P_1 G_2)] . \tag{60b}$$

This equation states that the sibling covariance varies directly with ρ through the genetic relationship between siblings. If the covariance between P_1 and P_2 is negative because parents allocate a fixed amount of parental resources between their children, the sibling covariance decreases. The opposite happens if parents invest more in their less fit children so that the gene-parenting covariance, $\text{cov}(P_1 G_2)$, is positive. The sibling covariance varies inversely with π if the covariances in equation 60b are negative.

If π_1 and π_2 differ, equation 60b becomes

$$\text{cov}(Y_1 Y_2) = \rho + \text{cov}(P_1 \pi_1)\text{cov}(P_2 \pi_2) + \text{cov}(P_1^* G_2) + \text{cov}(P_2^* G_1), \qquad (60c)$$

where $P^* = \pi P$ is the effect of parenting. Equation 60c is similar to equation 60b, except that the effect of parenting (P^*) matters rather than parenting itself (P) and there is a new term in the covariance between parenting and the return to parenting, i.e., $\text{cov}(\pi P)$. If parents invest more if the return to parenting is larger, $\text{cov}(\pi P)$ is positive, which increases the sibling covariance. If instead parents invest more in their less fit children, the opposite happens.

8.4   Multiple Phenotypes

So far we have been concerned with a single phenotype, Y. There are, however, numerous situations in which a number of phenotypes affect each other and are, therefore, jointly determined. A classic example is the joint determination of schooling and earnings, or of two or more health outcomes that are suspected of having a common genetic origin and for which comorbidity is suspected. A detailed analysis of the joint determination of schooling and earnings may be found in chapter 9. Here I illustrate matters using correlated health outcomes.

8.4.1   The Comorbidity Model

Let Y_A denote a latent variable for morbidity regarding disease A, and let Y_B denote the counterpart for disease B. If $Y_{Ai} > Y_A^*$, individual i catches disease A. This means that if i is sufficiently morbid with respect to some threshold Y_A^* he catches the disease, and if he is below the threshold he does not catch the disease. The threshold for disease B is Y_B^*. Individual i may catch either, both, or neither of the diseases. D_A is a dummy variable equal to 1 if disease A is caught and 0 otherwise. D_B is the counterpart for disease B. There are four possibilities:

$D_A = D_B = 0$ (i.e., neither disease is caught).

$D_A = D_B = 1$ (i.e., both diseases are caught).

$D_A = 1$ and $D_B = 0$ (i.e., only disease A is caught).

$D_A = 0$ and $D_B = 1$ (i.e., only diseases B is caught).

Morbidity cannot be observed; hence Y_A and Y_B are unobservable. That is why they are defined as latent variables. However, D_A and D_B are observable. In a logit model (with Y^* normalized to 0) the probability of catching the diseases is specified as follows:

$$P(D_{Ai} = 1) = \frac{1}{1+\exp(-Y_{Ai})}, \tag{61a}$$

$$P(D_{Bi} = 1) = \frac{1}{1+\exp(-Y_{Bi})}. \tag{61b}$$

These equations state that the probability of catching the diseases varies directly with morbidity. However, this effect is nonlinear; the marginal effect of morbidity increases initially and eventually decreases after the inflection point of the logistic curve is passed.[15]

The DGPs for morbidity are assumed to be the following:

$$Y_{cA} = \alpha_A Y_{cB} + \rho_A D_{pA} + \theta_A G_c + v_{cA}, \tag{62a}$$

$$Y_{cB} = \alpha_B Y_{cA} + \rho_B D_{pB} + \theta_B G_c + v_{cB}. \tag{62b}$$

These equations state that children's morbidity with respect to disease A depends on their morbidity with respect to disease B and vice versa. The α's are less than 1 in absolute value. If the α's are positive, morbidity is mutually reinforcing; if they are negative, they are mutually immunizing. In the latter case, exposure to A induces immunity to B and vice versa. If the parents had the disease, this may induce morbidity directly via ρ. Children may be more vulnerable simply because their parents had the disease. This causal channel is quite separate from heredity, through which parents affect genotypes as in equation 1. If parents with larger G_p happen to have a greater predisposition toward a disease, their morbidity Y_p increases, which increases the probability that $D_p = 1$. Therefore, G_c and D_p will be positively correlated in equations 62. Morbidity has a genetic basis if the θ's are nonzero. However, the effects of genotypes on morbidity differ if θ_A differs from θ_B. Finally, the v's in equations 62 are other random variables that affect morbidity. They have common variance σ_v^2 and are assumed for simplicity to be mutually independent. In the logit model the cumulative (Gumbel) distribution function for v is assumed to be $F(v) = -v\exp(-v)$.

8.4.2 Phenotype Correlations

Equations 62 are simultaneous equations in morbidity. Solving them gives their reduced forms:

$$Y_{cA} = \frac{\alpha_A \rho_B D_{pB} + \rho_A D_{pA} + (\theta_A + \alpha_A \theta_B) + \alpha_A v_{cB} + v_{cA}}{1 - \alpha_A \alpha_B}, \tag{63a}$$

$$Y_{cB} = \frac{\alpha_B \rho A D_{pA} + \rho_B D_{pB} + (\theta_B + \alpha_B \theta_A) + \alpha_B v_{cA} + v_{cB}}{1 - \alpha_A \alpha_B}. \tag{63b}$$

Notice that in the reduced forms parents' disease status for disease A indirectly affects their children's morbidity for disease B and vice versa. The same applies to the v's, which mutually affect morbidity. Notice, also, the "comorbidity multiplier"—the total effect of genotypes on morbidity is greater than the direct effects because $1 - \alpha_A \alpha_B < 1$.

Since our interest is in comorbidity, we can use the reduced forms to derive the sibling covariance for morbidity, $cov(Y_{cA}Y_{cB})$. However, to simplify the notation we can assume that the DGP is symmetrical, and hence that $\alpha_A = \alpha_B = \alpha$ and so on, and ignore the covariance between Dp and G_c. The covariance is equal to

$$
\begin{aligned}
&cov(Y_{cA}Y_{cB}) \\
&= \frac{\alpha\rho^2[var(D_{pA}) + var(D_{pB})] + \rho^2\alpha^2 cov(D_{pA}D_{pB}) + \theta^2(1+\alpha^2)var(G_c) + 2\alpha\sigma_v^2}{(1-\alpha^2)^2}.
\end{aligned}
\tag{64}
$$

This equation shows that parents are involved in the comorbidity of their children through several channels. First, comorbidity among parents induces comorbidity among children via $cov(D_{pA}D_{pB})$. Second, the greater are the variances of morbidity among parents the larger is comorbidity for children.[16] Third, comorbidity for children varies directly with the variance of their genotypes. However, the latter depends on the variance of genotypes among parents via equation 2. Finally, comorbidity varies directly (inversely) with the variance of v if α is positive (negative).

The variance of morbidity for children for both diseases is the same in the symmetric case and is equal to

$$\text{var}(Y_c) =$$
$$\frac{\alpha\rho^2\left[\text{var}(D_{pA})+\text{var}(D_{pB})\right]+\rho^2\alpha^2\,\text{cov}(D_{pA}D_{pB})+\theta^2(1+\alpha^2)\text{var}(G_c)+(1+\alpha^2)}{(1-\alpha^2)^2}$$

$$(65)$$

Finally, to obtain the correlation coefficient for comorbidity, equation 64 is divided by equation 65:

$$r_{AB} = \frac{\Omega + 2\alpha\sigma_v^2}{\Omega + (1+\alpha^2)\sigma_v^2}, \qquad (66a)$$

where

$$\Omega = \alpha\rho^2[\text{var}(D_{pA})+\text{var}(D_{pB})]+\rho^2\alpha^2\,\text{cov}(D_{pA}D_{pB})+\theta^2(1+\alpha^2)\text{var}(G_c).$$

$$(66b)$$

Since α cannot be larger than 1, the numerator in equation 66a must be smaller than the denominator, in which case the correlation is less than 1, as expected. If $\alpha = \rho = \theta = 0$, the correlation coefficient is 0, as expected.

8.5   Inequality and Mobility

Consider an outcome or phenotype Y, such as height or income, and let R_i denote the rank of individual i in the distribution for Y. If there are N individuals, then R is a number between 1 (the smallest value of Y) and N (the largest value for Y). If $R_i = N/2$, then Y_i is the median member of the distribution. Because individuals have different Y's, there is inequality; they have different heights or incomes. Inequality in height usually doesn't generate ideological sentiments about what the distribution should be. However, the same may not apply to economic variables, such as income. Egalitarians attach importance to equality *per se*. Or they may wish to attach particular importance to individuals who are in the tails of the income distribution—the very poor and the very rich. Perhaps there is no entirely ideology-free measure of inequality, but some measures of inequality that have been proposed are explicitly ideological, either because they assume that complete equality is desirable or because they assume that inequality is undesirable.

As we have seen, inequality and mobility are inextricably interwoven. So far, inequality has been measured by the variance or standard deviation and mobility by β. In this section, alternative measures of inequality and mobility are considered.

8.5.1   Measuring Inequality[17]

Let M denote a statistical measure of inequality such that if M increases there is more inequality. A satisfactory candidate for M should satisfy several criteria:

1. *The Weak Principle of Transfers (WPT)*   Consider two individuals i and j such that $Y_j = Y_i + d$, i.e., j is richer or heavier than i, since $d > 0$. If $y < \frac{1}{2}d$ is transferred from j to i, M should decrease for all values of d. WPT is common sense.

2. *The Strong Principle of Transfers (SPT)*   WPT does not attach any importance to the amount of reduction in inequality as measured by M. Common sense suggests that transferring y from the very rich to the rich should reduce inequality by less than transferring y from the very rich to the poor. Metrics with this property satisfy SPT.

3. *Scale Independence*   If Y increases proportionately for all individuals (i.e., everyone becomes heavier or richer by the same percentage), M should not change. This too is common sense. It means that inequality does not depend on the size of the cake.

4. *Principle of Population*   Nor should inequality depend on the number of cake- eaters (N). If two equally sized societies that are equally unequal ($M_1 = M_2 = M$) combine to form one large society with population $2N$, inequality has not changed, so M for the combined society should remain the same.

5. *Fixed Metric*   If there is complete equality, M should always have a lower bound equal to M_L. If there is complete inequality, M should always have an upper bound equal to M_H.

Some of these criteria are more important than others. The first is of primary importance. If the mean of Y and the population do not change, the third and the fourth aren't important. The fifth criterion is arguably the least important, since it simply sets upper and lower bounds to inequality for convenience.

Five common measures of inequality feature in table 8.2. The variance is, no doubt, the most familiar measure. It has a lower bound of 0 (complete equality, where everyone has the same), and an upper bound (complete inequality, where one person has all) that varies directly with N and $\bar{Y}$. The variance satisfies SPT, which encompasses WPT by definition. The coefficient of variation (CV), derived from the variance, is the standard deviation as a percentage of the mean. It is bounded between 0 and an upper bound that varies directly with N,

Table 8.2
Metrics for inequality.

Case	Metric		Perfect equality	Perfect inequality	Criteria satisfied
1	Variance	$\dfrac{1}{N}\sum\limits_{i=1}^{N}(Y_i - \bar{Y})^2$	0	$(N-1)\bar{Y}^2$	1,2
2	Coefficient of variation	$\dfrac{sd}{\bar{Y}}$	0	$\sqrt{N-1}$	1,3,4
3	Herfindahl's concentration index	$\dfrac{1}{N^2}\sum\limits_{i=1}^{N}\dfrac{Y_i^2}{\bar{Y}^2}$	$\dfrac{1}{N}$	1	1,2,3
4	Theil's entropy index	$\dfrac{1}{N}\sum\limits_{i=1}^{N}\left(\dfrac{Y_i}{\bar{Y}}\ln\dfrac{Y_i}{\bar{Y}}\right)$	0	$\ln N$	1,2,3,4
5	Gini coefficient	$\dfrac{1}{N^2\bar{Y}}\sum\limits_{i=1}^{N}\sum\limits_{i=1}^{N}|Y_i - Y_j|$	0	1	1,3,4,5

and it satisfies criteria 1, 3, and 4. Herfindahl's index of concentration (H) is the sum of the squared shares in the total. It has a lower bound of $1/N$ and an upper bound of 1, and it satisfies criteria 1, 2, and 3. Note that $H = (1 + CV^2)/N$, so metrics 1, 2, and 3 are related. In contrast, metrics 4 and 5 are not related. Theil's inequality coefficient (T) is bounded between 0 and $\ln N$, and satisfies all criteria except the fifth. Finally, the Gini coefficient (G) is based on the absolute differences between all pairs of individuals. It satisfies all criteria except SPT.

None of the metrics satisfy all the criteria. It is possible to fix this by attaching to Y_i weights that express aversion to inequality, which essentially imposes SPT on the metric. Atkinson's (1970) influential index satisfies all the criteria, but because it imposes ideological weights to Y_i it is not considered here. These weights are based on the principle that a dollar is worth more to a poor man than a dollar is worth to a rich man. In any case, it would be meaningless to calculate Atkinson indices for height and other ideologically neutral variables. A dollar may mean more to a poor man than to a rich man, but does a centimeter mean more to a short person than to a tall one? Therefore, the metrics features in table 8.2 are non-ideological.

8.5.2 The Gini Coefficient
The Gini coefficient G[18] satisfies four of the five criteria. Because it is based on absolute paired differences, it doesn't satisfy SPT. This means

that if y is transferred, as in criterion 1, it reduces G by more if the parties are in the middle of the distribution than if they are at either end. Therefore, the transfer of a dollar from someone with \$1,100 to someone with \$1,000 reduces G by more than the transfer of a dollar from someone with \$100 to someone with \$0, or from someone with \$10,100 to someone with \$10,000. Despite the fact that it does not satisfy SPT, G has proved to be the most popular measure of economic inequality. The reasons for this aren't obvious. After all, Theil's metric also satisfies four criteria, and like the Gini coefficient, can be conveniently decomposed into within-group inequality and between-group inequality. I think the reason behind the popularity of the Gini coefficient is that criterion 5 is more convenient than criterion 2. Practitioners prefer metrics that are bounded between 0 and 1. Because this enables them to compare inequality across time periods, countries and variables, they are prepared to sacrifice SPT.

This property of the Gini coefficient is more obvious if we use Schechter and Yitzhaki's (1987) formula for it:

$$G = 2\frac{\text{cov}(Y_i R_i)}{\overline{Y}}. \tag{67}$$

What matters in this formula is the covariance between Y and its rank. This covariance is naturally positive, because people with larger Y have bigger R. However, the covariance will be smaller if the distribution of Y is tight. R_i is greater than R_j even if Y_i exceeds Y_j by only a tiny amount. Perhaps the best way to understand the Gini coefficient is in terms of the Lorenz curve (illustrated in figure 8.3), in which the horizontal axis ranks individuals from lowest to highest in terms of percentiles and the vertical axis measures percentage shares in the total. In figure 8.3 the Lorenz curve is denoted by the curve ACB, which plots the shares in the total against shares in the population. At point C, for example, p_1 percent of the population owns y_1 percent of the cake. Note that p_1 is larger than y_1. At point B, p and y naturally tend to 100 percent, whereas at point A they are 0. The Lorenz curve must be increasing, since as p increases more of the cake is accounted for. However, it doesn't have to increase as smoothly as in figure 8.3. Suppose the Lorenz curve had been the straight line AB, which has a slope of 45°. Along AB there is complete equality, since y and p are the same. For example, when $p = p_1$, y equals y_2 instead of y_1. Since $p_1 = y_2$, there is complete inequality. In figure 8.3 the triangle ABD is divided into two areas: Q, which lies below (to the right of) the Lorenz curve, and H,

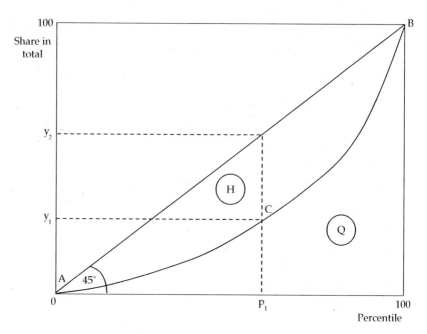

Figure 8.3
The Lorenz curve.

which lies above it but below the line AB. Intuition suggests that there is more inequality when H is larger. If H = 0, there is complete equality, since the Lorenz curve is AB. At the other extreme, where H = Q, there is complete inequality, since one individual has all the cake. The Gini coefficient is equal to the share of H in the triangle ABD; therefore, $G = H/(H + Q)$. The more distended the Lorenz curve (that is, the further ACB is from AB), the greater is H, and the larger is G.

8.5.3 Beta Convergence and Sigma Convergence

The concepts of beta convergence and sigma convergence were introduced in section 8.1. As we shall see, β measures absolute mobility, and sigma convergence and beta convergence are related conceptually. Therefore, mobility and sigma convergence must be conceptually related. In what follows, I examine this relationship—first by the method of least squares, which has been the dominant methodology. It turns out that this methodology entirely overlooks the concept of relative mobility. This is followed by a discussion of a methodology based on the Gini coefficient, which elegantly integrates the concepts of absolute mobility, relative mobility, sigma convergence, leveling up, and leveling down.

Consider equation 19a, which is repeated here for convenience:

$$Y_{ci} = \alpha + \beta Y_{pi} + G_{ci} + e_{ci}.$$

We are interested in estimating β from cross-section data on pairs of parents and children. The ordinary least squares (OLS) regression coefficient obtained by regressing Y_c on Y_p is defined as

$$\hat{\beta}_{OLS} = \frac{\mathrm{cov}(Y_c Y_p)}{\mathrm{var}(Y_p)}. \tag{68a}$$

Substituting for $\mathrm{cov}(Y_c Y_p)$ in terms of the intergenerational correlation coefficient gives

$$\hat{\beta}_{OLS} = r_{cp} \frac{\mathrm{sd}(Y_c)}{\mathrm{sd}(Y_p)}. \tag{68b}$$

Sigma convergence means that $\mathrm{sd}(Y_c) < \mathrm{sd}(Y_p)$; that is, Y is more equally distributed among children than it was among their parents. Beta convergence means that $0 < \beta < 1$; that is, there is regression toward the mean, or mean reversion in Y from one generation to the next. If $\beta > 1$, there is beta divergence; if $\mathrm{sd}(Y_c) > \mathrm{sd}(Y_p)$, there is sigma divergence. Equation 68b indicates the following results about the relationship between sigma convergence and beta convergence:

1. Sigma convergence necessarily implies beta convergence. Sigma convergence means that $\mathrm{sd}(Y_c)/\mathrm{sd}(Y_p) < 1$. Since $r_{cp} < 1$, β_{OLS} must be less than 1 in this case.

2. Sigma divergence does not necessarily imply beta divergence, since $r_{cp} < 1$.

3. Beta divergence necessarily implies sigma divergence, since $r_{cp} < 1$.

4. Beta convergence does not necessarily imply sigma convergence, since $r_{cp} < 1$.

These relationships between beta convergence and sigma convergence refer specifically to cross-section data on parents and children, i.e. to two consecutive generations. We have already seen (in section 8.2) that beta convergence implies sigma convergence over many generations. Therefore, the four relationships listed above refer to short-run mobility and inequality.

8.5.4   Beta Convergence, Gini Convergence, and Mobility

Beta has probably served as the most popular measure of mobility. Beta convergence, or mean reversion, means that phenotypes among children increase in families in which parents are relatively unfit, and decrease in families with relatively fit parents. This implies that children with less fit parents are upwardly mobile, whereas the children of fitter parents are downwardly mobile. Here "mobility" means absolute mobility. If outcomes were perfectly immobile, β would be 1 and the outcomes of children would be expected to be the same as those of their parents.

Let Y_{pi} denote an outcome for parent i, and let R_{pi} denote i's rank in the distribution of Y for parents. The corresponding outcomes for children are Y_{ci} and R_{ci}. Suppose, for simplicity, that parents have one child and that the means of Y for parents and children are the same too. If $Y_{ci} > Y_{pi}$, children are upwardly mobile in terms of Y—their outcome is larger than their parents'. Another measure of upward mobility is based on the rank of the outcome rather than the outcome itself. If $R_{ci} > R_{pi}$, children are upwardly mobile in terms of rank; the rank of the child in his distribution is higher than the rank of his parents in the distribution for parents. I shall refer to the former as *absolute mobility*, because what matters are comparisons between absolute values of Y. I shall refer to the latter as *relative mobility*, because rank, or pecking order, is inherently a relative concept. Therefore, if the phenotype is height or income, absolute mobility is measured in centimeters or dollars, whereas relative mobility is measured in terms of rank.

Absolute and relative mobility are fundamentally different concepts. Indeed, upward relative mobility may coexist with downward absolute mobility, and vice versa. A child can improve his rank in the distribution of Y for children relative to the rank of his parents, but he may nonetheless have a smaller Y than his parents. Therefore, $R_{ci} > R_{pi}$ may coincide with $Y_{ci} < Y_{pi}$. Of course, the two concepts of mobility may not be in conflict.

I follow Wodon and Yitzhaki (2001) in exploring the relationship between absolute and relative mobility. The OLS estimator for β is obtained by regressing Y_c on Y_p using cross-section data, as in equation 68b. However, since we use the Gini coefficient to measure inequality, we may prefer to use the Gini estimator for β, which uses the rank of Y_p, denoted by R_p rather than Y_p. The Gini regression estimator is

$$\beta_{Gini} = \frac{\text{cov}(Y_c R_p)}{\text{cov}(Y_p R_c)}. \tag{69}$$

The Gini estimator may be regarded as an instrumental-variables estimator,[19] since it uses the rank to instrument the level. The OLS estimator replaces R_p with Y_p. Since the rank of Y is typically measured more accurately than Y itself, the Gini regression coefficient is arguably a superior estimator than its OLS counterpart.

The intergenerational Gini correlation coefficients for Y are defined as follows:

$$\Gamma_{cp} = \frac{\text{cov}(Y_c, R_p)}{\text{cov}(Y_c, R_c)},$$
(70a)

$$\Gamma_{pc} = \frac{\text{cov}(Y_p, R_c)}{\text{cov}(Y_p, R_p)}.$$
(70b)

Unlike Pearson correlations, which are symmetrical, Gini correlations are asymmetrical. Therefore, the Gini correlation between children and parents in equation 70a is generally different from the Gini correlation between parents and children in equation 70b. Indeed, they may even have different signs. Equation 70a conditions on children's outcomes, and therefore measures backward mobility because it correlates outcomes for parents with their children's outcomes. Equation 70b conditions on outcomes for parents, and therefore measures forward mobility because it correlates outcomes for children with their parents' outcomes. So the direction of mobility matters. The two Gini correlations will be equal if the distributions of the data for Y_c and Y_p are "exchangeable"—that is, if their marginal distributions are similar and the relationships between Y_c and Y_p are symmetric.

Gini correlations, like Pearson correlations, are bounded between 1 and –1. Y is perfectly immobile when $\Gamma_{cp} = 1$. If $\Gamma_{cp} = 0$, there is random relative mobility, because it is not possible to infer R_c using information on Y_p. For all practical purposes, this represents the case of complete mobility. When $\Gamma_{cp} = -1$, there is perfectly reverse mobility: the child of the top-ranked parent has the lowest rank, and the child of the lowest ranked parent has the top rank. The child of the second-ranked parent is ranked second before the bottom, and so on. Note that when $\Gamma_{cp} = 0$, $\Gamma_{pc} = 0$, and that when $\Gamma_{cp} = 1$, $\Gamma_{pc} = 1$,

Substituting equations 67 and 70b into equation 65 gives rise to the following important decomposition theorem for β:

$$\beta_{\text{Gini}} = \Gamma_{cp} \frac{G_c}{G_p} \frac{\overline{Y_c}}{\overline{Y_p}}.$$
(71)

This equation shows that Gini β, which measures absolute immobility, varies directly with (backward) relative immobility (Γ_{cp}). It also varies inversely with the degree of Gini divergence as measured by G_c/G_p. Gini divergence is the counterpart of sigma divergence. And it varies directly with the rate of leveling up as measured by $\bar{Y}_c/\bar{Y}_p$, which exceeds unity in the event of leveling up and which is less than unity in the event of leveling down. Secular growth in the phenotype implies leveling up. If all three components happen to equal unity (i.e., there is no relative mobility), the Gini coefficient is stable and there is neither leveling up or down; then β_{Gini} is 1 and the rate of mean reversion is 0. When $G_c = G_p$ and $\bar{Y}_c = \bar{Y}_p$, equation 71 implies that $\beta_{Gini} = \Gamma_{cp}$, i.e., relative mobility and absolute mobility are identical when the Gini coefficient is stable and there is no leveling up or down. In general, however, the two measures of mobility differ. Indeed, beta may exceed unity when Γ is less than unity, and vice versa. If $\Gamma = 0$, then $\beta_{Gini} = 0$ regardless of the rates of Gini convergence and leveling. Equation 71 implies that the relationship between beta convergence and sigma convergence is essentially different from the relationship between beta convergence and Gini convergence. Because relative mobility and leveling are additional parameters, one cannot infer Gini convergence or Gini divergence from beta convergence or beta divergence.

As has been noted, in general Γ_{cp} differs from Γ_{pc}—that is, backward and forward measures of relative mobility differ. The problem is similar to the common index number effect, where, for example, the rate of inflation depends on the direction of measurement. Yitzhaki (2003) has suggested a symmetric "Gini Mobility Index" that weights the forward and backward measures of relative mobility. The index is defined as

$$S = \frac{G_p(1-\Gamma_{pc})+G_c(1-\Gamma_{pc})}{G_p+G_c}. \tag{72}$$

S is naturally bounded between 0 (no relative mobility) and 2 (perfectly perverse mobility). When $S = 1$, relative mobility is random. Numerical and empirical illustrations of equations 71 and 72 may be found in tables 4.6 and 4.7.

8.5.5   Rank Correlations
The Gini mobility index may be compared to other measures of relative mobility, which are concerned with the correlations for ranked data. Two popular candidates are r_S (due to Spearman) and r_K (due to Kendall):

$$r_S = 1 - \frac{6\sum_{i=1}^{N}(R_{ci} - R_{pi})^2}{N(N^2 - 1)}, \tag{73a}$$

$$r_K = \frac{2\sum_{i=1}^{N} k_i}{N(N-1)}. \tag{73b}$$

Spearman's rank correlation coefficient is bounded between −1 and 1. If the ranks are uncorrelated, $r_S = 0$. Kendall's rank correlation coefficient also is bounded between −1 and 1. It is calculated as follows: Rank the outcome for parents Y_p in descending order from $i = 1, 2, \ldots, N$. Define k_i as the difference between the number of children who are ranked below i and the number of children ranked above i. For example, if $N = 10$ and $i = 4$ there are six children of whose parents occupied ranks 5 to 10. If three of these six children occupy ranks below 4 (i.e., 5, 6, 7, 8, 9, or 10) and one occupies a rank above 4 (i.e., 1, 2, or 3), then $k_4 = 3 - 1 = 2$. If parents and children occupy the same ranks, then $k_i = N - i$, in which case $r_K = 1$. Equations 73a and 73b differ in the way they weight differences between R_c and R_p; whereas equation 73a weights them according to the squared difference, equation 73b simply weights them according to the number of children above and below the rank of their parents. Therefore, r_K is a non-parametric statistic, which makes it more attractive than r_S.

Relative mobility varies inversely with the rank correlation coefficient. If the rank correlation is 1, there is complete relative immobility, since the ranks of children are identical to the ranks of their parents. If the rank correlation is 0, there is complete relative mobility, since the ranks of children are uncorrelated with the ranks of the parents. If the rank correlation is −1, there is complete reverse mobility: the top-ranked parent has bottom-ranked children, the children of the second-ranked parent are ranked next to the bottom, and so on. When the ranked correlations are 1, 0, or −1, the Spearman and Kendall correlations are the same.

Another approach to measuring relative mobility, suggested by Bartholomew,[20] is denoted here by b. It is based on the transition matrix T_{pc}, which calculates the proportion p_{kj} of parents in percentile k whose children are in percentile j, where q denotes the number of percentiles. In the case of deciles, $q = 10$ and T_{cp} is a 10×10 matrix with elements p_{ki}. If there is no mobility, $p_{kk} = 1$ and $p_{ki} = 0$; that is, $T_{pc} = I$ is a diagonal matrix, and the children occupy the same percentile as their parents. In this case, $b = 0$. The formula for b is

$$b = \frac{2}{q(1+q)} \sum_{k=1}^{q} \sum_{j=1}^{q} p_{kj} |k - j|. \tag{74}$$

There is complete upward mobility when all the children of parents in percentile k occupy the top percentile, q; that is, $p_{kq} = 1$ and $p_{kj} = 0$, where $j \neq q$. In this case, $b = 1$. There is complete downward mobility when all the children of parents in percentile k occupy the bottom percentile, i.e., $p_{k1} = 1$ otherwise $p_{kj} = 0$. In this case too $b = 1$, since equation 74 is insensitive to the direction of mobility because the absolute value of $k - j$ is used. Therefore, relative mobility varies directly with b, which moves in the opposite direction to the rank correlations.

The main difference between b and the rank correlations is that b ignores intra-percentile mobility. It therefore understates relative mobility. Also, the number of percentiles q is arbitrary. In the limit, as $q = N$ and the number of percentiles equals the number of observations, equation 74 becomes

$$b = \frac{2}{N(1+N)} \sum_{i=1}^{N} |R_{\text{p}i} - R_{\text{c}i}|. \tag{75}$$

If instead of the absolute difference between ranks the simple difference were used, $1 - b$ would be a rank correlation coefficient, since $b = 1$ when the ranks of parents are identical to the ranks of children.

Finally, the difference between the Gini mobility index in equation 72 and the rank correlations is that the latter are exclusively reliant on the ranks of parents and children, whereas the Gini mobility index uses information on outcomes as well as ranks. Strictly speaking, therefore, the Gini mobility index is not a pure measure of relative mobility. However, it has the great advantage of being decomposable, so that relative mobility, absolute mobility, leveling up or down, and Gini convergence can be integrated both conceptually and statistically as in equation 72. No such integration is available for OLS estimates of β (which measure absolute mobility), for Spearman's rank correlation (which measures relative mobility), for the standard deviations for parents and children (which measure sigma convergence), or for leveling up or down.

9   Parenting Theory and Child Behavior

9.1   Axiomatic Theory

In chapter 1, I recalled the controversy over Wilson's suggestion that the sociobiology of animals might be applicable to humans. Sociobiologists axiomatized the theory of animal behavior by assuming that animals seek to maximize survival. The suggestion that human behavior and sex roles may be understood in terms of survivalism was received with derision and contempt. Wilson was accused of reductionism, sexism, and even racism. Though Wilson's suggestion attracted a great deal of criticism, economists entered the fray with virtual impunity. At approximately the same time that sociobiologists were developing their radical theories of animal behavior, Gary Becker and H. Gregg Lewis (1973) pioneered the "economic theory of human fertility." Superficially, the economic theory of fertility and sociobiological theory are similar: people instinctively desire to have children, and the tasks of parenting are allocated according to the comparative advantages of mothers and fathers. But whereas sociobiology is strongly evolutionary, the economic theory of fertility is not. For Becker, parents desire children simply because they enjoy being parents. Apart from children, parents have other aspects of life that are important to them, such as their careers and consumerism.

Although people may enjoy being parents for evolutionary reasons, economics seem to be more matter-of-fact about it than sociobiology. Treating the urge to procreate as an instinct that requires no explanation, economists focus on the price or cost of this instinct. In addition to the cost of raising children, the price of parenting includes what economists refer to as *opportunity costs*. These opportunity costs include opportunities forgone as a result of parenting, especially in terms of time forgone. Time spent on parenting is time not spent on other activities, since there are only 24 hours in a day.

Economics has traditionally been concerned with tradeoffs and with preferences or tastes. From this perspective, human fertility is just another "good" to be traded off with competing goods. Parents who choose to have more children have less of something else. Also, parents have different preferences for children and rival goods. Some get more pleasure out of children than others, and some get no pleasure at all.

Although the parenting instinct is central to the economic theory of fertility, it is not an absolute or exclusive instinct that supersedes all others. Instead, it is a relative instinct. It is no more or less important than the hedonist instinct to consume and to enjoy life in general. Perhaps sociobiology misjudged animals by assuming that their survival instinct reigns supreme and is absolute. Perhaps animals, like humans, are hedonists and trade off survivalism with hedonism. Perhaps sociobiology has something to learn from economics, just as economics has something to learn from sociobiology.

The Malthusian theory of population earned economics a bad name, "the Dismal Science," because it predicted that increased fertility induces mortality. Moreover, in this equilibrium people live at the margin of subsistence. Malthus predicted that an expansion of the population would increase pressure on economic resources, especially land, such that people would be forced to live below the margin of subsistence, and would eventually die as a result. In this way, the size of the population would be forced checked, and would be forced brought back into subsistence equilibrium. As Becker (1991, p. 136) noted, Darwin had read Malthus and was greatly influenced by him. In the Malthusian struggle to survive, Darwin predicted, natural selection would ensure that fitter children would survive to become parents, and, since fitness is inherited, future generations would be fitter. Natural selection would, therefore, increase the average fitness of the population.

"Although the Darwinian theory is highly relevant to nonhuman populations," Becker notes (p. 136), "it appears less applicable to human populations. Most families have controlled their fertility and have had fewer children than their capacities permit."

According to the economic theory of fertility, parents decide on both the quantity and the quality of their children. They invest in the quality of their children by investing in their health, their education, and their vocational training. Since these investments are costly, parents face a tradeoff between quantity and quality. If, with everything else equal, they have more children, they will invest less in each child, in which case the "quality" of the average child will be less than if they had fewer children.

This so-called Quality vs. Quantity Theory (QQT) is not just about fertility. Insofar as it seeks to explain parents' investment in their children's education, it contains the beginnings of an axiomatic treatment of parenting. There are, of course, many other aspects to parenting apart from educating children. However, the basic axioms of QQT may be extended to other aspects of parenting. Therefore, a second purpose of this chapter is to present an axiomatic theory of parenting according to which parents are concerned with the emotional and physical development of their children, but parents also have other objectives in life apart from their children. Parents face economic constraints, as in the QQT; the more they spend on their children, the less they have for other things. In addition, they face a time constraint: the more time they devote to their children the less time they have to spend on themselves. Whereas economic resources are storable and can be transferred from one period to the next, time is not storable. Economic resources may be borrowed and lent in the capital market, but parents' time cannot be borrowed or stored. Parents may sometimes wish that there were more than 24 hours in the day, and sometimes they may wish the opposite. An axiomatic theory of parenting must take account of both economic and temporal constraints.

I also mentioned in chapter 1 that evolutionary psychology became, to some extent, the acceptable face of sociobiology. An important component of evolutionary psychology is the Parental Investment Theory (PIT), which is concerned with parents' investments in their offspring. The QQT and the PIT seem to have much in common, insofar as both are concerned with parental investments in children. However, the two theories are quite different. The QQT is essentially a theory of fertility; the PIT is not. Also, in the PIT parents are motivated by survival of the fittest, whereas in the QQT they are simply motivated by their own happiness.

In the QQT, parents call the shots and children are assumed to be passive (Foster 2002). Parents make decisions, which children have to accept. To some extent, Becker's Rotten Kid Theorem justifies the passivity of children: it doesn't pay for children to upset their parents, on whom they depend. The Rotten Kid Theorem states that, if several conditions are met, the selfish interests of children coincide with those of their altruistic parents.[1] It doesn't pay for children to be rotten toward their parents. After all, parents are more powerful than their children. The Rotten Kid Theorem has a Victorian ring: children may be seen but not heard; they exist simply to satisfy their parents' sense of altruism. This is a very selfish sort of altruism.

However, it may pay for children not to be passive; it may pay for them to be "rotten." Although the relationship between parents and children is inherently asymmetric, children may be able to exploit their parents' love for them, and to cause their parents to change their behavior toward them. Children's pressure on parents is the stuff of family life, as is parents' pressure on children. Indeed, infants' complete dependence on their parents gives them bargaining power over their parents.

Although game theory has been avoided by developmental psychologists, it seems to be a natural way to think about parent-child interactions, as well as interactions between siblings. Parents and children may be regarded as players in a game in which each side forms a strategy for handling the other side. The same applies to siblings, who are natural rivals for their parents' attention and resources. Indeed, it is surprising that developmental psychologists have not exploited game theory, which has been adopted by biologists, zoologists, political scientists, lawyers, and economists. Therefore, below I also discuss how game theory may be used to theorize about child development and parenting.

To set the scene for the QQT, I begin with an axiomatic treatment of investment in education. Children differ in ability, which to some extent may be determined by heredity. One of the predictions of the model is that abler children will demand more education and will seek more financial help from their parents.

9.2 The Demand for Education[2]

In this section, I propose a two-period model in which the individual learns in the first period and earns in the second. As in previous chapters, the subscripts c refers to children and the subscript p to parents. During the first period, the child[3] invests in E_c units of education, which cost P per unit. Human-capital theory predicts that earnings in the second period (W_c) are assumed to vary directly with education and with innate ability (A) as follows:

$$W_c = A_c E_c^\delta, \tag{1}$$

where $0 < \delta < 1$. The latter implies that the marginal productivity of education (MPE) is positive but diminishes with the amount of schooling (E). The inter-temporal budget constraint is

$$(PE_c - Y)(1 + r) + C_c = W_c, \tag{2}$$

where r denotes the rate of interest, Y denotes parental financial support in the first period, and C denotes consumption, which takes place in the second period.

Mulligan (1997) reviews competing models of parental support (Y). Becker (1991) suggests that altruistic parents spend more on the education of their more able children because the return to education varies directly with ability. In contrast, I assume in this section that parents participate in the educational costs of their children regardless of their ability. They cover a proportion π of these costs, so that $Y = \pi PE_c$. Better-off parents (adjusted for family size) can afford to be more supportive; hence, $\pi = 1 - W_p^{-\delta}$, where W_p denotes parents' income. In short, parents regard schooling as being good for their children and are prepared to subsidize it irrespective of their children's ability. Whereas in Becker's model parents are completely paternalistic and decide for their children, in the present model children decide for themselves but respond to the incentives set by their parents. Perhaps children don't exercise choice in primary and secondary education, but they do in tertiary or higher education.

Individuals have only one independent decision to make: their investment in education. This decision determines their consumption as adults. Individuals are assumed to maximize consumption with respect to their investment in education. Therefore, C is maximized subject to equations 1 and 2. The model could be dynamized by allowing Y to be endogenous for both generations. However, the simple two-period model serves the purpose of revealing the underlying theoretical arguments. Maximizing consumption subject to equations 1 and 2 gives the optimal investment in schooling from the first-order conditions:

$$E_c^* = \left(\frac{(1+r)PW_p^{-\sigma}}{\delta A_c} \right)^{1/\delta-1}. \tag{3}$$

This equation states that children's demand for education varies directly with their ability (since $\delta < 1$) and with their parents' income,[4] and it varies inversely with the cost of education and the rate of interest. The unit cost of education (P) consists of school fees (P^*) and ancillary tuition costs. The former are common to all students, but the latter are assumed to vary inversely with ability and parents' education. This assumes that abler students and students with educated parents require less private tuition. I assume, therefore, that

$$P = P^* E_p^{-\varphi} A_c^{-1}. \tag{4}$$

This equation states that the unit cost of schooling varies proportionately with school fees, and varies inversely with parents' schooling and children's ability. Substituting equation 4 into equation 3 shows that more able children are twice blessed. P is lower because it is easier for them to learn, so they acquire more education and thus earn more. Since according to equation 4 having educated parents reduces P, the model implies that the demand for schooling by children varies directly with their parents' schooling.[5] Perhaps this is one of the reasons for the intergenerational correlation in education mentioned in chapter 2. Another reason is that if ability is inherited A_c and A_p will be correlated so that abler parents who are more educated have abler children who also become more educated.

Equation 3 assumes that the capital market is perfect, so individuals can finance their education by taking student loans. If the capital market is imperfect, a credit limit of $Z \geq PE - Y$ may prevent children from capitalizing their future earnings. In this case, $E = \min(E^*, E_{max})$, where $E_{max} = (Z + Y)/P$. Children with richer parents will be less credit constrained, but their E^* will still be greater according to equation 3.

9.3   The Quality vs. Quantity Theory[6]

The main purpose of this section is to develop a theory that predicts the relationship between the ability of parents and their fertility. This theory has "Beckerian" features, although Becker himself has not directly discussed the relationship between parents' ability and fertility. Continuing with the previous notation, and using N to denote the number of children, the utility function of parents is written as

$$U_p = \alpha \ln C_p + \beta \ln(NW_c) + \gamma \ln N. \tag{5}$$

In this equation, the utility of parents is hypothesized to vary directly with how much they consume (C_p), how many children they have (N) (i.e., quantity), and their children's combined income (NW_c) (i.e., quality). The altruism of parents is expressed by $\gamma > 0$ (which reflects their taste for children) and by $\beta > 0$ (which reflects their preference for better-off children). Their taste for consumption depends on $\alpha > 0$. These parameters are normalized by assuming that $\beta + \gamma + \alpha = 1$. These structural parameters are hard-wired and vary between parents. Completely selfish parents have $\beta = \gamma = 0$ and $\alpha = 1$; completely altruistic parents have $\alpha = 0$. The assumption that parents care about their children's income provides a motivation for having fewer children in whom they invest more. It is this that induces a tradeoff between quantity and quality.

According to equation 5, marginal utilities are positive, diminishing, and separable. For example, the marginal utility (MU) of consumption is equal to

$$\frac{\partial U_p}{\partial C_p} = \frac{\alpha}{C_p}. \tag{6}$$

This equation is positive and implies that marginal utility varies inversely with consumption. Separability means that the marginal utility of consumption depends only on consumption and not on the number of children (quantity) or the children's income (quality). Matters would have been different had the utility function been fully logarithmic instead of semi-logarithmic (that is, had the left-hand side of equation 5 been expressed as $\log U_p$). In this case the marginal utility of consumption is equal to

$$\frac{\partial U_p}{\partial C_p} = \frac{\alpha U_p}{C_p}. \tag{7}$$

Since U_p varies directly with N and NW_c, equation 7 states that the marginal utility of consumption varies inversely with consumption but varies directly with fertility.

In equation 5 parents are altruistic, but not as altruistic as in Barro and Becker 1988, where it is assumed that parents are altruistic toward their entire dynasty. Also, in contrast to Mulligan 1997, parents are concerned about their children's earnings rather than their consumption. They see their responsibility as setting their children up in life, without being concerned with how their children allocate resources between themselves and their grandchildren. Nor do our "puritanical" parents leave bequests because they have no direct interest in their children's consumption. For simplicity, their altruism is limited to helping their children acquire education so that they might earn more as adults.

Because they don't leave bequests, parents' consumption is equal to the income that they don't spend on rearing and educating their children. Hence,

$$C_p = W_p - aN - PE_cN, \tag{8}$$

where a denotes the unit cost of raising children and PE_cN is parents' outlay on their education, where, as in section 9.2, P denotes the unit cost of schooling. In this section it is assumed that parents cover the entire cost of their children's education, hence $\pi = 1$.

Parents assume that their children's wages are determined according to $W_c = J(E_c, A_c)$, that is, along the lines of equation 1. Parents don't know the true ability of their children (A_c) in advance of educating them and before they earn. However, if ability is partly inherited, they can predict their child's ability on the basis of what they know about their own ability. As in equation 1 in chapter 8, ability is assumed to be a genotype with a first-order intergenerational autoregressive process:

$$A_c = \rho A_p + \varepsilon_c, \tag{9}$$

where $\varepsilon_c \sim$ iid and $0 \le \rho \le 1$. Hence, parents can predict their children's ability provided $\rho \ne 0$. Since parents don't know ε_c *ex ante*, they expect each child to have the same ability. Parents therefore predict that their children's ability is ρA_p. Since this is the same for all their children, parents invest the same amount in each child. In a more general model, parents would learn about their children's ability and giftedness as discussed in section 9.4.

If the capital market were perfect, parents would invest in their children's education up to the point where the marginal product of human capital equaled the rate of interest ($MPE_c = r$). In this case, children's human capital (E_c) would vary directly with their parents' ability (A_p) and inversely with the rate of interest (r) and the cost of education. When capital markets are perfect, parents do not face a tradeoff between quality and quantity. They simply borrow to invest in quality, which is paid back once their children start earning. This means, in practice, that parents can borrow money simply on the promise of their child's ability. If, more realistically, the capital market is imperfect, parents will not be able to borrow on the collateral of their children's ability. They will consequently face a tradeoff between quality and quantity, because investment in their children's education must either be at the expense of the number of children or at the expense of their own consumption.

Parents make two independent decisions: family size (N) and schooling per child (E_c). They maximize utility in equation 5 with respect to these decision variables. The first-order conditions are

$$\frac{\partial U}{\partial N} = -\frac{\alpha(a + PE_c)}{C_p} + \frac{\beta + \gamma}{N} = 0 \tag{10a}$$

and

$$\frac{\partial U}{\partial E_c} = -\frac{\alpha PN}{C_p} + \beta \frac{MPE_c}{W_c} = 0. \tag{10b}$$

The second-order conditions for a maximum are as follows:

$$\frac{\partial^2 U}{\partial N^2} = -\frac{\beta + \gamma}{N^2} - \beta \frac{\alpha(a + PE_c)^2}{C_p^{\,2}} = B < 0, \tag{11a}$$

$$\frac{\partial^2 U}{\partial N \partial E_c} = -\frac{\alpha P}{C_p}\left(1 + \frac{N}{C_p}(a + PE_c)\right) = D < 0, \tag{11b}$$

$$\frac{\partial^2 U}{\partial E_c^{\,2}} = -\frac{\alpha P^2 N^2}{C_p^2} + \beta \frac{MPE'}{W_c} - \frac{MPE^2}{W_c^{\,2}} = F < 0. \tag{11c}$$

The second-order conditions for a maximum are $B < 0$ and $BF - D^2 = K > 0$. The former holds for sure; the latter is assumed to hold. Because $MPE' < 0$, F must be negative. Equation 10a states that the net marginal utility from the quantity of children is the gross marginal utility, ($\beta + \gamma)/N$, minus the marginal opportunity cost of having children in terms of consumption forgone. Equation 10b states that the net marginal utility from schooling per child, or quality, is the gross marginal utility minus the marginal opportunity cost of schooling in terms of consumption forgone. Optimization requires these net marginal utilities be 0.

The ability of children (A_c) enters the first-order conditions via equation 10b since the marginal product of schooling (MPE_c) depends on A_c as do wages (W_c). For convenience, the derivative of MPE_c/W_c with respect to A_c is denoted by ξ. If ability raises MPE by more than it raises W, then $\xi > 0$.[7] To determine how the ability of parents affects their fertility and their investment in schooling per child, the first-order conditions are totally differentiated with respect the ability of parents (A_p) using equation 9 to yield

$$\frac{dN}{dA_p} = \rho \frac{\beta \xi D}{K} < 0 \tag{12a}$$

and

$$\frac{dE_c}{dA_p} = -\rho \frac{\beta \xi B}{K} > 0. \tag{12b}$$

The model implies that if $\xi > 0$ abler parents have fewer children and invest more in their human capital. According to equations 12a and 12b, these effects vary directly with ρ. If $\rho = 0$, abler parents will not have lower fertility or invest more in their children's education, because they cannot predict their children's ability.

To determine the implications for fertility of an increase in child costs (a) and schooling per child, the first-order conditions are totally differentiated with respect to a to yield

$$\frac{dN}{da} = \frac{\alpha \beta}{C_p K}\left(1 + \frac{a + PE_c}{C_p}\right)\left(\frac{MPE'}{W_c} - \frac{MPE^2}{W_c^2}\right) < 0 \tag{13a}$$

and

$$\frac{dE_c}{da} = \frac{\alpha P}{C_p^2 K}\left[\frac{\alpha[1 + N(a + PH_c)]}{C_p} - (\beta + \gamma)\right] \gtreqless 0. \tag{13b}$$

According to equation 13a, fertility varies inversely with the cost of raising children. According to equation 13b, however, investment in schooling per child may either increase or decrease. If parents invest more in their children's human capital, it is because they trade off quantity against quality in view of the increase in the relative price of quantity as measured by a/P. If, instead, parents invest less, it is because they chose to increase their own consumption (C_p) and to spend less on parenting.

Finally, to determine the effect of the income of parents on fertility and schooling per child, the first-order conditions are totally differentiated with respect to parents' income (W_p) to yield

$$\frac{dN}{dW_p} = -\frac{\alpha \beta (a + PE_c)}{C_p^2 K}\left(\frac{MPE'}{W_c} - \frac{MPE^2}{W_c^2} + \frac{\alpha P^2 N}{C_p}\right) \tag{14a}$$

and

$$\frac{dE_c}{dW_p} = \frac{\alpha P}{C_p^2 K}\left(\frac{\beta + \gamma}{N} - \frac{\alpha(a + PE_c)}{C_p}\right). \tag{14b}$$

Since equations 14a and 14b cannot be signed, better-off parents may have more or fewer children, which they educate to a greater or lesser extent. The inability to sign these total derivatives stems from the arbitrariness of the income effect[8] on parenting. The greater the relative value of α, the more likely it is that the income effect is negative, because it implies that parents are less altruistic. As a result, they have fewer children and invest less in each child's education. If, however, parents are better off because they are more able, and if $\rho > 0$, they will chose to reduce quantity and raise quality, as already mentioned, because they predict that their children are more able too.

9.4 Discriminatory Parenting

In the preceding section, parents were strictly egalitarian in helping their children. Suppose, for example, that parents decide to have two children ($N = 2$) and to provide each one with 12 years of schooling ($E_c = 12$). If parents have no favorites, each child delivers the same utility or gratification. Also, *ex ante*, the ability of each child is assumed to be the same, namely ρA_p. Therefore, parents invest in each child the same amount of schooling. Suppose, however, that parents perceive that their children have different abilities. According to equation 9, the ability of the nth child is $A_{cn} = \rho A_p + \varepsilon_{cn}$.

Suppose that parents perceive A_1 and A_2 for their two children and that the utility function of parents is[9]

$$U = \alpha \ln W - \beta(W_1 - W_2)^2 - \gamma \ln E, \tag{15}$$

where $W = W_1 + W_2$ and $E = E_1 + E_2$. Equation 15 states that parents prefer their children to be better off because $\alpha > 0$ and prefer to outlay less on schooling because $\gamma > 0$. They also dislike wage inequality among their children because $\beta > 0$. We assume that wages are determined as in equation 1. How much schooling should parents give to each of their two children? If their children are unequally able, they should invest more in their abler child. On the other hand, parents dislike inequality, which means that they should go out of their way to help their less fit child.

Equation 15 is maximized with respect to E_1 and E_2. The first-order conditions are

$$\frac{\partial U}{\partial E_1} = \delta A_1 E_1^{\delta-1} \left(\frac{\alpha}{W} - 2\beta(W_1 - W_2) \right) - \frac{\gamma}{E} = 0 \tag{16a}$$

and

$$\frac{\partial U}{\partial E_2} = \delta A_2 E_2^{\delta-1}\left(\frac{\alpha}{W} + 2\beta(W_1 - W_2)\right) - \frac{\gamma}{E} = 0. \tag{16b}$$

Equating the first-order conditions and solving for the relative investment in schooling for the two siblings gives

$$\frac{E_1}{E_2} = \left(\frac{A_1}{A_2}\Omega\right)^{1/1-\delta}, \tag{17a}$$

where

$$\Omega = \frac{\alpha/W - 2\beta(W_1 - W_2)}{\alpha/W + 2\beta(W_1 - W_2)}. \tag{17b}$$

If parents don't care about equality (that is, if $\beta = 0$), equation 17b implies that $\Omega = 1$, in which case equation 17a states that relative schooling varies directly with relative ability because $0 < \delta < 1$. If child 1 is abler than child 2 ($A_1 > A_2$), his parents will invest more schooling in him, so that $E_1 > E_2$. The two siblings will get the same schooling if $A_1 = A_2$, i.e., they are equally able. If parents have an aversion to inequality because $\beta > 0$, equation 17b implies that $0 < \Omega < 1$, since $W_1 > W_2$. Therefore, aversion to inequality reduces sibling 1's relative schooling. If aversion to inequality is sufficiently strong, parents may even invest more in their less fit sibling, so that $E_2 > E_1$. This happens when $\Omega < \frac{1}{2}$. If parents aim for complete equality, so that $W_1 = W_2$, relative schooling must be equal to

$$\frac{E_1}{E_2} = \left(\frac{A_2}{A_1}\right)^{1/\delta} < 1. \tag{18}$$

In this equation, parenting (as represented by schooling) varies inversely with genotypes such as ability because parents practice reverse discrimination. Therefore, the abler child receives less schooling than the less able sibling. More generally, the response of relative schooling ($\varepsilon = E_1/E_2$) to relative ability ($\alpha = A_1/A_2$) is obtained by differentiating the first-order conditions with respect to α:

$$\frac{\partial \varepsilon}{\partial \alpha} = \frac{1}{1-\delta}\left(\Omega + \varepsilon\frac{\partial\Omega}{\partial\alpha}\right). \tag{19}$$

Here Ω is positive. However, $\varepsilon(\partial\Omega/\partial\alpha)$ is negative, because Ω varies inversely with α. Therefore, this equation may be negative or positive, depending on the strength of parents' aversion to inequality. More generally, this equation shows that endogenous parenting may be positively or negatively correlated with genotypes.

9.5 Strategic Children[10]

Thus far, children have been passive players. In accordance with the Rotten Kid Theorem, they accept what their parents decide for them, because it doesn't pay for children to upset their parents. This means that children who demand more from their parents are likely to end up with less. Parents care about their children, and are happy to help them, but they do not tolerate disobedience and recalcitrance.

In this section I present an alternative paradigm in which it pays for children not to be passive. By understanding what motivates their parents, children can maneuver them into giving them parental resources that they would not have received had they been passive. The basic assumption here is that parents care more about their children than children care about their parents. At birth, children don't care at all about their parents. As they get older, they begin to care about their parents and may even sacrifice their own interests to make them happy. At the end of life, these roles are reversed; altruistic children care for their elderly parents. However, mutual caring is typically asymmetric. This basic asymmetry enables children to behave strategically toward their parents.

Game theory[11] is the natural formal tool with which to analyze strategic interaction between parties having different and even conflicting interests. Children and parents may be regarded as players in what I am calling *the Heartstrings Game*. In this game, children exploit their parents' love by signaling distress. Parents don't want their children to be distressed, so they respond by offering more parenting than otherwise. To set the scene, it is assumed that there is only one child, so there is no sibling rivalry. But first the motivations of the parents and the child must be discussed.

9.5.1 The Motivation of Parents and Children

The basic model is essentially static. Everything takes place in a given time period, such as a day, a night, or an hour. If the unit of time happens to be a day, parents ignore what might happen tomorrow or what happened yesterday. In the jargon of game theory, this is a "one-shot game." In a dynamic setting, which is discussed later, today's decisions might depend on what happened yesterday and what might happen tomorrow. This would be the case if behavior is strategic so that parents or children act today to affect outcomes tomorrow. In the jargon of game theory, this is a "repeated game."

To simplify matters, parents are treated as a unit, and disagreements and tensions between parents are ignored. Parenting is denoted by X, which may take many forms. In sections 9.1–9.4, parenting consisted of paying for their children's schooling. Here it is treated generically. One way of thinking about X is as the time or attention that parents devote to their child. Parents allocate their time (T), which is naturally fixed, between themselves (T_p) and their child, so $T = T_p + X$. Parents therefore face a budget constraint on time rather than money.

As in sections 9.1–9.4, a utilitarian perspective is taken in which parents and children derive utility or satisfaction from their situation. Parents derive utility or pleasure (U_p) from the time they spend on themselves and from their child's happiness or utility (U_c). Children signal distress through Z, which may be thought of as acting out, crying, or arguing with parents. Z constitutes children's play or action in the game.

The utility function of parents is assumed to be semi-logarithmic and therefore separable, as in equation 5:

$$U_p = \alpha \ln U_c - (1 - \alpha) \ln X. \tag{20}$$

In equation 20, α is assumed to lie between 0 and 1. This equation states that parents are happier when their child is happier, but that parenting itself is costly to them. The more time they devote to parenting, the less time they have for themselves; hence U_p varies inversely with X. More altruistic or caring parents have larger α; that is, they attach less importance to spending time on themselves and are more concerned about their child's happiness. Pitiless or completely egocentric parents have $\alpha = 0$; that is, they don't care about their child's happiness at all, they care only about themselves. At the other extreme, completely selfless parents have $\alpha = 1$; that is, they care only about their child's happiness, and get no pleasure from spending time on themselves. Abusive parents have $\alpha < 1$; that is, they derive pleasure from making their child unhappy. In short, α is a structural, or exogenous, parameter that describes the hard-wired personality or tastes with which the parent is endowed.

The child's happiness or utility depends on two considerations. First, children derive pleasure from parental attention, as the object-relations theory of Winnicott (1960) suggests. Second, to draw parental attention children must act out (e.g. crying). In what follows, acting out is denoted by Z. Because the effort of acting out is distressful to children, they prefer that $Z = 0$, but they will act out if it is worthwhile.

The utility function for the child is assumed to be separable too:

$$U_c = \beta \ln X - (1 - \beta) \ln Z. \tag{21}$$

This equation states that children enjoy parental attention but don't like acting out. Here β, assumed to be positive but less than 1, measures the child's sensitivity to the parents' attention—that is, the child's gratifiability. More gratifiable children have larger β.

Notice that in equation 20 Z doesn't affect U_p directly. However, it affects parents indirectly through equation 21. I could have introduced a direct effect in equation 20, but for the sake of simplicity I have not done so. Notice also that in equation 21 U_c doesn't depend on U_p. This means that children don't care at all about their parents; they are completely selfish. I could have modified this, but in the interest of simplicity I assume that caring or altruism is a one-way street from parents to children.

9.5.2 Parenting with Passive Children

To set the scene, I investigate the case of a passive child, who does not cry to attract his parent's attention. To motivate this case, it is assumed that the child isn't distressed ($D = 0$) and therefore doesn't need to cry, in which case $Z = 0$. Since the child is passive, the outcome is entirely determined by the parent. The equilibrium can be represented simply as in figure 9.1, where adult time (T_p) is measured on the vertical axis and the child's happiness on the horizontal. When $T_p = T$, the parents spend no time on the child. At this point the happiness of the child is normalized to be 0. Equation 21 states that children are happier the more time their parents devote to them. In figure 9.1 this relationship is expressed by curve TT'. If parents spend all their time on their child, his happiness will be T'. Notice that curve TT' is concave toward the origin because the marginal utility of parenting is assumed to diminish.

In figure 9.1 the U_p curves are "indifference curves" for parents. These curves plot the combinations of parent time and child happiness that confer on parents the same level of utility. Therefore, along curve U_{p0} utility is the same. Along curve U_{p1}, utility is higher, but constant. Indifference slopes downward because parents want more parent time

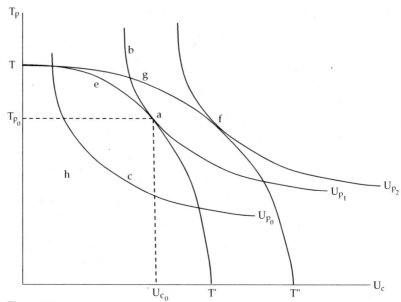

Figure 9.1
Optimal parenting with passive child.

to compensate them for less child happiness. Indifference curves are naturally convex toward the origin because marginal utility diminishes. Indifference curves cannot cross each other.

Parents are assumed to maximize their utility. Given their preferences as embodied in their indifference curves, and given curve TT', they maximize utility at point a where indifference curve U_{p1} is tangential to curve TT'. They allocate $T - T_{po}$ of their time to their child, as a result of which his happiness is U_{c0}. The equilibrium at a obviously depends on the shape of the indifference curves and the shape of curve TT'. More selfish parents, i.e., parents with larger α, will have flatter indifference curves so that the tangent of the highest indifference curve to TT' might be at e, where parents spend more time on themselves and their children are less happy than at a. If the child is more gratifiable because β is larger, curve TT' will shift to the right to say TT''. The new equilibrium will be at a point (such as f) at which parents are happier than at A, since they spend more time on themselves and their child is happier. However, there is nothing to stop the new equilibrium from being at, say, g, where the child is less happy than at a. In this case parents take advantage of their child's greater gratifiability by devoting less time to him.

Although figure 9.1 refers to a completely unrealistic situation, it sets the scene for much of what follows. However, it makes the obvious point that parents spontaneously devote time and attention to their children out of love. Children do not have to cry for their parents to devote attention to them. It shows that when the child is passive the parenting equilibrium depends on only two parameters: α and β. This can be shown more formally. Parents maximize their utility in equation 20 with respect to X subject to equation 21. Since $\log Z$ isn't defined when $Z = 0$, the term $(1 - \beta)\log Z$ in equation 21 is replaced by $z > 0$. The first-order condition for a maximum is

$$\frac{dU_p}{dX} = \frac{\partial U_p}{\partial U_c}\frac{\partial U_c}{\partial X} + \frac{\partial U_p}{\partial X} = 0 \tag{22a}$$

$$= \frac{\alpha}{U_c}\frac{\beta}{X} - \frac{1-\alpha}{X} = 0. \tag{22b}$$

X cancels out in equation 22b. Substituting equation 21 for U_c and then solving the result for X gives

$$\log X = \frac{\alpha}{1-\alpha} + \frac{z}{\beta}, \tag{23}$$

which states that parenting varies directly with α and inversely with β. This makes sense because if α is greater parents care more about their children, and if β is greater children are easier to gratify. The latter result depends on the specifics of the utility function. More generally, if β increases, parents may decide to be more generous to their children rather than less.

9.5.3   The Heartstrings Game

The set-up of the model implies that children set Z so as to attract parental attention X. How much will they act out, and how much attention will they get in return? To answer this question, it is necessary to determine the Nash equilibrium[12] of the game that characterizes parent-child interactions. Having obtained the Nash equilibrium, we can go on to ask what happens to the amounts of attention seeking and parental attention when external events distress the child. Also, how is the equilibrium affected by differences in such parameters as the child's capacity to cry, his resilience, his sensitivity, and the parents' altruism?

Parents pick X to maximize their utility. The first-order condition from maximizing equation 20 with respect to X is

$$\frac{\partial U_p}{\partial X} = \frac{\alpha}{U_c}\frac{\partial U_c}{\partial X} + \frac{\alpha-1}{X} = 0.$$

(24a)

From equation 21,

$$\frac{\partial U_c}{\partial X} = \frac{\beta}{X}.$$

(24b)

Substituting equation 24b into equation 24a and solving the result for X gives

$$X = \exp\left(\frac{\alpha}{1-\alpha}\right)Z^{1/\beta-1}.$$

(24c)

Equation 24c expresses the parents' optimal response to the child's acting out. It is the counterpart to equation 23 for the active child, i.e., when $Z > 0$. It states that X varies directly with Z because $0 < \beta < 1$. If $\beta > \frac{1}{2}$, the exponent of Z is less than 1, and convergent; otherwise, it is greater than 1, and divergent. The former means that equation 24c is convergent when children are more gratifiable, and divergent otherwise. Divergence means that the marginal reaction of parents to the acting out of their children varies directly with acting out. According to equation 24c, X varies directly with α, so more altruistic parents give more attention to their children.

The second-order condition for a maximum must be negative. This is satisfied because

$$\frac{\partial^2 U_p}{\partial X^2} = -\frac{\alpha^2 \beta^2}{U_c^3 X} < 0,$$

(25)

which holds for all values of β and α.

Next, we obtain the reaction of children to parenting—that is, the response of Z to X. Equation 21 is maximized with respect to Z. The first-order condition is

$$\frac{\partial U_c}{\partial Z} = \frac{\beta}{X}\frac{\partial X}{\partial Z} + \frac{\beta-1}{Z} = 0.$$

(26)

The second-order condition for a maximum is

$$\frac{\partial^2 U_c}{\partial Z^2} = \frac{1-\beta}{Z^2}\left[1 + \left(\frac{1}{\beta} - 2\right)\frac{\exp(\alpha/1-\alpha)}{X}Z^{1/\rho-1} - \frac{1-\beta}{\beta}\frac{\exp(2\alpha/1-\alpha)}{X^2}Z^{2(1/\beta-1)}\right]$$

$$= \Psi < 0.$$

(27)

Here the first term within the brackets is positive, the last term within the brackets is negative, and the second term within the brackets may be positive or negative. The latter will be negative when $\beta > \frac{1}{2}$, which happens when equation 24c is convergent. Therefore, equation 27 may be positive or negative. For a maximum, however, it must be negative.

To obtain the child's reaction to parenting, equation 26 is totally differentiated with respect to Z and X:

$$\Gamma dX + \Psi dZ = 0, \tag{28a}$$

where

$$\Gamma = \frac{\beta}{X}\left(\frac{\partial^2 X}{\partial Z^2} - \frac{1}{X}\frac{\partial X}{\partial Z}\right). \tag{28b}$$

If parenting is convergent, Γ must be negative, because the second partial derivative in equation 28b is negative. Γ will be negative provided parenting is not strongly divergent, which ensures that the term in brackets is not positive. From equation 28a we may solve for the reaction function of the child to parenting:

$$dZ = \Phi dX, \tag{29a}$$

where

$$\Phi = -\frac{\Gamma}{\Psi}. \tag{29b}$$

Since Ψ is negative according to equation 27, Φ is negative provided Γ is negative. Therefore, Z varies inversely with X; that is, children act out less when their parents pay them more attention. Just as parenting may be divergent or convergent, the same applies to acting out. If Φ becomes increasingly negative with X, acting out is divergent. This means that as X gets smaller, acting out (Z) becomes ever larger. This happens when the derivative of Φ with respect to X is negative. If the opposite happens, acting out is convergent.

In figure 9.2, curve P plots the reaction function of the parents from equation 24 and curve C plots the reaction function of the child from equation 29a. The two curves are drawn for the convergent case, which is why they are convex. In the divergent case they would be concave; that is, curves P and C would get steeper instead of flatter as X increased. X_0 denotes spontaneous parenting, which parents are happy to give

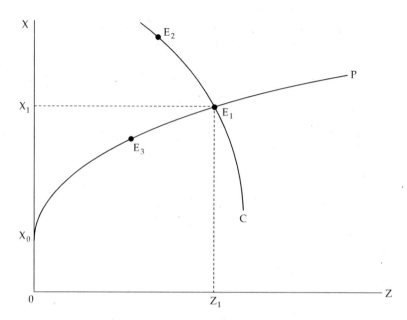

Figure 9.2
The Heartstrings Game.

even if their child doesn't act out (i.e., $Z = 0$). The passive child would receive X_0. The Nash equilibrium of the Heartstrings Game is determined where curves P and C intersect at E_1. Acting out is equal to Z_1, and parenting is equal to X_1. It pays for the child to act out, since $X_1 > X_0$. At E_1 both players are happy in the sense that neither wishes to diverge from this strategy.

If parents are more altruistic, X_0 will be larger, in which case curve P will shift upward. The new Nash equilibrium will be at a point, such as E_2, at which the child acts out less because Z is smaller and he gets more parenting. Because parents are more altruistic, the child benefits both ways: he gets more parental attention and he doesn't need to act out so much. If the child is more passive, curve C will shift downward and the Nash equilibrium will be at a point, such as E_3, at which the child acts out less and gets less parenting. If curves P and C don't intersect, either because curve P is very high in figure 9.2 or because curve C is very low, the child is passive, as in the Rotten Kid Theorem. He is satisfied with X_0 in the sense that he doesn't feel that acting out is worth the bother. In general, however, it pays for the child to be rotten, or normal.

9.5.4 Sibling Rivalry

I now introduce a rival sibling into the family, so that the family consists of triads: the parents, child A, and child B. The children compete for their parents' attention, so $X = X_A + X_B$. Child A and child B may also be envious of one another. Their envy is assumed to vary directly with relative parental attention. Child A is happier when he gets more attention than child B, in which case child B is unhappier. Equation 21 is extended by adding envy to each child's utility function:

$$U_A = \beta_A \ln X_A - (1 - \beta_A) \ln Z_A + \kappa_A \ln \frac{X_A}{X_B}, \tag{30a}$$

$$U_B = \beta_B \ln X_B - (1 - \beta_B) \ln Z_B + \kappa_B \ln \frac{X_B}{X_A}. \tag{30b}$$

Envy varies directly with κ, which, like β, is an exogenous, hard-wired personality trait. If $\kappa = 0$, equations 30a and 30b revert to equation 21, because there is no envy. If each child gets the same attention, so that $X_A = X_B$, the final terms in equations 30a and 30b are equal to 0. Parents are assumed to have no favorites and to be interested in the combined happiness of their children. Hence, $U_c = U_A + U_B$ in equation 20. This means, conveniently, that equation 24c continues to represent the parents' reaction to the combined acting out of their children. Each child understands that if he acts out, given the acting out of his sibling, his parents' reaction will be according to equation 24c. Therefore, $\partial X_A / \partial Z_A = \partial X_B / \partial Z_B = \Phi$. These are partial derivatives because Z_B is held constant in the case of child A and Z_A is held constant in the case of child B. In equilibrium, of course, if child A acts out more this will induce a response by child B, who probably will act out more too.

Child A maximizes U_A with respect to Z_A given Z_B. Equation 28b becomes

$$\Gamma_A = \frac{\beta_A}{X_A} \left[\frac{\partial^2 X_A}{\partial Z_A^2} - \left(1 + \frac{\kappa_A}{\beta_B}\right) \frac{1}{X_A} \frac{\partial X_A}{\partial Z_A} \right]. \tag{31}$$

When $\kappa_A = 0$, equation 31 reverts to equation 28b. Thanks to κ_A, equation 31 is more negative than equation 28b. The reaction functions for child A and child B are derived from Γ_A, Γ_B, and Ψ and are denoted by Φ_A and Φ_B respectively.

In the symmetric case,[13] $Z_A = Z_B$ and $X_A = X_B = \frac{1}{2}X$. The solution for this case is illustrated in figure 9.3. Curve P continues to apply for parents. Curve C' refers to the reaction function of child A or B since

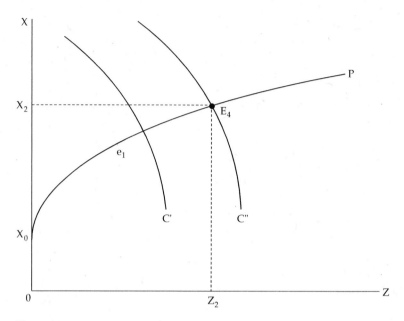

Figure 9.3
The Heartstrings Game with siblings.

in the symmetric case $\Phi_A = \Phi_B$. It lies to the right of curve C due to envy ($\kappa > 0$). Curve C" sums C' for the two siblings. Curve C" lies to the right of curve C', and it is less convex to the origin. The equilibrium is determined where curves C" and P intersect at E_4. For purposes of comparison E_1 in figure 9.3 replicates E_1 in figure 9.2. Parents devote X_2 of parenting to their children, whose combined acting out is Z_2. In the symmetric case, each sibling receives half the parental attention ($X_A = X_B = \frac{1}{2}X_2$), which is less than what his singleton counterpart received. Each sibling does half of the acting out in the symmetric case; hence, $Z_A = Z_B = \frac{1}{2}Z_2$, which is more than his singleton counterpart acted out. Needless to say, parents have less time for themselves than in the singleton case, and each child gets less attention.

In the asymmetric case, if $\beta_A > \beta_B$, child A is seeking more attention than child, in which case child A will get more than his share of parental attention by acting out more. Child A will also act out more if $\kappa_A > \kappa_B$, because child A's envy of child B exceeds child B's envy of child A. In equilibrium, combined crying will be greater than in the symmetric case, and parents will spend more time on their children, i.e., Z and X will be larger than in the symmetric case. Another source of asymmetry is favoritism, where for example parents favor child A over child B, either by preferring to spend more time with A or by being more responsive to A's acting out. Because child B is envious of child A, the equilibrium values of Z and X will be greater than in the symmetric case. It is therefore in the enlightened self-interest of parents to be even-handed toward their children. It doesn't pay for parents to be rotten, and fairness is its own virtue.

9.6 Dynamics

Thus far, parenting has been modeled in an entirely static context. Current parenting is assumed to be independent of past and future parenting. In some contexts, however, it might make sense to consider parenting as a sequence of static decisions, each day presenting itself as an occasion for static optimization. In this case, X_t has no implications for X_{t+1}, and X_{t-1} has no implications for X_t.

There are, no doubt, many instances in which rational agents take days one at a time. However, raising children is not in that category. Parents have to consider how their current behavior will affect the future development of their children. Infants are initially totally dependent on their parents, especially their mother. Infants have to learn how to "separate off" from their parents, develop resilience, and eventually grow into independent individuals. The separation process takes time. Parents have to be concerned about their child's resilience, both for the sake of their child and for their own sake. The child who succeeds in separating from his parents is more resilient and can cope better with stress. He is less needy of his parents to make him feel happy and can rely instead on his own psychological resources. Instead of resorting to crying to signal his distress, the separated child can satisfy his own needs with dignity. The separated child is less demanding of his parents, so his parents have more time to spend on themselves. Thus, separation is good for both sides. It is therefore in the enlightened self-interest of parents to promote the emotional development of their children.

The separation process has autonomous and non-autonomous components. The former derives from self-taught or spontaneous separation. Presumably even children without parents would learn to be self-sufficient[14] to some extent. The non-autonomous component, which is more important than the autonomous one, is parenting.[15] In this there is an inherent tension between (on the one hand) spoiling the child by making him happier in the short run and not encouraging separation and (on the other hand) being too strict in the belief that this will encourage separation. Parents are faced with a fine balancing act between excess and insufficiency in the time they devote to their children and the limits they set for them. Spoiling them might retard development, but so might excessive strictness.

This sounds like admitting that nurture by parents matters. However, this basic nurturing is not what the nature vs. nurture debate is about. All the protagonists, even Judith Rich Harris, admit that infants and children need parents for their healthy development just as surely as they need food. It is no coincidence that children are typically raised by their biological parents in warm and loving families. The nature-vs.-nurture debate is about the influence of parents beyond basic nurturing.

In this section I consider the dynamic strategy for parents in the Heartstrings Game. As before, it is assumed that parents and children are rational and act in their own best interests. However, parents are now required to act strategically in the best interest of their children.

9.6.1   Separation and Development

I begin by specifying the separation process. Let S_t represent a child's resilience at age t. At birth the child is endowed with resilience equal to S_0, which may vary from child to child according to his genotype. At the end of the separation process, the child achieves resilience equal to $S^* > S_0$, which may be greater or smaller depending on his genotype and on how the process is managed by his parents. Also, children vary by their innate ability to separate, so that otherwise identical children whose parents apply the same separation policy generally end up with different degrees of resilience. The separation process isn't necessarily monotonic; children may regress rather than progress, in which case S may decrease. On average, however, S increases.

As was mentioned above, there are two components to separation. Hence, $S = S_a + S_p$, where S_a denotes the autonomous component and S_p the component due to parenting.[16] It is assumed that the autonomous component depends on age and rises monotonically until it achieves a maximum (i.e., it is asymptotic or convex). The second component is hypothesized to depend on three main considerations. First, happier children develop more quickly. Second, given the child's happiness, parental attention makes children more dependent and may retard their development. Finally, because there is a natural upper limit to resilience, the rate of development varies inversely with its level. This simply means that separation is a convergent process rather than a divergent one.

In equation 32 it is assumed, for simplicity, that the separation process is linear:

$$\dot{S}_t = \frac{dS_t}{dt} = \mu + \sigma U_{ct} - \lambda X_t - \psi X_t - \psi S_t. \tag{32}$$

Here the parameter σ expresses the effect of the child's happiness on his development, and $\lambda > 0$ captures the retarding effect due to spoiling by parents. $\psi > 0$ ensures that separation is a convergent process, i.e., that S has an upper limit. The greater is ψ, the harder it is for the child to develop. To understand the mechanics of equation 32, consider what happens when $\sigma = \lambda = 0$, i.e., when parenting or nurture does not matter.[17] In that case, all the development is autonomous. The general solution to equation 32 is then

$$S_t = \frac{\mu}{\psi}(1 - e^{-\psi t}). \tag{33}$$

Equation 33 states that at birth[18] $S = 0$ and that at the end of the development process $S^* = \mu/\psi$. Therefore, the final level of resilience varies directly with μ and inversely with ψ. These parameters vary between children, so S^* varies between children. Equation 33 implies that the rate of growth of resilience is equal to

$$\frac{\dot{S}_t}{S_t} = \frac{\mu}{e^{\psi t} - 1}. \tag{34}$$

This equation states that the rate of development varies inversely with age and tends to 0 as the upper limit of resilience is approached. It also states that the rate of development varies inversely with ψ.

Suppose next that parenting matters, because σ and λ are positive, but parenting and the child's happiness are constant over time; that is, $U_{ct} = U_c$ and $X_t = X$. In this case, equation 33 becomes

$$S_t = \frac{\mu + \sigma U_c - \lambda X}{\psi}(1 - e^{-\psi t}). \tag{35}$$

If $\sigma U_c > \lambda X$, S^* increases relative to what it was in equation 33. Therefore, parenting promotes the long-term development of children. Happier and less spoiled children eventually achieve a higher level of development.

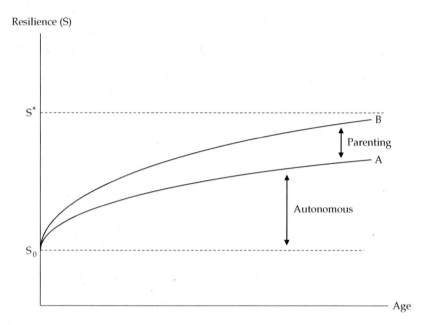

Figure 9.4
Development of resilience.

Figure 9.4 illustrates the development of resilience. Curve A plots autonomous development. The gap between curves A and B represents the contribution of parenting to the development of the child. There is a natural asymptote at S^*, which signifies the long-term resilience of the child. If the happiness of the child and parenting aren't constant over time, matters are more complicated. To see what happens in that case, we have to consider the determinants of parenting and those of child happiness over time. This is discussed in the next subsection.

9.6.2   Dynamic Optimization
To fix ideas, let us consider the simplest possible dynamic case: the case in which the child is passive, so that $Z = 0$. This means that Z may be dropped from equation 21. Since more resilient children are happier, equation 21 can be rewritten as

$$\log U_{ct} = \beta \log X_t + \phi \log S_t, \tag{36}$$

where ϕ is a structural parameter that expresses the effect of resilience on the happiness of the child. Since equation 36 is in logarithms, ϕ measures the elasticity of happiness to resilience, so an increase in resilience of 1 percent induces an increase in happiness of ϕ percent. Since equation 36 is fully logarithmic, the utility function is not separable in X and S; as was discussed above, this means that the marginal utilities of S and X vary directly with each other, i.e., S and X are complementary. Equation 20 is slightly modified too:

$$U_{pt} = \alpha \log U_{ct} + (\alpha - 1) \log X_t + \varphi X_t, \tag{37}$$

which implies that the marginal (dis)utility of X equals $(\alpha - 1)/X + \varphi > 0$. Like equation 20, equation 37 continues to be separable in X and U_c. The addition of φX makes the utility function slightly more general without changing its substance.

Substituting equation 36 into equation 37 gives

$$U_{pt} = \alpha \log X_t + b \log S_t + \varphi X_t, \tag{38}$$

where $a = \alpha (1 + \beta) - 1$ and $b = \alpha \varphi$.

The discounted utility of parents is defined as

$$V = \int_0^T U_{pt} e^{-\delta t} dt, \tag{39}$$

where δ is the rate of time preference of parents. It measures parents' impatience. If $\delta = 1$, future and current utility are valued the same. If $1 > \delta > 0$, future utility is valued less than current utility. If $\delta < 0$, future utility is valued more than current utility. Impatient parents will have larger δ. In the standard case, $1 > \delta > 0$—that is, parents are impatient.

For simplicity, let us re-write equation 32 in terms of X rather than U_c:

$$\dot{S}_t = \mu + c X_t - \psi S_t. \tag{40}$$

Parents choose X_t to maximize V. The dynamic aspect of the problem is induced by the fact that X_t affects S_{t+1} via equation 40, which in turn affects $U_{c(t+1)}$ via equation 38. Therefore, static optimization will be sup-optimal. The Hamiltonian of the system[19] is

$$H = U_{pt} e^{-\delta t} + \eta_t (\mu + c X_t - \psi S_t), \tag{41}$$

where η is a co-state variable which is equal to the shadow value of S, and which measures the marginal effect of resilience on the discounted utility of parents (V). Using the Maximum Principle due to Pontryagin, the first-order conditions for a maximum are

$$\frac{\partial H}{\partial X_t} = \left(\frac{a}{X_t} + \varphi \right) e^{-\delta t} + \eta_t c = 0 \tag{42a}$$

and

$$\frac{\partial H}{\partial S_t} = \frac{b}{S_t} e^{-\delta t} - \psi \eta_t = -\dot{\eta}_t. \tag{42b}$$

Equations 40, 42a, and 42b are nonlinear simultaneous differential equations that solve for the three unknowns X_t, η_t, and S_t. The roots of equation 42a and 42b may be obtained directly and are identically equal to $-\psi$. Since equations 42a and 42b are first-order differential equations, the characteristic equation of the system of simultaneous equations must be second-order. Therefore, there are two characteristic roots or eigenvalues, which are discussed further below. Because these equations are nonlinear, they unfortunately don't have analytical solutions. Substituting equation 42a for η and $d\eta/dt$ into equation 42b and solving the result for the rate of change of X gives

$$\frac{\dot{X}}{X} = \hat{X} = \frac{bcX_t}{aS_t} - \varphi\left(\psi + \frac{\delta}{a}\right)X_t - \psi - \delta. \tag{43}$$

This equation states that when parents behave optimally the rate of change of parenting varies inversely with the ratio of parenting to resilience (X/S). The latter is a measure of excess parenting, so parents cut back on parenting if they have over-parented. If $\varphi > 0$, equation 43 further implies that there is negative feedback from the absolute level of parenting. Finally, equation 43 states that the rate of growth of parenting varies inversely with $\psi + \delta/a$. More impatient parents have larger δ; thus, the future development of their child is less important to them, so they invest less in parenting. Larger ψ means that parenting is more difficult, so parents invest less in parenting.

Stationary-state values of parenting and resilience are denoted by X^* and S^* respectively. In the stationary state, $dX/dt = 0$ by definition. The stationary-state solution to equation 43 is obtained by setting $dX/dt = 0$, letting $X = X^*$ and $S = S^*$, and then solving the result for S^*:

$$S^* = -\frac{bc}{(\psi + \delta)/X^* + \varphi(\psi + \delta/a)}. \tag{44}$$

This equation states that in the stationary state S^* and X vary inversely with each other. This relationship is nonlinear. The inverse relationship is convergent if $2(\psi + \delta)/X^* < 1$; otherwise it is divergent. The stationary-state solution to equation 40 is obtained by setting $dS/dt = 0$, letting $X = X^*$ and $S = S^*$, and solving the result for S^*:

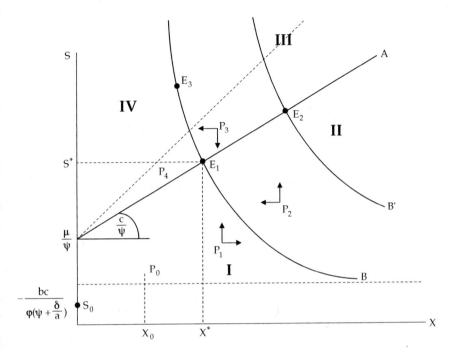

Figure 9.5
Phase diagram for optimal development.

$$S^* = \frac{\mu + cX^*}{\psi}. \tag{45}$$

Figure 9.5 is the phase diagram implied by equations 43–45. Curve A plots equation 45. Curve B plots equation 44 for the convergent case. The denominator in equation 44 is assumed to be negative, so that $S^* > 0$, which implies $\varphi < 0$. The stationary-state solutions are determined by the intersection of the two curves at E_1. The positions of curves A and B are determined by the structural parameters. For example, equation 44 implies that an increase in b (the satisfaction parents get from their child's resilience) would shift curve B to the right (to B') but curve A would remain unchanged. Therefore, the new stationary-state equilibrium would be at a point, such as E_2, at which S^* and X^* increase. An increase in μ (the convergence rate in resilience) shifts curve A upward but doesn't affect curve B, so the stationary-state equilibrium will at a point, such as E_3, at which S^* increases but X^* decreases. Other parameters (including c, the effect of parenting on resilience) are common to both curves. Equation 44 states that an increase in c shifts curve B to the right to B', and according to equation 45 curve A becomes steeper (curve A') so that the new equilibrium is E_4.

Equation 43 describes the dynamics of parenting. Children are, of course, born with almost no resilience, so S is initially very small and is denoted by S_0 in figure 9.5. The initial amount of parenting, which increases the resilience of the child, is denoted by X_0, so that P_0 denotes the initial equilibrium. At P_0, $X_0 < X^*$, so parents are under-parenting. Equation 43 states that in the next period they will increase their parenting, which increases resilience, so that P_1 (which is northeast of P_0) will be the new temporary equilibrium. The arrows indicate the direction of change in S and X. In quadrant I, the arrow points north for S and east for X.

This process continues until the temporary equilibrium is a point such as P_2. Notice that P_2 lies in quadrant II, in which parents are over-parenting. So parents reduce X, but S continues to increase because P_2 is below curve A. Therefore, in quadrant II the arrow points north for S but west for X. The next temporary equilibrium will be at a point like P_3, which is northwest of P_2. In quadrant III there is over-parenting and excess resilience; therefore the arrows drive the system in a southwesterly direction into quadrant IV.

If the roots are stable, the trajectory spirals in the counter-clockwise direction and eventually converges on E_1. If the trajectory spirals, it overshoots E_1 before converging. This typically happens when the roots are complex. If the roots are real, the trajectory will converge from below. To illustrate these roots, equation 43 is linearized around the stationary state:

$$\dot{X}_t = h - j(X_t - X^*) - k(S_t - S^*). \tag{46}$$

Equations 40 and 46 are linear first-order simultaneous differential equations with the following characteristic equation:

$$r^2 + (\psi + j)r + ck + \psi j = 0. \tag{47}$$

The roots or eigenvalues are the solution to equation 47. Since the equation is quadratic, there are two roots:

$$r = \frac{-(\psi + j) \pm \sqrt{(\psi + j)^2 - 4(ck + \psi j)}}{2}. \tag{48}$$

If the term inside the square root sign is negative, the roots are complex, in which case X and S converge to X^* and S^* in an oscillatory fashion. If this term is positive, the roots are real and are denoted by r_1 and r_2.

For stability and convergence to the stationary state, these roots must be negative. The general solutions for X and S are

$$X_t = X^* + A_0 e^{r_1 t} + A_1 e^{r_2 t} \tag{49a}$$

and

$$S_t = S^* + B_0 e^{r_1 t} + B_1 e^{r_2 t}, \tag{49b}$$

where the A's and the B's are arbitrary constants determined by either initial or terminal conditions. At time $t = 0$, $X_0 = X^* + A_0 + A_1$, and at $t = 1$, $X_1 = X^* + A_0 e^{r_1} + A_1 e^{r_2}$, which solve for A_0 and A_1:

$$A_0 = \frac{e^{r_2}(X_0 - X^*) - (X_1 - X^*)}{e^{r_1} - e^{r_2}}, \tag{50a}$$

$$A_1 = \frac{(X_1 - X^*) - e^{r_1}(X_0 - X^*)}{e^{r_1} - e^{r_2}}. \tag{50b}$$

Similarly, $S_0 = S^* + B_0 + B_1$ and $S_1 = S^* + B_0 e^{r_1} + B_1 e^{r_2}$, which solve for B_0 and B_1:

$$B_0 = \frac{e^{r_2}(S_0 - S^*) - (S_1 - S^*)}{e^{r_1} - e^{r_2}}, \tag{51a}$$

$$B_1 = \frac{(S_1 - S^*) - e^{r_1}(S_0 - S^*)}{e^{r_1} - e^{r_2}}. \tag{51b}$$

Substituting equations 50 and 51 into equations 49 provides the complete dynamical system for parenting and child development.

9.6.3 The Two-Period Developmental Model

In this subsection, the optimal developmental model of subsection 9.6.2 is simplified to reveal its underlying logic. To fix ideas, the simplest possible dynamic case is considered: the case in which the child suffers no distress, and hence $D = 0$. Because there is no distress, the child has no need to cry ($Z = 0$), in which event parental attention is entirely autonomous as it was in subsection 9.5.2. In subsection 9.6.2, time (age) was treated as a continuous variable; here, however, matters are simplified by treating time as a discrete variable. To simplify even more, it is assumed that there are only two time periods: the present (period 1) and the future (period 2). Two time periods are obviously the minimum required for dynamic analysis. In each time period, the parents' time constraint is normalized at $T = 1$. Therefore, $T_{p1} + T_{c1} = T = T_{p2} + T_{c2}$.

Also, in period 1 the child is endowed with resilience indexed by $S_1 = 1$ (represented by S_0 in subsection 9.6.1).

It turns out that matters are further simplified by assuming that the discrete time counterpart of equation 32 is loglinear. Therefore, the resilience of the child in the second period is equal to

$$S_2 = \mu U_{c1}^{\sigma} T_{c1}^{-\lambda} S_1^{\psi}. \tag{52}$$

This equation states that the child's resilience in the second period varies directly with his happiness in the first period and inversely with the spoiling effects due to excess parental attention and indulgence. It also depends on resilience in the first period; however, since, $S_1 = 1$, this term is equal to 1. In equation 52, σ, λ, and ψ lie between 0 and 1 for convexity; otherwise resilience would be explosive instead of convergent.

Parents are assumed to maximize their utility in both periods, but if they are impatient they may attach more importance to utility in the first period (U_{p1}) than in the second (U_{p2}). Parents are assumed to maximize discounted utility over the two periods:

$$V = U_{p1} + \delta U_{p2}. \tag{53}$$

Here the discount rate of parents, denoted by δ, is 1 when parents are patient and less than 1 when they prefer utility in period 1 over utility in period 2. If parents are completely impatient, $\delta = 0$; they don't care about the future.

Parents have only two decisions to make: how much time they allocate to their child in period 1 and how much they allocate in period 2. They therefore maximize V with respect to T_{c1} and T_{c2}.

The nature of the solution is illustrated in figure 9.6, where A denotes the utility coordinates for parents when they devote none of their time in the first period to their child. Along curve AcB in the direction from A to B, parents increase the time they devote to their child in the first period. At A they devote none of their time; at B they devote all of their time. As they devote time to their child, the child is happier in the first period, which makes the parents happier in the first period. If the child is happier in the first period, this will promote his development, and his resilience will be greater in the second period, which in turn will make the parents happier in the second period. Therefore, curve AcB may initially slope upward; time devoted to the child increases parents' utility in both periods. After a point, however, the slope of the curve becomes vertical, because the marginal utility of the time the parents

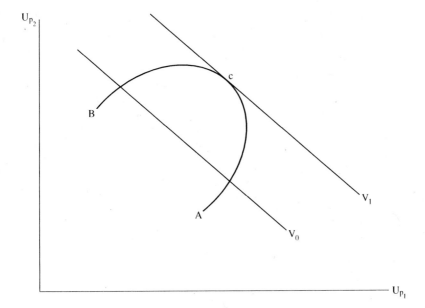

Figure 9.6
Parenting in the two-period model.

spend on themselves increases, and after a further point the slope turns negative. This happens when the parents stall the child's development through spoiling. Finally, the curve may bend backward so that utility in both periods falls as the parents devote more time to the child in the first period.

Curve AcB constitutes the inter-temporal "utility possibility frontier" for parents. It is inefficient for parents to be inside this frontier, and it is impossible for them to be outside it. They will therefore choose a point on the frontier that maximizes their lifetime utility, which in the two-period case is the discounted utility V over the two periods. Equation 53 implies that there is a family of linear indifference curves between utility in the two periods whose slope depends on δ. The highest attainable lifetime utility is $V^* = V_1$. Therefore, the parents choose point c on the utility possibility frontier, at which the tradeoff between utility in the two periods must be negative.

If the parents are more impatient because δ is smaller, the V curves will be steeper and the tangent between V^* and the utility possibility frontier will lie closer to A, implying that parents devote less time to their child in the first period. The shape of the utility possibility frontier depends on all the parameters of the model, which obviously determine the point of tangency.

Our attention has been focused on how parents allocate their time in period 1. What about period 2? Since in a two-period model there is by definition no period 3 or beyond, parents don't have to consider the future development of their child in period 2. It doesn't matter if they spoil him. Therefore, whereas the allocation of parent time in period 1 is a dynamic decision and parents had to consider the future consequences of their behavior, the allocation of parent time in period 2 is a static decision because the future doesn't exist. They simply allocate their time as in subsection 9.5.2. The two-period model is obviously unrealistic, but I hope its simplicity exposes the nature of the intertemporal tradeoffs that confront parents.

For simplicity it has been assumed that the child is passive. Suppose instead that the child is active because he is distressed (D is positive), so that the Crying Game is played in both periods. If the child cries in period 1, his parents give him more attention, so their utility is reduced in period 1. Also, the child's utility is generally lower, because, although he gets more attention, he has to cry for this, and he is distressed. Therefore, both U_{p1} and U_{c1} decrease when the child is not passive. The same applies in period 2. Consequently, the utility possibility frontier lies inside curve AcB in figure 9.6 when the child is not passive. However, its generic shape is not affected, and the optimal parenting strategy remains qualitatively the same. In any case whereas parents are concerned for their child's development needs and must therefore be forward-looking, it is unreasonable to assume that children are forward-looking, i.e., they cry in period 1 to induce their parents to devote more attention to them because they want their parents to promote their development. Parents think strategically, but children do not. Indeed, if children behaved strategically it would be impossible to dichotomize the short term and the long term.

9.6.4   Current and Future Parenting
Suppose that the outcome of the child depends both on current parenting and on lagged parenting:

$$Y_{ct} = \alpha X_t + \beta X_{t-1} + u_t, \tag{54a}$$

$$u_t = \varphi u_{t-1} + \varepsilon_t. \tag{54b}$$

According to equation 54a, the long-run effect of parenting on the outcome is $\alpha + \beta$. According to equation 54b, there is short-term inertia in the outcome variable, since $0 < \varphi < 1$. This means that if the outcome was above or below target, this difference is expected to persist for some time because u is autoregressive. Parents are assumed to be averse to effort, but since they have development targets for their child Y^*, which they do not wish to miss, they must make an effort to keep the outcome on target. The current loss function of the parent is therefore

$$L_t = \theta X_t^2 + (1-\theta)(Y_{ct} - Y^*)^2, \tag{55}$$

where θ expresses the relative weight that parents place on the effort of parenting. Parents are assumed to minimize expected discounted loss:

$$V = E_t\left(\sum_{i=1}^{T}\delta^{i-1}L_{t+i}\right), \tag{56}$$

where E_t denotes the expected value operator at the beginning of period t. The first-order condition for a minimum with respect to X_t is

$$\frac{dV}{dX_t} = E_t\left(\frac{dL_t}{dX_t} + \delta\frac{dL_{t+1}}{dX_t}\right) = 0 \tag{57a}$$

$$= 2\theta X_t + 2\alpha(1-\theta)E_t(Y_{ct} - Y^*) + 2\beta(1-\theta)E_t(Y_{ct+1} - Y^*) = 0. \tag{57b}$$

Equation 57b solves for optimal parenting:

$$X_t = -\frac{\alpha(1-\theta)}{\theta}E_t(Y_{ct} - Y^*) - \frac{\beta(1-\theta)}{\theta}E_t(Y_{ct+1} - Y^*). \tag{58}$$

Equation 58 states that current parenting varies inversely with the expected overshoot of the outcome above target at time t and time t + 1. Since current parenting affects the future as well as the current outcome, equation 58 contains both terms. Had equation 54a included higher-order lags, equation 58 would have contained higher-order expected leads. An important thing to note is that, in addition to being influenced by the child's current behavior, current parenting is partly influenced by the child's expected future behavior.

Equation 58 can be rewritten in terms of past parenting and expected future parenting. Substituting equations 54 into equation 58 for $E_t(Y_{ct})$ and $E_t(Y_{ct+1})$ and solving the result for X_t gives

$$X_t = \pi_1 E_t(X_{t+1}) + \pi_1 X_{t-1} + \pi_2 u_{t-1}, \tag{59}$$

where

$$\pi_1 = -\frac{\alpha\beta(1-\theta)}{\theta + (\alpha^2 + \beta^2)(1-\theta)}$$

and

$$\pi_2 = -\frac{\varphi(1-\theta)(\alpha + \beta\varphi)}{\theta + (\alpha^2 + \beta^2)(1-\theta)}.$$

Equation 59 states that current parenting varies inversely with expected future parenting and with past parenting, since $\pi_1 > 0$. It also varies inversely with u_{t-1}, since this induces the outcome to be above the target. Like equation 58, from which it is derived, equation 59 states that current parenting depends on expected future parenting as well as on past parenting.

In chapter 3, I criticized developmental psychologists for ignoring the potential effect of expected future parenting on current parenting. In terms of equation 59, they specify X_{t-1} but ignore $E_t(X_{t+1})$. Their empirical models are therefore entirely backward-looking. By ignoring forward-looking behavior, their models' risk being misspecified. Since in general parents' current expectations of their future actions depend on their expectations of their children's future behavior, this means that the empirical analysis of parents' actions cannot be conducted in isolation from their expectations of the children's future behavior.

10 Empirical Methodology

10.1 Data Errors

Data on outcomes for parents and children may contain measurement errors. For example, if the outcome happens to be schooling, the recorded data on years of schooling may not be accurate. Or the heights of parents and children may be over-recorded or under-recorded. As we shall see, misrecording of data on parents has much more serious statistical consequences than misrecording of data on children. Indeed, measurement error in outcomes for parents induces "attenuation bias" in both β and the intergenerational correlation coefficient. This creates the statistical illusion that β and the intergenerational correlation are smaller than they really are. In contrast, measurement error in the outcomes of children induces attenuation bias in the intergenerational correlation coefficient but not in β. The solution to the attenuation bias problem is to apply the "errors-in-variables" method to the estimation of β.[1]

A related but quite different problem is concerned with transitory or short-term intergenerational correlations and their permanent or long-term counterparts. Broadly speaking there are two types of variables, those that fluctuate such as weight, and those that do not fluctuate such as height. Weight may increase after Christmas or decrease during Lent, but height remains unchanged. Therefore, recorded weight depends on when it is measured whereas recorded height does not. In the case of economic data, income is generally lower in a recession than in a boom. Income may contain both cyclical and seasonal components, which make current income, as measured, differ from what economists refer to as *permanent income*. The latter is more representative of long-term income, which is arguably of greater interest than current income. The trouble is that permanent income is not generally measured, and only current income is measured. Survey data that are collected on outcomes for parents and children (and indeed, for data in general) typically refer to the time at which the survey took place. At this date the outcome may have been unusually high or low. Ideally, we would like the data to refer to some average that smooths out short-term fluctuations, which would be more representative than the "snapshot" data collected in surveys.

In retrospective surveys individuals are asked to recall their outcomes in the past as well as the present. However, retrospective data are naturally less reliable than current data; it is harder to recall your weight a year ago than it is to recall your present weight. In longitudinal surveys individuals are observed repeatedly, and fluctuating variables such as weight or income may be averaged.[2] However, longitudinal surveys are rare, and in any case may involve attrition bias due to non-random attrition of the sample. Most surveys collect current snapshot data, which may not be representative of the underlying phenomena that they are supposed to measure.

Just as measurement error induces attenuation bias, so the use of current data tends to induce attenuation bias in permanent intergenerational correlations. In the absence of data error, the current intergenerational correlation is estimated without bias, but it tends to be smaller than the permanent intergenerational correlation because these data may not be representative. The solution to this problem is to estimate the intergenerational correlation using the "errors-in-variables method." In general, therefore, two types of instrumental variables are required. The first is for measurement error in the data. The second is for misrepresentation that may arise in current survey data for fluctuating phenomena. Sometimes the same instrumental variable may serve both purposes, for example, height in the case of weight, especially in the case of adults who have reached their permanent height.

10.1.1 Measurement Error

Suppose the objective is to estimate Galton's beta[3]:

$$Y_{ci} = \beta Y_{pi} + \varepsilon_{ci}, \tag{1}$$

where, for simplicity, ε_c is an iid random variable that is independent of Y_p. Suppose further that the Y's are mismeasured so that

$$\tilde{Y}_{ci} = Y_{ci} + v_{ci} \tag{2a}$$

and

$$\tilde{Y}_{pi} = Y_{pi} + v_{pi}, \tag{2b}$$

where $\tilde{Y}$ denotes the data and v denotes measurement error. It is assumed that measurement error is independent of the underlying truth, i.e., $E(Yv) = 0$, and that $E(v) = 0$, i.e., there is no systematic bias in data recording. Substituting equations 2a and 2b into equation 1 gives

$$\tilde{Y}_{ci} = \beta \tilde{Y}_{pi} + u_i \tag{3a}$$

and

$$u_i = \varepsilon_{ci} - v_{ci} - \beta v_{pi}. \tag{3b}$$

We cannot estimate β from equation 1, since the true data do not exist. Therefore, β is estimated from equation 3a using actual data. Notice, however, that, according to equation 3b, $\tilde{Y}_p$ in equation 3a is not independent of u. In fact, $E(\tilde{Y}_p u) = -\beta \operatorname{var}(v_p)$, so that

$$E(\hat{\beta}_{OLS}) = \beta - \beta \frac{\operatorname{var}(v_p)}{\operatorname{var}(\tilde{Y}_p)} = \beta \frac{\operatorname{var}(Y_p)}{\operatorname{var}(\tilde{Y}_p)}. \tag{4}$$

According to equation 2b, $\operatorname{var}(\tilde{Y}_p) = \operatorname{var}(Y_p) + \operatorname{var}(v_p)$. Since $\operatorname{var}(Y_p) < \operatorname{var}(\tilde{Y}_p)$, equation 4 states that the absolute value of the OLS estimator of β is biased downward. Since the ratio of these variances is a positive fraction, the OLS estimate of β must be a fraction of its true estimate. Therefore, the estimate is said to be attenuated. If β is positive its estimate is biased downward. If β is negative its estimate is biased upward. Attenuation bias cannot produce the wrong sign of β since the bias is proportionate to its true value.

The noise-to-signal ratio, $\operatorname{var}(v_p)/\operatorname{var}(\tilde{Y}_p)$, varies inversely with $\operatorname{var}(Y_p)/\operatorname{var}(\tilde{Y}_p)$. If the noise-to-signal ratio is 1, the data are entirely noisy, i.e., $\operatorname{var}(Y_p) = 0$ and $\operatorname{var}(\tilde{Y}_p) = \operatorname{var}(v_p)$, in which case equation 4 states that the estimate of β is 0. At the other extreme, if the noise-to-signal ratio is 0, so that $\operatorname{var}(v_p) = 0$, equation 4 states that the estimate of β is equal to its true value. Figure 2.3 plots the relationship between attrition bias and the noise-to-signal ratio.

Notice that the mismeasurement of Y_c plays no direct role here. However, it plays an indirect role since the variance of u in equation 3a increases with $\operatorname{var}(v_c)$, which in turn increases the variance of the estimate of β. Therefore, data errors in Y_c do not induce bias but they reduces statistical efficiency. Nevertheless, data error in Y_c is clearly a less serious matter than data error in Y_p.

In chapter 8 it was noted that β and the intergenerational correlation coefficient (r) are related. This means that attenuation bias in β induces attenuation bias in r. Using the definition of the correlation coefficient, it is simple to show that

$$\hat{r} = r\frac{\text{sd}(Y_p)\text{sd}(Y_c)}{\text{sd}(\tilde{Y}_p)\text{sd}(\tilde{Y}_c)}, \tag{5}$$

where $\hat{r}$ denotes the attenuated intergenerational correlation and r denotes its true value. Since $\text{sd}(Y) < \text{sd}(\tilde{Y})$ for both Y_p and Y_c, it must be the case that if r is positive the attenuated correlation coefficient is less than its true value. Notice that attenuation bias in the intergenerational correlation coefficient is induced both by measurement error in the outcomes of children as well the outcomes of their parents. Therefore, the noise-to-signal ratios for children as well as parents matters for the intergenerational correlation coefficient, whereas in the case of β only the noise-to-signal ratio for parents matters.

Attenuation bias is illustrated numerically in table 10.1 for different assumptions about the noise-to-signal ratio. In case 1 there is no mismeasurement so the estimates equal their true values. In case 2 measurement error is assumed to apply to data on children but not to parents' data. The noise-to-signal ratio for children is 16 percent since $\text{var}(v_c) = 0.16$. The estimate of the intergenerational correlation as attenuated by 7.2 percent, but β is not affected. In case 3 both sets of data are mismeasured, but to the same degree. Therefore, both β and r are attenuated to the same extent, by 13.8 percent. In case 4 data on parents are assumed to be more mismeasured than data on children, in which the noise-to-signal ratio is 4 percent. Attenuation bias in β is greater than in r. Case 5 reverses case 4. Attenuation bias in β decreases because it is not affected by measurement error in data on children. However, attenuation bias in r does not change because it depends on the products of the true standard deviations relative to their false counterparts.

Table 10.1
Attenuation bias. (True β and r are 0.5.)

Case	$\text{sd}(v_p)$	$\text{sd}(v_c)$	$\tilde{\beta}$	$\tilde{r}$
1	0	0	0.5	0.5
2	0	0.4	0.5	0.4642
3	0.4	0.4	0.4310	0.4310
4	0.4	0.2	0.4310	0.4552
5	0.2	0.4	0.4808	0.4552

10.1.2 Errors-in-Variables Estimation

The solution to this errors-in-variables problem is to find an instrumental variable for parents Z_p which is correlated with Y_p and is independent of its measurement error (v_p). Suppose, for example, that height of parents (H_p) is measured accurately and that Y_p is the body mass of the parent. There is every reason to expect that taller people have greater body mass, therefore Y_p should depend directly on H_p. Also, there is no reason to suspect that measurement error in body mass should be correlated with height, unless height is mismeasured too. Therefore, $E(H_p v_p) = 0$, in which case height may serve as an instrumental variable for body mass. Matters would be different if height featured in equation 3a because the instrumented estimate of body mass would be perfectly correlated with height, and the parameters of the model would cease to be identified. The IV estimator is

$$\hat{\beta}_{IV} = \frac{\operatorname{cov}(\tilde{Y}_c Z_p)}{\operatorname{cov}(\tilde{Y}_p Z_p)}, \tag{6}$$

where $H_p = Z_p$. Substituting equation 3a into equation 6 gives

$$\hat{\beta}_{IV} = \frac{\beta \operatorname{cov}(\tilde{Y}_p Z_p) + \operatorname{cov}(\varepsilon_c Z_p) - \operatorname{cov}(v_c Z_p) - \beta \operatorname{cov}(v_p Z_p)}{\operatorname{cov}(\tilde{Y}_p Z_p)}. \tag{7}$$

Since by definition Z_p is independent of measurement error,

$$E[\operatorname{cov}(v_p Z_p)] = E[\operatorname{cov}(v_c Z_p)] = 0.$$

Also, ε_c is, by definition, independent of outcomes for parents; hence,

$$E[\operatorname{cov}(\varepsilon_c Z_p)] = 0.$$

Therefore, equation 7 reduces to

$$E(\hat{\beta}_{IV}) = \beta,$$

in which case the expected value of the IV estimator of β is equal to its true value.

10.1.3 Instrumental Variables Estimation and the Generalized Method of Moments

A generalization of the IV estimator is GMM (Generalized Method of Moments), which since its development in the early 1980s has become a standard feature of econometrics textbooks.[4] Suppose there are $M > 1$ instrumental variables denoted by $Z_1, Z_2, \ldots, Z_M$, which by definition are independent of v and therefore of u in equation 3. The IV estimator removes measurement error (v_p) from $\tilde{Y}_p$ by regressing $\tilde{Y}_p$ on the Z variables. Since the Z variables are independent of measurement error the fitted value of $\hat{Y}_p = \tilde{Y}_p$ from this regression is free of measurement error and is therefore expected to equal Y_p. In fact it may be shown that $\hat{\beta}_{IV}$ in equation 6 is equivalent to regressing $\tilde{Y}_c$ on $\hat{Y}_p$.

The mechanics of the GMM estimator are different. GMM uses the individual moment restrictions for each instrumental variable. According to each of these restrictions, $cov(uZ_m) = 0$. Since there are M instrumental variables, there are M such moment conditions. Each of these restrictions may be used to form an IV estimate of β, denoted by $\beta_{IV}(m)$, by replacing Z_p in equation 6 with Z_m. The GMM estimator, β_{GMM}, weights the M moment restrictions in an optimal fashion. In special cases IV and GMM are equivalent, but they are generally different, especially in the presence of heteroscedasticity.

10.1.4   Current vs. Permanent Correlations

Suppose, once more, that our objective is to estimate β in equation 1 where the Y's are permanent or long-term measures. However, the data do not reveal Y but Y^* where asterisks denote the current data for Y. Y and Y^* generally differ so that

$$Y_c^* = Y_c + \omega_c, \tag{8a}$$

$$Y_p^* = Y_p + \omega_p, \tag{8b}$$

where the ω's are iid random variables that denote the gaps between current and permanent values of Y. Substituting equations 8 into equation 1 gives rise to an equation that is similar to equation 4:

$$E(\hat{\beta}_{OLS}) = \beta \frac{var(Y_p)}{var(Y_p^*)}. \tag{9}$$

According to equation 8b, $var(Y_p^*) = var(Y_p) + var(\omega_p)$, in which case $var(Y_p) < var(Y_p^*)$. Therefore, here too, there is attenuation bias and the absolute value of β is underestimated. As in the case of measurement error, attenuation bias is induced by transitory components in the outcomes for parents; the transitory component in the case of children reduces efficiency but does not induce bias. Finally, it should be emphasized that the OLS estimate of β is unbiased and efficient for Y^* (current values of Y), but not, of course, for permanent values of Y.

The solution to this problem is similar to the solution for the errors-in-variables problem. We need to find instrumental variables that are correlated with permanent value of Y_p, which are uncorrelated with ω_p. Suppose, once more, that Y denotes body mass, which, however, is measured accurately. Currently measured body mass may differ from permanent body mass for a variety of reasons. For example, we may have put on weight over Christmas. Height, on the other hand does not depend on Christmas, and current and permanent height are the same. Therefore, height may serve as an instrumental variable to estimate β using the method of instrumental variables.

In practice both types of problem might arise simultaneously. The data refer to current rather than permanent measurements and these measurements happen to be inaccurate. In this case both types of attenuation bias would occur simultaneously. The presence of both types of bias could seriously understate the strength of the intergenerational β coefficient. Under the assumption that measurement errors (v) and transitory components (ω) are independent, it is straightforward to show that when both types of bias are present:

$$E\left(\hat{\beta}_{OLS}\right) = \beta \frac{\text{var}(Y_p)}{\text{var}(Y_p) + \text{var}(v_p) + \text{var}(\omega_p)}. \tag{10}$$

The denominator in equation 10 is larger than its counterpart in equation 4 because of the additional presence of $\text{var}(\omega_p)$. The OLS estimate of β is therefore doubly attenuated.

10.2   Bias in Intergenerational Autoregressions

Recall the first-order intergenerational AR^3 model discussed in detail in chapter 8:

$$Y_{ci} = \alpha + \beta Y_{pi} + G_{ci} + e_{ci}, \tag{11a}$$

$$G_{ci} = \rho G_{pi} + \varepsilon_{ci}, \tag{11b}$$

$$e_{ci} = \varphi e_{pi} + \mu_{ci}, \tag{11c}$$

where G denotes genetic endowment, or genotype, e is an unobserved environmental component, and ε and μ are mutually independent random iid draws from the gene pool and environments respectively. The absolute values of ρ and φ are assumed to lie between 1 and -1.

Suppose that the main research objective is to estimate β, the mean reversion coefficient. A secondary objective is to estimate ρ, the coefficient of heredity in the intergenerational transmission of genetic endowment. A third objective might be to estimate φ. As was discussed in chapter 8, β captures the causal effect of parenting or nurture on the outcome of children, while ρ captures the effect of nature. Therefore, equations 11 constitute the simplest nature-nurture model.

The OLS estimator of β is

$$\hat{\beta} = \frac{\text{cov}(Y_c Y_p)}{\text{var}(Y_p)}. \tag{12}$$

Substituting equation 11a into equation 12 gives

$$\hat{\beta} = \beta + b, \tag{13a}$$

$$b = \frac{\text{cov}(Y_p G_c) + \text{cov}(Y_p e_c)}{\text{var}(Y_p)}. \tag{13b}$$

Equation 13a states the OLS estimator contains the true values of β and bias, b. If the outcome for parents is independent of G_c and e_c, the OLS estimator of β is unbiased and consistent because $b = 0$. However, equations 11b and 11c imply that these variables are not independent due to heredity in genetic endowments, and shared environmental exposure. In fact the covariance between them is expected to be as follows:

$$\text{cov}(Y_p G_c) = \beta \rho \, \text{cov}(Y_g G_p) + \rho \, \text{var}(G_p), \tag{14a}$$

$$\text{cov}(Y_p e_c) = \beta \varphi \, \text{cov}(Y_g e_p) + \varphi \, \text{var}(e_p). \tag{14b}$$

If ρ and φ are positive, equations 14a and 14b are positive, in which case b is positive. However, b might be negative. It would only be by chance that $b = 0$, i.e., when the two covariances just happen to cancel each other out. In general, therefore, the OLS estimator of β is biased and inconsistent. Tables 5.1 and 5.2 provide numerical illustrations of the bias in estimates of β induced by G_p and e_p respectively. The next three sections discuss methodological solutions to this problem.

10.3   The Generated-Regressor Methodology

Had data been available on the genetic endowments of parents (G_p) and the environments of parents (e_p) the problem of bias would not have arisen in the first place. This phenomenon is therefore referred to as *omitted-variable bias*. To see this, we can substitute equations 11b and 11c into equation 11a to obtain

$$Y_c = \alpha + \beta Y_p + \rho G_p + \varphi e_p + v_c \tag{15a}$$

and

$$v_c = \varepsilon_c + e_c. \tag{15b}$$

Equation 15a may be estimated by OLS because it satisfies the classical regression assumptions:

$$E(v_c) = E(v_c Y_p) = E(v_c G_p) = E(e_p v_c) = 0.$$

Since the regressors are independent of the residuals (v_c), OLS estimates of β and ρ are unbiased and consistent.

10.3.1 Implementing the Generated-Regressor Methodology

Of course the problem is that data for genotypes and environments of parents aren't available. Suppose, however, that somehow we managed to generate an unbiased estimate of G_p, denoted by $\hat{G}_p$, which is expected to equal G_p itself:

$$\hat{G}_p = G_p + \omega_p, \tag{16}$$

where ω denotes measurement error and $E(\omega) = 0$. The missing regressor is generated, hence the name "generated regressor" methodology (Pagan 1984). Similarly, a regressor may be generated for e_p, however, in what follows the methodology is illustrated with respect to unobserved genotypes. Substituting equation 16 into equation 15a gives

$$Y_c = \alpha + \beta Y_p + \rho \hat{G}_p + w_c, \tag{17a}$$

$$w_c = v_c - \rho \omega_p. \tag{17b}$$

$E(Y_p w_c) = 0$ because $E(Y_p v_c) = E(Y_p \omega_p) = 0$. However, the same does not generally apply to the estimate of the genotypes of parents:

$$E(\hat{G}_p w_c) = E[(G_p + \omega_p)(v_c - \rho \omega_p)] = -\rho \, \mathrm{var}(\omega_p). \tag{18}$$

Because equation 18 is negative, OLS estimates of ρ suffer from attenuation bias, which is negative. Since Y_p and G_p are positively correlated the bias in the estimate of ρ induces bias in the estimate of β. If, however, $\mathrm{var}(\omega_p) = 0$ because the genotypes of parents is estimated with perfect accuracy, equation 18 is 0 and there is no attenuation bias.

Equation 18 establishes that the generated-regressor methodology swaps omitted-variable bias for attenuation bias. However, the latter is typically smaller than the former because whereas OLS omits all of the genotypes of parents, the generated-regressor methodology omits only some of the genetic endowment of parents. Half a loaf is better than no bread. Therefore, the generated-regressor methodology is superior to OLS. And if the generated regressor is accurately estimated, so that $\text{var}(\omega_p) = 0$, it goes all the way in removing the bias induced by unobserved genetic endowments.

The generated-regressor methodology in this context requires data on children, parents, and grandparents. Equation 11a is estimated by OLS for parents, i.e., Y_p is regressed on Y_g to obtain an estimate of v_p, which (assuming $\alpha = 0$ for convenience) is equal to

$$\hat{v}_p = Y_p - \hat{\beta}_p Y_g = Y_p - (\beta_p + b)Y_g = v_p - bY_g. \tag{19}$$

Due to omitted-variable bias for G_g, the estimated residuals are biased. However, the source of the bias is known and is equal to $-bY_g$. Equations 11b and 19 imply the following relationship between the estimated residuals and the unobserved genetic endowment of parents:

$$G_p = \hat{v}_p - e_p + bY_g . \tag{20}$$

Substituting equation 20 into equation 15a gives

$$Y_c = \alpha + \beta Y_p + \rho \hat{v}_p + \rho bY_g + h_c , \tag{21a}$$

$$h_c = \varepsilon_c + e_c - \rho e_p. \tag{21b}$$

In equation 21a all the parameters appear to be identified, including the bias b. However, Y_p is not independent of h_c, because the latter comprises e_p. In fact,

$$E(Y_p h_c) = -\rho \, \text{var}(e_p), \tag{22}$$

which induces negative attenuation bias in the estimate of β. Nevertheless, equation 21b makes the point that if environmental influences on the outcome happened to be observable, i.e., if e_p was observable and specified as a covariate in the model, attenuation bias would disappear, and all the parameters in equation 17a would be identified.

10.3.2   The Cochrane-Orcutt Method
The generated-regressor methodology requires cross-section data on children, parents and grandparents. An alternative but related

procedure[5] with such data is to apply the Cochrane-Orcutt method to estimate models with serial correlation in the residuals. In what follows, generation c is denoted by t, generation p by t − 1, generation g by t − 2, and so on. As in the generated-regressor methodology environments are ignored for simplicity. Equations 11a and 11b are therefore written as follows:

$$Y_t = \alpha + \beta Y_{t-1} + G_t \text{,} \tag{23a}$$

$$G_t = \rho G_{t-1} + \varepsilon_t \text{.} \tag{23b}$$

Substituting equation 23b into equation 23a gives

$$Y_t = \pi_0 + \pi_1 Y_{t-1} + \pi_2 Y_{t-2} + \varepsilon_t \text{,} \tag{24}$$

where

$$\pi_0 = (1 - \rho)\alpha \text{,}$$

$$\pi_1 = \beta + \rho \text{,}$$

and

$$\pi_2 = -\beta\rho \text{.}$$

In equation 24 the residual for children (ε_t) is independent of the outcomes for parents (Y_{t-1}) and grandparents (Y_{t-2}). Therefore, OLS estimates of π_1 and π_2 are unbiased and consistent. Equations 21a and 24 are similar in that they both use data on parents and grandparents. However, equation 21a uses a generated regressor whereas equation 24 does not. Also, equation 21a is linear in the structural parameters (β and ρ) whereas equation 24 is not. Notice that when β and ρ are positive the conditional effect of the outcome for grandparents on the outcome of their grandchildren is negative.[6] In equation 21a, β is estimated directly; in equation 24, it is the solution to

$$\hat{\beta} = \frac{\hat{\pi}_1 \pm \sqrt{\hat{\pi}_1^2 + 4\hat{\pi}_2}}{2} \text{.} \tag{25}$$

The estimate of ρ is then $\hat{\rho} = \hat{\pi}_1 - \hat{\beta}$. In principle, there are two solutions, but only one of these solutions will be acceptable in terms of stationarity.

Equation 24 establishes that the Cochrane-Orcutt method identifies the structural parameters in the AR^2 model. Matters are unfortunately different in the AR^3 model in which equation 11c is not ignored and the intergenerational AR coefficient φ for environments is a structural parameter to be estimated together with ρ and β. In the AR^3 model the counterpart of equation 24 is

$$Y_t = \psi_0 + \psi_1 Y_{t-1} + \psi_2 Y_{t-2} + \psi_3 Y_{t-3} + v_t, \tag{26a}$$

$$v_t = \varepsilon_t - \varphi\varepsilon_{t-1} + \mu_t - \rho\mu_{t-1}, \tag{26b}$$

where

$$\psi_0 = \alpha(1-\rho)(1-\varphi),$$

$$\psi_1 = \beta + \rho + \varphi,$$

$$\psi_2 = -\rho\varphi - \beta(\rho + \varphi).$$

and

$$\psi_3 = \beta\rho\varphi.$$

The good news is that the three structural parameters are determined by the estimates of ψ_1, ψ_2, and ψ_3 in equation 26a. Notice that the coefficient for grandparents (ψ_2) continues to be negative as in equation 24, but the coefficient for great-grandparents (ψ_3) is positive. As in the AR^2 case, there may be multiple solutions to the structural parameters, since the ψ's are nonlinear in β, ρ, and φ. There are two pieces of bad news. First, equation 26a includes Y_{t-3}, so data are also required on great-grandparents. Therefore, the intergenerational cross-section data involve four generations rather than (as in equation 24 for the AR^2 model) three. Second, because according to equation 26b v_t varies inversely with ε_{t-1} and μ_{t-1}, v_t in equation 26a is not independent of Y_{t-1}. Therefore, OLS estimates of the ψ's in equation 26a will be biased downward and inconsistent, especially in the case of ψ_1.

In the case of time-series data this problem is easily overcome. Equation 26a would be estimated by Generalized Least Squares (GLS) rather than OLS. However, in the case of intergenerational cross-section data GLS is not feasible. Therefore, the Cochrane-Orcutt method works for the AR^2 model but not for the AR^3 model.

10.3.3 "Mincer Residuals" as Generated Regressors

Genetic endowments express many phenomena including ability. Juhn et al. (1993) were the first to suggest that unobserved ability may be proxied by the residuals from "Mincer Models." The Mincer Model, one of the workhorses of labor economics,[7] hypothesizes that wages

(W) are the return to acquired human capital, which is hypothesized to vary directly with years of schooling (E) and labor-market experience, proxied by age (A). Wages are also hypothesized to vary directly with innate human capital, or ability (a), which, unlike acquired human capital is typically unobserved. The basic Mincer Model is specified as follows:

$$\ln W_i = \delta_0 + \delta_1 E_i + \delta_2 A_i - \delta_3 A_i^2 + \delta_4 X_i + a_i, \tag{27}$$

where X denotes a set of demographic controls, such as sex and ethnic origin, that might determine wages. Since the dependent variable is a logarithm, the return to a year's schooling is δ_1, which is hypothesized to be positive. There is an empirical consensus among labor economists that this return falls in the range of 7–12 percent. There is also an empirical consensus that wages vary over the life cycle. At first they increase with age, but eventually (after about 45 years) they decrease. This ∩-shaped relation is captured by the negative coefficient on age squared.

The residual in equation 27 is hypothesized to express unobserved components of human capital and measures the return to innate ability. This assumes that the data do not contain measurement error, for otherwise a would embody the return to innate ability as well as measurement error. The estimated residuals of equation 27 constitute generated regressors for unobserved ability. Since R^2 for Mincer Models is typically about 0.35, the majority of wage inequality is attributed to inequality in ability.

Equation 27 generates unbiased estimates of ability if the covariates in the Mincer Model are independent of unobserved ability a. Since equation 27 is usually estimated using data from labor-market surveys that refer to some specific year, workers who are older in the sample were born earlier. Since there is no reason to suspect that ability varies by birth cohort it is reasonable to assume that A and a are independent in equation 27. The same applies to the components of X, such as sex and ethnic group. However, it is unlikely to apply to schooling, since, as was discussed in chapter 9, abler individuals are likely to acquire more schooling, in which case $E(Ea) > 0$, and the generated regressor for ability will be biased.

There are two solutions to this problem. The first is to estimate equation 27 by IV rather than OLS, as will be discussed in the next section. The second is based on bias correction as in equation 21a. Applying this correction to equation 27 gives

$$\hat{a} = a + b, \tag{28a}$$

$$b = b_1 E + b_2 A + b_3 A^2 + b_4 X. \tag{28b}$$

Typically, equation 27 is estimated using data on parents to generate a regressor for their unobserved ability, $\hat{a}_p = a_p + b$. Suppose we wish to estimate equation 17a using $\hat{a}_p$ instead of $\hat{G}_p$. The bias-corrected estimator would be

$$Y_c = \alpha + \beta Y_p + \rho \hat{a}_p + b_1 E_p + b_2 A_p + b_3 A_p^2 + b_4 X_p + w_c, \tag{29}$$

in which the generated-regressor model is estimated together with the auxiliary variables for parents used to generate estimated ability for parents. These auxiliary variables estimate b in terms of equation 28b, as a result of which the estimates of β and ρ are unbiased.

10.4   Instrumental Variables

A very different strategy for solving the genetic bias problem is to estimate equation 11a using the method[8] of instrumental variables (IV). In this context an instrumental variable (Z) is hypothesized to affect Y_p directly but which is independent of u_c, i.e., $E(Y_pZ) \neq 0$ but $E(u_cZ) = 0$. The latter means, via equation 11b, that $E(G_cZ) = E(e_cZ) = 0$, i.e., Z is independent of unobserved genetic endowments and environments of children. Since G_c and e_c depend on G_p and e_p, Z must also be independent of G_p and e_p. If Z exists, the IV estimator of β is defined as

$$\hat{\beta}_{IV} = \frac{\text{cov}(Y_cZ)}{\text{cov}(Y_pZ)}. \tag{30}$$

The IV estimator instruments Y_p with Z; that is, it replaces Y_p with its expected value given Z. The latter must be independent of the regression residual because Z is independent by definition. In short, Z identifies β.

It will also identify ρ in the AR^2 model. Having obtained an unbiased estimate of β, we can estimate ρ as follows: Compute the estimates of u_c and u_p from

$$\hat{u}_c = Y_c - \hat{\alpha}_{IV} - \hat{\beta}_{IV} Y_p \tag{31a}$$

and

$$\hat{u}_p = Y_p - \hat{\alpha}_{IV} - \hat{\beta}_{IV} Y_g \tag{31b}$$

and substitute these estimated residuals into equation 11c to estimate
ρ. Because the residuals are unbiased, so is the estimate of ρ. If data on
grandparents aren't available, equation 31b cannot be calculated, in
which case ρ cannot be estimated. What is important here is that IV
does not require data on grandparents to obtain unbiased estimates of
β. In the AR^3 model, ρ and φ are not identified even if data are available
for grandparents. Since $u = G + e$, G and e cannot be decomposed
from u.

10.4.1 Natural Experiments and Instrumental Variables

Suppose hypothetically that β could be estimated under laboratory
conditions. Controlled experiments would be conducted in which parent-child dyads were randomly selected, and Y_p would be varied randomly for these dyads. Subsequently, the data for Y_c may be used to
estimate β without bias. In these hypothetical laboratory conditions the
results of the experiment cannot be confounded by unobserved genetic
effects, since the dyads in the experiment were chosen independently
of their genetic endowments and the treatments for Y_p were also administered independently of genetic endowments. Obviously laboratory
experiments or randomized trials aren't feasible in the present context.

Natural experiments mimic laboratory experiments insofar as they
randomize the variable, whose causal effect is the object of interest.[9] In
the present context, this variable is Y_p, whose causal effect on Y_c, or
"treatment effect," represented by β, is the object of interest. In a natural
experiment spontaneous occurrences serve to randomize Y_p. These
occurrences must fulfill two main requirements. First, they must
directly affect Y_p. Second, they must not directly affect the outcome of
interest, which in the present context is Y_c. This means that these occurrences have nothing to do with genotypes, for otherwise the second
requirement would not be satisfied. These random occurrences randomize Y_p and mimic naturally or spontaneously the randomization
that would take place in a laboratory.

Instrumental variables (Z) were defined as variables that affect Y_p
directly but do not affect Y_c directly. Such variables behave like occurrences in natural experiments. Therefore, IVs are synonymous with
natural experiments (Angrist and Krueger 2002). The problem, of
course, is to find convincing candidates for Z. If Y is schooling, labor
economists have suggested a variety of ingenious IVs, including month
of birth (Angrist and Krueger 2000) and the "draft lottery" (Angrist
1990). If Y is illicit drug use, Beenstock and Rahav (2002) use cigarette

price data to represent Z. If Y is class size, Angrist and Lavy (1999) use school enrollment to represent Z. If Y is vocational training, Eyal and Beenstock (2008) use course availability to represent Z. If Y is the income of parents, Shea (2000) uses trade union status and sectoral wage rates to represent Z.

10.4.2   Relationship between IV and Generated Regressors

Suppose a vector of exogenous controls is added to the basic intergenerational AR model so that outcomes of children depend on other observable exogenous factors (X_c) apart from outcomes of parents:

$$Y_c = \beta Y_p + \gamma X_c + u_c, \tag{32a}$$

$$u_c = \rho \mu_p + \varepsilon_c. \tag{32b}$$

OLS estimates of β continue to be biased because Y_p and u_c are correlated. The counterpart of equation 32a for parents is

$$Y_p = \beta_p Y_g + \gamma_p X_p + u_p, \tag{33}$$

where X_p is a vector of exogenous controls for parents. Equation 33 allows β and γ for parents to differ from their counterparts for children; hence β_p and γ_p may differ from β and γ respectively. X_c and X_p may partially overlap if the outcomes of parents and children are affected by common variables (such as a common religion). However, a subset of the X_p variables, denoted by Z_p, does not affect the outcomes of children, i.e., the Z_p variables are omitted from X_c. These Z_p variables may serve as IVs to identify the parameters in equation 32a because they directly affect Y_p, but do not directly affect Y_c. Note that Y_g cannot serve as an IV: unlike Z_p, it is not independent of u_p, since both u_p and Y_g depend on u_g and u_c depends on u_p. Matters would be different if $\rho = 0$, which demonstrates that the genetically induced relationship between u_c, u_p, and u_g rules out Y_g as an instrumental variable.

The generated-regressor methodology is based on the substitution of equation 32b into equation 32a:

$$Y_c = \beta Y_p + \gamma X_c + \rho u_p + \varepsilon_c. \tag{34}$$

Since in equation 34 Y_p and u_p are independent of ε_c, estimates of β and ρ are unbiased and consistent. If X_p happened to equal X_c, there would be no omitted variables, in which case β ceases to be identified because the set of IVs, Z_p, is empty. In this case IV is not feasible. The generated-regressor methodology, in contrast, identifies β in this case, because Y_p

is independent of ε_c. However, γ is not identified, because X_c and u_p are perfectly collinear.

10.5   Multiple Phenotypes and Single Genotypes

So far a single outcome or phenotype Y has been considered. Suppose that there are K phenotypes (labeled $k = 1, 2, \ldots, K$) and that they depend on only one genotype, as follows:

$$Y_{cki} = \alpha_k + \beta_k Y_{pki} + u_{cki},$$ (35a)

$$u_{cki} = \pi_k G_{ci} + \mu_{cki},$$ (35b)

$$G_{ci} = \rho G_{pi} + \varepsilon_{ci}.$$ (35c)

Equation 35a has the same form as equation 11a and allows each outcome to have separate structural coefficients, i.e., β varies by outcome. The phenotype residual (u_{ck}) has a genetic component (G_c) and an environmental component (μ_{ck}). For simplicity it is assumed that the latter are not intergenerationally correlated. Therefore, equations 35 constitute an AR^2 model. The genotype affects phenotypes differentially so that π varies by phenotype. Since Y_{pk} depends on G_p, and G_c depends on G_p,

$$E(Y_{pk} u_{ck}) = \pi_k \rho \text{var}(G_p).$$

Therefore, OLS estimates of equation 35a are biased and inconsistent.

The multiple phenotype model may be used to generate unbiased estimates of β_k in the absence of data for G_p. According to equation 35b, the residuals for individual i are dependent because

$$E(u_{ji} u_{ki}) = \pi_j \pi_k \text{ var}(G_{ci}).$$ (36)

Equation 36 states that the residuals are correlated within individuals because i's genotype affects phenotypes j and k. However, the residuals aren't correlated between individuals, because their genetic endowments are independent.

10.5.1   Panel-Data Model

Equations 35 have a panel structure. In the standard panel-data model[10] the same individuals are observed over time. Here the same individuals are observed not over time but across outcomes. Nevertheless, we may exploit panel-data econometrics to estimate unbiased estimates of β. The bias in equation 35a stems from the fact that according to equation 35b there is a missing variable, G_p. Substituting equations 35b and 35c into equation 35a produces

$$Y_{cki} = \beta_k Y_{pki} + \rho \pi_k G_{pi} + \omega_{cki},\qquad(37a)$$

$$\omega_{cki} = \pi_k \varepsilon_{ci} + \mu_{cki}.\qquad(37b)$$

Equations 37 establish that had data been available for G_p there would have been no problem of bias since ω_{ck} would have been independent of Y_{pk} and G_p. The β coefficients are directly estimated. However, ρ and π_k are not separately identified. According to equation 37b the covariance between the residuals for outcomes k and j is expected to be

$$E(\omega_{ck}\omega_{cj}) = \pi_k \pi_j \operatorname{var}(\varepsilon_c^2).\qquad(38)$$

Therefore, given the variance of ε_c, equation 38 is informative of $\pi_k \pi_j$.

The two-way specific effects panel-data model approximates the missing variable in equation 37a by $\rho \pi_k G_{pi} = \alpha_i + \theta_k$, where α_i denotes a specific effect for child i and θ_k denotes a specific effect for outcome k. Strictly speaking these effects should be multiplicative rather than additive. However, in log-linear models $\ln(\rho \pi_k G_{pi}) = \ln(\rho \pi_k) + \ln G_{pi}$, in which case $\theta_k = \ln(\rho \pi_k)$ and $\alpha_i = \ln G_{pi}$. The panel-data model is

$$Y_{cki} = \alpha_i + \theta_k + \beta_k Y_{pki} + w_{cki},\qquad(39)$$

in which the residuals w are now independent of Y_{pk} since the specific effects have been estimated. Therefore, equation 39 identifies β_k and delivers unbiased estimates of the β coefficients. However, ρ and π_k remain unidentified. Notice that equation 39 allows for heterogeneity in the β coefficients across the different outcomes. The specific affects may be specified to be fixed or random. Typically, the latter is more appropriate for random samples of the population. Although the number of families N is potentially infinite, K (the number of phenotypes) is likely to be small and finite, i.e., the panel is "short." If K is fixed, the random effects estimator is root-N consistent for all parameters in equation 39. Taylor (1980) has shown that the finite sample properties are satisfactory when N is about 50 for $K = 5$. In contrast, the fixed effects estimator is root-N consistent for β_k but not for α_i and θ_k.

10.6   Heterogeneity

So far it has been assumed that β and other parameters do not vary across individuals, i.e., these parameters are homogeneous. This section deals with heterogeneity,[11] in which these parameters may vary across individuals. This means, for example, the children may vary in their sensitivity to their parents' treatment, in which case the causal effect of parents on children is heterogeneous. Consider the following simple "random coefficients" model for some outcome Y:

$$Y_i = \alpha_i + \beta_i X_i + u_i, \tag{40a}$$

$$\beta_i = \beta + v_i. \tag{40b}$$

where $E(u) = E(v) = 0$. Equations 40 constitute a heterogeneous effects model because the effect of X on Y varies between individuals. Equation 40b states that the expected or average effect of X on Y equals β. However, if v_i is positive individual i is more sensitive to X than the average individual. If v_i is sufficiently negative, β_i may be 0 or even negative. The residual (u) in equation 40a captures unobserved phenomena such as genotypes and environments. It may be that u and v are dependent. This will arise, for example, if sensitivity is partly genetic so that genotypes and sensitivity are correlated. Finally, X and u may be dependent due to gene-environment correlation, i.e., because X is endogenous rather than exogenous. The same applies to X and v.

For example, if Y is earnings and X is schooling, u is unobserved earning ability and v is unobserved learning ability. Earning and learning ability are unlikely to be independent; therefore $E(uv) \neq 0$. Also, as was noted in chapter 9, abler individuals are expected to acquire more education, i.e., $E(Xu) > 0$ and $E(Xv) > 0$. Therefore, X, u, and v are dependent.

Substituting equation 40b into equation 40a gives

$$Y_i = \alpha + \beta X_i + w_i. \tag{41a}$$

$$w_i = u_i + X_i v_i. \tag{41b}$$

It is obvious that X in equation 41a is not independent of w, since w depends on X in equation 41b. Multiplying equation 41b by X and taking the expected value of the result gives

$$E(Xw) = E(X^2 v) + E(Xu), \tag{42}$$

which will not be 0 unless X and u and X^2 and v are independent. Therefore, OLS estimates of β are biased and inconsistent. The solution to this problem is to estimate equation 41a by IV, which involves finding instrumental variables that affect X directly but do not affect Y directly.

Here and on other occasions, it is necessary to express expected values, variances, and covariances involving products of random variables. For example, Xv in equation 41b involves products of two random variables. To aid exposition, the rules for calculating these expressions are listed, where A and B are two random variables and $\Rightarrow$ denotes their expressions when $E(A) = E(B) = 0$:

$$E(AB) = E(A)A(B) + \text{cov}(AB) \Rightarrow \text{cov}(AB), \tag{43a}$$

$$\begin{aligned} \text{var}(AB) &= \text{var}(A)\text{var}(B) + \text{cov}(A^2B^2) - E(A)E(B) - [E(A)E(B) + \text{cov}(AB)]^2 \\ &\Rightarrow \text{var}(A)\text{var}(B) + \text{cov}(A^2B^2) - \text{cov}(AB)^2, \end{aligned} \tag{43b}$$

$$E(A^2B^2) = E(A^2)E(B^2) + \text{cov}(A^2B^2), \tag{43c}$$

$$\text{cov}[A(AB)] = E(A^2B) - E(A)A(AB) \Rightarrow E(A^2B) = \text{cov}(A^2B). \tag{43d}$$

The variance of Y according to equation 41a is

$$\text{var}(Y) = \beta^2 \text{var}(X) + \text{var}(w) + 2\beta \text{cov}(Xw). \tag{44}$$

According to equation 41b, $\text{var}(w)$ is equal to

$$\text{var}(w) = \text{var}(u) + \text{var}(X)\text{var}(v) + \text{cov}(X^2v^2) - \text{cov}(Xv)^2 + 2\text{cov}[(Xv)u]. \tag{45}$$

Equation 45 uses the rule that the variance is equal to the expected value of the square minus the square of the expected value, and the rule that the expected value of a product of random variables is equal to the product of the expected values plus the covariance. The variance of w varies directly with the variances of u and v, and it depends on the covariances between X^2 and v^2, between X and v, and between u and Xv. If X, u, and v are independent, all the covariances in equation 44 are 0, because the gene-environment correlation is 0.

In this case equation 44 states that the variance of Y equals the variance due to X, $\beta^2\text{var}(X)$, the genotypic variance $\text{var}(u)$, and the variance due to heterogeneity in β, $\text{var}(v)\text{var}(X)$. However, the gene-environment correlation implies that X, u, and v are not independent, in which case the variance of Y also depends on the constellation of covariances.

10.7   Sibling Effects

The discussion so far has been limited to parent-child dyads. Let us now consider triads comprising parents and two siblings, denoted by subscripts 1 and 2. The model is based on equations 32:

$$Y_1 = \beta_1 Y_p + \gamma_1 X_1 + \lambda_1 Y_2 + u_1, \tag{46a}$$

$$u_1 = \rho_1 u_p + \varepsilon_1, \tag{46b}$$

$$Y_2 = \beta_2 Y_p + \gamma_2 X_2 + \lambda_2 Y_1 + u_2, \tag{46c}$$

$$u_2 = \rho_2 u_p + \varepsilon_2, \tag{46d}$$

where λ denotes the sibling interaction coefficient discussed in chapter 8. Equations 46 allow for the parameters to vary between siblings, e.g., due to birth order. For example, if sibling 1 is born before sibling 2 and firstborns receive more parental attention, β_1 may be bigger than β_2. However, since both siblings bear the same genetic relationship with their parents, ρ_1 is expected to equal ρ_2. X_1 and X_2 are vectors of exogenous variables hypothesized to affect siblings 1 and 2 respectively.

10.7.1 IV estimation

In equation 46a Y_2 is not independent of u_1 since Y_2 depends on u_1 via λ_2. Similarly, in equation 46c Y_1 is not independent of u_2. Therefore, OLS estimates of the parameters of equations 46a and 46c are biased and inconsistent, in addition to the bias due to ρ discussed in section 10.2. For example, if λ_2 is positive the estimate of λ_1 will be biased upward because Y_2 and u_1 vary directly with each other. The solution to this problem is, as usual, estimation by IV. This requires that the X_1 variables are not identical to the variables in X_2. Specifically X_2 must omit variables in X_1, and X_1 must omit variables in X_2. Suppose, for example, that there are three X variables: A, B, and C. If sibling 1 is affected by A and B and sibling 2 is affected by A and C, this condition is satisfied because B is omitted from X_2 and C is omitted from X_1. However, if sibling 1 is affected by C the condition is not satisfied and estimation by IV is not possible. Since siblings share backgrounds, X_1 and X_2 are likely to be very similar if not identical, in which case it is difficult to identify the parameters. An example of an IV might be illness experienced by one sibling but not the other, or some family event that affected one sibling but not the other.

10.7.2 Seemingly Unrelated Regression

Suppose for argument's sake that there are no IVs at all, because $X_1 = X_2 = X$; that for simplicity the parameters of equations 46 are homogeneous, so that $\lambda_1 = \lambda_2 = \lambda$ and so on; and that $\rho = 0$. The solutions to the simultaneous equations 46a and 46c then are

$$Y_i = \frac{\beta(1+\lambda)Y_{pi} + \gamma(1+\lambda)X_i}{1+\lambda^2} + v_i \qquad (47a)$$

and

$$v_i = \frac{u_i + \lambda u_g}{1+\lambda^2}. \qquad (47b)$$

Equation 47a contains the same variables as equation 32a, however, the parameters are different because they are affected by sibling interaction. Also, according to equation 47b the residuals are correlated between siblings. This correlation induces the phenomenon of "seemingly unrelated regression" (SUR) since the equations for pairs of siblings are related through their residuals.[12] If SUR is ignored, the estimates of the parameters in equation 47a are unbiased and consistent, because Y_p and X are independent of v, but they aren't efficient.

Using equation 47b it can be shown that the correlation coefficient between the residuals of sibling pairs is

$$r = \frac{2\lambda}{1+\lambda^2}. \qquad (48)$$

The solution for λ from equation 48 is

$$\lambda = \frac{1 \pm \sqrt{1-r^2}}{r}. \qquad (49)$$

Using the estimated residuals to calculate the estimate of r, equation 49 can be used to solve for the estimate of λ. There are two solutions to equation 49, because it is a quadratic equation, but solutions in which the absolute value of λ exceeds 1 are ruled out. For example, if $r = 0.5$ the solutions for λ are 3.732 and 0.268. The correct solution for λ is therefore 0.268.

Having thus estimated λ, we can derive the estimates of the β and γ from the parameter estimates of equation 46a, since the coefficient of Y_p identifies β and the coefficient of X identifies γ. In short, all the parameters are identified even if there are no IVs.

10.8   Peer-Group Effects

Suppose that the outcome for an individual is hypothesized to depend on the average outcome in his peer group. If the are M exclusive groups and N individuals, there is an average of N/M members per group. However, groups need not be exclusive, and individuals may belong to more than one group. The groups are assumed to be exogenous, so individuals do not choose their group. Therefore, issues concerning peer-group selection (see section 10.11) do not arise for now. Since parents do not affect the argument here, I simplify by ignoring parents and by setting $\beta = \rho = 0$. The model is

$$Y_i = \alpha + \gamma X_i + \theta \bar{Y}_i + u_i, \tag{50}$$

where $\bar{Y}_i$ denotes the average outcome in i's peer group and θ is the peer-group effect. The peer-group effect has a number of interpretations. First, there may be knowledge spillovers between members of the group, so members learn from each other. Second, herding behavior may induce members to be influenced by the group as a whole. This will happen if members of the group do not like to stand out, in which case the group average affects their behavior. For the moment, the estimation of θ is our concern, rather than its interpretation.

Models such as equation 50 are affected by the "Reflection Problem" (Manski 1995). Since each individual is his peers' peer, the average outcome for the group is a reflection of the outcome of the individuals that form the group. To show this equation 50 implies that the average outcome for Y in group m is

$$\bar{Y}_m = \frac{\alpha + \lambda \bar{X}_m + \bar{u}_m}{1 - \theta}, \tag{51}$$

i.e., it depends on the mean of X in the group and the group's average ability as measured by $\bar{u}_m$. Since u_i is part of $\bar{u}_m$, $\bar{Y}_i$ in equation 50 is not independent of u_i and the parameters aren't identified. In fact,

$$E(\bar{u}_m u_i) = \text{var}(u)M/N > 0.$$

Numerical illustrations of parameter bias induced by reflection are presented in table 5.4.

The solution to the reflection problem requires IVs that affect the group average but do not directly affect the individuals in the group. For example, if abler individuals happened to join the group randomly, the group average would increase independently of the outcomes of the incumbent members in the group.

10.9   Neighbor Effects

Neighbor effects are a special case of group effects. Proximity did not matter in section 10.8, but it matters here. In this section, equation 50 is replaced by the "spatial lag" model (Anselin 1988):

$$Y_i = \gamma X_i + \theta \tilde{Y}_i + u_i,$$ (52a)

$$\tilde{Y}_i = \sum_{j=1}^{N} w_{ij} Y_j .$$ (52b)

In equation 52b, $\tilde{Y}_i$ denotes the mean of Y among i's neighbors. The weights w sum to 1 and $w_{ij} = 0$ if j is not a neighbor of i. It is assumed for now that individuals do not choose their neighbors, i.e., neighbors are exogenous. The issue of selectivity is deferred to section 10.11. The parameters in equation 52a are not identified because each individual is his neighbors' neighbor. Therefore, $\tilde{Y}_i$ is not independent of u_i, and the estimate of θ will be biased upward. The problem sounds similar to the peer-group problem, but it is essentially different because there are natural IVs to identify the "spatial lag" coefficient θ. To demonstrate this, we can vectorize equations 52:

$$Y = \gamma X + \theta WY + u,$$ (53)

where $Y = (Y_1, Y_2, \ldots, Y_N)$, X is a column vector of X_i, u is a column vector of residuals u_i, and W is an $N \times N$ matrix with elements w_{ij} with zeros on the diagonal since $w_{ii} = 0$. By matrix algebra, the solution for Y is

$$Y = A(\gamma X + u),$$ (54a)

$$A = (I_N - \theta W)^{-1} = I_N + \theta W + \theta^2 W^2 + \cdots,$$ (54b)

where I_N is an $N \times N$ unit diagonal matrix. Equation 54b inverts the polynomial in $(I_N - \theta W)$. Since $\tilde{Y} = WY$ equations 54 may be used to express $\tilde{Y}$ as follows:

$$\tilde{Y} = WY = \gamma(WX + \theta W^2 X + \theta^2 W^3 X + \cdots) + WAu.$$ (55a)

Therefore, the expected value of $\tilde{Y}$ may be written as

$$\tilde{Y} = \gamma \left(\tilde{X} + \theta \tilde{\tilde{X}} + \theta^2 \tilde{\tilde{\tilde{X}}} + \cdots \right) + WAu.$$ (55b)

In equation 55b, $WX = \tilde{X}$ is the X vector among first-order (immediate) neighbors, $W^2 X = \tilde{\tilde{X}}$ is the X vector among second-order neighbors, and so on. These are the natural IVs for identifying the parameters in equation 52a. Variation in the X variables among first-order and higher-order neighbors solves the identification problem. Equation 55b is estimated, and $\hat{\tilde{Y}}$ is used to instrument $\tilde{Y}_i$ in equation 52a, which provides unbiased estimates of γ and θ. Alternatively, these parameters may be estimated by GMM rather than IV (subsection 10.1.3), or by maximum likelihood (Anselin 1988).

10.10   Endogenous Behavior

In this section, two types of endogenous behavior that affect the identification of the parameters of the model are considered. (These types of behavior were discussed in more detail in chapter 9.) In the first, parents are hypothesized to behave in a way that improves their children's outcomes. In the second, children behave in a way to attract more parental resources. For simplicity, it is assumed here that parents have only one child. (Extension to the case of more than one child may be found in chapter 9.)

10.10.1   Endogenous Parenting

Let P denote parental behavior (parenting for short), which influences the child via the intergenerational AR model:

$$Y_c = \beta Y_p + \varphi P + u_c. \tag{56}$$

Following the discussion of parenting theory in chapter 9, parents' preferences are defined in terms of the outcome for their child (Y_c) and in terms of their effort at parenting:

$$U_p = \alpha \ln Y_c - \gamma \ln P. \tag{57}$$

Equation 57 states that parents prefer less parenting to more, but they prefer their child to achieve a greater outcome for Y_c. The optimal solution for P is obtained by substituting equation 56 into equation 57 and then differentiating the result with respect to P. This partial derivative is set to 0 to obtain the first-order conditions from which the optimal solution for P is obtained. The first-order and second-order conditions for a maximum are respectively

$$\frac{\partial U_p}{\partial P} = \frac{\alpha \varphi}{Y_c} - \frac{\gamma}{P} = 0 \tag{58a}$$

and

$$\frac{\partial^2 U_p}{\partial P^2} = \frac{\gamma}{P^2} - \frac{\alpha^2}{Y_c^2} < 0. \tag{58b}$$

Substituting equation 56 into equation 57 and solving the result for P gives

$$P = \gamma \frac{\beta Y_p + u_c}{\varphi(\alpha - \gamma)} + v_p ,$$ (59)

where v_p denotes an optimization error with $E(v_p) = 0$. If parents aren't too altruistic, so that $\gamma > \alpha$, the denominator of equation 59 is negative, in which case parenting varies inversely with Y_p and u_c. In this model, parents who see that their child is genetically fitter (he has a larger u_c) need to devote less effort to parenting. Importantly, P in equation 56 is therefore not independent of u_c. Consequently, the parameters in equation 56 are not identified, since parenting and the outcome of the child are jointly determined. This result is generic and does not depend on the specifics of equations 56 and 57.

The solution to this identification problem is, as usual, the IV estimator. Instrumental variables are required that determine parenting but do not directly determine the outcome of the child. According to equation 59, the outcome of parents (Y_p) is a determinant of parenting; however, since Y_p affects Y_c directly in equation 56, it cannot serve as an instrumental variable. The optimization error (v_p) affects Y_p directly but does not affect Y_c directly. Proxies for optimization error could serve as instrumental variables, provided they are independent of Y_p and u_c.

10.10.2   Endogenous Child Behavior

Suppose that P in equation 56 varies directly with attention seeking by children, which is denoted once more by Z:

$$P = \mu Z + \pi ,$$ (60)

where π denotes here the random component of parenting and $E(\pi) = 0$. Children prefer larger outcomes, but they dislike attention seeking. The objective function of children is assumed, as in chapter 9, to be

$$U_c = \phi \ln Y_c - \eta \ln Z .$$ (61)

Children set Z to maximize equation 61 subject to equations 60 and 56. Following the optimization procedure in the subsection 10.10.1 (i.e., solving for optimal Z and then substituting equations 56 and 60 into the result) gives the solution for P:

$$P = \eta \frac{\beta Y_p + \phi \pi + u_c}{\phi \mu(\varphi - \eta)} + v_c ,$$ (62)

where v_c denotes an optimization error for children with $E(v_c) = 0$. Equation 62 shows that P depends on u_c, in which case P is not independent of u_c in equation 56. Therefore, the parameters of equation 56 are not identified if children act strategically with respect to their parents.

In summary, endogenous parenting induced by parents themselves or their children establishes dependence between P and u_c in equation 56. The parameters β and φ are consequently not identified by OLS. The solution to the identification problem involves, as usual, instrumental variable that directly affect Z and P, but which do not directly affect outcome Y_c.

10.11   Selectivity

The issue of selectivity has arisen on several occasions. Individuals may choose their peers and neighbors. Parents may choose their adopted children, adoption agencies may choose parents, and parents might choose not to adopt. The implications of selectivity with respect to identification[13] are discussed in the context of adoption. For these purposes, the random utility model discussed in chapter 9 is used. Let V_{ij} denote the utility of parent i who adopts child j. Parents also have an option not to adopt, which delivers them utility equal to V_{i0}, which is an unobserved random variable.

V is assumed to depend additively on the observed and unobserved characteristics of parents and prospective adoptees:

$$V_{ij} = \alpha_j X_{pi} + \eta X_{cj} + w_{ij}, \tag{63}$$

where $\eta X_{cj} + w_{ij}$ denotes the random utility if child j is adopted by parent i. Parents are assumed to maximize V_{ij}. If $\text{argmax}(V_{ij}) < V_{i0}$ parents are better off if they do not adopt. Otherwise they will adopt the child who maximizes their V_{ij}. Therefore, the choice of child and the decision to adopt depend on the observed characteristics of parents and children, X_p and X_c, and their unobserved characteristics w_{ij}.

Adoption is more complicated than this because the adoption agency also has a say by matching children to parents, and the children themselves might have a say too, if they are old enough. Therefore, data on adoptees have gone through a very complex process of selection over which the investigator has no control and perhaps little understanding. The set-up used here is simplified and treats parents as if they are choosing between cars, or not to buy a car at all. This has the advantage of being a widely studied discrete choice problem.[14]

Suppose the objective is to estimate equation 11a using data on adoptees. Since the children are adoptees, they are genetically unrelated to their adoptive parents, so that $\rho = 0$. Therefore, the genetic endowment of the child is $u_c = \varepsilon_c$. (environments e are ignored for simplicity). It is most unlikely that ε_c and w are independent since the unobserved (by the investigator) characteristics of the adopted child and his unobserved genotype are very likely to be positively correlated. Matters would be different if adoptees were randomly assigned to parents in which case w would play no role in the adoption decision. Since ε_c and w are dependent, β in equation 11a is not identified. It would be identified only if adoptees were randomly assigned.

This problem arises because the sample of adoptees is not a random sample. It is a selective sample. Estimation of equation 11a must therefore allow for sample selection bias, which is based on a model for selectivity. It is assumed that v and w, which aren't observed by the investigator, are independent, and have logistic distributions so that, for example, $F(w) = (1 + e^{-w})^{-1}$. Parents choose between $j = 0, 1, \ldots, K$. If $j = 0$ they choose not to adopt. The conditional logit model for this discrete choice problem is

$$P_{ij} = \frac{\exp(\alpha_j X_{pi} + \eta X_{cj})}{\sum_{k=0}^{K} [\exp(\alpha_k X_{pi} + \eta X_{ck})]}, \tag{64}$$

where P_{ij} denotes the probability that parents i will adopt child j. If they choose to adopt, the child they adopt is denoted by $j = i$. Estimation of the conditional logit model by maximum likelihood provides consistent estimates of the parameters in equation 64.

Having obtained these parameters, we can estimate equation 11a with a correction term ξ for sample selectivity[15]:

$$Y_{ci} = \alpha + \beta Y_{pi} + \psi \xi_i + \varepsilon_{ci}, \tag{65a}$$

$$\zeta_i = \frac{\phi(H_i)}{\Phi(H_i)}, \tag{65b}$$

$$H_i = \Phi^{-1}(P_{ii}), \tag{65c}$$

where $\phi()$ denotes the density of the standard normal distribution and $\Phi()$ denotes its cumulative density (CDF). In equation 65c P_{ii} is the probability that parents i choose the child that they adopted, which is used to construct ξ_i. Its coefficient ψ in equation 65a depends on the covariance between ε and w denoted by $\text{cov}_{\varepsilon w}$. If $\text{cov}_{\varepsilon w} = 0$ then $\psi = 0$

and adoption is quasi-random. Omitting ξ in equation 65a would constitute model misspecification unless $\psi = 0$, and would induce bias in the parameter estimates. On the other hand, specification of ξ corrects potential bias due to sample selection.

The above serves to illustrate how sample selection in adoption induces bias in parameter estimates. Table 5.4 presents numerical illustration of selection bias. It was assumed that selectivity arises only because of adoptive parents. In real life, selectivity arises also because of the behavior of the adoption agencies as well as the decision of biological parents to give up their children for adoption. The adoption process therefore has three consecutive hurdles; the adoption decision by biological parents, the placement decision by adoption agencies, and the adoption decision by adoptive parents. Hurdle models of selection have been discussed by Labeaga (1999).

10.12   Partial Identification

The previous sections have been concerned with full identification of the parameters of interest. For example, β is fully identified when a specific unbiased number such as 0.4 has been estimated. However, complete identification may not always be feasible because instrumental variables required for identification may not happen to be available. In any case some of the identifying assumptions might be arbitrary if not questionable. For example, in section 10.11 identification of the selection coefficient ψ assumed that what the investigator does not observe in adoption choice (v and w) has a logit distribution. Also, the model was assumed to be linear. If either or both of these identifying assumption is invalid, identification would be spurious.[16] Of course, some identifying assumptions may be tested empirically. For example, misspecification tests are available for linearity and even for different parametric assumptions, such as logit vs. the normal distribution.[17] However, not all identifying assumptions are testable.

The methodology of partial identification (Manski 2003) is essentially conservative in that it avoids making arbitrary parametric assumptions about what we do not observe. Some would say that it is more honest because it gives more expression to the data and less to the assumptions of the investigator. The critics of partial identification counter-argue that partial identification is typically too incomplete, and is not practical or useful. For example, if β is naturally bounded between 1 and –1, the partial identification of β about to be described will bound it between, say, 0.6 and –0.4. This means that we cannot even conclude whether β is positive or negative. On the other hand, we can rule out that β exceeds 0.6 and is smaller than –0.4.

10.12.1 Counterfactuals

As in equation 11a, let β be the parameter of interest, the identification of which is confounded by unobserved genetic endowments and environments. To make matters simple let the outcome Y be 0 or 1, i.e., it is dichotomous. There are therefore two groups of children. Group A children have parents with $Y_p = 1$ and group B children have parents with $Y_p = 0$. A fraction n of the children belong to group A. Let P_A and P_B denote the proportion of children in groups A and B respectively, with $Y_c = 1$.

If β exceeds 0, one might expect P_A to exceed P_B because Y_p is larger for children in group A. On the other hand, the fact that P_A exceeds P_B might have nothing to do with Y_p. It might simply be the case that group A is genetically fitter than group B. Group A children may have inherited their parents' favorable genes, which explains why $Y_p = 1$ for group A parents and why P_A is larger than P_B. Ideally, we would like to observe the children in group A twice. Once when their parents have $Y_p = 1$, which the data reveal, and once when $Y_p = 0$, which the data do not reveal. The latter is the counterfactual for group A. We would also like to observe group B twice. In the case of group B, the data reveal what happens to them when $Y_p = 0$, but their counterfactual ($Y_p = 1$) is not revealed. Had these counterfactuals been revealed by the data, we would have been able to calculate the unconditional expectation of Y_c for both groups. Since children in group A have parents with $Y_p = 1$ and children in group B have parents with $Y_p = 0$, the difference between these unconditional expectations is informative about the causal effect of Y_p on Y_c, which is equal to β.

The obvious problem is that the counterfactuals are unknown. However, they may be bounded. For example, in the case of group A, had Y_p been 0 instead of 1, perhaps the entire group would have had a zero outcome ($Y_c = 0$). This cannot be ruled out because the truth might be that β is positive and group A is genetically less fit, so that but for the fact that their parents had $Y_p = 1$, Y_c would have been 0 for all of group A. On the other hand, the entire group might have obtained a unit outcome ($Y_c = 1$) under the counterfactual. This cannot be ruled out because the truth might be that β is negative and group A is fitter. The counterfactual for group B is similarly bounded between 0 and 1.

10.12.2 Non-Parametric Bounds

Beta may be bound using Bayes' Rule, which states that the unconditional expectation is the sum of the conditional expectations multiplied by their probabilities. Thus, if C and D are mutually exclusive events, the unconditional expected value of X, which depends on these events, is

$$E(X) = E(X/C)P(C) + E(X/D)P(D).$$

The data reveal $P_A = P_A(Y_c = 1/Y_p = 1)$, which is the proportion of high phenotypes among group A, i.e., the children of high-phenotype parents. The data also reveal $P_B = P_B(Y_c = 1/Y_p = 0)$, which is the proportion of high phenotypes among group B, i.e., the children of low-phenotype parents. Therefore, P_A and P_B are conditional probabilities. When Bayes' Rule is applied, the unconditional probabilities are

$$P_A^* = P_A(Y_p = 1)P_A(Y_c = 1/Y_p = 1) + [1 - P_A(Y_p = 1)]P_A(Y_c = 1/Y_p = 0) \quad (66a)$$

and

$$P_B^* = [1 - P_B(Y_p = 0)]P_B(Y_c = 1/Y_p = 1) + P_B(Y_p = 0)P_B(Y_c = 1/Y_p = 0). \quad (66b)$$

Equations 66 use the fact that since there are only two states of the world for Y_p $P_A(Y_p = 0) = 1 - P_A(Y_p = 1)$ and similarly for group B. The unbiased estimate of β is $P_A^* - P_B^*$ rather than $P_A - P_B$. To see this, suppose that children had been taken away from their biological parents at birth and had been randomly assigned to parents. In this case, $P_A(Y_p = 1) = 1 = P_B(Y_p = 0)$. Therefore equation 66a simplifies to $P_A = P(Y_c = 1/Y_p = 1)$ and equation 66b simplifies to $P_B = P(Y_c = 1/Y_p = 0)$. Under such random assignment, $\beta = P_A - P_B$, as expected, because random assignment severs the genetic link between parents and children. Therefore, any difference between the outcomes of groups A and B must be due to the causal effect of Y_p on Y_c.

In the data, $P_A(Y_p = 1) = n$ and $P_B(Y_p = 0) = 1 - n$. The counterfactuals between A and B are naturally bounded between 0 and 1. Substituting this information into equations 66 bounds the unconditional probabilities:

$$P_{AL}^* = nP_A, \quad (67a)$$

$$P_{AH}^* = nP_A + (1 - n), \quad (67b)$$

$$P_{BL}^* = (1 - n)P_B, \quad (67c)$$

$$P_{BH}^* = (1 - n)P_B + n. \quad (67d)$$

Equations 67a and 67c assume that the counterfactuals are 0, which provide lower bounds to the unconditional probabilities and labeled L, and equations 67b and 67d assume that the counterfactuals are 1, providing upper bounds to the conditional expectations, labeled H. The bounds for β are therefore equal to

$$\beta_H = P_{AH}^* - P_{BL}^* = nP_A + (1-n)(1-P_B) \tag{68a}$$

and

$$\beta_L = P_{AL}^* - P_{BH}^* = (n-1)(P_A + P_B). \tag{68b}$$

The empirical data alone rule out that β is larger than β_H and less than β_L. However, the true value of β lies within these bounds. Notice that $\beta_H - \beta_L = 1$. Without any data at all, this range is 2 as noted above. Therefore, the data reduce the range of ignorance from 2 to 1, and β is partially identified. Since the range is 1, partial identification here does not even determine the sign of β, except in the unlikely case the lower or upper bound happens to equal 0. See table 5.2 for numerical illustrations.

10.12.3   Placebo

It might be argued that it cannot hurt children to have high phenotype parents. In this case it would be unreasonable to argue that group A children could have been better off had their parents been of low phenotype, and that group B children could have been worse off had their parents been of high phenotype. This placebo assumption bounds the counterfactuals for group A between 0 and P_A (instead of 1), and bounds the counterfactuals for group B between P_B (instead of 0) and 1. Substituting the placebo bounds into equations 66 gives an upper bound for β of $\beta_H = P_A - P_B$ and a lower bound of $\beta_L = n(P_A - 1) - (1 - n)P_B$. Notice that the upper bound is equal to what it would be under random assignment and the range between the bounds is reduced from 1 to $(1 - n)P_A - nP_B$. Making placebo assumptions narrows the bounds for β and reduces the ambiguity of partial identification. However, it might reasonably be argued that the placebo assumption assumes away what should have been tested empirically.

Whereas complete identification is defined uniquely, the same does not apply to partial identification. Partial identification comes in a great many varieties and forms. There are different degrees of partiality, as exemplified by the placebo assumption.[18]

10.13 Behavioral Genetics

Behavioral genetics is mainly concerned with identifying the genetic component of the variance of outcomes or phenotypes. The starting point of behavioral genetics[19] is the additive decomposition of an outcome of interest, or phenotype, Y, into genetic (G), environmental (E), and random components (R):

$$Y_i = G_i + E_i + R_i. \tag{69}$$

Alternatively, E denotes environments that are shared by siblings, and R denotes their unshared environments. Equation 69 may be generalized to allow for *gene-environment interaction*, in which case G_iE_i would also feature in equation 69, which would no longer be linear and additive. This extension will be discussed shortly.

10.13.1 Decomposing the Phenotype Variance
The variance of Y according to equation 69 has the following decomposition:

$$\mathrm{var}(Y) = \mathrm{var}(G) + \mathrm{var}(E) + \mathrm{var}(R) + 2[\mathrm{cov}(GE) + \mathrm{cov}(GR) + \mathrm{cov}(ER)]. \tag{70}$$

The main preoccupation of behavioral genetics is to estimate heritability, defined as $h^2 = \mathrm{var}(G)/\mathrm{var}(Y)$, i.e., the genotypic share of the variance. It is typically assumed that some or all of the covariance terms in equation 70 are 0, and can be ignored. Since R is entirely random, it might be reasonable to assume that $\mathrm{cov}(GR) = 0$, although even this is not obvious.

In behavioral genetics, $\mathrm{cov}(GE)$ is referred to as the *gene-environment covariance*. The *gene-environment correlation* ($r_{GE} = \mathrm{cov}(GE)/\mathrm{sd}(G)\mathrm{sd}(E)$) refers to the phenomenon where genetics plays a role in the selection of environments by individuals. For example, genetically fitter individuals are more likely to attend college or university. Or genetically gifted children are more likely to be sent to schools that will enable them to flower. Whereas the gene-environment correlation involves the role of genetics in exposure to environments, the gene-environment interaction involves the genetic sensitivity or impact of the environment on outcomes. For example, a person genetically predisposed to hay fever will avoid flower gardens. If, however, he is exposed to a flower garden he will sneeze more. The former involves the gene-environment correlation, while the latter involves the gene-environment interaction. There is an obvious behavioral link between the two phenomena.

To explore the implications of gene-environment interaction, let us write equation 69 as $Y = G + E + GE$ and, for simplicity, ignore R. In this case, equation 70 becomes[20]

$$\text{var}(Y) = \text{var}(G) + \text{var}(E) + \text{var}(EG)$$
$$+ 2\{\text{cov}(EG) + \text{cov}[G(EG)] + \text{cov}[E(EG)]\}, \tag{71a}$$

$$\text{var}(EG) = E(G^2)E(E^2) + \text{cov}(E^2G^2) - [E(G)E(E) + \text{cov}(EG)]^2, \tag{71b}$$

$$\text{cov}[G(EG)] = E(G^2E) - E(G)\text{cov}(EG), \tag{71c}$$

$$\text{cov}[E(EG)] = E(E^2G) - E(E)\text{cov}(EG). \tag{71d}$$

Equation 71b shows that according to equation 43b the variance of gene-environment interaction varies inversely with the gene-environment covariance. If the means of G and E are assumed to be 0, equation 71b simplifies to $\text{var}(G)\text{var}(E) - \text{cov}(EG)^2$. Equations 71c and 71d show that the covariance between G or E and EG also varies inversely with the gene-environment covariance. If the means of G and E are 0, equations 71c and 71d simplify to $E(G^2E)$ and $E(E^2G)$ respectively. If, in addition, we are prepared to assume that these expected values are also 0, equation 71a simplifies to

$$\text{var}(Y) = \text{var}(G) + \text{var}(E) + 2r_{EG}\text{sd}(G)\text{sd}(E) + \text{var}(G)\text{var}(E)(1 - r_{EG}^2), \tag{72}$$

where r_{EG} denotes the gene-environment correlation. Differentiating equation 72 with respect to r_{EG} and simplifying gives

$$\frac{\partial \text{var}(Y)}{\partial r_{EG}} = 2\text{sd}(G)\text{sd}(E)[1 - \text{cov}(EG)]. \tag{73}$$

If the gene-environment covariance is negative, gene-environment interaction increases the phenotypic variance. If, however, the gene-environment covariance is positive and greater than 1, gene-environment interaction reduces the phenotype variance. Table 3.2 reports numerical illustrations of equation 72 in the determination of heredity.

The covariance between G and E shows that the nature-nurture dichotomy is too simplistic since the gene-environment correlation expresses the "nature of nurture," and the gene-environment interaction expresses the "nurture of nature." Although behavioral genetics draws attention to the covariance between G and E, it is for the most part ignored in practice. Finally, behavioral genetics overlooks $\text{cov}(ER)$ because luck is implicitly assumed to be part of the environment. Since much of life depends on luck and is neither to do with genes or environments, this omission is not merely semantic.

The methodological workhorses in behavioral genetics are quasi-experiments based on comparisons between MZ (identical) twins and DZ (fraternal) twins, and comparisons between adopted children and biological children. The basic idea is that MZ twins share more common genes than DZ twins, therefore a comparison between correlations between the outcomes of MZ twin pairs and DZ pairs identifies the genetic contribution to these outcomes. Similar considerations apply to comparisons of biological siblings and pairs of adopted and biological siblings. The former are genetically related to their parents and each other whereas the latter are not. Therefore, a comparison between correlations between pairs of biological siblings and pairs involving adopted children identifies the genetic contribution to these outcomes.

An important identifying assumption that is common in behavioral genetics is the equal-environments assumption (EEA), according to which sibling correlations for environments are identical for all types of siblings, including MZ twins, DZ twins, biological siblings, and adopted siblings. This means, for example, that parents relate to identical and fraternal twins in exactly the same way, and that they relate to their adopted and biological children in the same way too.

The comparison between adopted and biological siblings is more complicated than the comparison between MZ and DZ twins, since parents do not choose their biological children but the same does not apply to adopted children. Indeed, behavioral genetics typically ignores the issue of sample selection bias discussed in section 10.11. Behavioral genetics makes many strong assumptions to identify the genetic component in the study of identical twins and adoptees. These identifying assumptions are discussed in subsection 10.13.3.

10.13.2 Heterogeneity in Sensitivity to the Environment

Behavioral genetics treats the environment as an aggregate E, which conceals the fact that two individuals can be exposed to identical environments but respond differently. Suppose for example that the environment itself is E^* and the effect of the environment on individual i is $E_i = (\alpha + a_i)E_i^*$, where a_i is a random variable with a mean of 0 and $\alpha_i = \alpha + a_i$ is the sensitivity of individual i to the environment. The variance of E is defined as follows:

$$\text{var}(E) = \text{E}[\alpha[E^* - \text{E}(E^*)] + aE^* - \text{E}(aE^*)]^2$$
$$= \alpha^2 \text{var}(E^*) + \text{var}(aE^*) + 2\text{cov}[E^*(aE^*)], \tag{74a}$$

$$\text{var}(aE^*) = \text{var}(a)\text{var}(E^*) - \text{cov}(aE^*) + \text{cov}(a^2 E^{*2}), \tag{74b}$$

$$\text{cov}[E^*(aE^*)] = \text{E}[E^*(aE^*)] - \text{E}(E^*)\text{E}(aE^*) = \text{E}(aE^{*2}) = \text{cov}(aE^{*2}). \tag{74c}$$

In equations 74a–74c it is assumed that E^* has a mean of 0. Therefore, the variance of E varies directly with the variance of the environment, with the product of the variances of a and E^*, and it varies inversely with $\text{cov}(aE^*)$. The latter will be positive if more sensitive individuals seek more exposure to the environment, or parents invest more in their more responsive children. Finally, if there are nonlinearities in this relationship $\text{cov}(aE^{*2})$ will not be 0. Table 3.3 in chapter 3 presents numerical illustrations of equation 74a, which show the sensitivity of the variance of E to various assumptions about the correlations between a and E^*, between a and E^{*2}, and between a^2 and E^{*2}.

The sibling covariance for E is obtained by using the rules in equations 43:

$$\text{cov}(E_c E_s) = \alpha^2 \text{cov}(E_c^* E_s^*) + \text{cov}[(a_c E_c^*)(a_s E_s^*)] + 2\alpha \text{cov}[(a_c E_c^*)E_s^*], \tag{75a}$$

$$\text{cov}[(a_c E_c^*)(a_s E_s^*)] = \text{cov}(a_c a_s)\text{cov}(E_c^* E_s^*) + \text{cov}[(a_c a_s)(E_c^* E_s^*)]. \tag{75b}$$

The sibling covariance for E varies directly with the covariance between sibling environments, the covariance between siblings' sensitivity to their environments, as well as other covariance terms, such as between the products of the a's and the E^*'s.

Dividing equation 75a by equation 74a gives the sibling correlation for the concept of environment in behavioral genetics (r_E) when siblings vary in their sensitivity to their environments. This shows that the sibling correlation depends on no less than nine independent variances and covariances featured in equations 74 and 75. If, to simplify matters, the last terms in equations 74 are assumed to be zero, the sibling correlation for E equals

$$r_E = r_{E^*} \frac{\alpha^2 + r_a \text{var}(a)}{\alpha^2 + \text{var}(a) + r_{aE^*}\text{sd}(a)}, \tag{76}$$

where r_{E^*} and r_a denote the sibling correlations for environments (E^*) and sensitivity to them (a), and r_{aE^*} denotes the environment-sensitivity correlation. Notice that if the sibling correlation for environmental exposure is zero ($r_{E^*} = 0$), the sibling correlation for E is zero as expected.

Also, if siblings are perfectly correlated for sensitivity ($r_a = 1$) and the environment-sensitivity correlation is zero ($r_{aE^*} = 0$), equation 76 states, as expected, that $r_E = r_{E^*}$. Finally, even if sibling environments happen to be perfectly correlated ($r_{E^*} = 1$), the sibling correlation for environments from behavioral genetics (r_E) is less than 1 because siblings' sensitivity to these environments are less than perfectly correlated ($r_a < 1$).

Table 10.2 illustrates the relationship between the sibling correlation of behavioral genetics (r_E) and the correlation for actual environments (r_{E^*}) under various assumptions about the sibling correlation for sensitivity to environments and the environment-sensitivity correlation. In table 10.2 it is further assumed that $\alpha = \text{var}(a) = 1$. In case 1 the two sibling correlations are the same because sensitivities are perfectly correlated (no heterogeneity) and the environment-sensitivity correlation is zero. In case 2 sibling sensitivities are uncorrelated and r_E is only half of r_{E^*}. Cases 3 and 4 show that when sensitivity to the environment is heterogeneous r_E is less than r_{E^*}. Case 5 shows that if the environment-sensitivity correlation is positive r_E is even smaller. Cases 6 and 7 show that if the environment-sensitivity correlation is sufficiently negative r_E may exceed r_{E^*}.

Table 10.2 ignores several other parameters that affect the relationship between the sibling correlation for environments in behavioral genetics and the actual sibling correlation. These include the variance of heterogeneity, $\text{var}(a)$, which according to equation 76 reduces r_E relative to r_{E^*}.

Table 10.2
Sibling correlations with heterogeneity in environmental effects.

Case	r_{E^*}	r_a	r_{aE^*}	r_E
1	0.5	1	0	0.5
2	0.5	0	0	0.25
3	0.5	0.5	0	0.375
4	0.5	−0.5	0	0.125
5	0.5	0.5	0.3	0.326
6	0.5	0.5	−0.3	0.441
7	0.5	0.5	−0.6	0.536
8	0.4	0.5	0.3	0.261

10.13.3   Goldberger's Critique

For more than 30 years Arthur Goldberger persuasively argued that the methodological workhorses of behavioral genetics are fundamentally lame. Let us begin with equation 70 under the standard assumption of behavioral genetics that the covariance terms happen to be 0, i.e., the gene-environment correlation is ignored. Subsequently, the argument is extended to the case in which the gene-environment correlation is not assumed to be 0. According to equation 69, the phenotype covariance for pairs of siblings (c and s) is equal to

$$\mathrm{cov}(Y_c Y_s) - r_G \sigma_G{}^2 + r_E \sigma_E{}^2 + 2[\mathrm{cov}(G_c E_s) + \mathrm{cov}(E_c R_s)] \ . \tag{77}$$

In equation 77, r_G denotes the sibling correlation for genotypes and r_E denotes the sibling correlation for environments. It is assumed that $\mathrm{cov}(R_c G_s) = 0$, since R and G are independent, and it is assumed that the sibling covariance terms are symmetrical, for example that $\mathrm{cov}(G_c E_s) = \mathrm{cov}(G_s E_c)$. Since parenting is a component of E, these covariances will be negative if parents invest more in their fitter children, i.e., fitter children are preferred by their parents at the expense of their less fit siblings. Since the gene-environment correlation is assumed to be 0, the cross-sibling covariances are 0 too, as in Goldberger 1979.

The sibling phenotype correlation under all these assumptions is therefore equal to

$$r_Y = \frac{r_G \sigma_G{}^2 + r_E \sigma_E{}^2}{\sigma_Y{}^2} = r_G h^2 + r_E e^2 \ . \tag{78}$$

Behavioral geneticists are interested in estimating heritability ($h^2 = \mathrm{var}(G)/\mathrm{var}(Y)$). The contribution of the environment to the variance of Y is denoted by $e^2 = \mathrm{var}(E)/\mathrm{var}(Y)$. In the case of twin studies the standard genetic assumptions are that r_G equals 1 for MZ twins and it equals a half for DZ twins in the absence of assortative mating, and it is slightly higher than this if mating is assortative. It is standard to make the behavioral assumptions that r_E is 1 if siblings are reared together and 0 if they are reared apart. When these assumptions are substituted into equation 78, the sibling correlations for DZ and MZ twins reared together are

$$r_{MZ} = h_{MZ}^2 + \frac{\mathrm{var}(E_{MZ})}{\mathrm{var}(Y_{MZ})} \tag{79a}$$

and

$$r_{DZ} = \tfrac{1}{2}h_{DZ}^2 + \frac{\mathrm{var}(E_{DZ})}{\mathrm{var}(Y_{DZ})}. \tag{79b}$$

If we are prepared to make the further assumption (also made by Goldberger) that $\mathrm{var}(E)$ and $\mathrm{var}(Y)$ are the same for MZ and DZ twins, equations 79 solve for heritability:

$$h^2 = 2(r_{MZ} - r_{DZ}). \tag{80}$$

This estimate of heritability is as robust as the numerous behavioral assumptions that have been made. If, for example, $r_{MZ} = 0.6$ and $r_{DZ} = 0.4$ for some phenotype, then $h^2 = 0.4$ and $e^2 = 0.6$. Heritability accounts for 40 percent of the variance; the other 60 percent is due to the environment.

More generally, the solution for heritability—even with the assumptions that the gene-environment correlation is 0, the sibling covariances are 0, and σ_E and σ_Y are the same—is

$$h^2 = \frac{r_{E(DZ)}r_{MZ} - r_{E(MZ)}r_{DZ}}{r_{G(MZ)}r_{E(DZ)} - r_{G(DZ)}r_{E(MZ)}}. \tag{81}$$

Owing to epigenetics, $r_{G(MZ)}$ is less than 1 and $r_{G(DZ)}$ is less than ½. Also, the equal-environments assumption, according to which $r_{E(DZ)} = r_{E(MZ)} = 1$, is unlikely to hold. Indeed, it is possible to concoct defensible assumptions about the parameters in equation 81 which imply that heritability is 0 (Goldberger 1979). The basic methodological problem is that equations 79 are not two simultaneous equations in two unknowns. Apart from h^2 and e^2, the unknown parameters include r_G and r_E for DZ and MZ twins. Thus, we have two equations in at least six unknowns. The parameters are under-determined. In econometric parlance, heritability is not identified.

Goldberger (1977) extended his critique to the case in which the gene-environment correlation is not 0. For simplicity, we continue to assume that $\mathrm{cov}(ER) = \mathrm{cov}(E_cR_S) = 0$. Equation 78 now becomes

$$r_Y = \frac{r_G\,\mathrm{var}(G) + r_E\,\mathrm{var}(E) + 2r_{GcEs}\mathrm{sd}(G)\mathrm{sd}(E)}{\mathrm{var}(Y)} = r_G h^2 + \Omega, \tag{82a}$$

$$\Omega = \frac{r_E\,\mathrm{var}(E) + 2r_{GsEc}\mathrm{sd}(G)\mathrm{sd}(E)}{\mathrm{var}(Y)} = r_E e^2 + 2her_{GsEc}. \tag{82b}$$

The numerator includes the sibling covariance term and the denominator includes a term in the gene-environment correlation $r_{GE}\mathrm{sd}(G)\mathrm{sd}(E)$.

It is obvious that if Ω is assumed to be identical for MZ and DZ twins, equation 80 continues to be the solution for hereditability. Goldberger (1977) points out that this is how Jencks and Brown (1977) "identified" heritability. The arbitrary behavioral assumptions they made about the components of Ω led them back to the same solution for heritability as the behavioral genetic model in which the gene-environment correlation is 0 as in case 7 in table 3.4.

Jencks and Brown focus their attention on the gene-environment correlation, but they overlook the sibling covariances in equation 77. They completely ignore the role of parenting in balancing the needs of their children. This is a surprising omission especially for sociologists. Assuming heroically as in equation 80 that $r_G = 1$ for MZ twins and a half for DZ twins and that r_E is the same for MZ and DZ twins the solution for heritability becomes

$$h^2 = 2[(r_{MZ} - B_{MZ}) - (r_{DZ} - B_{DZ})],$$ (83a)

$$B = 2her_{GsEc}.$$ (83b)

If B is assumed to be the same for DZ and MZ twins, equation 83a reverts to where we started in equation 80. The crucial parameter in B is the sibling gene-environment cross-correlation denotes by r_{GsEc}. Parents probably are the most important component of the shared environment of siblings. Parent investment theory predicts that this correlation probably is positive, and it is unlikely to be the same for MZ and DZ twins because the latter are more genetically different from the former.[21]

Behavioral geneticists typically make the strong behavioral assumption that the gene-environment correlation is 0. As a sociologist, Jencks (1972) rightly attaches importance to the gene-environment correlation.[22] He uses sibling correlations for biological and adopted children, denoted here by r_B and r_A respectively, rather than MZ and DZ twins. However, the identification problem is essentially the same. His three equation system is

$$h^2 + e^2 + 2her_{GE} = 1,$$ (84a)

$$r_B = r_G h^2 + r_{EB} e^2 + 2her_{B(GsEc)},$$ (84b)

$$r_A = r_{EA} e^2 + 2her_{A(GsEc)},$$ (84c)

where r_{GE} denotes the gene-environment correlation. Jencks ignores the gene-environment cross-correlation between siblings, which I have added in equations 84b and 84c. Since adopted siblings are genetically uncorrelated ($r_{GA} = 0$) equation 84c has two components rather than three.

Jencks makes the standard behavioral assumptions that r_E is the same for adopted and biological siblings, which assumes, for example, that parents treat their biological and adopted children identically. He also assumes that the gene-environment correlation is identical for adopted children and non-adopted children. Finally, by omission, Jencks assumes that the gene-environment cross-correlation between siblings is the same regardless of whether children are adopted or not. There are many other identifying assumptions that are made implicitly. For example, e^2 is the same for adopted and non-adopted children. He also assumes that adopted children are randomly assigned to parents, who are themselves representative of parents as a whole. Finally, because equation 84a sums to 1, Jencks implicitly assumes that the variance of R is 0, i.e., there is no unshared environment.

Under all these behavioral assumptions, the solutions for heritability, environmentability, and the gene-environment correlations are

$$h^2 = \frac{r_B - r_A}{r_G}, \tag{85a}$$

$$e^2 = \frac{r_A}{r_E}, \tag{85b}$$

$$r_{GE} = \frac{1 - h^2 - e^2}{2he}. \tag{85c}$$

Notice that to solve these equations it is necessary to make further assumptions about r_G and r_E. Note that the solution for heritability is same as it was in equation 80. This is because equations 85 have a recursive or triangular structure. The solutions for h and e do not depend on the gene-environment correlation.

If $r_A = 0.4$, $r_B = 0.6$, and $r_G = \frac{1}{2}$, equation 85a implies that heritability is 0.4. If $r_E = 1$, e^2 is also 0.4. This means that the contribution of the gene-environment correlation is 0.2, which implies that the gene-environment correlation is 0.25. By now it should be needless to say that these numbers are as arbitrary as the many behavioral assumptions that have been made.

10.14   The Structural Social Science Model

Often, as in Purcell 2001, equation 69 is written without R, so that the "environment" is defined as everything else that is not genetic. This practice largely reflects the fact that E and R are "nuisance parameters" to behavioral geneticists. A "nuisance parameter" is a parameter that is not the object of interest but is suspected of inducing bias in the estimate of the object of interest. For example, if β is the object of interest in equation 11a, ρ is a nuisance parameter since it induces bias in the estimate of β. Social scientists, in contrast, focus on various components of E, including household, family, neighborhood, cultural, and peer-group effects. To social scientists these various aspects of E are what is really interesting. For some social scientists genetics is a nuisance parameter that obscures the effects of these components of E on the outcome of interest. Therefore, the research agendas in social science and behavioral genetics are different, and one man's nuisance parameter is another man's raison d'être.

Another way of framing this methodological dichotomy follows Goldberger 2005. Social scientists are concerned with structure whereas behavioral geneticists are concerned with analysis of variance. Structuralists are concerned with modeling human behavior, a good example of which is the Quality vs. Quantity Theory, discussed in chapters 3 and 9, which starts by establishing axioms of human behavior and finishes by specifying empirically testable hypotheses. Behavioral genetics simply lumps all non-genetic phenomena into the "environment," a black box with no clear structure. "It is ironic," Goldberger aptly remarks, "that the assumptions of the behavior-genetic model refer so directly to social behavior, rather than biological processes."

Behavioral genetics gives behavior short shrift, and emphasizes genetics. It would have been just as arbitrary to give genetics short shrift and to assume that everything is behavioral.

Social scientists are mainly interested in testing hypotheses of the type

$$Y_{ci} = \beta Y_{pi} + \lambda Y_{si} + \gamma X_{ci} + \delta C_{ci} + \theta P_i + u_{ci}, \tag{86a}$$

$$u_{ci} = \rho \mu_{pi} + \varepsilon_{ci}, \tag{86b}$$

where Y_p and Y_s are outcomes for i's parents and sibling respectively, X is a vector of demographic controls, C is a vector of contextual or environmental variables, and P is a vector of variables that represent "parenting" (as discussed in section 10.10). Indeed, equation 86a brings together the main phenomena that have been discussed in this chapter. These five types of variables are elements of i's environment and are observable. The coefficients λ, β, γ, δ, and θ are causal and constitute the parameters of interest. And u_c is a residual that, according to equation 86b, is related to u_p, since genotypes are not observed but may be inherited. For some, ρ may also be a parameter of interest.

Equations 86 constitute a "Structural Social Science Model" (SSSM) in that they incorporate the behavioral implications of axiomatic theory regarding the behavior of parents and children. The model is structural in the sense of Goldberger 2005. This model should not be confused with the Standard Social Science Model critically discussed in chapter 3 above. The latter ignores heredity and genetics, and is the polar extreme of behavioral genetics, which ignores behaviorism. In contrast, SSSM integrates genetics and behaviorism axiomatically.

Because genotypes and some environmental variables aren't observable, empirical testing of SSSM is not straightforward. Also gene-environment correlation induces dependence between variables such as P and u in equation 86a. The previous sections have discussed a wide variety of methodological problems in estimating the parameters of interest in equation 86a, all of which threaten the identification of the parameters of interest. These include intergenerational serial correlation (section 10.2), parameter heterogeneity (section 10.6), sibling dependence (section 10.7), neighborhood and peer-group effects (sections 10.8 and 10.9), endogenous parenting (section 10.10), and selectivity (section 10.11).

Suppose that all these methodological problems were successfully overcome and unbiased estimates of the parameters in equations 86 were obtained. The estimated structural model could be used to decompose the variance of Y. In terms of equation 69 the environmental variables (E) comprise Y_p, Y_s, X_p, C, and P, the genetic component $G = \rho u_p$, and the residual component $R = \varepsilon_c$. Therefore, social science carries out the same decomposition of variance as in behavioral genetics, but the means are radically different. What behavioral genetics lumps together under E is what social science is all about. This would not matter if the methodology of behavioral genetics delivered unbiased estimates of E. However, since this is most unlikely, the estimate of the variance of G in equation 71a will be biased since behavioral genetics underestimates and even ignores altogether the role of the environment. In what follows, several methodological difficulties in testing SSSM are discussed.

10.14.1   Gene-Environment Correlation and Interaction in SSSM

The gene-environment correlation implies that observables such as C_p in equation 86a are jointly determined with the outcome variable, since C_p depends on u_c. For example, if schooling is a component of C_p and abler children acquire more schooling, schooling will be positively correlated with u_c which varies directly with genetic ability. The methodological solution to this problem is to find instrumental variables, which directly affect schooling but which do not directly affect the outcome of interest (Y_c).

Gene-environment interaction may be understood in terms of parameter heterogeneity discussed in section 10.6. For example, γ in equation 86a may vary between children:

$$\gamma_i = \gamma + \delta u_i + v_i, \tag{87}$$

where δ denotes the coefficient of the gene-environment interaction. Substituting equation 87 into equation 86a and ignoring for simplicity the other parameters gives

$$Y_i = \gamma X_i + w_i, \tag{88a}$$

$$w_i = u_i + \delta u_i X_i + v_i X_i. \tag{88b}$$

The gene-environment interaction is expressed by $u_i X_i$. Also, $v_i X_i$ is the interaction between the environment and heterogeneity in γ. The expected value of w is (recalling equations 43)

$$E(w) = E(u) + \text{cov}(Xv) + \delta \, \text{cov}(Xu),$$

since $E(u) = E(v) = 0$. If the gene-environment correlation is 0, then $\text{cov}(Xv) = \text{cov}(Xu) = 0$, in which case $E(w) = 0$. However, gene-environment interaction induces threefold dependence between X and w in equation 88a, because

$$E(wX) = E(uX) + \delta \, \text{cov}(uX^2) + \text{cov}(vX^2).$$

The first and second dependences are induced by the gene-environment correlation. The third is due to gene-environment interaction. If the gene-environment correlations and interactions are strictly linear so that, for example $\text{cov}(uX^2) = 0$, then $E(wX) = E(uX)$. In any case, γ in equation 88a ceases to be identified since the gene-environment correlation implies that $E(uX)$ is not 0.

To estimate this feature (γ) of SSSM requires instrumental variables for X. These variables affect X directly but do not affect Y directly. For example, if X refers to school attended and Y refers to years of schooling, the instrumental variable must affect the former but not the latter. Empirical examples of such instrumental variables are discussed in chapter 6.

10.14.2 Sibling Correlations

This subsection focuses on the implications of SSSM for sibling correlations. To simplify matters all other parameters are ignored except θ. This includes the sibling interaction coefficient λ, which induces sibling correlation directly. Let Y_1 and Y_2 denote outcomes for pairs for siblings in family i, where the data-generating process is as follows:

$$Y_{1i} = \theta_{1i} P_{1i} + u_{1i}, \tag{89a}$$

$$Y_{2i} = \theta_{2i} P_{2i} + u_{2i}. \tag{89b}$$

As in section 10.10, P denotes an environmental impulse such as parenting, that favorably affects Y, through the child's sensitivity to his parent (θ). The DGP is heterogeneous, since siblings are hypothesized to respond differently to parenting, so θ_{1i} does not necessarily equal θ_{2i}. The θ's are random variables that are independent between sibling pairs but are correlated within pairs since θ may be partly genetic. In the homogeneous case, θ is fixed within pairs (so that $\theta_{1i} = \theta_{2i} = \theta_i$) but not between pairs (so that θ_i varies between families). According to equation 86b the covariance between u_1 and u_2 is equal to $\rho^2 \mathrm{var}(u_p)$, which is genetic.

P is determined endogenously, as discussed in section 10.10. Therefore, P_{1i} and P_{2i} will generally differ, so that the EEA is violated. However, P_{1i} and P_{2i} will tend to be correlated, since these variables are determined by the same parent. Since parents in different families are unrelated, EGEA (the equal-gene-environments-assumption, defined in subsection 3.2.3) will generally be violated too; there is no reason why discriminatory parenting policy should be similar across families.

According to equation 86, the sibling covariance is equal to

$$\mathrm{cov}(Y_1 Y_2) = \mathrm{cov}[(\theta_1 P_1)(\theta_2 P_2)] + \rho^2 \, \mathrm{var}(u_p) + 2\mathrm{cov}[u_2(\theta_1 P_1)], \tag{90a}$$

$$\theta_1 = \theta + a_1, \tag{90b}$$

$$\theta_2 = \theta + a_2, \tag{90c}$$

$$\mathrm{cov}[(\theta_1 P_1)(\theta_2 P_2)] = \mathrm{cov}(P_1 P_2)\mathrm{cov}(a_1 a_2) + \mathrm{cov}[(a_1 a_2)(P_1 P_2)], \tag{90d}$$

$$\mathrm{cov}[u_2(\theta_1 P_1)] = \theta \mathrm{cov}(u_2 P_1) + \mathrm{cov}[u_2(a_1 P_1)]. \tag{90e}$$

In equation 90a it is assumed that $\text{cov}[u_2(\theta_1 P_1)]$ and $\text{cov}[u_1(\theta_2 P_2)]$ are symmetrical. In equations 90b and 90c, a is a random variable with $E(a) = 0$ that may be correlated between siblings. In equation 90d it is assumed that $\text{cov}[(a_1 P_1)P_2]$ and $\text{cov}[(a_2 P_2)P_1]$ are symmetrical. Equations 90 embody eight behavioral covariance terms, which refer to different aspects of parenting and the responsiveness of siblings to parenting. For example, $\text{cov}(P_1 P_2)$ and $\text{cov}(a_1 a_2)$ refer to differential parenting between siblings and the differential sensitivity of siblings to parenting.

According to equations 89 and 86b, the phenotypic variance depends on three behavioral covariances:

$$\text{var}(Y) = \theta \rho \, \text{cov}(u_p P) + \theta \, \text{cov}(\varepsilon P) + \rho \, \text{cov}[u_p(aP)]. \tag{91}$$

Since the sibling correlation coefficient is defined as equation 90a divided by equation 91, it depends on no less than twelve behavioral phenomena. All these phenomena arise in the highly simplified version of SSSM represented by equations 89. Matters would naturally be much more complex in the case of SSSM in equations 86. Indeed, this is why the simplified version of SSSM is used here, for otherwise the number of behavioral covariances would become intractably large.

What do equations 90 and 91 imply about comparisons between sibling correlations for MZ and DZ twins, or for adopted and biological siblings? In behavioral genetics the EEA means that these twelve covariances are assumed to be identical for MZ and DZ twins and adopted and biological siblings. These empirical restrictions may be related to some important covariances.

(i) $\text{Cov}(P_1 P_2)$ refers to differential parental treatment between siblings, which according to the EEA is the same for MZ and DZ twins and adopted and biological siblings. If parents behave more or less attentively to adopted children the EEA is violated. The same applies if they treat MZ twins differently than DZ twins (for example, by dressing them identically).

(ii) $\text{Cov}(a_1 a_2)$ refers to the correlation in sensitivity of siblings to parenting. If MZ siblings have more correlated sensitivities than DZ siblings, the EEA will be violated. In the case of adopted and biological siblings this covariance is expected to be 0.

(iii) $\text{Cov}(u_2 P_1)$ refers to the cross-covariance in parenting when rival siblings happen to be fitter. This covariance will be negative if parenting is egalitarian. The EEA requires that parents' egalitarianism is the same for all types of siblings.

(iv) $\text{Cov}(uP)$ refers to the gene-environment correlation for parenting. If fitter children need less parenting the covariance is negative. The EEA assumes that this covariance is the same for all types of siblings.

(v) $\text{Cov}(aP)$ refers to the response of parenting to children's responsiveness to parenting. If more responsive children requires less parenting, this covariance will be negative. If parents respond differently to the sensitivity of adopted children than they do to their biological children, the EEA will be violated.

(vi) $\text{Cov}(u_pP)$ refers to the relationship between the genotype of parents and their parenting. If fitter parents make better parents this covariance is expected to be positive. If fitness matters more for parents who adopt, the EEA will be violated.

10.14.3 Sibling Interaction in SSSM

This subsection focuses on the sibling interaction in SSSM, which in the previous subsection was ignored. To explore the implications of sibling interaction P and C are ignored in equation 86a and X is assumed to be exogenous but correlated between siblings. Since Y_1 and Y_2 depend on each other, the reduced form solution for SSSM may be obtained as in equation 48a.

The sibling covariance and the variance are respectively

$$\text{cov}(Y_1Y_2) = \frac{\beta^2(1+\lambda)^2 \text{ var}(Y_p) + \gamma^2(1+\lambda)^2 \text{ cov}(X_1X_2) + \rho^2 \text{ var}(u_p)}{(1-\lambda^2)^2} \quad (92a)$$

and

$$\text{var}(Y) = \frac{\beta^2(1+\lambda)^2 \text{ var}(Y_p) + \gamma^2(1+\lambda)^2 \text{ var}(X) + \rho^2 \text{ var}(u_p) + \sigma^2}{(1-\lambda^2)^2}, \quad (92b)$$

where σ^2 denotes the variance of ε. The sibling correlation is equation 92a divided by equation 92b which varies directly with the sibling interaction coefficient λ and the sibling correlation for X. The EEA will be violated in the following instances:

(i) Sibling interaction is different between MZ and DZ twins, i.e. λ_{DZ} differs from λ_{MZ}. If MZ twins interact more strongly than DZ twins, behavioral genetics will over-estimate hereditary. The same applies to differences in sibling interaction between adopted and biological siblings, i.e. if λ_A differs from λ_B.

(ii) X is more correlated for MZ twins than DZ twins. This will cause behavioral genetics to over-estimate heredity.

(iii) The genotypic variance, var(u_p), for parents who adopt is different from its counterpart for biological parents. The same applies to the phenotypic variance of parents, var(Y_p).

(iv) If biological parents interact more or less closely with adopted children than with biological children, so that β_A differs from β_B, the EEA will be violated. The same might apply to the parents of MZ and DZ twins, i.e., if β_{DZ} differs from β_{MZ}.

10.14.4 Orphans

The methodology of behavioral genetics "controls" for genetics by comparing the outcomes of MZ twins or adopted and biological siblings. MZ twins are genetically identical, whereas adoptees are genetically unrelated to their siblings. Gould and Simhon (2011) have suggested a third type of comparison based on orphans. If children are orphaned at birth, they obviously cannot be nurtured by their deceased parents. Therefore, any correlation between the phenotypes of deceased parents and their orphaned children cannot be due to nurture and parenting. It can only be genetic. More generally, nurture and parenting vary directly with the age at which children are orphaned. A child who is orphaned at 13 naturally receives more nurturing from his deceased parent than a child orphaned aged 6.

Sooner or later, we all have to lose our parents. However, the loss of a parent in childhood has two main developmental costs, which do not apply to adults. First, the trauma of losing a parent at a young age may have developmental implications. The developmental implications of this trauma may vary with the age at which the child becomes orphaned. Second, the deceased parent can no longer nurture the orphaned child. Perhaps the first effect is zero if the child is orphaned at birth. In this case only the second effect matters for the child. In general, the death of a parent induces both effects, and they are difficult to disentangle empirically.

This proposition can be illustrated with the following simple model, based on behavioral genetics, in which S denotes schooling and G and E denote genotypes and environmental effects not related to schooling. Subscripts o and c refer to orphaned and non-orphaned children, and, as usual, subscript p refers to parents. The phenotypes of orphans and other children are determined as follows:

$$S_o = G_o + \alpha E_o, \tag{93a}$$

$$S_c = G_c + \theta S_p + E_c. \tag{93b}$$

Notice that in equation 93a orphans' schooling doesn't depend on parents' schooling, whereas in equation 93b the causal effect of parents' schooling on other children is denoted by θ. Since the effect of the environment might be different for orphans, α might not equal 1 in equation 93a. According to equations 93, the intergenerational covariances for schooling for orphans and other children are respectively

$$\text{cov}(S_o S_{po}) = \text{cov}(G_o S_{po}) + \alpha \, \text{cov}(E_o S_{po}) \tag{94a}$$

and

$$\text{cov}(S_c S_p) = \text{cov}(G_c S_p) + \theta \, \text{var}(S_p) + \text{cov}(E_c S_p). \tag{94b}$$

In the spirit of behavioral genetics, θ is identified if we are prepared to make the following identifying assumptions:

(i) $\alpha = 1$

(ii) $\text{cov}(G_o S_{po}) = \text{cov}(G_c S_p)$

(iii) $\text{cov}(E_o S_{po}) = \text{cov}(E_c S_p)$.

Assumption i states that orphans respond to the environment in the same way as other children. For example, schools are part of the environment. This assumption means that school choice is independent of orphan status. If orphans happen to be more sensitive or less self confident they might attend different schools to non-orphaned children. Or if they attend similar schools their progress might be different. In short, bereavement and the trauma of losing parents have no behavioral implications for school choice or pedagogic achievement.

Assumption ii states that the covariance between the schooling of deceased parents and the genotypes of their children is the same as the covariance for living parents. If deceased parents are less fit than living parents (which explains why the former died but the latter lived) and fitness matters for parents' schooling, assumption ii will be violated. Technically this happens because S_{po} and S_p are different. I have shown that the earnings of otherwise identical workers are 12 percent lower if they happened to die within 10 years (Beenstock, Chiswick, and Paltiel 2010). This "shadow of death" effect suggests that these workers were less fit to begin with. Their lower productivity and their premature demise stem from a common cause. If the same phenomenon applies to schooling, the schooling of deceased parents might be inferior in quantity and in quality to that of living parents.

Assumption iii states that the covariance between the environments of children and their parents' schooling is the same for orphans and other children. This assumption is bound to be violated, since the death of parents probably has serious repercussions for children's environments. The environments of orphaned children are turned upside down when parents die. Apart from anything else, orphans may become stepchildren.

Nevertheless, using these assumptions in the spirit of behavioral genetics, equations 94 imply that

$$\hat{\theta} = \frac{\text{cov}(S_c S_p) - \text{cov}(S_o S_{po})}{\text{var}(S_p)} = \frac{\text{sd}(S_c) r_{cp} - \text{sd}(S_o) r_{op}}{\text{sd}(S_p)}. \tag{95}$$

This equation identifies the causal effect of parents' schooling on children's schooling by making strong behavioral assumptions. Table 10.3 simulates some illustrative estimates of θ that are obtained from equation 95. The intergenerational correlation for schooling is assumed to be 0.4 and the standard deviation of parents' schooling is normalized at 1. In case 1 it is assumed that the standard deviation of children's schooling is the same as their parents', i.e., there is neither intergenerational sigma convergence nor divergence. However, since equations 93 imply that the variance of schooling for orphans must be less than for other children, the standard deviation for orphans is assumed to be 0.8. In case 1 the intergenerational correlation for orphans is assumed to be zero, in which case θ is 0.4. This means that if parents' schooling is increased by one year this causes the schooling of children to increase by 0.4 year.

This effect is reduced to 0.24 if the intergenerational correlation for orphans is 0.24, as in case 2. Case 3 shows that sigma convergence

Table 10.3
Identifying the causal effect of parents' schooling using data for orphans.

Case	r_{cp}	r_{op}	sd_p	sd_c	sd_o	θ
1	0.4	0	1	1	0.8	0.4
2	0.4	0.2	1	1	0.8	0.24
3	0.4	0.2	1	0.8	0.6	0.2
4	0.4	0.4	1	1	1	0
5	0.4	0.4	1	1	0.8	0.08

further reduces θ to 0.2. Case 4 shows that if the intergenerational correlations for orphans is the same as for other children θ is zero because the correlation has an entirely genetic explanation. If, additionally, there is more equality in the schooling of orphans (case 5), it must be because there is causal effect of schooling. Therefore, in case 5 θ is 0.08.

The estimates of θ reported in table 10.3 are as robust as the identifying assumptions upon which they are based. Suppose, for example, that assumption i is violated. In this case, equations 94 imply

$$\theta^* = \hat{\theta} + (\alpha - 1)\frac{\text{cov}(E_c S_p)}{\text{var}(S_p)}, \tag{96}$$

where $\hat{\theta}$ is the estimate of θ from equation 95. Notice that if α is 1, $\theta^* = \hat{\theta}$ as expected. Notice also that the multiplicand of $\alpha - 1$ is equal to the regression coefficient of E_c on S_p. If this regression coefficient happens to be 1 and α is 0.8, equation 96 states that the estimates of θ in table 10.3 are over-estimated by 0.2. In case 3 this means that θ is in fact zero. The greater the regression coefficient and the smaller is α, the greater is the over-estimate of θ. If, in addition, assumptions ii and iii are violated, the bias in the estimate of θ becomes yet more complicated.

10.15   Genome-Wide Association Studies (GWAS)[23]

10.15.1   Statistical Testing
Suppose that the true GWAS model is

$$Y_i = \alpha + \beta X_i + \gamma Z_i + u_i, \tag{97}$$

where X and Z are genetic markers or genotypes, Y is a phenotype, i labels individuals, and u is assumed to be an iid residual with variance equal to σ^2. Equation 97 is the simplest multiple-gene model. The OLS estimates of β and γ are

$$\hat{\beta} = \frac{\text{sd}(Y)\text{sd}(Z)(r_{YX} - r_{YZ}r_{XZ})}{\text{sd}(X)\text{sd}(Z)(1 - r_{XZ}^2)} \tag{98a}$$

and

$$\hat{\gamma} = \frac{\text{sd}(Y)\text{sd}(X)(r_{YZ} - r_{YX}r_{XZ})}{\text{sd}(X)\text{sd}(Z)(1 - r_{XZ}^2)}, \tag{98b}$$

where, e.g., r_{XZ} denotes the correlation between X and Z. The null hypothesis for equation 97 is that β and γ are jointly 0. The null hypothesis may be tested by calculating the F statistic defined as

$$F = \frac{[\text{var}(Y) - \text{var}(\hat{u})](N-3)}{2\text{var}(\hat{u})}, \tag{99}$$

where $\hat{u}$ denotes the estimated residuals and N denotes the number of observations. If F exceeds the critical value of the F statistic with 2 degrees of freedom in the numerator and $N - 3$ degrees of freedom in the denominator, the null hypothesis may be rejected.

In a more conservative context, the null hypothesis is that β and γ are individually 0. In this case, the model is rejected if either of the estimates of β and γ is not statistically significant. To apply this test, the t statistics of the estimates of β and γ may be used.

The variances of the estimates of β and γ are defined as follows:

$$\text{var}(\hat{\beta}) = \frac{\sigma^2}{N \, \text{var}(X)(1 - r_{XZ}{}^2)}, \tag{100a}$$

$$\text{var}(\hat{\gamma}) = \frac{\sigma^2}{N \, \text{var}(Z)(1 - r_{XZ}{}^2)}. \tag{100b}$$

Therefore, the t statistics are

$$t_{\hat{\beta}} = \frac{\hat{\beta}}{\text{sd}(\hat{\beta})} \tag{101a}$$

and

$$t_{\hat{\gamma}} = \frac{\hat{\gamma}}{\text{sd}(\hat{\gamma})}. \tag{101b}$$

If the t statistic exceeds its critical value in the case of the estimate of β but is less than its critical value in the case of the estimate of γ, the conservative null hypothesis cannot be rejected. If X and Z are uncorrelated, the two tests are identical because the F statistic depends on the two t statistics. In this case, if β and γ are jointly statistically significant they are also individually statistically significant. However, if, as in the case of genetic markers, X and Z are correlated, β and γ might be jointly significant but not individually significant. In this case, the conservative test will over-reject equation 97. Clearly the joint test is appropriate.

As was noted in chapter 7, the majority of GWAS research tests one gene at a time, or marker by marker. In terms of equation 97, Y is regressed sequentially on individual genetic markers. Suppose the marker is X and the following model is estimated:

$$Y_i = \alpha' + \beta' X_i + v_i. \tag{102}$$

If equation 97 is the true model, it must be the case that the residuals of this single-gene model are equal to

$$v_i = \gamma Z_i + u_i. \tag{103}$$

Using equation 103 to calculate the expected value of the estimate of β', we obtain

$$E(\hat{\beta}') = \beta' + \gamma r_{XZ} \frac{\text{sd}(Z)}{\text{sd}(X)}, \tag{104}$$

which shows that if X and Z are correlated, as they are, the estimate of β' is biased. In fact the estimate of β' is equal to its true value plus omitted-variable bias, which is equal to the indirect effect of Z on Y through its correlation with X.

Now that we have estimated β', the next step is to determine whether it is statistically significant using the t statistic for the estimate of β':

$$t_{\hat{\beta}'} = \frac{\hat{\beta}'}{\text{sd}(\hat{\beta}')} \tag{105a}$$

$$\text{var}(\hat{\beta}') = \frac{\sigma_v^2}{N \text{ var}(X)} = \frac{\gamma^2 \text{ var}(Z) + \sigma^2}{N \text{ var}(X)}. \tag{105b}$$

If γ is not 0 because Z is a genotype for Y, the t statistic for β decreases. In fact, as shown in table 7.3, it is easy to reject the hypothesis that X is a genotype for Y when the opposite is true. The probability of making this mistake varies directly with γ and the variance of Z since these parameters increase the standard deviation of the estimate of β', and it varies inversely with the omitted-variable bias in the estimate of β'.

Therefore, the marker-by-marker GWAS methodology in which individual genotypes are tested one at a time runs the risk of missing the correct model except in the most unlikely event that genotypes are uncorrelated. The sequential methodology not only runs the risk of false negatives; it also runs the risk of false positives. False positives arise when X is in fact not a genotype for Y, but the estimate of β' in equation 100 is artificially positive or negative due to omitted-variable bias induced by the correlation between X and Z.

10.15.2 Stratification Bias

Suppose that there are two populations, A and B, and that equation 97 is the true GWAS models for these populations:

$$Y_{Ai} = \beta_A X_i + \gamma_A Z_i + u_{Ai},$$ (106a)

$$Y_{Bi} = \beta_B X_i + \gamma_B Z_i + u_{Bi}.$$ (106b)

Notice that genotypic sensitivity will vary between the two populations if β_A does not equal β_B and if γ_A does not equal γ_B. If $\gamma_B = 0$, Z is a marker for population A but not for population B.

If the data are pooled, as they are in practice, the correct model will be as follows:

$$Y_i = \beta_B X_i + \gamma_B Z_i + D_i(b X_i + g Z_i) + u_i,$$ (107a)

$$u_i = D_i u_{Ai} + (1 - D_i) u_{Bi},$$ (107b)

where D_i is a dummy variable if individual i belongs to population A and 0 if he belongs to population B. When $D = 0$, equation 107a refers to population B. When $D = 1$, equation 107a refers to population A, in which case $\beta_A = \beta_B + b$ and $\gamma_A = \gamma_B + g$. Equation 107a may be used to estimate the correct GWAS model provided data are available for D. The trouble is, of course, that D is not observed.

Price et al. (2006) developed the EIGENSTRAT method to take account of population stratification, which decomposes the data into principal components. The intuition behind EIGENSRAT is that in heterogeneous populations there will be principal components that do not exist in homogenous populations. Indeed each stratum of the population should have its own principal component. In our example, one of the principal components should pick up the difference in correlation between the genotypes of population A and B.

EIGENSTRAT involves the following three steps. First, data on M genetic markers are used to estimate principal components. Price et al. suggest that when there are two populations the first principal component contains information on population stratification. Let the first PC be used to proxy population stratification, with

$$PC_i = \sum_{n=1}^{N} \lambda_n X_{ni} ,$$ (108)

where λ_m denotes the loading of the first PC on marker X_m. Second, phenotypes and markers are regressed on PC to obtain their residuals denoted by y and x_m:

$$Y_i = \varphi PC_i + y_i ,$$ (109a)

$$X_{ni} = \theta_n PC_i + x_{ni} .$$ (109b)

These residuals adjust the data for population stratification; they are ancestry-adjusted transformations of Y and X. As such they are supposed to represent Y and X that would hypothetically have been observed in a homogeneous population. Third, y is regressed on x_m to estimate genotypic sensitivities:

$$y_i = \sum_{n}^{K} \delta_n x_{ni} + v_i ,$$ (110)

where K is a subset of M. Substituting equations 105 into equation 110 gives

$$Y_i = \sum_{n}^{K} \delta_n X_{ni} + \psi PC_i + v_i ,$$ (111a)

$$\psi = \phi - \sum_{n}^{K} \delta_n \theta_n .$$ (111b)

EIGENSTRAT, as represented by equation 111a, is supposed to be equivalent to equation 107a. However, it is obvious that equations 111a and 107a are different. First, the genotypic sensitivities (δ_m) in equation 111a are assumed to be the same for the two populations, whereas they differ in equation 107a. Second, the genotypic markers are assumed to be the same for the two populations, whereas they are different in equation 107a. Third, PC is collinear with the genotypic markers in equation 111a whereas D is not collinear in equation 107a. If $K = M$, PC and genotypes may be perfectly collinear, in which case the parameters of equation 111a aren't identified. More generally, because PC depends on genotypes through equation 108 estimation of δ_m in equation 111a is biased unless λ_m happens to be 0. In this unlikely case, PC does not depend on X_m and δ_m entirely reflects genotypic sensitivity. In short, identification in EIGENSTRAT "works" for technical reasons rather than substantive reasons. If PC just happens to be sufficiently independent of $\Sigma \delta_m X_m$, EIGENSTRAT "works." But even in this case the estimates of δ_m are biased.

The basic methodological problem with EIGENSTRAT is that genotypic marker data are used for two purposes, to stratify populations and to estimate genotypic sensitivities. One ideally needs to stratify using data that are independent of genotypes. Also, there is no reason to believe that the first principal component expresses population stratification. Even in homogeneous populations there will be statistically significant principal components simply because genetic markers are correlated between themselves. The first principal components are therefore more likely to be due to genetics than to population stratification. Therefore, a major methodological problem with EIGENSTRAT concerns the identification of the principal components that are induced by population stratification and the principal components that are induced by genetics.

10.16   Sequencing vs. Causality[24]

If event A happens before event B and if these events are correlated, does this mean that A causes B? If events A and B occurred simultaneously the answer is obviously "no" because correlation does not establish causality. However, the fact that A occurred before B seems to suggest causality from A to B, since B (which happened after A) cannot affect A. This argument is false, as a simple example demonstrates. If A is cooking and B is eating, the correlation between cooking and eating does not establish that cooking causes eating. Hunger is the common cause of both cooking and eating. A precedes B in this case because there is a natural sequence which starts with hunger, which is followed by cooking and is completed by eating. If a power outage prevented cooking, so that event A did not occur, event B would still occur because eating would involve uncooked food. This establishes that cooking does not cause eating. Cooking predicts eating because A precedes B, but prediction and causality are different phenomena.

In chapter 6 it was noted that developmental psychologists confuse prediction and causality. In this case event A is mothering when the child is 1 month old and event B is infant irritability at 3 months. If mothering at 1 month is motivated by its affect on her child at 3 months

A is not independent of B despite the fact that it precedes B. The correlation between A and B embodies reverse causality from B to A.

The purpose of this section is to answer the following question. When is prediction or sequencing causal? The answer is: When A is "weakly exogenous." Let B denote the outcome and A denote the hypothesized cause of B where A occurs before B. The argument is illustrated with the following simple, first-order dynamic model, where subscript t refers to time and where ε and e are iid random variables:

$$B_t = \alpha + \beta B_{t-1} + \theta A_{t-1} + u_t, \tag{112a}$$

$$A_t = \mu + \lambda A_{t-1} + \varphi B_{t-1} + e_t, \tag{112b}$$

$$u_t = \rho u_{t-1} + \delta e_t + \phi e_{t-1} + \varepsilon_t. \tag{112c}$$

Notice that equation 112a allows, for generality, that B depends on its own past in addition to the past of A. In fact, if $0 < \beta < 1$, beta convergence applies to B. The same applies to A in equation 112b. If $0 < \lambda < 1$, beta convergence also applies to A. Equation 112b also allows for feedback from B to A via φ. This might not make much sense in the case of cooking and eating, but it makes sense in the case of mothering and infant irritability. Finally, equation 112c allows the residuals in equation 112a to be autocorrelated via ρ and correlated with the residuals in equation 112b via δ and ϕ.

The parameter of interest is θ. This parameter will have a causal interpretation if A_{t-1} in equation 112a is independent of u_t. In this case A_{t-1} is weakly exogenous. It is obviously not strongly exogenous because A depends on lagged B according to equation 112b. Two conditions are required for weak exogeneity. First, according to equation 112c, if ϕ is non-zero u_t depends on e_{t-1}. Since according to equation 112b A_{t-1} depends on e_{t-1}, A_{t-1} and u_t are dependent. Weak exogeneity therefore requires $\phi = 0$. Notice that it does not require $\delta = 0$ because A occurs before B. Second, lagging equation 112b one period implies that A_{t-1} depends on B_{t-2}. Lagging equation 112c one period implies that u_{t-1} depends on u_{t-2} via ρ. Since B_{t-2} depends on u_{t-2} according to equation 112a and u_t depends indirectly on u_{t-2}, A_{t-1} and u_t are dependent via ρ. Therefore, the second requirement for weak exogeneity is $\rho = 0$. If $\rho = \phi = 0$, A_{t-1} is weakly exogenous and the estimate of θ has a causal interpretation. If A_{t-1} is not weakly exogenous, because either or both ϕ and ρ are non-zero, A_{t-1} predicts B but does not cause it. To establish that θ is causal and not merely predictive, it is therefore necessary to show that ρ and ϕ are 0.

In equations 112, A is said to "Granger cause" B if θ is statistically significant. Granger causality arises when conditional on lags of B, lags of A help predict B. If, in addition, φ is statistically significant, B "Granger causes" A. There may be one-way or two-way Granger causality. Notice that Granger causality is not about causality, it is about conditional prediction. If, however, A_{t-1} is weakly exogenous in equation 112a, Granger causality is synonymous with causality.

Equation 112b involved feedback from B to A. Suppose that, in addition, there is feedforward from B to A because A_t depends on expectations of B_{t+1} as in equation 59 in chapter 9. For example, mothering at time t depends on mothers' expectations of their children's behavior in the next period. In this case, equation 112b becomes

$$A_t = \mu + \lambda A_{t-1} + \varphi B_{t-1} + \psi E_t(B_{t+1}) + e_t, \tag{113}$$

where ψ denotes the feedforward parameter. According to equation 112a,

$$E_t(B_{t+1}) = \alpha + \beta B_t + \theta A_t. \tag{114}$$

Substituting equation 114 into equation 113 gives the following relationship for A_t:

$$A_t = \frac{1}{1-\theta\psi}(\mu + \alpha\psi + \lambda A_{t-1} + \beta\psi B_t + \phi B_{t-1} + e_t). \tag{115}$$

According to this equation, A_t depends on B_t and not just B_{t-1} in equation 112b. Therefore, A_{t-1} in equation 112a requires a further condition for weak exogeneity. The additional requirement is $\delta = 0$.

Notes

Chapter 1

1. See Bowlby 1969, p. 40.

2. Bellman invented dynamic programming in the 1950s, and Pontryagin developed the Maximum Principle in the 1960s. For an introduction to control theory, see Hocking 1991.

3. For the full story, see Laland and Brown 2002 and Pinker 2002.

4. Pinker (2002) argues that Locke's tabula rasa was political and not intended as a statement about human nature—that Locke was attacking the received wisdom about the Divine Right of Kings and the dominance of the Church. This interpretation is too narrow, because Locke directly referred to knowledge more generally, including moral and physical knowledge.

5. Popper (1966, volume 1) accuses Plato of racism and of supporting eugenics.

6. See, for example, Galor and Moav 2002.

7. For a history of this cultural war, see Weintraub 2002.

8. "I have come to feel that Marshall's dictum that 'it seems doubtful whether anyone spends his time well in reading lengthy translations of economic doctrines into mathematics, that have not been made by himself' should be exactly reversed. The laborious literary working over of essentially simple mathematical concepts such as is characteristic of much of modern economic theory is not only unrewarding from the standpoint of advancing the science, but involves as well mental gymnastics of a particularly depraved kind." (Samuelson 1947, p. 6)

9. On the development of econometrics in the twentieth century, see Morgan 1990 and Hendry and Morgan 1995. "Indeed," Hendry and Morgan write, "econometrics was not welcomed with open arms in the late 19th and early 20th century; rather it was received with derision, suspicion and some outright hostility." (p. 40) The Cowles approach built on methodological developments of the 1930s and the 1940s. Econometrics probably would have continued to develop as it did even without the Cowles Commission. Therefore, Cowles serves here as a metaphor for testing hypotheses with non-experimental data.

10. Daniel Kahneman and Vernon Smith (an economist) were awarded the Nobel Prize in economics in 2002.

11. The Royal Geographical Society had been out of contact with Dr. Livingstone for 2½ years when Stanley met Livingstone in Africa. Stanley sold his story to the press, and the news was sensational. Galton chaired a packed meeting of the RGS at which Stanley was due to speak. Stanley, who was the illegitimate son of a Welsh farmer and had been adopted by an American, pretended that he was born in America. In his opening remarks, Galton asked Stanley to clear up certain mysteries about his origins. For more on the Stanley Affair. see chapter 7 of Forrest 1974.

12. Quoted in Keynes 1993 and in Bulmer 2003.

13. To be fair, eugenics was popularized in Britain by George Bernard Shaw, Karl Pearson, and R.A. Fisher, among others. In the US, Charles Davenport founded the Cold Spring Harbor Laboratory to promote research into eugenics. In the end it was left to the Nazis to discredit eugenics.

14. Although the word was first used by Bateson in 1906 and by Johannsen in 1909.

15. Galton 1875a.

16. Galton 1875b.

17. Indeed, Plomin et al. (2001, p. 163) write that Galton "can be considered the father of behavioral genetics."

18. First reported in Galton 1877 but reported in greater depth in Galton 1889.

19. Galton referred to r as "co-relation."

20. When Y is regressed on X, the sum of squared residuals is minimized with respect to Y. When X is regressed on Y, the sum of squared residuals is minimized with respect to X. Therefore, the direction of the regression matters.

21. First reported in Galton 1885 but discussed in greater depth in Galton 1889.

22. Galton 1885, p. 272.

23. Textbooks in psychology, such as *Hilgard's Introduction to Psychology* (Atkinson et al. 2000), usually refer critically to Galton's ideas on heredity and to the debate about nature vs. nurture.

24. Diamond 1977, reprinted on p. 234 of Benjamin 1997.

25. Benjamin 1997, p. 238.

26. For example, Gazzaniga and Heatherton 2006.

27. Atkinson et al. 2000, p. 424.

28. Miller 1993, p. 432.

29. Hacohen (2000, p. 92) mentions that Adler's daughter told him about this conversation. In fact, Popper mentions it himself.

30. For a post-modernist critique of economics, see McCloskey 1983.

31. To be fair, Sacerdote has also been a major contributor to the economic literature on peer-group effects and related effects.

32. See, e.g., Juhn, Murphy, and Pierce 1993 and Heckman 2001.

33. Herrnstein and Murray based their research on data from the National Youth Longitudinal Study for 1990, which included IQ scores provided by the US military. Their appendix 4 reports numerous OLS and logistic regression models in which the main independent variables are IQ, SES (socioeconomic status of parents) and age. The dependent variables cover schooling, idleness, family matters, crime and civility. Their appendix 6 includes regression models for income and wages. Surprisingly, significance tests were not reported. I contacted Murray about this. He told me that the original results have not been preserved, so he cannot tell me whether the effect of IQ on wages was statistically significant.

34. See Herrnstein and Murray 1994, p. 279.

35. Rawls 1970; Nozick 1974; Hayek 1960.

Chapter 2

1. In this case, $\ln Y_c = \alpha + \beta \ln Y_c + u$, which may be written as $Y_c = e^{\alpha + u} Y_p^\beta$. The expected value of Y_c is $Y_p^\beta e^{\alpha + \sigma^2/2}$, and $\partial Y_c / \partial Y_p = \beta(Y_c / Y_p)$. Therefore, "marginal beta" varies directly with the ratio of the outcome of children to the outcome of parents.

2. The estimation controls for birth cohort, immigration cohort, and continent of birth.

3. Using a sample of 1,873 men, they regress age-adjusted AFQT scores on the following variables: black –0.57, Hispanic –0.22, mother high school graduate 0.26, mother college graduate 0.16, father high school graduate 0.25, father college graduate 0.3, mother professional 0.17, father professional 0.23, sibship –0.05, no reading material –0.19. The numbers refer to size effects, and $R^2 = 0.415$. See Neal and Johnson 1996, table 5.

4. The first principal component of psychometric tests is referred to as g. It is intended to measure the general level of intelligence.

5. Apart from AFQT scores, Gould also uses IQ test scores reported on high school transcripts.

6. Jencks' estimates aren't original; they are derived from secondary data. See Jencks 1972, appendix A.

7. Solon used data from the Panel Study on Income Dynamics; Peters (1992) and Altonji and Dunn (1991) used data from the National Longitudinal Study of Youth (NLSY). Both studies are nationally representative. The different data sets generate slightly different results.

8. Income is defined as earnings plus non-labor income such as interest, transfers and rent.

9. Data on wealth are problematic for two reasons. First, it is more difficult to measure than income or consumption. Second, the data typically come from unrepresentative samples, such as probate records.

10. Israelis are callable for reserve duty until they are about 40 years old. Since 2005 recipients of religious exemptions from the army are permitted to work when they are 24 years old. However, so far this controversial reform has had only a small effect on participation in the labor market by the ultra-orthodox.

Chapter 3

1. Mincer (1974) and Ben Porath (1967) probably were the first economists to attach importance to the role of the family in economics, and to the role of economics in the family.

2. See, e.g., Ehrenburg and Smith 2006 and Ermisch 2003.

3. As was mentioned in chapter 1, this criticism has been made forcibly by Goldberger (1979, 2005).

4. During the 1950s and the 1960s macroeconomics became temporarily detached from the mainstream of economic theory. It became a different subject based on *ad hoc* ideas about the determination of wages and inflation. That was a very confusing time intellectually. Today this renegade macroeconomics is known disparagingly as "old-style Keynesianism." Patinkin (1966) brought this breakaway macroeconomics back into the intellectual fold. I have told the story about this intellectual counter-revolution in macroeconomics in Beenstock 1980. Since the 1970s macroeconomic theory has returned to its axiomatic roots.

5. On the effect of parenting on cognitive development, see Van Geert 1991. On the effect of mothers' response on the dynamics of child irritability, see Olthof, Kunnen, and Boom 2000. For a comprehensive discussion of the "mechanization" of infant development theory, see Schultz 2003.

6. For example, for Newton gravity is axiomatic while the inverse-square law is the mechanical implication of the axiom. Deductive theory begins from primitive axioms (Popper 1963).

7. For examples of variable-based modeling, see Van Geert 1991, Olhof, Kunnen, and Boom 2000, and Schultz 2003.

8. Since E denotes the shared environment and R denotes the unshared environment, the sibling correlation for the environment is equal to
$r_E = \mathrm{var}(E)/[\mathrm{var}(E)+\mathrm{var}(R)+2\mathrm{cov}(RE)]$.

9. In chapter 5 I show that the empirical data may nevertheless reveal something about the role of genetics, but this is quite different from claims of behavioral genetics.

10. On program evaluation, see Lee 2006.

11. See, e.g., Plomin et al. 2001, pp. 298–299.

12. Atkinson et al. 2000, p. 104.

13. For a useful introduction to evolutionary psychology, see Workman and Reader 2008.

14. A different kind of theory of fertility is based on the demand for children as providing insurance for their parents, especially when they are unable to work. In industrialized countries these insurance services are provided either by the state or through private insurance. Therefore, this issue is not considered here.

15. See also Mcnown and Ridao-cano 2004 and Gauthier and Hatzuis 1997.

16. For an accessible introduction to game theory, see Dixit and Nalebuff 1999.

Chapter 4

1. There are a number of distinguished longitudinal surveys, including the Panel Study of Income Dynamics (PSID) and the National Longitudinal Study of Youth (NLSY) in the US, the British Household Panel Survey (BHPS) in the UK, the German Socioeconomic Panel (GSOEP) in Germany, and the Survey of Labour Income Dynamics (SLID) in Canada. Their sample sizes tend to be small, and for many countries (e.g. Israel) there are no longitudinal surveys at all.

2. Rousseau's personal life echoed these beliefs!

3. For a more detailed discussion of the relationship between beta convergence and sigma convergence in this context, see subsection 8.5.3.

4. Because $cov(Y_p u)$ is assumed to be 0 in ordinary least squares, it does not feature in equation 2. For further details, see subsection 8.1.2.

5. Strictly speaking, this is "narrow-sense heritability," since the model is linear. Nonlinear models give rise to "broad-sense heritability."

6. This subsection is based on subsection 8.1.4.

7. This subsection is based on subsections 8.2.1 and 8.2.2.

8. In figure 8.2, curves 1 and 3 illustrate monotonic sigma convergence from above. Curve 2 illustrates monotonic sigma convergence from below. Curve 4 illustrates sigma convergence with overshooting.

9. This subsection is based on subsections 8.5.2 and 8.5.4.

10. This section is based on section 8.3.

11. The following equations are based on equation 47 in chapter 8.

12. This section is based on section 8.4.

Chapter 5

1. Sugden (2008) interprets Hume along the lines I suggest. This is strange because Sugden is a co-author of Bardsley et al. 2010. Indeed, in private correspondence Sugden writes that he authored the relevant chapter in Bardsley et al. 2010. But when he wrote that "David Hume is another candidate for the experimental economists' Hall of Fame" (ibid., p. 4), he was referring to Hume's discovery of anomalies in rational decision-making behavior, rather than to the "idea that controlled experiments can contribute to economics."

2. For the story behind this development, see Bruni and Sugden 2007.

3. Other examples involve randomized trials in schooling in India (Duflo 2007) and Colombia (Angrist et al. 2002). Indeed, much of "new development economics" consists of carrying out randomized trials in developing countries. Angrist and Pischke (2009) make an enthusiastic case for randomized field trials. However, even they recognize that problems of compliance turn randomized trials into quasi-experiments in which assignment to the treatment group or control group serve merely as instrumental variables for the identification of treatment effects. Surprisingly, Angrist and Pischke don't mention Hawthorne effects as a problem in social experimentation.

4. Jones (1992) questions whether Hawthorne effects are indeed present in the Haw-thorne Works data. Even if they aren't, Hawthorne effects remain a genuine methodologi-cal problem for experiments involving humans. They may apply to participants in the ultimatum game. They may also be present in random field trials, such as the de-worm-ing experiment in Kenya. The de-wormed children probably were aware that they were guinea pigs. If they improved their sanitary behavior to contribute to the experiment's success, de-worming would appear more effective than it was.

5. In his Nobel lecture, Heckman (2001) attributes partial identification to Smith and Welch (1986), but it is mostly associated with Manski (1989, 2003).

6. See equation 1 in chapter 2 and the discussion in section 8.2.

7. See section 10.2.

8. The bias equals $\rho(1-\beta^2)/(1+\rho\beta)$.

9. See subsection 10.3.2.

10. The classical regression assumptions are that X is independent of the residuals, that the variance of the residuals is constant, and that the residuals are independent of each other.

11. For example the Central Bureau of Statistics in Israel has matched the censuses of 1972, 1983, 1995, and 2008. People who were parents in 1972 may have been great-grandparents by 2008.

12. See section 10.4.

13. Most econometric textbooks include a chapter on GMM. See, e.g., Greene 2008.

14. This section draws on section 10.3.

15. Beenstock 2007, 2008, 2010a.

16. This section draws on section 10.12.

17. This section draws on section 10.5.

18. See Angrist and Evans 1998.

19. Angrist and Lavy 1999.

20. This section draws on section 10.11.

21. See equations 67 in chapter 10.

22. I have assumed in table 5.5 that the variance of ε for siblings is identical. The OLS estimate of λ is equal to the sibling correlation as defined in equation 49 in chapter 10.

23. Methodological issues involved in identifying peer-group effects are discussed in section 10.8.

24. $P = PP_1 + (1 - P)P_0$; therefore $P = P_0/(1 - P_1 + P_0)$.

25. See Crowley 2000.

26. The phenomenon of spurious regression was discovered by Yule (1896). Subse-quently, Yule (1926) discovered the nonsense regression phenomenon, which arises when, although the means don't vary over time, the variances depend on time. However, it took many years until Phillips (1986) provided the statistical theory for these

phenomena, which arise when the data are non-stationary. For an advanced treatment of this topic, see Hamilton 1994; for an intermediate treatment, see Enders 2010.

27. Beenstock, Paldor, and Reingewertz (2010) show that the greenhouse-gas effect is spurious.

28. Calibration was introduced into macroeconomics by Kydland and Prescott (1982), who used calibration to develop a new theory of business cycles. The methodology of calibration was subsequently adopted by many macroeconomists (Dave and DeJong 2007). Many economists, including Heckman (1996) and Pagan (1994), remain skeptical about the contribution of calibration to hypothesis testing. So do I.

Chapter 6

1. Data mining is discussed in chapters 7 and 10.

2. See, e.g., Hack et al. 1995; Conley and Bennett 2000; Behrman and Rosenzweig 2003.

3. Had they been marginally not significant, would they have been published?

4. Chaloupka and Warner 2000. Econometric estimates of the price elasticity of demand for cigarettes are typically of the order of –0.7; an increase in the price of 1 percent lowers demand by 0.7 percent.

5. Unfortunately their evidence is weakened by large standard errors of the coefficients. In their first-stage regressions, R^2 is only about 0.03. Therefore, smoking status is weakly related to cigarette taxes, and the instrumental variables may be "weak." Weak instruments may induce spurious identification of treatment effects in natural experiments (Bound, Jaeger, and Baker 1995). Staiger and Stock (1997) suggest that the instrumental variables are weak if the F statistic of the first-stage regression is less than 10. Evans and Ringel do not discuss this issue. Since their sample size is enormous (10.5 million), I calculate the F statistic to be about 65,000, which is clearly significant. Therefore, technically the instruments aren't weak. The t statistics in the second-stage regressions are barely significant; they vary between –2.04 and –2.65 for birth weight and less than this for low and very low birth weight. Evans and Ringel argue that this results from the fact that cigarette taxes don't vary much (the standard deviation is 7.8 cents in 1982–1984 dollars).

6. Discussed in chapters 5 and 10.

7. The results refer to the pooled estimates for all four states. However, the results are statistically significant only for Michigan in the case of birth weight and only for Michigan and Arizona in the case of low birth weight.

8. See chapters 5 and 10 on fixed-effects and panel-data methods.

9. In model 3 in table 1 of Conley and Bennet 2000 there are 8,213 observations, whereas in the fixed-effects model there are 987 observations. Since the samples of the two models differ, it is not possible to calculate a likelihood ratio test. To compare the two models it is necessary to estimate model 3 using the same observations as in the fixed-effects model. Since the two models are non-nested, a comparison of the two models may be carried out using non-nested tests.

10. Strictly speaking fetal growth which is the rate of fetal weight gain allowing for the fact that gestation varies.

11. To see this, let Y_{is} denote mortality of sibling s in family i, and denote birth weight by X_{is}. The family fixed-effects model is $Y_{is} = \alpha_i + \beta X_{is} + u_{is}$, where the family fixed effect α_i measures parenting ability. Abler parents have lower α_i, and if mortality varies inversely with birth weight then β is expected to be negative. The OLS residual is $v_{is} = \alpha_i + u_{is}$. If α_i varies inversely with birth weight (i.e., abler parents have lighter babies), v_{is} and X_{is} are inversely related and the OLS estimate of β is biased downward.

12. In principle, it is possible to take account of sample selection bias. (See chapter 10.) This would involve using data on the non-consenting mothers as well as the consenting mothers. However, developmental psychologists working in this area generally ignore the matter, and even seem to be unaware of the issue.

13. Based on a 34-item questionnaire completed by mothers.

14. They also report that fussiness, time-to-calm, and mother's involved contact vary inversely with parity. Also, mothers' time-to-intervene is shorter for irritable girls than for boys.

15. Prediction is equivalent to Granger causality (discussed in section 10.16).

16. This means that in equation 2 Y_1 varies directly with v.

17. Their table 1 doesn't distinguish between parents who received PTT and parents who didn't.

18. See their table 3.

19. He shows that specifying IQ in a human capital model for earnings reduces the return to schooling, which implies that schooling varies directly with IQ.

20. Let S_i denote years of schooling of individual i and let N_i denotes sibship. The OLS regression is $S_i = \alpha + \beta N_i + u_i$, where embodies learning ability. If $\beta = 0$, its OLS estimate will be negative if the covariance between N and u is negative.

21. Bingley et al. report that the causal effect of fathers' schooling on their children's schooling is negative.

22. Examples include Dearden et al. 1997, Sacerdote 2002 and 2007, Plug 2004, Björklund et al. 2006, and Holmlund et al. 2008.

23. For a discussion of related natural experiments, see Björklund and Salvanes 2010.

24. See Beenstock 2007 and Pagan 1986.

25. Table 6.2 implies that $Y_c = 0.089 Y_p + x$. Therefore, $\text{cov}(Y_c Y_p) = 0.089 \text{ var}(Y_p) + \text{cov}(x Y_p)$. Since $r_{cp} = \text{cov}(Y_p Y_c)/\text{sd}(Y_c)\text{sd}(Y_p)$, we get that $r = 0.089\text{sd}(Y_p)/\text{sd}(Y_c) = 0.17$, assuming $\text{cov}(x Y_p) = 0$ and given the decrease in inequality in schooling between the generations.

26. According to table 6.2 the variance of the logarithm of earnings is equal to $0.115^2 = 0.013$ times the variance of schooling.

27. The size effects are much smaller, which suggests that households in which both spouses worked in 1983 behave differently than households in which only the head of household worked.

28. See the discussion in chapter 3.

29. Maybe there is less policing in "good" neighborhoods, and therefore the probability of arrest is smaller.

30. If MTHC housing were randomly assigned, this result would be expected, since the treatment effect should be independent of observable heterogeneity.

31. The t statistics are –1.71 for dropping out before twelfth grade, 2.1 for matriculation, and 2.33 for attending a good high school.

32. The t statistics are 2.14 for math scores and 2.57 for verbal scores. Other results are on the verge of significance. For example, probability of reaching eleventh grade without grade repetition (t statistic = 1.74 for math score), probability of dropping out before completing twelfth grade (t statistic = –1.74 math score and –1.94 verbal score), quality of high school attended (t statistic = 1.58), and probability matriculation (t statistic = 2.1 for high-percentile math scores). Nevertheless, Gould et al. conclude: "Overall, our results indicate that Ethiopian immigrant children who were placed in a better elementary school environment . . . tend to perform better in high school, both in terms of progressing through the system without repeating grades, and in terms of achievements in matriculation exams." (2004, p. 520)

33. The same authors, Gould et al. (2011), use a similar research design to study the long-term causal effects of environments on a variety of social and economic outcomes. Operation Magic Carpet airlifted over 50,000 Yemenite Jews during 1949–1951. They too were allocated rather haphazardly across the country. In 2006 Gould et al. interviewed nearly 3,000 Magic Carpet immigrants who were between 56 and 61 years old and found that female immigrants who had grown up in better environments (home with running water, toilet, and electricity, and not in an immigrant enclave) were more likely to matriculate, to obtain higher education (college or university), to have fewer children, and to be more assimilated into Israeli society.

34. The regression coefficient is 0.068 with a t statistic of 2.34.

35. Similar results have been found by Zimmerman (2003) for freshmen at Williams College. Here too the peer-group effect is small. Students in the middle of the verbal SAT distribution do worse if their roommate is in the bottom 15 percent of the SAT distribution.

36. See equation 8.4, which assumes that genes and environments play no role in the intergenerational transmission mechanism. See also table 3.1.

37. By solving for b from $b^2 + [2(1 - r_{cp}^2)/(r_{cp}^2 - r_{cs})]b + 1 = 0$.

38. See equation 53 in chapter 8.

39. Since $r_c = 2\lambda/(1 + \lambda^2)$, the solution for λ is $(1 - \sqrt{1 - r_c^2})/r$.

Chapter 7

1. Backward stepwise regression proceeds by successively eliminating covariates that are statistically insignificant. Forward stepwise regression proceeds by successively adding covariates that are most statistically significant. It is well known that, because the final model is path-dependent, the arbitrariness of the search process influences the results. The LASSO method (Tishbirani 1996) refines forward stepwise regression by optimally updating the parameter estimates of the incumbent covariates at each stage. This means that some covariates might be subsequently dropped form the model. LASSO models are therefore less path-dependent. The "general-to-specific" method (Hendry 1995; based on Leamer 1987) is also a stepwise specification search procedure in which hypotheses are tested. All these stepwise procedures are infeasible in the case of

genome-wide association studies, since the number of parameters exceeds (by far) the number of observations.

2. $t = [\sqrt{N}\,(\bar{Y} - \mu_0)]/\text{sd} = [\sqrt{20}\,(12 - 10)]/2 = 4.4721$.

3. $z = [(10 + 2.093) - 15]/2 = -1.4535$, where Prob $z < 1.4535 = 0.073$.

4. Such as Beauchamp et al. (2011).

5. This model is discussed in subsection 10.15.1.

6. White shows that much of the "evidence" against the Efficient Markets Hypothesis in financial economics results from data mining. Researchers obtained spurious results by using naive p values rather than corrected p values.

7. Details of this case are discussed in section 10.15.

Chapter 8

1. For a useful introduction to time-series models, see chapter 2 of Enders 2010. Almost every introductory textbook on econometrics includes a chapter on time-series models; for an example, see chapter 12 of Stock and Watson 2003.

2. For a discussion of stationarity, see Enders 2010.

3. For useful descriptions of the algebra of lag operators, see Enders 2010 and Sargent 1976.

4. This specification was originally suggested by Becker and Tomes (1976).

5. If the variance is constant, ε is said to be *homoscedastic*. If the variance is not constant, ε is said to be *heteroscedastic*.

6. Kurtosis is measured by the fourth moment, defined as $E[(\varepsilon - E(\varepsilon)]^4$, divided by the variance squared. For the normal distribution this ratio is 3. If the ratio exceeds 3, there is excess kurtosis.

7. If the distribution is symmetric, the third moment, defined as $E[(\varepsilon - E(\varepsilon)]^3$, is 0. The distribution is skewed to the right when the third moment is positive.

8. See the analogous discussion relating to figure 2.1, in which $Y^* = 0$.

9. For more on Wold representation theory, see Enders 2010.

10. The conditional variance is conditional on $\text{var}(G_p)$. The unconditional variance is the variance that is not conditional on $\text{var}(G_p)$.

11. On solution techniques for second-order stochastic difference equations, see Sargent 1976 and Enders 2010. By partial fractions,

$$\frac{1}{(1 - \lambda_1 L)(1 - \lambda_2 L)} = \frac{1}{\lambda_1 - \lambda_2}\left(\frac{\lambda_1}{1 - \lambda_1 L} - \frac{\lambda_2}{1 - \lambda_2 L}\right).$$

12. Autoregressive moving average models are denoted by ARMA(p, q), where p refers to the autoregressive order and q to the moving average order.

13. Here too the arbitrary constants of integration, which tend to 0 over time, are omitted for convenience.

14. Note that $\sigma_\epsilon^2/\text{var}(Y_c) = 1 - r_{cp}^2$.

15. The probit model is the main alternative to the logit model. The probit model assumes that unobservables such as genetic endowments are normally distributed, whereas the logit model assumes them to have a logistical distribution. See, e.g., chapter 14 of Cameron and Trivedi 2005.

16. Because D_A and D_B are dummy variables, $\text{var}(D_A) = P_A(1 - P_A)$, $\text{var}(D_B) = P_B(1 - P_B)$ and $\text{cov}(D_A D_B) = P_A P_B$.

17. Cowell 1977 is a useful reference.

18. As was noted in chapter 4, the coefficient was first published by Corrado Gini in 1912.

19. The instrumental-variables estimator is discussed in chapter 10.

20. Spearman and Kendall rank correlations are standard features in most textbooks on statistics. On b, see Bartholomew 1982.

Chapter 9

1. On the Rotten Kid Theorem, see pp. 8–14 and chapter 8 of Becker 1991.

2. This section draws on Beenstock 2010a.

3. Becker (1991) assumes paternalism since parents decide their children's schooling. Here I assume that parents cannot force schooling on their children, especially not secondary and tertiary education.

4. In Becker 1991, parental income doesn't determine schooling when the capital market is perfect. In the present model, parents' income matters because it determine the rate of subsidy (π) and children decide their schooling instead of parents.

5. The same result may be obtained if children's preferences for education depend on their parents' schooling.

6. This section draws on Beenstock 2007.

7. If $J()$ is log-linear (Cobb-Douglas) so that $W = A^a H^h$, then $\xi = 0$. If $J()$ is CES so that $W = [aA^d + hH^d]^{1/d}$, with $d \leq 1$, then $\xi = -had(HA)^{d-1}[\ ]^{-2}$, which is positive when $d < 0$.

8. When a price happens to fall, purchasing power increases. The "income effect" refers to how this extra purchasing power is spent on rival goods or activities.

9. This generalizes the polar allocation rules discussed by Sheshinsi and Weiss (1982). In the first of those rules, parents are *ex ante* egalitarian; they maximize the combined utilities of their children. In the second, parents are *ex post* egalitarian; they maximize the minimum utility of their less fit child. The former implies that $\beta = 0$. The latter implies that $\beta = \infty$.

10. This section draws on Beenstock 2010b.

11. For an introduction to game theory, see Dixit and Nalebuff 1991.

12. Nash equilibrium arises when players in a game do not wish to deviate from their plays or their behavior.

13. When $\kappa_A = \kappa_B$ and $\beta_A = \beta_B$.

14. Recall François Truffaut's film *L'enfant sauvage*.

15. See, e.g., Cassidy 1994 or Thompson 1994.

16. S_a captures "nature"; S_p captures "nurture."

17. As claimed by Harris (1998).

18. For convenience, S_0 has been normalized to 0.

19. On the dynamic optimization techniques used here, and especially on the Maximum Principle, see Hocking 1991.

Chapter 10

1. For a discussion of attenuation bias, see Cameron and Trivedi 2005.

2. Longitudinal surveys such as the Panel Study of Income Dynamics were discussed in chapter 2.

3. In this chapter, as elsewhere, p labels parents, c labels children, g labels grandparents, gg labels great-grandparents, s labels siblings, and i labels individuals.

4. See, e.g., Greene 2007 or Cameron and Trivedi 2005.

5. Attributed to Cochrane and Orcutt (1949). The Cochrane-Orcutt procedure features in most econometrics textbooks.

6. This result has also been noted by Becker and Tomes (1986).

7. See, e.g., chapter 7 of Borjas 1996.

8. Details about IV may be found in any textbook on econometrics, such as Cameron and Trivedi 2005. For a comparison of IV and GMM, see subsection 10.1.3.

9. For a more detailed discussion of the relationship between natural experiments and IV, see Angrist and Pischke 2009.

10. The econometrics of panel data is discussed in section v of Cameron and Trivedi 2005, in chapter 9 of Greene 2008, and in Baltagi 2005.

11. For further discussion of heterogeneity and the random coefficients model, see p. 97 of Cameron and Trivedi 2005.

12. For further discussion of seemingly unrelated regression, see pp. 209–210 of Cameron and Trivedi 2005.

13. For further discussion of selectivity and selection bias, see chapter 16 of Cameron and Trivedi 2005 and chapter 24 of Greene 2008.

14. On discrete choice, see chapters 14 and 15 of Cameron and Trivedi 2005, chapter 23 of Greene 2008, Ben Akiva and Lerman 1985, and Train 2003.

15. In equations 67 w is assumed to be normally distributed, whereas in equation 66 it is assumed to have a logistic or Gumbel distribution. For the case in which w has a logistic distribution in equation 67a, see Dubin and McFadden 1984.

16. Eyal and Beenstock (2008) show that arbitrary parametric assumptions in the specification of selectivity and discrete choice can even reverse the sign of the estimated parameter of interest.

17. A popular misspecification test for linearity is due to Ramsey (1969). Silva (2001) discusses tests of parametric alternatives in discrete choice models.

18. These varieties and forms are discussed in Manski 2003, where equations 73 are also extended to the case where Y is continuous rather than discrete. On partial identification in the treatment of drug addicts, see Beenstock 2010c.

19. For a useful summary and review, see Purcell 2001.

20. Using the rule $E(YX) = E(Y)E(X) + cov(YX)$.

21. Goldberger (1977) does not discuss the sibling gene-environment cross-correlation.

22. See Jencks 1972, appendix A. Here I present the basic outline of Jencks' model, in the same simplified spirit in which Goldberger (1977) presented the related model of Jencks and Brown (1977).

23. For further details about GWAS, see chapter 7 above.

24. The concepts of weak exogeneity and Granger causality that are used in this section are discussed in Enders 2010.

Terms and Concepts

Absolute intergenerational mobility   The change in an outcome relative to the mean between two generations. For example, upward mobility occurs when years of schooling for children relative to mean schooling for children exceeds years of schooling for parents relative to mean schooling for parents. In contrast to *relative intergenerational mobility*.

Assortative mating   Spouses choose each other on the basis of their characteristics. For example, fitter or more educated men mate with fitter or more educated women. In contrast to *random mating*.

Attenuation bias   A statistical bias that is induced by mismeasurement in correlated data. If the correlation is positive, attenuation bias induces under-estimation of the correlation. If the correlation is negative, attenuation bias induced over-estimation of the correlation. Attenuation bias does not affect the direction of the correlation.

Attrition   The loss of subjects from longitudinal data.

Autocorrelation   Dependence of random variables on their previous values. For example, first-order autocorrelation occurs when the current value depends on the first lagged value.

Axiomatic theory   Theory that is based on primitive axioms, such as rationality and survival of the fittest. In contrast to *ad hoc theory*, which is based on empirical observation.

Behavioral genetics   Study of the phenotypes of identical and fraternal twins and adopted and biological siblings with the objective of quantifying heritability.

Beta convergence   The process by which variables converge on a fixed mean over time. In contrast to *beta divergence*, in which variables do not converge on a fixed mean. Also known as *mean reversion*.

Compliance   In randomized trials it is not possible to force people to comply. The control subjects might obtain the treatment independently, and the trial subjects might refuse to take the treatment.

Conditional inequality   Inequality in the current generation conditional on (given) inequality in the previous generation. In contrast to *unconditional inequality* and *structural inequality*.

Data-generating process (DGP)   A stochastic (random) process by which time-series data are generated. For example, genotypes of children depend on their parents' genotype plus a random draw from the gene pool.

Data mining   Searching data for statistical models that maximize goodness of fit.

Developmental psychology (developmentalism)   Study of the psychological development of infants, children, and youths.

Econometrics   Statistical theory designed to test causal hypotheses with observational data.

Elasticity   The percentage change in one variable induced by a percentage change in another.

Endogenous   Correlated with the regression residuals. The opposite of *exogenous*.

Endogenous parenting   An axiomatic theory of parenting that predicts how parents behave toward their children.

Epigenetic drift   The process by which identical twins become genetically dissimilar as they age.

Equal-environments assumption (EEA)   An assumption in behavioral genetics according to which the correlation between sibling environments is the same for identical and fraternal twins and adopted and biological siblings.

Equal gene-environment assumption (EGEA)   The assumption that the gene-environment correlation is the same for pairs of identical twins and pairs of fraternal twins. Also the assumption that the gene-environment correlation is the same for pairs of adopted siblings and pairs of biological siblings.

Errors-in-variables estimation   Estimation of parameters that takes account of measurement error in the data.

Exogenous   Independent of the regression residuals. The opposite of *endogenous*.

Gene-environment correlation   A concept in behavioral genetics referring to the correlation induced by the dependence of environments on genotypes. For example, musically gifted children are more likely to attend music school.

Gene-environment interaction   A concept in behavioral genetics referring to the sensitivity of phenotypes to the interplay of genotypes and environments. For example, individuals genetically predisposed to hay fever sneeze more in flower gardens.

Generated regressor   A regressor that cannot be observed directly and is represented by an estimate.

Genome-wide association study (GWAS)   Statistical searching of the genome for genetic markers that are correlated with phenotypes.

Genotype   Genetic characterization of individuals' genetic endowments.

Gini coefficient   A measure of inequality that is bounded between 0 (complete equality) and 1 (complete inequality). In contrast to the *variance*, which has no upper bound.

Gini regression   Regression in which the dependent variable is regressed on the rank of the independent variable. In contrast to *ordinary least squares*.

Hawthorne effect   The effect of an experiment on the participants in the experiment such that the results of the experiment are distorted.

Identically and independently distributed (iid) variables   Random variables, with fixed variance, that are not autocorrelated.

Identification   The process by which a causal effect is estimated without bias using observational data.

Innatism   A concept, invented by John Locke, that refers to the belief that humans are born with pre-existing knowledge. The opposite of *tabula rasa*.

Instrumental variable   A variable that is correlated with an endogenous regressor but is not directly correlated with the dependent variable.

Instrumental variables (IV) estimator   An estimator that uses instrumental variables to randomize the covariates, in contrast to the *ordinary least squares* method.

Longitudinal data   Samples consisting of repeated observations over time of the same individuals or families. Also known as *panel data*.

Mean reversion   See *beta convergence*.

Nash equilibrium   When players in a game have no incentive to deviate from their plays.

Observational data   Data based on observing actual behavior outside an experimental setting.

Ordinary least squares (OLS) estimate   The estimate of the regression slopes and intercept that minimizes the residual sum of squares.

Natural experiment   A natural occurrence that differentially randomizes covariates that are hypothesized to affect outcomes. For example, twin births randomize family size, since twin births are unplanned.

Nature vs. nurture   The dichotomy between outcomes' being determined by heredity and genetics (nature) and outcomes' being by environments such as parenting, family, and neighborhoods (nurture).

Nuisance parameter   A parameter of no intrinsic interest that may bias estimates of the parameters of interest.

Phenotype   An outcome such as health, income, or fertility.

Phenotype-environment sensitivity   The reaction of phenotypes to environments, which differs between individuals—that is, people respond differently to identical environments.

Panel data   See *longitudinal data*.

Partial identification   Using observational data, a causal effect is identified ambiguously to fall within a bound. In contrast to *point identification*, which is unambiguous.

Pure sibling correlation   Correlation between siblings induced solely by their mutual influence.

Quality vs. Quantity Theory (QQT)   An axiomatic theory of fertility according to which parents decide on the number of children (quantity) and their investment in each child (quality). More quantity means less quality, so parents trade off quality and quantity.

Quasi-experiments   Occurrences that induce randomness in participation in treatments and programs. For example, the fact that cigarette taxes reduce smoking in a way that is independent of smoking reveals the effect of smoking on an outcome of interest (e.g., health).

Randomized trial   To evaluate the effect of a program on some outcome, the program is offered to a random sample of the population (the trial group) but is withheld from the population as a whole (the control group).

Reflection bias   Statistical bias in the estimate of a parameter induced by the fact that two or more individuals are mutually influential.

Relative mobility   Refers to the change in the rank (position in the distribution) of an outcome, such as income or height, between two points in time for the same individual, or between generations. In contrast to *absolute mobility*.

Resilience   The ability of children to cope with life's problems.

Rotten Kid Theorem   A theorem that predicts that it is in the enlightened self-interest of children to cooperate with their parents. More generally, it is in the self-interest of beneficiaries to cooperate with their benefactors.

Selection bias   Statistical bias induced by samples that are not random.

Sigma convergence   A process by which the standard deviation decreases over time.

Sociobiology   Study of animal behavior based on the axiom of fitness maximization.

State of nature   A concept, invented by Rousseau, that refers to a situation that would arise if children did not have parents or families.

Structural inequality   The average level of inequality toward which inequality tends over many generations. Also called *unconditional inequality*.

Symmetry   The simplifying assumption that different individuals have the same parameters.

Tabula rasa   A concept invented by John Locke and also referred to as *blank slate*. The belief that people are born with no knowledge, and that knowledge is acquired only through experience. The opposite of *innatism*.

Variables, Subscripts, and Greek Letters

Variables

cov covariance

E environment

e random component of the environment

G genotype

L lag operator

r correlation coefficient

sd standard deviation

u regression residual

var variance

X covariate

Y phenotype

Subscripts

c children

g grandparents

gg great-grandparents

i family

j degree of ancestry

p parents

s sibling

t time (measured in generations)

Greek Letters

β   mean reversion coefficient

ε   random draw from the gene pool

φ   intergenerational transmission coefficient of environments

λ   sibling interaction coefficient

ρ   coefficient of genotypic heredity

σ   standard deviation of ε

Bibliography

Akabayashi, H. 2006. An Equilibrium Model of Child Maltreatment. *Journal of Economic Dynamics & Control* 30: 993–1025.

Altonji, J. G., and T. A. Dunn. 1996. Using Siblings to Estimate the Effect of School Quality on Wages. *Review of Economics and Statistics* 78: 665–671.

Angrist, J. D. 1990. Lifetime Earnings and the Vietnam Era Draft Lottery: Evidence from Social Security Administrative Records. *American Economic Review* 80: 313–335.

Angrist, J. D. 2001. Instrumental Variables and the Search for Identification: From Supply and Demand to Natural Experiments. *Journal of Economic Perspectives* 15: 69–85.

Angrist, J. D., E. Bettinger, E. Bloom, E. King, and M. Kremer. 2002. Vouchers for Private Schooling in Colombia: Evidence from a Randomized Natural Experiment. *American Economic Review* 92: 1535–1558.

Angrist, J. D., and W. N. Evans. 1998. Children and Their Parents' Labor Supply: Evidence from Exogenous Variation in Family Size. *American Economic Review* 90: 431–442.

Angrist, J. D., and V. Lavy. 1999. Using Miamonides' Rule to Estimate the Effect of Class Size on Scholastic Achievement. *Quarterly Journal of Economics* 114: 533–575.

Angrist, J. D., V. Lavy, and A. Schlosser. 2010. Multiple Experiments for the Causal Link Between the Quantity and Quality of Children. *Journal of Labor Economics* 28: 1–52.

Angrist, J. D., and J.-S. Pischke. 2009. *Mostly Harmless Econometrics: an Empiricist's Companion*. Princeton University Press.

Anselin, J. L. 1988. *Spatial Econometrics*. Kluwer.

Ashenfelter, O., and C. Rouse. 2000. Schooling, Intelligence, and Income in America. In *Meritocracy and Economic Inequality*, ed. K. Arrow, S. Bowles, and S. Durlauf. Princeton University Press.

Atkinson, A. B. 1970. On the Measurement of Inequality. *Journal of Economic Theory* 2: 244–263.

Atkinson, A. B., A. K. Maynard, and C. G. Trinder. 1983. *Parents and Children: Incomes in Two Generations*. Heinemann.

Atkinson, R. L., et al. 2000. *Hilgard's Introduction to Psychology*, thirteenth edition. Harcourt College Publications.

Balatagi, B. 2009. *Econometric Analysis of Panel Data*, fourth edition. Wiley.

Bandura, A. 1977. *Social Learning Theory*. Prentice-Hall.

Bardsley, N., R. Cubitt, G. Loomes, P. Moffat, C. Starmer, and R. Sugden. 2010. *Experimental Economics: Rethinking the Rules*. Princeton University Press.

Barro, R. J., and G. S. Becker. 1988. A Reformulation of the Economic Theory of Fertility. *Quarterly Journal of Economics* 103: 1–25.

Barro, R.J. and Sala-I-Martin, X. 2004. *Economic Growth*, second edition. MIT Press.

Bartholomew, D. J. 1973. *Stochastic Models for Social Processes*, third edition. Wiley.

Beauchamp, J. P., D. Cesarini, M. Johannesson, M. J. H. M. van der Loos, P. D. Koellinger, P. J. F. Groenen, J. H. Fowler, J. N. Rosenquist, A. R. Thurik, and N. Christakis. 2011. Molecular Genetics and Economics. *Journal of Economic Perspectives* 25.

Becker, G. S. An Economic Analysis of Fertility. 1960. In *Demographic and Economic Change in Developing Countries*, ed. G. Becker. Princeton University Press.

Becker, G. S. 1964. *Human Capital: A Theoretical and Empirical Analysis with Special Reference to Education*. Columbia University Press.

Becker, G. S. 1965. A Theory of the Allocation of Time. *Economic Journal* 75: 493–517.

Becker, G. S.1991. *Treatise on the Family*, second edition. Harvard University Press.

Becker, G. S., and H. Gregg Lewis. 1973. On the Interaction Between the Quality and Quantity of Children. *Journal of Political Economy* 81: S279–S288.

Becker, G. S., and N. Tomes. 1986. Human Capital and the Rise and Fall of Families. *Journal of Labor Economics* 4: S1–S39.

Beenstock, M. 1980. *Neoclassical Theory of Macroeconomic Policy*. Cambridge University Press.

Beenstock, M. 2004. Rank and Quantity Mobility in the Empirical Dynamics of Inequality. *Review of Income and Wealth* 50: 519–541.

Beenstock, M. 2007. Do Abler Parents Have Fewer Children? *Oxford Economic Papers* 59: 430–457.

Beenstock, M. 2008. Deconstructing the Sibling Correlation: How Families Increase Inequality. *Journal of Family and Economic Issues* 29: 325–345.

Beenstock, M. 2010a. The Intergenerational Transmission of Inequality in Schooling and Earnings. *Journal of Income Distribution* 18: 118–141.

Beenstock, M.2010b. Crying Games in the Theory of Child Development. *European Journal of Developmental Psychology* 7: 717–745.

Beenstock, M. 2010c. Partial Evaluation with Observational Data: The Treatment of Drug Addicts. *Journal of Experimental Criminology* 6: 83–113.

Beenstock, M., and G. Rahav. 2002. Testing Gateway Theory: Do Cigarette Prices Affect Illicit Drug Use? *Journal of Health Economics* 21: 679–698.

Beenstock, M., Y. Reingewertz, and Paldor N. 2010. Polynomial cointegration tests of anthropogenic impacts on climate change. Mimeo, Hebrew University of Jerusalem.

Beenstock, M., B. R. Chiswick, and A. Paltiel. 2010. Testing the Immigrant Assimilation Hypothesis with Longitudinal Data. *Review of Economics of the Household* 8: 7–27.

Behrman, J. R., and M. R. Rosenzweig. 2002. Does Increasing Women's Schooling Raise the Schooling of the Next Generation? *American Economic Review* 92: 323–334.

Behrman, J. R., and M. R. Rosenzweig. 2001. The Returns to Increasing Body Weight. PIERS working paper 01-052, University of Pennsylvania.

Behrman, J. R., and M. R. Rosenzweig. 2004. Returns to Birthweight. *Review of Economics and Statistics* 86: 586–601.

Behrman, J. R., and P. Taubman. 1985. Intergenerational Earnings and Ability in the United States: Some Estimates and Tests of Becker's Intergenerational Endowments Model. *Review of Economics and Statistics* 67: 144–151.

Behrman, J. R., and P. Taubman. 1989. Is Schooling "Mostly in the Genes"? Nature-Nurture Decomposition Using Data on Relations. *Journal of Political Economy* 97: 1425–1446.

Bell, S. M., and M. D. Salter Ainsworth. 1972. Infant Crying and Maternal Responsiveness. *Child Development* 43: 1171–1190.

Ben Akiva, M. E., and S. R. Lerman. 1985. *Discrete Choice Analysis: Theory and Application to Travel Demand*. MIT Press.

Benjamin, L. T. 1997. *A History of Psychology*, second edition. McGraw-Hill.

Ben-Porath, Y. 1967. The Production of Human Capital over the Life Cycle. *Journal of Political Economy* 75: 352–365.

Bevan, D. L. 1979. Inheritance and the Distribution of Wealth. *Economica* 46: 381–402.

Bingley, P., K. Christensen, and V. M. Jensen. 2009. Parental Schooling and Child Development: Learning from Twin Parents. Working Paper 07, Danish National Centre for Social Research.

Björklund, A., and M. Jäntti. 1997. Intergenerational Income Mobility in Sweden Compared to the United States. *American Economic Review* 87: 1009–1018.

Björklund, A., T. Eriksson, M. Jäntti, O. Raum, and E. Österbaka. 2002. Brother Correlations in Earnings in Denmark, Finland, Norway and Sweden Compared to the United States. *Journal of Population Economics* 19: 757–772.

Björklund, A., M. Lindahl, and E. Plug. 2006. The Origins of Intergenerational Association: Lessons from Swedish Adoption Data. *Quarterly Journal of Economics* 121: 999–1026.

Björklund, A., M. Jäntti, and M. Lindquist. 2009. Family Background and Income during the Rise of the Welfare State: Brother Correlations in Income for Swedish Men Born 1932–1967. *Journal of Public Economics* 93: 671–680.

Björklund, A., and K. G. Salvanes. 2010. Education and Family Background: Mechanisms and Policies. Discussion Paper 5002, Institute for the Study of Labor (IZA).

Bjorklund, D., and T. K. Shackelford. 1999. Differences in Parental Investment Contribute to Important Differences Between Men and Women. *Current Directions in Psychological Science* 8: 86–89.

Black, S. E., P. J. Devereux, and K. G. Salvanes. 2005. The More the Merrier? The Effect of Family Size and Birth Order on Children's Education. *Quarterly Journal of Economics* 120: 669–700.

Black, S. E., P. J. Devereux, and K. G. Salvanes. 2005b. Why the Apple Doesn't Fall Far: Understanding Intergenerational Transmission in Human Capital. *American Economic Review* 95: 437–449.

Black, S. E., P. J. Devereux, and K. G. Salvanes. 2007. From the Cradle to the Labor Market? The Effect of Birth Weight on Adult Outcomes. *Quarterly Journal of Economics* 122: 409–439.

Black, S. E., P. J. Devereux, and K. G. Salvanes. 2008. Like Father Like Son? A Note on the Intergenerational Transmission of IQ Scores. NBER Working Paper 14274.

Booth, A. L., and H. J. Kee. 2009. Intergenerational Transmission of Fertility Patterns. *Oxford Bulletin of Economics and Statistics* 71: 183–208.

Borjas, G. J. 1996. *Labor Economics.* McGraw-Hill.

Bouchard, T. J., and M. McGue. 1981. Familial Studies of Intelligence: A Review. *Science* 212: 1055–1059.

Bound, J., D. Jaeger, and R. Baker. 1995. Problems with Instrumental Variable Estimation When the Correlation Between the Instruments and the Endogenous Variables Is Weak. *Journal of the American Statistical Association* 90: 433–450.

Bowlby, J. 1969. *Attachment and Loss.* Hogarth.

Bowles, S., and H. Gintis. 2002. Intergenerational Inequality. *Journal of Economic Perspectives* 16: 3–30.

Branãs-Garza, P., T. Garcia-Munõz, and S. Neuman. 2010. The Big Carrot: High Stakes Incentives Revisited. *Journal of Behavioral Decision Making* 23: 288–313.

Bronfenbrenner, U. 1979. *The Ecology of Human Development: Experiments by Nature and Design.* Harvard University Press.

Bruni, L., and R. Sugden. 2007. The Road Not Taken: How Psychology Was Removed from Economics, and How It Might Be Brought Back. *Economic Journal* 117: 146–173.

Bulmer, M. 2003. *Francis Galton: Pioneer of Heredity and Biometry.* Johns Hopkins University Press.

Cameron, C., and P. Trivedi. 2005. *Microeconometrics.* Cambridge University Press.

Caspi, A., J. McClay, T. E. Moffit, J. Mill, J. Martin, I. W. Craig, A. Taylor, and R. Poulton. 2002. Role of Genotype in the Cycle of Violence of Maltreated Children. *Science* 297: 851–854.

Carmichael, C. M., and M. McGue. 1994. A Longitudinal Study of Personality Change and Stability. *Journal of Personality* 62: 1–20.

Cassidy J.1994. *Emotion Regulation: Influences of Attachment Relationships.* Monographs of the Society for Research in Child Development 59 (2–3, serial no 240).

Cawley, J., J. Heckman, J. Lochner, and E. Vytlacil. 2000. Understanding the Role of Cognitive Ability in Accounting for the Recent Rise in the Economic Return to Education. In *Meritocracy and Economic Inequality*, ed. K. Arrow, S. Bowles, and S. Durlauf. Princeton University Press.

Cesur, R., and I. Rashid. 2008. High Birth Weight and Cognitive Outcomes. National Bureau of Economic Research, Working Paper 14524.

Chadwick, L., and G. Solon. 2002. Intergenerational Income Mobility among Daughters. *American Economic Review* 92: 335–344.

Chaloupka, F. J., and K. E. Warner. 2000. The Economics of Smoking. In *Handbook of Health Economics*, ed. J. Newhouse and A. Culyer. North Holland, Elsevier Science.

Christensen, K., T. E. Johnson, and J. W. Vaupel. 2006. The Quest for Genetic Determinants of Human Longevity. *Nature Reviews. Genetics* 7: 436–448.

Conley, D. 2004. *The Pecking Order*. Pantheon Books.

Conley, D., and N. G. Bennet. 2000. Is Biology Destiny? Birth Weight and Life Chances. *American Sociological Review* 65: 458–467.

Conley, D., and R. Glauber. 2008. All in the Family? Family Composition, Resources, and Similarity in Socioeconomic Status. *Research in Social Stratification and Mobility* 26: 297–306.

Corak, M., and A. Heisz. 1999. The Intergenerational Earnings and Income Mobility of Canadian Men: Evidence from Longitudinal Income Tax Data. *Journal of Human Resources* 34: 504–533.

Couch, K. A., and T. A. Dunn. 1997. Intergenerational Correlations in Labor Market Status: A Comparison of the United States and Germany. *Journal of Human Resources* 32: 210–230.

Cowell, F. A. 1977. *Measuring Inequality: Techniques for the Social Sciences*. Wiley.

Crockenberg, S. B., and P. Smith. 2002. Antecedents of Mother-Infant Interaction and Infant Irritability in the First 3 Months of Life. *Infant Behavior and Development* 25: 2–15.

Crook, M. N. 1937. Intra-family Relationships in Personality Test Performance. *Psychological Record* 1: 479–502.

Crowley, J. T. 2000. Causes of Climate Change over the Past 1000 Years. *Science* 289: 270–279.

Daniels, M., B. Devlin, and K. Roeder. 1997. Of Genes and IQ. In *Intelligence, Genes and Success*, edited by B. Devlin, S. Feinberg, D. Resnick, and K. Roeder. Springer-Verlag.

Dave, C., and D. DeJong. 2007. *Structural Macroeconomics*. Princeton University Press.

Davies, G., et al. 2011. Genome-Wide Association Studies Establish That Human Intelligence Is Highly Heritable and Polygenetic. *Molecular Psychiatry*, in press.

Dawkins, R. 1976. *The Selfish Gene*. Oxford University Press.

Dearden, L., S. Machin, and H. Reed. 1997. Intergenerational Mobility in Britain. *Economic Journal* 107: 47–66.

Diamond, J.1997. *Guns, Germs and Steel: the Fates of Human Societies*. Norton.

Diamond, S. 1997. Francis Galton and American Psychology. In *A History of Psychology*, second edition, ed. L. Benjamin. McGraw-Hill.

Dixit, A. K., and B. F. Nalebuff. 1991. *Thinking Strategically*. Norton.

Downs, A. 1957. *An Economic Theory of Democracy*. Harper.

Duflo, E. 2007 Remedying Education: Evidence from Two Randomized Experiments in India. *Quarterly Journal of Economics* 122: 1235–1264.

Easterlin, R. A. 1966. On the Relation of Economic Factors to Recent and Projected Fertility Changes. *Demography* 3: 131–153.

Eaves, L. J., P. K. Hatemi, E. C. Prom-Womley, and L. Murrelle. 2008. Social and Genetic Influences on Adolescent Religious Attitudes and Practices. *Social Forces* 86: 1623–1646.

Edin, P.-A., P. Fredriksson, and O. Åslund. 2003. Ethnic Enclaves and the Economic Success of Immigrants: Evidence from a Natural Experiment. *Quarterly Journal of Economics* 118: 329–357.

Enders, W. 2010. *Applied Econometric Time Series*, third edition. Wiley.

Ermisch, J. 2003. *An Economic Analysis of the Family*. Princeton University Press.

Ernst, C., and J. Angst. 1983. *Birth Order: Its Influence on Personality*. Springer-Verlag.

Etzel, B. C., and J. L. Gewirtz. 1967. Experimental Modification of Caretaker-Maintained High-Rate Operant Crying in a 6 and 10 Week Old Infant. *Journal of Experimental Child Psychology* 5: 303–317.

Evans, W. N., and J. S. Ringel. 1999. Can Higher Cigarette Taxes Improve Birth Outcomes? *Journal of Public Economics* 18: 135–154.

Eyal, Y., and M. Beenstock. 2008. Sign Reversal in the LIVE Treatment Effect Estimates: The Effect of Vocational Training on Unemployment Duration. *Labour Economics* 15: 1102–1125.

Farrington, D. P., J. W. Coid, and J. Murray. 2009. Family Factors in the Intergenerational Transmission of Offending. *Criminal Behaviour and Mental Health* 19: 109–124.

Feldman, R., C. Greenbaum, and N. Yirmiya. 1999. Mother-Infant Affect Synchrony as an Antecedent of the Emergence of Self-Control. *Developmental Psychology* 35: 223–231.

Flynn, J. R. 2000. IQ Trends over Time: Intelligence, Race and Meritocracy. In *Meritocracy and Economic Inequality*, ed. K. Arrow, S. Bowles, and S. Durlauf. Princeton University Press.

Foster, E. M. 2002. How Economists Think about Family Resources and Child Development. *Child Development* 73: 1904–1914.

Forrest, D. W. 1974. *Francis Galton: The Life and Work of a Victorian Genius*. Taplinger.

Galor, O., and O. Moav. 2002. Natural Selection and the Origin of Economic Growth. *Quarterly Journal of Economics* 117: 1133–1192.

Galton, F. 1869. *Hereditary Genius: An Enquiry into Its Laws and Consequences*. Macmillan.

Galton, F. 1874. *English Men of Science: Their Nature and Nurture*. Macmillan.

Galton, F. 1875. The History of Twins, as a Criterion of the Relative Powers of Nature and Nurture. *Journal of the Anthropological Institute* 5: 391–406.

Galton, F. 1883. *Inquiries into Human Faculty and its Development*. Macmillan.

Galton, F. 1885. Regression towards Mediocrity in Hereditary Stature. *Journal of the Anthropological Institute* 15: 246–263.

Gauthier, A. H., and J. Hatzius. 1997. Family Benefits and Fertility; an Econometric Analysis. *Population Studies* 51: 285–306.

Gazzaniga, M. S., and T. F. Heatherton. 2006. *Psychological Science*, second edition. Norton.

Glueck, S., and E. Glueck. 1950. *Unraveling Juvenile Delinquency.* Harvard University Press.

Goldberger, A. S. 1977. Twin Methods: A Skeptical View. In *Kinometrics: Determinants of Socioeconomic Success within and between Families*, ed. P. Taubman. North-Holland.

Goldberger, A. S. 1979. Heritability. *Economica* 46: 327–347.

Goldberger, A. S. 2005. Structural Equation Models in Human Behavior Genetics. In *Identification and Inference for Econometric Models: Essays in Honor of Thomas Rothenberg*, ed. D. Andrews and J. Stock. Cambridge University Press.

Goodall, J. 1986. *The Chimpanzees of Gombe: Patterns of Behavior.* Harvard University Press.

Gottesman, I. I. 1991. *Schizophrenia Genesis: The Origins of Madness.* W.H. Freeman.

Gottlieb, D., R. Frish, E. Toledano, and N. Zussman. 2009. The Effect of Child Benefit on Fertility. Discussion Paper 2009.13, Research Department, Bank of Israel. In Hebrew.

Gould, E. D. 2005. Inequality and Ability. *Labour Economics* 12: 169–189.

Gould, E. D., V. Lavy, and M. D. Paserman. 2004. Immigrating to Opportunity: Estimating the Effect of School Quality Using a Natural Experiment on Ethiopians in Israel. *Quarterly Journal of Economics* 119: 489–526.

Gould, E.D., Lavy, V and Paserman, M.D. 2011. Sixty Years after the Magic Carpet Ride: The Long-Run Effects of Early Childhood Environment on Social and Economic Outcomes. *Review of Economic Studies.*

Gould, E. D., and A. Simhon. 2011. Does Quality Time Produce Quality Children? Evidence on the Intergenerational Transmission of Human Capital using Parental Deaths. Discussion Paper 8258, Centre for Economic Policy Research.

Gould, S. J., and R. C. Lewontin. 1979. The Spandrels of San Marco and the Panglossian Program: A Critique of the Adaptionist Program. *Proceedings of the Royal Society of London* 205: 281–288.

Grawe, N. D., and C. B. Mulligan. 2002. Economic Interpretations of Intergenerational Correlations. *Journal of Economic Perspectives* 16: 45–58.

Greene, W. H. 2008. *Econometric Analysis*, sixth edition. Pearson Prentice Hall.

Guo, G., and L. K. VanWey. 1999. Sibship Size and Intellectual Development: Is the Relationship Causal? *American Sociological Review* 64: 169–187.

Hack, M., N. K. Klein, and G. Taylor. 1995. Long-Term Developmental Outcomes of Low Birth Weight Infants. *Future of Children* 5: 19–34.

Hacohen, M. H. 2000. *Karl Popper—The Formative Years, 1902–1945 Politics and Philosophy in Interwar Vienna.* Cambridge University Press.

Hagan, J., and A. Palloni. 1990. The Social Reproduction of a Criminal Class in Working-Class London, Circa 1950–1980. *American Journal of Sociology* 96: 265–299.

Hamilton, J. 1994. *Time Series Analysis*. Princeton University Press.

Hansen, L. P., and J. J. Heckman. 1996. The Empirical Foundations of Calibration. *Journal of Economic Perspectives* 10: 87–104.

Harris, J. R. 1998. *The Nurture Assumption: Why Children Turn Out the Way They Do*. Touchstone.

Harris, J. R. 2006. *No Two Alike*. Norton.

Hausman, J. A., and D. A. Wise, eds. 1985. *Social Experimentation*. University of Chicago Press.

Hayek, F. 1960. *The Constitution of Liberty*. Routledge & Kegan Paul.

Heckman, J. J. 1976. The Common Structure of Statistical Models of Truncation, Sample Selection, and Limited Dependent Variables and a Simple Estimator for Such Models. *Annals of Economic and Social Measurement* 5: 475–492.

Heckman, J. J. 2001. Microdata, Heterogeneity, and the Evaluation of Public Policy: Nobel Lecture. *Journal of Political Economy* 109: 673–748.

Hedges, L. V., and I. Olkin. 1985. *Statistical Methods for Meta-analysis*. Academic Press.

Hendry, D. F. 1995. *Dynamic Econometrics*. Oxford University Press.

Hendry, D. F., and M. Morgan, eds. 1995. *Foundations of Econometric Analysis*. Cambridge University Press.

Herrnstein, R. J., and C. Murray. 1994. *The Bell Curve: Intelligence and Class Structure in American Life*. Free Press.

Hertz, T., T. Jayaserunda, P. Piraino, S. Selcuk, N. Smith, and A. Veraschagina. 2007. The Inheritance of Educational Inequality: Intergenerational Comparisons and Fifty-Year Trends. *B.E. Journal of Economic Analysis and Policy (Advances)* 7: 10.

Hocking, L. M. 1991. *Optimal Control*. Clarendon.

Holmlund, H., M. H. Lindahl, and E. Plug. 2008. The Causal Effect of Parents' Schooling on Children's Schooling: A Comparison of Estimation Methods. IZA Discussion Paper 3630.

Hume, D. 1739. *A Treatise on Human Nature*. John Noon. Second edition, revised and annotated: Clarendon, 1978.

Insel, P. M. 1974. Maternal Effects on Personality. *Behavior Genetics* 4: 133–144.

Ioannides, J. P. A. 2005. Why Most Published Findings Are False. *PLoS Medicine* 2: 696–702.

Jahromi, L. B., S. P. Putnam, and C. A. Stifter. 2004. Maternal Regulation of Infant Reactivity from 2 to 6 Months. *Developmental Psychology* 40: 477–487.

Jäntti, M., and E. Österbacka. 1996. How Much of the Variance of Income Can Be Attributed to Family Background? Evidence from Finland. Working paper, Åbo Academy University.

Jencks, C. 1972. *Inequality: A Reassessment of the Effect of Family and Schooling in America*. Harper and Row.

Jencks, C., and M. Brown. 1977. Genes and Social Stratification. In *Kinometrics: Determinants of Socioeconomic Success within and between Families*, ed. P. Taubman. North-Holland.

Jones, S. R. G. 1992. Was There a Hawthorne Effect? *American Journal of Sociology* 98: 451–468.

Joseph, J. 1998. The Equal Environment Assumption of the Classical Twin Method: A Critical Analysis. *Journal of Mind and Behavior* 19: 325–358.

Juhn, C., K. M. Murphy, and B. Pierce. 1993. Wage Inequality and the Rise in Returns to Skill. *Journal of Political Economy* 101: 314–342.

Kamin, L. J., and A. S. Goldberger. 2002. Twin Studies in Behavioral Research: A Skeptical Review. *Theoretical Population Biology* 61: 83–95.

Kaufmann, R. K. and Stern, D. I. 2004. A Statistical Evaluation of Atmospheric-Ocean General Circulation Models: Complexity v Simplicity. Rensselaer Working Papers in Economics 0411.

Keynes, M., ed. 1993. Sir Francis Galton, FRS: The Legacy of His Ideas. Macmillan.

Kling, J. R., J. Ludwig, and L. F. Katz. 2005. Neighborhood Effects on Crime for Female and Male Youth: Evidence from a Randomized Housing Voucher Experiment. *Quarterly Journal of Economics* 120: 87–130.

Kochanska, G., and R. A. Thompson. 1997. The Emergence and Development of Conscience in Toddlerhood and Early Childhood. In *Parenting and Children's Internalization of Values: A Handbook of Contemporary Theory*, ed. J. Grusec and L. Kuczynski. Wiley.

Korenman, S., and C. Winship. 2000. A Reanalysis of The Bell Curve: Intelligence, Family Background, and Schooling. In *Meritocracy and Economic Inequality*, ed. K. Arrow, S. Bowles, and S. Durlauf. Princeton University Press.

Kraft, P., E. Zeggini, and J. P. A. Ioannidis. 2009. Replication in Genome-Wide Association Studies. *Statistical Science* 24: 561–573.

Kremer, M. 2003. Randomized Evaluations of Educational Programs in Developing Countries. *American Economic Review* 93: 102–106.

Kuhn, T. S. 1970. *The Structure of Scientific Revolutions*, second edition. New American Library.

Kydland, F., and E. S. Prescott. 1982. Aggregate Fluctuations and the Time to Build. *Econometrica* 50: 1345–1370.

Labeaga, J. S. 1999. A Double Hurdle Rational Addiction Model with Heterogeneity: Estimating the Demand for Tobacco. *Journal of Econometrics* 93: 49–72.

Lach, S., Ritov, Y. and Simhon, A. 2006. The Transmission of Longevity across Generations. Discussion Paper 06.01, Falk Institute for Economic Research in Israel.

Laland, K., and G. Brown. 2002. *Sense and Nonsense: Evolutionary Perspectives on Human Behaviour*. Oxford University Press.

Lander, E. S., and N. J. Schork. 1994. Genetic Dissection of Complex Traits. *Science* 265: 2037–2048.

Lazear, E. 2000. Economic Imperialism. *Quarterly Journal of Economics* 115: 99–146.

Leamer, E. E. 1978. *Specification Searches*. Wiley.

Lee, M.-J. 2005. *Microeconometrics for Policy, Program and Treatment Effects*. Oxford University Press.

Lien, D. S., and W. N. Evans. 2005. Estimating the Impact of Large Cigarette Tax Hikes: The Case of Maternal Smoking and Infant Birth Weight. *Journal of Human Resources* 40: 373–392.

Lillard, L. E., and R. J. Willis. 1994. Intergenerational Educational Mobility: Effects of Family and State in Malaysia. *Journal of Human Resources* 29: 1126–1166.

Liu, Y.-J., C. J. Papasian, J. Hamilton, and H.-W. Deng. 2008. Is Replication the Gold Standard for Validating Genome-Wide Findings? *PLoS ONE* 3: 1–7.

Lizzeri, A., and M. Siniscalchi. 2008. Parental Guidance and Supervised Learning. *Quarterly Journal of Economics* 123: 1161–1195.

Loeber, R., and T. Dishion. 1983. Early Predictors of Male Delinquency: A Review. *Psychological Bulletin* 94: 68–99.

Loehlin, J. C. 1992. *Genes and Environment in Personality Development*. Sage.

Loehlin, J. C. 2005. Resemblance in Personality and Attitudes between Parents and their Children: Genetics and Environmental Contributions. In *Unequal Chances, Family Background and Economic Success*, ed. S. Bowles, H. Gintis, and M. Osborne-Groves. Princeton University Press.

Long, C. D. 1958. *The Labor Force under Changing Income and Employment*. Princeton University Press.

Luce, R. D. 1959. *Individual Choice Behavior: a Theoretical Analysis*. Wiley.

Lynn, R., and T. Vanhanen. 2002. *IQ and Global Inequality*. Summit Publishers.

Maccoby, E. E. 2000. Parenting and Its Effects on Children: On Reading and Misreading Behavior Genetics. *Annual Review of Psychology* 51: 1–27.

Manski, C. F. 1989. Anatomy of the Selection Problem. *Journal of Human Resources* 24: 343–360.

Manski, C. F. 1995. *Identification Problems in the Social Sciences*. Harvard University Press.

Manski, C. F. 2003. *Partial Identification*. Praeger.

Manski, C. F., J. Pepper, and C. Petri. 2001. *Informing American Policy on Illegal Drugs*. National Research Council, National Bureau of Science.

Martin, M. A. 2008. The Intergenerational Correlation in Weight: How Genetic Resemblance Reveals the Social Roles of Families. *Journal of American Sociology* 114: 567–605.

Matheny, A. P. 1990. Developmental Behavior Genetics: Contributions from the Louisville Twin Study. In *Developmental Behavior Genetics: Neural, Biometrical and Evolutionary Approaches*, ed. M. Hahn, J. Hewitt, N. Henderson, and H. Benno. Oxford University Press.

Mayer, S. 1997. *What Money Can't Buy: Family Income and Life's Chances*. Harvard University Press.

Mazumder, B. 2008. Sibling Similarities and Economic Inequality in the US. *Journal of Population Economics* 21: 685–701.

McCloskey, D. 1983. The Rhetoric of Economics. *Journal of Economic Literature* 21: 481–517.

McGue, M., B. Hirsch, and D. Lykken. 1993. Age and the Self-Perception of Ability: A Twin Study Analysis. *Psychology and Aging* 8: 72–80.

Mcnown, R., and C. Ridao-cano. 2004. The Effect of Child Benefit Policy on Fertility and Female Labor Force Participation in Canada. *Review of Economics of the Household* 2: 237–254.

Medlund, P., R. Cederlof, B. Floderus-Myrhed, L. Friberg, and S. Sorensen. 1977. A New Swedish Twin Registry. *Acta Medica Scandinavica* 201, S600.

Mednick, S. A., W. F. Gabrielli, and B. Hutchings. 1984. Genetic Influences in Criminal Convictions: Evidence from an Adoption Cohort. *Science* 25: 891–894.

Menchik, P. L. 1979. Intergenerational Transmission of Inequality: An Empirical Study of Wealth Mobility. *Economica* 46: 349–362.

Miguel, E., and M. Kremer. 2003. Worms: Identifying Impacts on Education and Health in the Presence of Externalities. *Econometrica* 72: 159–217.

Miller, P. H. 1993. *Theories of Developmental Psychology*, third edition. Freeman.

Mincer, J. 1974. *Schooling, Experience and Earnings*. Columbia University Press.

Morgan, M. 1990. *The History of Econometric Ideas*. Cambridge University Press.

Mulligan, C. B. 1997. *Parental Priorities and Economic Inequality*. University of Chicago Press.

Murphy, M., and L. B. Kudsen. 2002. The Intergenerational Transmission of Fertility in Contemporary Denmark: The Effects of Number of Siblings (Full and Half), Birth Order, and Whether Male or Female. *Population Studies* 56: 235–248.

Neal, D. A., and W. R. Johnson. 1996. The Role of Pre-Market Factors in Black-White Wage Differences. *Journal of Political Economy* 104: 869–895.

Newcombe, R., B. J. Milne, A. Caspi, R. Poulton, and T. E. Moffit. 2007. Birth-Weight Predicts IQ: Fact or Artefact? *Twin Research and Human Genetics* 10: 581–586.

Nozick, R. 1974. *Anarchy, State and Utopia*. Basic Books.

Olneck, M. 1977. On the Use of Sibling Data to Estimate the Effects of Family Background, Cognitive Skills and Schooling: Results from the Kalamazoo Brothers Study. In *Kinometrics: Determinants of Socioeconomic Success within and between Families*, ed. P. Taubman. North-Holland.

Olkin, I., and S. Yitzhaki. 1992. Gini Regression Analysis. *International Statistical Review* 60: 185–196.

Olthof, T., E. S. Kunnen, and J. Boom. 2000. Simulating Mother-Child Interaction: Exploring two Varieties of a Nonlinear Dynamic Systems Approach. *Infant and Child Development* 9: 33–60.

Österbacka, E. 2001. Family Background and Economic Status in Finland. *Scandinavian Journal of Economics* 103: 467–484.

Oreopoulos, P. 2003. The Long-Run Consequences of Living in a Poor Neighborhood. *Quarterly Journal of Economics* 118: 1533–1575.

Oreopoulos, P., M. E. Page, and A. H. Stevens. 2006. Does Human Capital Transfer from Parent to Child? The Intergenerational Effects of Compulsory Schooling. *Journal of Labor Economics* 24: 729–760.

Pagan, A. 1984. Econometric Issues in the Analysis of Regressions with Generated Regressors. *International Economic Review* 25: 221–247.

Pagan, A. 1994. Calibration and Econometric Research: An Overview. *Journal of Applied Econometrics* 10: S1–S10.

Patinkin, D. 1965. *Money, Interest and Prices*, second edition. Harper & Row.

Patterson, G. R., and M. S. Fogatch. 1995. Predicting Future Clinical Adjustment from Treatment Outcome and Process Variables. *Psychological Assessment* 3: 275–285.

Permutt, T., and J. R. Hebel. 1989. Simultaneous Equation Estimation in a Clinical Trial of the Effect of Smoking on Birth Weight. *Biometrica* 45: 619–622.

Peters, H. E. 1992. Patterns of Intergenerational Mobility in Income and Earnings. *Review of Economics and Statistics* 74: 456–466.

Phelps Brown, H. 1988. *Egalitarianism and the Generation of Inequality*. Clarendon.

Phillips, P. C. B. 1986. Understanding Spurious Regressions in Econometrics. *Journal of Econometrics* 33: 311–340.

Pinker, S. 2002. *The Blank Slate: The Modern Denial of Human Nature*. Penguin.

Plomin, R., J. DeFries, G. E. McLearn, and P. McGuffin. 2001. *Behavioral Genetics*, fourth edition. Worth.

Plug, E. 2004. Estimating the Effect of Mothers' Schooling on Children's Schooling Using a Sample of Adoptees. *American Economic Review* 94: 358–368.

Plug, E., and W. Vijverberg. 2003. Schooling, Family Background and Adoption: Is It Nature or Nurture? *Journal of Political Economy* 111: 611–641.

Pluzhnikov, A., D. K. Nolan, Z. Tan, M. S. McPeek, and C. Ober. 2007. Correlation of Intergenerational Family Sizes Suggests a Genetic Component of Reproductive Fitness. *American Journal of Human Genetics* 81: 165–169.

Popper, K. R. 1963. *Conjectures and Refutations*. Routledge.

Popper, K. R. 1966. *Plato*, fifth edition, volume 1: The Open Society and Its Enemies. Routledge.

Price, A. L., N. J. Patterson, R. M. Plenge, M. E. Weinblatt, N. A. Shadwick, and D. Reich. 2006. Principal Components Analysis Corrects for Stratification in Genome-Wide Association Studies. *Nature Genetics* 38: 904–909.

Purcell, S. 2001. Statistical Methods in Behavioral Genetics. In *Behavioral Genetics*, fourth edition, ed. R. Plomin, J. DeFries, G. McLearn, and P. McGuffin. Worth.

Ramsay, J. B. 1969. Tests for Specification Errors in Classical Linear Least Squares Regression Analysis. *Journal of the Royal Statistical Society. Series B. Methodological* 31: 350–371.

Rawls, J. 1972. *A Theory of Justice*. Harvard University Press.

Reiersøl, O. 1941. Confluence Analysis by Means of Lag Moments and Other Methods of Confluence Analysis. *Econometrica* 6: 1–24.

Rodgers, J. L., H.-P. Kohler, K. O. Kyvik, and K. Christensen. 2001. Behavior Genetic Modelling of Human Fertility: Findings from a Contemporary Danish Twin Study. *Demography* 38: 29–42.

Rostow, W. W. 1960. *The Stages of Economic Growth: a Non-communist Manifesto*. Cambridge University Press.

Rousseau, J.-J. 1992. *The Collected Writings of Rousseau*, volume 3, ed. R. Masters and C. Kelly. University Press of New England.

Rowe, D. C., and D. P. Farrington. 1997. The Familial Transmission of Criminal Convictions. *Criminology* 35: 177–202.

Rutter, M. 2006. *Genes and Behavior: Nature-Nurture Interplay Explained*. Blackwell.

Rutter, M. 2007. *Scholastic Attainment following Severe Institutional Deprivation: A Study of Children Adopted from Romania*. Institute of Psychiatry, King's College.

Sacerdote, B. 2001. Peer Effects with Random Assignment: Results from Dartmouth Roommates. *Quarterly Journal of Economics* 116: 681–704.

Sacerdote, B. 2002. The Nature and Nurture of Economic Outcomes. *American Economic Review* 92 (2): 344–348.

Sacerdote, B. 2007. How Large Are the Effects from Changes in Family Environment? A Study of Korean-American Adoptees. *Quarterly Journal of Economics* 122: 119–157.

Samuelson, P. A. 1947. *Foundations of Economic Analysis*. Harvard University Press.

Sargent, T. 1976. *Macroeconomic Theory*. Academic Press.

Schechtman, E., and S. Yitzhaki. 1987. A Measure of Association Based on Gini's Mean Difference. *Communications in Statistics Theory and Methods* A16: 207–231.

Schott, J. R. 2005. A High-Dimensionality Test for the Equality of the Smallest Eignevalues of a Covariance Matrix. *Journal of Multivariate Analysis* 96: 827–843.

Schultz, T. W. 1963. *The Economic Value of Education*. Columbia University Press.

Schultz, T. R. 2003. *Computational Development Psychology*. MIT Press.

Sen, A. K. 1976. Poverty: An Ordinal Approach to Measurement. *Econometrica* 44: 219–231.

Sexton, M., and J. R. Hebel. 1984. A Clinical Trial of Change in Maternal Smoking and Its Effect on Birth Weight. *Journal of the American Medical Association* 251: 911–915.

Shea, J. 2000. Does Money Matter? *Journal of Public Economics* 77: 155–184.

Sheshinski, E., and Y. Weiss. 1982. Inequality Within and Between Families. *Journal of Political Economy* 90: 105–127.

Shields, C. L., and J. A. Shields. 1962. *Monozygotic Twins Brought- up Apart and Brought-up Together*. Oxford University Press.

Sieben, I., J. Huinink, and P. M. de Graaf. 2001. Family Background and Sibling Resemblance in Educational Attainment: Trends in the Former Federal Republic of Germany, the German Democratic Republic and the Netherlands. *European Sociological Review* 17: 401–430.

Siegmund, D., and B. Yakir. 2007. *The Statistics of Gene Mapping*. Springer.

Siegler, R., J. Deloache, and N. Eisenberg. 2003. *How Children Develop*. Worth.

Silva, J. 2001. A Score Test for Non-Nested Hypotheses with Applications to Discrete Response Models. *Journal of Applied Econometrics* 16: 577–598.

Sims, C. 1996. Macroeconomics and Methodology. *Journal of Economic Literature* 10: 105–120.

Skinner, B. F. 1953. *Science and Human Behavior*. Macmillan.

Smith, J. P., and F. Welch. 1986. *Closing the Gap: 40 Years of Economic Progress for Blacks*. Rand Corporation.

Smith, E., and F. Conrey. 2007. Agent-Based Modeling: A New Approach for Theory Building in Social Psychology. *Personality and Social Psychology Review* 11: 1–18.

Solon, G. 1992. Intergenerational Income Mobility in the United States. *American Economic Review* 82: 393–408.

Solon, G. 1999. Intergenerational Mobility in the Labor Market. In *Handbook in Labor Economics*, ed. O. Ashenfelter and D. Card. Elsevier.

Squire, L., and H. Van der Tak. 1984. *Economic Analysis of Projects*. Johns Hopkins University Press.

Sroufe, L. A. 1997. Psychopathology as an Outcome of Development. *Development and Psychopathology* 9: 251–268.

Staiger, D., and J. Stock. 1997. Instrumental Variables Regression with Weak Instruments. *Econometrica* 65: 557–586.

Stanley, T. D. 2005. Beyond Publication Bias. In *Meta-Regression Analysis: Issues in Publication Bias in Economics*, ed. C. Roberts and T. Stanley. Blackwell.

Stern, D. N. 1985. *The Interpersonal World of the Infant: A View from Psychoanalysis and Developmental Psychology*. Basic Books.

Stock, J. H., and M. H. Watson. 2003. *Introduction to Econometrics*. Addison-Wesley.

Sugden, R. 2008. Hume's Non-Instrumental and Non-Propositional Decision Theory. *Economics and Philosophy* 22: 365–392.

Taylor, W. E. 1980. Small Sample Considerations in Estimation from Panel Data. *Journal of Econometrics* 13: 203–233.

Thompson, R. 1994. Emotion Regulation: A Theme in Search of a Definition. *Monographs of the Society for Research in Child Development* 59 (2–3): 25–52.

Thornberry, T. P., A. Freeman-Gallant, A. J. Lizotte, M. D. Krohn, and C. A. Smith. 2003. Linked Lives: The Intergenerational Transmission of Antisocial Behavior. *Journal of Abnormal Psychology* 31: 171–184.

Tishbirani, R. 1996. Regression Shrinkage and Selection via the LASSO. *Journal of the Royal Statistical Society. Series B. Methodological* 58: 267–288.

Train, K. E. 2003. *Discrete Choice Methods with Simulation*. Cambridge University Press.

Tschacher, W., and H. Haken. 2007. Intentionality in Non-Equilibrium Systems? The Functional Aspects of Self-Organized Pattern Formation. *New Ideas in Psychology* 25: 1–15.

Trivers, R. L. 1972. Parental Investment and Sexual Selection. In *Sexual Selection and the Descent of Man, 1871–1971*, ed. B. Campbell. Aldine.

Trivers, R. L. 1974. Parent-Offspring Conflict. *American Zoologist* 14: 249–264.

Trivers, R.L. 1985. *Social Evolution*. Benjamin/Cummings.

Van den Boom, D. C., and J. B. Hoeksma. 1994. The Effect of Infant Irritability on Mother-Infant Interaction: A Growth Curve Analysis. *Developmental Psychology* 30: 581–590.

Van Egeren, L. A., M. S. Barratt, and M. A. Roach. 2001. Mother-Infant Responsiveness: Timing, Mutual Regulation, and Interactional Context. *Developmental Psychology* 37: 684–697.

Van Geert, P. 1991. A Dynamic Systems Model of Cognitive and Language Growth. *Psychological Review* 98: 3–53.

Van Ijzendoorn, M. H., and F. O. A. Hubbard. 2000. Are Infant Crying and Maternal Responsiveness During the First Year Related to Infant-Mother Attachment at 15 Months? *Attachment & Human Development* 2: 371–391.

Vaupel, J. 1988. Inherited Frailty and Longevity. *Demography* 25: 277–287.

Watson, J. B. 1928. *Psychological Care of Infant and Child*. Norton.

Watson, J. B. 1930. *Behaviorism*. Norton.

Watson, J. D. 2003. *DNA: The Secret of Life*. Knopf.

Weintraub, E. R. 2002. *How Economics Became a Mathematical Science*. Duke University Press.

West, D. J., and D. P. Farrington. 1997. *The Delinquent Way of Life*. Heinemann.

White, H. 2000. A Reality Check for Data Snooping. *Econometrica* 68: 1097–1126.

Wilson, E. O. 1975. *Sociobiology: The New Synthesis*. Harvard University Press.

Winnicott, D. W. 1960. The Theory of Parent-Infant Relationship. *International Journal of Psycho-Analysis* 41: 585–595.

Working, E. J. 1927. What Do Statistical Demand Curves Show? *Quarterly Journal of Economics* 41: 212–235.

Workman, L., and W. Reader. 2008. *Evolutionary Psychology: an Introduction*, second edition. Cambridge University Press.

Wright, P. G. 1928. *The Tariff on Animal and Vegetable Oils*. Macmillan.

Yitzhaki, S. 2003. Gini's Mean Difference: A Superior Measure of Variability for Non-Normal Distributions. *Metron* 61: 285–316.

Yitzhaki, S., and E. Schechtman. 2004. The Gini Instrumental Variable or the Double Instrumental Variable Estimator. *Metron* 62: 287–313.

Yitzhaki, S., and Q. Wodon. 2003. Mobility, Inequality and Horizontal Equity. *Research in Economic Inequality* 12: 177–198.

Yule, U. 1897. On the Theory of Correlation. *Journal of the Royal Statistical Society*, A, 60,: 812–854.

Yule, U. 1926. Why Do We Sometimes Get Nonsense Correlations between Time Series? A Study in Sampling and the Nature of Time Series. *Journal of the Royal Statistical Society*, A, 89: 1–69.

Zimmerman, D. 1992. Regression towards Mediocrity in Economic Stature. *American Economic Review* 82: 409–429.

Zimmerman, D. 2003. Peer Effects in Academic Outcomes: Evidence from a Natural Experiment. *Review of Economics and Statistics* 85: 9–23.

Ziv, Y., and J. Cassidy. 2002. Maternal Responsiveness and Infant Irritability: The Contribution of Crockenberg and Smith's "Antecedents of Mother-Infant Interaction and Infant Irritability in the First 3 Months of Life." *Infant Behavior and Development* 25: 16–20.

Index